Massacres, Resistance, Protectors

Muslim–Christian Relations
in Eastern Anatolia during World War I

Massacres, Resistance, Protectors

Muslim–Christian Relations in Eastern Anatolia during World War I

DAVID GAUNT
with the assistance of
JAN BEṮ ṢAWOCE
and an appendix of documents prepared by
RACHO DONEF

GORGIAS PRESS
2006

First Gorgias Press Edition, 2006

Copyright © 2006 by Gorgias Press LLC.

All rights reserved
under International and Pan-American Copyright Conventions
Published in the United States of America by Gorgias Press LLC, New Jersey

ISBN 1-59333-301-3

GORGIAS PRESS
Piscataway, New Jersey
www.gorgiaspress.com

Printed and bound in India by Replika Press

Summary

Table of Contents	vii
List of Maps	xi
List of Tables	xiii
Preface	xv
Abbreviations	xvii
1 Introduction and Background	1
2 Setting the Stage: Kurds and Turks, Armenians and Syriacs	29
3 The Road to the Fatal Solution	53
4 Playing with Fire: Occupied Urmia	81
5 The Ethnic Cleansing of the Hakkari Mountains	121
6 Anatolia's Heart of Darkness	151
7 The Destruction of Midyat	181
8 Sayfo: The General Massacre of Northern Mesopotamia	197
9 The Battle for Azakh	273
10 Implications and Conclusions	295
11 Notes on the Sources	317
Appendix 1 Oral Testimony on Tur Abdin 1914–15	327
Appendix 2 Documents on the Syriac Population	405
Appendix 3 Documents on the Number of Victims	433
Appendix 4 Turkish Archival Documents on Deportations and Sieges	445
Bibliography	495
Indexes	507

Table of Contents

Summary v
List of Maps xi
List of Tables xiii
Preface xv
Abbreviations xvii
1 Introduction and Background 1
    The Development of the Religious and Ethnic Groups 2
    Christians Go East 5
    The Origins of the Syriac Orthodox Church 8
    Under Muslim Rule 11
    Christian Missionaries 15
    Pre-war Population of the Oriental Churches 18
    Chaldeans 24
2 Setting the Stage: Kurds and Turks, Armenians and Syriacs 29
    The Kurdish Question 29
    The Armenian Question 38
    A Heritage of Massacres 41
    The Great Powers 46
    Ideology 48
3 The Road to the Fatal Solution 53
    Preparations for War in the Caucasus 53
    War and the Minorities 56
    The First Campaign 58
    Jihad and Iran 62
    Deportation as a Military Tactic 64
    Ottoman Deportations 65
    The Failure of Diplomacy 71

4 Playing with Fire: Occupied Urmia...81
   "Atrocities Committed by the Ottoman Troops".................................82
   The Occupation of Iran 85
   Iranian Weakness and Foreign Intrigues 89
   The Christian Minorities 92
   Border Provocations...94
   The Calm before the Storm 100
   Under Occupation..103
   The "Armenian Revolt" Scare..106
   Emergency in Urmia 110
   Missions and Refugees..112
   International Reactions..119
5 The Ethnic Cleansing of the Hakkari Mountains..................................121
   The Assyrian Homeland...124
   The Pre-War Deportation Order 127
   Bashkale 130
   The Road to Disaster..138
   Assessing the Damage 144
6 Anatolia's Heart of Darkness...151
   Preparations for Genocide..154
   The First Steps 160
   A Climate of Fear 165
   Disaster 170
   Was Anyone Safe?..175
   "Either Them or Us"..177
7 The Destruction of Midyat..181
   Tur Abdin: The West Syriac Heartland 183
   A Week-long Massacre 188
   Solidarity Breaks Down 192
   Annihilation of the Syriacs...194
8 Sayfo: The General Massacre of Northern Mesopotamia......................197
   A Catalogue of Massacres 200
9 The Battle for Azakh...273
   The "Midyat Rebellion" 275
   Naji and Scheubner-Richter...280
   Syriacs or Armenians?..282
   Naji's Defeat...288
   Enver Intervenes 290

10 Implications and Conclusions	295
The Number of Victims	300
Intentions	303
Ethnic Cleansing	308
11 Notes on the Sources	317
General Sources	317
Sources on Urmia	320
Sources on Hakkari and Van	322
Sources on Diyarbekir Vilayet	323
Appendix 1 Oral Testimony on Tur Abdin 1914–15	327
A. General Statements	328
B. Midyat	331
C. 'Ayn-Wardo	348
D. Kfar-Boran	364
E. Kfar-Gawze	367
F. Kafro-Elayto	371
G. Kfarze	372
H. Bote	374
I. 'Urnes	377
J. Saleh	378
K. Habses	379
L. Basibrin	379
M. Anhel	380
N. Mor Awgin	381
O. Mor-Malke	383
P. M'are	384
Q. Mizizah	384
R. Hazakh	387
S. Nsibin and Gozarto	392
T. Miyafarqin	394
U. Tel-Ghaz	395
V. Sa'irt	395
W. Gziro	397
X. Diyarbekir, Midyat, 'Ayn-Wardo	397
Appendix 2 Documents on the Syriac Population	405
1. Statistics Provided by the Assyro-Chaldean Delegation to the Peace Conference	405
2. Liste des villages, des habitations et nationalités	406
3. The Size of the Chaldean Church in June 1913	429

Appendix 3 Documents on the Number of Victims...................................433
    1. The Approximate Number of Victims
       Belonging to the Vilayet of Diyarbekir...433
    2. Hecatombs and More Hecatombs..436
    3. Christian Massacres of 1915 in Diyarbekir Vilayet 441
Appendix 4 Turkish Archival Documents on Deportations and Sieges....445
    1. The Deportation of the Assyrians in Ottoman Documents 445
    2. Documents Related to the Siege of Azakh
       in the Turkish Military History Archives 450
Bibliography 495
Indexes 507
    Towns and Villages 507
    Places of Execution..522
    Persons..523
    Authors Cited...533

List of Maps

Map 1: The Upper Tigris region 10
Map 2: The Eastern Syriacs of Hakkari and neighboring regions
    at the beginning of the twentieth century. 14
Map 3: Map of the Chaldean Church. 26
Map 4: Northwestern Persia, showing principal Christian towns destroyed
    by Turks and Kurds; also line of flight to the Russian border 86
Map 5: The tribes and districts of the Hakkari Mountains 124
Map 6: Kurdish tribes of the Upper Jezire. 186
Map 7: Plan of Midyat. 189
Map 8: Tur Abdin region at the start of World War I 198–99
Map 9: Azakh (İdil) township and surrounding villages 274

LIST OF TABLES

Table 1: Number of Assyrian, Armenian, Jewish, and Kurdish households within the Nestorian dioceses in the Hakkari, Urmia, and Bohtan regions 21
Table 2: Assyro-Chaldeans living in Diyarbekir vilayet and Urfa sanjak 23
Table 3: Population figures for the Syriac Orthodox Church, 1920 24
Table 4: Size of the Chaldean Church in June 1913 25
Table 5. Population on the eve of World War I for the Oriental churches in northern Mesopotamia and adjacent regions 28
Table 6: Approximate population of Assyro-Chaldeans lost in battle or massacred between 1914 and 1919 300
Table 7: Population of the Mosul, Diyarbekir vilayets; Aleppo, Urfa, Deyr-Zor, Sa'irt, Hakkari sanjaks; and Urmia, Salmas regions, in 1914 406
Table 8: District Haute Baroude 407
Table 9: District Jilou 408
Table 10: District de Nirwa 408
Table 11: District de Doustican 408
Table 12: District de Baz 409
Table 13: District de Livon-Bas 409
Table 14: District Haut Livon 409
Table 15: District de Noddiss 409
Table 16: District de Sarii et Temou 410
Table 17: District Chamisdinon 410
Table 18: District de Zazon 411
Table 19: District de Guardian 411
Table 20: District de Galia de Derianai 412
Table 21: District de Valtou 413
Table 22: District de Tal 414
Table 23: District Tiari Haute 414
Table 24: District de Albac 415
Table 25: District de Gavar 416

Table 26: District d'Ourmiah 417
Table 27: District de Gavar (all listed villages are Assyrian) 418
Table 28: District de Haut Barwar 418
Table 29: District of Tkhouma 419
Table 30: District de Barwar de Bohtan 420
Table 31: District d'Ispirad 420
Table 32: Ville de Diarbekir et des environs 422
Table 33: Kaza (District de Silivan) 422
Table 34: Kaza (district) Lédjé 423
Table 35: Kaza (district) Dérék 423
Table 36: Argana Madan (sandjak) 423
Table 37: Kaza (district) de Palou 423
Table 38: Sandjak (département) Severak 423
Table 39: Kaza (district) de Veran-Chéhér 424
Table 40: Sandjak (département) de Mardine 424
Table 41: Kaza (district) de Avnié (ou) Savour 424
Table 42: Kaza (district) de Nissibin 425
Table 43: Kaza (commune) de Habab (attaché à Nissibin) 425
Table 44: Kaza (district) de Djeziret-ibn-Oumar 426
Table 45: Kaza (district) de Midiat (Djébel Tour Abédine) 427
Table 46: Kaza (district) de Bechérie 427
Table 47: Nahie (commune) de Bafavoi 428
Table 48: Sandjak (département) d'Ourfa 428
Table 49: Statistique générale de l'archidiocèse patriarcal 429
Table 50: Statistique de l'archevêché d'Amida et de ses villages 429
Table 51: Statistique de l'archevêché de Kerkouk 430
Table 52: Statistique du diocèse de Séert 430
Table 53: Statistique de l'archevêché d'Urmiah 430
Table 54: Statistique de l'évêché d'Akra 431
Table 55: Statistique du diocèse d'Amadia 431
Table 56: Statistique du diocese de Gézirah 431
Table 57: Statistique du diocèse de Mardin 431
Table 58: Statistique du diocèse de Salmas 432
Table 59: Statistique du diocèse de Séna 432
Table 60: Statistique du diocèse de Van et des Missions nestoriennes ... 432
Table 61: Statistique du diocèse de Zakhô 432
Table 62: Christians of Diyarbekir vilayet who disappeared
during the persecution of 1915–16 434
Table 63: Disappeared Christians in the Sanjak of Mardin
during the persecution of 1915–16 435

Preface

This book began as a documentation of what had happened to the East and West Syriac Christians of northern Mesopotamia and northwestern Iran during World War I. Over the course of research, the theme has expanded greatly, because the fate of Syriacs was so inextricably mixed up with that of the Syriac Catholics, Chaldeans, Nestorian Assyrians, and Armenians (of all denominations) that it did not make sense to exclude them. This book documents events that happened in previously poorly researched regions, and to relatively little known religions and ethnic groups. However, this approach has led to the discovery of a great many new sources. The quality of the sources is so impressive that they permit a degree of concretion around the treatment of Oriental Christians during World War I that has been lacking until now. This has made for fascinating research, and it has also been a powerful personal experience.

David Gaunt has written the main text of the book. Jan Bet-Şawoce is responsible for appendix 1 on the oral history of Tur Abdin. Dr. Racho Donef has done the translations in appendix 4 of Ottoman documents from the Presidential Archive and from the Military History Archive.

Without the help and support of others, the completion of this book would not have been possible. We would like to thank the following people for much practical help during our research: Professors Elena Melkumian and Grigorii Kosach of Moscow, Viktoria Aivazova of Munich, Zeki Yalcin of Södertälje, and Kurosh Hormozd Nazlu and Juliana Jawaro of the United States. We have received so much spiritual support from so many people that it is impossible to thank each and every one. Please accept our collective thanks.

We especially express gratitude to the Baltic Sea Foundation for making this research possible and the publication committee at Södertörn University College.

David Gaunt
Jan Bet-Şawoce
Racho Donef

ABBREVIATIONS

ATAŞE   Askeri Tarih ve Ştratejik Etut Başkanlığı (Turkish General Staff Military-Historical and Strategic Study Archives, Ankara)
AVPRI   Arkhiv vneshnei politiki rossiiskoi imperii (Archive of the Foreign Policy of the Russian Empire, Moscow)
BOA   Başbakanlik Osmanli Arşivi (Prime Ministerial Ottoman Archives, Istanbul)
CUP   Committee for Union and Progress
PAAA   Politisches Archiv des Auswärtigen Amtes (Political Archive of the Foreign Office, Bonn)
RGVIA   Rossiiski gosudarstvennyi voenno-istoricheskii arkhiv (Russian State Military-Historical Archive, Moscow)
PRO FO   Public Record Office Foreign Office, London

The components of a Turkish archival designation are as follows: Kol., *koleksiyon* "collection"; BDH, *Birinci Dunya Harbi* "World War I"; Kls., *klasör* "file"; Dos., *dosya* "dossier"; Fih., *fihrist*, "catalogue number."

1 INTRODUCTION AND BACKGROUND

The events discussed in this book took place in Northern Mesopotamia during World War I. This is an area where today Arab, Iranian, Kurdish, and Turkish interests coincide. Historically it has formed a complicated mosaic made up of many separate cultures and religions—some of these were very large, but some were small, such as the Armenian Catholic, Syriac, Assyrian, and Chaldean Christians which are the subject of this book.

The history of this region is not a matter of general knowledge, so it is necessary to paint a broad background to the wartime activities of "ethnic cleansing"[1] and genocide, which will be described in considerable detail further on. By the 1920s, the multidenominational Christian populations of the region were radically depleted and almost entirely displaced from their historic settlements. Representatives of the remnants of these groups insist that they were the victims of a genocide planned and carried out by the wartime leadership of the Ottoman Empire. The Assyrian, Chaldean, and Syriac groups have proposed the term *Sayfo*, meaning "year of the sword," as a name for this catastrophe. In many countries, parliamentary bills have been considered which would brand Sayfo as an act of genocide of the same rank as the slightly better known case of the Armenian genocide.

Methodologically, this monograph describes events on a local level in order to reach a new level of accuracy about who was doing the killing, and who were the victims, and what were the circumstances. Thus it can serve as a complement to previous academic work on World War I genocide, which has often focused on national politics, the highest decision-makers,

---

[1] "Ethnic cleansing" is the forced displacement of an entire population, defined as an ethnic, religious, or racial group, from a particular territory. It is usually, but not always, perpetrated in wartime and is considered a war crime. In general the intention is to destroy the practical possibility of carrying on cultural traditions, even if part of the group survives its displacement. It was orginally coined by the Serbian side, evidently as a euphemism, during the wars that accompanied the breakup of Yugoslavia in the early 1990s. Some people may consider ethnic cleansing to be a legitimate part of nation-building because the term seems free of evil connotations. However, it has come to be used in the literature, and it is used in this book, to designate a crime against humanity.

and the question of ultimate responsibility for what happened.[2] Most previous studies have focused on deportations, while the focus here is on massacres and other forms of face-to-face violence. Concentration on a regional level also enables a combination of archival, oral, and printed sources in Turkish, Arabic, Syriac, as well as Russian, German, French, and English-language sources. A large number of these sources have never been cited before, and some of them are printed here in the appendixes.

The region examined here is the Ottoman provinces (*vilayets*)[3] of Van (foremost Hakkari), Diyarbekir, and Bitlis (foremost Bohtan) in southeast Anatolia, plus the Iranian province of Azerbaijan during its occupation by Ottoman troops. Almost all of the events related here took place during a twelve-month period from November 1914 to November 1915. By the end of 1915, Sayfo had resulted in the nearly total disappearance of the native Christian population from places they had inhabited since time out of mind.

This book cannot pretend to be the definitive work on the Syriac Sayfo. First, it deals only with 1914 and 1915, and although this is the most intensive genocidal period, killing continued throughout the war and even spilled over into the era of the Turkish Republic. Second, new source materials turn up constantly both from the private papers of Syriac families and in the increasing accessibility of Turkish archives.

THE DEVELOPMENT OF THE RELIGIOUS AND ETHNIC GROUPS

The aboriginal Syriacs of north Mesopotamia and Persia were among the very first people to convert to Christianity. For reasons hidden by the mist of history, they split off from mainstream Christendom and formed unique churches with special theologies and rites. The Christian churches known as the Syriac Orthodox (headed by the "Patriarch of the God-protected City of Antioch and of All the Domain of the Apostolic Throne"), the Assyrian

---

[2] Vahakn Dadrian, *The History of the Armenian Genocide: Ethnic Conflict from the Balkans to Anatolia to the Caucasus* (1995); Peter Balakian, *The Burning Tigris: the Armenian Genocide and America's Response* (2003); Taner Akçam, *Armenien und der Völkermord: Die Istanbuler Prozesse und die türkische Nationalbewegung* (1996); Donald Bloxham, *The Great Game of Genocide: Imperialism, Nationalism and the Destruction of the Ottoman Armenians* (2005).

[3] In descending order of importance, the Ottoman administrative territories were the *vilayet* or province, governed by a *vali*; the *sandjak* or district, governed by a *mutasarrif*; the *kaza* or subdistrict, governed by a *kaymakam*; and the *nahiya* or commune, governed by a *mudir*.

Church (headed by the "Venerable and Honored Father of Fathers and Chief Shepherd, the Catholicos and Patriarch of the East"), the Chaldean Church (headed by the "Patriarch-Catholicos of Babylon of the Chaldeans"), and the Syriac Catholic Church (headed by the "Patriarch of Antioch") are sometimes collectively called the Oriental Churches.[4] Intertwined historically and geographically with the former are the Armenian Apostolic Church (also termed Gregorian after its founder Gregory the Illuminator) and its uniate branch the Armenian Catholic Church. To complete the picture, mention should be made of the Melkite Syriacs who remained within the Greek Orthodox Church (hence their name taken from *malik* or king). Most Melkites lived in provinces along the Mediterranean coast, but there were a few in the major cities of southeast Anatolia.

In the West Syriac dialect, individuals use the word *Suryoyo* (in East Syriac the same word is *Suryaya*) to designate their ethnic identity. For some reason, European sources have tended to conflate all of the Syriac language–speakers and employ a confusing battery of terms. Until the late nineteenth century, European writers often used the term "Chaldean" to cover all of the Syriac-speaking peoples. Toward the end of that century, the English term "Assyrian" and the Russian term *Aisori* came into use, and during World War I it made its worldwide breakthrough in the newspapers. After the war, the combined term "Assyro-Chaldeans" was used by the delegations attending the peace conferences; perhaps this term has a Russian origin, as *Sirokhaldeitsy* was used in a religious historical book in 1899.[5] As a generic term, I use "Syriac" here to designate all of the Christians who use a variant of the Aramaic language. Other more specific terms are used to distinguish the various churches.

The Ottoman state was a theocracy, so it seldom had a use for terms that mixed the separate religions. On the contrary, it consistently distinguished *Nasturiler* (Nestorians) from *Keldanleri* (Chaldeans) and *Süryaniler* (Syriacs) and may not have been aware that they all had a common history. The Syriacs in their turn were subdivided into *Süryani kadim* or *eskim* (both mean Old Syriacs), *Protestanlar* (Protestants), and *Katolikler* (Catholics). Every

---

[4] Donald Attwater, *The Churches of the East* (1961).

[5] Adolphe D'Avril, *La Chaldée chrétienne: Étude sur l'histoire religieuse et politique des Chaldéens-Unis et des Nestorians* (1864); I. Babakhanov, *Sirokhaldeitsy, ikh istoriya i zhizn'* [Syro-Chaldeans: Their history and life] (1899); William Walker Rockwell, *The Pitiful Plight of the Assyrian Christians in Persia and Kurdistan* (1916); Joseph Naayem, *Les Assyro-Chaldéens et les Arméniens massacrés par les Turcs: Documents inédits recueillis par une témoin oculaire* (1920).

so often, the Ottomans would use the term *Jakobiler* (Jacobite) for the Syriac Orthodox.

As they emerge in historical documents, the Mesopotamian Christians are believed to have used Aramaic (which is the root of Syriac) as a common language. In ancient times this Semitic language was widespread throughout the Middle East from Petra to Persia. Judging from a few probable direct quotations in the New Testament, Jesus spoke a Palestinian variant of Aramaic. For a period, Persia used Aramaic as its administrative language. The Oriental Churches retained Syriac as their liturgical language, while Greek and Latin became the languages of Christianity everywhere else.

Syriac-speakers are divided into two main dialects. At the start of the twentieth century, the East Syriac–speakers lived along the Turkish-Iranian border and the east bank of the Tigris River valley with its tributaries flowing from the east. Literally they lived in the heart of Kurdistan. The West Syriac–speakers lived along the Euphrates River valley and its left-bank tributaries. The West Syriac–speaking area thus lies between the two great rivers of Mesopotamia.[6] An important local dialect of Neo-Syriac is known as Turoyo, which is spoken in the Tur Abdin district of Diyarbekir province in Turkey. In late Ottoman times, numerous Syriacs in the southernmost outposts of Anatolia along the Tigris River had begun speaking Kurdish or Arabic.

The core identification for Syriacs and Armenians has been their unique Churches. The history of the churches is staggeringly complicated and the main cult centers have shifted many times, perhaps reflecting population retreats from repression and ethnic cleansing toward more isolated areas, but perhaps also reflecting a general decimation through conversion in the accessible settlements. Cultural isolates remained in some of the most remote places. In comparison, the Armenian Apostolic church has had a more stable development, but population movement has brought this religion to places far from the original Armenian state, and isolation has caused friction. The Catholic Armenian Church grew up basically among Armenians who lived outside of the Armenian heartland.

The Aramaic-speakers were among the very first populations in which Christianity gained hold. Since the time of the Babylonian Captivity, there had been many Jews living in the towns in the region, and they also spoke Aramaic. After the early churches were established, there were conversions of individual Syriacs, Armenians, Persians, and Arabs. Even before the Ro-

---

[6] Mark Sykes, "Journeys in Northern Mesopotamia" (1907).

man Empire became officially Christian, large congregations could be found in and around the urban center of Antioch in northern Syria. Antioch was then one of the largest cities in the entire Roman Empire, and its rural upland was very populous. In Persia, a Christian presence emerged very early, although the official Zoroastrian religion did not always tolerate them. The Armenian kingdom adopted Christianity about the year 300, and from the start Armenian theologians found inspiration among the Syriac theologians of Edessa.

Before Christianity became an official religion in the Roman Empire, the early Christians were subject to various degrees of persecution depending on the inclination of the emperor. During this period, many local variants of Christian theology grew up and gained followers. Particular theologies and unique forms of religiosity developed in the patriarchy of Antioch, which later on set these Christians in full conflict with co-religionists elsewhere in the Empire. Briefly put, the conflicts revolved about whether and how Christianity could combine its Jewish-origin roots with the widespread Greek philosophic tradition. Whereas the Europeans found it easy to invent such new combinations, the Syriacs as a rule would reject them. Thus theological strife went hand in hand with geopolitical friction between the Asian and Greco-Roman spheres.

Once it was legal, the Christian Church in the Roman Empire sought to shape its fragments into a single unified creed and ritual. This process squeezed many of the major Eastern theologians out of positions of influence, and their teachings were condemned as unorthodox or even as heresy. One of the major tasks of this unification process was to take a common stand on the divinity and humanity of Jesus. The prevailing view was that Christ was one person but combining two natures, both a godlike nature and a human nature. This interpretation stood in conflict with the widespread monophysite (Greek for "single nature") concept of the Antioch patriarchy and the Armenian Church. This line argued that Jesus had either divine nature, or human nature, but not both and definitely not at the same time. Ecumenical councils in 431 in Ephesus and 451 in Chalcedon resulted in the condemnation of monophysitism as taught by the theologian Eutyches, whose doctrine formed the basis of the Syriac Orthodox and Armenian Churches, as well as Nestorius, whose doctrine was adopted by the Assyrian Church of the East.

CHRISTIANS GO EAST

Once the teachings of Nestorius and Eutyches were condemned, their followers could be persecuted as heretics. They were particularly numerous in northern Mesopotamia and present-day Syria and Turkey. Many congregations simply seceded from Roman Catholicism and rejected outright the new creed of Chalcedon.[7] The dissidents managed to survive without a formal structure for many generations. Other followers of Nestorius eventually found asylum in the Persian Empire, which from 363 had its western border running through the middle of northern Mesopotamia, and its territory encompassed much of Iraq and parts of eastern Anatolia. The heavily fortified frontier ran between the towns of Mardin, on the Roman side, and Nisibin, on the Persian side. Although the Armenian Church was just as monophysite as the Syriac, it flourished in an independent vassal state just outside the reach of the Romans.

Over the following centuries, the East Roman emperors fluctuated between repression and reconciliation in order to resolve this confrontation, but religious and political opposition to Rome held a firm grip on the Syriac people. For a short period the town of Edessa (later named Urfa, now Sanliurfa) became the major intellectual center for heretical theologies. In 489, the followers of Nestorius were driven out of Edessa, and they fled eastward across the Persian border to the town of Nisibin. As enemies of the Byzantines, they were welcomed and tolerated as allies by the Persians. Persia developed one of the few native Christian Churches ever to emerge outside of the Roman Empire. Already by the third century it contained important communities of Christians. Their numbers increased when defeated Roman soldiers were taken as captives to Persia. Great confusion marked the initial Persian approach to the Christians: sometimes they were tolerated and sometimes they were persecuted. At any rate, the hostility between the empires meant that Syriac Christianity in Persia grew in isolation from co-religionists within the Roman Empire. There were, however, a number of convents and schools in Edessa and Nisibin, and they evolved into places where Persian, Syriac, and Armenian Christians might meet. Attempts to reconcile the Persian with the Roman church were unsuccessful due to Persian politics. In 424, a synod was called and it formed an imperial organization which raised the status of the Catholicos of Ctesiphon to that of Patriarch of the East and thereby severed all ties with the Patriarch of Antioch, who previously had some residual authority over the Christians of Persia.[8]

---

[7] Steven Runciman, *A History of the Crusades* 1 (1951), 7.

[8] Robin E. Waterfield, *Christians in Persia: Assyrians, Armenians, Roman Catholics and Protestants* (1973), 18–19.

The Sassanid rulers of Persia were in perpetual confrontation with Byzantium, and this obviously encouraged the decision of the Persian Christians to openly accept Nestorian theology, because it reduced the risk that the Christians would be accused of sympathy with the Byzantines. The Persian congregations were concentrated along the valley of the Tigris River.[9] The Church drew its membership from a mixed ethnic base of Syriac, Jewish, Persian, and Arab elements. The Arab element came from the Lakhamid tribe (living mostly in northern Iraq), who were loyal to the Persian emperors and who adhered to the Persian Church.

The Islamic conquest of Persia was complete by 637. Under both Zoroastrian and Muslim rule, the Nestorian church was tolerated and could build new churches.[10] Under Persian protection, the Nestorian church perfected the classical form of the East Syriac dialect. Even more important, the church began an impressive missionary expansion. At its greatest extent, in the thirteenth century, there was a network of Nestorian churches in Central Asia and China along the Silk Road as well as along the Malabar Coast of India.

The Nestorian mission in Central Asia influenced the leaders of many Mongol tribes to convert.[11] Many Mongol khans married women who were Nestorians. There was hope in some quarters that all of the Mongols would convert from Buddhism to Christianity, but in the end the Khans opted for Islam. At the start of the fifteenth century, Timurlane devastated the Middle East and shattered most of the Nestorian and Jacobite organizations. The churches never truly recovered from this blow, and they were reduced to relatively isolated toeholds struggling to avoid oblivion.

The Christian survivors of the Mongol invasion were left scattered and decimated. What followed was a very confused and poorly documented era lasting many centuries. It is very difficult to make sense of the various splits within the East Syriac Church. It would seem that the Mongol destruction stripped the Church of unquestioned authority, and instead tribal, clan, and regional rivalry reduced the Christians to law-of-the-jungle civil war. At various times, one side or the other sought the support of the Pope and in return promised to unite with Roman Catholicism, only to relapse after a few generations.

---

[9] Hubert Jedin, *Atlas zur Kirchengeschichte* (1970), 10.
[10] Chase Robinson, *Empire and Elites after the Muslim Conquest: The Transformation of Northern Mesopotamia* (2000).
[11] Jedin, *Atlas zur Kirchengeschichte*, 27.

Internal strife resulted in permanent social, political, and geographic splits, and rival churches grew out of the same Nestorian and Persian root, but for a long time they were locked in mutual enmity. After much vacillation, one side permanently united with the Vatican, while the other opted for continued autonomy. An East Syriac breakaway organization united with the Roman Catholic Church in 1681 and the Pope dubbed it "Chaldean," in memory of the biblical kingdom. It kept its Syriac-language ritual and ancient customs such as married parish clergy. Over the centuries, the main residence of the patriarch of the autonomous Nestorian Church shifted many times, but in the late Middle Ages the Nestorian patriarch chose the hamlet of Kochanes deep inside the Hakkari Mountains, and here the patriarchal seat remained until the summer of 1915. The Uniate Chaldean Church's patriarchs lived in Diyarbekir from 1681 to 1830, when they moved for good to Mosul. Gradually a territorial division emerged. The Old Church had a relatively concentrated settlement in the Hakkari Mountains and adjacent plains in northwestern Iran as far as Lake Urmia. The Chaldean Church was just as densely settled; although it had its core in Mesopotamia north of Mosul, it also intermingled with traditional Nestorians in Iran.[12]

The two East Syriac churches had separate social spheres. The Chaldeans had a significant urban base, but the traditional church was locked in feudal agrarian settings. The leader of the Nestorian Church resided at Kochanes in the midst of a tribal society of mountaineers who were led by hereditary chiefs called *malek*s, who formed a rudimentary noble class. New patriarchs were always chosen from the Shimun dynasty and always bore the title *Mar Shimun*, or Lord Simon, followed by their given name. Others of their co-religionists lived in the plains of northern Mesopotamia in serfdom under landlords. The Nestorians developed a day-to-day symbiosis with the neighboring Kurds; occasionally travelers had trouble distinguishing them, except for the obvious religious difference.

THE ORIGINS OF THE SYRIAC ORTHODOX CHURCH

While the Syriac followers of Nestorius were welcome in the Persian Empire, the monophysite Syriacs chiefly stayed in place in the patriarchy of Antioch and fiercely stood their ground. Although denounced as heresy, an underground organization succeeded in holding its own under the outward guise of Orthodoxy. However, at certain times repression eased and the

---

[12] Michel Chevalier, *Les Montagnards Chrétiens du Hakkâri et du Kurdistan septentrional* (1983).

monophysites could work openly. Under the protection of Emperor Anastasius, Severus served as patriarch of Antioch from 512 to 518, and he was able to spread monophysitism openly. One generation later, the time proved ripe to create the structure that grew into the Syriac Orthodox Church. Under the influence of his Syriac wife Theodora, Emperor Justinian appointed Jacob Baradaeus (d. 578) bishop of Edessa in 541. Using this high position, he recruited other declared monophysite theologians to church offices in his diocese. It is said that he anointed hundreds of priests. In fact he was so successful that for a long time Europeans always, and Ottomans sometimes, termed this the Jacobite Church.

By about 500, the future Syrian Orthodox homeland in northern Mesopotamia (map 1) was already well represented in the form of dioceses for metropolitans (archbishops) in Edessa, Amida (the Syriac name for Diyarbekir), Malatya, and Dara (outside of Mardin).[13] In the sixth century, the Arabs of the Ghassanid kingdom (vassals of the Roman Empire who patrolled the Syrian desert against the Persians) converted to the monophysite branch of Christianity. Gradually the seat of the monophysite religion shifted away from the Mediterranean coast and inland toward northern Mesopotamia.

According to the church history of Michael the Syrian (patriarch 1166–1199), by the ninth century most of the coastal communities no longer existed and Jacobite settlement was concentrated in a swath of territory north of Aleppo, reaching the upper Euphrates River and continuing on into Tur Abdin.[14] By Michael's time, the center of the Jacobite Church was no longer even within the Byzantine Empire, but rather in Muslim-ruled territory.[15]

---

[13] Jedin, *Atlas zur Kirchengeschichte*, 8.
[14] Ibid., 26.
[15] Ibid., 38.

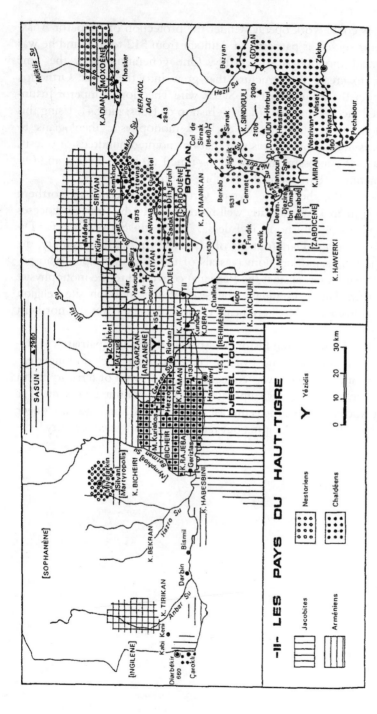

Map 1: The Upper Tigris region. From Michel Chevalier, *Les Montagnards Chrétiens du Hakkâri et du Kurdistan septentrional* (1983), map III.

Under Muslim Rule

According to a tradition as old as the conquests of Muhammad, Muslims considered Christians and Jews living in a Muslim country to be worthy of respect as fellow "peoples of the book." The legal term used to designate a protected non-Muslim was *dhimmi*, from an Arabic word for protection. As long as they paid a special personal tax and observed detailed rules of submissive behavior (these codes changed over time and were not always enforced in full), showing proper deference toward Muslims, the Christians and Jews were allowed religious and cultural autonomy plus freedom from persecution. The so-called Contract of Omar has been considered an agreement drawn up between Caliph Omar and the Christians of Syria, and it specifies how the latter should dress and how they should behave in order to be worthy of Muslim protection.[16] In principle, their highest religious leaders became their main public representatives and the Christians could observe their own family and religious laws, run their own charities, courts, and schools, and collect their own taxes. Although the Muslim standpoint was that non-Muslims might not hold public office or be part of the military, at the beginning of Arab rule caliphs resided in Damascus with its large Christian population and sophisticated administration, so many Syriac Christians filled vital functions. The monophysites probably marked an improved social and religious status, being no longer harassed heretics.

This favorable relationship lasted as long as the caliphs used Damascus as their capital. The Abbasid caliphs transferred their capital to Baghdad, and they were much more strict Muslims than the Umayyads. Baghdad lay in an area that had been part of the Persian Empire, and so many Nestorians lived there.[17] However, some monophysite Syriacs also moved to the cities of Baghdad, Mosul, and Tikrit, where bishoprics had been established.[18]

After the Mongol invasions of the mid thirteenth century, a long dark age set its stamp on Mesopotamia. This was reinforced by the irreparable damage done in 1402 by Timur, who destroyed as much as possible, displacing many peoples. Baghdad was left in ruins, and Antioch ceased forever to have any importance. Defensive walls and fortresses were pulled down, and public buildings burned. In the ensuing power vacuum, Turkmen tribes fought incessantly over the spoils, each trying desperately to form a state that could last.

---

[16] Hugh Goddard, *A History of Christian–Muslim Relations* (2000), 34–50.

[17] Runciman, *History of the Crusades*, 1:26–27.

[18] Jedin, *Atlas zur Kirchengeschichte*, 26.

Meanwhile, in western Anatolia, the Ottoman Empire was beginning to take shape. At first the Ottoman dynasty expanded in Balkan Europe. But early in the sixteenth century, the sultans turned their eyes eastward to conquer territories held by the Turkman tribes, Persians, and Arabs. Little by little, the Ottomans pressed on into Mesopotamia. A series of wars with the Safavids shoved the Persian border back and forth over Syriac settlements. Throughout these conflicts the decimated Nestorians remained linked with the destiny of the Persian Empire, but this empire gradually lost ground to the Ottomans. When the new border was finalized, the Nestorians found themselves split between the two empires, and Hakkari with the homes of the Mar Shimun and the tribes was on the Ottoman side.

The Ottoman rulers adopted the original Islamic *dhimmi* institution but went some steps further by integrating non-Muslims within the state apparatus. A semiformal structure of religious corporations called *millet*s, after the modern Turkish word for nation, developed. The sultan appointed the highest religious officials for the non-Muslim religions, and these persons aided in the collection of taxes, guaranteeing the congregations' loyalty and overseeing religious courts and education. The main Ottoman innovation was state-recognized and legitimized corporate autonomy for the major non-Muslim religious groups. Historians have adopted the term "millet system" even though the word was not used in that particular sense until the nineteenth century and even though the practice was a far cry from systematic.[19] The chief claim to "systemhood" lies in its universality as Christians and Jews were now treated alike—no better, but also no worse, and neither religion could harass the other. Supposedly, there were three original non-Muslim millets: the Greek Orthodox headed by the Patriarch of Constantinople, the Jewish headed by the Chief Rabbi of Constantinople, and the Armenian headed by the Armenian Patriarch of Constantinople. The Greek Patriarch was also expected to represent the interests of the few Roman Catholics. The Armenian Patriarch also represented the interests, as fellow monophysites, of the Syriac Orthodox Church. The situation for the Nestorians is less clear, as the Mar Shimun was also the leader of recognized autonomous tribes (termed *ashiret*) and was therefore legally independent of Ottoman government as long as he delivered the yearly tribute.

The *dhimmi* could reside wherever they wished and they could observe their religion, although always in a low key. They should in principle dress differently from Muslims, not carry weapons, not ride horses, not build new

---

[19] *Christians and Jews in the Ottoman Empire: The Functioning of a Plural Society*, ed. Benjamin Braude and Bernard Lewis (1982).

churches or synagogues, and so on. They were forbidden to hold public office and could not be soldiers, and they had to pay the *jizye* (poll tax) in return for their status. The size of the tax varied over time and between regions, and there were many exemptions. Religious leaders, priests, and monks, as well as those in some sort of obligatory civil or border guard service, were tax-free, but each ordinary household or adult male bachelor had to pay a set sum each year.

Gradually millets were formed for the minor religious groups, and they became very numerous during the nineteenth century. A millet for Armenian Catholics was set up in 1830.[20] Closely related to the Armenian Catholics, but not quite a millet, was the agreement for the Chaldeans which came into being October 21, 1844.[21] A document issued that day took the form of a joint contract regulating the civil and administrative union of Chaldeans within the general framework of the Armenian Catholic millet. The Armenian Catholic Patriarch would continue to be the person who would negotiate for the Chaldeans living in Constantinople at the Sultan's court. The Armenian Catholic patriarch agreed not to interfere with the inner organization of the Chaldean Church. In return, the Chaldean patriarch paid a yearly sum of money as a reimbursement for services. In May 1845, the Syriac Catholics signed a similar mutual contract with the Armenian Catholic Patriarch. From necessity, a permanent form of cooperation developed among the Catholic churches, particularly among the highest leadership.

The Protestants received their millet in 1850, and this represented the few Syriac and Armenian converts to Protestantism.[22] The Porte is said to have granted a millet for the Syriac Orthodox in 1882.[23] This would imply that it broke away from the long-standing vassal relationship under the Armenian Patriarch. No millet document has yet been discovered concerning the Nestorians, and there was no representative in Constantinople, although the Mar Shimun definitely filled the role of a millet representative in relation to the governor of Van province.

---

[20] Hagop Barsoumian, "The Dual Role of the Armenian *Amira* Class within the Ottoman Government and the Armenian *Millet* (1750–1850)" (1982), 180.

[21] D'Avril, *La Chaldée chrétienne*, 86–88.

[22] John Joseph, *Muslim–Christian Relations and Inter-Christian Rivalries in the Middle East* (1983), 76; Suavi Aydin et al., *Mardin: Aşiret – Cemaat – Devlet* (2000), 244.

[23] Hanna Aydin, *Die Syrisch-Orthodoxe Kirche von Antiochien* (1990), 96.

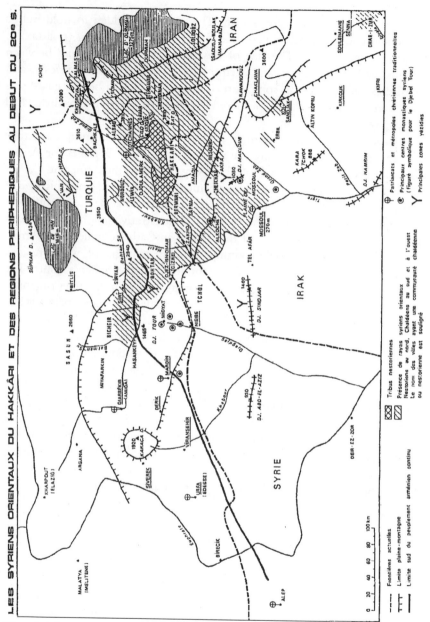

Map 2: The Eastern Syriacs of Hakkari and neighboring regions at the beginning of the twentieth century. From Michel Chevalier, *Les Montagnards Chrétiens du Hakkâri et du Kurdistan septentrional* (1983), map I.

CHRISTIAN MISSIONARIES

Catholic missionaries had been sporadically working in northern Mesopotamia since the Middle Ages. During the Early Modern period, Diyarbekir became a center of Catholicism for the various Syriac clergymen who had converted from Nestorianism. However, in the nineteenth century the number of missionaries and the extent of their work increased greatly and the Catholics were no longer unchallenged. Protestant missionaries came from many countries, representing a wide variety of denominations. In response the Dominicans, Capuchins, Lazarists, and Jesuits opened permanent Catholic missions. Since it was forbidden on pain of death for a Muslim to convert to another religion, the missionaries targeted the indigenous Christian and Yezidi populations but secretly wooed heterodox Muslims like the Alevites. It was inevitable that missionaries began to compete with each other. There has been much suspicion that European, Russian, and American missionaries had an overall negative impact on the situation of the native Christians, particularly in the decades leading up to World War I.

Roman Catholic priests and missionaries settled in Mesopotamia in the eighteenth century and made a permanent presence. Most of them were French Dominicans who worked not just among the Chaldeans, who were an already established uniate Church, but also with the Syriacs and Armenians, among whom they made many converts. An important cultural center was the Dominican mission and seminary in Mosul. By 1915, the Armenian Catholics were reported to identify themselves primarily as "Catholics and actually could not speak Armenian" but rather spoke Arabic.[24] Early in the twentieth century, the Catholics had begun making many converts among some of the Assyrian tribes, particularly the Jilu. The Eugène Boré Lazarists and the Sisters of Saint Vincent de Paul established a misson at Urmia in Iran during the 1830s. It was active among the Chaldeans, Nestorians, and Armenians and made some converts. This mission existed through World War I and played an important role as a sanctuary for refugees of all faiths during the Ottoman occupation of western Persia (map 2).

There was a sizable Syriac group of Catholics who had left the Syriac Orthodox Church, causing a schism. Afterward the Catholics and the Orthodox Syriacs remained in deep conflict and were not on speaking terms. A formal Syriac Catholic Church organization emerged in the last half of the seventeenth century.[25] In Mesopotamia the Armenian Catholic Church

---

[24] Ishaq Armalto, *Al-Qusara fi nakabat al-nasara* [The calamities of the Christians] (1919), 30.

[25] Joseph, *Muslim–Christian Relations*, 40–54.

was centered on Mardin. From the appointment of Malkun Tazbaz in 1708 there was an unbroken succession of archbishops. The diocese of the Mardin archbishop extended southward to Baghdad, Basra, Mosul, and Deyr-Zor.

American Protestant missionaries began working in the region in the mid 1830s, when missions in Mosul and Urmia were founded. At first the Protestant missionaries were particularly attracted to the Nestorian tribes. At least one of them speculated that he had found the lost tribes of Israel.[26] Also, it was hoped that the young Nestorians could be trained as missionaries and that through their mediation Christianity could once again spread throughout Asia, repeating their accomplishments in medieval times.[27] The American mission in Urmia was taken over by the Presbyterian Board of Missions in 1870. However, there were also American Baptists and German and Swedish Lutheran missions active in the Urmia neighborhood. Within Anatolia, American missionaries were based in Mardin, Midyat, Diyarbekir, Van, and Bitlis and some other places. Sometimes a foreign mission had many domestic employees and grew into a large complex of adjacent buildings containing clinics, hospitals, primary schools for boys and girls, colleges, dormitories, and orphanages as well as chapels. In Van and Urmia, the mission hospital was the primary medical institution in the town. As a rule, Protestant converts belonged to the wealthy merchant families. Swedish missionaries considered the Syriacs easier to convert than the Armenians.[28]

The Anglican Church began its missionary activities in the 1840s when English clergymen were sent to make official contact with the Nestorian and Chaldean leaders. The Archbishop of Canterbury created a mission to the "Assyrians" in 1886. A. C. Tait, Archbishop of Canterbury, was the first major English-language opinion-builder to use the term "Assyrians" for the Oriental Christians. He did this in a fund-raising appeal in 1870 to set up the "Assyrian Christians Aid Fund." The reason given for the use of "Assyrian" was that it was considered more neutral compared with the negative-sounding Nestorian, with its intimation of heresy.[29]

---

[26] Asahel Grant, *The Nestorians; or, the Lost Tribes* (1845).

[27] John Joseph, *The Modern Assyrians of the Middle East: Encounters with Western Christian Missions, Archaeologists, and Colonial Powers* (2000), 67–68.

[28] John Hultvall, *Mission och vision i Orienten: Svenska Missionsförbundets mission i Transkaukasien-Persien 1882–1921* (1991), 59–61.

[29] J. F. Coakley, *The Church of the East and the Church of England: A History of the Archbishop of Canterbury's Assyrian Mission* (1992), 65–66, 5. According to Coakley, the term may have come from the pen of the missionary George Percy Badger,

Missionary activities accelerated after the 1895–96 massacres. Because of the great number of orphans, widows, handicapped, refugees, and destitute, there was need for hospitals, orphanages, and sheltered workplaces. German missionaries and philanthropists were active in the central provinces of Anatolia. Particularly important was the Deutschen Hülfsbundes für Armenien, founded in 1896, with its leader Johannes Lepsius. This began its work in Aleppo, Harput, Van, and Urfa building mission stations, orphanages, and hospitals. About the same time, Lepsius also created the Deutsche Orient-Mission, which had stations in Varna in Bulgaria and Urmia in Iran.[30] Some of the female personnel of the German mission orphanages had been recruited in Scandinavia by the Women's Mission Union based in Copenhagen.

The Russians established a Russian Orthodox spiritual mission in Urmia in 1898. This mission was integrated into an overall foreign policy strategy to increase Russian influence in the area. The propagandizing was particularly focused on the Nestorians along the Iranian–Turkish border regions. The Russian ambassador in Constantinople, M. N. Girs, wrote that the "Nestorians appear essential instruments to enable the spreading of our influence in Kurdistan."[31] The energetic Archimandrate Sergei led the mission, and by World War I he had established a teacher training college, a school for girls, and sixty-three village schools educating 1,845 pupils. He succeeded in enticing Mar Ilya, the bishop of Supurgan, to convert to Russian Orthodoxy. On the eve of World War I, Sergei made many contacts with Mar Shimun and traveled throughout the Hakkari Mountains. He reported an agreement for the conversion of the Assyrian tribes to Orthodoxy on July 8, 1914, but the outbreak of war made it impossible to follow up this step.[32] It was claimed that twenty thousand Assyrians belonged to the Orthodox Church.

By the early twentieth century, interreligious conflict had polarized. The tolerance implied by the traditional millet system was a dead letter, and in face-to-face confrontations the non-Muslims risked being called *gawur*, infidels.

---

who was Tait's expert on East Syriac matters.

[30] Hans-Lukas Kieser, *Der verpasste Friede: Mission, Ethnie und Staat in den Ostprovinzen der Türkei 1839–1938* (2000), 160–63.

[31] M. S. Lazarev, *Kurdistan i kurdskaya problema (90-e gody XIX veka – 1917 g.)* [Kurdistan and the Kurdish question, 1890–1917] (1964), 232.

[32] Ibid., 162, 234.

Pre-war Population of the Oriental Churches

Reckoning the size of the Oriental Christian population was never a straightforward matter. The Ottoman Empire did not have a standing bureau of the census or a statistical central bureau. Instead, counts of the population were made at varying intervals. Classifications of ethnic and religious groups differed inexplicably between counts. In the absence of stable and reliable statistics, every serious observer, and even some who were not so serious, made calculated guesses, the accuracy of which it was not easy to check. Because the size and percentage of the non-Muslim population was a sensitive international political issue, publishing statistics concerning them was not an innocent practice.

There exist some principles of source criticism in historical studies of population. One is to use sources that are as close as possible in time to the era being studied. Another is that the person supplying the figures should be in a position to know at first hand the situation of the population described. A third is that the figures should be based on the lowest level, if possible from lists of individuals or households. If that is not possible, then the level of individual villages, parishes, or towns is the next best alternative. It should be possible to crosscheck figures with data coming from other sources.

There do exist some aggregate province-level statistics, but they cannot be accepted at face value. The Assyro-Chaldean delegation at the Paris peace conference published a table designed to supplement the Armenian Patriarch's statistics.[33] The Armenian Patriarch had published figures for the central and northern Armenian provinces but had omitted the southeast, reasoning that few Armenians lived there. The region delimited by the Assyro-Chaldean delegation was "the vilayets of Mosul, Diyarbekir, the sanjaks of Aleppo, Urfa, Deyr-Zor, Sa'irt, Hakkari and the regions of Urmia and Salmas in Persia"; it further delimited the region as the parts of the named territorial units that were on the left bank of the Murad Su and the left bank of the Euphrates River. This resulted in a total Christian population for the designated part of the Ottoman Empire amounting to 620,200 individuals, of which 118,200 were Armenian (chiefly Catholic) and 485,000 Assyro-Chaldeans. This contrasts with the Armenian Patriachate's 1,018,000 Armenians and 123,000 "Nestorians, Jacobites, and Chaldeans." It is possible that the two tables can be combined.[34]

---

[33] This table is reprinted in appendix 2 below.

[34] *La question assyro-chaldéenne devant la conférence de la paix.* This is a 16-page pamphlet dated July 19, 1919, signed by Said A. Namik and Rustem Nedjib, the main

It is not clear where the Armenian Patriarchate and the Assyro-Chaldean delegation found their statistics, but they must have come from sources assembled by the Ottoman bureaucracy, rather than from their own dioceses and deaneries. First, the figures cover many more groups than just the Armenians and Syriacs. Second, those who made the tables were able to divide up provinces along lines that corresponded to contemporary Ottoman administrative boundaries, rather than to the century-old bishoprics. Further, the total populations are subdivided into narrow ethnic rather than religious categories. The Christian churches would have had no reason to count the number of Muslim Turkmen, Circassians, sedentary Kurds, nomadic Kurds, Zazas, Lazes, Kamavends, Gypsies (Roma), and so on. The diverse category of non-Muslims is subdivided into Jews, Kizilbash, Yezidis, Shabaks, Sarlis, Babis, and so on. All these anomalies indicate a source within the Ottoman administration that had been gathering information on ethnic minorities. Another sign that the source does not originate in a church context is that the important religious distinction between Orthodoxy, Catholicism, and Protestantism is completely missing. We have thus to judge figures that in all probability were produced by a government ethnographic investigation. Both the Armenian and the Assyro-Chaldean leaders ignored the official Ottoman census of 1914, which gave figures for non-Muslims that were thoroughly misleading and inaccurate. As a token of the confused nature of the official census-taking and the lack of coordination between the local correspondents, the Syriac Orthodox population is shown in three separate categories: *Süryaniler*, *Eski Süryaniler*, and *Jakobiler*.[35] Under-registration of minorities was a fact of life in Ottoman statistics. Contemporaries knew about the defective registration. When the Chaldean Church described the extent of the massacres in the town of Sa'irt, it pointed out that although the government registers only included the names of 767 of its congregation, many more than that number had been annihilated at a single slaughter in that town, and there was a series of massacres.[36]

Assyro-Chaldean delegates. "Statistical Analysis of the Racial Elements in the Ottoman Vilayets of Erzeroum, Van, Bitlis, Mamouret-ul-Aziz, Diarbekir, and Sivas, Drawn Up 1912 by the Armenian Patriarchate at Constantinople," in *The Treatment of the Armenians in the Ottoman Empire, 1915–1916*, ed. James Bryce and Arnold Toynbee (1916), uncensored edition (2000), 656.

[35] This gives 54,750 Syriacs, 4,133 Old Syriacs, 13,211 Chaldeans, 6,932 Jacobites, and 8,091 Nestorians in the entire Ottoman Empire in 1914. Kemal H. Karpat, *Osmanlı Nüfusu (1830–1914) Demografik ve Sosyal Özellikleri* [Ottoman population 1830–1914, demographic and social characteristics] (2003), 226–27.

[36] Note addressée au Consulat de France en Mésopotamie par un ecclésiastique

These aggregate statistics need to be checked against an independent source on a lower level of aggregation. One suitable document for scientific analysis that gives village-level figures for the pre-war Syriac population was presented by Agha Petros, the head of the Assyro-Chaldean delegation, at the peace conference in Lausanne in 1922.[37] It contains 30 pages and covers more than nine hundred villages grouped either by district (kazas) or by church diocese. There are two separate parts to this document: part A, of 17 pages, deals with the Syriac populations of Van, Bitlis, and Urmia (in Iran) provinces; part B, of 13 pages, gives the Syriac population of Diyarbekir province and the sanjak of Urfa. These are the absolute core areas for Syriac settlement, but tens of thousands of Syriacs lived outside them in other parts of Anatolia like Sivas, Harput, Adana, Adiyaman (Hassanmansur), Marash, and Anteb, as well as farther south in the provinces of Aleppo and Mosul. In addition, an untold number of Syriacs had moved to the expanding Russian Empire towns of Baku and Tbilisi.

In Part A, "Liste des villages, des habitations et nationalites," all of the names of the villages are typewritten according to French principles of transcription. Alongside the names, ethnicity is designated in the categories Assyrians, Kurds, Armenians, or Jews. For the districts of Upper Baroude, Baz, Sarai, and Urmia, the number of households was typewritten at the same time the list was drawn up. Thus the group that started the list should have hailed from those districts. For the other districts, the number of households is written in ink with the same pen and slanted style as used by Agha Petros in signing the cover letter. He entered the number of households; his numbers can at times be sloppy and he sometimes changes the ethnic classifications from Assyrian to Kurd and vice versa. Accuracy is problematic: at times the figures for an entire district are rounded off to the nearest ten and sometimes they are exact.

Part B has the official stamp in Syriac script, "Assyrian Chaldean Delegation Paris" and bears the heading "Nombre des villes, bourgs et villages, habités totalement ou partiellement par les Assyro-Chaldéens en 1914 dans tout le vilayet de Diarbekir et le sandjak d'Ourfa." This register differs considerably from Part A in being free from changes and additions. It only lists Syriac villages, and it gives the population rather than number of households. However, all of the figures are rounded off rather than exact. It

---

chaldéen," in Arthur Beylerian, *Les Grandes Puissants: L'Empire Ottoman et les arméniens dans les archives françaises (1914–1918)* (1983), 478.

[37] Petros to Mr. Adam (British Delegation Lausanne), November 25, 1922, PRO FO 371 839/23 82893; published in appendix 2 below.

is evident that the list intends to include all religions: Orthodox, Catholic, and Protestant.

Analysis of the lists results in the figures seen in table 1, presented by district. The 38,148 listed households in nearly 600 villages can be multiplied by an average household size to get a figure for the total population. Five is a normal multiplier for pre-modern households. Given the low ages at marriage, high fertility, and close kin relations, there seems no apparent reason to use a smaller household size. Thus this list results in an Assyrian or East Syriac population of 190,740, or rounded off, 190,000.

Table 1: Number of Assyrian, Armenian, Jewish, and Kurdish households within the Nestorian dioceses in the Hakkari, Urmia, and Bohtan regions

Diocese	Number of Assyrian villages	Number of Households			
		Assyrians	Armenians	Jews	Kurds
Upper Baroude	26	608	200		100
Jilu	21	1,683			
Nerwa	4	315			346
Doustican	8	212			169
Baz	7	370			70
Lower Livon	9	399			
Upper Livon	19	757			
Noduz	11	710			
Sarai	16	660			1,000
Shamdinan	20	826			
Zazon	13	713		30	379
Guardean	5	260			
Galia	34	2,374			2,822
Waltou	54	2,699			275
Chal	9	843			
Upper Tiyyari	26	3,107			432
Albak	12	659	481		893
Gawar (Hakkari part)	26	1,040	310	100	1,068
Urmia	91	10,148			
Gawar (Persian part)	17	1,089			
Upper Barwar	51	2,788		49	1,947
Thkuma	14	2,484			50
Barwar (in Bohtan)	15	727	691		668
Inspirad	48	2,577			2,488
Total	**594**	**38,148**	**1,682**	**179**	**12,707**

Is there any corroborating evidence from other sources that the East Syriac population was between one hundred and two hundred thousand? The Russians showed great interest in the Assyrians as a potential military and political resource. Therefore the Russian military intelligence commissioned several investigations to ascertain the strength of the group. Just before the start of the war, Laloyan, a Russian geographer, estimated the size of the Assyrian population in the Ottoman Empire at 135,000 for 1914.[38] A report by Major General P. I. Aver'yanov, the Russian General Staff expert on Kurdistan, in 1912 asserted that there were about 100,000 Nestorians in all of the Ottoman territories and that 75,000 of them lived in the Hakkari sandjak, where they made up from one fourth to three fourths of the population of the districts of Julamerk, Albak, Gawar, and Oramar.[39] Mar Shimun gave the total figure of 150,000 in 1912.[40] As for the East Syriac population of Iran, the Assyro-Chaldean delegation to the Paris Peace Conference stated that the pre-war population of Iran was 78,000, and this is very close to the figure 76,000 supplied by Laloyan, the Russian geographer.[41] Surprisingly, Laloyan's count for Urmia province is much higher than Agha Petros's figure of 55,000 because the latter omits the entire northern sector including the Chaldean diocese of Salmas and many Nestorian settlements such as Ganganchin, Yagmrali, Zomala, Tebatan, Shirbat, and Karadjalu.

A possible reason behind Agha Petros's omission indicates the political use of this list. Its purpose was probably not to give the entire Assyro-Chaldean pre-war population at all. Rather, it was to give the pre-war population for those tracts that the delegation believed it had a fighting chance of including within the borders of a future Assyro-Chaldean state. Thus areas that would be outside its anticipated borders were not relevant.

The Assyro-Chaldean delegation's list B concerning the West Syriac population gives the breakdown by district seen in table 2. This list totals 133,000 Assyro-Chaldeans. From the title it presumably includes not just the Syrian Orthodox Church, but also Syriac Catholics and Protestants. It is not clear from the text whether or not it includes members of the uniate

---

[38] E. A. Laloyan, "Aisori vanskago vilaiet" [Assyrians in Van vilayet] (1914), 4.

[39] P. I. Aver'yanov, *Etnograficheskii i voenno-politicheskii obzor' aziatskikh' vlad'nii ottomanskoi imperii* [Ethnographic and military-political description of the Asian provinces of the Ottoman empire] (1912), 24.

[40] Vladimir Genis, *Vitse-konsul Vvedenski sluzhba v Persii I Bukharskom khanstve (1906–1920 gg.) Rossiskaya diplomatiya v sud'bakh* [Vice-Consul Vvedenski's service in Persia and the Khanate of Bukhara, 1906–1920] (2003), 339.

[41] *La Question Assyro-Chaldéenne*, 15–16; Laloyan, "Aisori vanskago vilaiet," 4.

Table 2: Assyro-Chaldeans living in Diyarbekir vilayet and Urfa sanjak, 1914

District	Number of villages	Population Size
Diyarbekir central	32	14,450
Silvan	14	4,000
Lije	10	4,100
Derek	1	500
Argana Maden	1	100
Palu	1	50
Severek	33	7,750
Viranshehir	16	3,700
Mardin	9	14,100
Saur	7	3,700
Nisibin	58	16.700
Habab	9	2,600
Jezire	55	17,800
Midyat	47	20,550
Beshiri	28	4,890
Bafaya	15	2,000
Urfa	11	16,000
Total	**347**	**133,000**

Chaldean Church. But its congregations in Dara and Tel-Arman and the entire diocese of Sa'irt are not mentioned.

A way to check whether the population contains more than just Syriac Orthodox is to compare with statistics for that church that were prepared for the Paris peace conference in 1920 (table 3). They were presented by the archbishop of Syria, Severius A. Barsaum.[42]

Six of the districts lie outside of the Diyarbekir vilayet; if they are excluded, the number of Syrian Orthodox families in Diyarbekir becomes 11,535. It is not obvious what sort of multiplier to use. Although 5 is common for households, here the measure is "families." Families in Mesopotamia tended to be very large, and they could include kin even though they lived in separate households.[43] A high Ottoman tax official, Ali Emîri, who had served in many of the eastern provinces, wrote that Christian families, and particularly the families of rural poor, had very many children—often as many as eight or ten. Perhaps it is not improbable that 10 could be a suitable multiplier, and this would give a total size of the Syrian Orthodox

---

[42] Severius A. Barsaum, Memorandum No. 23 February 1920 PRO FO 371 E-1221/ 110-112.

[43] Ali Emîri, *Osmanlı Vilâyât-i Şarkiyyesi* [The Otttoman eastern vilayets] (2005), 24.

Table 3: Population figures for the Syriac Orthodox Church, 1920

District	Number of villages	Number of families
Diyarbekir	30	764
Silvan	9	174
Lije	10	658
Derek	1	350
Severek	30	897
Viranshehir	16	303
Mardin	8	880
Sawro	7	880
Nisibin	50	1,000
Jezire	26	994
Beshiri	30	718
Bafaya	15	282
Midyat	47	3,935
Bitlis	12	130
Sa'irt (Bitlis vilayet)	1	100
Shirvan (Bitlis vilayet)	9	283
Garzan (Bitlis vilayet)	22	744
Harput (Mamuret ul-Aziz)	24	508
Urfa (Aleppo vilayet)	1	50
Total	**345**	**13,350**

population of 133,350, of which 115,350 resided in the province of Diyarbekir. Thus it would appear that Part B of the Assyro-Chaldean delegation list and the list presented by Barsaum solely for the Orthodox Church have similar totals. It is highly likely that the Catholics and Protestants are not counted in list B and must be added.

CHALDEANS

The largest number of Catholics was in the uniate Chaldean Church with its patriarch of Babylon, residing in Mosul. Just before the war, Joseph Tfinkdji, a Chaldean priest from Mardin, published statistics that he had collected for the entire Chaldean Church in 1913 (table 4; map 3).[44] This was a massive job for one man and very time-consuming, but it resulted in a systematic count. The published figures are by diocese and broken down into villages. For each village he rounds off the population. A few uncertain figures are indicated with question marks. His study revealed a church that was stagnating, and in places like Tel-Arman, Viranshehir, and Derike, the small

---

[44] Joseph Tfinkdji, "L'Eglise chaldéenne catholique autrefois et aujourd'hui" (1914).

Table 4: Size of the Chaldean Church in June 1913*

Diocese	Number of parishes	Size of population
Amid (Diyarbekir)*	9	4,180
Sa'irt (Bohtan)*	37	5,380
Jezire*	17	6,400
Mardin*	6	1,670
Van*	10	3,850
Urmia (Iran)*	21	7,800
Salmas (Iran)*	12	10,460
Sena (Iran)*	1	900
Kirkuk (Irak)	9	5,840
Mosul (Patriarchy)	26	42,890
Akra (Iraq)	19	2,390
Amadia (Iraq)	17	4,970
Zakho (Iraq)	15	4,880
Total	**177**	**101,610**

*Asterisk indicates a place within the zone of widespread massacres.

number of parishioners was forced to attend services led by Armenian Catholic or Syriac Catholic priests. In Midyat and Nisibin, the office of priest had been vacant for many years. Other parishes had disappeared owing to "bad times."[45]

As a small church, the Chaldean dioceses covered a wide territory and seldom corresponded with Ottoman administrative boundaries. Thus the diocese of Diyarbekir included far-away Urfa. Tkfindji's figures indicate a slight population increase compared with the only previous attempt, in 1896, to establish the number of souls. At that time there were 78,790 Chaldeans in both the Ottoman Empire and Persia.[46]

Returning to Tfinkdji's statistics, they reveal that slightly more than 40,000 Chaldeans lived within the zone of the most intense anti-Christian activity, which are marked in the table by an asterisk. The main part of the Chaldean population lived outside the killing fields. Many independent sources state that the valis prohibited massacres in the province of Mosul.[47]

---

[45] Ibid., 511.

[46] J.-B. Chabot, "État religieux des diocèses formant le patriarcat chaldéen de Babylone au 1er janvier 1896" (1896).

[47] Jacques Rhétoré, *"Les chrétiens aux bêtes": Souvenirs de la guerre sainte proclamée par les Turcs contre les chrétiens en 1915*, 170–73, 348, 352; Holstein to Wangenheim, June 10, 1915, in Johannes Lepsius, *Deutschland und Armenien: Sammlung diplomatischer Aktenstücke* (1919), document 78.

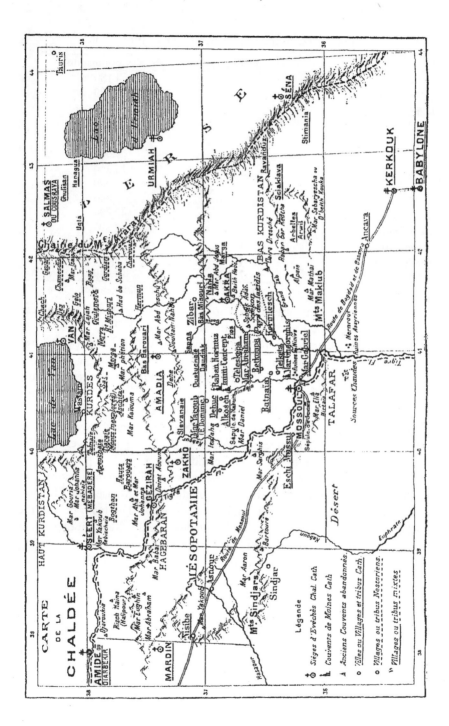

Map 3 *[opposite]*: Map of the Chaldean Church. From Joseph Tfinkdji, "Église chaldéenne catholique autrefois et aujourd'hui" (1914), 451.

The only known exception was an attack on the village and monastery of Mar Yacoub near Zakho, but the responsible Kurdish chief was executed for that. Also, the province of Aleppo, with the exception of Urfa and the terrible extermination of refugee camps around Deyr-Zor in 1916, witnessed relatively few armed attacks.

There is some risk that Tfinkdji's and Agha Petros's lists overlap. Tfinkdji's list is focused on the Chaldean religion, Agha Petros purports to focus on a secular Assyro-Chaldean national identity and should thus be free from religious considerations. Apparently, however, Agha Petros's list does have a religious element since it does not even consider the Chaldean regions of Sa'irt and Salmas. There is a risk of double counting in Diyarbekir, Mardin, Jezire, and Van, as some (but not all) of the same villages appear on both lists. Even so, the Chaldean statistics do record Catholic villages that are absent from the Assyro-Chaldean delegation's list. It is not possible to give the size of the overlap with any accuracy, but is surely a few thousand.

There are no similar village-by-village statistics for the Syriac Catholic, Armenian Catholic, or Protestant churches. This forces the use of aggregate numbers, and they must be handled with caution, as the sources are not transparent. From December 1914 to November 1916, some French Dominican monks were interred under house arrest in a building that belonged to the Syrian Catholic Patriarchy in Mardin. As scholars they tried to make accurate estimates about the size of the Catholic population. Jacques Rhétoré stated that in the province of Diyarbekir there were 12,500 Catholic Armenians, 11,120 Chaldeans, and 5,600 Syriac Catholics.[48] Rhétoré's figures for the Chaldeans are very close to what a reworking of Tfinkdji's statistics gives, and it is likely that the two priests were able to consult with each other in Mardin. The figures for the Catholic Armenians probably came from the office of Archbishop Ignatius Maloyan, who before his death was a frequent guest at the Syrian Catholic Patriarchy in Mardin.

Rhétoré also mentioned 725 Protestants, but he was in no position to know much about that organization. The American Protestant missionaries found their converts in successful merchant families of Syriac Orthodox background, and the tax collectors paid close attention to their numbers and

---

[48] Rhétoré, *"Les chrétiens aux bêtes,"* 136.

Table 5. Population on the eve of World War I for the Oriental churches in northern Mesopotamia and adjacent regions*

Group	Source	Population Size
Assyro-Chaldeans (East Syriac)	Assyro-Chaldean delegation list A	190,000
Assyro-Chaldeans (West Syriac)	Assyro-Chaldean delegation list B	133,000
Chaldean Church	Tfinkdji	101,000
Syriac Catholic (Diyarbekir only)	Rhétoré	5,600
Armenian Catholic (Diyarbekir only)	Rhétoré	12,500
Syriacs in northern parts of Van, Bitlis-Sivas, Harput	Armenian Patriarchate	56,000
Assyro-Chaldeans in southern parts of Diyarbekir, Van, Bitlis plus Urfa, Der Zor, Mosul, and Urmia	Assyro-Chaldean delegation	563,000

* Note: The numbers should not be combined.

wealth. Tfinkji, the local priest, estimated that there were 1,000 Protestants in Mardin and 450 in Midyat.[49]

Table 5 assembles various population estimates for the pre-war Aramean populations of Anatolia and northern Mesopotamia. These are all contemporary, made before or just after the war. They indicate that the sizes of the different Oriental Churches were quite small. The Nestorians made up the largest church, with just under 200,000 members. It is not possible to add all of the statistics together because there is a risk of double counting. However, the figures presented by the Armenian Patriarchate and the Assyro-Chaldean delegation should complement each other, and thus can be summed. This results in a total figure of 619,000. Whether or not even this figure gives total coverage for Anatolia and Mesopotamia is hard to judge, but it does exclude the Aramean populations in the greater part of Syria, Lebanon, and Palestine.

---

[49] Joseph Tfinkdji, "Le Catholicisme à Mardin (Meopotamie)" (1914), 30; "Le Christianisme à Tour-Abdin," 453.

2 SETTING THE STAGE: KURDS AND TURKS, ARMENIANS AND SYRIACS

THE KURDISH QUESTION

With few exceptions, the Syriac and Armenian settlements in southeast Anatolia were in regions where Kurds made up the majority of the population and Kurdish chiefs, called *agha*s, held local political power. In premodern times, Syriacs and Kurds lived on close footing. Traditionally, the Assyrian religious leader Mar Shimun was second in command to the emir of Hakkari and ruled in his absence. Many Kurdish tribal confederations in Diyarbekir province had Syriac members.[1] The tribes of the Nisanai in northwest Iran, the permanently settled Muhallemi and Omerli of Mardin sanjak, had originally been Christians and had some remembrance of this, and some kept up ties with their Christian relatives.[2] Kurdish folklore also talks of friendly attitudes toward the Syriacs, but not toward the Armenians. One Kurdish proverb about the Nestorians is, "Between us there is but a hair's breadth, but between us and the Armenians a mountain." Love affairs between Kurdish men and Nestorian women were not unheard of.[3] Travelers sometimes classified the Nestorian tribesmen as "Christian Kurds." Basile Nikitine pointed to the common racial background when he studied the great number of abandoned churches and minuscule enclaves (including bishops' dioceses) squeezed among a Muslim population. In his view this was caused by the conversion to Islam and assimilation into Kurdish cul-

---

[1] Ziya Gökalp, *Kürt Aşiretleri Hakkinda Sosyolojik Tetkikler* [Sociological studies of Kurdish tribes] (1992).

[2] PRO FO 371 248/1223 W. A. Wigram intelligence report, March 1, 1919; Pierre Rondot, "Les tribus montagnards de l'Asie antérieure: Quelques aspects sociaux des populations Kurdes et Assyriennes" (1937).

[3] Edward Noel, "The Character of the Kurds as Illustrated by Their Proverbs and Popular Sayings" (1920), 90; Edgar T. A. Wigram, "The Ashiret Highlands of Hakkiari (Meopotamia)" (1914), 49–50; G. R. Driver, "The Religion of the Kurds" (1922).

ture of a previously much larger and more widespread Nestorian community.[4]

However, most Christians in eastern Anatolia were not free-living tribesmen, but instead lived from agriculture and herding and were the subjects of feudal Kurdish *agha*s or in a few cases equally feudal Nestorian *malek*s. Thus the Armenian and Syriac Questions became part and parcel of the complex Kurdish Question. Throughout the nineteenth century the bloody inter-ethnic and inter-religious conflicts were basically those between Sunni Kurds and members of the various Oriental Christian churches. The Christians found support in marginal Kurdish groups like the non-Muslim Yezidi, who were ostracized for worshipping the Devil, and the Dersim, who were heterodox Shi'a-believing Alavites, often termed *kizilbashi* (redheads) in Turkish.

Until the middle of the nineteenth century, the Kurdish population was divided into large, territorially based, tribal confederations ruled by hereditary emirs. Official emirates had been formed after Sultan Selim the Grim conquered Kurdistan in the early sixteenth century. An emirate was independent of the Ottoman government, but the emir had responsibility for unifying the peoples within his territory and mediating between the chiefs of rival tribes and clans. Depending on the power of the central government, the emirs would either pay a set tribute to the sultan or be themselves paid a yearly income by the sultan. Slowly the Ottoman government increased its activity in the area to gain control over the larger towns, set up a juridical system, started collecting taxes, and reduced the independence of the emirs. After the fall of the emirs, Kurdish society was shattered. One of the few unifying forces was the leadership of the dervish orders, particularly the Nakshbandi order.

Chaos reigned througout northern Mesopotamia and Kurdistan during the early nineteenth century. Ottoman control, which had seldom been very strong anyway, disintegrated after the armies of the rebel Egyptian ruler, Muhammad Ali, won battles and occupied Syria, with the collaboration of some local Kurdish tribes. His foremost Kurdish supporters were the Kurdish-Arab tribal confederation of the Milli that lived between Diyarbekir and Aleppo. Later, under their paramount leader Ibrahim Pasha, they emerged as the most important confederation on the western fringe of Kurdistan. They fought continually against their main rival the Shammar Arabs, who lived in the steppe south of Jezire; and by pressing back the

---

[4] Basile Nikitine, "Les Kurdes et le Christianisme" (1922).

Shammar, the Milli moved into that area. Ibrahim displayed full loyalty to the sultan and was richly rewarded.[5]

Once the short-lived Egyptian occupation was over, awareness of Ottoman impotence inspired Kurdish chiefs to enlarge their rule. Some strove after autonomy similar to that achieved in Egypt. The more ambitious of them hoped eventually to create their own independent states. Although the Ottoman government made a priority of subduing the local tribes, it was no match for them.[6] Badr Khan, the Emir of Bohtan, a member of the Aziz dynasty, came very close to succeeding in the 1840s and made the town of Jezire his capital. Uniting the chiefs of Van, Hakkari, Miks, Kars, and Ardelan, he instituted a government, set up a standing army, and issued his own coins until he was defeated in 1845.[7] Even if these were mainly internal conflicts within the Kurdish nation, they had consequences for the Christian peoples, because they were pressed to take sides; the Assyrian tribes in particular had no hesitation in participating on the battlefield together with their Kurdish allies.

The Kurdish Emirate of Hakkari, which ruled fourteen Kurdish and Christian tribes, fell into turmoil as two members of the ruling house fought to become emir. The Assyrian highland tribes were integrated into the emirate, and Mar Shimun was the emir's second in command. A bloody conflict became unavoidable when the main body of the Assyrians supported the losing side in a struggle for the throne. They were loyal to the son of the previous emir. When the usurper Nur-Allah became the emir of Hakkari, he determined to take stronger control over the Christians living within his jurisdiction. He even attacked Kochanes in 1841, and this resulted in a permanent breach between the emirate and the Assyrians.[8] In this conflict the majority of the Assyrians supported Mar Shimun throughout, but there were some who, seeing the folly of opposition, broke with him and joined Nur-Allah's side. Thus the Nestorians began to divide and the political authority of Mar Shimun was no longer unquestioned.[9]

In 1843, a large-scale Kurdish revolt broke out when Nur-Allah and Badr Khan invaded Assyrian territory. In July of that year, Badr Khan at-

---

[5] Rondot, "Les tribus montagnards de l'Asie antérieure," 34–35.

[6] William Ainsworth, "An Account of a Visit to the Chaldeans, inhabiting Central Kurdistan; and of an Ascent of the Peak of Rowánduz (Túr Sheikhíwá) in the Summer of 1840" (1841), 21–22.

[7] "The Azizan or the Princes of Bhotan," (1949), 249–50.

[8] David McDowell, *A Modern History of the Kurds* (1996), 45.

[9] John Joseph, *The Modern Assyrians of the Middle East* (2000), 76–77.

tacked the Nestorians living in and near the town of Jezire and in the district of Barwar in the western approach to the Hakkari Mountains. Massacres continued over several years, and the number of Christians killed reached an estimated ten thousand persons.[10] Mar Shimun fled with his family to Mosul. A similar attack took place in 1846. Badr Khan's activities against the Nestorian Christians became internationally known through newspaper articles, and the Great Powers put pressure on the Porte to intervene.[11] These conflicts and the international attention resulted in a serious reassertion of Ottoman power in the area and the piecemeal destruction of the autonomy of the Kurdish emirates.[12] In themselves, the Christian massacres woke European politicians and public opinion to the "victimization" of the Ottoman Christians, the hostility of the Kurds, and the suspected collusion of the government authorities. It was an important milestone for public opinion concerning international protection for religious minorities.

After the destruction of the Kurdish emirates, Kurdistan dissolved into small-scale struggles at a low level. Gradually, Kurdish religious leaders called s*haykh*s took over the role of mediator between tribes and legitimate political unifying forces. The rise of the shaykhs, however, introduced a high degree of religiosity into the previously merely political struggles of Kurdistan. This combination of religion and politics made it more difficult for Kurdish leaders to ally with the Assyrian Nestorian Christians, the Yezidis, and Shi'a Kurds. In the wake of the Russo-Turkish war of 1877–78 there came a minor revolt of the Kurds of Hakkari and Bohtan headed by some of the many sons of Badr Khan. A more important incident, however, was the religiously inspired revolt of Shaykh Ubaydallah, which aimed to create an independent Kurdistan uniting Turkish and Persian Kurds. This major revolt actually achieved some territorial success. Ubaydallah hailed from Nihri, a border village in the Shamdinan district of Hakkari, where his very influential family led the Nakshbandi mystic order. Ubaydallah's forces invaded western Iran in 1880 and seized the rural areas west of Lake Urmia and even threatened the city of Tabriz.[13] At the time of World

---

[10] V. Minorsky, "Kurds, Kurdistān, iii: History, A: Pre-Islamic History; B: The Islamic Period up to 1920" (1981), 462.

[11] "Massacre of the Nestorian Christians," *Times of London*, September 6, 1843; "Nestorian Christians – Kurdistan," January 5, 1844; "The Nestorian Christians – Urmia," January 29, 1845.

[12] McDowell, *Modern History of the Kurds*, 46–47.

[13] Minorsky, "Kurds, Kurdistān," 465; M. M. van Bruinessen, "Shamdīnān" (1996); McDowell, *Modern History of the Kurds*, 53–59.

War I, the descendants of Badr-Khan (foremost among many rivals was the pro-Russian Abdul Razzek) and Shaykh Ubaydallah (his sons Abdul Khadir and Muhammed Sadiq and grandson Taha) would use the memory of these exploits to claim to be the natural leaders of the Kurdish independence movement. They also placed the union of Ottoman and Persian Kurds on the political agenda and made the border strip a magnet attracting spies, adventurers, and guerillas.

High religious and political tension imperiled Muslim–Christian relationships. The traditional division into a favored Muslim population and an underprivileged but tolerated Christian population eroded. Tolerance withered particularly in rural areas, where inherent conflicts between Christian farmers and nomadic Kurdish herders turned cruel. The Anglican minister W. A. Wigram authored a book on a journey he made through northern Mesopotamia just before World War I broke out. The Assyrian tribesmen told him that lately endemic inter-ethnic and inter-religious violence assumed more brutal proportions. He wrote that among the Muslim and Christian tribesmen the situation was

> by no means intolerable a generation ago … arms were approximately equal; and the Christians, though outnumbered, had strong positions to defend, and were of good fighting stock, as men of Assyrian blood should be. So, until Abdul Hamid's day, the parties were fairly matched on the whole; and generations of "cross-raiding" had evolved an understanding in the matter, capable of summary statement as "Take all you like, but do not damage what you leave; and do not touch the women." Thus livestock were fair lot, and so were carpets and other house-furniture, and arms of course. But the house must not be burnt, and standing crops and irrigating channels not touched, while a gentlemanly brigand would leave the corn-store alone. Women were never molested when a village of *ashirets* was raided, until a few years ago. And this was so thoroughly understood that it was not necessary even to guard them. … Of late things have changed for the worse in this respect. Women are not always respected now; and the free distribution of rifles among the Kurds has done away will all the old equality. This was done, when the late Sultan raised the "*Hamidiye*" battalions; partly for the defense of his throne, partly perhaps with the idea of keeping the Christians in subjection. Now when to odds in numbers you add the additional handicap implied in the difference between Mauser and flintlock, the position becomes impossible; and the balance has since inclined steadily against the Christian tribes.[14]

---

[14] W. A. Wigram and Edgar Wigram, *The Cradle of Mankind: Life in Eastern Kurdi-*

A proven technique of imperial rule is to divide and conquer. The Ottoman government sought to gain the loyalty of certain Sunni Kurdish tribes who were not previously known for rebellion. They could be flattered and given privileges, while the rebellious former emirs were ignored. Thus the traditional leading dynasties like the Badr Khan were pushed into nearly permanent opposition, while new tribes or tribes that had moved into new areas became the object of government favoritism. The aim, naturally, was to undermine traditional leaders and to attach groups that for various reasons needed state support in order to flourish. One aspect of this policy was an attempt to integrate the elite of certain selected Kurdish tribes into the Ottoman establishment. One example of this selection was the southern part of the province of Diyarbekir. Historically this was controlled by a confederation called the Haverkan, which was large enough to include Arab Bedouin tribes and Syriac Christians. Under the emirate era, the chief of this confederation was a vassal of the emir of Bohtan. As part of the crushed Bohtan state, the Haverkan tribes were anti-government and kept up a chronic low-intensity local rebellion. Into this area moved new tribes belonging to the Dakshuri confederation. They were strangers to the area and had no previous relation to Bohtan. However, the Dakshuri had the support of the Ottoman government. Thus small conflicts over villages and grazing lands quickly turned into a conflict between the Haverkan and the authorities.[15] Up to and through World War I, part of the Haverkan was always in a state of revolt against the government. During the Christian massacres, some of the Haverkan in Tur Abdin had the courage to protect their Christian neighbors just as much from defiance of the government as from humanitarian morality.

Starting in 1891, a Cossack-like military force, *Hamidiye* irregular cavalry regiments (named after the reigning Sultan Abdul Hamid II), was recruited from select loyal Kurdish tribes. The chiefs became the commanding officers. Each regiment had between 512 and 1,152 soldiers, who were given modern rifles, ammunition, dashing uniforms, and ranks. Big confederations could form more than one regiment, while small tribes formed only a few companies. The regimental officers and the sons of tribal chiefs were educated in military schools.

A stated aim of the Hamidiye regiments was to reinforce the border areas in case of attack. Thus the first regiments were set up in the north-

---

stan (1914), 167–68.

[15] Martin van Bruinessen, *Agha, Shaykh and State: The Social and Political Structures of Kurdistan* (1992), 101–3.

eastern areas around Erzincan, Hinis, Malazgirt, and Van in 1891, where the brunt of a Russian attack could be expected. In 1898, similar regiments were set up in northern Mesopotamia, which was not under threat of invasion. Obviously the regiments had functions that were not connected with military defense, and during World War I their war record was abysmal; some galloped home in panic already in the war's second week.[16] In peacetime, the regiments proved highly disruptive of civilian life. Tribes with regiments realized they had an insurmountable superiority over rival tribes that did not. The soldiers could be used to settle scores in local vendettas. The Ottoman authorities dared not intervene, because they needed to be able to call on the loyalty of the Hamidiye regimental tribes in case of a major crisis. Further, as the Ottoman state had great financial problems and could not always pay wages, the regiments were assigned certain Christian villages from which they could collect or extort taxes. This was a situation that naturally encouraged abuse.[17] The regiments had a bad influence on local politics and proved to have little worth on the battlefront.

In the Mardin region, the main Hamidiye regiments were the 41st, 42nd, and 43rd, which were camped in Viranshehir and recruited from the Milli confederation. Among the commanders of the Milli regiments were the paramount leader Ibrahim Pasha (41st) and his two sons Abdulhamid (42nd) and Mahmud (43rd). The 44th regiment was based in Siwerak, and it recruited from the Karakechi tribe headed by Halil. The 45th regiment recruited from the Kiki-Kikan tribe under Reshid. The 46th was based in Siwerak and recruited from the Bucak tribe, whose leader was Yusuf Agha. The 47th regiment recruited from the Tayy, who were Bedouin Arabs living near Nisibin. Finally, the 48th and 49th regiments recruited from the Miran tribe headed by Mustafa Pasha and his son Abdulkarim Bey.[18] In the Hakkari Mountains, the Kurdish regiments were formed among the loyal Artoshi confederation: the 50th regiment was led by Haji Bey of Hadzhan, the 56th by Hassan Bey of Shepefanli, the 59th by Hurshid Bey of the Pinyanish tribe (a direct descendent of Nur-Allah, the last emir of Hakkari), and the 60th by Omer Bey of Shidan.[19]

Tribes with Hamidiye regiments were normally loyal to the Sultan, and so they naturally opposed the Young Turk revolution of 1908. They had a

---

[16] Ishaq Armalto, *Al-Qusara fi nakabat al-naasara* (1919), 109.
[17] McDowell, *Modern History of the Kurds*, 59–60.
[18] Suavi Aydin et al., *Mardin. Aşiret – Cemaat – Devlet* (2000), 318.
[19] R. I. Termen, *Otchet' o poezdke v sandzhak Khekkiari, Vanskago vilaiet v 1906 gody* [Report of travel in the sanjak of Hakkari, Van vilayet in 1906] (1910), 147–50.

considerable stake in keeping him in power. The Sultan had given them arms, money, and superior status, and the commanders assumed lifestyles reminiscent of the old emirs. Several of these leaders chose exile in Iran at the autonomous Khanate of Maku, rather than stay in the new constitutional regime, and lived there on banditry in the border regions. The Young Turk movement was composed of many career military officers, and as such they were against the very idea of irregular cavalry units outside military discipline and normal chains of command. Ibrahim Pasha, leader of the Milli, attempted a revolt with the three regiments recruited from his tribe, and he died during this campaign.

The Kurdish attitude toward the new constitutional regime was far from favorable. Talk of reducing the number of Hamidiye regiments and placing them under direct military control discredited the Young Turks in the eyes of the tribes that would be affected. Also, traditional anti-Sultan Kurdish leaders aspiring for independence felt little attraction to the Young Turk policies. Instead, the latter identified with Pan-Kurdish nationalism and tried even to bind together the various tribes of Turkish and Iranian Kurdistan.[20] Continually in opposition, Amin Ali Badr Khan was a founding member of the political party *Kurdistan Ta'ali we Taraqi Jamiyati* (Society for the Rise and Progress of Kurdistan), founded in 1908. Midhat Badr Khan started the journal *Kurdistan* in 1889 in Cairo, and Abdur Rahman Badr Khan and Sureya Badr Khan served as editors.[21] Throughout Kurdistan, a political movement began about 1911 under the slogan *Ev khulli – khulli yammae*, meaning "This land – our land." Traditional leaders adhered to the Kurdish nationalist movement that called for autonomy and opposition to the government. Many would-be leaders dealt secretly with the Russians. Among them were the cousins Husayin and Abdul Rezzak Badr Khan of Bohtan, Shaykh Taha of Nihri, and Shaykh Abdul Salam of Barzan. Russia also had contacts with Mar Shimun of the Assyrians and with some of the Yezidi leaders. Russia offered to help the Kurds gain autonomy, and this lured the Ottomans into making similar commitments. In this game the Kurdish nationalists switched sides between the Russians and the Ottomans depending on their perception of which of them was more likely to fulfill their promises.[22]

Events culminated after the *Bab-i Ali* military coup of January 23, 1913, brought on the dictatorship of the warlords Enver, Talaat, and Jemal.

---

[20] M. S. Lazarev, *Kurdistan i kurdskaya problema* (1964), 155.
[21] "The Azizan," 250; McDowell, *Modern History of the Kurds*, 90–95.
[22] Lazarev, *Kurdistan*, chaps. 5–6, pp. 138–250.

Inspired by the recent success of the Albanians in achieving their own Muslim state, Kurdish political leaders made a concerted effort to secede similarly. Within a short time there were serious Kurdish revolts in the area around Bitlis, with the involvement of Badr Khan's descendants; north of Lake Van led by Huseyin, the leader of the Haydaranli Kurds; and in Iraq, led by Shaykh Said Barzani. In the spring of 1913, a new uprising had its epicenters in the towns of Jezire, Midyat, and Hasankeyf, and it gained some Syriac participation. In March 1914, a mass rising of Kurds took place in the province of Bitlis, and the capital was besieged. The Ottomans had to bring together large armies in order to crush these uprisings, and twelve leaders were executed in Bitlis on May 7, 1914.[23]

Faced with escalating Kurdish nationalist feelings, the Young Turk government reversed its previous rejection of the irregular Kurdish cavalry. Former regimental chiefs who had gone into exile in Iran could now return. New units were formed under the new designation Tribal Light Cavalry Regiments. To increase loyalty to the government, some Kurdish aghas and their sons were recruited into the local branches of the Committee for Union and Progress. This succeeded in splitting the Kurds into oppositional nationalists and loyal regime supporters.[24] Many Kurdish leaders were in exile, in hiding, or in prison when World War I broke out. Ottoman overanxiety resulted in reports of Kurdish revolts or the mass desertion of Kurdish soldiers to the Russian side.[25] The dream of Russian help in the struggle for independence induced Abdul Rezzak to ally with the Russians throughout the war, and he and some of his kin collaborated with the Russian occupation as provisional governors. In July 1915, Abdul Rezzak marched with Kurdish and Armenian volunteers toward his home base in Bitlis province, where he in fact did start a short-lived rebellion.[26]

---

[23] Lazarev, *Kurdistan*, 210–15; McDowell, *Modern History of the Kurds*, 100-101; Bergfeld to Bethmann Hollweg June 21, 1913, in *Die armenische Frage und der Genozid an den Armeniern in der Türkei (1913–1919)*, ed. Vardges Mikaelyan (2004), 46.

[24] McDowell, *History of the Kurds*, 99.

[25] Jevdet to Ministry of Interior November 17/30, 1914 document no. 1996 in *Askeri Tarih Belgeleri Dergisi* vol. 32, no. 83 (March 1983); Kazim to War Office November 21/22, 1914 document no. 1813 in ibid. vol. 31, no. 81 (1982).

[26] Mahmut Kamil to Enver July 22, 1915 document no. 2012 in *Askeri Tarih Belgeleri Dergisi* vol. 43, no. 85 (October 1983); Holstein to Deutsche Botschaft July 28, 1915 in Johannes Lepsius, *Deutschland und Armenien 1914–1918: Sammlung diplomatischer Aktenstücke* (1919), 114.

THE ARMENIAN QUESTION

Although they were important steps toward modernization, the *Tanzimat* reforms, which began in the 1830s, were generally ineffective, causing great frustration. The urban Christian elite probably experienced some improvement of status, but for the hundreds and thousands of farmers there was little change, except in the form of rising expectations of equality. In eastern Anatolia they lived in increasing insecurity. Suddenly, the situation of the Christian minorities became the focus of the European diplomatic corps.

Russia and the Ottoman Empire once again waged war in 1877 and 1878. That time it was primarily because Orthodox Christians in the Balkans wanted to break away and form their own states, and Russia intervened in their favor. The Ottomans lost this war very decisively, and Russia dictated a harsh peace treaty at San Stefano in which the Turks would cede much territory not just in the Balkans but also some Armenian provinces in northeastern Anatolia. The other Great Powers were taken by surprise and summoned a new international peace conference in Berlin with the underlying purpose of limiting the Russian gains. Uninvited, an Armenian delegation arrived at the Berlin Peace Conference and, though they were never recognized as a party to the conference, the final treaty included a clause to guarantee the minority status of the Armenians. Article 61 obliged the Sultan to introduce reforms to improve the condition of the Armenians, and to safeguard them against Circassian and Kurdish aggression. The article also called for monitoring the effect of these reforms in eastern regions with Armenian populations. This article was composed without consulting the Armenians, and they protested; it turned the Armenian Question into an international concern for generations to come. It also resulted in a backlash as Muslim opinion insisted on equating reforms for the non-Muslims with foreign plots to carve up the Ottoman Empire.

As a step along the diplomatic route to solving the Armenian Question, six provinces were singled out as the "six Armenian *vilayets*" in international law. The region where reforms were to be introduced was composed of the provinces of Bitlis, Diyarbekir, Erzurum, Mamuret-el-Aziz (Kharput), Sivas, and Van. Still, not all of the Armenians in the Ottoman Empire lived within these provinces, as there was a dense Armenian settlement in Trabzon and Cilicia and in most large cities throughout the Empire. This reform territory also affected a large number of the Syriac, Chaldean, and Assyrian Christians who were concentrated in the provinces of Bitlis, Diyarbekir, and Van. A prime intention was to create joint Muslim and Christian governance in these provinces along the lines that had been recently introduced after a Muslim–Christian civil war in Lebanon. However, no effort was made to implement the Lebanon model of joint rule in any of the designated provinces.

The Great Powers interpreted article 61 to mean that they could intervene to monitor the process of reform in the Armenian provinces. Thus it came about that consulates and vice-consulates of foreign countries were set up in the major cities of Mesopotamia. There were American, British, French, German, Italian, and Russian consular representatives throughout the region. They reported infringements of the rights of non-Muslims and they reported back to their home countries on the plight of the Christians. Thus the issue of the "Armenian Question" became a major theme of foreign policy discussion throughout the world.

After the Berlin conference, the pace of reforms halted, and most observers point to the personal rule of Sultan Abdul Hamid II (1876–1909) as the key hindrance. Early on, he dissolved the recently instituted National Assembly and suspended the new constitution. The first session of the National Assembly met in 1876–77 and had 115 deputies: 67 Muslims and 48 non-Muslims, which gave nearly proportional representation. Abdul Hamid's reactionary measures closed a promising line of reform that was to be revived at the Young Turk revolution of 1908. Still there remained an official rhetoric of equality among all Ottoman subjects irrespective of religion, and of combating remnants of timeworn *dhimmi*-type anti-Christian discrimination. In Constantinople and some other cities, non-Muslims were accepted in central administration and in tasks that required higher education.[27] In reality, outside the large cities, progress was slow, and this caused discontent particularly among the Armenians, who began to organize their own separatist political movements. Because of Ottoman intransigence, some of these Armenian nationalists drifted toward revolutionary ideas. Several political organizations emerged, among the most important being the socialist *Hunchak* (the Bell) Party, founded in 1887, and the *Dashnaktsutiun* (Armenian Revolutionary Federation, usually referred to with the short form *Dashnak*), founded in 1890. In frustration over slow improvement, a small group of Armenian revolutionaries seized the Ottoman Bank building in Istanbul in August 1896 and began throwing bombs. This caused a popular backlash, and Armenian shops and homes were sacked and Armenians were killed. Until the Young Turk revolution of 1908 reinstated the constitution, the Dashnaks functioned in secret, trained guerilla fighters, and stockpiled weapons for a coming revolutionary situation. But it

---

[27] Carter Findley, "The Acid Test of Ottomanism: The Acceptance of Non-Muslims in the Late Ottoman Bureaucracy" (1983).

also cooperated with the Young Turks, a similar revolutionary secret organization.

The Young Turk movement agitated for reinstituting the constitution, reducing the importance of religion, and reforming institutions. Many of the founders of the Young Turk movement were military and civil officials with European education and experience. Many were not ethnic Turks and most did not hail from Anatolia, but they shared a dream of a common Turkish identity and a vision of Anatolia as a Turkish homeland. The Young Turks sought contact across ethnic and religious barriers with Jews and Armenians. The Committee for Union and Progress (CUP) emerged as a militant branch within the Young Turk movement, seeking contact with the equally militant Dashnak party, and tight Turkish–Armenian friendships developed. After the revolution of 1908, the Dashnaks converted into a parliamentary democratic party, with elected members of the National Assembly.

When a new National Assembly was elected in 1912, it included nine Armenians, two of whom belonged to the CUP and three to the Dashnak party; the rest were independents. There were no National Assemby members who were Syriacs, Chaldeans, or Assyrians.[28] As far as is known, there were no political party organizations among the latter before the war, but the war experience stimulated the growth of embryonic Assyrian political parties.[29]. Most noteworthy among them was *Khoyada Atouraïa* (Assyrian Unity), which had a democratic republican ideology. Among individual efforts, Feridoun Bit-Abraham published the journal *Nakocha* (the Bell) in Tbilisi, and Benyamin Arsanis edited *Kochab d'Denkha* at Urmia.[30] These movements engaged Iranian Assyrians, so their activities had little bearing on the Syriacs living in the Ottoman Empire.

Only after they had come to full power in the coup of 1913 did the CUP reveal themselves committed to the idea of homogenizing the population and dissipating minorities by planned ethnic cleansing. In the wake of Turkey's defeat in the First Balkan War, in January 1913 the CUP staged a bloody military coup, seized power, and eliminated their political rivals. A dictatorship came to power composed of Talaat, Minister of the Interior; Enver, from 1914 Minister of War; and Jemal, Marine Minister and Gover-

---

[28] Aykut Kansu, *Politics in Post-Revolutionary Turkey, 1908–1913* (2000), 445–97.

[29] Yoab Benjamin, "Assyrian Journalism: a 140-Year Experience" (1993); Gabriele Yonan, *Journalismus bei den Assyrern: Ein Überblick von seinem Anfängen bis zur Gegenwart* (1985).

[30] Basile Nikitine, "Une petite nation victime de la guerre: les Chaldéens" (1921), 614.

nor-General of Syria. This triumvirate had as a major goal regaining territory recently lost in the Balkan wars. On the initiative of Russia, an international conference was held to discuss the possibility of international monitoring of the deteriorating conditions of the Christian populations in Eastern Anatolia. The conference resulted in the appointment of two inspectors, one from Holland and one from Norway. They had just begun their inspection tours when World War I broke out. Behind the scenes, Talaat designed plans for the homogenization of the population by moving ethnic minorities from their core homelands and scattering them in regions where they had never previously lived. Thus Kurds, Armenians, and Arabs were to be sent to western Anatolia; and Bosniaks, Circassians, and other Muslim refugees to eastern Anatolia. In no place were these ethnic groups to become more than 10 percent of the population, and it was assumed that the uprooted would quickly assimilate into Turkish culture, as the Turkish language would be their only common means of communication. From the spring of 1914, Greeks were forcibly deported from strategically important parts of the west coast.[31] Thus when the World War broke out, the country was witnessing the process of mass deportations of many different ethnic groups. Some of the leading figures with greatest responsiblity for the later massacres had prior experiences as instruments of the expulsion of the Greeks.

A Heritage of Massacres

Since the 1890s the world had been aware that conflicts between Ottoman Muslims and Christians were getting out of hand. There was even a growing suspicion that local authorities were involved and that the government was passive. In 1895, a public demonstration, the largest Armenian display of dissatisfaction ever in Istanbul, was attacked by a mob. As news of this riot spread from the capital, a wave of plundering and killing of Christians struck throughout Anatolia. The motive given for the violence was the widely held belief that the Armenians had attacked the Muslims first.

Within a short space of time, riots and plundering broke out in Diyarbekir, Kharput, Sivas, Urfa, and other towns and untold villages. Disturbances throughout the province of Diyarbekir occurred from the autumn of 1895 through the first months of 1896. In November 1895 in the town of Diyarbekir the riots began with the burning of the commercial districts. Mobs struck mainly against the large Armenian community (of whom a

---

[31] Fuat Dündar, *İttihat ve Terakki'nin Müslümanları İskân Politikası (1913–18)* [CUP Muslim settlement policy 1913–18] (2001).

thousand were killed and a full two thousand shops destroyed), but aggression also affected the other Christian denominations. The French vice-consul reported to his ambassador that for Orthodox Syriacs there were 150 deaths, 25 houses plundered, and 200 shops plundered and burned. The Syriac Catholic losses were 3 deaths, 6 houses plundered, and 30 shops plundered and burned. The Chaldean losses amounted to 14 deaths, 58 houses plundered, and 78 shops plundered and burned.[32] These riots give the appearance of being more focused on damaging or destroying property than on outright killing and thus resemble the contemporary anti-Jewish pogroms of the Russian Empire.

There are differences of opinion as to the degree to which the Ottoman authorities were involved in the Hamidiye massacres. Some officials, police, and military actually did protect Christian lives and property, but some did participate. An official Ottoman investigative team arrived in Diyarbekir in December 1895. A statement by this group to local Christian notables indicates the ruler's position and purported to contain a message from the Sultan himself, placing the blame on the victims.

> For our Lord Sultan, we have investigated the unrest which has occurred in some parts of Anatolia, such as Samsun, Sivas, Mamuret-ul-Aziz, and Diyarbekir as a consequence of the Armenian uproar and the request of leading men in His Imperial Majesty's provinces. We have seen the atrocities which have occurred and which exceed what happened in Diyarbekir. We were much aggrieved by that. It stands clear that what has happened is a result of the intrigues of certain foreign powers, primarily England. They have spread destructive ideas in the hearts of the Armenians. They have caused unrest in the capital city and raged against the Sublime Porte in the hope of winning success with their evil intentions. This does not lie in the interest of the Armenians, but rather in that of the English, who are trying to devour this country for themselves. Those who have listened to them tread a dangerous path, dedicated to crushing the High State's throne against the will of our Lord Sultan and Our Lord Jesus Evangelium, as it is written in your books: "He who rises against Caesar, rises against God." The enemies of the state have started unrest in some of our empire's protected peoples. This has brought damage to both the state and to the religious communities, both Muslim and Christian, despite the fact that the state only desires calm for all of its subjects. However, all non-Muslims have rights and there is, as Muslim law and the Sunni tradition prescribe, no

---

[32] Gustave Meyrier, *Les Massacres de Diarbekir. Correspondance diplomatique du Vice-Consul de France 1894–1896* (2000), 134–35.

difference between Muslim and Christian. This is confirmed by the favor His Highness our Sultan Abdul Hamid Khan II has shown the Christians in the form of high office and signs of honor. For Muslims and Christians are, in his view, equal. There is no difference between Muslims and Christians. What we say here we have heard directly from His Majesty.[33]

From this quote it is apparent that the government, instead of searching for the perpetrators, blamed the Christians for their sorrowful condition. They were accused of being duped by foreign powers into making demands of a political nature that would not help them but could only rock the foundations of the Ottoman state. The government insisted that there was no need to demand political reforms, as personal equality between Muslims and non-Muslims already existed. As stated, some non-Muslims had already achieved high office. Note that this statement places no blame on the rioters who plundered, burned, and killed; nor does it promise to bring them to justice. It also affirms that the Sultan at that moment perceived Great Britain as his major enemy and as the power with the greatest influence over Armenian opinion. This accusation of being the instruments of foreign powers would later shift focus. During World War I, the Armenians and Assyrians would be accused of helping the Russians, while the various Armenian and Syriac Catholic groups as well as the Chaldeans were believed to be collaborating with the French.

The disturbances in Diyarbekir province were worst in the provincial capital and its immediate surroundings. This part of the province had many Armenians. In the southern part of the province, however, there were very few Armenians (and the Armenians who did live there were overwhelmingly Catholic). In this region there were many instances when authorities managed to constrain the riots and killings. There were also examples of local Muslims who protected their Christian neighbors. Ottoman soldiers protected Christians who sought asylum in the monastery of Za'faran (close to Mardin) against Kurdish attacks. The village of Mansouriya was similarly protected by soldiers who fired with artillery against large contingents of attacking tribesmen. In Nisibin, a riot began with plundered shops and five Christian murders, but the chief of the Arab Tayy tribe sent the mob fleeing. At Midyat, soldiers aided the Christian inhabitants. In Mardin, the local Kurdish clans of Mishkawiya and Mandalkaniya protected the Christians. Thus in those parts of Diyarbekir province where there was a concentration of Syriac Christians they experienced considerable protection from their

---

[33] Manuscript of Habib Jarwe, published in Armalto, *Al-Qusara*, 47.

Muslim neighbors. The degree to which the Christians were protected reflected the degree to which they were integrated into local society, whereas in economically more developed Diyarbekir the religious groups were segregated, and economic rivalry triumphed over neighborly solidarity.

When in 1915 violence once again threatened the Oriental Christians, it was probably natural for the Syriacs of Diyarbekir province to hope that they would come relatively unscathed out of a conflict that was described by authorities as chiefly Armenophobic. There were serious attempts in the Mardin district by local Muslim civilians and Ottoman officials in 1915 to protect the Christians. However, circumstances proved different, and these officials were replaced; the soldiers, instead of guarding against the Kurds, cooperated and participated in the attacks. Kurdish chiefs who offered protection were forced to change sides. This difference reflects changes brought about by the Young Turk rise to power, the development of new nationalistic Turkish ideologies, which contributed to the identification of all Christians—no longer just Armenians—as subversive elements and allies of the enemy. In many ways, this worsening of Muslim–Christian relations agrees with Michael Mann's theory that ethnic cleansing is part of the early democratic experience of modernizing societies.[34]

As a result of the massacres of 1895 and 1896, European countries stepped up their philanthropic activities. Tens of thousands of Christian orphans were placed in children's homes, schools, and hospitals manned by missionaries, doctors, and nurses that opened throughout eastern Anatolia. This, of course, also increased the amount of information available in Europe about conditions for the Ottoman Christians.

A geographically limited, but nevertheless very bloody, massacre occurred in the vicinity of Adana, provincial capital of Cilicia. This took place during the two-week-long attempt in 1909 by Sultan Abdul Hamid to regain power and revoke the new constitutional rule. The mob wanted to show its support for the sultan. This massacre is important because, possibly for the first time, no distinction was made between Armenians and other Oriental Christians. The disturbances broke out in Adana on April 14. Local mobs focused on Armenian and other Christians in that town and its immediate neighborhood. One political reason behind the massacres was that at that time the Young Turks were closely allied with the Armenian Dashnak Party, and the rioters were showing support for the sultan.

Apparently the riots and killing did not spread to other regions. In an official report afterward, the following figures for deaths were given for the

---

[34] Michael Mann, *The Dark Side of Democracy: Explaining Ethnic Cleansing* (2005).

town of Adana: 2,093 Armenians, 133 Chaldeans, 418 Syriac Orthodox, and 63 Syriac Catholics. However, contemporaries deemed these figures an understatement and believed that up to 20,000 Christian deaths should be counted for the entire province, and among the victims were 850 Syriacs and 422 Chaldeans.[35] The National Assembly delegate for Adrianople, Agob Babikyan, presented a report shortly after. According to him, the events in Adana marked a change in the previous anti-Christian policy, since for the first time it was not just the Armenians who were the target.

> During the Abdul Hamid regime, the women and children were spared, and the Christians of other nationalities were not attacked, not even Armenian Catholics and Armenian Protestants. But as at Adana, no distinction was made between the Christians. The Syrian Orthodox and the Syriac Catholics who do not have any similarity with the language of the Armenians—because they speak Arabic—were killed: of the first, 400 victims, and of the second 65; the Chaldeans there were 200; and the Greeks [probably meaning Melkites], a hundred in the town of Adana.[36]

Abdul Hamid's counterrevolution floundered after only two weeks, and he was deposed and sent into internal exile. The new Sultan Mehmed V (r. 1909–1918) was a figurehead monarch. When the constitutional government investigated the events in Adana, it blamed them on the old despotic regime. Trials were held and several persons were hanged for organizing the mayhem. Babikyan judged the inclusion of non-Armenian Christians among the victims as a new departure and an escalation of Armenophobia into a general anti-Christian feeling. Even though only a small number of Syriacs were victims, and even though the pogroms were limited to one province, the massacres of 1909 signified a change in attitude, and from that moment on, nationalistic attention turned against all Christians, not just the Armenians.

In 1915, memories of 1895 and 1909 were still fresh, and many Christians see the massacres and ethnic cleansing as an unbroken process of escalating harassment going on for twenty years that culminated in 1915. Very early in the war, and particularly from early 1915, the Christian population feared the outbreak of new massacres. Their leaders urged them to be calm and ignore provocations and endure the various outrages. Among some Muslims a desire developed to commit a more complete massacre than was possible previously. For instance, Feyzi, a CUP National Assembly Member

---

[35] Raymond Kévorkian, "La Cilicia (1909–1921) des Massacres d'Adana au Mandat Français" (1999), 100–101.
[36] Ibid., 167.

for Diyarbekir and one of the chief instigators of the 1915 massacres, was the son of Arif Effendi, who as mayor masterminded the 1895 pogroms.[37] On the first occasion, the Great Powers pressured the sultan to stop the massacres, but during the war the situation was different, and military and civil authorities created the preconditions for a general massacre and gave the killers free reign.

THE GREAT POWERS

Without doubt, Russia was the greatest threat to Ottoman control in the area. Since the time of Tsar Peter I it had been forcing its way through the Caucasus, often displacing the native Muslim population. In the eighteenth century at the Treaty of Kücük Kaynarca in 1774, Russia assumed the role of protector of Orthodox Christians living in the Ottoman Empire. However, Russia's prime ambitions were territorial. By 1801 it had annexed Georgia in the southern Caucasus. One long-term goal was to get an outlet to the sea. The main alternative was to get hold of the straits, but this met with all sorts of opposition from the other Great Powers. A secondary alternative was to extend its influence from Transcaucasia further south and reach the Persian Gulf.

Russia waged nearly constant war with the Ottomans and the Persians, and often these led to invasions. In 1827, there was a Russo-Persian war; in 1828–29, Russia temporarily occupied the Ottoman city of Erzurum, and when the Russian armies withdrew, a number of Armenians and Assyrians followed along. They settled in the provinces of Erivan and Zakavkaz. In the late nineteenth century, there were 1,250 Assyrian "immigrants" living in Erivan *gubernia*.[38] During the Crimean War of 1855–56 there was another Russian invasion of Eastern Anatolia. And in 1878 the Ottomans in the treaty of Berlin gave up the provinces of Kars, Ardahan, and Batum—where there were many Armenians and some Assyrians. Through these conquests, many Armenians and Assyrians became acquainted with Russia and went there to work as seasonal laborers.

Historically, Great Britain had been the Ottoman Empire's most reliable ally. Unfailingly it had supported the Ottomans against the expansion of the Russians. However, resenting the British occupation of Cyprus in

---

[37] Joseph Alichoran, "Un dominicain témoin du génocide de 1915" (2005), 314; Yves Ternon, "Mardin 1915: Anatomie pathologique d'une destruction" (2002), 113.

[38] A. Arutinov', "K' antropologii aisorov'" [On the anthropology of the Assyrians] (1902), 89.

1878 and Egypt in 1882, Abdul Hamid began to seek other allies. The major new friend was Germany, which as a united state since 1871 very quickly stepped in to help the Sultan modernize the army. In 1878, Bismarck had convened the peace congress in Berlin to obtain a more favorable peace treaty for the Ottomans. Germany gave considerable military aid and in 1883 sent General Colmar von der Goltz to head the military college in Constantinople; this prepared the way for a stream of German military advisors and munitions. The Germans had economic ambitions in the Middle East, and the most symbolic aspect of this economic thrust was the Berlin-to-Baghdad railway, which was nearly complete by the outbreak of World War I. German diplomats, particularly the Foreign Office Undersecretary Kiderlen-Wächter, liked to stress that Germany had only economic interests in Turkey and no political or territorial ambitions.[39] This contrasted their position with that of the more "imperialistic" great powers, who were not bashful about their territorial dreams. Drawing a demarcation between economic and political interests put Germany at a disadvantage when working with Turkish governments. During Abdul Hamid's reign, Germany had presented itself as the "Friend of the Sultan," and it had some difficulty in adapting to the Young Turk revolution. The Young Turks, who at least initially were French-oriented, saw Germany as the main foreign supporter of the fallen reactionary regime. Relations between Germany and Turkey gradually improved through necessity, but they failed to reach the closeness of Abdul Hamid's era. Throughout the World War, Germany experienced friction in dealing with its ally—for many months Turkey hesitated to enter the war on the side of the central powers, despite a secret agreement with Minister of War Enver. The Turkish leaders also proved intransigent when the Germans tried to persuade them to abandon the anti-Christian massacres and deportations.

German and Russian rivalry also extended to Kurdistan, and each country had agents in place trying to curry favor with the local inhabitants. Neither power appears to have scored great success, but much time and effort were put into the task. One of the Russian strategies was to urge an alliance of all potential opposition forces in the region. Thus they tried to create a union of Armenian, Syriac, and Kurdish politicians, but they made little progress beyond preliminary discussions.[40] Within the Kurdish nationalist movement a pro-Russian faction emerged under the leadership of Ab-

---

[39] Ernst Jäckh, *Kiderlen-Wächter der Staatsmann und Mensch: Briefwechsel und Nachlass* (1924), 2:214–29.
[40] Lazarev, *Kurdistan*, 235ff.

dul Rezzak, and this resulted in growing cultural and political ties. Substantial support for the Russians did not evolve, as the various Kurdish chiefs had their own local agendas. One Russian intelligence officer reported in 1913 the existence of what he called a "Holy alliance" of Kurds, Turks, and Persians to drive the Russians out of northern Iran.[41]

IDEOLOGY

With the realization that it was falling behind the European powers, starting in the reign of Sultan Mahmud II (1808–1839) attempts were made to reform the institutions of the Ottoman state. The chronic military and financial problems peaked at the revolt of Muhammad Ali Pasha in Egypt, who defeated the Ottoman armies sent out to fight him and managed to occupy territory as far north as Syria. The *Tanzimat* reform period, which extended from the first major decrees until the ascension of Sultan Abdul Hamid II in 1878. The initial reform of the *Hatt-i Sherif* of Gulhane in 1839 and of Hümayun in 1856 placed, in principle, all subjects, regardless of religion, on an equal basis. This gave promise of removing discriminatory rules of conduct regarding *dhimmi* status that no longer could be accepted, as a sign of religious tolerance. They would thus pay the same taxes as Muslims and be free from denigrating customs—but would also be subject to military conscription. The object of the reforms was to strengthen the Empire by reinforcing the institutions of the state and modernizing the military. But the citizens had to be motivated to pay taxes, be obedient to state decrees, and identify and participate in its military exploits.

A name given to this concept of citizenship was Ottomanism (in Turkish *Osmanlilik*), an ideology with roots in the reform period. This line of thinking was intended to shape a common multicultural citizenship for all who lived within the borders of the Empire irrespective of religion and ethnicity. Ottomanism was a policy for furthering equality between all the Sultan's subjects, Muslim and non-Muslim alike, and the voluntary allegiance of all subjects to the dynasty of Osman and the Sultanate. It portrayed the Sultan as a patriarch of a large family but concerned with all of his children regardless of their faith. The *Tanzimat* program was primarily secular, and consequently the millet system, which meant rule through religious leaders, had to be replaced. Some Muslims realized that they had much to lose and little to gain if non-Muslims were raised to equal status, so reaction to the reforms had a religious twist. In the final analysis, the main problem with

---

[41] Ibid., 281–85.

the reforms was that they were not introduced by shock therapy and simply did not produce the promised equality fast enough.

The autonomous millets of the major minority religions had to be reorganized. Previously leadership was in the hands of the religious hierarchy. The reforms provided intellectuals, artisans, and other laymen a place in the governing bodies. For instance, in 1863 the Armenians established an assembly of 140 members, the vast majority of whom were laymen. Similar developments brought laymen to power in the Greek and Jewish millets.[42] On the basis of these reforms and political declarations, Christian and Jewish groups began to be visible and raised demands for implementation of the long-promised equality and civil rights.

Against this background a constitution was written which gave parliamentary representation to all citizens in a National Assembly. The increased public visibility and self-confidence of the non-Muslims, however, caused an immediate backlash, and Sultan Abdul Hamid suspended the constitution; the promises of political and civic equality were not to be fulfilled. This resulted in political movements particularly among the Greeks and Armenians. It also resulted in great pressure on Turkey from the Great Powers to implement the principles of equality and nondiscrimination. Various international schemes were drawn up to secure the situation of the non-Muslims and they nearly always infringed on Ottoman sovereignty, which was much resented by Muslim opinion.

A reaction grew against the perceived rising status and welfare of the non-Muslims. A leading political journalist and dramatist, Namik Kemal (1840–1888), criticized the Tanzimat reforms. To him, they symbolized the weakness of the Empire, since the reforms were brought about by foreign pressure and with the complicity of the non-Muslim inhabitants. Instead, Kemal proposed the rejuvenation of the political integrity of the empire through unification based on religious *shari'a* law. Only the sharia could serve as a foundation for a just and equitable state; therefore a constitution must reinstate Islamic religious law, and all Ottomans, regardless of faith, must be subject to these laws.[43] The Young Ottomans, predecessors of the Young Turks, criticized the Tanzimat as far too autocratic and the creation and symbol of foreign hegemony.

A later development was Pan-Islamism. This vision came to dominate during the rule of Abdul Hamid. It intensified in response to the steady loss

---

[42] R. H. Davison, "Tanẓīmāt" (1998), 204ff.

[43] Joseph G. Rahme, "Namik Kemal's Constitutional Ottomanism and Non-Muslims" (1999), 31–32.

of territory as Christian populations in the Balkans organized national liberation movements and succeeded in carving out their own states. Waves of destitute Muslim refugees flooded into Anatolia as a result of what was perceived as Christian aggression. In northeast Anatolia, Russia annexed the provinces of Ardahan, Batum, and Kars and was believed to desire to swallow the entire swath of Armenian settlement. Concerned over imperialistic expansionism disguised as protecting Christianity, Muslims rallied behind their religion.

What could instead unify the major part of the peoples of the Ottoman Empire was the Muslim faith. Thus Turks, Albanians, Arabs, and Kurds were believed capable of a common identity that would give the state greater strength than Ottomanism. One factor that underpinned Pan-Islamism was a growing emphasis on the Sultan as the true Caliph with a religious authority that was separate from and greater than his political authority.[44] Pan-Islam brought religious polarization into political life.

Turkism and Pan-Turkism developed within groups with roots in central Asia who conceived of a greater Turkish-speaking nation called Turan.[45] The first really influential Turkist ideologist was Yusuf Akçura, who was born in central Russia. In 1904 he published an influential article, "Three Types of Policy," in which he contrasted Islamism with Turkism. He argued that Islamism was doomed to failure and that only Turkism had a chance of political success.[46] This vision called for the Ottoman Empire to liberate ethnic Turkish peoples living in the Caucasus, Crimea, and Central Asia from Russian rule. It promised to form a large Turkic ethnic state including Azeris, Chechens, Circassians, Tatars, Turkmen, and many others. The reverse side of this is that it excluded important Muslim groups that lived in the Empire, but who were not Turkish: Albanians, Arabs, and Kurds. With the growth of separatist nationalism among the Albanians, who fought their way to independence in 1913, and the Kurds, Pan-Turkism emerged as the only viable policy, although Pan-Islamism continued to get lip-service. Of the wartime dictators, Enver Pasha was particularly attracted to an expansionistic version of this idea and on several occasions ordered the army to advance through the Caucasus.

On the international level, the Pan-Turkist activists sent agents into countries with Turkic-speaking populations like Iran and Russia. They also had considerable literary and journalistic production. Many Circassians were

---

[44] M. E. Yapp, *The Making of the Modern Near East 1792–1923* (1987), 181–82.
[45] Jacob Landau, *Pan-Turkism: From Irredentism to Cooperation* (1995).
[46] Erik J. Zürcher, *Turkey: A Modern History* (1998), 133–34.

recruited as agents of the Special Organization *Teskilat-i Mahsusa*, which organized deportations, executions, and massacres. The main thrust of this activity was directed against Russia, which contained many Turkic-speaking ethnic minorities, and Iran with its Turkic peoples the Azeri and Afshar. In domestic politics, Turkism meant abandoning the traditional multicultural pluralism of Ottomanism, and the imposition of a unified scheme of one language, Turkish, and one religion, Islam. The Minister of the Interior, Talaat, was oriented toward creating a smaller nation—a Turkish heartland limited to Anatolia—and he developed his population relocation schemes with that in mind.[47]

On the eve of World War I, the Ottoman leaders could alternate between Pan-Islamism and Pan-Turkism in their propaganda war. The CUP's main organizer in Iran, Ömer Naji Bey, was a convinced Pan-Turkist. When agitating in Iran he preached Pan-Islamism to the Persians and Kurds, but with the local Azeris and Afshars he spoke of Turkic solidarity.[48] With the support of Germany, the Sultan, acting as Caliph, together with the Shaykh-ul-Islam, declared jihad against the enemy. It was a rare instance of an official rather than local and unauthorized fatwa proclamation of jihad. Its aim was to encourage the Muslims in Russia and in the French and English colonies to revolt from "Tunis and Algiers, from Egypt to India, from Persia into the Caucasus and further to Bukhara and Afghanistan." Germany also portrayed itself as the friend of Muslims, never having conquered a Muslim land. "With this Pan-Islamic zeal the military march of Turkey spreads out against Russia and against England," wrote Ernst Jäckh, Germany's leading expert on Turkey and a major war apologist. "If the Turks could take Egypt and with it the Suez Canal, that would break the back of the British Empire." However, "In war against England, against Russia, and against France, the Turks must win. ... Turkey is fighting for its existence or nonexistence."[49] For many Ottomans, the fight for survival was also coupled with a need to revive Islamic values, a necessity even in the eyes of the German ally. This set the stage for the fatal solution for the non-Muslims living within the borders of the Ottoman Empire.

---

[47] Dündar, *İttihat ve Terakki'nin Müslümanları İskân Politikası*.
[48] Fethi Tevetoğlu, *Ömer Naci* (1987), 88–89, 93.
[49] Ernst Jäckh, *Die deutsch-türkische Waffenbrüderschaft* (1915), 25–26.

3 THE ROAD TO THE FATAL SOLUTION

Military necessity, it was said, motivated the suffering that will be described in later chapters of this book. It is therefore important to begin with a short narrative about the campaigns along the Caucasus front, the origin of the deportation decrees, and the international repercussions.

In the early twentieth century, militarism was almost unquestioned in Europe. Enormous armies prepared for total war, which nearly everyone expected. According to strategists, wars were to be won through the complete annihilation of the enemy's military resources. War was thus unlimited, and just about any actions that reduced the potential strength of an enemy could be seen as wise precautionary steps. However, early in the course of the war, civilians too could become the "objects of military necessity" if they belonged to the wrong ethnic or religious group. For governments at war, military necessity itself could be turned into a catchall phrase for whatever the high military command considered important; for the politicians in power it became a trump card to play whenever and wherever political or juridical values seemed at risk.[1]

PREPARATIONS FOR WAR IN THE CAUCASUS

Germany almost had to drag the Ottoman Empire into World War I.[2] Opposition to participating in the war was widespread, and in the government only Enver Pasha, the pro-German Minister of War, proved enthusiastic. Turkey was exhausted after having recently fought and lost three wars in rapid succession—against Italy in Libya (1911–12) and the two Balkan wars (1912–13). The national debt was astronomical, the railroad network was small and several sectors of the heralded Baghdad line years from completion, the armaments industry was insufficient, and the thrice-defeated army

---

[1] Isabel V. Hull, *Absolute Destruction: Military Culture and the Practices of War in Imperial Germany* (2005).

[2] Ulrich Trumpener, *Germany and the Ottoman Empire 1914–1918* (1968); Frank Weber, *Eagles on the Crescent: Germany, Austria and the Diplomacy of the Turkish Alliance* (1970); Wolfdieter Bihl, *Die Kaukasus-Politik der Mittelmächte*. part 1: *Ihre Basis in der Orient-Politik und ihre Aktionen 1914–1917* (1975).

was spread thin defending the vast borders of the empire. The Ottoman Empire did not have any immediate war aims and direly needed time to lick its wounds and restructure its army. After the Balkan wars, many senior officers had been forced to retire and younger, less experienced officers assumed commands. For all these reasons, and many more, the Triple Entente powers (Britain, France, and Russia) expected Turkey to keep its repeated assurances of neutrality.

Germany needed Turkey to open up the Caucasus front against the Russians and thereby tie down divisions that otherwise could have been pitted against Germany in central Europe. Further, if transport through the Suez Canal could be disrupted, Britain would be seriously weakened. Germany even conceived a wild design of invading India overland through Persia and Afghanistan, but to accomplish this it needed a staging ground on Ottoman soil. From the start of the war, Germany pressured the Ottoman government to join; and Enver and the German ambassador, Baron von Wangenheim, signed a secret alliance treaty on August 2, 1914, without the full knowledge of the cabinet. When Grand Vizier Sait Halim heard of the treaty, he attempted to get some concessions from Germany. The primary issues were the removal of international agreements that favored foreign citizens (the so-called capitulations), that Greece return certain islands in the Aegean Sea, that Germany support the long-standing claim of Turkey to annex those parts of northwest Iran where Turkish was spoken and Sunni Kurds lived, war indemnities, and so on. The Ottoman government kept on hesitating to join the war. However, the Entente powers heard of the existence of a secret alliance with Germany and began to make hasty plans for a probable war in the Middle East. Together Enver and the German military advisors, without informing the rest of the government, initiated provocations against Russia in order to make Russia declare war on Turkey first. The best-known provocation was the bombardment at the end of October of Odessa and some Crimean ports by ships from the German Navy's Mediterranean Squadron but flying the Ottoman flag, after which Russia did declare war on November 2, 1914. There were other provocations in the relative obscurity of the Turkish-Iranian border, with military-orchestrated atrocities on Christian villages.

General mobilization, known as the time of *seferbelik*, began early in August 1914. Many oral narratives of the persecution of Christians start with mobilization, because it drained the villages of their young men and because of the simple fact that so few recruits managed to return home. All males in certain age groups were obliged to register for the draft. Soldiers were placed in separate units according to their religious beliefs. Christian conscripts between the ages of 20 and 45 were placed in the regular army. Males in the age ranges 15–20 and 45–60 were placed in unarmed labor battalions as bearers of equipment and supplies. Most of the railroad stations were located several weeks' march from the Russian border, and provisions had to be brought over poor roads to the forts. In many areas, roads were so bad that wheeled vehicles were out of the question. So the need for labor battalions was insatiable. Labor battalions also worked on fortifications, digging ditches, road repair, road construction, and harvesting crops. Mobilization was brutal, and recruits had sometimes to be chained together to prevent desertion.[3] Twenty young men from the Rhawi clan of Midyat were taken and only two or three returned safely, while one escaped to Russia.[4] One of the conscripts observed the murder of recruits before they arrived at boot camp:

> In 1914, the Turkish army took me at mobilization. The officers saw that I was rather short, so they rejected me and put me aside and I was forgotten. However, I was able to witness how the others were killed on the way.[5]

Besides the regular army, the Ottomans had recourse to the irregular Kurdish cavalry set up during the reign of Sultan Abdul Hamid II that was still known as *Hamidiye* regiments, despite a recent name change. These were recruited from within certain loyal tribes, and a tribal chief headed each. They were modeled on the Cossacks of the Russian army. In 1910 they had been reformed and renamed Light Reserve Cavalry Regiments and placed under the command of the Third Army, which was based in Erzurum. As poorly trained irregulars they had a bad military reputation ever since the Balkan wars as unreliable in the face of the enemy and undisciplined at most other times. In addition, the Ottomans sent out a general call to all the Kurdish tribes for volunteers for the front; a number of tribes responded and most were placed in the province of Van.

Another reserve force was the *Jandarma* (Turkish for gendarmerie), based in every province. These gendarmes were often veteran soldiers, sometimes including a few non-Muslims. One of the few Christian gendarmes was Isa Polos of Kfar-Boran, who was the sole non-Muslim in his unit of 22 soldiers. He was so well integrated that his unit helped him to get

---

[3] Rume Lahdo-Antar, interviewed July 1993 (appendix 1, no. 3).
[4] Yawsef Babo-Rhawi, interviewed June 1993 (appendix 1, no. 5).
[5] Eliyo Gares, interviewed January 1999 (appendix 1, no. 61).

to safety. In Midyat, Afremo Salma-Gawwo served as a gendarme.[6] Responsibility for the gendarmes lay with the Ministry of the Interior; their function was internal security and guarding the border. Two forms existed: stable regiments who were billeted in the major towns and villages and never left the province, and mobile regiments that could be sent to other provinces if need be. Under mobilization these battalions were transferred to the Ministry of War, and they were deployed along less vital sectors of the front. Several east Anatolian mobile gendarme units were part of the Turkish occupation forces in Iran. During the deportations, the local gendarmes also served as guards.

WAR AND THE MINORITIES

Both the Ottomans and the Russians organized units for guerilla war behind the front lines. Preparations started long before the war. The Russians recruited Armenian, Kurdish, and Assyrian volunteers among Ottoman subjects, while the Ottomans looked for allies among the Armenians and Muslims in the Russian Caucasus provinces. The Russians had about 100,000 Armenians in the regular army, mostly Russian citizens, plus an estimated 10,000 Ottoman Armenian volunteers recruited through the Armenian National Bureau.[7] The Russians promised that they would aid in liberating Armenia.

The Young Turks tried to do the same thing and approached the Dashnak party, the Kurds, the Iranian Azeris, and the Assyrians to entice them to form guerilla bands. The Ottoman government tried to gain the allegiance of the Armenians by offering them an autonomous state. The condition was that the Turkish Armenians organize a revolt of their brothers living beyond the border in the Russian provinces and coordinate this with a planned uprising of Muslims. If the rebellion succeeded, the Armenians would be given a territory encompassing the province of "Kars, the province of Erivan, a part of Elizavetpol, a fragment of the province of Erzeroum, Van and Bitlis." This vassal state was envisioned as an autonomous Turkish protectorate. An assembly of Armenian politicians in Erzurum listened to the plan, but they refused, advising the Young Turks instead to remain neutral and not enter the war at all. This was taken as a sign of

---

[6] Hanna Polos, interviewed November 1993 (appendix 1, no. 42); Karmo Salma-Gawwo, interviewed July 1993 (appendix 1,no. 7).

[7] Peter Gatrell, *A Whole Empire Walking: Refugees in Russia during World War I* (1999), 18–19.

disloyalty.⁸ The idea had been presented by two members of the CUP central committee, Eastern Anatolia's political boss Ömer Naji Bey and Behaeddin Shakir, to a congress of the Dashnak party in Erzurum in August 1914.⁹ In all probability, similar proposals and promises had been presented by vali Tahsin Bey to Mar Shimun on August 3, 1914. The Patriarch returned from Van and sent letters to the congregations to remain quiet, "and to fulfill strictly all their duties to the Turks. He was, in fact, waiting till he should see how far the Turks would or could fulfill their covenant."¹⁰

Immediately after the declaration of war, CUP negotiators were sent to Erzurum and Van to test the loyalty of the Armenians and to see once again if they would agree to stage an uprising in the Russian Armenian provinces. Part of this scheme was to form bands of partisans, *çete*s (Turkish for gangs or bandits), from the Armenians, and these bands would work in secret behind the Russian lines in union with Transcaucasian Muslims. In Van, once again the Young Turk negotiators were the former vali of Erzurum Tahsin Bey and Naji. Again the Armenians refused.¹¹ By this time pogroms against Armenians had already begun, although not on a large scale and not everywhere in the province. The ruling vali, Jevdet, met with the prominent Armenians to hear their complaints. He warned them that hostility in the province could come to affect all Armenians and that the situation could change rapidly. The Armenians protested over the Armenophobic agitation among the Muslim tribes. Jevdet accused them of exaggerating and threatened them with punishment for that. Writing to Talaat, he concluded, "I believe that the Armenians will be a problem."¹²

From November on, rumors were rife that an Armenian revolt was expected to break out at Van. Kazim Karabekir was stationed nearby and

---

⁸ Statement by Roupen of Sassoun to the Armenian Community of Moscow and narrative of Y. K. Rushdouni, in *The Treatment of the Armenians in the Ottoman Empire 1915–1916*, ed. James Bryce and Arnold Toynbee (1916; uncensored edition, 2000), 116, 94.

⁹ Johannes Lepsius, *Le rapport secret du Dr. Johannes Lepsius sur les massacres d'Arménie* (1918), 200–201.

¹⁰ Surma d'Beit Mar Shimun, *Assyrian Church Customs and the Murder of Mar Shimun* (1920), 66–67.

¹¹ Statement of Roupen, in Bryce and Toynbee, *Treatment of the Armenians*, 116–17; "Obrona Vana" [The defense of Van], originally published by Armyanskii natsional'nym Byuro in 1917 and reprinted in *Genotsid armyan i russkaya publitsistika* [The Armenian genocide in Russian publications] (1998), 147.

¹² Jevdet to Minister of Interior November 30/December 1, 1914, document no. 1996, in *Askeri Tarih Belgeleri Dergisi*, vol 34, no. 85 (October 1985).

communicated that his soldiers had intercepted two Armenian agents at the Iranian border. Under interrogation they admitted that there would soon be a revolt in Van. Kazim added a personal reflection: "And the present situation shows it too."[13]

THE FIRST CAMPAIGN

Enver was fond of undercover operations and special task forces—death squads—outside ordinary military command. These could be used for retaliation, provocation, sabotage behind the lines, and liquidation of party dissidents and political opponents. Long before the Balkan wars, he founded in secret the *Teşkilat-i Mahsusa* (Special Organization), which became a state organ on October 15, 1911.[14] He recruited its original members, among them Ömer Naji, and it took orders from Enver. When World War I began, the Special Organization swelled and fulfilled not just military but also party political tasks. Special Organization operatives were intelligence officers, undercover agents, spies, saboteurs, or professional cutthroats.[15] Naji used the Caucasian Revolutionary Society as the cover for his section, and it had local cells in Erzurum, Trabzon, and Van. In Van he recruited a militia from the surrounding Kurdish tribes.[16] The Special Organization in Anatolia was placed under the Third Army command. Often, volunteers were recruited among criminal elements. On several occasions Talaat Pasha order the release of convicts from prisons in order to man the *çete* gangs that made up the bulk of Special Organization members. Laz and Circassian were the preferred ethnic background for the thugs who were used for creating havoc to coincide with deportations.[17] Regular army officers despised the Special Organization operatives.

> Enver Pasha trusted these groups of tramps. He knew that they created mayhem and plundered villages. That he did not suppress these groups

---

[13] Kazim to Commander of Third Army November 29, 1914, document no. 1812, in ibid., vol. 31, no. 81 (December 1982).

[14] Fethi Tevetoğlu, *Ömer Naci* (1987), 129; Erik J. Zürcher, *Turkey: A Modern History* (1998), 114, gives a later date for the formalization.

[15] Vahakn Dadrian, "The Role of the Special Organization in the Armenian Genocide during the First World War" (1993), 50–82.

[16] Abdulla Muradoğlu, "Teşkilat-i Mahsusa" [Special Organization], in the newspaper *Yeni Şafak*, November 23, 2005; Shakir was the chairman of the central board that steered the special organization.

[17] BOA. DH. ŞFR 46/134 November 2, 1914, 47/196 November 27, 1914, and 54/65 July 19, 1915.

was his weakness. All who belonged to these special organizations were bandits, shaikhs, dervishes and deserters. We made great opposition to forming these organizations. But we could not stand up against Enver Pasha and the CUP strong man Behaeddin Shakir.[18]

Defense along the Caucasus front was the task of the Ottoman Third Army, about 150,000 soldiers, based in the heavily fortified garrison town of Erzurum.[19] The front was very long, running about 500 kilometers from the Black Sea to the Turkish-Iranian border and beyond. The frontier traversed mountains up to 3,000 meters high with deep snow and bitter cold winters. It was thus much more suited for defense than for aggressive action. The easiest approach for the Russians would be through the Aras River valley leading in the direction of Erzurum. On the Caucasus front, the war began with a Russian offensive on November 5 that gained some insignificant strips of border territory a few kilometers inside enemy territory. It was called the Köprüköy operation and resulted in the quick but short occupation of some towns close to the border, including Bayazit, Sarai, and Bashkale to the north and east of Lake Van.

On December 22, with the enthusiastic encouragement of the German military advisors, Ottoman troops under the personal leadership of Enver Pasha began a major offensive directed against the key railhead of Sarikamish just across the Russian border on the railroad to Kars, the capital of the Russian province with the same name. This was of course conceived as a surprise attack, since actions at that time of the year were a sheer gamble. At the start, luck was on the Ottoman side; up to the last week in December, the Turkish Third Army made good progress uphill, but in relatively good weather. Then their luck turned in the last days of December. In the nick of time, the Russians unexpectedly succeeded in reinforcing Sarikamish, and the Russian chain did not break down in panic as Enver had hoped.

---

[18] Aziz Samih, "Umumi Harpte Kafkas Cephesi Hatıraları" [The World War: Caucasus Front memoirs] (1935); Rafael de Nogales, *Four Years beneath the Crescent* (1926), 73–74.

[19] Genelkurmay Başkanlığı, *Birinci Dünya Harbi'nde Türk Harbi Kafkas Cephesi 3 ncü Ordu Harekâti* [World War I, Turkish War on the Caucasus Front, Third Army operations] (1993), is a multivolume work dealing with the Caucasian front through Turkish documents. Edward J. Erickson, *Ordered to Die: A History of the Ottoman Army in the First World War* (2001), is based mostly on that work and some additional Turkish documents. N. G. Korsun, *Alashkertskaya i Khamadanskaya operatsii na kavkazskom fronte mirovoi voiny v 1915 gody* [The Alashkert and Hamadan operations on the Caucasus Front in World War I in 1915] (1940), is based on Russian documentation.

And the weather turned execrable. On the night of January 2–3, the Third Army suffered a catastrophe, with an estimated 90,000 killed, wounded, captured, missing in action, or deserted. According to Felix Guse, a German serving as chief of staff, only 30,000 soldiers returned.[20] After this the Third Army had to be reconstructed from scratch, and it never regained its original strength. Fortunately for the Ottomans, even the Russians were exhausted by the battle over Sarikamish and they could not stage a counteroffensive, so troops on both sides settled into defensive positions and waited for the spring thaw. The front line was almost the same as the prewar border, except that Russia occupied Alashkirt and Bayazit, district capitals north of Lake Van. Russia evacuated the occupied towns of Sarai and Bashkale, where the Christian inhabitants were accused of collaboration and punished.

The Sarikamish offensive resulted in a Turkish disaster, but it did help the Central Powers in the long run. Because of the fear of attack in Transcaucasia, the Russians poured armies and provisions into this region, thus deploying significant military resources far away from Germany's eastern front. Also, at the height of battle the Russians appealed to London for the opening of a new front along the Dardanelles, thus forcing the allied disaster at Gallipoli. Turkey, despite its weak and decimated army, succeeded in tying up numerically superior Entente forces and holding them far distant from the European theater of war.[21]

The Ottomans did have one breakthrough, although it was probably a total surprise given their first reaction and the course of events. The Russians pulled back their garrisons from the Iranian border strip on New Year's Day 1915, and with literally no opposition rag-tag Turkish forces headed by the vali of Van Jevdet Bey, Kazim Karabekir, and Ömer Naji occupied the region, for a short time holding Tabriz. This force included the Van Jandarma, Hamidiye irregulars, and tribal volunteers from both sides of the border. The Turkish occupation lasted from January until May 1915. The Ottomans had long dreamed of annexing this part of Iran, since it would put them in direct land contact with the Turkic-speaking Muslims in Russian Azerbaijan and could be seen as a foundation-stone for a future Pan-Turanian state. It was one of the important war aims listed by the Grand Vizier. In the long run, the Turkish invasion forces proved inade-

---

[20] *Die Europäischen Mächte und die Türkei während des Weltkrieges: Konstantinopel und die Meerengen* (1930–32), 2:179, 4:21; Felix Guse, *Die Kaukasusfront im Weltkrieg bis zum Frieden von Brest* (1940), 49–50.

[21] Ibid., 50–52.

quate to hold the province, and they were in place only because the Russians had evacuated. When the Russians returned with a force that included Armenian and Assyrian militia, the Ottman troops were seized with panic and massacred local Armenian and Assyrian villages. They continued these massacres even when they returned to their own territory.

After Sarikamish, the Russian Caucasian army was also badly shaken and had to compete for needed replacements and supplies with the hard pressed divisions on the European front. Apparently there was no plan beyond limited action on the Caucasus front for the spring of 1915. It took some effort to regain the parts of Iran that were occupied by the Ottomans. What was worse, along the German and Austrian fronts the Russian army had collapsed during the spring and summer of 1915, with the loss of nearly two million soldiers and vast territory, so the distant Caucasus front assumed low priority. However, news arrived in late April 1915 of the desperate situation of the besieged Armenians in the city of Van and of the ongoing massacres throughout that province. Units of the Caucasian Army in Iran were rerouted to Van in order to relieve the Armenians. The Russians, along with Armenian volunteers, arrived there about May 20 and withdrew after only two months, taking the Christians with them.

Further north, the Russian General Yudenich started an offensive on May 6 aimed toward Erzurum, but this was beaten back. He restarted hostilities on July 10 directed against Mush, but the defenders put a halt to this and tried to push the Russians back to the border. This Turkish counterattack failed and the front stabilized in the middle of August, but with the Russians still holding territory along the northeastern rim of Van province. As the Russians pulled back from the city of Van, the Ottoman armies returned and even mounted a halfway successful counteroffensive north of the lake. During the second half of 1915 there was little military threat on the Caucasus front or even on the Turkish-Iranian border. The Russians had to consider their front in Eastern Europe, and the Ottomans needed to deploy resources for the successful but costly defense of Gallipoli.

The military experience of 1915 indicates that, if the Russians had planned on support from an Armenian revolt, it had not materialized. If the events in Van really were attempts to start a large-scale revolt, it was surprisingly limited to just one place with limited strategic value at a time when the Russian army was nowhere near. The Russian generals, many of whom were Armenophobic, have even been accused of neglecting the potential importance of Armenian local knowledge and therefore had difficulty traversing unknown terrain. According to one military history, General Yudenich refused to use the "numerous and pro-Russian Armenian elements in the area of action."²² The rising in Van appears to be an isolated occurrence that caught the Russians unawares and probably was a response to provocation on the side of the Ottoman authorities rather than a revolt tactically planned to aid a European victory. The nearest Russian forces were so far distant that it took their units a month to relive the besieged. Similarly accused of rebellion to aid the enemy, the Assyrians lived in an isolated region that the Russian army did not care to enter.

JIHAD AND IRAN

On November 12, 1914, Sultan Mehmed V, in his capacity as Caliph, proclaimed holy war and appealed to the Muslim subjects of the Entente powers to join in a common struggle with the Ottoman Empire. The Sultan's proclamation was immediately posted on government buildings, in Mardin for instance on the courthouse door. This proclamation was confirmed in a fatwa issued by the Shaykh-ul-Islam on November 14. This fatwa specified that the holy war was directed against the enemies of Islam, particularly Britain, France, and Russia. On November 21, the Sultan renewed the proclamation in an appeal to non-Ottoman Muslims that they join the jihad. Iran in particular was named.

Because of the heavy-handed Russian and British influence in Iran there was great public resentment against them, and the Ottomans hoped to channel Iranian frustration into a military resource. However, the Sultan had religious authority only among the Sunni Muslims; his proclamations pulled little or no weight in overwhelmingly Shi'ite Iran, other than among the Sunni Kurdish tribes. To overcome this handicap, the major Shi'ite leaders on Ottoman territory in the holy cities of Najaf and Kerbala also issued a fatwa of jihad.²³ The Russians and British realized that they were sitting on a powder keg in Iran if a jihad ignited the pent-up anti-Russian and anti-British feelings. The Persian government promised them they would not permit the distribution of the Najaf fatwa and would destroy any copies that could be discovered. However, the fatwa spread through secret channels while the government was passive.²⁴

---

²² W. E. D. Allen and Paul Muratoff, *Caucasian Battlefields: A History of the Wars on the Turco-Caucasian Border, 1828–1921* (1953), 311, cited in Erickson, *Ordered to Die*, 107.

²³ Ulrich Gehrke, *Persien in der deutschen Orientpolitik während des ersten Weltkrieges* (1961), 1:32, 2:22.

²⁴ Russian Ambassador in Tehran Vasili Korostovez to Russian Foreign Minister Sergei Sazonov November 16/29, 1914, and December 15/28, 1914, in *Die*

On Persian territory, appeals to jihad were posted even before war was officially declared. In September, a call for jihad signed by an Ottoman mufti was posted in the strategically important Kurdish town of Sawuj Bulak, south of Lake Urmia. In October, the Iranian authorities in Urmia observed that kinsmen of shaykh Abdul Khadir of Nihri were agitating for holy war and loyalty to the Sultan among the border tribes.[25] In November a new fatwa, signed by three Turkish shaykhs residing in Turkey, among them Abdul Khadir, appealed to the Iranian tribes to come to the aid of the Sultan in the name of religion.[26] In February 1915, early in the Turkish occupation of Urmia, a declaration of jihad was printed and widely distributed by the Ottoman authorities as part of a successful campaign to recruit volunteers.[27] At Meshed, fifty Turkish "missionaries" arrived in January and spread leaflets and preached holy war.

Probably as a sheer provocation, the occupation authorities repeatedly demanded that the French mission at Urmia use its printing press to print the jihad fatwa. Each time, Jacques Sontag, the head of the mission, refused.[28] In Turkish-occupied Iran, the jihad apparently did have importance in creating a common front against the Russians and the local Armenian and Syriac Christians, who were seen as their allies. Basile Nikitine, a Russian vice-consul in Urmia, published captured Ottoman documents that used the expression "Great Jihad" for the ethnic cleansing of Christians from the Turkish-Iranian border region. The document in question was a letter from Suto Agha, the head of the Oramar tribe, to Haydar Bey, the vali of Mosul. Suto spoke of their cooperation in "the time of the Great Jihad when the army attacked Tiyyari and T'khuma." Nikitine believed that the

---

Internationalen Beziehungen im Zeitalter des Imperialismus. Dokumente aus den Archiven der Zarischen und der Provisorischen Regierung, ed. Otto Hoetzsch, ser. 2, vol. 6 (1934), documents 570 and 704.

[25] Kargozar of Urmia to Ministry of Foreign Affairs October 13, 1914; Minister of Foreign Affairs to Persian Ambassador Constantinople October 27, 1914, in Empire de Perse, *Neutralité Persane* (1919), 10 and 17, documents 18 and 30.

[26] Abdul Khadir was a well-known figure in this part of the world. He took a leading part in his father Ubaydalla's revolt in 1880. He was a member of the Ottoman Senate and President of the Council of State (McDowell, *A Modern History of the Kurds* [1996], 53, 94).

[27] Florence Hellot-Bellier, "Chronique de massacres annoncés: Les Assyro-Chaldéens de Perse, la Perse et les puissances européennes 1896–1919" (1998), 103–6; McDowell, *Modern History of the Kurds*, 103.

[28] Joseph Alichoran, "Un dominicain témoin du genocide de 1915 le père Jacques Rhétoré (1841–1921)" (2005), 294.

jihad was a cover-up for more basic interests having to do with property and getting rid of foreign dominance.[29]

DEPORTATION AS A MILITARY TACTIC

Armies in the early twentieth century considered the relocation of minority populations through involuntary deportation to be standard procedure. This was a technique practiced by colonial powers in Africa. As a military tactic it was always accompanied by a high degree of brutality, since removal had to go swiftly and tolerated no opposition. The British during the Boer war and the Germans in their conflict with the Herero of Southwest Africa applied collective punishment in this way. The Balkan wars also resulted in widespread ethnic cleansing. Organized forced relocation became part and parcel of the strategies taught in military schools. It was said to be a matter of security for the army to be free from espionage and uprisings of the disloyal. At military academies, officers were taught to identify potential security risks, such as minorities, and to remove them. One aim was to prevent men from the targeted population from sneaking across the front and joining the enemy. During World War I, the Germans cleared the front lines in Belgium and France of conquered people who could be expected to be disloyal. At times the deportations began with brutal atrocities, as in Belgium, aimed at causing the populations to panic and flee or at least at terrifying them.[30]

Russia also employed forced population movements. On July 25, 1914, the general staff ordered the evacuation of "enemy-subject males of military service age" residing near the border. In Russia, the German- and Austrian-origin settlers "physically capable of carrying a weapon" were sent to central Russia. Jews were also suspected of sympathies with the Germans and Austrians and were thought to be potential spies. Thus Jewish populations near the front were exiled to distant regions. Often the Russian army used Cossack troops to do the rounding up and transportation. They were usually quite brutal, and a deportation order could easily devolve into a village pogrom against the Jews. An alternative to the mass relocation of an entire tract was to seize the rabbis and hold them as hostages, threatening to kill them if anything was done to help the enemy.

In January 1915, along the Caucasus front, Viceroy Vorontsov-Dashkov ordered the relocation of thousands of "refractory" Muslims from

---

[29] Basile Nikitine, *Kurdy* (1964), 229; "Une petite nation victime de la guerre: les Chaldéens" (1921), 623.

[30] Hull, *Absolute Destruction*, passim, esp. "The Armenian Genocide," 263–90.

Kars and Batum hundreds of miles northward to central Russia. Later, other Muslims were interned on an uninhabited island in the Caspian Sea. They were accused of aiding Ottoman troops during the Sarikamish campaign. There was also a short-lived idea that after the war the entire Muslim population of the Caucasus would be deported to Turkey and their land given to Russians. However, the deportation issue quickly became complicated as the Georgian Duma deputies complained that those affected were Adjzars, ethnic Georgians of the Muslim faith, who were fully loyal to Russia. After this intervention, Russian army relocation ceased. Overall the Russians deported about 10,000 Muslims from the Caucasus, and most of them arrived at their destinations.[31]

OTTOMAN DEPORTATIONS

By the end of January, Russian authorities reported the number of known Christian refugees from the Caucasus war zones that they were caring for. These totaled 49,838 Armenians, 8,061 Assyrians, 9,345 Greeks, and 113 of other nationalities.[32] Most came from Turkey and Persia. But they represented only the tip of an iceberg in relation to all population displacement that was underway. Other refugees had not made it across the battle lines, and some had died in the attempt.

It is possible that the Ottoman deportations were planned to be brutal but not fatal, to be limited and not global; to target only Armenians and not the other Christians. But designs and reality are separate phenomena. There were three separate phases of forced migration during the war era. The first was the slow-paced exchange of minority populations begun by Talaat as Minister of the Interior before the war. The second was the "military necessity" banishments of Armenian men started by Enver early in 1915 and carried out by the army. The third was the total removal of entire Christian populations in the summer of 1915 on the order of Talaat and organized by the local civil administrations together with death squads of local militiamen.

Talaat initiated a scheme of forced migration in the spring of 1914, beginning with minorities living in strategic military areas. The coastal Greek

---

[31] Gatrell, *A Whole Empire Walking*; Eric Lohr, *Nationalizing the Russian Empire: The Campaign against Enemy Aliens during World War I* (2003).

[32] Yerevanskaya statisticheskaya komissiya, *Odnodnevnaya perepis bezhentsev iz Turtsii, Persii i iz mest pogranichnikh s Turtsiei (armyan, aisorob, grekov i pr.)* [One-day count of refugees from Turkey, Persia, and places near the Turkish border: Armenians, Assyrians, Greeks, and others] (1915), 68–69.

population of western Anatolia was the first priority, and many persons were removed from the mainland to the Aegean islands. Plans were made to move Kurds and Arabs to western and central Anatolia. Muslim refugees from Albania, Bosnia, and other parts of the Balkans were to be placed in Diyarbekir, Adana, and Sivas. Circassians were settled in Urfa and Diyarbekir, while Chechens would be sent to Aintab. Armenians were sent from eastern to western provinces. Some of this was under way or in advanced preparation when World War I began.[33] Two persons who would later organize genocidal activities in Diyarbekir coordinated the pre-war expulsion of coastal Greeks: vali Reshid Bey served in the sanjak of Karesi, and his vice-vali Bedreddin Bey served in the town of Biga, near the Dardanelles.

Talaat's peacetime involuntary deportations could be considered, with some stretch of the imagination, to be population exchanges, as the intention then was not to kill, although most deportations did involve the shooting of those who refused. But in peacetime, deportations even of small groups of people involve a degree of force; and the long-term aim was to undermine the cultural integrity of the minority cultures, even the Muslim, resulting into full assimilation.

Military evacuations differ greatly from population exchange. They have no other goal that removing a specific population in its entirety from a specific area. The work must be done quickly, and thus the element of violence and intimidation accelerates. Since it is not a matter of resettlement, an army usually does not care about where the displaced population goes or whether it physically survives. Military actions against Ottoman Armenians began on February 25, 1915. The Ottoman General Staff sent Directive 8682 on "Increased Security Precautions." The directive pointed to disloyal Armenian behavior in Bitlis, Aleppo, Dörtyol, and Kayseri and coupled it with treasonous aid to the Russians and French. The Third and Fourth Armies were ordered to increase security and watch for signs of dissent. As a first step, ethnic Armenian soldiers and officers were to be removed from headquarters staffs and important command posts. The intelligence service asserted that the Armenian Patriarchy in Istanbul was transmitting military secrets to the Russians. This triggered a spy panic, and ever-increasing accusations of Armenian treason snowballed.[34] Everywhere, suspicions grew of preparations for an Armenian rising if and when the Russians mounted a

---

[33] Fuat Dündar, *İttihat ve Terakki'nin Müslümanları İskân Politikası (1913–1918)* [CUP Muslim Settlement Policy 1913–1918] (2001), 117–21, 131–33.

[34] ATAŞE First Division, Turkish General Staff February 25, 1915, cited in Erickson, *Ordered to Die*, 98.

spring offensive. Ethnic Armenian soldiers were disarmed. In some units the Armenian soldiers were shot outright; this is known to have happened in occupied Iran. But military necessity also affected civilian Armenians, particularly those who lived along the railroad or along the few roads suited for motor vehicles. Risings there could cut off deliveries of food, medicine, and armaments, which were always in short supply. The harder authorities searched for signs of Armenian disloyalty, the more they found them, or at least so it seemed. Little evidence was needed to gain permission to impose severe repression against supposed rebels.

With the siege of Van and the purported discovery of arms caches and bombs in many cities and towns, the long-prophesied concern over a full Armenian "rebellion" panicked out of all proportion. An important initiative came from the War Office. Staff officer Ismet[35] wrote in top secrecy to Talaat to express the army's concern. "

> About Lake Van and in Van itself, as we know, there has been a center for continual Armenian revolts. I think that we must remove them from this revolt-nest and scatter them. The Third Army informed us that on April 7, the Russians forced their Muslim villagers to cross our border in a state of nakedness. In order to stop this and what I just told about, I want to say the following. Either the above-mentioned Armenians with their families should be forced into the Russian side, or we should force them to the innermost parts of Anatolia. I ask you to choose one of these alternatives. If it is not any security risk, I desire to send the bandits with their families outside of the area of rebellion, and instead of them I would like to move in Muslim people.[36]

The War Office's concern was not over a general Armenian rising, but only the situation in Van, and thus it spoke for a limited deportation to central Anatolia.

Panic seemed to know no end. House searches were ordered among all "Christians," not just the Armenians, in the hunt for enemy collaborators. The search was to encompass even their "Muslim partners," whom Talaat ordered sent to military courts if they were caught hiding Christians.[37]

---

[35] (1884–1973) He later took the surname Inönü and was prime minister 1923–24, 1925–37 and president 1938–50.

[36] Ismet to Talaat May 2, 1915, document no. 1830 in *Askeri Tarih Belgeleri Dergisi* vol. 31, no. 81 (December 1982).

[37] BOA. DH. ŞFR 53/85 Talaat to Fourth Army May 23, 1915.

When the response to Ismet came from the Minister of the Interior, it was in the form of a much more radical solution. On May 27, 1915, Talaat issued the "Regulation for the Settlement of Armenians Relocated to Other Places because of War Conditions and Emergency Political Requirements." This regulation called for the deportation of Armenian civilians for the duration to the sparsely settled Syrian steppe and desert region. Considering Ismet's telegram, resettlement to inner Anatolia was assumed to be a security risk. The organization was to be done by the civil administration in the provinces under the surveillance of a special department within the Ministry of the Interior. Responsibility for transport was placed on the civil authorities, which also had to protect the lives of the Armenians. The banished persons were to be resettled in places that were at least 25 kilometers from the Baghdad railroad. Armenian civilians who were en route to resettlement in central and western Anatolia suddenly were redirected to the province of Aleppo. Between 5 and 10 percent of a minority might be left in place, and artisans pursuing crafts important to the army could remain: these included a few bootmakers, saddlemakers, and metalworkers, but even they led a precarious life. Deportation orders arrived at different times in the various provinces. The eastern provinces were the first affected and the western the last. Deportees in the eastern provinces had the least chance of survival.

Talaat Pasha's family preserves a notebook in which Talaat kept essential data about the effect of his deportation order of May 27, 1915.[38] One page contains a list of the number of Armenians deported from the various provinces. It gives a total of 924,158 persons, and thus must have been made when the deportations were more or less over. However, one province, Van, is totally missing; this is explicable, as it was outside Ottoman control for several months of 1915 and the Armenians fled as refugees to Russia. Thus, the number of Armenians who left their homes was much greater. This notebook may not include the Armenians who were killed in their home towns and villages, and it may ignore victims belonging to other faiths. The Talaat notebook exceeds somewhat the total figure of 835,600 victims supplied by Armenian sources in August 1915.[39] At the end of 1915

---

[38] Murat Bardakçı, "Tehcir edilen Ermeniler 924 bin 158 kişiydi" [The deported Armenians were 924,158], *Hürriyet*, April 24, 2005. The notebook is in the possession of Talaat's wife and grandchild. The handwriting is not Talaat's, but is probably that of an official in the Ministry of Interior.

[39] The figures are included a letter from Ghévond Tourian, the Armenian Prelate in Bulgaria, to Boghos Nubar Pasha, the president of the Armenian National Delegation, August 12/25, 1915, in Beylerian, *Les Grandes Puissants: L'Empire Ottoman et les arméniens dans les archives françaises (1914–1918)* (1983), 133; *Armyanskii Vest-*

the Armenian patriarch of Constantinople, Zaven, calculated that the number of victims from his church were "not less than one million" and that the valis of Bitlis, Diyarbekir and Erzurum had reported that there were no longer any Armenians in those provinces.[40] Confirmation of this assertion comes from a telegram sent by the vali of Diyarbekir in August 1915 stating that there were "no longer any Armenians left to deport."[41] Knowledge of this and similar telegrams indicates that the Armenian patriarchy had high-placed informers inside the Ministry of the Interior.

For the province of Bitlis, Talaat noted 109,251 Armenian deportees, and this was a sizeable percent of the 180,000 that the Armenian Patriarch in Constantinople estimated lived there in 1912. Beside Diyarbekir, he wrote, 61,002 deportees. The Armenian Patriarch noted 105,000 Armenians living there in 1912.[42] It is known that the vali, Reshid Bey, telegraphed on September 28, 1915, that he had so far deported 120,000 persons.[43] Thus it is probable that the statistics in the notebook were made before that date. Talaat's telegrams to the provincial governors often asked for statistics, but he asked for differentiation between Catholic, Protestant, and Apostolic Armenians as well as Syrian Catholics and Protestants.

When he was confronted with the horror of what had happened to the Armenians, he responded that they were a military necessity. In an interview for a correspondent of the *Berliner Tageblatt* he said:

> The Armenian deportation was a military necessity. While being deported to Mesopotamia they were attacked by the Kurds on the way and partly massacred. It was likewise necessary, last year in March, during the Dardanelles campaign, to remove the Armenians from Constantinople and neighborhood to distant regions. The Government had ordered their deportation to [Deyr-Zor]. Unhappily, bad officials into

---

nik 1916, no. 2, in *Russkie istochniki o genotside armyan v Osmanskoi imperii 1915–1916 gody* [Russian sources on the Armenian genocide in the Ottoman Empire 1915–1916], ed. G. A. Abraamyan and T. G. Sevan-Khachatryan (1995), 88–90.

[40] Patriarch Zaven to Archimandrate Vegunin December 28, 1915 in *Genotsid armanyan v osmanskoi imperii. Sbornik dokumentov i materialov*, ed. by M. G. Nersisiyan (Erevan: Izdatel'stvo Aiastan 1982), p. 338.

[41] BOA. DH. EUM. 2Şb 68/71 Reshid to Ministry of Interior September 18, 1915, referring to a telegram sent on August 18/31, 1915.

[42] Figures given in Bryce and Toynbee, *Treatment of Armenians*, 657.

[43] Nejdet Bilgi, *Dr. Mehmed Reşid Şahingiray'in Hayatı ve Hâtıraları: İttihâd ve Terakki Dönemi ve Ermeni Meselesi* [Dr. M. R. S.'s life and memory: The CUP period and the Armenian Questions] (1997), 48; BOA. DH. EUM 2Şb 68/71 Reshid to Talaat September 18, 1915.

whose hands the execution of these orders had been committed went into unreasonable excesses in doing their duty.

The correspondent added: "Here, Talaat Bey paused a moment, passed his hand over his eyes as if he wished to drive away a bad vision, and then continued: We are not savages. The reports of these tragic events have caused me more than one sleepless night."[44] Some other sources indicate that Talaat was disturbed by the news coming through. The chairman of the National Assembly, Halil Menteshe, found Talaat one morning in the spring of 1915 with eyes red and skin pale, and near fainting. When he asked what was wrong, Talaat said he had just received telegrams from the vali of Erzurum. "I received many telegrams about the Armenians and became agitated. I could not sleep all night. This is something that a human heart cannot bear. But if we hadn't done it, they would have done it to us. Of course we started first, that is the fight for national existence."[45] One wonders just who the "bad officials" were that Talaat mentioned, since he kept Reshid in office despite diplomatic protests and even promoted him to governor of Ankara. Reshid's vice-vali Bedreddin, who was just as bloody-minded, was appointed his successor. So Talaat cannot have been too disappointed with these repressive officials. In September 1915, a tribunal was established to try the culpability of officials and gendarmes who had handled the deportations badly.[46]

As the following chapters will discuss, the circumstances of the "deportations" were very peculiar. First, the actions, particularly in the first two months, encompassed all Christians in the eastern Anatolian provinces, not just the Armenians. Second, the deportations could not reasonably be deemed resettlement, since so few actually arrived at the stated destination. Many people were killed directly in or outside their hometowns and villages; others were killed while en route by foot. Men had the greatest risk of being killed immediately. Women and children formed the bulk of the caravans walking south to the desert. These were invariably attacked, women raped, children abducted, and a great number killed and left lying beside the road. Third, the provincial authorities did not establish any organization for the provision of food, water, and shelter for the Christians en route. Instead,

---

[44] Report from the British Intelligence Service, Cairo May 20, 1916, in Beylerian, *Les Grandes Puissants*, 206.

[45] Halil Menteşe, *Halil Menteşe'nin Anıları* [H. M.'s memoirs] (1986), 216.

[46] General Commander of the Jandarma Major Rasim to Enver, September 26 1915, document no. 2018 in *Askeri Tarih Belgeleri Dergisi* vol. 43, no. 85 (October 1985).

high civil officials and local politicians recruited killing squads in order to effectuate the expulsions. They seized the property of the Christians and sent part of it to the Ministry of the Interior and kept part of it for themselves. Fourth, very early the German consuls could name the officials, politicians, and military who instigated atrocities against the Christians, and they insisted on their removal and punishment. However, in Diyarbekir the only Ottoman officials who were replaced were those who protested against the anti-Christian measures; the worst perpetrators, such as the vali, stayed at their posts and continued the massacres in the face of foreign protests.

THE FAILURE OF DIPLOMACY

Almost from the very beginning, the German diplomats feared that the reprisals against the Armenians would degenerate into a general massacre of all Christians. In this matter they had little influence over the CUP government.[47] However, the testimony of their protests gives important insights into what was shared knowledge among the members of the Central Powers.

Between Enver's decree in February and Talaat's deportation regulation of May 1915, awareness grew of the extreme nature of the treatment of the Christian populations in Turkey and in Turkish-occupied Iran. Although the possibility of an Armenian revolt had been discussed almost from the start of the war, the exaggerated hostilities, extensive arrests, and atrocities were out of proportion to the shaky evidence that had been assembled of a full-scale and substantive Armenian rebellion threatening the fiber of the Empire. Instead, it looked more like decisions made in panic by a suspicious and jittery regime willing to believe loose accusations stemming from the distant provinces.

From April and May 1915, the international press started to make public a stream of information about a considerable number of atrocities perpetrated on the Assyrians and Armenians during the Ottoman occupation of Urmia and about the artillery bombardment of the Armenian quarters in Van.[48] On May 24, 1915, the Entente powers published a solemn proclamation stating that in consideration of the Ottoman regime's "crimes against humanity and civilization" they would hold personally responsible "all members of the Turkish Government, ... together with its agents impli-

---

[47] Hull, *Absolute Destruction*, 279–85; Vahakn Dadrian, *German Responsibility in the Armenian Genocide* (1996).

[48] Much of this early information is published in Bryce and Toynbee, *Treatment of Armenians*.

cated in the massacres." At the end of the war, trials would be held for the atrocities as crimes against humanity and civilization. This pronouncement was printed in major newspapers throughout the world.[49]

At first the Germans appeared to have given the Ottoman government its tacit permission to pursue their harsh treatment of the Armenians. After all, it was wartime and the Germans and Russians were doing the same thing in the European theater of war. But they clearly had no idea of the Pandora's box that was being opened. At first, the German ambassador, Baron von Wangenheim, agreed with the Ottoman version that the Armenians were allied with the Russians and posed a grave threat to the survival of Turkey. The ambassador sent a telegram to the German Foreign Office, explaining that the treatment of the Armenians was a consequence of their anti-Turkish insurgency. Although he regretted the brutality of the methods, he stated, "I am of the opinion that we must make the form [of treating Armenians] milder, but we ought not basically hinder them." He appealed to the Foreign Office to try to persuade the pro-Armenian opinion-makers in Germany that the "chosen means are unavoidable given the present military and political condition of Turkey" and to stop their criticism.[50]

Germany's initial permissive attitude, however, soon cracked as the extent of the atrocities began to be known among the German consuls, who were more sensitive to the plight of civilians than were the army officers. They were particularly enraged when it became clear that the policies were not just directed against the Armenians, but also against other Christian groups who lacked contacts with the enemy, even encompassing Protestant and Catholic converts connected to the German missionaries. A major turning point in German opinion was the public humiliation and murder of the Armenian Catholic archbishop of Mardin, Ignace Maloyan, in mid June 1915. News of this outrage spread very quickly.

On June 15, 1915, the second column of Christian prisoners from Mardin and Tel-Arman was trudging, tied together with ropes and chains in groups of five, northward toward the provincial capital Diyarbekir, where it was said they would face trial. In charge of the column was Abdul Khadir, the head of the Mardin gendarmerie, and Tewfik, the assistant to Reshid

---

[49] *New York Times* May 24, 1915, front page. See Beylerian, *Les Grandes Puissants*, documents 33, 34, 36, 37, 38, 40. The original Russian initiative contained the phrase "crimes against Christianity and civilization," but after French and British objections this was changed to "crimes against humanity and civilization."

[50] Wangenheim to Foreign Office May 31, 1915, in Lepsius, *Deutschland und Armenien 1914–1918: Sammlung diplomatischer Aktenstücke* (1919), 79.

Bey, the vali of Diyarbekir. The prisoners had been 255 as they shuffled through the gate to take the main road: 181 Armenian Catholics, 50 Syriac Catholics, 19 Chaldeans, and 4 Protestants. Among them were twelve priests of various denominations. Halfway to Diyarbekir, a selection was made at the caves of Sheikhan and the guards murdered 84 prisoners. A second selection led to the execution of 15, including some of the priests. Probably no prisoner held any hope of reaching Diyarbekir alive, since they all knew that the previous column sent from Mardin on June 11 had been slaughtered down to the last man. Just as the prisoners were being lined up for a new selection and execution, from afar came Ottoman cavalry officers wildly gesticulating and blowing a trumpet. As the riders approached they yelled, "Halt! Halt! Pardon from the Sultan!" A cavalry officer then took command and escorted the surviving prisoners to Diyarbekir, where they were kept under guard. It turned out that the pardon did not concern the Armenians, but only members of the other religions, mostly Syriacs of various faiths. No prisoner was actually released, and the whole group marched back to Mardin and was again locked up. Then unexpectedly on June 26, Memduh, the provincial chief of police, appeared. "All Syriacs, Chaldeans, and Protestants, hold up your hands and give us your names!" This group was allowed to go home. As they left, the Armenian prisoners appealed to the departing: "Have mercy! Remember us and try to save us!" Some of those released had to be carried home.[51]

By June, the German diplomats were fully aware that the deportations and massacres affected more than the Armenians. Perhaps the best-informed German consuls were Holstein, in Mosul, and Rössler, in Aleppo. They received news directly from survivors who managed to escape from Anatolia. The consuls spoke of the need to prevent the Ottoman regime from setting loose a "general massacre" and demanded that their government force a change. This resulted in a reaction from Talaat, who on July 12, 1915, sent a telegram to the vali of Diyarbekir.

> It has been reported to us that the Armenians of the province of Diyarbekir, along with other Christians, are being massacred, and that some 700 Armenians and other Christians were recently slaughtered in Mardin like sheep after having been removed from the city through nightly operations. The number of people slain through such massacres is estimated to be 2,000. It is feared that unless these acts are stopped definitely and swiftly, the Muslim population of the region may proceed to massacre the general Christian population. The political and disciplinary

---

[51] Ishaq Armalto, *Al-Qusara fi nakabaat an nasara* (1919), 224.

> measures adopted against the Armenians are absolutely not to be extended to other Christians, as such acts are likely to create a very bad impression on public opinion. You are ordered to put an immediate end to these acts lest they threaten the lives of the other Christians without discrimination.[52]

The background to Talaat's July 12 telegram was a protest from Germany. The telegram even takes some of its exact wording from a message sent on July 10 by Walter Holstein, the German consul in Mosul, to ambassador Wangenheim in Constantinople.

> The former mutasarrif of Mardin, who is presently here, gave me the following information: the vali of Diyarbekir, Reshid Bey, is raging like a crazed bloodhound against the Christians of his vilayet. Recently he has let gendarmes sent from Diyarbekir slaughter like sheep 700 Christians from Mardin (mostly Armenians) including the Armenian bishop in the night at a place outside the town. Reshid Bey is continuing his bloody work against the innocent, and their number is today over two thousand. Unless the government immediately takes energetic measures to stop Reshid Bey, the common Muslim population in the vilayet will also begin to massacre Christians. Day by day the situation here is growing more threatening. The government must recall Reshid Bey immediately and thereby document that it does not approve of these atrocities, which is the common opinion here.[53]

The identity of Holstein's informant is not clear because the Germans believed that there were two consecutive mutasarrifs of Mardin who were replaced for opposition to the Christian massacres.[54]

Albert Guys, who was living in Aleppo as a private person after retiring as French consul in Diyarbekir, supplied similar news to the Entente.[55] He composed a long report and wrote that a few days after Reshid took over, mass arrests of Christians began and about 1,600 were imprisoned and tortured. Every day new bodies could be seen outside the ancient Roman walls: about one hundred prominent Armenian merchants died of torture. In the city, "ferocious and barbaric" house searches for weapons con-

---

[52] BOA. DH. ŞFR, nr 54/406 Ministry of Interior to Diyarbekir vilayet, also printed in Turkish Republic. Prime Ministry. *Armenians in Ottoman Documents (1915–1920)* (1995), 75.

[53] Holstein to German Embassy July 10, 1915, in Lepsius, *Deutschland und Armenien*, 101–2.

[54] Rössler to Bethmann Hollweg September 27, 1915, in Mikaelyan, *Armenische Frage*, 208.

[55] Report of Guys July 24, 1915, in Beylerian, *Les Grandes Puissants*, 48–52.

tinued for six weeks. In Mardin, "a great part of the Armenian Catholics, Jacobites, Chaldeans, and Syriac Catholics have met the same horrible end as those in Diyarbekir. When the Armenian Catholic Patriarchy sent a telegram to the archbishop in Mardin, they received the response that the latter no longer existed."

On July 12, Ambassador Wangenheim presented Germany's formal protest to Talaat about the fears of a general massacre of all Christians.

> On the orders of Reshid Bey, the gendarmes of Diyarbekir went to Mardin and there arrested the Armenian bishop along with a great number of Armenians and other Christians, in all seven hundred persons. During the night, all of them were taken outside the city and butchered like sheep. The total number of victims of these massacres is estimated at 2,000 souls. If the imperial government does not take measures against Reshid Bey, it is feared that it will not be possible to stop the lower classes of the Muslim population in the region of the vilayet from committing a general massacre of all of the Christian inhabitants.[56]

On the same day as the German protest, Talaat sent his telegram to Reshid. Obviously the intention was to please the German ambassador; since these events were a month old, Talaat must have already been well informed by his own ministry. But there were some differences between the two versions. The Germans named the provincial governor as the mastermind and knew that the gendarmes acted on his orders. Talaat's telegram excludes that. The Germans demanded that Reshid be replaced; however, he remained in his position until 1916 and was never reprimanded for his anti-Christian activities. Also, Talaat specifies that the negative treatment should be confined to Armenians only, which is not exactly the thrust of Holstein's argument that the Turkish authorities were butchering completely innocent people, including the Armenians. This was a far cry from the "documented disapproval of the atrocities" that Holstein demanded. Reshid Bey and the provincial government in Diyarbekir resumed killing Christians of all denominations as soon as they felt they were not being observed, but it was done less publicly than before.

On August 4, 1914, Talaat sent a ciphered telegram to various valis and mutasarrifs ordering them to cease the deportations of the Catholic Armenians and to send him statistics of their number.[57] On August 15 he

---

[56] Kaiserlich Deutsche Botschaft to Talaat July 12, 1915, in Lepsius, *Deutschland und Armenien*, 102–3.

[57] BOA. DH. ŞFR, nr 54-A/252.

sent a similar telegram stopping deportations of Protestant Armenians and requiring statistics.[58] The content of these telegrams was to demarcate that the target population was the "Gregorian" Armenians who belonged to the Apostolic Church. But what about the other Oriental Christians? Did the Sultan's pardon and Talaat's telegrams really result in full amnesty? Apparently some sort of order had arrived in Diyarbekir earlier than Talaat's telegram. The Mardin prisoners who were Syrian, Chaldean, and Protestant were released on June 26. The same thing happened on June 27 to the non-Armenian prisoners in Nisibin and Derike, where all Christian prisoners were released, but all were rearrested. Through various compilations there is written evidence of massacres and attacks against Christians in 178 small towns and villages in Diyarbekir province and its nearest neighboring regions (see chapter 8).[59] These are a mixture of Armenian, Syriac, and Chaldean populations. Only a minority of testimonies date the events, but in 54 cases dates are given that are before Talaat's July 12 telegram. Massacres in April and May took place mostly in villages and towns near the city of Diyarbekir. Those in June and early July took place in the sanjak of Mardin. Thus when the telegram of July 12 came, the lion's share of the destruction had already taken place and there were not many left to save.

Large-scale attacks on rural towns and villages appear to have ceased after mid July, probably in connection with the month of Ramadan. A clear exception is the border town of Jezire, with a mixed Armenian, Syriac, and Chaldean population that had been relatively free from persecutions until August. In the Christian enclave of Urfa, in Aleppo province, massacres did not start until the middle of September. In the major towns of Diyarbekir and Mardin the amnesty appears to have been respected, although the few surviving Christians there continued to be harassed, arrested, tortured, and killed. But the mass character of the previous atrocities was seldom present. There are, however, exceptions. In the town of Midyat, with 25,000 inhabitants, which was half Syriac Orthodox, soldiers encircled the Christian quar-

---

[58] BOA. DH. ŞFR, nr 55/20.

[59] Malfono Abed Mschiho Na'man Qarabasch, *Vergossenes Blut: Geschichten der Greuel, die an den Christen in der Türkei verübt, und der Leiden, die ihnen 1895 und 1914–1918 zugefügt wurden* (2002); Süleyman Hinno, *Günhe d Süryoye d Turabdin* [The massacre of the Syriacs of Tur Abdin] (1987); Jacques Rhétoré, *Les Chrétiens aux bêtes": Souvenirs de la guerre sainte proclamée par les Turcs contre les chrétiens en 1915* (2005); Hyacinthe Simon, *Mardin la ville heroique: Autel et tombeau de l'Arménie (Asie Mineure) durant les massacres de 1915* (1991); Joseph Naayem, *Les Assyro-Chaldéens et les Arméniens massacrés par les Turcs: Documents inédits recueillis par un témoin oculaire* (1920); Armalto, *Al-Qousara* (1919).

ters on 19 July and began to shoot into the houses. The battle of Midyat went on for more than a week.[60] The mass murder of the Syriac Orthodox population of the town of Nisibin took place on August 16 (the Armenian population having been killed in mass executions on June 15 and June 28). Other places in Diyarbekir province that experienced mass extermination after Talaat's telegram were Derike, Sawro, and Ras al-'Ayn.

Despite the official declarations excluding them from the "deportations," non-Armenian Christians kept on being the object of mass murder. The German consuls repeatedly informed their embassy that Catholics and Protestants were being slaughtered. On August 13, the consul in Aleppo, Rössler, reported that the order freeing the Armenian Catholics had been rescinded and that the vali said that all were to be deported without exception.[61] Mordtmann, the dragoman of the German embassy, heard from the Armenian Catholic Patriarch that the order had been reversed.[62] Temporary Ambassador Hohenlohe-Langenburg also learned that the Turkish government had changed its orders for both Catholics and Protestants. He had taken some diplomatic countermeasures but did not think they would have any success.[63] Throughout the region, the Germans began to realize that the Turks considered the given orders excluding Protestants and Catholics not as universal decrees, but only referring to limited places—for instance, the city of Aleppo, but not the province.[64] Later it was explained that the orders only had relevance for the few Catholics and Protestants who had not yet been deported from their homes and that the deportees would never be permitted to return home. Those who were in the midst of transport would continue to the designated destinations.[65]

By August 1915, the German diplomats were particularly anxious that it not appear that Germans could be observed taking any part in the anti-Christian events. A temporary Ambassador in Istanbul, Prince Hohenlohe-Langenburg, issued an appeal to the *Reichskanzler* to release to the German public statements to the effect that all Germans should distance themselves from and assume no responsibility for the Turkish government's policy of "extermination" and "measures forced" on the Armenians and express the

---

[60] Commander of Third Army Mahmut Kamil to Enver July 22, 1915, document no. 2012 in *Askeri Tarih Belgeleri Dergisi* vol. 34 no. 85 (October 1985), 81.

[61] Rössler to Bethmann Hollweg August 13, 1915, in Lepsius, *Deutschland und Armenien*, 129.

[62] Mordtmann annotation of August 21, 1915, ibid., 137.

[63] Hohenlohe-Langenburg to consulate in Adana August 24, 1915, ibid., 138.

[64] Hohenlohe-Langenburg to consulate in Aleppo August 27, 1915, ibid., 143.

[65] Rössler to Deutsche Botschaft September 12, 1915, ibid., 153.

opinion that the German authorities did not approve of what was happening.[66]

The opinion is widespread that the Germans could have done more than just pressure their ally with diplomatic notes. They hesitated because Turkey quite obviously was more important to Germany than Germany was to Turkey. Turkey succeeded in tying down Russian troops that otherwise could have been used on the east European front. The Ottomans had less need for the Germans. They were doing rather well on their own with their few German advisors: they stopped the allies in their tracks at Gallipoli, they won a victory over the British south of Baghdad, and the front against Russia in the Caucasus was stable. This was no small accomplishment for a country that was unprepared for war. The *quid pro quo* was that Germany made only feeble efforts to stop the "deportations."

Armenian Patriarch Zaven was kept continually informed of the repeated attempts by the neutral countries to influence the Ottoman government. On many occasions, both the United States and the Bulgarian ambassadors had tried to intervene, but their words fell on deaf ears. Talaat would always respond that the treatment of the Christians was an internal affair and that after the repeal of the capitulations, no foreign power had any right to interfere in such matters.[67]

During the autumn, the Vatican began to put pressure on the Austro-Hungarian government to use its influence over their Ottoman ally to end the persecutions of and atrocities against the Christians. On October 24, 1915, the ambassador of the Vatican to the Viennese court approached Foreign Minister Stephan von Burian to intervene at the Sublime Porte on behalf of the Armenians. Burian replied that the Austrians had been trying for several months to make an impression on the Ottoman government. But they had made no progress, as the Turks always maintained that "Armenian attacks on the peaceful Turkish population motivated such measures."[68]

Energetic Vatican involvement was triggered by the murder of the archbishop of Mardin, Maloyan, since he was a Catholic and had been to

---

[66] Hohenlohe-Langenburg to Bethmann Hollweg August 12, 1915, ibid., 126–27.

[67] Partiarch Zaven to Archimandrate Vegunin December 28, 1915, in *Genotsid armyan*, 343.

[68] Artem Ogandzhanyan, *1915 god neosporimye svidetel'stva: Avstriiskie dokumenty o genotside armyan* [The year 1915 unquestionable evidence: Austrian documents on the Armenian genocide] (2005), 189.

Rome. In July, Monsignor Dolci, the Vatican agent in Istanbul, was called to a meeting with the Armenian Apostolic Patriarch in Istanbul to discuss the "general massacre in Mardin."[69] Trying to correspond as the highest Catholic leader with the highest Muslim leader, Pope Benedict XV sent a personal letter to Sultan Mahmud V on September 10, 1915, protesting that innocent Christians were being treated barbarously and appealing to the Sultan for clemency.[70] Other dispatches of Vatican diplomats indicate a deep concern for a "threatening destruction of an entire people." It had become a case of collective punishment with no distinction as to religion or whether the victims were women, children, or priests.[71] The Austrian diplomats even had difficulty in getting a meeting to give the Pope's letter personally to the Sultan because of Young Turk obstructionism. But when this finally happened, on November 19, 1915, the Sultan replied that it was unfortunately not possible to distinguish the "peaceful elements from those who were in rebellion"; thus the punishment had to collective.[72] However, the mounting international pressure did seem to be having an effect, and in December Dolci could report that the persecutions has "nearly completely ceased" and that there was a "substantial improvement of the situation."[73] By the end of 1915, the major expulsions and massacres had ceased, but the greatest part of the Christian population in eastern Anatolia had ceased to exist. Persecution did not subside but continued with less intensity throughout the war.

---

[69] Dolci to Cardinal Gaspari July 29, 1915, cited in Andrea Riccardi, *Mediterraneo: Cristianesimo e islam tra coabitazione e conflitto* (1997), 116.

[70] Benedict XV to Mahmud V September 10, 1915, ibid., 122.

[71] Cardinal Gaspari to Monsignor Scapinelli September 15, 1915, ibid., 121.

[72] Ibid., 122.

[73] Dolci to Cardinal Gaspari December 12, 1915, in ibid, 123.

4 PLAYING WITH FIRE: OCCUPIED URMIA

On March 10, 1915, the Russian consul, Pavel Vvedenski, became the first civilian official to inspect a horrifying atrocity in an out-of-the-way spot on the plain of Salmas, near several small Iranian towns. This was the village of Haftevan, between Khosrowa, the center of the Chaldean Catholic minority, and Dilman, an Armenian town. This was the first consciously planned mass execution of civilians committed by the Ottoman army in its Caucasus campaigns, the first of many. Before his eyes were the remains of the adult Christian male population of an entire district. Vvedenski found hundreds of corpses lying exposed everywhere. All of the bodies were mutilated and, as far as he could see, most had been decapitated. Vvedenski particularly noted several horrendous scenes. The massacre took place some days before the Russian troops arrived. Locals said that Ottoman soldiers had cordoned off the village and those who tried to enter had been beaten.[1]

The vice-commander of Russia's First Caucasus Army, K. Matikyan, counted the corpses and came up with a total of 707 Armenians and Syriacs (or Aisori as he called them) who had been murdered by Ottoman soldiers and Kurdish volunteers on the orders of the kaymakam. He wrote that he saw "with my own eyes hundreds of mangled corpses in pits, stinking from infection, lying in the open, I saw headless corpses, chopped off by axes, hands, legs, piles of heads, corpses crushed under rocks from fallen walls."[2] A Russian newspaper immediately categorized this event as a pogrom.[3]

---

[1] Vladimir Genis, *Vitse-konsul Vvedenski sluzhba v Persii I Bukharskom khanstve (1906–1920 gg.) Rossiskaya diplomatiya v sud'bakh* [Vice-Consul Vvedenski's service in Persia and the Khanate of Bukhara, 1906–1920] (2003), 44.

[2] K. Matikyan letter of February 24/March 9, 1915, in *Genotsid armyan v osmanskoi imperii: Sbornik dokumentov i materialov* [The Armenian genocide in the Ottoman Empire: Collection of documents and materials], ed. M. G. Nersisiyan (1982), 276–77, and *Russkie istochniki o genotside armyan v Osmanskoi imperii 1915-1916 gody* [Russian sources on the Armenian genocide in the Ottoman Empire 1915–1916], ed. G. A. Abraamyan and T. G. Sevan-Khachatryan (1995), 9–10.

[3] *Tiflisskii listok* March 15, 1915, cited in K. P. Matveev and I. I. Mar-Yukhanna, *Assiriiskii vopros vo vremya i posle pervoi mirovoi voiny* [The Assyrian Question during and after World War I] (1968), 50.

The American Presbyterian missionary F. N. Jessup wrote on March 17, 1915:

> A few days before the return of the Russian army to Salmas, when the Turks saw that they would be compelled to flee, they secured the names of all Christians by a ruse, pretending that all who registered would be protected. Then they gathered all the men into one place and carried them out in companies of about twenty-five, each to be shot down in cold blood. Others were tied with their heads sticking through the rungs of a ladder and decapitated, others hacked to pieces or mutilated before death. In this way practically every Christian man remaining in Salmas was massacred. You can imagine the fate of girls and women. The most detailed report received, signed by a number of men now on the ground, stated that from 712 to 720 men were thus killed in Salmas.[4]

"ATROCITIES COMMITTED BY THE OTTOMAN TROOPS"

Iran's Minister of Foreign Affairs registered a formal protest on March 5 with the Ottoman ambassador in Tehran over what he termed the calamities that had struck the people through the "atrocities committed by the Ottoman troops" that had occupied the northwest corner of his country. He complained that the powerless provincial officials had been forced to watch repeated

> acts of violence committed by your soldiers, who in the course of battle have pillaged many villages, torched many others, and reduced all of the inhabitants to a state of misery. This violence is most noted in the areas where there are many villages inhabited by Christians, where the population has been violated and mercilessly massacred.

In the experience of the Foreign Minister, the extreme form of these massacres was unmatched even in enemy territory, much less within a neutral country like Iran. The Minister had also received official protests over the conduct of the Ottoman occupants on March 3 and 19 from the legations of Britain, France, and the United States. The Turkish ambassador in Tehran was lectured on the absolute necessity of damping the "hatred sown by the Turks among the tribes of Azerbaijan." The Iranians insisted that Turkey pull back its troops and during the withdrawal exercise restraint, conducting themselves "with less ferocity, particularly the Kurdish irregulars."[5] In response the units commanded by Jevdet, who were responsible

---

[4] F. N. Jessup March 17, 1915, in James Bryce & Arnold Toynbee, *The Treatment of Armenians in the Ottoman Empire, 1915–1916* (1916; uncensored ed., 2000), 153.

[5] Minister of Foreign Affairs Moaven od-Dowleh to Turkish Ambassador

for the worst excesses, drew back to Van, where they transplanted their acquired taste for anti-Christian ferocity.

What is known about Haftevan barely affords a clue as to why it was selected as the place for a major massacre. Perhaps it was because it was near a crossroads for north–south and east–west travel. Perhaps it was just too close to the Ottoman headquarters. Perhaps it was because for decades it had served as a base for American Presbyterian and Swedish Lutheran missionary activities among the Armenians and Assyrians. The Americans had begun in 1884, and the Christian population expanded as an asylum for Ottoman refugees fleeing from the 1895–96 pogroms. The Swedish missionary society was present from 1902 to 1907 and ran an orphanage, an infirmary, activities for the disabled, and a small carpet-weaving factory.[6]

In nearby Khosrowa, which was overwhelmingly Chaldean Catholic, the French mission complex served as the headquarters of the Ottoman commander Jevdet, who was on leave from his post as vali of Van. The murders were said to have had been committed jointly by the Ottoman troops and local Shikak tribesmen under the notorious border bandit Simko Agha, his brother Shukri, and Omar Khan. Jevdet had realized that the Russians were on their way and could not be stopped by the relatively weak troops and unreliable Kurdish cavalry under his command. Promised reinforcements, under general Halil Bey, had failed to arrive. The Russian detachments advancing against them were known to have an Armenian commander and to include Armenian and Assyrian volunteer brigades. Perhaps feelings also ran high because of the Ottoman origin of some of the Armenians in Haftevan. Occupation authorities summoned all Christian males in surrounding rural districts to come to the village of Haftevan on the pretext of their needing to be registered. In addition to these villagers, all of the Armenian and Syriac males in the market town of Dilman and its closest villages were arrested and taken to the place of execution. Orders had recently arrived from the War Office that Armenian soldiers in Ottoman service could be shot if they did not follow orders, and some of the victims belonged to this category.[7]

March 5, 1915; Minister of Foreign Affairs Moaven od-Dowleh to Persian Ambassador in Constantinople March 18, 1915; Ambassador of the United States Caldwell to Minister of Foreign Affairs March 19, 1915, documents nos. 266, 301 and 306 in Empire de Perse, *Neutralité Persane: Documents diplomatiques* (1919), 139, 153, 155.

[6] N. F. Höjer, "Till armeniernas vänner" (1897); Elin Sundvall, "Missionen i Persien" (1911), 60; John Hultvall, *Mission och vision i Orienten: Svenska missionsförbundets mission i Transkaukasien-Persien 1882–1921* (1991), 224–34.

[7] See also the following statements in Bryce and Toynbee, *Treatment of Armeni-*

Over two days, somewhere between 700 and 800 adult males were executed under hair-raising circumstances. Jevdet's army ran low on ammunition, so the soldiers were told not to use bullets. In one farmyard Vvedenski found a covered well and from its roof hanging upside down was a headless body; the well itself was full of corpses, all of them decapitated. The victims had been hung upside down by their feet and had their heads chopped off before being dropped into the well. In groups of a dozen, men had been made to face a wall while they were killed one by one with pickaxes smashing the backs of their skulls. In another place, men were forced to put their heads between their legs and then their heads were cut off as if slaughtering sheep. In another place prisoners stuck their heads through rungs in a ladder and after that the heads were chopped off. Vvedenski counted fifteen wells filled with bodies, and in addition there were several barns filled with corpses. Vvedenski had great difficulty keeping the Armenians and Syriacs, who had begun to return to their homes, from taking revenge on their Muslim neighbors.[8] Even the Ottoman high command was stunned by the news of these excesses. The Turkish General Staff's military history of the war calls it an "unfortunate incident" and puts the blame on undisciplined troops, volunteers, and tribes.[9]

However, this was a catastrophic result that could have been predicted. The Turkish-Iranian border strip had been loaded like an explosive device, a region already marked by ethnic and religious conflict. The Ottomans had been fishing for collaborators. They found many among the Sunni Kurdish tribes, the Turkmen inhabitants, as well as the constitutionalist opposition to the Shah. There were many disgruntled Muslims who had benefited far less from the growing Russian trade than had the Christians. The border strip was filled with CUP organizers and Teskilat-i Mahsusa agents who conspired with local political adventurers and bandit chiefs. Into this, the torch of jihad was thrown. In all likelihood the Ottomans intended to create as much chaos as possible and then move in and reinstate calm, proving that the Iranian government was no longer respected and that only the Ottomans could guarantee law and order. In that way they could strengthen

---

ans: William Shedd, 139; Robert M. Larabee, 146; Paul Shimmon, 197, 587. The Turkish denialist historian Salahi Sonyel states that the "claim" of a massacre at Haftevan was "refuted by the British consul in Tabriz" (*The Assyrians of Turkey: Victims of Major Power Policy* [2001], 88).

[8] Genis, *Vitse-konsul Vvedenski*, 44.

[9] ATAŞE 4/3671, Kls. 2950, H-11, F-139, cited in Genelkurmay Başkanlığı, *Birinci Dünya Harbi'nde Türk Harbi Kafkas Cephesi 3 ncü Ordu Harekâtı* [World War I, Turkish War on the Caucasus Front, Third Army operations], 2:1 (1993), 582.

their international credibility for permanent annexation and at the same time gain the loyalty of the locals. But the forces they set in motion proved impossible to control, and their own troops ceased to be the solution to the mayhem but rather its cause.

THE OCCUPATION OF IRAN

The Shah of Iran declared the neutrality of Iran on November 1, 1914. Iran needed to be on good terms with the Ottomans and Germans as well as the British and Russians and dared not side with either. However, none of these powers respected Iranian neutrality. Some of the blackest marks in the history of Christian–Muslim violence took place in the Iranian province of Azerbaijan during the first part of 1915 (map 4). In the muddle that was Iranian politics, the entire northern zone had been under Russian protection for some years. The Russians ruled through a puppet governor and garrisoned small numbers of troops in the important towns. But at the beginning of January, the Russian garrisons suddenly pulled out. The background was the Iranian insistence on respect for its neutrality. Although Azerbaijan was already in a state of turmoil and de facto war, the Shah's government claimed that the main cause was the Russian presence, which increased local sympathies for the Sultan. The Iranian government assured the British ambassador that it could guarantee the safety and property of the Christian minorities. The Iranian army would move in, and that would assuredly calm the ongoing "religious effervescence." [10]

---

[10] Account of meeting between Mostovfi el-Memalik, the President of the Council of Ministers, the Minister of Foreign Affairs, and the Ambassadors of Russia and Great Britain December 23, 1914; Account of meeting with the President of Council of Ministers and Ambassador of Great Britain December 29, 1914, documents nos. 137 and 148, in Empire de Perse, *Neutralité Persane*, 78–82, 88–89.

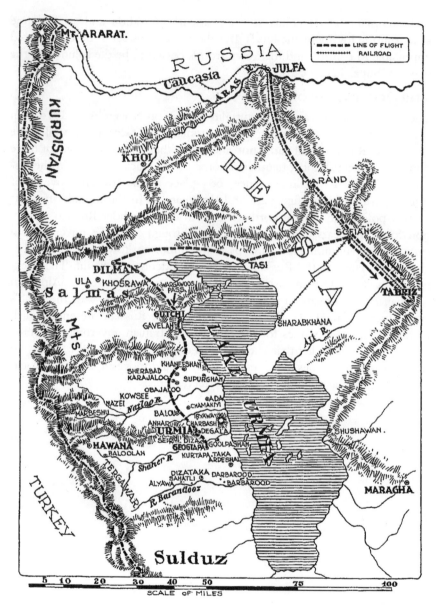

Map 4: Northwestern Persia, showing principal Christian towns destroyed by Turks and Kurds; also line of flight to the Russian border. From Yonan Shahbaz, *The Rage of Islam* (1918), 1.

After the Iranian government succeeded in pressuring the Russians out, they also repeatedly demanded the evacuation of Ottoman forces from their soil.[11] Strangely, this did not happen. The Russian retreat initiated a number of days of anarchy, during which time many Christians fled to Russian territory while local Persian and Kurdish Muslims perpetrated pogroms, shot refugees, raped women, and committed countless terrible deeds. Instead of respecting Iranian neutrality, the Ottomans moved in troops and assembled masses of tribal volunteers on a wide front; after a short interim of sheer chaos, the army of occupation attempted to restore a semblance of order—a complete failure. Because the Ottoman army was fighting on three fronts already and would soon open an attack on Egypt, it had difficulty finding adequate trained troops for occupied Azerbaijan. Instead they relied on a skeleton crew of a few hundred soldiers backed up by an enormous collection of tribal nomads attracted to the many appeals from the authorities to engage in holy war.

The Turkish forces composed of mobile regiments of the Van Jandarma, Teskilat-i Mahsusa operatives, tribal volunteers, and local Muslims were apparently surprised by the unexpected opportunity. Their subsequent behavior showed that they were mentally unprepared for occupation and peaceful rule over alien civilians. Fired up by holy war rhetoric, the occupation forces and their associated tribesmen treated the local Christians badly, as it was taken for granted that they wholeheartedly supported the Russians. At an early stage, the Iranian government had to protest to Turkey and Germany over the brutality of the occupation. On February 11, the German ambassador in Istanbul hosted a meeting between War Minister Enver and the Iranian ambassador to air complaints about the Ottoman troops.[12]

It is not easy to see who was actually in charge, as the invasion was split into several free-ranging detachments. The first phase of occupation rule was purely military, but a civilian occupation government led by Raghib Bey, the former Turkish consul in Urmia, took over in late February and ruled until mid May. Initially, the highest-ranking military and political leader appears to have been Ömer Naji Bey, the CUP's unchallenged expert on Iran and a field commander of the Teskilat-i Mahsusa. He had been in Iran several times in the past decade preparing for a local pan-Islamic upris-

---

[11] Minister of Foreign Affairs to the Persian Ambassadors in London and Petrograd January 6, 1915; Minister of Foreign Affairs to Persian Ambassador in Constantinople January 7, 1915, documents nos. 155 and 156, in ibid., 94–95.

[12] Ulrich Gehrke, *Persien in der deutschen Orientpolitik während des Ersten Weltkrieges* (1961), 2:309.

ing and at one time even ran his own guerilla band. He was identified as leader when the troops (an ad hoc unit called the "Mosul detachment") entered Urmia (now renamed Rezaiyeh) on January 4 and Tabriz on January 14. He appears to have returned to his post as inspector over east Anatolia after the invasion was completed.[13] The missionaries witnessed his attempts to restore law and order. He personally supervised the execution of twelve Kurdish brigands caught red-handed plundering the French mission complex in Urmia.[14] A complicated character, at one moment he conversed with the missionaries amicably in the French he had picked up in Parisian exile, while at the next he preached holy war. Using what sounds suspiciously like a false name, a certain Ibrahim Fouzi or Ibrahim Effendi sent out appeals calling himself alternately commander of the Turkish troops, or chief of the mujahedin, or the representative from Mosul. He appealed for local volunteers to follow the road into Russia and as "true partisans of Islam act sincerely and unite yourselves against the infidel."[15]

Another leader of the makeshift Turkish occupation was the aforementioned Jevdet, vali of Van province, who was Minster of War, Enver's brother-in-law and thus a member of his inner circle. Westerners, like some German military advisors, found Jevdet hard to judge. However, it appears that he held the view that the Turks should at least solve the Armenian question even if they did not stand a chance of winning the war. He was seen as an exponent of a policy dedicated to "the promulgation and expansion of Islam."[16] According to the Ottoman view, Jevdet Bey commanded "an ad hoc regiment-sized force."[17] They occupied a bulge from the Turkish border extending over the Salmas plain to the administrative center of Dilman. This was a farming region with many Armenians and Chaldeans.

---

[13] Genelkurmay, *Birinci Dünya Harbi'nde*, 581–82; Fethi Tevetoğlu, *Ömer Naci* (1987), 165; Florence Hellot-Bellier, *Chronique de massacres annoncés: Les Assyro-Chaldéens de Perse, la Perse et les puissants européennes 1896–1919* (1998), 106.

[14] Lazarist missionary Abel Zayia cited in Eugène Griselle, *Syriens et Chaldéens: Leur martyre, leurs espérances* (1917), 36, 47; Statement of the superior of the mission at Khosrowa, M. Georges Decroo, "En Perse: Pillages et massacres" (1915).

[15] Minister of Foreign Affairs to Russian Ambassador January 7, 1915; Minister of Foreign Affairs to Persian Ambassador in Constantinople February 10, 1915, documents nos. 157 and 214, in Empire de Perse, *Neutralité Persane*, 96, 119.

[16] Paul Leverkuehn, *Posten auf ewiger Wache: Aus dem abenteuerreichen Leben des Max von Scheubner-Richter* (1938), 33; see also Clarence D. Ussher, *An American Physician in Turkey: A Narrative of Adventures in Peace and War* (1917), 260ff.

[17] Edward J. Erickson, *Ordered to Die: A History of the Ottoman Army in the First World War* (2001), 65.

After his first taste of genocide at Haftevan, Jevdet returned to Turkey, where he led the siege of the Armenians of Van during April and May and the horrendous atrocities in the towns of Sa'irt and Bitlis in June.

A third leader was Kazim (Karabekir), who commanded a force of Jandarma and tribal volunteers. What was termed the First Expeditionary Force under Kazim was seldom more than units of gendarmes and unreliable tribal volunteers. This regiment camped along the border strip and advanced into Iran only to take the nearby town of Kotur, which was just north of Jevdet's position. The Kotur corridor stretched into Iran. From there "detachments of irregulars" patrolled the main caravan road leading to Khoi.[18] Kazim's units were all but permanently based in the Kotur River valley and around Bashkale in order to guard the likeliest approaches to Van from the points of easiest entry.[19]

A Persian official, the powerless governor of Urmia, Azim al Saltaneh Sardar, lacked words to describe conditions during the occupation. Instead he wrote that the Turks "had instigated the mujahedin and the agents of Satan to perpetrate that which may not be written with a pen nor spoken by a tongue."[20]

IRANIAN WEAKNESS AND FOREIGN INTRIGUES

During World War I, the town of Urmia, with about 50,000 inhabitants, changed hands several times. When the Russians abandoned the city on January 2, 1915, the Turks took control. The last Ottoman forces left a few days before the Russians marched back on May 24, 1915.[21] In the wake of the Russian revolutions of 1917, the Russian army began to break up and then disappeared. The Christians organized their own defensive forces out of locals and the many refugees. A new Ottoman invasion, with new atrocities, forced them all out of Urmia in 1918, but that is a different story.

The Ottomans had long desired to annex the Urmia region and had spoken with the Germans and Iranians about this goal. They had occupied the border strip as late as 1912, and the exact border was a subject of contention. On several occasions the Iranians noted that the stones marking

---

[18] Paléologue to Delcassé December 30, 1914, in Arthur Beylerian, *Les Grandes Puissants: l'Empire Ottoman et les armeéniens dans les archives françaises (1914–1918)* (1983), 6.

[19] Felix Guse, *Die Kaukasusfront im Weltkrieg bis zum Frieden von Brest* (1940), 33, 60.

[20] Cited in Basil Nikitine, "Une apologie kurde du sunnism" (1933), 122.

[21] Basile Nikitine, "Urmiya" (1934), 1121.

the border had been removed.²² In late October 1914, Enver and Talaat met with the Iranian ambassador in the presence of the German ambassador. They proposed a project to assemble, with German support, a joint Ottoman-Iranian army of 100,000 men. In exchange, Iran was to surrender to Turkey the region of Urmia.²³ The Iranians refused, but obviously some of the activities of the Ottoman authorities during the occupation of Azerbaijan, such as moving border markers, were inspired by these ideas. When diplomacy failed, the Ottomans began to conspire with the adventurous Iranian opposition politician Prince Salar al-Dawla to start a revolt in the western provinces.²⁴

Regardless of who was in power, Ottoman governments in the decade prior to the Great War followed a policy of trying to annex this province. Taking advantage of the weakness of Russia after its defeat by Japan, the Ottomans pushed forward their position in the Caucasus. The Turkish army invaded Persian Azerbaijan in 1905 and, although it left some parts earlier, kept troops in place until October 1912 when the First Balkan War erupted. In 1907, the CUP sent Ömer Naji Bey straight from exile in Paris to Iran, where he disguised himself as a schoolteacher. He propagated pan-Islamic brotherhood between Turks and Iranians, found allies among the Shah's enemies, formed a guerilla band, and managed to get caught but was pardoned in the nick of time from facing a firing squad.²⁵

German missionaries testified to repeated attacks on Christian villages during this period.²⁶ The Ottoman diplomats claimed not only all areas where Turkish was spoken, but also areas inhabited by Sunni Kurds. This overlapped the regions where the Armenians and East Syriacs lived. Ottoman expansionism met head on with Russian expansionism, as the Tsar's government had longstanding interests in the same region. Following religious and political divisions, the Ottomans sought support among local Muslims, while the Russians favored the local Christians. Both countries vied for the support of the fickle Kurdish tribes, in particular the Shikak, who since the 1880s had formed a growing confederation living in the

---

²² Circular to all Persian foreign legations November 12, 1914; Kargozar of Tabriz to Minister of Foreign Affairs February 26, 1915, documents nos. 77, 247, in Empire de Perse, *Neutralité Persane*, 45–46, 132.

²³ M. S. Lazarev, *Kurdistan i kurdskaya problema (90-e gody XIX veka- 1917 g.)* [Kurdistan and the Kurdish Question, 1890–1917] (1964), 299.

²⁴ Gehrke, *Persien in der deutschen Orientpolitik*, 1:40, 2:29.

²⁵ Tevetoğlu, *Ömer Naci*, 88–94.

²⁶ Gabriele Yonan, *Ein vergessener Holocaust: Die Vernichtung der christlichen Assyrer in der Türkei* (1989), 67–77.

Turco-Iranian no-man's-land. Always difficult, their chief Simko, a bandit with nationalistic instincts, waged partisan wars on both sides of the border and married into the family of the traditional power-holders, the shaikhs of Nihri.[27]

In July 1909, the Shah had been deposed and sent into exile. A new constitution, which he had annulled, was restored and Nasir-ul-Mulk ruled as regent. Upon this crisis, Russia and Britain reached an agreement to divide Iran into zones of influence. The Russians received the northern part, the British the southern part, and in the middle was a neutral zone. Each of the powers moved in some troops and tried to build up a local police force. The neutral zone was patrolled by a gendarmerie commanded by Swedish officers, who were blatantly pro-German during the war.[28]

The German ambassador in Constantinople, Baron Wangenheim, feared that Russia aimed to annex the province of Persian Azerbaijan and, if possible, all of Kurdistan.[29] Persian Azerbaijan fell into the Russian sphere, and Russia slowly took charge by garrisoning small numbers of troops in Tabriz in 1909 and in Urmia and Khoi in 1910 and by extending its protectorate as far as Sawuj Bulak (south of Lake Urmia and now renamed Mahabad) in 1911. It also created a Persian Cossack regiment. Within their zone of influence, the main Russian interest was in the northern sector running from Tabriz to Khoi, which was settled with Armenians and Kurds. The Kurdish tribes of the Shikak and Haydaranli overlapped the borders. Agents of Russia, Turkey, and the Shah constantly courted the tribal leaders, particularly Simko, who lived off raiding the farmers on the frontier around Salmas, and who was given the position of district governor of Kotur in a fruitless attempt to tame him.[30] The Turkish-Kurdish refugee Abdul Rezzak, of the Badr Khan dynasty, entered Russian service, and he was given the task of creating cooperation between the Kurds and the Armenian and Syrian Christians in the northern borderlands.[31]

The Russians and the Ottomans vied with each other to win the allegiance of influential local personalities. After its coup in January 1913, the CUP sent a thirty-man undercover mission to the area to prepare for future

---

[27] Lazarev, *Kurdistan*, 201; Farideh Koohi-Kamali, *The Political Development of Kurds in Iran: Pastoral Nationalism* (2003); Martin van Bruinessen, "Kurdish Tribes and the State of Iran: the Case of Simko's Revolt" (1983).

[28] Markus Ineichen, *Die Schwedischen Offiziere in Persien (1911–1916)* (2002).

[29] Lazarev, *Kurdistan*, 236.

[30] Ibid., 180, 201; van Bruinessen, "Kurdish Tribes," 383.

[31] ATAŞE, Kol.: BDH, Kls.: 1488, Dos.: 32/-, Fih.: 3-6. Confidential letter No. 262 Caucasus Military Command to Caucasus Governor March 26, 1914.

expansion. A leading figure was the military officer Halil Bey, an uncle of Enver who later returned to Azerbaijan as the head of the Fifth Ottoman Expeditionary Force.[32] Other members of the group were Ömer Naji, who was fluent in Persian, and Kazim Karabekir. Most, if not all, of the group were Teskilat-i Mahsusa operatives. In his memoirs Halil mentioned that they particularly tried to curry the favor of Simko and that he believed that they had become friends.[33]

THE CHRISTIAN MINORITIES

According to the Russian general staff, the population of the Urmia province was nearly 300,000, and 40 percent were Christian. About 50,000 were Armenians, the 75,000 Syriacs were mostly Nestorians, but among them were 30,000 Russian Orthodox, 3,000 Chaldeans, and 1,000 Lutherans.[34] These figures are not entirely accurate, probably exaggerate the size of the Russian Church, and definitely underestimate the Catholic and Protestant presence. The list Agha Petros presented to the Peace Conference (see chap. 1) gave the figure of 11,237 "Assyro-Chaldean" households for the dioceses of Urmia and Gawar. However, despite the claim, that list excluded the Chaldean and even some of the Nestorian population.

There was a very large Nestorian community with a metropolitan residing in Urmia and bishops in Ada, Gogtapa, Gyarvilan, and Supurgan. The Chaldean community was also large. The Chaldean bishop of Salmas resided in the town of Khosrowa and in that and eleven other congregations had a flock numbering about 10,500, which made it the largest Chaldean diocese outside of the Patriarchy of Mosul. There was also a Chaldean bishop residing in Urmia, with 7,800 persons living in twenty-one congregations in his diocese.[35] Missionaries had been working in the area since the mid nineteenth century, and there were over a thousand converts to Roman Catholicism and several thousand converts to various branches of Protestantism—Presbyterians, Methodists, Anglicans, and Lutherans were all active.

---

[32] He became known as Halil Pasha of Kut, after the victory of Kut al-Amara over the British in July 1916.

[33] Taylan Sorgun, *İttihad ve Terakki'den Cumhuriyet'e Halil Paşa Bitmeyen Savaş* [From the CUP to the Republic: Halil Pasha's unfinished war] (2003), 46.

[34] Genis, *Vvedenskii*, 13.

[35] Joseph Tfinkdji, "L'Eglise chaldéenne catholique autrefois et aujourd'hui" (1914), 498, 515.

The Russian Orthodox Church claimed between 12,000 and 20,000 converts, mostly in the Supurgan diocese.³⁶ The Russian presence in Iran was significant and growing. Propinquity to the booming economy of the Russian Transcaucasian province created many economic opportunities and promised future prosperity. It also gave the Russian Orthodox Church a particular attraction, and a mission led by Archimandrate Sergei was quite successful in the pre-war period in villages straddling the border. It focused primarily on the Nestorians and was so successful that the Anglican mission considered closing down their own activities. Sergei had close contacts with the Nestorian Patriarch Mar Shimun, and just before the war there was a decided possibility that he and his flock would go over to Orthodoxy.³⁷

The American missionary William A. Shedd presented a geographic description of the area in 1903 and described the conditions of the Syrian population. They

> live in the three plains of Urmia, Salmas and Sulduz, bordering on Lake Urmia, and in the three little plains of Mergawar, Tergawar, and Baradost, just under the lofty mountains that form the boundary between Persia and Turkey. The largest numbers are farmers, working the lands of the feudal nobility. The direct taxes paid by them are insignificant in amount, but the amount that goes to the landlords is excessive. In irrigated lands the amount paid by the farmer is generally two-thirds of the produce of grain fields, if the seed is furnished by the landlord, and one half if he furnishes the seed himself.... Besides this, he has also to furnish the landlord a very indefinite amount of unpaid labour.

As a result of this heavy burden, the men had begun to travel in order to find work.

> The most marked feature of their industrial condition, to which is due much prosperity and also much demoralization, is the wholesale migration of men to Russia for temporary employment. Every year thousands of Syrians cross into Russia to find work. The development of Transcaucasia, with the building of the cities of Tiflis, Batumi, and Baku, has created a demand for labourers, skilled and unskilled, and Syrian carpenters, masons, and day-labourers have found lucrative employment. Not a few, too, have become contractors and employers of labour, some on a large scale. The recently completed Tiflis-Kars-Erivan railroad was

---

³⁶ I. Babakhanov, *Sirokhaldeitsy, ikh istoriya i zhizn'* [Syro-Chaldeans: Their history and life] (1899), 13.

³⁷ J. F. Coakley, *The Church of the East and the Church of England: A History of the Archbishop of Canterbury's Assyrian Mission* (1992), 320, 326.

built very largely by Syrian workmen and Syrian contractors, who are now looking forward eagerly to the extension of the line to the Aras river, and ultimately across the border into Persian territory. Others find work as porters and water-sellers in various Russian cities. Hundreds more are small shopkeepers or itinerant peddlers.[38]

The picture that Shedd gives is of a quickly modernizing rural population in feudal conditions that was integrated into the commercial economy of neighboring Russia and in all likelihood was swiftly differentiating itself from its Muslim neighbors in commercial and work experience, and some self-made men had obviously acquired new wealth. Not all of this labor migration was temporary, and some Syriac families established themselves firmly in Tbilisi and Erivan.

Most of the East Syriac population was concentrated into an agrarian upland with the city of Urmia as its main capital. Urmia had several tens of thousands of inhabitants representing all faiths. There were two Christian quarters: the Mart-Maryam with about 100 houses of Nestorians, and the Faitlachen quarter, which was predominantly Syriac but also included between 30 and 40 Armenian families. There was also a Jewish quarter with 300–400 families.[39]

The Urmia region was bordered on the east by Lake Urmia, which is a salt lake below sea level surrounded by marshes with much bird life. To the west ran high mountains that made up the Ottoman-Iranian frontier. The city of Urmia was a major market for well-irrigated agricultural plains and valleys, with cereals, vegetables, grapes, melons, and other fruit and nuts as specialties. Produce was exported to Russia over a railway that went from Tabriz to Julfa at the Russian border and then farther through the Caucasus Mountains. There were several very large plains, each thickly populated with farming villages. Besides the commercial center of Urmia there were several small and medium-sized market and administrative towns, such as Dilman, Khoi, and Supurgan; among the richest agrarian settlements were Gogtapa and Gulpashan.

BORDER PROVOCATIONS

Basing his narrative on German diplomatic sources, Ulrich Gehrke points out some parallels with the well-known Turkish provocations by surprise attack on Odessa and some other Russian Black Sea ports in late October 1914. He compares them with the less well known state of de facto war that

---

[38] William A. Shedd, "The Syrians of Persia and Eastern Turkey" (1903), 4.
[39] C. F. Lehmann-Haupt, *Armenien Einst und Jetzt* (1910), 1:303.

unfolded in Persian Azerbaijan in the very same month.[40] In reality, this small corner of the war turned into a killing field for punitive military action and reprisals against civilians. The Iranian towns of Dilman in the north and Urmia in the east, and Turkish Bashkale in the west, set the limits of this triangle. Within this space a confusing array of forces made up of regular army, irregular cavalry, volunteers, and brigands ran amok, slaughtering defenseless civilians. Eventually the locals responded by forming village militia units; they received some rifles from the Russian army. Near Dilman, a camp was established for training Armenian and Assyrian volunteers.

These invasions sparked a spiral of ethnic cleansing in villages on both sides of the border. In August, some Ottoman Assyrian Christians had been deported from their villages near Bashkale. Then, Kurds and other Sunni Muslims were expelled from villages near Urmia. The Turks in response expelled several thousand Assyrians from the Ottoman border regions, and these were settled in the houses of the expelled Muslims. According to an Ottoman account, the Russians crossed several times into Turkish territory and committed "cruel attacks." The Ottoman imperial army, it was explained, had to retaliate because "Russia's operation was the kind which endangered our security."[41]

Because of the relatively easy terrain and the agricultural surplus, this was a region that was particularly attractive to military strategists, who dreamed of marching armies up from Iraq through it to get to the oil fields of Baku on the Caspian Sea. Marching a large army through the Turkish side was nearly impossible because the high and precipitous chains of mountains hindered wheeled vehicles, and provisions were hard to come by from the sparse population.

The first Turco-Russian skirmishes occurred in August and September 1914, several months before the formal declaration of war and while there were few Russian troops around. Clarence Ussher, an American physician based in Van, noted that Jevdet Bey was absent and "took bands of volunteers across the border to stir up the Persians against Russia and, by destroying and plundering many Christian villages, to arouse their lust for blood so that they might be incited to join in a holy war."[42] Since Jevdet was Enver's brother-in-law, it is likely that the Minister of War was pulling the strings behind the scene. If Russia could be brought to declare war on

---

[40] Gehrke, *Persien in der deutschen Orientpolitik*, 1:20.

[41] ATAŞE Kol.: BDH, Kls.: 1488, Dos.: 32/-, Fih.: 3-2, 3-3.

[42] Ussher, *American Physician*, 226; Vvedenskii also noted these actions and attributed a similar aim, see Lazarev, *Kurdistan*, 297.

Turkey first, it would ease the problems that Enver had with the cabinet majority who hesitated to join the war. In order to be effective, provocations must, by nature, be outrageous enough to cause headlines. The first atrocities occurred in Christian villages with converts to the Russian Orthodox Church.

Ottoman documents accuse the Russians of many small border violations. According to them, they invaded from Iran on August 27 to attack the border region of Muradiye (the main town here is Sarai), where they "began oppression and intrigue."[43] The Ottomans accused the Russians of sending a detachment of soldiers on September 8 into the village of Kerboran 26 kilometers east of the town of Bayazit and shooting at the border guards. There is no mention of casualties. The Russians were also blamed for attempting to entice the Kurdish tribes to revolt. When the tribesmen refused, the Russians were said to have destroyed their villages, seized property, massacred males, and raped women. The Ottomans asserted that the aim of the carnage was to intimidate the neighboring tribes into subservience to Russian interests.[44]

In August 1914, the first wave of Nestorian refugees began to pour over the border from Turkey. Early in August, the Russians discussed the need for a local militia of both Kurds and Christians for self-defense, because the small Russian garrisons were deemed inadequate. The Russian Foreign Minister Sazonov sent a telegram on August 13/26 to the Viceroy of the Caucasus, Vorontsov-Dashkov, discussing the necessity of setting up a militia composed of Assyrian, Kurdish, and Armenian volunteers. 25,000 rifles and twelve million cartridges were ready for distribution. General Vorovpanov, Colonel Andrievski, and vice-consul Vvedenski were to select the leaders of the volunteers. On September 20, a plan was presented to form small bands of Armenians under Russian command and to train them in camps at Dilman and Khoi.[45] The Turks observed that in Salmas a contingent of 400 Armenian volunteers was in training and had even tried to slip over the border but had been repulsed. Because of their established network of informers, the Ottomans knew of most of these preparations and spread the news among the army officers that Russia was arming Assyrians and Armenians.[46]

---

[43] ATAŞE Kol.: BDH, Kls.: 1488, Dos.: 32/-, Fih.: 3-1.

[44] ATAŞE Kol.: BDH, Kls.: 1488, Dos.: 32/-, Fih.: 3-1. The name Kerboran is Syriac.

[45] Gehrke, *Persien in der deutschen Orientpolitik*, 1:17, 2:6–7.

[46] Matveev and Mar-Yukhanna, *Assiriiskii vopros*, 44–45; Lazarev, *Kurdistan*, 301.

Escalating Turkish and Kurdish invasions of Iran took place a month before the Ottoman Empire joined the war. Border skirmishes were a daily occurrence, with losses on both sides. There was also intertribal warfare as tribes loyal to the shaykhs of Nihri set out to settle outstanding scores with Simko's Shikak. At the start of October, troops and tribes started massive killing and plundering of border villages and forced the rural population to flee into Urmia.[47] Iranian authorities estimated the core to have been 200 Turkish soldiers joined by local Kurdish tribes. A reported 60 tribesmen, one Turkish officer, and an unknown number of Ottoman soldiers were killed in the attacks when self-defense militia and troops made up of Russian-Armenian subjects shot back.[48] This invasion reached as far as the so-called Jewish Hill cemetery just outside the town before Russian and Syriac defenders forced them to halt. After surveying the damage to the Christian villages and considering the destruction of Orthodox and Catholic churches, Vvedenski found the term "jihad" appropriate.[49]

The first, mainly Kurdish, attacks were soon followed by a new provocation.[50] The missionary William Shedd wrote that serious fighting started in Azerbaijan weeks before the formal declaration of war.

> Disturbances at once began along the border and at the beginning of October 1914, a determined attack was made on Urmia, ostensibly by Kurds. It was afterwards clear, from statements made by Persians and Turks who were engaged in the attack, that the nucleus of the fighting force was made up of Turkish soldiers and that the attack was under the command of Turkish officers. It was also clear from statements made by Persians friendly with the Turks and unfriendly towards the Russians,

---

This is also one of the telegrams the Ottomans captured, see ATAŞE Kol.: BDH, Kls.: 1488, Dos.: 32/-, Fih.: 3-1; Kol.: BDH, Kls.: 1488, Dos.: 32/-, Fih.: 3-5; Genis, *Vvedenskii*, 26–27.

[47] Jacques Sontag to Père Fiat November 30, 1914, in *Saint Vincent de Paul Annales de la Mission* 80 (1915): 528; Gehrke, *Persien in der deutschen Orientpolitik*, 1:20.

[48] Minister of Foreign Affairs to Turkish Ambassador in Tehran October 7, 1914; Minister of Foreign Affairs to Persian Ambassador in Constantinople October 7, 1914; Kargozar of Tabriz to Ministry of Foreign Affairs October 9, 1914; Kargozar of Tabriz to Foreign Ministry October 10, 1914, documents nos. 10, 11, 12, 13, in Empire de Perse, *Neutralité Persane*, 7–9.

[49] Genis, *Vvedenskii*, 30–31.

[50] Lazarev, *Kurdistan*, 299; Salahi R. Sonyel, *The Assyrians of Turkey: Victims of Major Power Policy* (2001), 87, speaks only of a battle between "tribal Kurds" and the Christians and Russians and omits the Turkish officers.

that the result of success in this attack would have been the looting of the Christian population, with probable loss of life.[51]

The Catholic missionary Abel Zayia gave another version, reporting that the Turkish and Kurdish invasion had taken Urmia by surprise, since the troops had come over the high mountains to the west.

> The Russians retreated to Urmia and left all of the Christian villages of the plain of Tergawar, such as Mawana, Korana, Baloulan, Chibane, etc., at the mercy of the Turco-Kurds. All of the inhabitants fled to the city, where they sought refuge in the French and American missions. After descending into the plain of Urmia, the Turco-Kurds burned all the Christian villages which they found in their way, such as Anhar, Alwatshe, and massacred the columns of refugees.

The Turks came to within a few kilometers of Urmia before stopping at Jewish Hill. There a unit of Cossacks stopped them, but because the invaders were so many, it took several days to force them out, and for a short time the Turkish and Kurdish units perpetrated massacres in the villages that fell into their hands.[52]

According to information gathered by Vvedensky, the force combined a small number of Turkish army units together with a large number of Turkish and Iranian Kurds, the invasion being headed by Jevdet Bey.[53] After the retreat, Iranian authorities found the bodies of seven uniformed Ottoman officers and soldiers. Inspection of the documents in their clothes revealed the identity of Abdullah, a Circassian from Bitlis (passport no. 1221), sergeant, first battalion, third regiment of the Fourth Army; Omar, a Circassian from Bitlis (passport no. 1295), private, seventh battalion, third regiment of the Fourth Army, carrying on his person a letter addressed to a Circassian officer in the ninth company based at Karakilisa in Erzurum vilayet. Their dead officer, Hachem, carried the Ottoman military law code, a map, a plan of action, and a letter from a soldier asking for news about his brother who was reported killed in action.[54] If these men belonged to the

---

[51] Statement by the Rev. William A. Shedd, in Bryce and Toynbee, *Treatment of Armenians*, 136–40.

[52] Eugène Griselle, *Syriens et Chaldéens*, 41–42.

[53] Lazarev, *Kurdistan*, 298–99.

[54] Report from vice-governor of Azerbaijan October 14, 1914; Russian Ambassador in Tehran to Minister of Foreign Affairs October 19, 1914; Minister of Foreign Affairs to Ottoman Ambassador in Tehran October 29, 1914; Report from Kargozar of Tabriz to Minister of Foreign Affairs November 1, 1914, documents nos. 20, 26, 34, 39, in Empire de Perse, *Neutralité Persane*, 11, 14, 19–20, 23–24.

Fourth Army Corps, they should at that time have been in Thrace; and if they belonged to the Fourth Ottoman Army, then they should have been in Sinai preparing for the assault on Suez. There was no explanation as to why they would be in contact with the Third Army headquarters in Erzurum unless, as is probable, these soldiers had been recruited into Teskilat-i Mahsusa, as their Circassian ethnicity and correspondence with Karakilisa indicates. Just prior to the outbreak of war, Russia protested over the incursions of Ottoman Kurds into Iran and the massacre and pillaging of Christian villages.[55]

The Ottoman version of these events was that the Russians by themselves

> destroyed the Mergawar and Tergawar districts and parts of all the districts between Beradost and Somay ... and started to slaughter the Muslim population, chasing the members of tribes, which arrived destitute and disheveled, to our borders. On October 21, 1914, they attacked our border posts Gelenkano and Khatune and conducted violent battles. On the other hand, the Nestorian bands, in concert with the Russians, attacked the Ottoman consulate in Russia [*sic*] and slaughtered its guards and hanged the most important Muslim merchants of the people of Balad-Sini on the gallows they prepared in the vicinity of the consulate.[56]

The Iranians reported that the Russians staged reprisals on villages near Mawana and Anhar.[57] The Turkish consul accused Assyrian self-defense units made up of members of the Jilu tribe of committing an atrocity in one of these reprisals. They had been assaulted by neighboring Kurds and in return attacked two villages that had fired on them. The villages were said to have been totally pillaged, with the slaughter of 50 persons. The Iranian authorities were skeptical and noted that the alleged attack had not been confirmed, but still added that such incidents show the danger of "engendering religious hatred."[58] This might have happened, for the Jilus were sel-

---

[55] BOA. DH. ŞFR 45/242 Ministry of Interior to Van and Mosu vilayets October 12, 1914. Salahi Sonyel gives the selective information that "tribal Kurds" participated in the attacks on Urmia in September and October, but he omits all mention of the Ottoman officers and soldiers (*Assyrians of Turkey*, 87).

[56] ATAŞE Kol.: BDH, Kls.: 1488, Dos.: 32/-, Fih.: 3-1.

[57] Kargozar of Tabriz to Ministry of Foreign Affairs October 9, 1914, document no. 12, in Empire de Perse, *Neutralité Persane*, 8.

[58] Report of Kargozar of Azerbaijan to Minister of Foreign Affairs November 1, 1914, document no. 40, ibid., 24–25.

dom known to turn the other cheek; but then again, the Ottomans sorely needed a case that would show that they were not alone in committing atrocities.

THE CALM BEFORE THE STORM

After the October provocations there was a period of two months free of further attacks in the Urmia area. Both the Ottomans and the Russians had reason to keep on their best behavior and not estrange the Iranian government. The Ottomans, on the one hand, were trying to entice the Iranians to join their side for a combined attack on Baku.[59] The Russians, on their side, were aware of the rising Muslim hostility against them and did not want to risk a conflict that would devastate Azerbaijan, one of their prime economic interests.[60] Russia had even proposed enticing Iran with an offer of the Shi'a holy cities Najaf and Kerbala. In the final analysis, neither the Turks nor the Russians could afford the troops and resources that a major operation on Iranian territory would entail.

However, in December the two enemies could be observed gathering strength. A few thousand Russian troops arrived to reinforce the defenses, and they included contingents of Armenian volunteers, estimated to number 1,300.[61] Major General F. G. Chernozubov was appointed head of the army in Azerbaijan in December 1914. Because their main armies were assembled near the straits and at Erzurum, the Ottomans lacked regular troops available for immediate deployment in Iran. Enver ordered the rapid formation of the ill-fated Fifth Expeditionary Corps, to be commanded by Halil Bey (Enver's uncle), and rushed from Constantinople to Iran with instructions to push on as far as Dagestan. But as this corps had to be recruited, transported, assembled, and trained, they were not in place until late April.[62]

Meanwhile, along the border strip Shaykh Abdul Khadir of Nihri and other Ottoman leaders fired up the latent religious fanaticism of the nomad tribes. They were invited to fight with the Ottomans and received arms and ammunition. An unavoidable conflict took shape.

---

[59] Gehrke, *Persien in der deutschen Orientpolitik*, 1:38–43.

[60] Russian Foreign Minister to Viceroy in Caucasus Vorontsov-Dashkov October 20/November 2, 1914, document no. 450, in *Die Internationalen Beziehungen im Zeitalter des Imperialismus*, ed. Otto Hoetzsch (1934), 393–94.

[61] Minister of Foreign Affairs to Persian Ambassador in Constantinople October 27, 1914, document no. 30, ibid., 17.

[62] Gehrke, *Persien in der deutschen Orientpolitik*, 1:44.

Armenian and Assyrian volunteers from Urmia fought at the Köprüköy front in a battle lasting from early November to early December and then participated in the Sarikamish front, where fighting went on from mid December 1914 to January 18, 1915.⁶³ Crossing the Iranian border, Russian units passed into Turkey on November 3 and advanced on Sarai and Bashkale, the nearest towns; but after a short occupation, they were repulsed and retreated back to Iran. Ottoman troops were given orders to pursue the Russians into Iranian territory.

Most Ottoman attention was directed toward the town of Sawuj Bulak just south of Lake Urmia. Here began a snowballing of Kurdish tribes volunteering to accompany a small contingent of regular troops. Iranian officials watched helplessly as the mutasarrif of Kirkuk, Mohammed Ahmed, established a base with a few hundred soldiers and five hundred tribesmen.⁶⁴ Subsequently, they were joined by the mutasarrif of Suleymaniya with some officers. Assorted Turkish and local tribes volunteered. Among the leaders and tribes were: Bayezid Agha, Mohammed Amine Agha of the Piran tribe, Shaykh Ala al Din of the Tawila, and Shaykh Najm ed Din and leaders of the Debokri tribe. From the villages of Rayete, Darband, and Pasvah came Calipha Samad, Saleh, and Shaykh Mohammed of the Herki confederation. To the horror of the Iranians, some of the Persian Kurds insisted they were Ottoman subjects and agitated for a general Kurdish revolt.⁶⁵

Russian and Iranian forces confronted the Ottomans in December 1914, when there were two battles near Sawuj Bulak. The second battle ended in a complete Turkish and Kurdish victory. The Russian consul in Sawuj Bulak, A. I. Ias, was killed in the rout, and many sensitive documents concerning the arming and organization of the Armenian and Assyrian volunteers and self-defense militia fell into Ottoman hands.⁶⁶

---

⁶³ Matveev and Mar-Yukhanna, *Assiriiskii vopros*, 47.

⁶⁴ Telegraphic report from Sawuj Bulak December 12, 1914, document no. 116, in Empire de Perse, *Neutralité Persane*, 66; Russian Consul-General in Tabriz to Russian Foreign Minister November 26/December 9, 1914, document 632, in Hoetzsch, *Internationalen Beziehungen*, 540.

⁶⁵ Telegraphic Report from Sawuj Bulak December 12, 1914; Minister of Foreign Affairs to Turkish Ambassador Tehran December 7, 1914; Vice-Governor of Azerbaijan to Foreign Minister December 13, 1914; Foreign Minister to Turkish Ambassador Tehran December 20, 1914, documents nos. 120, 126, 128, 134, in ibid., 67–72, 75–76.

⁶⁶ Some of these documents are part of a report on the state of the war up to about March 1915: ATAŞE, Kol.: Bhd., Kls.: 1488, Dos.: 32/-, Fih.: 3-1, 3-2, 3-3,

Fear spread among the Russians, as some of them jumped to the conclusion that they were facing Halil's strong expeditionary force, by which they were vastly outnumbered. Not until the Turkish and Kurdish forces marched into Tabriz in the second week of January did the Russians realize that they had been fooled. On that day, a few hundred Kurds in national costume on horse and foot accompanied by a detachment from the Turkish army entered the city. They announced the "reign of the Christians is over" and seized weapons and ammunition from the Iranian armory. The German consul, Wilhelm Litten, termed it a "giantic bluff." But from that moment on, the Russians poured in reinforcements and began a steady series of victories against the poorly organized and trained occupation forces.[67]

The panic was not the only reason for the quick Russian evacuation. The Russians had realized that the Ottomans were increasingly successful in their pan-Islamic agitation among the local Muslims and that part of the Iranian government secretly supported anti-Russian activities. This undermined Russian prestige, made it the object of political intrigues, and hindered it from defending the province. The evacuation of Russian troops that previously protected the Turkish-Iranian border was a calculated risk. With luck, it would force Iran to mount a defense using its own army against the Ottoman invader. Armed conflict between Iran and Turkey would in a single stroke defuse the power of the pan-Islamic propaganda, and the Ottomans would become as unpopular as the Russians.[68] The only problem with this thinking was that Iran was not even close to being able to push the Ottoman army out of Azerbaijan. After two weeks of anarchy, the Russians turned around as news came of their victory at Sarikamish and they realized the actual weakness of the army of occupation. In February, Russian and Ottoman troops dug in and prepared for battle near the town of Khoi. It was a grave situation, and the Russians had the advantage over the Ottomans of being able to bring in reinforcements while the Turks looked on as the tribal volunteers packed up and left.[69]

3-4, 3-5, 3-6, 3-7, 3-8, 3-9, 3-10, 3-11, 3-12, 3-13.

[67] Gehrke, *Persien in der deutschen Orientpolitik*, 1:47, 2:34; Hellot-Bellier, *Chronique de massacres*, 103.

[68] Russian Ambassador in London (Benkendorff) to Russian Foreign Minister December 25, 1914/January 7, 1915, in Hoetzsch, *Internationalen Beziehungen*, ser. 2, vol. 6, document 731.

[69] Kargozar of Tabriz to Minister of Foreign Affairs February 5, 1915, document no. 207, in Empire de Perse, *Neutralité Persane*, 116–17.

UNDER OCCUPATION

Because the Russians kept secret their plans to withdraw, the Christians were taken by surprise and fled in panic in the middle of winter. The large Christian population in the rural districts of Urmia and Salmas was undefended. Mass panic prevailed and thousands of people fled. Some walked barefoot through the snow, slush, and mud. They left their animals and property behind. It took a march of seven days to cross the Russian border. Georges Decroo, the French Lazarist superior of the mission at Khosrowa, estimated that 20,000 Christians crossed the Russian border.[70] Because of flight, labor migration, and serving in volunteer brigades, many adult males found themselves behind Russian lines while their families remained in the occupied zone. The anguish this separation caused can hardly be exaggerated.

Urmia was swiftly overrun by Ottoman troops, and Kurdish tribal forces, not meeting opposition, began to pillage, burn villages, destroy farmsteads, slaughter Christians, and fulfill any other obligations conceivably intrinsic to jihad. Between the retreat of the Russians and the arrival of the Turkish occupation authorities there was a short interval of two or three days of sheer anarchy, during which local Iranian Muslims staged pogroms against their Christian neighbors. Advance units of the Turkish army officially took Urmia on January 5, and on January 8 they occupied the plain of Salmas, which the army controlled until the middle of May.[71]

Some of the Assyrian villages raised resistance and shot back at their attackers. In Gogtapa, villagers fortified the Russian Orthodox Church, which was at the top of a hill, and defended themselves for several days until their ammunition ran out. In the nick of time, the medical missionary Packard arrived waving the American flag and saved the villagers. Negotiations with the Kurdish leaders resulted in permission to lead the survivors to safety in Urmia. Other Syriac villages that attempted to resist were Hay-Tepe and Ardichay on the shores of Lake Urmia. The Russian vice-consul, Nikitine, reported that on "December 20 [January 2] Russian troops and consulate abandoned Urmia. Among local Christians a panic immediately occurred. Christian Syriacs tried to organize resistance in the villages of

---

[70] Letter of Georges Decroo March 12, 1915, in *Les Missions catholiques* 10 (September 1915): 207.

[71] E. F. Ludshuveit, *Turtsiya v gody pervoi mirovoi voiny 1914–1918gg. Voenno-politicheskii ocherk* [Turkey in the years of World War I 1914–1918: Military-political study] (1966), 76.

Ardichay and Hay-Tepe."⁷² An American Methodist medical missionary, Jacob Sargis, sent a dispatch on February 12, 1915, in which he described the destruction of Ardichay. "At Ardichay 75 women and girls ran into the sea [Lake Urmia] to escape the Turks. They refused to trust promises of safety if they came out, and all were shot as they stood in the water."⁷³

It was estimated that the total Turkish occupation forces numbered 15,000.⁷⁴ According to German officers, these troops were composed of two corps of Kurdish volunteers and one division of gendarmes.⁷⁵ The Russians decided not to try to return immediately to Urmia, which was defended by sizable Ottoman forces that were daily building up their strength. Rather, the Russian army directed its counteroffensive against Sofian, where Naji was badly defeated on January 15/28.⁷⁶ The Russians retook Tabriz two days later. They then pushed south toward Dilman. However, progress grew slow, and they regained Dilman on the Salmas plain only on February 21/March 5, finding evidence of massacres.⁷⁷

But massacres were not confined to the Ottoman side. There were repeated reports that Armenian and Syriac volunteers were taking revenge on local villages. The highest local Iranian official in Khoi asserted that Armenian soldiers looted and burned the entire tract between Salmas and Julfa and had massacred a great number of villagers. He stated that he had spoken with their Russian commandant but got in reply "the situation is complicated." Officials in Tabriz also reported destruction caused when the Russian army advanced from Khoi into the Salmas plain, where villages again were burned. Assyrian Jilu tribesmen were accused of perpetrating massacres. Surveying the damage, the Iranians insisted that the assassins and plunderers were not solely the Kurds, but also the Armenian volunteers.⁷⁸ These accusations are vague since they do not name villages or give

---

⁷² Niktitine` to Russian Imperial Mission in Teheran January 1916, AVPRI, 1. Y.F. Persian Table "B", des 489, 1910-1916, dossier 529, list 34-40.

⁷³ Narrative of Dr. Jacob Sargis February 12, 1915, in Bryce and Toynbee, *Treatment of Armenians*, 191.

⁷⁴ Lazarev, *Kurdistan*, 322.

⁷⁵ Leverkuehn, *Posten auf ewiger Wache*, 23.

⁷⁶ Genelkurmay, *Birinci Dünya Harbi'nde*, 582.

⁷⁷ N. G. Korsun, *Alashkertskaya i Khamadanskaya operatsii na kavkazskom fronte mirovoi voiny v 1915 gody* [The Alashkert and Hamadan operations on the Caucasus Front in World War I in 1915] (1940), 34.

⁷⁸ Kargozar of Tabriz to Minister of Foreign Affairs February 4 and 21, 1915; Kargozar of Azerbaijan to Minister of Foreign Affairs March 20, 1915, documents nos. 202, 236, 312, Empire de Perse, *Neutralité Persane*, 115, 127, 158.

dates, and they speak of vast regions. However, the Russian commander did not stop them, and vice-consul Vvedensky at Haftevan said he had difficulty in controlling the Armenians and Assyrians.

Beginning in late February, when the Turkish troops retreated, they plundered and burned villages and slaughtered inhabitants. When the Russians retook the Salmas plain, they found evidence of the recent atrocities perpetrated on Christian villages, particularly the already described atrocities at Haftevan. News reaching the West from the area that had been occupied by the Turkish troops created shock waves. A telegram sent to Petrograd and referred to in the *New York Times* stated:

> Prior to the evacuation of the towns between Julfa and Tabriz the Turks and Kurds, who were retreating before the Russian advance pillaged and burned villages and put to death some of the inhabitants. At Salmas, Pagaduk and Sarna orders are said to have been given for the destruction of the towns. All the Armenians of Antvat were collected and according to this message 600 males were put to death.[79]

In Istanbul, the German ambassador and the CUP leadership realized that events in Urmia had gotten out of hand. On February 11, 1915, Wangenheim arranged a meeting between Enver, General von der Goltz, and the Persian ambassador to assess the situation. The Persian ambassador spoke of the impossibility of trusting the tribes. He added that the local Turkish officers were doing a disservice by alienating opinion, and that the high command should punish them. Enver said that the need for tribal volunteers would cease, since Halil's expedition with more than 10,000 regular troops would soon arrive. He promised to discipline the officers who had behaved badly.[80]

In mid March, the Iranian government reported finding the corpse of a uniformed Turkish cavalry officer killed in battle near Kirmanshah. Among his papers was a letter he was carrying to the Turkish consul. It contained detailed instructions about the aims of Ottoman troops in the area. Among the points was one of particular relevance, warning the consul to avoid repeating "the imprudent maneuvers taken in Azerbaijan."[81]

---

[79] "Whole Plain Strewn by Armenian Bodies," *New York Times*, March 20, 1915.

[80] Wangenheim to Foreign Office February 13, 1915, in Gehrke, *Persien in der deutschen Orientpolitik*, 2:309–10.

[81] Commander of Expedition Hossain-Rauf to Ottoman Consulate Kirmanshah March 12, 1915 included in Kargozar of Kirmanshah to Minister of Foreign Affairs March 18, 1915, document no. 302, in Empire de Perse, *Neutralité Persane*, 153.

The "Armenian Revolt" Scare

The disorganized Ottoman occupation force found itself face to face with a trained Russian army and brigades of Armenian and Syriac volunteers thirsting for revenge. Some less motivated volunteers began to slide away. The Kurdish tribesmen were the first to evaporate. Jevdet reported that the new Russian divisions included Armenian volunteers and jumped to the conclusion that this was the first stage in an Armenian revolt. On March 1, Enver responded, telling him to take special steps with Armenian soldiers serving in the Ottoman army. Those who "do not follow orders ... shall be shot without warning." When on March 3 Jevdet lost a battle to Russians, he reflected that the Turkish loss would "stimulate by a hundred percent" the local Armenians to revolt and advised that his own units had begun to disintegrate. The Russians attacked again a few days later, and Enver stated that he believed that the entire aim of the Russian offensive was to reach Van and give the Armenians living there the opportunity to rebel.[82] In their minds, Enver and Jevdet had already decided that an Armenian revolt was inevitable and under way. Even though it was forced to retreat, the occupation army could at least reduce the potential strength of the Christian volunteers.

In mid March, newspapers throughout the world were flooded with news about atrocities in Urmia and the towns and villages of its province. The situation definitely worsened as the Turkish army prepared to return home. Beliayev, the Russian chargé d'affaires in Tabriz, communicated the immediate danger to his government in a secret telegram sent March 1/14, 1915. It began by reference to the killings in Haftevan and indicated that the mayhem was spreading throughout the province.

> According to received information, before our troops arrived at Salmas, the Turks-Kurds had killed 800 men. According to rumors and a letter of American missionary [William] Shedd from Urmia, Kurds and [Turkish] soldiers slaughtered and killed Christians in the surroundings of Urmia. There is a risk that they will breach the sanctuary of the American mission and before they leave Urmia, they will massacre the Christians who are protected by the Americans.[83]

He repeated this message with more urgency on March 9/22.

---

[82] ATAŞE 4/3671, Kls. 2950, H-11, F 1-206; 6/4517, Kls. 5249, H-1, F. 1-16; 6/4517 Kls. 5240, H-1, F 1-19, in Genelkurmay, *Birinci Dünya Harbi'nde*, 583–85.

[83] AVPRI, III. F. 133, 1915, des. 470, dossier 49, vol. II, list 438.

The Turks are preparing to massacre the Christians in Urmia. There is an evident threat to American and French missionaries, and also for the 15,000 Christians who are hidden in the missions. The Assyrian Orthodox priest and Nestorian Assyrian priests were taken from the missions and were tortured. I request that you send troops immediately. This is also the request of the Americans and French.[84]

News of the widespread massacres spread rapidly. The American missionary Larabee lamented on March 12:

Sad news. The Kurds driven back from Khoi massacred 800 Syrian and Armenian men with cruel torture. This was in the plain of Salmas. In Urmia the biggest and wealthiest Syrian village, Gulpashan, which had been spared by payments of large sums of money was given over to plunder by the returning Kurds. The men of the village were all taken out to the cemetery and killed; the women and girls treated barbarously.[85]

Vvedensky was equally dismayed. He let the Russian government know on March 1/14,

I have begun to investigate the Christian villages. I have investigated 20 villages. Everywhere there is complete ruin and devastation. Churches, schools, and libraries have only walls [standing]. Icons and sacred items are lying in the mud, torn and riddled with bullets. Some churches were transformed into stables or supply rooms for food or plunder. The villages are full of corpses of the poor victims of massacres, which were carried out by Turks and Kurds everywhere in Salmas. ...The corpses bear the marks of cruel killing with axes, daggers, and blunt objects.[86]

The next day, Vvedensky sent another secret telegram:

I received a message from an American missionary in Dilman. About 1,000 people were massacred, 2,000 persons died from hunger and disease. There is threat of a new massacre. During the last week one hundred persons were massacred. In the American mission there are about 15,000 people. The Turkish consul [in Urmia] Raghib Bey is very cruel.[87]

Aware that their makeshift forces were inadequate, the Turks were rushing reinforcements to Azerbaijan. Lieutenant Colonel Halil Bey was sent with some elite units to command the occupation. Until early Decem-

---

[84] AVPRI, III. F. 133, 1915, des. 470, dossier 49, vol. II, list 444.
[85] Statement of Larabee, in Bryce and Toynbee, *Treatment of Armenians*, 146.
[86] AVPRI, III. F. 133, 1915, des. 470, dossier 49, vol. II, list 580.
[87] AVPRI, III. F. 133, 1915, des. 470, dossier 49, vol. II, list 586.

ber 1914, Halil served as military governor of Istanbul; Enver then ordered him to form the Fifth Expeditionary Force in order to invade the Caucasus through Iran and reach Dagestan.[88] These troops (later renamed the 51st and 52nd divisions of the Sixth Army) amounted to 248 officers, 10,920 soldiers, 6 machine guns, and 12 mountain howitzers. The force also came to include local gendarmes and 12,000 irregular Kurdish cavalry. Halil would have known this part of Iran from his intelligence mission in 1913.

Halil's troops arrived in Azerbaijan on April 15 after an exhausting forced march from Rowanduz. He expected to confront the Russian forces commanded by General Nazarbekov (as Nazarbekian served as general in the Armenian Republic army) together with Syriac and Armenian volunteers forming a brigade headed by Antranik Ozanian.[89] The Nestorian militia organized the previous autumn also fought on the Russian` side.[90] In size and training, Halil's was definitely the superior army (10–12 battalions plus thousands of nomadic tribesmen, compared to 10 battalions and a volunteer brigade), and furthermore the enemy did not yet know he was in place.

Halil's original plan was to take the Russians by surprise. However, by the time he had arrived, the events in Van were getting out of hand, and part of his expedition had to be rerouted to Van to help out there. With a decimated force he could not complete his mission, and his army was badly mauled in fierce battles near Dilman that left thousands of casualties on the battlefield. Turkish sources give the losses for May 1, the first day of battle. They name 15 officers and 453 soldiers dead, 28 officers and 1,200 soldiers wounded, and 370 missing in action. Many of the badly injured were abandoned in the field, so the casualties may have been much greater; Russian and local sources speak of 3,500 Ottoman dead.[91] The Armenian and Syriac volunteers under Antranik played a decisive role in repulsing the Turks.[92] Apparently, on the first day of the battle the Turks succeeded in occupying Dilman, and the Russians had heavy losses. But the next day, determined

---

[88] Vahakn Dadrian, "Documentation of the Armenian Genocide in Turkish Sources" (1991), 116; Genelkurmay, *Birinci Dünya Harbi'nde*, 570–77; Ludshuveit, *Turtsiya v gody pervoi mirovoi voiny*, 76–79; Erickson, *Ordered to Die*, 62–63.

[89] Korsun, *Alashkertskaya i khamadanskaya operatsii*, 42.

[90] Genelkurmay, *Birinci Dünya Harbi'nde*, 597.

[91] ATAŞE 6/4517, Kls. 5240, H-6, F 1-28, 30, cited in Genelkurmay, *Birinci Dünya Harbi'nde*, 597–98; Griselle, *Syriens et Chaldéens*, 55.

[92] Vakharshak Ovakiyan, "V pokhode s Andranikom" [On the road with Antranik] (1916).

Armenian opposition resulted in a Turkish defeat with thousands of casualties.[93]

Halil did not comment on this defeat in his memoirs but wrote merely that he had to disengage because Van had fallen to the Armenians, which actually did not happen until two weeks later. At any rate, he blamed his defeat (or forced withdrawal) on the Armenians.[94] He followed the example of Jevdet and executed the Armenian officers, troops, and medical personnel in the Expeditionary Force. The exact date for this is not known, but it probably went on for some days. The German advisors knew that Halil while in Persia ordered the execution of several hundred unarmed Armenian soldiers and officers who were in the labor squads. A German officer, Scheubner-Richter, stated that "Halil Bey's campaign in northern Persia included the massacre of his Armenian and Syrian battalions and the expulsion of the Armenian, Syrian, and Persian population out of northern Persia, and consequently there was great bitterness toward the Turks." One Turkish officer wrote later "upon orders of General Halil 800 Armenians and another time 1,000 soldiers, officers, and medical doctors in the Expeditionary Force were disarmed and killed by the Turkish soldiers of that force."[95] The Syrian-American Jacob Sargis, a doctor at the missionary hospital in Urmia, recorded a conversation with the district governor of Gawar, who had just refused an order to kill all of the Armenian soldiers. Others had stepped in and executed them instead. Killed were 29 soldiers at Kharmad, and 8 Armenian officers were taken to a place outside Urmia where they were shot. One badly wounded survivor made his way to Sargis's hospital. In the corps "commanded by Halil, there were about 400 Armenians.... They were all doomed to be butchered."[96]

On May 13, Halil telegraphed that he would abandon Iran and march toward Van across Gawar and Bashkale.[97] By that time, casualties had re-

---

[93] Korsun, *Alashkertskaya i Khamadanskaya operatsii*, 42; testimony of Abraham Shlemon in William Walker Rockwell, *The Pitiful Plight of the Assyrian Christians in Persia and Kurdistan* (1916), 32; Andranig Chalabian, *General Andranig and the Armenian Revolutionary Movement* (1988), 237–43.

[94] Sorgun, *İttihad ve Terakki'den Cumhuriyet'e*, 97.

[95] Scheubner-Richter report of December 4, 1916, in Johannes Lepsius, *Deutschland und Armenien 1914–1918: Sammlung diplomatischer Aktenstücke* (1919), 308; Vahakn Dadrian, "The Armenian Genocide: An Interpretation" (2003), 64–65.

[96] Narrative of Dr. Jacob Sargis February 16, 1916, in Bryce and Toynbee, *Treatment of Armenians*, 190.

[97] Holstein to Deutsche Botschaft May 14, 1915, in Lepsius, *Deutschland und Armenien*, 67.

duced his army to half its original size.[98] On May 15, the Turks, Kurds, and Persian volunteers were observed to have left Urmia, with the Russians in hot pursuit.[99] The loss of the battle of Dilman and the subsequent Ottoman abandonment of Azerbaijan coincided with on-going massacres of the local Assyrian and Armenian population in Van. Halil and other Turkish occupation functionaries, who were forced to leave, began to take revenge on Ottoman citizens of Christian faith. A Venezuelan mercenary in Ottoman service, Rafael de Nogales, observed that afterward Halil did "as he pleased in wreaking his own vengeance on the Christians for the moral and material aid they had lent the Russians during the Battle of Dilman."[100]

EMERGENCY IN URMIA

The Russian consul-general at Tabriz, Orlov, reported on January 24/February 5:

> After the retreat of Russian troops from Urmia, a Turkish consulate opened and with it came a unit of Turkish forces with 4 mortars and 1,500 armed Kurds. Christians of the city were hidden at the [missions of the] Catholics and Protestants. Christians from villages had either run away or been killed. The region has been devastated.[101]

An estimated 20,000 to 25,000 Christian refugees—mostly Syriacs—had been left stranded in Urmia. Almost from the start of the occupation, there were massacres in neighboring villages, forcing survivors into the town.

Having had no military value for the Russians, the city of Urmia was not liberated until May 24, 1915. From February, when the Russians started their counteroffensive, until their pullout in May, the Turkish authorities began mass executions, kidnapping and extorting large amounts of ransom money, and plundering and looting Christian property. The American missionaries witness a worsening of the situation with the arrival of a civil governor, Raghib, in late February.[102] The powerless Persian authorities could do no more than register destruction and protest.

---

[98] Genelkurmay, *Birinci dünya harbi'nde*, 654.

[99] Griselle, *Syriens et Chaldéens*, 55 ; Johannes Lepsius, *Les Massacres d'Arménie* (1918), 114–15.

[100] Rafael de Nogales, *Four Years beneath the Crescent* (1926), 134.

[101] AVPRI, III. F. 133, des. 470, dossier 49, vol. II, list 425.

[102] Mary Lewis Shedd, *The Measure of a Man: The Life of William Ambrose Shedd, Missionary to Persia* (1922), 169–73.

The unfortunate inhabitants of Urmia have been plundered many times and they are without means of subsistence, the stocks of merchandise have been stolen. The population lives confused and consternated, their misfortune aggravated by each moment. The insecurity has reached its peak ... there is no perspective of a return to order.

They appealed to recall the Turkish troops to put a stop to the carnage.[103]

Yonan Shahbaz, an American citizen of Syriac origin, was eyewitness to the sacking and looting of the village of Gogtapa, where his home Baptist church was located. This village was 10 kilometers south of Urmia. On the morning after the Russian retreat, Muslims stood waiting outside the village walls to rob Christians who tried to flee. Some young Christians who had weapons made barricades in preparation for an attack. Because of its wall, Christians fled into Gogtapa from surrounding villages. A Kurdish attack began on January 3. It was said that the aggressors were 25,000 Kurds and a few thousand Iranian Muslims. Some had sacks and wagons prepared to carry away loot. The inhabitants panicked. Shahbaz and his wife raised a large American flag over their building, and many people sought protection there. By that time, the Kurds had entered the village; its southern quarters were on fire, and people were being shot in the streets. Many women and children were shot at the open gate as they tried to reach the Baptist church compound just outside the walls. Shahbaz led one large group who decided to escape. As they were running, the aggressors shot at them. Shahbaz and his family managed to get to Urmia, where the American mission gave them shelter.[104] A Catholic missionary reported that in Gogtapa, more than one hundred persons were killed and a Catholic priest had been decapitated. In the villages of Diza-Tékia, Atlakandi, Tazakend, and Ardichay, Catholic clerics had met a similar death or had been crucified.[105]

---

[103] Kargozar of Tabriz to Minister of Foreign Affairs February 26, 1915; Undersecretary of State to Persian Ambassador in Constantinople March 3, 1915; Minister of Foreign Affairs to Ottoman Ambassador Tehran March 5, 1915; Minister of Foreign Affairs to Turkish Ambassador Tehran March 5, 1915, documents nos. 247, 261, 264, 266, in Empire de Perse, *Neutralité Persane*, 132, 137–39.

[104] Yonan H. Shahbaz, *The Rage of Islam: An Account of the Massacre of the Christians by the Turks in Persia* (1918), 73–84.

[105] Letter of Abel Zayia, *Les Missions catholiques*, May 19, 1916, 234–36.

MISSIONS AND REFUGEES

Chronicles written in the American and French missions in Urmia provide the ability to reconstruct the build-up of fear and panic among those who had sought asylum in the mission compounds. The American compound was quite large, and during the occupation it also took over the neighboring English mission, which was abandoned. The compound had a good supply of running water. The missionaries had a sum of money in a bank account and thus could buy food in the local market. American flags were placed on many of the buildings. As the United States was neutral at that time, the situation for the American missionaries was better than for most others. Mary E. Lewis, who was the head of the American School of Modern Girls in Urmia, wrote the chronicle in the form of a diary.[106]

The Catholic French Lazarist mission compound had 3,000 refugees, and the French Filles de la Charité sheltered 700. Since Turkey was at war with France, people hiding there were particularly at risk. A collective of nuns of the Sisters of Saint-Vincent-de-Paul wrote a journal. Also in the French mission was the Catholic missionary Abel Zayia, who published his own chronicle.[107] The Russian Orthodox compound had been abandoned, and the Turkish consul, who was the head of the occupation civil government, used it as his headquarters and jail.

> JANUARY 2, FRENCH JOURNAL: From the first hour, the news of the departure of the Russians spread through the city. ... All of the sisters showed the resolution to remain at their posts ... the missionaries and sisters stay in order to save the lives of the Christians if this is possible; if not, they will die with them.
>
> JANUARY 3, FRENCH JOURNAL: It is true! The Russian troops have left the city. ... Voilà, Urmia is delivered to the Kurds ... the Persian Moslems themselves fear the approach of the Kurds. ... Many families have followed the Russian troops and not having found carriages have left on foot; they prefer to die of cold along the route rather than expose themselves to the atrocities of the Kurds.
>
> JANUARY 5, ZAYIA JOURNAL: The Kurdo-Turks have made their entry into the city and in the morning, the Kurds cast themselves over the Christian quarters and began to pillage. This activity was already under way when two Turkish officers, Naji Bey and Reshid Bey, accompanied by some soldiers, showed up in the places and killed a dozen of the

---

[106] *The War Journal of a Missionary in Persia*, ed. Mary Schauffler-Platt (1915); selections in Bryce and Toynbee, *Treatment of Armenians*, 154–82.

[107] Both are published in Griselle, *Syriens et Chaldéens*, the nuns on pp. 29–39 and Zayia on pp. 40–59.

brigands. The others went away. Notice that despite the war between the Turks and France, most of their officers have great sympathy for the French.

JANUARY 8, FRENCH JOURNAL: The house of the missionaries is full: schoolrooms, dormitories, storerooms, and corridors are in use; one can count more than two thousand refugees.

JANUARY 9, LEWIS JOURNAL: At once, as soon as the Russians had gone, with large numbers of Syrians and Armenians leaving at the same time, the evil-minded Moslems all over the plain began to plunder the Christian villages. When the people were trying to flee to the missionaries in the city, they were robbed on the roads of everything they had, even of their outer clothing. In some of the villages, the Moslem masters placed guards to prevent people from going themselves or bringing their possessions to the city, saying that they would protect them. When they tried to get away, these guards robbed and stripped them. The crowds began to pour in at our gates on Sunday [January 3]; the city people were taken in by night and many others from near by. On Sunday morning we put up the American flags over the entrances.

JANUARY 10, FRENCH JOURNAL: The family of one of our priests has arrived in a state that is impossible to describe; the priest is massacred with seven members of his family. The American Protestant mission is again full of refugees; there they are more crowded than we are, and the mortality there is frightening.

JANUARY 13, LEWIS JOURNAL: There are hundreds of mountaineers [Turkish Nestorian refugees] who have no place to go to. Before this affair they were distributed among the villages, and we had established a number of schools especially for them. These people had been driven from their homes by the Kurds early in the autumn [of 1914]. ... They are chiefly crowded into the church and our large schoolroom. The people who are suffering most are those who have been accustomed to the comforts and decencies of life, who are crowded together like cattle, without sufficient clothing or food.

JANUARY 14, LEWIS JOURNAL: Mr. Allen returned last evening from his journey to the villages of the Nazlu river [south of Urmia and the first line of attack]. Several thousand fled towards Russia; many have hidden with Moslems who are now trying to force them to become Mohammedans and to give their girls in marriage to Moslems. In Ada perhaps as many as a hundred were killed, most of them young men. It is told that they were stood up in line, one behind the other, by the Kurds, to see how many one bullet would kill. I went down to see the woman in the room under mine who had received word of the killing of her brother in Karadjalu. Everywhere there is wailing and sadness.

JANUARY 19, FRENCH JOURNAL: Continuation of the pillage. ... If the poor people try to defend their [property], they are threatened with death. The Persian authorities have assured the security, the effects however do not correspond with their promises; even in broad daylight people who walk in the streets can be robbed of their clothes.

JANUARY 23, LEWIS JOURNAL: Yesterday we counted three thousand three hundred in the church, and many have gone out, so there must have been four thousand people there these last two weeks. Is it any wonder that children are dying by the score? Morning and afternoon there are burials; at other times the bodies are collected and laid in a room near the gate. ... Dr. Packard has been gone for several days to the Nazlu villages, to gather together the remnants of the people scattered in the Moslem villages, or in hiding, and to see if it be possible to put them into a few of their own places again. Most of the Kurds have left, but the Syrians are unarmed, and, just as from the beginning, their Moslem neighbours are their greatest enemies. If it isn't Djihad, it is very near it. It must have been planned beforehand, for there has been some concerted action from one end of the plain to the other, though here and there some Moslems have been friendly throughout, have done many kindly deeds and saved many lives.

FEBRUARY 1, FRENCH JOURNAL: Of all the villages of the plain, only three are intact today. ... The Muslims of the countryside have been agitated to the final point against the Christians: there is a large part who have committed many atrocities.

FEBRUARY 5, LEWIS JOURNAL: Pretty soon there was quite a commotion in our front yard. I jumped up, and saw in the yard a dozen or more Turkish soldiers, who entered through our front door and went up to the roof through our halls. ... The Turks searched the house, but took nothing. ... It is maddening to have our premises and houses invaded in this way, and by such a lot, but we are helpless, and, for the sake of what we may be able to do for the safety of the people, our gentlemen have to smile and try to turn away their wrath with soft words, even though they are threatened and called liars by the representatives of the invading Government. ... Still the ghastly procession of the dead marches on. Between seven and eight hundred have died so far.

FEBRUARY 12, LEWIS JOURNAL: Last week, the Shahbandar, or Turkish Consul, who is now the chief authority, demanded six thousand *tomans* [Iranian money] of the Syrians. With great trouble this was partly collected and partly borrowed by the help of the Sirdar [actually Sardar, a Persian Governor], who demanded six hundred more for his share. The Shabandar promised that, if this were given, the shops and houses of the Syrians in the city would not be disturbed. It remains to be seen how much his word is worth.

FEBRUARY 12, FRENCH JOURNAL: The Turkish authorities asserted that the missionaries have caches of arms and military munitions. On this false pretext, today at about 10 o'clock, the secretary of the Turkish consulate, one officer, and twenty soldiers came into the Mission in order to make a search. ... They were evidently concerned to arrest the male refugees hiding at the Lazarists and the Sisters. ... Finally they separated a group of twenty, and took them to prison. ... This group was imprisoned for "having hidden arms" and having "fought with the Russians against the Turks."

FEBRUARY 12, ZAYIA JOURNAL: Two Turkish officials, one civil, Sami Bey, and one military, Bedri Bey, accompanied by 30 soldiers came in order to search both us and the sisters [nuns], 3,000 refugees squeezed one against the other; they occupied all of the space of the house, they searched in detail even the house of the sisters. They did not find anything that compromised us [but] they seized 154 men and transported them to the Turkish consulate in groups of 30 or 40. Among them are to be found 6 priests and one Nestorian bishop who, even he, sought refuge in the French mission. On the 13th the majority returned, except 61 men.

FEBRUARY 17, LEWIS JOURNAL: A few days ago the Turkish Consul arrested all the men at the French Mission. After some examination, a hundred were sent away, leaving about sixty-three at the Consulate. A gallows with seven nooses was erected at the "Kurdish Gate" of the city, the one near us, and on Sunday the ropes were put in place. The people here on Sunday [14 February] were very badly scared. ... As yet no one has been hanged, but the Turkish Consul is demanding money for their release... The Turkish Consul has demanded the ten thousand tomans of English bank money committed to us when the banker fled. The matter has been referred to our Consul in Tabriz. If it should have to be surrendered, we should be in straits, for that is all we have to buy bread with for these thousands of hungry people.

FEBRUARY 21, FRENCH JOURNAL: Decidedly the hatred of France is obvious among the Turks. Today the Mission was again invaded by a group of Kurds accompanied by Turkish soldiers. They went into a cellar full of the property of our Christians. The plundering was total.

FEBRUARY 23, LEWIS JOURNAL: Last night one of the most terrible things that has yet happened occurred. In the evening ten or a dozen of the prisoners from the French Mission, taken ten days or more ago by the Turkish Consul, were discharged, and we all felt that probably the rest would soon be set free, as there is no special charge against them. But this morning five men, two of them Moslems, were found hanging from the gallows at the Kurdish Gate, and forty-eight others were shot beyond the Tcharbash Gate. No one has dared to go out yet and get the bodies. ... Today a terrible fear has fallen on the people. There is much silent weeping, but little violent demonstration, though the mothers, wives and families of the murdered men are here. The question in everybody's mind is: "What will the Turks do next?" Forty or fifty shots were distinctly heard in the night between one and two o'clock, but no one guessed what they meant.

FEBRUARY 23, FRENCH JOURNAL: In the night four were hanged and the others shot. ... Permission to go and bury the dead has been refused. From 7 to 9 o'clock, we saw numbers of Muslims who made a spectacle of the place of execution. ... They were executed near the Jewish cemetery.

FEBRUARY 23, ZAYIA JOURNAL: About 1:30 A.M. the servant who stayed on the roof heard shots coming from the direction of the Jewish Hill about 2 kilometers northwest of the city. He did not think that it was anything but a battle between Kurds, but rather the execution of the persons detained at the Turkish consulate. They were tied in groups of five, six, or ten, arm to arm. They let them believe that they were being conducted to Van; but when they arrived at the fatal place, their killers commanded that they sit down to eat a bit. ... As they sat on the ground the fusillade began and fifty-one of them were found dead.

FEBRUARY 24, LEWIS JOURNAL: The French missionaries and the nine nuns were very much alarmed for their personal safety. They asked that one of our men should go there and put up an American flag; but, of course, we could not do that. Yesterday the Turkish Consul sent word that if we wanted the bodies of the three Christians hanging at the gate, we had permission to take them.

FEBRUARY 27, LEWIS JOURNAL: When Mr. McDowell returned from the burial of those shot on Jewish Hill, he reported that they had found forty bodies and identified all but five or six. On Wednesday [February 24] night, a still more horrible deed was committed at Gulpashan. This village and Iriawa had been shielded, partly through the efforts of a German; but on Wednesday night a band of Persian volunteers, arriving from Salmas or beyond, went there, took fifty men, and, according to reports, shot them in the graveyard near by. They then plundered the village, took girls and young women, outraged them, and acted in general as one might expect Satan to do when turned loose.

FEBRUARY 28, LEWIS JOURNAL: The reports of Mr. Allen from Gulpashan were too black to be written. The soldiers sent out by the [Turkish] Consul to protect the villages against Kurds and Moslem looters left unviolated hardly a woman or girl of those remaining in the village, and a number of girls were carried off. It seemed quite apparent that they understood that the whole business of protecting was to be a farce. When on Sunday morning Mr. Allen returned and wanted to bring people with him, he was not permitted. Those who had been murdered in the cemetery a few nights previously had been buried under a few inches of earth, and when he wanted to have them uncovered to identify them and bury them deeper, he was refused. The soldiers had made them all sit down on the ground and then shot them. They looked them over, and any who were found to be breathing were shot the second time. The only reason for all this was that they bore the name "Christian." ... Mr. McDowell went to Iriawa and found similar conditions there.

MARCH 19, FRENCH JOURNAL: Today everyone trembled; yesterday the Turks, having got news of defeat at Van which has been taken by the Russians [obviously a false rumor]—went and shot fifty of their own soldiers. The latter were Turkish subjects, but Christians. They were shot out of revenge, because at Van the Russians had been seconded by the Armenians.

APRIL 6, LEWIS JOURNAL: We have dwelt so long in the valley of death with the sick, the starving, the dying, with the unending procession of little bodies sewn up in a piece of cloth, friendless corpses carried out on ladders, with gaping mouths and staring eyes, crude unpainted coffins, coffins covered with black chintz, the never-ceasing wail, and eyes of the mourners that never dried, hands outstretched for what we cannot give.

JUNE 3, LEWIS JOURNAL: On Sunday, the 24th May, the advanced guard of the Russian army entered Urmia, and in the afternoon the commander came to call on our gentlemen. When we learned that the army would not remain, but were ordered to follow the enemy, there was consternation and great fear. And when the army moved on, the Moslems immediately began to annoy and rob the Syrians who had returned to their villages. There was great fear of a Moslem uprising against the Christians, and hundreds fled in the direction of Salmas. Finally, the Russians left a small guard of about two hundred men. Three days ago about six thousand Russian troops, with artillery, came in from the south and marched through the city. ... We shall try now to empty our yards of refugees.

American and French Catholic missionaries in Urmia gave protection to large numbers of refugees over a period of five months. The American mission compound contained between 15,000 and 17,000 persons, the French Lazarist mission compound had 3,000, and the French Filles de la Charité sheltered 700.[108] The people in these compounds lived under great

---

[108] Letter of Decroo March 12, 1915, in *Les Missions catholiques*, September 10, 1915, 207.

hardship and were afflicted by hunger and disease.[109] Those who sought shelter in the compounds were never free from danger.

On several occasions, adult males were seized from the American and French compounds, taken out, and summarily executed. Abel Zayia asserted that 150 persons, including 6 priests and a Nestorian bishop, had been seized from the French mission and taken to the Turkish consulate, but only a hundred returned the next day. Afterward an American missionary later found a mass grave with 42 cadavers, many badly mutilated.[110] Speaking of this and other killings of refugees, Shedd gave the following description:

> During this period the Turks were guilty not only of failure to protect the Christians effectively, but also of direct massacres under their orders. One hundred and seventy men thus massacred were buried by the American missionaries, their bodies lying in heaps where they had been shot down and stabbed, tied together and led out to be murdered by Turkish agents. These massacres took place on three different occasions. Once men were seized by Turkish officers in the French Mission and sent out from Turkish headquarters to be killed; once there were men seized in a village which was under the protection of Turkish soldiers and had its safety pledged repeatedly by the highest Turkish officials; and once there were men from just over the border in Turkey who had been forced to bring telegraph wire down to Urmia and were taken out and killed. In each of these cases some escaped and crawled out, wounded and bloody, from the heaps of dead and dying, to find refuge with the American missionaries. Besides these, the Armenian soldiers in the Turkish army, previous to the arrival of Halil Bey, were shot. In Urmia, the total losses of this period, from the evacuation of the town by the Russians on the 2nd January until their return on the 24th May, were the murder of over one thousand people—men, women and children; the outraging of hundreds of women and girls of every age—from eight or nine years to old age; the total robbing of about five-sixths of the Christian population; and the partial or total destruction of about the same proportion of their houses.

About 3,000 to 4,000 of those who sought shelter at the American mission died of disease, mainly from typhus; and 600 of those who fled to the

---

[109] Statement by Shedd, in Bryce and Toynbee, *Treatment of Armenians*, 138; letter of Decroo from late January 1915 published in *Saint Vincent de Paul Annales de la Mission* 80 (1915): 529.

[110] Abel Zayia, *Les Missions catholiques*, May 19, 1916, 234–36.

Catholic mission met the same fate.[111] In addition, an estimated 6,000 persons had been killed in the slaughter and raiding of the rural villages.[112]

In January 1916, Basile Nikitine, the new Russian vice-consul in Urmia, submitted a report that summarized briefly the major features of the period of Turkish occupation.

> Russian troops and the consulate abandoned Urmia. Immediately panic occurred among the local Christians. Syriac Christians tried to mount a defense in the villages of Ardichay and Hay-Tepe. After the Russian troops left, Christians found protection in the American and French missions. In the American mission during the winter about four thousand people died from disease, and in the French about five hundred. Turks performed mass executions of Christians from the French mission on the Jewish Hill outside Urmia. They also made mass executions in the villages of Gulpashan, and in the village of Kowsi, where Jacobites from Mosul were killed. Turks also extorted large sums. For example, the French paid six thousand tumans for Mar Ilya, the bishop of Urmia.[113]

INTERNATIONAL REACTIONS

In the wake of the formal protests of the British, French, and United States legations, news of conditions in Turkish-occupied Azerbaijan spread throughout the world. A flood of newspaper articles began to be published in late March in most major countries. There were separate articles in the *New York Times* on March 22, "Turkish Consul led Mob to our Mission"; March 24, "Massacre in Urumiah"; March 26, "Hang a Bishop in Our Mission";[114] March 28, "Turks Continue Slaying in Urumiah"; and March 31, "Urumiah Physician Here. Dr. Yuseff Tells of the Horror of the Flight from the City." After these news articles came a flood of letters to the editor, publication of private letters sent to the relatives and friends of mis-

---

[111] Michael Zirinsky, "American Presbyterian Missionaries at Urmia during the Great War" (1998); Statement by Shedd, in Bryce and Toynbee, *Treatment of Armenians*, 139; *Les Missions catholiques*, May 19, 1916, 234–36.

[112] Y. M. Nisan to F. N. Heazell May 25, 1915, in Bryce and Toynbee, *Treatment of the Armenians*, 187.

[113] AVPRI, I U. F. 144, Persidskii stol B, des. 489, 1910-1916, dossier 529, list 34-40.

[114] This headline turned out not to be true, ; it refers to the Russian Orthodox bishop Mar Ilya, who was not killed but was seized and held for ransom by the Turkish consul.

sionaries. Wide-ranging campaigns to collect money began under the aegis of the "American Committee for Armenian and Syrian Relief."

The Ottoman government began a policy of disinformation and denial of atrocities. Such denial, of course, made diplomacy very difficult. On March 30, the *New York Times* reported that the Grand Vizier had called in the American ambassador in Istanbul, Henry Morgenthau, and told him, "No acts of violence had been committed at Urumiah." He also explained that alleged atrocities were "grossly exaggerated.". The Turkish War Office "denied that there had been any disorders whatever. The reports of attacks upon foreigners have virtually all come from Tiflis, which is far from Urumiah, and between the two places communication is said to be so difficult that error was to be expected."[115] On March 31 there was news of a new assurance of protection of "not only foreigners, but natives as well ... by the Turkish regular troops, due at Urmiah last Saturday. Apparently no advices had been received in Constantinople from Urumiah after the regulars had reached that place as no mention was made of their arrival." The Turkish government scored some initial success in their disinformation campaign, and Secretary of State Bryan stated that news of atrocities was similar to the "game of Gossip" and that "tales relayed through many messengers ... were certain to be distorted out of all resemblance to the original report."[116] Thus, the Ottoman government was at first given the benefit of the doubt, and throughout the world many remained skeptical about the information filtering through Russian hands.

Much later, on May 8, 1917, William Shedd summarized in a letter to Basile Nikitine the experiences of the last two years.

> It is nearly two years now since you came to Urmia and it is not necessary for me to remind you of the vicissitudes of these eventful years. When you came we had just emerged from the perils and sufferings of the months of Turkish occupation. Hundreds of Christians have been massacred, thousands have died of disease, their villages were in ruins, and the people were weak from privation and emaciated from hunger. I am sure that neither you nor I will forget the visits we made together to the ruined villages. The Moslem population has suffered also, but many of them had been guilty of cruel wrong to the Christians, murder, rape and robbery. The ruin was moral as well as material and [left] a residue of hate and revenge.[117]

---

[115] *New York Times*, "Turkish Army Due At Urumiah," March 30, 1915.
[116] *New York Times*, "New Promise By Turkey," March 31, 1915.
[117] AVPRI, UI. F. Persidskii stol, des. 490c, 1917, dossier 15c, list 5.

5 THE ETHNIC CLEANSING OF THE HAKKARI MOUNTAINS

In July 1915, Mar Shimun XXI Benyamin penned yet another desperate note to the Russians begging for help and describing the hopeless situation of the Assyrian tribes fighting in the mountains above the Zab River valley.

> During a month when our people were fighting against Kurds, Haydar Bey, the Governor of Mosul, came with Turkish units and cannons. ...The Turks occupied our villages and burned them down. Now Assyrians live on the mountain peaks from Tiyyari, Tkhuma, to Diz. They are dying from hunger, because they have no food. We have no bullets, we are surrounded by the Turks, and we have no solution.[1]

This siege had continued throughout the summer until the Assyrians left their homeland and crossed the nearby border to join with the other Christian refugees massed in northwest Iran. After they left, all their houses, churches, and relics were destroyed. Few signs of Assyrian culture remained—they were never to return.

The Assyrian tribes were the prime target among all the Syriac groups in the Ottoman Empire, and the CUP spoke of them with the same degree of suspicion as they did the Armenians. The ethnic cleansing of Hakkari was a consequence of a series of government decrees, some of which predated the war. The eradication of the autonomous Assyrian tribes had been a favorite idea of Talaat Pasha, the Minister of the Interior, because they made up an almost solid non-Muslim eagle's nest on an important border. When war became imminent, ethnic cleansing began on a small scale and then spiraled after a few months to a full-scale operation. Talaat made the final decision at the moment it was clear that the Assyrian tribes were being defeated. He wrote to the valis of Mosul and Van accusing the Nestorians of cooperating with the Armenians and Russians. He proposed: "We should not let them return to their homelands."[2]

---

[1] AVPRI III. F. 133, 1915, des. 470, dossier 49, vol 2. list 468 Secret telegram No 201, July 11, 1914, contains Mar Shimun's letter.

[2] BOA. DH. ŞFR 54/240 Talaat to valis of Mosul and Van June 30, 1915.

From his vantage point in Iran, Akimovich, the Russian chargé d'affaires at Dilman, noted, "In early August, Assyrian refugees from Urmia and the province of Van were arriving in Dilman. They are [now] about 18,000. Among them are many sick people dying from hunger and exhaustion."[3] The first wave of Assyrian refugees who arrived on the Salmas plain was estimated at 35,000. About 5,000 remained in Bashkale as a rear guard, and an unknown number perished as they kept fighting in the mountains. The plain of Salmas in Iran turned out to be a bad location for so many refugees. As a rural district with small villages and towns, there was little shelter, so the people stayed in the open air. Farming had been disrupted by the war, so food was scarce, and signs appeared of the famine that was to last several years.[4] When the unavoidable epidemics broke out, there was little medical care to be had. Very many died that winter.

The Assyrians attempted to fight their way back to their ancient homeland several times during the war and even after, but they never succeeded. Here is the story behind their exodus, which also amounted to one of the most complete cases of ethnic cleansing. This is a tale of government plans for deportation, harassment, and massacres by local Kurdish chiefs—all leading up to a full war between the well-armed Ottoman army and the traditional Assyrian tribal warriors. This is a difficult story to narrate, not only because it is the tale of escalating violence, but also because the Assyrians themselves were kept in the dark about what was being planned for them, and ethnic cleansing had not been part of their previous experience. The documentation is sparse, consisting of news of massacres, executions, attacks, invasions, and retreats, without much clarification. The Assyrians had no long-range strategy except defense and survival. There were no foreigners present who could make independent observations as the missionaries could in Mardin and Urmia. The massacres in the sanjak capital Baskale were so many that it gives the impression of containing a combined concentration and death camp where refugees were held captive until their execution. However, no one managed to escape from Bashkale, and thus we lack information about what went on inside the town and how the captives were treated.

In the Syriac experience, Hakkari is in many respects a unique case. First, for a long time it was near or on the front line, with Russian and Ottoman troops wreaking havoc on the civilian population. Second, a deporta-

---

[3] AVPRI, P.F. 144, des 490, 1915-1917, dossier 22c, list 18-20.

[4] Mohammed Gholi Majd, *The Great Famine and Genocide in Persia, 1917–1919* (2003).

tion decree was issued in October 1915, before war broke out. In it the Assyrians were marked for destruction because of collaboration with the Russians. Third, the Assyrians actually did have contacts with the Russians and had been led to expect some military support, and they did receive a small amount of arms and ammunition. Fourth, the Assyrians were so provoked by the repeated massacres and slaughter that a tribal council made some sort of declaration of war in May 1915. Fifth, the annihilation of the Assyrians did not occur through deportations, but rather through an enormous military invasion that pushed them out of their ancestral homes.

Discussions of the events of 1915 have only rarely found evidence that the jihad fatwa of November 1914 had any effect. However, in referring to the ethnic cleansing of Hakkari, local Kurdish tribes spoke of it as the time of the "great jihad." In 1917, an Assyrian raid resulted in the capture of some correspondence with Ottoman officials. Among them was a letter from Suto, the agha of Oramar, to Haydar Bey, vali of Mosul and highest commander of the forces that fought against the Assyrians. "I had the honor of presenting myself to Your Excellency last spring during the Great Jihad, when the soldiers went against Tiyyari and Tkhuma."[5] This is a reference to the massive campaign against the heartland of the Assyrian tribes in June 1915.

The Hakkari mountain range makes up the southeastern sandjak of the province of Van; for centuries it was the heartland of the Nestorian Church and the Assyrian tribes. But it was also smack in the middle of Kurdistan. The fate of the Armenians and Assyrians is intertwined with that of the Kurds and the Turks. On April 20, 1915, Ottoman forces began bombarding the Armenian sections of Van, announcing that they were trying to put down an "Armenian revolt." On April 23, other units of the Ottoman army reported that a "Nestorian revolt" was under way.[6] Since the start of the World War, the government had prophesied the coming of an Armenian revolt, and it acted as if it expected the same from the Assyrians.

---

[5] Cited in Jacques Rhétoré, *"Les Chrétiens aux bêtes": Souvenirs de la guerre sainte proclamée par les Turcs contre les chrétiens en 1915* (2005), 279.

[6] ATAŞE 4/3671, kls. 2950, H-13, F 1-110, cited in Genelkurmay Başkanlığı, *Birinci Dünya Harbi'nde Türk Harbi Kafkas Cephesi 3 ncü Ordu Harekâtı* [World War I, Turkish War on the Caucasus Front, Third Army operations], 2:1 (1993), 592.

Map 5: The tribes and districts of the Hakkari Mountains (tribal districts in capitals). From Surma, *Assyrian Church Customs and the Murder of Mar Shimun* (1920), n.p.

THE ASSYRIAN HOMELAND

> The Mountain region between the upper course of the River Zab and the Persian border is very rugged, and contains only very deep and narrow valleys, except the lofty plain of Gawar. These valleys are inhabited by Kurdish and Syrian clans that own their allegiance to the Sultan within their mountain country only by paying an irregular and very inconsiderable tribute. Disputes between individuals and communities are settled by a primitive code of tribal law, enforced by the strong arm of the people themselves. Their wealth consists almost entirely of sheep, and these are the objects of frequent inter-tribal raids. Unlike the Kurds, none of the Christians are nomadic, although they spend the summer months as much as possible in the mountain encampments, where sheep are kept. The narrow valleys are terraced, and so fields are made, which are sown with millet, Indian corn, potatoes, and other products. ... Instead of going to Russia for work, the men go for the winter to the plains to the south and find work in the large cities, from Mosul to Aleppo and Damascus, especially as stonemasons and basket-makers. ...

Most miserable of all are the Syrians living in or near the mountain districts under more complete Government control. During the past fifty years the Turkish Government has gradually extended its authority in the mountain districts. The power of the great Kurdish chiefs has been broken, and, one after another, districts have become *rayat* instead of *ashiret*.[7]

According to a Russian intelligence agent who traveled throughout the area in 1904, the Assyrians made up 37 percent of the population of Hakkari, and they were 95 percent of the population in the enclave designated the "Assyrian ashiret," that is, the area of the independent tribes (map 5). A report by P. I. Aver'yanov, a major-general serving in the Russian general staff, estimated in 1912 that there were about a hundred thousand Nestorians in the whole Ottoman Empire and that 75,000 of them lived in Hakkari. Mar Shimun himself believed the combined size of his flock in Turkey and Iran numbered 150,000 souls.[8]

A hereditary religious and secular leader, the Patriarch of the Nestorians was always named Mar Shimun and was always selected from the Shimun dynasty. The patriarchs lived in celibacy, and at the death of a Mar Shimun, he was always succeeded by a nephew. For centuries the patriarch resided in the mountain hamlet of Kochanes not far from the government center of Julamerk, a town that was mainly Kurdish. The second highest religious leader was the Metropolitan or *Matran* of Shamdinan, who always bore the title Mar Khnanisho and resided in a border village. He was more or less a neighbor to the most influential Kurdish leader, the shaykh of Nihri.

In the past, most Assyrians in the Van vilayet belonged to the Nestorian Church with Mar Shimun as religious and secular leader. There were literally hundreds of Nestorian villages and hamlets scattered throughout the mountains and valleys of the Upper Zab River. However, the Catholic Chaldean Church also had considerable presence, and its influence grew in the decades before World War I. In recent times, a Catholic mission in Van had organized a reported 3,850 souls in the Van and Hakkari areas. There

---

[7] William A. Shedd, "The Syrians of Persia and Eastern Turkey," 5–6.

[8] V. T. Maevskii, *Voenno-statisticheskoe opisanie vanskogo i bitlisskogo vilaetov'* [Statistical report on Van and Bitlis vilayets] (1904), 230–43; P. I. Aver'yanov, *Etnograficheskii i voenno-politicheskii obzor' aziatskikh' vlad'nii ottomanskoi imperii* [Ethnographic and military-political description of the Asian provinces of the Ottoman Empire] (1912), 24; Vladimir Genis, *Vitse-konsul Vvedenski sluzhba v Persii I Bukharskom khanstve (1906–1920 gg.) Rossiskaya diplomatiya v sud'bakh* [Vice-Consul Vvedenski's service in Persia and the Khanate of Bukhara, 1906–1920] (2003), 339.

were several communities of Chaldeans in the immediate vicinity of Van. The leader of the Jilu tribe, Nimrod Shimun (an elder cousin and bitter rival of the Patriarch), and Mar Sargis, the tribe's bishop, converted to Roman Catholicism in 1904.[9] There were also a few Protestant converts made by missionaries.

Two socio-economic types of Assyrians lived in Van province. Foremost were the highland Assyrians belonging to the independent ashiret tribes of Tiyyari, Tkhuma, Jilu, Ishtazin, Baz, and Diz, who lived in the Hakkari Mountains. Despite the term "tribe," they were settled in villages, but they did have large flocks and moved them according to the seasons. Secondary to them were the more numerous lowland Assyrians living on permanently settled farms along the valleys and on the plateaus.

The highlanders were autonomous of Ottoman government and even possessed some influence over neighboring Kurdish tribes; they were used as outside mediators in intertribal feuds. Members of ashirets did not pay personal taxes, so the Ottoman authorities never attempted to count the population, and even the Mar Shimun had only an approximate idea of the size of his people. Most of the tribes paid a small tribute to the government of 30 to 50 liras per year.[10] However, the annual tribute paid by the Jilu tribe was much larger, amounting to 800 liras.[11] The Jilu tribe was semi-independent from the rest of the Nestorian tribes and often went its own way; at least one traveler mistook them for a Kurdish tribe.

The Assyrians in the lowlands were subject to most of the Ottoman laws and regulations and paid some, but not all, of the taxes and dues that other non-Muslims had to pay.[12] Many nomadic and seminomadic Kurdish tribes were regularly present in the area: the Artoshi, Oramar, Shamdinan, Herki, Zebari, Ruzhaki, Shernakli, Khizan, Barzan, Girdi, Bahdinan, Missuri, Bohtan, Hasankeyf, Nauchai, Jelali, Rawan, and many other small groups.[13] However, according to the Assyrians, the most destructive element during World War I was the Oramar Kurdish tribe headed by Suto Agha. This tribe lived between Gawar and the mountains on the Persian

---

[9] Joseph Tfinkdji, "L'Eglise chaldéenne catholique autrefois et aujourd'hui" (1914), 516.

[10] In 1911, 1 lira (or Turkish pound) was valued at £0, 18s. 0d. or $4.40 (*Encyclopædia Britannica*, 11th ed., 18:706, s.v. "Money").

[11] R. I. Termen, *Otchet' o poezdke v sandzhak Khekkiari, Vanskago vilaiet v 1906 gody* [Report of travel in the sanjak of Hakkari, Van vilayet in 1906] (1910), 78–88.

[12] Surma D'Bait Mar Shimun, *Assyrian Church Customs and the Murder of Mar Shimun* (1920), 55–66.

[13] Ely Bannister Soane, *To Mesopotamia and Kurdistan in Disguise* (1926), 406.

frontier. During the war it perpetrated massacres both in Turkey and in Iran and was considered by the Assyrians to have been responsible for most of the worst atrocities. An Assyrian expedition of retribution was organized in the summer of 1917 to capture Suto and destroy his forts.[14]

THE PRE-WAR DEPORTATION ORDER

On account of their position on the main roads leading to the nearby Iranian border, at the outbreak of World War I the Christians of the district centers of Sarai (in kaza Mahmudie of Van sanjak) and Bashkale (the capital of Hakkari sanjak) were strategically important to both sides. A recent Russian investigation had found that Sarai had 105 Assyrian and 46 Kurdish households, while Bashkale had 161 Armenian, 158 Kurdish, and 150 Jewish households; and there were many Christian villages in the vicinity.[15] Bashkale was to have an unfortunately bloody history during World War I as the scene of repeated large massacres of Christians in the period between September 1914 and May 1915.

Long before the Ottomans entered the war, the Christians, beginning with border villages, were being cleansed out of the region. One important observer of these events was the Russian vice-consul stationed at Urmia, Basile Nikitine. After the war he became famous for cultural and historical research about the Kurds. When the Ottomans declared general mobilization in early August 1914, the Assyrians dodged conscription, like everyone else. Nikitine discovered on August 2/15, 1914, that

> Turkish Syriacs refused to be mobilized in the Turkish army, and this was followed by repression and requisition of their property. As a result, Syriacs fled to Persia. On July 25/August 6, Turks detained about two thousand Syriacs near the Turkish-Persian border, but 500 managed anyhow to get into Iran, and the Kurds informed on them to the Turkish authorities.[16]

Quickly, repression increased and a growing number of refugees turned up in Iran. Nikitine reported on August 15/28,

> Turkish authorities have imposed severe control over the territory of the Turkish Syriacs and take reprisals against their leaders. Mar Shimun was called to Van and the bishop of Shamdinan, Mar Khnanisho, was ar-

---

[14] Joel E. Werda, *The Flickering Light of Asia; or, the Assyrian Nation and Church* (1924), 69–80.
[15] Maevskii, *Voenno-statisticheskoe opisanie*, 49, 53.
[16] AVPRI, I.F. 293, des. 571, dossier 420, list 5-6.

rested. But the people nevertheless demand autonomy. Now Syriacs from the villages of Sheitan, Bitlo, Serarlu, Bitkare, Nerdish, Segin, Hilanek, Derboder, and Diru have been deported to Persia. The Turks burned down the Syriac villages and confiscated the property of the inhabitants.[17]

It has not been possible to identify all of these place names, but those that can be were located along the border in Shamdinan and Jilu. Most of the refugees arrived in the town of Urmia, where they were cared for in the missions. Thus began an exodus of Nestorians from Turkey that continued through the entire year 1915.

The Ottoman government was disturbed by doubts about Nestorians' loyalty and was concerned over the possibility that more of them would move into Iran and join the self-defense units established by the Russians. They were a risk, as the Ottomans planned an invasion of Iran. In October 1914, Talaat Pasha sent a decree to the vali of Van ordering the deportation of the Assyrians on the border. They would be resettled much further west, in central Anatolia. Like other ethnic groups being evacuated, they were to be portioned out among many villages so that they would be submerged in a world of Turkish-speaking Muslims. Thus they would not be able to maintain their traditional language and customs, but instead would have to assimilate. The motivation behind the order was that

> the Nestorians have always remained suspect to the government [due to] their predisposition to be influenced by foreigners and become a channel and an instrument [for them]. Because of the operation and efforts in Persia, the concern of the government over Nestorians has increased, particularly about those who are found along our border with Iran. The government's lack of trust of them results in their chastisement—their deportation and expulsion from their locations to suitable provinces such as Ankara and Konya. They are to be transferred and dispersed so that they henceforth will not live together in a mass, but will live exclusively among Muslim people, and in no location are they to exceed twenty dwellings. ... The government will not undertake to provide any type of support [while they are on their way], to be permitted to stay and transmitted to the appropriate province and after preparations of the matter [they are] to depart from Van.[18]

This project was not just a simple resettlement, since the dispersal of the Assyrians in the manner described was designed to destroy their culture,

---

[17] AVPRI, I.F. 293, des. 571, dossier 420, list 59-61.
[18] BOA. DH. ŞFR 46/78, Ministry of Interior to Van vilayet October 26, 1914.

language, and traditional way of life. At the end of October, Talaat also ordered the arrest of Nestorians in and around the district center of Julamerk, on no other grounds than that they appeared to be purposefully gathering.[19]

Unaware of government decisions, Mar Shimun's elder sister Surma noted with surprise and consternation that the Turkish authorities had arrested Assyrian farmers and artisans in the borderland Gawar plateau.[20] She also reported the murder by the government of 50 men who had been brought from Gawar to Bashkale. Even in the westernmost district, Berwar, peasant dwellings were sacked and the women abducted. Obviously, these actions must be seen in light of the deportation telegram and their refusal to abandon their homes. According to Surma, some friendly Kurds had informed Mar Shimun that he must set himself in safety since the authorities planned his arrest. She clarified: "It must be clearly understood that the atrocities of which we have given instances did not take place without the knowledge of high officials. On every occasion, the fullest details were sent in writing by Mar Shimun to the Vali of Van, and to the Kaim-makam concerned."[21] It was not yet apparent to the Assyrians that the government was pulling the strings and rigging a trap.

Prior to the declaration of war, Turkish troops violated the border with Persia and laid Christian villages to waste. In Van province, regiments of Hamidiye irregular cavalry had been concentrated, as well as volunteers taken from diverse Kurdish tribes. Several volunteer brigades were destined to cross into Iran, where they were to wage guerrilla warfare. According to the French vice-consul in Van, the intention was to create incidents so that Russia would declare war.[22] Sometimes they battled with Russian troops and local Christian self-defense units posted in the border settlements. Large-scale attacks occurred in late September and October, and on one occasion Turkish and Kurdish forces came within sight of Urmia. In response, the Iranians shut down the Turkish consulates in Khoi, Tabriz, and Urmia. They also expelled some Kurds and other Sunni Moslems to Turkey. In retaliation, the Turkish authorities expelled several thousand Christians from Hakkari.[23] They were settled in farming villages along the west-

---

[19] BOA. DH. ŞFR 46/102 Ministry of Interior to Van vilayet October 28, 1914.

[20] Gawar was divided between Turkey and Iran, so there are provinces with the same name in both countries.

[21] Surma, *Assyrian Church Customs*, 67.

[22] Barthe de Sandfort to Bompard September 19, 1914, in Arthur Beylerian, *Les Grandes Puissants: L'Empire Ottoman et les Arméniens dans les archives françaises (1914–1918)* (1983), 4.

[23] Yonan Shahbaz, *The Rage of Islam: An Account of the Massacre of Christians by the*

ern border and received arms from the Russians. The self-defense of the Iranian Assyrians convinced the Ottomans that there was no prospect that the Ottoman Assyrians would suddenly become more loyal.[24]

BASHKALE

Located in the narrow Great Zab River valley and surrounded by high mountains, Bashkale, whose name means Main Fort, had local military importance. People traveling from Van or Hakkari to Iran could hardly avoid it. The town was on the frontier of an ethnic divide, with Armenians to the north and Assyrians to the south, and Kurds everywhere. Throughout the early war years, Bashkale filled with waves of refugees trying to escape who were not able to get much farther. It became the scene of numerous mass executions of Christians. At the start of the war, a large and diverse Ottoman expeditionary force camped there and at outposts in order to patrol the border. Kazim Karabekir, who later became a famous general and politician, was in charge; he sometimes had the advice of Ömer Naji, who supervised the Teskilat-i Mahsusa operatives based there.

When war began in early November 1914, many skirmishes took place between Ottoman and Russian troops in the far northeast corner of present-day Turkey. On the first days of hostilities, the Russians captured the towns of Sarai and Bashkale and held the latter for a few days while the local Christians apparently collaborated with them. That could have opened the road to Van for the Russians, if they had possessed the strength necessary to follow up these quick victories.[25] But the invasion was very short, and when the Ottomans re-entered Sarai and Bashkale, they punished the local Christians as traitors. Hearing news of the reprisals, Y. K. Rushdouni wrote, "Twelve villages in the Gargar [Gawar] district on the Persian frontier, Bashkale and Sarai with the Nestorian and Armenian villages round, were ruthlessly wiped out after the Russian retreat. ... News of this sort was constantly being brought to the town [Van] by refugees from distant places."[26]

Turks in Persia (1918), 58.

[24] BOA. DH. ŞFR 46/195 Ministry of the Interior to Van vilayet November 4, 1914.

[25] Paléologue to Delcassé November 5, 1914, in Beylerian, *Les Grandes Puissants*, 5.

[26] Statement of Y. K. Rushdouni June 7, 1915, in Bryce and Toynbee, *Treatment of Armenians*, 88, 96.

According to the testimony of Sbordoni, who served as an Italian consular agent in Van, new retributive massacres took place in Bashkale in the first week of December. Ahmed Bey, the head of 160 gendarmes, and Sheref Bey, commander of a Hamidiye unit, were accused of the slaughter.

> They pillaged and burned the Armenian houses, killed all of the men and left their cadavers in the street, captured the beautiful girls, and abandoned the women and children without food or shelter. The neighboring Armenian villages were subjected to the same thing. The Armenians of the villages of Paz, Arak, Piss, Alanian, Alas, Soran, Rasoulan, and Avak were assembled. They were conducted to a place where all were massacred. According to the latest statistics, there were in Bashkale and the named villages 1,600 Armenians (of which a small part are Nestorians).[27]

Not all of the villages were completely Armenian, and Alanian at least contained 30 Assyrian households.[28] Witnesses stated that the families were not allowed to bury the bodies.

What was going on? In late November, Ottoman authorities in Van grew frantic over the expected Armenian revolt. Families of Turkish officials packed and fled to safety in far away Bitlis.[29] From their border positions, Kazim Karabekir's troops had just captured two agents who had tried to cross the border. Under interrogation they confessed that an Armenian revolt would soon break out in Van.[30] Ömer Naji, along the border, examined a letter that his men had taken from a Kurdish guide who was smuggling it from the Armenian military leader Antranik (who was training volunteers just across the border) to Van's political leaders Vramian (the deputy to the National Assembly) and Ishkhan. This letter was a response to a message sent by Vramian to keep the Armenian volunteers calm so as not to provoke the increasingly jittery Ottoman authorities. Antranik sent back nothing more than his greetings. Ömer seized the occasion to send a sarcastic telegram to Vramian wondering about contact with the Russian army. "Congratulations to you on learning from Bakunin, Marx, and Kropotkin

---

[27] Henry Barby, *Au pays de l'épouvante: L'Arménie martyre* (1917), 234.

[28] Foreign Office FO 839/23 82893 "Liste des villages, des habitations et nationalites" sent by Agha Petros to British delegation Lausanne November 26, 1922.

[29] Jevdet to Minister of Interior November 17/30, 1914, document 1996, in *Askeri Tarih Belgeleri Dergisi*, vol. 34 (1983); see also statement of Y. K. Rushdouni, in Bryce and Toynbee, *Treatment of Armenians*, 95.

[30] Kazim to Commander of 3rd Army November 29, 1914, document 1812, in *Askeri Tarih Belgeleri Dergisi*, vol. 31 (1982).

your new role as provocateur. Congratulations to the revolutionary Ishkhan, to whom the Russian despot sends his greetings."[31] Ömer's telegram was just one more warning that the Armenian leaders were stigmatized in the eyes of the CUP as revolutionaries and traitors.

For a second time, a Russian force slogged its way to Bashkale and held it briefly. Weapons that were captured from the Ottoman soldiers were distributed among the local Armenians. The Van Jandarma found one of these armed groups at a place named Bellu in the Gawar plateau. They surrounded the house but were shot at, and some of the gendarmes died. More troops were brought in, leading to more casualties. Hurshid, the commander of the local Hamidiye regiment, was one of the slain.[32] This event was interpreted as the first concrete sign of the awaited Armenian revolt. About this time, Karabekir decided to disarm the soldiers of Armenian birth under his command.[33] Most likely, "disarm" was a euphemism for more severe treatment. News arrived at Van that the Ottoman troops were running amok in the vicinity of Bashkale and that unarmed Armenian soldiers had been slaughtered. This did nothing to calm anxiety among the Christians, who took it as a premonition of worse to come. Vramian made many protests to Talaat, but to no avail. Rather than deal with the issues, the Minister of the Interior ordered him expelled from Van.[34]

Thus the lines of ethnic and religious confrontation began to be drawn in November and December 1914. Behind the scenes, many other Christian villages were meeting terrible fates. A Nestorian survivor gave the following testimony to a Russian court investigating war crimes:

> In 1914 I lived in the village of Gose [a Russian transliteration of Houzi] close to the town of Bashkale. In the winter of that year ... at about six o'clock in the evening, I saw that the Turks were approaching. I went out into the plain to find my brother Aywaz, who was tending the cattle, to tell him. I had not gone far before I saw my brother running toward me. He was totally covered in blood, his mouth was sliced open, and his half cut off tongue hung from his mouth. Since he could not speak, he began to explain with his hands. From this explanation I understood that the Turks had done it. But who exactly and why, and under whose

---

[31] Obrona Vana [The defense of Van], in *Genotsid armyan i russkaya publitsistika* [The Armenian genocide in Russian publications] (1998), 153.

[32] Ibid., 156–57.

[33] Telegram from Van Mobile Jandarma received at War Office December 5, 1914, document no. 1813, in *Askeri Tarih Belgeleri Dergisi*, vol. 31 (1982).

[34] Obrona Vana, in *Genotsida armyan*, 158–59; see Talaat's attempt to follow up BOA. DH. ŞFR 48/38 and 48/39 December 18, 1914.

orders, my brother could not tell. ... I went up the Ashan Hill and hid. From the mountain I had a good view of Gose village. On the next morning, after the Turkish troops had left Gose and gone on, I came down from the hill and went to my house. I found my brother's corpse in the road beside my house. He had a piercing wound passing all the way through the neck and another through the stomach. I cannot say what had caused these wounds. The village was completely empty, and I later learned that the inhabitants had been taken captive. I was so shocked that I did not notice if there were any other dead than my brother. ... Later my neighbor Benjamin Lovkoev said that Taher Pasha and Hurshid Bey were the commanders of the Turkish troops.[35]

Houzi was a village with 78 Assyrian households and Hurshid was the commander of the local irregular cavalry regiment made up of the Pinyanish tribe.

According to testimony from a cousin of Mar Shimun and the widow of the village headman Yuhannan Abdarov, the Turkish forces entered his village of Ardshi in November 1914. According to Maevskii, Ardshi had 57 households, all of them "Nestorians."[36] The widow was one of the few known survivors. She was saved to deliver a warning in person to Mar Shimun. Her husband and two sons were cut down before her eyes; the whole village was burned and the church destroyed. All the women, about 150 persons, were distributed among relatives of a Kurdish chief. The priest was murdered. The leader of the Turkish force was the well-known figure Hurshid Bey in command of a group of death squad volunteers. Her testimony was:

> The Turks attacked the village of Ardshi in November 1914. These Turks were not regular *askeri* [soldiers] but the Sultan's special volunteers, called the "Group Hamidiye." The Head of the group was officer Hurshid Bey. As soon as they invaded Ardshi village, they set the house of Yuhannan Abdarov on fire and arrested my husband and sons. They were tortured to death. They were beaten from all sides and ordered to become Muslims, but they refused. Before my eyes Hurshid Bey shot my sons with a pistol. As I saw what happened, I tried to protect my husband, but Hurshid Bey kicked me in the face, knocking out two teeth. Then he shot my husband with six bullets. The corpses of the dead, even that of my husband, were left lying in the road. We were not allowed to bury the dead. Hurshid Bey ordered that the corpses be

---

[35] RGVIA, Extraordinary Investigation Commission Taganrog, No. 11329, Testimony of Simon Lazarev March 9, 1916.

[36] V. T. Maevskii, *Voenno-statisticheskoe opisanie* (1904).

smeared with excrement. Over the following four days the dogs ate the corpses. Then Hurshid Bey ordered that the corpses be thrown in the latrine, where even the cross of the village church got thrown. Then Hurshid had the whole village burned and twelve people killed. ... All the women, virgins, and children were taken captive and brought to the village of Atis. There they had to choose: Islam or death. 150 women and girls were forced to become the wives of Hurshid Bey's relatives. ... Of all the prisoners, only I remained, because Hurshid Bey knew that I was the cousin of the patriarch Mar Shimun. When I was freed, I went by foot to my parents in Kochanes, near Julamerk. I was on the road for two days. I was so tired that I had to leave two of my small children under a tree. To this day I know nothing of their fate. My small daughter died of hunger on the way. I arrived at my parents' half crazy from my terrible experiences.[37]

Lady Surma remarked on this event in her war chronicle and wrote the date as November 14, but she may have meant November 27 given that there were two calendar systems in use. From a separate source, Mar Shimun learned that Hurshid had murdered Yuhannan Abdarov on government orders. A scout had been sent, and he revealed:

As for the Christians of Albak, most of the young men have been killed, all the villages and houses plundered, and the women and young children carried captive and now kept in the house of a Kurd, Shahin Agha. He has used them kindly and has prevented any attempts to make them embrace Islam by force. The wife of Shamasha [deacon] Yukhannan [Yuhannan] and her two younger sons (ages nine and eleven) have been carried off by Khurshad Beg [Hurshid Bey] and are now kept in one of their own stables. Her two children were begging in the village for bread for their mother and themselves.[38]

Another witness to the same massacre testified that the Turkish officers demanded that Abdarov give them money and that he gave some, but they demanded more, as well as gold items. He was tortured by first having his ring finger chopped off, then his hand, then his mouth was cut open ear to ear and his tongue cut out.[39]

On one occasion, the Ottoman forces at Sarai ordered all the Christian men in the district to come to town to rebuild the ruined barracks. But in-

---

[37] RGVIA, Fund 13159, dossier 1428, list 22, testimony of Judad Abdarova August 27 and 30, 1916.

[38] Surma, *Assyrian Church Customs*, 69.

[39] RGVIA, Extraordinary Investigation Commission Taganrog, testimony of Benjamin Leshkoiev 17 February 1916.

stead of repairing buildings, when they arrived on December 30 the gendarmes staged a massacre. Twenty-eight of the youngest men were led out of the town and shot. Then the elder men were slaughtered in the same way. The organizers were identified as Mehmed Ali with his sons, as well as Hüseyin Bey's sons Taher and Mustafa.[40]

Ceaseless ethnic cleansing by means of ruthless attacks and panic plagued the Turkish-Iranian border strip. As soon as the Russians left a village or town undefended, Kurdish irregulars or volunteers moved back in and punished the population for alleged collaboration. Often the Russians would appoint some local Christians, Ottoman subjects, to administrative posts. Acceptance of a position under the Russian occupation was interpreted as an act of treason. Y. K. Rushdouni reported that when the Russians disappeared,

> different fragments of the Turkish army rallied and then instead of pursuing the enemy they exterminated the Armenian and Syrian population of Bashkale, Sarai and the surrounding villages. ... Twelve villages in Gawar district, on the Persian frontier, Bashkale, and Sarai with Nestorian and Armenian villages round, were ruthlessly wiped out after the Russian retreat.[41]

Near the Turkish-Iranian border, the Ottoman forces once more pillaged the Christian villages in the Albak valley around the town of Bashkale.[42] The German observer Johannes Lepsius received information that the villages in the Albak valley were destroyed on the order of the kaymakam of Sarai.[43] He stated that the massacres began on or around December 22, 1914, as the Turkish army began its retreat, but that news of these massacres did not become known until February 1915.[44] The German Ambassador, Wangenheim, informed the Reichskanzler on April 15, 1915, that two "complete slaughters" of Christians had occurred in districts in Van province with the connivance of the local civil authorities.[45]

---

[40] Barby, *Au pays de l'épouvante*, 235–36.
[41] Letter of Y. K. Rushdouni June 7, 1915, in Bryce and Toynbee, *Treatment of Armenians*, 88, 96–98.
[42] RGVIA, Fund 13159, opis 6, dossier 1428 list 16-17, witnesses Benjamin Leshkoiev and Simon Lazarev.
[43] Johannes Lepsius, *Les massacres d'Arménie* (1918), 91–92.
[44] Ibid., 209–10.
[45] Wangenheim to Bethmann Hollweg April 15, 1915, in Lepsius, *Deutschland und Armenien: Sammlung diplomatischer Aktenstücke* (1919), 47.

The existing Ottoman forces were insufficient to mount a direct attack on the Assyrian tribes, but they could cause much local damage in towns and villages in the valleys and plains. Jandarma, local Hamidiye irregulars, and Kurdish volunteers manned the Turkish frontline in Van province. According to Entente military intelligence, these were "detachments of irregulars, reservists." The intelligence service found it impossible even to identify the division or corps to which they belonged.[46] When refugees from these areas came into contact with the Russian army, they informed them about the massacre of "nearly the entire male Christian population of Gawar and Bashkale. ... The Christian villages have been burned and sacked."[47]

Several sources mention that in January 1915, leading Syriac notables and merchants from Bashkale and the surrounding region of Gawar were arrested and forced to be beasts of burden carrying heavy loads across to Urmia. These were bundles of wire. One source believes that it was barbed wire, another that it was telegraph wire, and it could well have been both. The size of the group was about 60 males, "all well-to-do, some of them noted men of that place." After they had completed the task of carrying these loads to Urmia, they were murdered at a desolate spot near the border known as Ismail Agha's Kale. The Board of Foreign Missions of the Presbyterian Church in the U.S.A. termed this to be the "most diabolically cold-blooded of all the massacres." E. T. Allen, an American medical missionary, heard of the massacre from three wounded survivors who had managed to turn up at the mission hospital in Urmia, where they told their story. In November 1915, Allen began to look for the place of execution, to give the bodies a Christian burial.

> Yesterday I went to the Kala of Ismael Agha and from there to Kasha, and some men went with me up the road to the place where the Gawar men were murdered by the Turks. It was a gruesome sight—perhaps the worst I have seen at all. There were seventy-one or two bodies; we could not tell exactly, because of the conditions. It is about six months since the murder. Some were in fairly good condition—dried like a mummy. Others were torn to pieces by the wild animals. Some had been daggered in several places, as was evident from the cuts in the skin. The majority of them had been shot. The ground about was littered with empty cartridge-cases. It was a long way off from the Kala, and half-an-hour's walk from the main road into the most rugged gorge I

---

[46] M. Paléologue to M. Delcassé December 30, 1914, in Beylerian, *Les Grandes Puissants*, 6.

[47] French embassy in Russia to Department of Foreign Affairs May 5, 1915, in Beylerian, *Les Grandes Puissants*, 17.

have seen for some time. I suppose the Turks thought no word could get out from there—a secret, solitary, rocky gorge. How those three wounded men succeeded in getting out and reaching the city is more of a marvel than I thought at the time.[48]

As the Ottoman border defense degenerated into increasingly retributive barbarity and punitive acts of extreme cruelty, the Christians began to understand that they were being targeted by the local tribes with the blessing of the local government. Mar Shimun noted that the poorly armed lowland Assyrian villages were attacked first. "When we saw many Christians of Gawar and Albak killed without reason, we thought our turn would come."[49] Mar Shimun called a council of the tribal chiefs and made contact with the Russians through Agha Petros, an Assyrian serving as a translator for the Russian consulate in Urmia.[50] Vice-consul Vvedenski reported that he had received a letter from Mar Shimun on November 10/23 asking whether he should open hostilities against the Turks and proposing a strike on Bashkale.[51]

On the political level, the government in Istanbul was still hoping that the Assyrians might be somehow enticed or coerced into joining their side. A new mutasarrif had been appointed, namely Shefik Bey, who was moved from Mardin with the specific task of convincing the Assyrian tribes to join the Ottoman side. He left Mardin on November 24.[52] Joel Werda, an American member of the Assyro-Chaldean delegation to the Paris Peace Conference, recorded that Mar Shimun had been called to Bashkale to meet with Shefik in December 1914. Once again,

> The patriarch and his people were promised absolute protection, together with a large sum of money to be distributed among the warriors of the mountains, on the precondition that the head of the Assyrian Church should pledge himself in writing that he would not allow the

---

[48] Statement of E. T. Allen November 8, 1915; Narrative of Dr. Jacob Sargis February 12. 1915, in Bryce and Toynbee, *Treatment of Armenians*, 193–94, 190; Griselle, *Syriens et Chaldéens*, 51. Ismail Agha's Kale was a new settlement of Christian refugees from the 1895–96 pogroms.

[49] Surma to W. A. Wigram September 26, 1915, in Bryce and Toynbee, *Treatment of Armenians*, 206.

[50] Hazqiyel Rayyis Gabriyel Beth-Malik Babane, *Tash'ita d Aturaye* [Assyrian history] (1975), 30.

[51] Genis, *Vvedenski*, 35.

[52] Ishaq Armalto, *Al-Qusara fi nakabat al-nasara* [The calamities of the Christians] (1919), 112. This person should be Mehmet Şefik, see Suavi Aydin et al., *Mardin: Aşiret – Cemaat – Devlet* [Mardin: Tribes, community, state] (2000), 242.

Nestorian tribes to take up arms against the Turkish government, and also pledge himself under oath that he would not side with Russia.[53]

This proposal was then discussed with the tribal chiefs, who rejected it.

Ever since the beginning of 1915, the Assyrian tribes had been preparing for an attack by a large invasion. Defenses were prepared to meet a frontal attack. In the middle of January, the Assyrians reacted when straggling survivors reached Kochanes. At the end of January, Malek Ismael of Upper Tiyyari sent 500 young warriors to guard the patriarch. A council was held under the leadership of Mar Shimun, and it decided to send the women and children to safer places near Chamba in Upper Tiyyari. Only those who were able to mount a defense remained.[54]

THE ROAD TO DISASTER

Small-scale Turkish and Kurdish assaults on tribal Assyrians happened quite frequently and more or less forced the Assyrians to increasingly see Russia as their only possible savior. Already-established Assyrian contacts with the Russians intensified throughout early 1915. By March, the Russians had steadily advanced in Azerbaijan, pushing the Ottoman forces before them. Falling back into home territory, the undisciplined and disorganized troops had just participated in the massacres of Gulpashan, Gogtapa, Haftevan, the French mission compound in Urmia, and other villages.

While his forces were being regrouped, Jevdet was in Van soliciting support among Muslim notables for a general massacre of the Armenians and Assyrians in his province. His attitude toward the non-Muslims had clearly been affected by his recent experience that troops could be taught to exterminate unarmed civilians. Rumor spread far and wide that Jevdet nicknamed his guard the "butcher battalion" (*kassablar taburu*). Lepsius had heard that when Jevdet came home, he assembled a meeting of Van's leading Muslims and allegedly bragged: "We made a clean sweep with the Armenians and Syriacs in Azerbaijan. We must do the same with the Armenians of Van."[55] The Archbishop of the Chaldean Church in Van, Jacques-Eugène Manna, had heard nearly the same and wrote that Jevdet uttered: "I

---

[53] Werda, *Flickering Light*, 5.
[54] Rudolf Macuch, *Geschichte der spät- und neusyrischen Literatur* (1976), 234; Surma, *Assyrian Church Customs*, 70.
[55] Lepsius, *Deutschland und Armenien*, xiv, 471; Lepsius, *Les Massacres d'Arménie*, 94.

have cleansed the Christians from the country of Bashkale and Sarai. I would like to cleanse them from Van and its surroundings."[56]

According to the physician Clarence Ussher, preparations were made to begin general massacres on April 19. On that day, irregular Kurdish units attacked many places. In the town of Van, the assault started on April 20, 1915.[57] The Armenians put up armed resistance lasting a month, when Russian troops and Armenian volunteers came to their relief. The Syriac population was just as troublesome for Jevdet, and on April 23 he reported that they also had rebelled. Local tribes were sent to put down the "Nestorian revolt."[58]

News of destruction spread quickly. Vvedensky, chargé d'affaires in the Russian consulate in Khoi, reported, "In Gawar and Bashkale almost all of the male Christian population was massacred. The Christian villages are being burnt and destroyed."[59] Based on testimony from refugees streaming over the border, the Russians informed the French Government, "The entire male Christian population of Gawar and Bashkale has been massacred. At Shatak, the Turks have similarly organized massacres. The Christian villages are burned and pillaged."[60] A letter sent by a missionary to the Presbyterian Mission Board in New York on April 19 also talked of massacres:

> The news that comes to us from across the Turkish border is far from pleasant. The many hundreds (and perhaps some thousands) of Armenians and Syrians in the region of Bashkale have been massacred. ... In the mountains Mar Shimun is said to have gathered the independent tribes about him, and they are battling for their lives against great odds. These are the near-by places. What is going on inside Turkey, God only knows.[61]

In Hakkari, Kurdish attacks became more lethal with the arrival of troops bent on revenge. Regular army soldiers retreating from Iran and Van

---

[56] Cited in Eugène Griselle, *Syriens et Chaldéens: Leur martyre, leurs espérances* (1917), 24.

[57] Clarence D. Ussher, *An American Physician in Turkey: A Narrative of Adventures in Peace and War* (1917), 236–45.

[58] Genelkurmay, *Birinci Dünya Harbi'nde*, 592; urgent telegram of Kazim (Karabekir), Commandant Van Jandarma April 29, 1915, document no. 2005, in *Askeri Tarih Belgeleri Dergisi*, vol. 34 (1985).

[59] AVPRI, III. F., 1915, des. 470, dossier 49, vol. II, list 597.

[60] Communication de l'Ambassade de Russie au Département May 5, 1915, in Beylerian, *Les Grandes Puissants*, 17.

[61] Robert M. Larabee to Presbyterian Missions Board April 19, 1915, in Bryce and Toynbee, *Treatment of Armenians*, 147.

gathered nearby to regroup after the military defeats. The first unit to arrive was the remainder of Halil Bey's expeditionary force, which was drawing back from Urmia trying to follow the valley of the Zab River. After Jevdet was ordered to abandon Van, he was ordered to combine forces with Halil at Tergawar (Nogales called it Tokaragua) just on the Iranian frontier. Here Kazim Bey, who had pulled back from the north, set up headquarters with the Van Jandarma division and some Kurdish volunteers. As the Turks pulled out of Bashkale, one more massacre took place. A group of "three hundred to four hundred Armenian women and children, and some fifteen artisans, likewise Armenians," were slaughtered in nearby caves with the collusion of the mutasarrif.[62] From there, in the face of massive Russian and Armenian volunteer presence, the Turkish troops retreated over the plain of Berwar westward in early June.

A telegram from Walter Holstein, the consul in Mosul, to the German embassy in Constantinople broke the news on May 8 that the

> Christian population of Van province for several days has found itself in uproar. ... Nestorian tribes of Tiyyari in the district of Bashkale rose at the same time. 2,000 well-armed Tiyyari attacked Moslem villages and fortified themselves north of Julamerk. [Halil's] troop reinforcements are on their way to Van and Bashkale.[63]

From the other side of the Iranian border, Halil notified his superiors that he was redirecting his army to Gawar, Bashkale, and Van, where he perceived that the "situation seems to have worsened."[64] Units of the Russian army were hot on their heels. The British missionary W. A. Wigram, a member of the Archbishop of Canterbury's Mission to the Assyrians, asserted that a meeting of the Assyrian tribal leaders on May 10, 1915, resulted in a declaration of war against the Ottoman authorities.[65] No text of a declaration has ever been made public. Basile Nikitine, the Russian vice-consul in Urmia, stated instead that the meeting resulted in an order for general mobilization.[66] The Assyrian mobilization revealed their isolation,

---

[62] Rafael de Nogales, *Four Years beneath the Crescent* (1926), 100, 102–3.
[63] Wangenheim to Auswärtiges Amt May 10, 1915, in Lepsius, *Deutschland und Armenien*, 65.
[64] Holstein to German Embassy May 14, 1915, in ibid., 67.
[65] W. A. Wigram, *Our Smallest Ally* (1920); Joseph Alichoran, "Assyro-Chaldeans in the 20th Century: from Genocide to Diaspora," 54–55; Salahi Sonyel, *The Assyrians of Turkey: Victims of Major Power Policy* (2001), 92.
[66] Basile Nikitine, "Nestorianen" (1936), 977.

and the promised Russian aid was not forthcoming. Instead the Kurdish tribes were given a free hand to deal with the Nestorians as they saw fit.

On May 18, Holstein reported that Mar Shimun expressed fears that the Muslims were in the course of perpetrating a general massacre of Christians.

> The Lord of the Nestorians, Mar Shimun in Kochanes, told me that the anti-Christian movement in Amadia district [the southernmost in the Hakkari region] is growing daily. Moslems there plan a general massacre of Christians and have partially already begun. Today the Chaldean Patriarch here delivered the same message.

Haydar Bey, the vali of Mosul, admitted that a general massacre was a possibility but, according to the German consul, put no effort into preventing it. Holstein pleaded with ambassador Wangenheim to pressure the Ottoman government to force the vali to intervene with the "Kurdish shaykhs."[67]

Around this time, a major breach emerged within the Nestorian camp. Nimrod Shimun, the head of the Jilu tribe, had been a difficult rival to several Nestorian patriarchs. Although the conflict was not new, the risks were growing. He continued his opposition even during these trying times. Mar Shimun organized the assassination of Nimrod and six other leading members of his party at an ambush on May 22, 1915. The exact background is not known, but it must have had to do with issues of uniting the tribes for common defense. There was suspicion that Nimrod, who had good relations with the Ottoman authorities, was in contact with the government and could not be trusted.[68] However, the course of events, which defeated the Jilu first of all, proved that they had no secret deal with the Ottomans. The assassination put a stop to future military cooperation between the Jilus and the other tribes. The Jilu went their own way under their new leader, Malik Cambar. According to Cambar, when the war broke out, an estimated 800 young men from the tribe were absent working in other countries, and thus the tribe's war-making capacity was very weak. After losing several battles in quick succession, they left Hakkari on their own on June 20, 1915, and entered Persian territory, where most of the warriors volunteered to join the Russian army.[69]

---

[67] Holstein to German Embassy May 18, 1915, in Lepsius, *Deutschland und Armenien*, 72–73.

[68] Babane, *Tash'ita d Aturaye*, 32.

[69] Malik Cambar, *Vie et coutumes des Maliks* (1924), 8, 22; "Autobiography"; Sam Parhad, *Beyond the Call of Duty: The Biography of Malik Kambar of Jeelu* (1986), 16–17.

On May 25, Halil's rear guard left Urmia. Before the various Turkish detachments managed to regroup, the Russians attacked in the vicinity of Bashkale. Halil was forced to take his army westward into the desolate high mountains. Again the Russians attacked, on June 4 at Liva. From there, Halil's decimated expeditionary force struggled on to reach Sa'irt.[70] There he reassembled whatever was left of his two divisions and orchestrated a bloody massacre of Assyrians and Chaldeans in the town and the neighboring villages.

A plan was set in motion for the ethnic cleansing of Hakkari. War Minister Enver and Interior Minister Talaat coordinated their preparations, as this needed to be a combined civil and military effort. In the absence of other alternatives, responsibility for the operation against the Assyrian tribes was placed under the command of the vali of Mosul, Haydar Bey. He knew the area well after once serving as kaymakam in Gawar.[71] He had fresh reserves that could march up from Mosul, and he mobilized the local Kurdish tribes, planning an invasion from three points of the compass. He was in Kirkuk and had an easy attack route through the Zab River valley. In order to make Haydar's expedition fully legal, the districts of Julamerk, Gawar, and Shemdinan were temporarily transferred into the jurisdiction of Mosul province.[72] Haydar began with an attack on the large Assyrian villages of Ashita and Sarespido in Tiyyari. The Turkish troops tried to cross the Jamany Bridge but were repulsed. Then Haydar's force struggled against the Assyrians over the bridge at Bet-Khiyo, which was one of the few bridges over the Great Zab River. An advance force of three thousand Turks and Kurds attempted to take the pass between the Mountains of Tiyyari and Tkhuma and occupied the top of Mont White.[73] They were repulsed, but with great losses. Again Haydar Bey's forces were in battle at the bridge at Bet-Khiyo. They simultaneously attacked Chamba in a battle that lasted several days. There was a second attack on Tkhuma. Although most of these Turkish attacks were unsuccessful, the Assyrians paid a very high price for their victories.[74]

---

[70] Lepsius, *Les massacres d'Arménie*, 116; Taylan Sorgun, *İttihad ve Terakki'den Cumhuriyet'e Halil Paşa Bitmeyen Savaş* [From the CUP to the Republic: Halil Pasha's unfinished war] (2003), 99.

[71] Haydar had been mutasarrif in Urfa prior to his appointment as vali in February 1915. Rhétoré, *"Les chrétiens aux bêtes"*, 172–73.

[72] BOA. DH. ŞFR 53/276 Ministry of the Interior to Mosul vilayet June 7, 1915.

[73] Werda, *Flickering Light*, 10.

[74] Eva Haddad, *The Assyrian, Rod of My Anger* (1996), 43, 45, 46, 50. The dates

Shlemon, son of Malek Ismael, of Upper Tiyyari elaborated the ill-fated Assyrian defense with further details. Haydar had engaged the services of the following Kurdish tribes and gave them specific targets. From the west, the Emir of Upper Berwar, Reshid Bey, with his tribes and Turkish troops marched against Ashita, the Lizan valley, and Lower Tiyyari. Said Agha from the village of Chal marched against one valley in Lower Tiyyari. Ismael Agha marched against Chamba in Upper Tiyyari. Said Agha from Julamerk marched on Mazrago in Upper Tiyyari. From the east, Suto Agha of Oramar was directed against the Jilu, Dez, and Baz tribes. The first coordinated attack came on June 11, with thrusts against Ashita and Sarespido and the entire valley of Lizan. The two first-named villages were lost immediately on the first day, but most of the population managed to flee. The Assyrians destroyed a bridge in Lizan in order to keep it from falling into Ottoman hands. Also on the first day, Lower Tiyyari was invaded. Although the Assyrian defense was strong and the Kurds had great losses, many houses were burned and sacked. Small battles were waged throughout the mountains, and even when the Assyrians won, it often proved a costly victory, weakening their already limited capabilities and wasting their ammunition. Shlemon confirms that the Jilu were badly beaten in the first stage of the campaign and retreated to Iran. Suto Agha of Oramar, together with other Kurdish tribes, attacked their main settlement of Zirne. Despite support from the Baz tribe, the Assyrians lost 70 persons in that single battle. Suto continued to attack and destroy the other villages, and the losses were enormous. The Assyrians had only their traditional weaponry, while the Kurds had modern German-manufactured rifles, machine guns, and artillery.[75]

Around June 20, the government prepared to play its ultimate trump card, having captured Mar Shimun's brother Hormuz. Talaat Pasha informed the vali of Mosul about this hostage.[76] On June 27, Haydar Bey sent a letter to Mar Shimun: "All of Tiyyari is destroyed. ... The battle continues. May I inform you that your brother Hormuz finds himself in captivity in Mosul. If you and all your tribes do not capitulate, your brother will be murdered."[77] This younger brother had been studying in Istanbul when the war broke out. His sister Surma printed her version of the message from Haydar to Mar Shimun: "Hormuz, your brother, is in my hands; if you do

---

given for battles are incorrect.

[75] Babane, *Tash'ita d Aturaye*, 47.
[76] BOA. ŞFR 54/81 Ministry of Interior to Mosul vilayet June 20, 1915.
[77] Macuch, *Geschichte der spät- und neusyrischen Literatur*, 235–37.

not order your people to lay down their arms, your brother will be put to death." Mar Shimun is said to have replied, "My people are my sons, and they are many, Hormuz my brother is but one. Let him therefore give his life for the nation."[78] Shlemon records hearing news of Hormuz's death sometime toward the end of July.[79]

The Turkish troops received support from the Kurds of the Barzan tribe, who plundered Tkhuma, Tiyyari, Jilu, and Baz. In Jilu the main church, Mar Zaya, from the fourth century, was destroyed together with all its priceless contents, including antique Chinese vases dating from the time of the great Nestorian missions.[80] By late June, the Assyrians were in a sorrowful plight. They were surrounded by Ottoman troops.[81] On June 30/July 12, chargé d'affaires Beliayev in Tabriz reported a message delivered from Mar Shimun by Agha Petros on the crisis. He

> asks to say from the Patriarch that the Turks from Mosul and Revanduz attacked Tiyyari, Tkhuma, and Jilu. There are many wounded and killed, ammunition is running out, and the situation is critical. He asks for 3,000 soldiers with artillery in order to prevent the combination of Turkish troops with Persian Kurds. If not, they will [all] be murdered.[82]

The Russians were never able to send much help, and the Assyrians retreated higher and higher up into their mountains, where there was neither shelter nor food. In the end there was no alternative but to leave Hakkari and cross into Russian-held territory to find safety.

Assessing the Damage

Paul Shimmon, the representative of Mar Shimun in Britain, summarized the Nestorian experience in an article published in the Armenian Journal *Ararat* in November 1915. Among other things, he gave news about the situation in Hakkari.

> The troubles of Mar Shimun's independent tribes of Tiari, Tkhuma, etc., in Kurdistan, south of Van, began last June. Mar Shimun's seat in the village of Kochanes was attacked by regular troops and Kurds, destroyed and plundered. Most of the people escaped to Salmas. Mar Shi-

---

[78] Surma, *Assyrian Church Customs*, 72–73.
[79] Macuch, *Geschichte der spat- und neusyrischen Literatur*, 239.
[80] Nikitine, "Nestorianen," 977.
[81] Statement of Mr. Paul Shimmon, in Bryce and Toynbee, *Treatment of Armenians*, 200.
[82] AVPRI, III. F. 133, 1915, des 470, dossier 49, vol. II, list 465.

mun at the time was in the interior with the main body of his congregation. A regular Turkish force with artillery and some 30,000 Kurds, etc., marched on the Christians. The forty villages of Berwar, those nearest towards Mosul, were destroyed first, and only seventeen of them are known to have escaped. The women of many of the others have been forced to become Moslems. For forty days the people defended themselves against superior forces, and that only with flintlocks and antiquated rifles. At last, unable to withstand the onslaught of modern artillery, with which the Turks also bombarded the Church of Mar Sawa, the people withdrew to the interior of the mountains with the Patriarch's family in their center; and here they subsisted on herbs and some sheep they had taken with them, while many were daily dying of starvation. Mar Shimun came to Salmas—I had an interview with him there, and he has sent me to speak for him and his—to effect the escape of his people, or at least of as many of them as could be saved. All this happened in the latter part of September, when ... some 25,000 had already arrived, and with them Mar Shimun, himself as destitute as the rest, while 10,000 more were to follow. The condition of the remnant, for in all there are over 100,000, is very precarious, but let us hope not hopeless.[83]

In an extended version of his report, Shimmon adds: "The larger part of the Syrians are still in the mountains wandering about from place to place, without food, and with no hope of anyone coming to their relief." He also listed the various villages that had been destroyed; for the Hakkari district his list was very brief: "All Tiari. All Tkhoma except Mazra'a. All Barwar."[84]

The Archbishop of the Chaldean Church, Jacques-Eugène Manna, tried to investigate the situation of those Assyrians in Van who had converted to Catholicism. Manna named

> sixty Assyro-Chaldean villages in the vicinity of Van that had been subjected to atrocities. The village of Kharachique, composed of 37 families, lost 103 persons. Khinno, 32 families, lost 51 persons. Ermans, 22 families, of which half were massacred. Sele, 50 families, Kharafsorique, 20 families were completely annihilated. Akhadja and Rachan, 30 families, there are no more than 2 males and the females escaped, etc., etc. In the district of Gawar, likewise in the province of Van, the Assyro-Chaldeans made up some twenty villages where nearly everyone has been massacred, except the women and the small children.[85]

---

[83] Reprinted in Bryce and Toynbee, *Treatment of Armenians*, 198.
[84] Ibid., 587–89.
[85] In Griselle, *Syriens et Chaldéens*, 22–24.

The Russian vice-consul in Dilman, Akimovich, sent word on September 16/29, 1915, of the arrival of yet one more wave of refugees.

> Nestorians from the mountains were arriving in Salmas. They informed us that they could no longer continue to fight against the Turks and Kurds. Because they had insufficient quantity of arms and ammunition and so they were forced to escape. About 50,000 Nestorians together with Mar Shimun came to Bashkale.[86]

Akimovich had a conversation with Mar Shimun on September 18/31.

> Mar Shimun, who came yesterday to Dilman, was today at my home and he told me that about 20,000 Nestorians are coming to Salmas, the others are continuing to fight in the Mountains of Nestoria [Assyria], which are surrounded by the troops of Haydar Bey, who has about 1,500 soldiers with two artillery pieces and about 8,000 Kurds. Mar Shimun asks us to send our army to Julamerk, in order to save its people from massacre. And if that is not possible, he asks for help to the Nestorians who came to Salmas and to prevent those who escaped from massacre by the Turks from dying of hunger here. I request that you do all that you can for the Nestorians, who merit your help.[87]

The American Presbyterian E. T. Allen wrote to his employer, the American Board of Foreign Missions:

> As you know, the first attack by the combined force of Turks and Kurds was made in June and was partially successful. The people were driven out of their valleys into the high mountains central to Tiari, Tkhoma, Tal and Baz. In this movement not many lives were lost, but many villages were destroyed. The hostile forces were for some reason withdrawn, and for some weeks there was comparative quiet, broken only be spasmodic attacks by local forces. About three weeks ago there was another concerted attack made by the Turks and Kurds on their stronghold in the mountain top, and they were driven out. Between fifteen and twenty thousand, with great difficulty, made their escape, part of their road being held by the Kurds. They came down the Tal and Kon valleys, followed by the Kurds, and attempted to turn up the [Great] Zab to get by way of Julamerk. They found the Kurds in force at the Julamerk bridge, and were forced to turn down stream. At the head of Tiari they crossed the Zab and went up into the hills, which they found deserted by the Kurds, who had gone to war. They then

---

[86] AVPRI, P. F., des. 490, 1915-1917, dossier 22c, list 26.

[87] AVPRI, III.F. Persian table. 144, des 490, dossier 22c list 27, Secret telegram No 88, Akimovich to Third Political department September 18, 1915.

made their way round behind Julamerk, meeting no hostile force until they reached the ridge between Kochanes and the Zab. Here again they found a force of Kurds waiting for them. They had quite a sharp fight between them and the Kurds were worsted. From there on they had no more trouble, reaching Bashkale in safety, and later coming down to Salmas. These are the people I found in Salmas. They number, according to my estimate between fifteen and twenty thousand. Among them are Mar Shimun and his family and all our helpers, with one or two exceptions. With reference to those who were left in the mountains, perhaps a thousand more succeeded in getting through. There are still some thousands shut up there, and their fate is still uncertain. How many were killed in this last attack, I have found no one who could give even an estimate, but undoubtedly the number must be large.[88]

A joint refugee relief organization for the Syriacs took shape on the Salmas plain, where many of the Nestorians lived in great misery. A relief committee distributed aid parcels. A Russian philanthropic organization provided medical care in field hospitals at Dilman and Haftevan. The Americans also established a Relief Committee, which gave food and medical care. "As it was cholera, typhoid and pneumonia did their worst among a people wasted by hardship, unprotected from cold and without shelter."[89] The situation was hopeless, and little could actually be done to save the refugees. Philips Price, an American war correspondent, wrote:

> At the end of September, 25,000 mountain Nestorians from the Tkhuma, Baz and Tiari [Tiyyari] regions, who had been fighting with the Kurds all summer and had fled for lack of ammunition, came pouring into the plain led by their Patriarch, Mar Shimun, and began to plant themselves down in the orchards and gardens round the villages. All the villages of the plain were already occupied, and, as the winter was just setting in, their condition without housing, food and clothing was desperate. Meanwhile relief committees were organized under the Russian Consul Akimovich, the Armenian Bishop Nerses, who lent funds from the Armenians of the Caucasus, and an American Missionary from Urmia. … As regards the medical side of the relief, I am inclined to doubt the possibility of making effective provision under the circumstances.

---

[88] E. T. Allen letter of November 8, 1915, in Bryce and Toynbee, *Treatment of Armenians*, 203–4.

[89] "Report on the Distribution of Relief," in Bryce and Toynbee, *Treatment of Armenians*, 219.

There are not sufficient skilled doctors, and it is impossible to get drugs through from the Caucasus in sufficient quantity to do much good.[90]

On January 3/16, 1916, Mar Shimun addressed another appeal for help to the Russian viceroy of the Caucasus.

> We and our Assyrian people, at the request of the Most Puissant Master of the Russian Lands, and following the example of the brave Christian Russian army, joined it and began to fight with arms in our hands against its enemies for four months in the mountains of Kurdistan, which are very hard to cross. Our fight against the enemies was very difficult and it cost us many losses on our side, but unfortunately after the retreat of the Russians from the province of Van ... the Turks who marked our sympathy for Russia and its army made all effort to take revenge on us for our feelings for Russia. For this purpose, they combined a large and well-organized army, attacked us, cutting off all roads that linked us with Russia, and determined to kill all of us. We fought bravely until all our ammunition was spent. ... We and our people abandoned our native mountains and all our property, which contained precious monuments of the oldest Christian culture, and escaped to find safety and protection in the regions of Persia that were occupied by Russian forces. ... The love for Russia and the Most Puissant Master of Russian Lands and Defender of the Christians of the East requested us to organize a volunteer unit from our people, which number a few thousand men, to fight the enemies of Russia. ... Our people are ruined. Some of our people were killed at the hands of Russia's enemies in Kurdistan and in the Urmia region, when the Russian army retreated; and others, most important, died from disease and hunger in various places in Turkey and Iran.[91]

A high prelate of the Chaldean Church reported in 1918

> the enormous losses that our Chaldean Church has suffered in the Nestorian mountains. Alas, all of the work of the Catholics in that country ... has been destroyed. The Nestorian mountains themselves are totally empty of their inhabitants. On the pretext that nests of Armenian deserters and Russian soldiers dwelt there in the mountains with the connivance of the Nestorians, [planning] to strike against the province of Mosul, the Turkish government directed its troops and cannons at these

---

[90] Statement February 22, 1916, ibid., 222.
[91] AVPRI, P. F. des 490, 1915-1917, dossier 22c, list 40-42.

unfortunates, destroying and burning their villages and forcing the inhabitants to leave their place to the Muslims of Van.[92]

Remembering a ride along the border strip, the German officer Paul Leverkuehn gave his impression of the results of the Turkish policy.

> Besides Armenians there were also other Christian sects, who had lived for centuries along the Turkish-Persian frontier—and they were not excepted from the persecution. Thus the vali of Mosul in his vilayet crushed a purported uprising of the Nestorians (a Christian sect that had emerged about the year 500) and he destroyed their valuable culture. And by driving them out he of course gave the Russian army in Persia a fine group of volunteers. Perhaps, I have never before seen so clearly this entire military-political madness, until we were on the weary ride on the path along the Persian frontier.[93]

---

[92] "Note adressée au Consulat de France en Mésopotamie par une ecclésiastique Chaldéen," in Beylerian, *Les Grandes Puissants*, 479.

[93] Paul Leverkuehn, *Posten auf ewiger Wache: Aus dem abenteuerreichen Leben des Max von Scheubner-Richter* (1938), 102.

6   Anatolia's Heart of Darkness

Two Kurdish brigands, Mustafa and Omar, sat in a cave by the Tigris and divided up the loot from the Armenians they had just murdered. This was not the first time they had taken Diyarbekir Armenians on rafts downriver and killed them at this spot—a desolate place where the river follows a deep ravine with caves at the bottom of the cliffs. This time it was a bit different. The usual deal with Reshid Bey, the vali, was to divide up the booty fifty-fifty, the bandits taking half while the vali pretended to give his share to the Red Crescent. This time they had been asked to bring back a special golden bracelet with many precious stones. One diamond was as big as a hazelnut. This was meant as a trophy for Reshid's wife, who had seen it and demanded it of her husband. As a reward, they could keep all the other cash, gold, and jewels. It was not so hard to get hold of the bracelet, since it had been the pride and joy of Diyarbekir's wealthiest man. But it was so large, so heavy, and so obviously costly that the chiefs thought first that they should keep it for themselves. Then they realized that if they kept it, word would spread and Reshid was sure to find out and have them killed. However, it seemed just too much to hand it over to the governor. So in a bold moment of moral economy, they kept the bracelet and told Reshid that it had fallen in the water when they searched the bodies.

Mustafa and Omar were brothers, sons of the female chief Perihan of the Rama (Rema) Kurds. When Reshid called them to Diyarbekir the first time, they were outlaws hiding from justice after murdering a rival. Reshid had promised them a full pardon if they would help him do a necessary task that he as governor could not do—namely, kill the treasonous Armenians. As vali he was bound to protect all citizens, even the non-Muslims; but, he explained, the Armenians were aiding the Russians who were fighting against the loyal Kurdish volunteers under Karabekir's command. Among them was their brother Emin, and he was in great danger. Reshid claimed to have consulted many muftis, and they had all agreed that killing non-Muslims was no crime, but rather a good deed, and that those who did so would come to heaven with "green hands" and assume a place of honor. He would like to kill 500 with his own hands but could not as long as he was a high civil servant. Would Mustafa and Omar agree to help?

They made a deal and prepared a fleet of the peculiar rafts called keleks, made of inflated skins, the only type of vessel that could travel the river from Diyarbekir to Mosul. Within a few days the first transport took place, as Reshid ordered about 600 imprisoned Armenian men to be deported, ostensibly to Mosul where they could begin a new life. Mustafa and Omar turned up with their band and guided the fleet downriver quite some way, to a place near their hideout. They killed the men and threw their bodies into the river. Some days later, the people of Hasankeyf, Jezire, and Mosul were horrified to see the bloated corpses floating in the stream. The Rama tribe repeated this procedure a few more times, but then the provincial government began deportations overland. In June Reshid sent spies to find and kill Mustafa and Omar, and the rest of the Rama tribe ran away to the desert of Syria. At least, this is the story told by their nephew Hüseyin, the son of Emin, who had heard the legend told many times.[1]

Reshid amassed great riches, as did many other local administrators and politicians. They held the cities of Diyarbekir and Mardin in a state of terror during the summer and autumn of 1915. It was reported at the end of August that 120,000 "Armenians" had been deported from the province and there were none left.[2] The majority of the deportees were dead; the victims included Christians of all denominations. As one of the main crossing-points for caravans of Christians deported from northern provinces, roads along the countryside in Diyarbekir province were littered with the corpses of those who succumbed along the way. Riding horseback on the road to Diyarbekir, an Ottoman official noted:

> Half-way on the road we saw a terrible spectacle. The corpses of the killed were lying in great numbers on both sides of the road; here we saw a woman outstretched on the ground her body half veiled by her long hair; there women on their faces, the dried blood blackening their delicate forms; there again, the corpses of men, parched to the semblance of charcoal by the heat of the sun. As we approached Siverek, the corpses became more numerous, the bodies of children being in great majority … as we approached Diyarbekir the corpses became more numerous … we had not expected to find corpses of the killed near to the walls of Diarbekir, but we were mistaken, for we journeyed among the bodies until we entered the city gate.[3]

---

[1] Hüseyin Demirer, "Haver Delal" [Help, my dear] (1983), 77–80.
[2] BOA. DH. EUM. 2Ş69/71 Reshid to Talaat September 18, 1915, referring a telegram first sent on August 31.
[3] Fâ'iz El-Ghusein, *Martyred Armenia* (1917), 19–23.

In most of the Ottoman Empire, the story of genocide is the climax to the story of deportation; but in Diyarbekir province, people were killed in or near their homes and only the urban women and children were formed into deportation caravans (and even these were attacked). The original Armenian deportation decree of May 27, 1915, actually exempted Diyarbekir because of its distance from the front line.[4] In the absence of a public deportation order it proved difficult to use the subterfuge of "deportation" due to military necessity. Instead, efforts were made at proving that the Christians were planning a revolt, and that was used as the pretext for the first wave of arrests and massacres. Finally, Talaat sent a general order for the deportation of the Armenians on June 21 to the valis of Diyarbekir, Trebizond, Harput, and Sivas. It read:

> All Armenians living in the villages and towns of the province will be resettled to Mosul, Urfa, and Zor, with no exceptions. Necessary measures will be taken to secure their lives and property during the deportation.[5]

In fact, by the time the order arrived, mass extermination of Christians of all faiths had been going on for several weeks throughout the length and breadth of the province, and the guarantee of safety of life and property must have rung hollow. Whether or not Reshid received personal orders from Istanbul to start the massacres at an earlier date is a matter of speculation. However, he was appointed vali in February 1915 because of his previous history of willingness to work closely with local Diyarbekir CUP politicians in anti-Armenian violence.

The town of Mardin, capital of a sanjak with the same name, clung to the slopes of a plateau; from the roofs one could see far and wide. On July 23, 1915, from the rooftop of a building in the Syriac Catholic religious complex, the priest Ishaq Armalto could see in the distance how a caravan of Armenian women and children was being attacked on the main road from Diyarbekir.

> We saw a long column come from Diyarbekir, surrounded by Kurdish bandits. They attacked, stole, humiliated, and starved them. They offered them Islam before they butchered them; otherwise they would kill them outright. These mountains and wilderness became the Christians' graves. We were informed by a reliable source that soldiers sold their captives to the Kurds for very low prices. ... The Kurds haggled over

---

[4] BOA. DH. ŞFR 53/129 Ministry of Interior to several vilayets May 27, 1915.
[5] BOA. DH. ŞFR 54/87 Ministry of Interior to several vilayets June 21, 1915.

the prices as if it were a question of wares in a market. The military had little time and needed to sell quickly so that the "capital" did not lose value. They sold whole columns for 1,000 pounds, another for 600, and a third for 500. The Kurds led them out in the wilderness and valleys, divided them up, removed their clothes, and shot them. But it did not stop there: they cut open their stomachs, pulled out entrails, searched through the women's hair, clothes, and shoes so as not to miss anything of value. And pity those who had a gold tooth, for that was pulled out before the owner was killed. All this effort gave a good result.[6]

PREPARATIONS FOR GENOCIDE

Diyarbekir province has a unique position within the "treatment of Armenians." There were few soldiers here, as it was far from any front lines. Instead, all of the evidence singles out the role of the highest administration—the vali, the vice-vali, the chief of police—and the local political elite—elected members of the National Assembly and the local leaders of the CUP clubs.

Until late winter 1915, there had been very little evidence of systematic attempts to eradicate the local Christian population. There had indeed been much harassment, and hard words were spoken, but little killing of civilians. It was said that the vali Hamid Bey was very sympathetic to the situation of the Christians. However, to make a symbolic gesture, 12 Syriac youths from the village of Karabash (close to the provincial capital), who had hidden in the nearby hills to evade conscription, were tried on trumped-up charges of desertion in the face of the enemy on the Dardanelles front and sentenced to death. They were hanged in official ceremonies throughout the area. Two of them were hanged in Diyarbekir on February 18 in the presence of the vali and Ömer Naji Bey, CUP "inspector" or party boss for Eastern Anatolia and a special organization *Teskilat-i Mahsusa* organizer.[7] In what very much looks like a protest, on the day before the hanging, Hamid asked (or

---

[6] Ishaq Armalto, *Al-Qusara fi nakabat al-nasara* (1919), 292; for the sale of entire deportation columns, see also El-Ghusein, *Martyred Armenia*, 35–36.

[7] Malfono Abed Mschiho Na'man Qarabasch, *Vergossenes Blut: Geschichten der Greuel, die an den Christen in der Türkei verübt, und der Leiden, die ihnen 1895 und 1914–1918 zugefügt wurden* (2002), 58–59; Joseph Naayem, *Les Assyro-Chaldéens et les Arméniens massacres massacrés par les Turcs: Documents inédits recueillis par un témoin oculaire* (1920), 152; Armalto, *Al-Qusara*, 128; A. H. B., "Mémoires sur Mardine (1915ss)" (1998), 177.

was forced) to be transferred and immediately accepted a lower-ranking position as financial inspector in one of the Arabian provinces.[8]

Now a complicated process began of finding a new vali who was willing to do whatever it was that Hamdi had refused to do. Diyarbekir's deputies in the National Assembly, Feyzi Bey and Zulfi Bey, accused Hamdi of favoring the Armenians and of being a close friend of their bishop.[9] Reshid, then serving as vali of Mosul, was not the first choice. Rather, the first appointee was the vali of Bitlis, Mustafa Bey, who even accepted the position on February 21. However, renewed pressure from local CUP politicians paved the way for their candidate.[10] After considerable correspondence, they obtained the appointment of Reshid, who had previously been their willing instrument; during a one-month stint as vali the year before, he had orchestrated the burning and plundering of Christian shops in the bazaar.[11] Feyzi was the son of Arif, who had organized the 1895 pogroms and massacres in Diyarbekir.

All contemporary observers pointed to Reshid Bey as the mastermind behind the massacres and mayhem, so it is worth knowing something of his life and character. There is the possibility of gaining some insight into his motives as he formulated a defense before he committed suicide to avoid a trial for war crimes. Reshid was educated as a military doctor and early in his career became involved in the first Young Turk clubs founded in the 1880s. He later became a member of the exclusive Committee for Union and Progress and took the code name Shahin Giray, which his descendents have adopted as a surname. Unscrupulous, violent, corrupt, and well-connected, perhaps he needed no prompting to instigate ethnic cleansing in his jurisdiction.

Reshid was born in the Caucasus in 1872 but came to Turkey as an infant. Because of his political activities he was exiled to North Africa, where he met with exiled Kurdish political activists. He married Mazlume, a granddaughter of Badr-Khan, Pasha of Bohtan.[12] Thus he had relatively

---

[8] BOA. DH. ŞFR 50/24 Ministry of Interior to Diyarbekir vilayet February 17, 1915; 50/53 Ministry of Interior to Diyarbekir vilayet February 21, 1915.

[9] Yves Ternon, "Mardin 1915: Anatomie pathologique d'une destruction" (2002), 83–84.

[10] Aykut Kansu, *Politics in Post-Revolutionary Turkey, 1908–1913* (2000), 478.

[11] BOA. DH. ŞFR 50/72 February 23, 1915; 59/94 February 25, 1915; 50/95 February 24, 1915; 59/108 February 27, 1915; 50/129 February 28, 1915; 50/143 March 1, 1915; 50/144 March 2, 1915.

[12] Nejdet Bilgi, *Dr. Mehmed Reşid Şahingiray'ın Hayatı ve Hâtıraları: İttihâd ve Terakki Dönemi ve Ermeni Meselesi* [Dr. M. R. S.'s life and memory: The CUP period

good contacts with the loyalist branches of the Badr-Khan dynasty and, through them, the Milli and the Karakechi tribes.

He was a loyal CUP member without personal political ambitions but willing to do the party's dirty work behind the scenes, first as a hit-man and then as an official. After the Young Turk revolution of 1908, he returned from exile and began an administrative career, serving as kaymakam of Istanköy from October 1909, as mutasarrif of Humus, Kozan, Rize, and Karesi. In the last-named place he was in office from July 8, 1913, to July 23, 1914, and organized the forced deportation of the Greeks, ordered by Talaat. Prior to his second appointment in Diyarbekir, Reshid governed Basra, where he instigated the murder of several high-ranking officials, among them his predecessor. He served in Basra until the end of November 1914; from November 24 he was provisional vali in Baghdad, and from January 10 to February 25, 1915, he held the post of vali in Mosul. While in Iraq he formed a small private army composed of Circassian volunteers, part of which he took with him to Diyarbekir. In particular, Harun and Aziz were identified as ruthless leaders of the various bands (contemporaries used the Turkish term *çete*) that attacked villages or assassinated opposition Muslim notables.[13]

After the war, Reshid was brought to trial for his crimes. In his defense he wrote that upon arrival in Diyarbekir he found the Armenians, Nestorians, and Yezidis in revolt.

> It was the most sensitive time of the war. The enemy occupied large areas of Van and Bitlis. Inside the province and its surroundings were revolts of Yezidis and Nestorians. There was need for quick action. The Armenian stance humiliated us and the situation for the government was serious because we had no regular forces. We had a reserve Jandarma that was inadequate and poorly equipped. The general Muslim population was concerned over the war, and the Armenian murders and insults caused fear.[14]

He proposed to the government the creation of paramilitary *çete* units to take care of the rebellious elements. They could be recruited from the ranks of army deserters; perhaps he was thinking of his already extant private army, since observers state that he came with a retinue of 40 Circassian bodyguards.[15] However, he met with opposition from the central govern-

---

and the Armenian Questions] (1997), 7–17.

[13] Abidin Nesimi, *Yılların İçinden* [During the years] (1977), 36–37.

[14] Bilgi, *Şahingiray*, 24.

[15] Naayem, *Les Assyro-Chaldéens*, 153.

ment. Not to be stopped, he created the innocent-sounding "Committee for the Investigation of the Armenian Question," which also performed a networking function for anti-Christian activities. Deputy Feyzi (leader of the local CUP club), identified by Naayem as the main local instigator of the massacres, served as the vice-chairman. Other members of this group were the provincial secretary Ibrahim Bedreddin (always called Bedri for short) Bey, the commander of the gendarmes Rushtu (a Circassian), Shevki (the son of a mufti), Sheref, Tahir Effendi, and many others, amounting to nearly thirty persons of various levels—from members of parliament to local merchants, administrators, and religious figures.[16]

Bedreddin was believed to be the only person who could influence Reshid's decisions. He was more fanatical than Reshid and pushed him to extremes. Yves Ternon suggests that it was Bedri who orchestrated the expansion of the anti-Armenian policy to encompass all Christian religions, and as mutasarrif of Mardin he was in the right location for such a scheme, since that sanjak was a mosaic of many diverse Christian churches. He was appointed mutasarrif of Mardin in the summer of 1915.[17] Later, in March 1916, he succeeded Reshid as vali of Diyarbekir. After the war he, along with deputies Feyzi and Zulfi, was held by the British under arrest on the island of Malta charged with war crimes, but all of them managed to escape and return to Turkey.[18]

Reshid received direct advice and orders from Talaat Pasha, and a direct telegraph line went from city hall to the Minister of the Interior.[19] When the mercenary Rafael de Nogales met with Reshid for a conversation on June 26, the vali intimated that the anti-Christian atrocities were committed on the orders of Talaat himself through a telegram containing only three words: *Yak-Vur-Öldür*—that is, "burn, demolish, kill."[20] It is hard to believe that Talaat would actually use such blunt language in an official telegram, but Reshid had done his utmost to convince the government that he was in the midst of a full revolt, so such a telegram may have been sent.

When Reshid arrived, Diyarbekir was no longer a garrison town of the regular army. Instead, it had a small mobile gendarme unit, the Diyarbekir

---

[16] Ibid., 153–55, Bilgi, *Şahingiray*, 26; for more on these persons see Uğur Ü. Üngör, "A Reign of Terror: CUP Rule in Diarbekir Province 1913–1923" (2005).

[17] BOA. DH. ŞFR 53/291 Ministry of Interior to Diyarbekir vilayet June 8, 1915; 54/214 June 28, 1915; 56/192 September 29, 1915.

[18] Bilâl N. Şimşir, *Malta Sürgünleri* [The Malta exiles] (1976), 58, 76, 109, 219, 228, 354, 385.

[19] Ternon, "Mardin 1915," 85–86.

[20] Rafael de Nogales, *Four Years beneath the Crescent* (1926), 147.

Jandarma, composed of elderly career soldiers, that was used for internal order. Under the command of the Minister of the Interior, this unit became a subdivision of the Van Jandarma division, and it had been sent to Van on February 24, 1915, in anticipation of an Armenian rising and was thus no longer in place. All that remained in Diyarbekir was the stationary gendarme regiment.[21]

As the example of the Nazi Holocaust shows, organizing mass extermination is not simple and demands a complex apparatus. The preparations included more than the formation of a trusted group of collaborating genocidal administrators and politicians. Reshid also needed to remove many Ottoman officials who were opposed to the anti-Christian policies. Some officials insisted on the loyalty of the Ottoman Christian citizens in their jurisdiction. A further complicating factor for Reshid was that there was no deportation order until the final week of June, whereas he began his anti-Christian measures in April, so during the critical initial period he was acting only in concert with the local CUP deputies. Throughout the war, Feyzi and Zulfi were active as enthusiastic agitators for the anti-Christian campaign. According to Armalto, their message was "Do not leave a single Christian! Whoever does not do this duty is no longer a Muslim!"[22] Feyzi particularly was known as a fanatic Pan-Turk nationalist. Zulfi became Reshid's chief negotiator for recruiting the Kurdish brigands for the Tigris River atrocities.[23]

In what seems to have been a provocation, the mutasarrif of Maden-Argana, an important mining district with many Armenian miners and manufacturers, was removed.[24] Reshid had Hilmi Bey, the mutasarrif of Mardin, replaced by his right-hand man, Bedri Bey, on June 8, 1915. This enabled the arrest and killing of Christian notables over the following days. Hilmi protested publicly and was transferred to a new post in Iraq. Members of Reshid's Circassian guard liquidated the journalist Ismail Mestan and some middle-level officials. Çerkez Harun murdered the kaymakam of Lije, Hüseyin Nesimi, and the kaymakam of Derike. Nesimi's family asked Talaat to investigate, and Reshid responded by blaming Armenian rebels for the

---

[21] Edward J. Erickson, *Ordered to Die: A History of the Ottoman Army in World War I* (2001), 62.

[22] Armalto, *Al-Qusara*, 150.

[23] Ibid., 383.

[24] BOA. DH. ŞFR 51/54 Ministry of Interior to Diyarbekir vilayet March 18, 1915.

killing, an explanation that Talaat, but not Nesimi's family, accepted.[25] Çerkez Aziz assassinated the substitute kaymakam of Beshiri, Ali Sabit es-Süweydi. Word of the assassinations spread throughout the administration; a high tax official, Ali Emîri, emphasized that these assassins were "non-Turks."[26] The fate of the kaymakam of Midyat, Nuri Bey, is not known. Contemporaries speculated that he was killed for refusal to follow orders to lead a massacre.[27] However, judging by documents at the Ministry of Interior, he may have been held hostage for some period of time, suddenly turning up in Iraq. Talaat sent telegrams inquiring as to his whereabouts.[28] Other kaymakams transferred out of the province for opposition were Mohammed Hamdi Bey of Chermik, Mehmed Ali Bey of Sawro, and Ibrahim Hakki Bey of Silvan.[29]

Reshid also needed collaborators for large-scale actions requiring local knowledge, contacts, and great numbers of armed volunteers. The solution was to secretly go ahead with his original plans to create paramilitary units that could coordinate activities in local towns and villages. He established what he called militia regiments, each with 50 volunteers taken from the local Muslims who were given uniforms or a red armband and rifles; their leaders had officer rank. Because they consisted of 50 militiamen, they were termed by most of the inhabitants the *Al-Khamsin*, Arabic for "the fifty." The militia head for the whole province was Mustafa Bey. Each death squad had its own assigned territory. The southernmost group was under the command of lieutenant Refik Nizamettin Qaddur Bey, a Muhallemi,[30] who devastated Nisibin and the many small villages of the southeast with the assistance of Hassan Hajo and his subsection of the Haverkan confederation. The central death squad was based in Mardin under the leadership of Nuri Badlisi; the northernmost death squad was based in Diyarbekir under Sidki, a relative of the CUP delegate Feyzi. Ahmed Nazo was in charge of the death squad in Jezire. Sometimes the Al-Khamsin militia carried out

---

[25] BOA. DH. ŞFR 54A/117Ministry of Interior to Diyarbekir vilayet July 28, 1915; 56/361 October 13, 1915 Talaat called Nesimi a martyr. See, however, the book by his son, Nesimi, *Yılların İçinden*, 37.

[26] Bilgi, *Şahingiray*, 34; Ali Emîri, *Osmanlı Vilâyât-i Şarkiyyesi* [The Otttoman eastern vilayets] (2005), 93.

[27] Holstein to Deutsche Botschaft July 16, 1915, in Lepsius, *Deutschland und Armenien: Sammlung diplomatischer Aktenstücke* (1919), 104.

[28] BOA. DH. ŞFR 54/210 Ministry of Interior to Bitlis vilayet June 27, 1915.

[29] Bilgi, *Şahingiray*, 87–88.

[30] Gawriye Maqsi-Hanna Hamra, interviewed November 1997 (appendix 1, no 70).

the massacres single-handedly, but for the most part they needed the support of swarms of mounted warriors from the Kurdish tribes. Because there were death squads in each district, the anti-Christian reign of terror could go on simultaneously throughout the province; and, except for a few pockets of resistance, the Christians were close to annihilated by August. The prime strategy was to assemble a massive force and surround a village in order to frighten the inhabitants into passivity, then disarm them and slaughter the adult males before looting the houses. In villages where they expected opposition, such as 'Ayn-Wardo, they could assemble more than 10,000 Kurds from many separate tribes.

The adherence of Kurdish tribal collaborators was not a straightforward matter, as many of the Christians were actually semi-feudal peasants belonging to Kurdish landlords, who had no direct reason to kill off their own laborers and clients. In the 1895 massacres, the Kurds protected many Syriac Christians. Early in 1915, many aghas of the Haverkan confederation had already begun to pledge protection. The branch headed by Chelebi and his relatives Sarokhano and Sarohan protected Christians throughout the war, while Hassan Hajo cracked under government pressure, reneged on his promises, and collaborated.[31] Reshid sought contact with Kurds who had nothing to lose. He sought out bandits and promised them pardon for their previous crimes if they collaborated. He persuaded the Rama tribe to be the first strikers. This tribe participated in assaults on many villages: 'Ayn-Wardo, Dayro da Ṣlibo, Dufne, Habses, Hasankeyf, the many Christian villages in the Hawar river valley, and Ka'biye. When in mid July the supply of cutthroats seemed to be drying up during Ramadan, Talaat allowed the convicts of Siwerek Prison to be set free.[32] Immediately, this region just south of Diyarbekir became one of the most dangerous tracts for the deportation caravans to cross.

THE FIRST STEPS

The first action that Reshid took against the Christians in the city of Diyarbekir began in the middle of April 1915 with house searches for deserters. This action took place at the same time as the bombardment of the Armenian quarter in Van. Together the two events reflected a coordinated effort to stamp out Christian opposition to the war. Since the beginning of mobilization, several hundred Armenian youths who refused enrollment or deserted from the army had been living on the roofs in Diyarbekir's Armenian

---

[31] On Sarohan, see the interviews in appendix 1, nos. 26, 67.
[32] BOA. MB HPS.M 15/19 July 16, 1915.

quarter. Up on the roofs the authorities could not get hold of them, and they called themselves "the battalion on the terraces." On April 16, the Armenian quarter was cordoned off by troops and its gates were locked. Soldiers went house to house searching for weapons and deserters. They checked not only private homes, but also schools and churches. By the end of the day, three hundred young males had been arrested and were marched off to the central prison. The town crier announced that the Christians had one day to turn over all of their weapons. When there was little compliance, soldiers used the pretext of searching for weapons to break into homes and churches.

Religious and lay leaders of various Armenian denominations, including Gregorians, Catholics, and Protestants, met to discuss the possibility of mounting an armed resistance, for they did have a few weapons saved for self-defense. This meeting ended, however, without agreement. One group wanted to fight back at any cost; the other said that resistance would be impossible for any length of time. After this failure to form a united front, the local authorities had an easy task of making individual arrests. On April 27, Reshid telegraphed the government announcing the result of his actions.

> Over the past ten days I have taken the most serious measures against the deserters, and at the same time we searched the Armenian houses and took important steps. We have found masses of weapons and military uniforms and ammunition and different weapons and much powder to make dynamite. We have imprisoned 120 notable persons so far in the central part of the province. The majority have been members of committees [revolutionary parties] and about a thousand deserters. Our raids and searches continue.[33]

The next day, the local commander communicated that the searches had uncovered a single hidden cache amounting to 7 German Mausers, 1 Bulgarian Manliheri rifle, 1 English Martini rifle, 2 rifles of Ottoman manufacture, an unstated number of revolvers, 16 bombs, 30 unfinished bombs, plus some dynamite and gunpowder. They also found instruction manuals on how to care for rifles and how to construct bombs.[34] The cache of 11 rifles, some revolvers, and a few bombs might be just enough for a suicidal last-ditch defense lasting an hour but was a contrast to Reshid's claim of masses of weapons suitable for a revolt.

---

[33] Cited in Bilgi, *Şahingiray*, 27; also printed as document no. 1912, in *Askeri Tarih Belgeleri Dergisi*, vol. 32 (1983).

[34] Hakki, Commander Eleventh Army Corps to War Office April 28, 1915, document no. 1913, in *Askeri Tarih Belgeleri Dergisi*, vol. 32 (1983).

Photographs were taken of the collected weapons and published in newspapers. If the deserters really had been conscripted soldiers, it would not be surprising that the authorities found uniforms and rifles in the raids; the Mauser rifle was the army's standard. The Venezuelan mercenary Nogales reacted as follows when he was shown the photographs by the commander of the Diyarbekir Jandarma, Mehmed Asim Bey.

> A close contemplation of those interesting photographs revealed plainly that the park [sic] therein represented was composed almost entirely of fowling-pieces easily disguised by a thin layer of army guns. I fear very much therefore that all this ostentatious collection of elements of war was nothing more or less than the work of Mehmed Asim Bey himself, in his attempt to mislead and impress the public.[35]

Nogales' testimony has extra value as he had just retreated from Van, where he had been in charge of artillery, so he knew precisely what sort of arms the Armenian defenders in Van were using. That arsenal was obviously different from the pile revealed in the photograph. Naayem also reported that the photographs were manipulated.[36]

By late May, 1,600 Diyarbekir notables had been jailed to avert the alleged revolt. Most of them were Armenians, but there were also a number of Syriac Catholics and Chaldeans among them. Many of the most prominent persons were interrogated under torture, but they were never brought to trial. They were questioned about where stockpiles of weapons and explosives had been hidden. They were also offered conversion to Islam, which would gain them a pardon. During this time, persons in authority extorted enormous sums of money from the families of the prisoners. Several prisoners died of the torture. On May 25, the surviving prisoners were assembled in the courtyard of the prison. A mufti read a telegram that had purportedly come from the government:

> The Government, with its customary beneficence, despite your attitude in this regard, has given you a pardon for your aggressive actions and will not inflict any punishment on you. Only, it orders your deportation to Mosul. You may return to your homes once the war is terminated. You are delivered from a great responsibility. You are commanded to give property and money to us so that we can make preparations for your departure.[37]

---

[35] Nogales, *Four Years beneath the Crescent*, 140, 76.
[36] Naayem, *Les Assyro-Chaldéens*, 155.
[37] Ternon, "Mardin 1915," 88.

After that, the prisoners were again locked in their cells. They were told they were lucky to get sent to Mosul rather than the desert.

On May 30, a large group of prisoners was taken from their cells. They were roped or chained together and either placed in wagons or tied behind vehicles. They were marched through the main street of Diyarbekir, and on their way they sang songs of farewell to families who gazed from windows and roofs. After the prisoners passed through the city gates, they were led down to the river harbor. Their valuables were seized, but authorities assured the deportees that their property would be returned upon arrival in Mosul. Different figures are given for the number of persons deported on this day—1,200 (Rhétoré), 1,060 (Simon), 700 (Naayem), 680 (Armalto)—but it was obviously a huge group. They got on the rafts and set off along the river and were slaughtered at Shekevtan in the valley of Besvan. But false good news was sent back to their family and friends that they arrived safe and sound.

Other contingents were sent within a few days and met the same fate. On June 10, the German Consul, Holstein, reported from Mosul that empty rafts were seen abandoned on the river, and the next day bodies and parts of bodies floated by. Locals told him that they were the remains of a contingent of 614 Armenian men, women, and children who had been banished from Diyarbekir. Officials placed the blame for the deed directly on the provincial government. When Holstein went to city hall in Mosul to register his "deep detestation of this crime," the vali there told him that Reshid alone should be held responsible.[38]

Hüseyin Demirer elaborated on what the Rama tribe told of the slaughter. Reshid had tricked a group of very wealthy Armenians into paying him a large bribe to change their deportation destination from Urfa to Mosul, where they believed it would be easier to emigrate. The Armenians boarded the rafts in good spirits and even celebrated by playing music and singing songs. Obviously, they believed that they were saved through their special deal with Reshid. They even offered Mustafa and Ömer food and drink. The next day, the Kurds stopped the rafts, saying that the river was dangerous at night and that they should camp on the shore where there were suitable caves. The Armenians stepped ashore and continued their festivities, and most became drunk on alcohol, which made the task of the guards much easier. Then the men were escorted in groups of two or three and were killed. Before the corpses were thrown into the river, the stom-

---

[38] Holstein to Deutsche Botschaft June 10, 1915, in Lepsius, *Deutschland und Armenien*, 82.

achs were ripped open and heavy stones were placed inside in hopes that this would keep them from surfacing.[39]

At one point, the prison authorities tortured an Armenian prelate to get him to sign a statement that all of the Armenian prisoners who were killed had died of natural causes. When he refused he was murdered outright—most testify that he was doused with gasoline and set aflame.[40] Large numbers of Christian soldiers serving in the forced-labor battalions were killed along the Diyarbekir–Urfa and Diyarbekir–Harput main roads. About 1,800 soldiers were slaughtered near Argana. Qarabash called the place the "Fort of Laborers" and dated three of the many labor battalion massacres (the first he mentioned had 190 victims, the second 112, and the third an unknown number) to June 16/29 and the following days. Two survivors managed to make it to Diyarbekir. The perpetrators were units of the death squad commanded by Sidki plus Kurdish volunteers.[41]

Few details are known of the further deportations from Diyarbekir. The Rama tribe participated in four convoys of rafts sent down the Tigris River. These were mostly the Diyarberkir Christian notables. The usual columns of women and children went by foot and faced extermination at suitable isolated places. The French Dominican priest Hyacinthe Simon listed 52 principal massacres in the Diyarbekir region with the approximate number of victims and the dates. His list begins in June and stops in October. It includes attacks on places in Diyarbekir province plus neighboring areas like Sa'irt (in Bitlis province) and Urfa (in Aleppo province). It also includes the major attacks on deportation caravans passing through the province on their way south. Among the largest single massacres, he noted Midyat, where 7,000 were killed during a week in the middle of July; Jezire, where 15,000 were killed on August 8 and a further 6,000 were killed on August 20; and Brahimie, where 4,000 were killed on June 25. Among the large-scale attacks on columns of Armenian deportees passing through the area: 12,000 Armenian exiles were killed on the road between Diyarbekir and Mardin on June 20; 7,000 exiles were killed at Dara on July 11; 12,000 of a

---

[39] Demirer, *Haver Delal*, 74–76.

[40] Report of Guys July 24, 1915; article in *Hayasdan* cited in Tchobanian to French Foreign Minister August 16, 1915; "Note du Département sur les massacres arméniens" December 1915, in Beylerian, *Les Grandes Puissants*, 50, 56, 153; El-Ghusein, *Martyred Armenia*, 25.

[41] Letter of Chevront Tourian, Armenian bishop of Bulgaria appendix to cover letter of October 22, 1915; "Note du Département sur les massacres arméniens" December 1915, in Beylerian, *Les Grandes Puissants*, 130, 152–53; Qarabasch, *Vergossenes Blut*, 65–68.

large convoy of women and children were exterminated on the road between Diyarbekir and Mardin on September 10; and the final survivors of that were murdered at Nisibin on September 14.[42]

A CLIMATE OF FEAR

The nature of the sources means that we can obtain more information about the genocide in Mardin than in perhaps any other place. As capital of a sanjak, Mardin was the seat of the district governor, the mutasarrif. Mardin was an ancient settlement dwarfed by a fortress on a high plateau, with the rest of the town sprawling like an amphitheater downward on the slopes. It was a supply center for caravans going east, west, north, and south. It was the seat of an archbishop of the Armenian Catholic Church, Ignatius Maloyan; an archbishop of the Syriac Catholic Church, Gabriel Tappouni; the patriarch of the Syriac Orthodox Church, 'Abdalla Sattuf; Israel Audo, bishop of the Chaldean Church; an American Protestant Mission led by Alpheus Andrus; and religious centers for the Capuchins, Franciscans, and the Filles du Charité. Surrounding the town of Mardin was its agricultural upland, with more than a hundred villages and the large Syriac Orthodox monastery of Za'faran and the Syriac Catholic monastery Mar Efram.

Reshid sent some of his own staff to organize the anti-Christian campaign in Mardin. Among them was Shakir Bey, his aide-de-camp, who temporarily took charge of the gendarmerie in Mardin; Bedri Bey, the vice-vali; Memduh Bey, the commissioner of police; Çerkez Harun, captain of the gendarmes and member of Reshid's bodyguard; and Halil Adib, president of the criminal law court in Mardin.[43] Halil Adib was also the Mardin representative of the Committee for Unity and Progress. According to Armalto, he ordered the militia assaults on the large villages of Tel-Arman and Kesor.[44] There was a local "subcommittee" headed by Khzar Koomeli, the mayor of Mardin, which ran the practical aspects of the genocide.[45]

Fears of an impending massacre grew from the very onset of the war. The mobilization of young and adult males began in August 1914, and Christians were included. Almost none of the conscripts who were marched

---

[42] Hyacinthe Simon, *Mardine la ville heroique: Autel et tombeau de l'Arménie (Asie Mineure) durant les massacres de 1915* (1991), 133–42 (reprinted in appendix 3 below).

[43] Ibid., *Mardine*, 47–48.

[44] Armalto, *Al-Qusara*, 151.

[45] Ara Sarafian, "The Disasters of Mardin during the Persecutions of the Christians, Especially the Armenians, 1915" (1998), 263.

away to the front or to training camps ever returned, and after a short while desertion became widespread. House searches for deserters and the public execution of deserters who were caught were daily events. The military confiscated the contents of Christian shops in the bazaars and took draft animals to supply the army. Armalto records a number of instances of random violence and killing of Christians. One of the few positive events in Mardin was the appointment of Hilmi Bey as mutasarrif in December 1914. He went out of his way to be seen as officially supportive toward Archbishops Maloyan and Tappouni and promised to "help them in all their problems." Thus began a degree of cooperation between the highest Christian leaders and the district governor. When accusations spread that Christians had deserted from the army and were hiding in the area, the two archbishops went to city hall and met with the head of the local garrison and Hilmi. They asked for a list of names so that they could help in searching for the runaways. This was taken by Hilmi as a "sign of upright love of the state." The mutasarrif also attended a dinner held at Tappouni's residence on February 11, at which Maloyan was also a guest. Throughout the winter and early spring of 1915, Maloyan missed few occasions to express the loyalty of himself and his congregation to the Ottoman state. For these declarations and other acts of loyalty, Maloyan received news that the government awarded him a medal in recognition of his services to the state.[46] This medal arrived on April 20 along with a diploma from the Sultan, and they were presented to him in a public ceremony. In his acceptance speech Maloyan "wished the Sultan success and that his ministers would win the war."[47]

However, despite the official recognition, Maloyan was deeply worried. As the Entente powers in March 1915 started their attacks along the Straits, rumors began to spread in Mardin of plans to exterminate the Christians. On March 23, in the nearby town of Kesor, soldiers arrested the priest Girgis Sham'i and local Syriac notables, bound them together with a rope, and marched them to the town court. Tappouni had to intervene with Hilmi and arrange to get them freed after they pledged "upright submission and loyalty to the state." On Palm Sunday, soldiers were sent into all of the churches to arrest any deserters they could find as well as the church deacons, who as religious functionaries had until then been free from military obligations. Two men were taken from the Syriac Church and sent to Diyarbekir. The soldiers harassed the churchgoers throughout Holy Week and

---

[46] Armalto, *Al-Qusara*, part 2, chaps. 14, 17, 19.
[47] Ibid., p. 131.

made arbitrary arrests of Christians caught in the streets. Armalto wrote: "We are unable to list all of the violence that the soldiers committed against the Christians, all of the bitterness they had to taste and the cup of sorrow and misery they had to empty."[48] The Christians spent Easter Sunday plagued by "trembling, scared hearts, and fearful, restless minds." Aiming to calm feelings, Hilmi Bey visited the various churches on the day after Easter and tried to console the priests.

Maloyan was greatly troubled by the anti-Christian propaganda being spread in the area by a certain Hajji Zaki, who was distributing a pamphlet with the prophetic title "Refugee Columns" that, according to Armalto, insulted the Christians and agitated the Muslims against them. In April, Maloyan invited Hajji Zaki to dinner to persuade him to cease his anti-Christian rage, but this step proved unavailing. Zaki wrote to the villages and encouraged the Kurdish leaders to "pull up the Christians by the roots and exterminate them." He continued this propaganda until Hilmi Bey expelled Zaki, who then moved to Diyarbekir but continued his campaign through other Mardin residents.[49]

Another very disturbing event was the creation on April 13 of an Al-Khamsin death squad recruited from local Muslim volunteers who had somehow been able to avoid the army. Armalto noted: "We did not know the purpose of this mobilization, but we were pessimistic and our worry grew." On April 22, church leaders were tipped off by a high official that they should "hide the letters, papers, and books that you have, which contain political news or which are written in French or Armenian. The government intends to search diligently for such material and to punish very severely those who have it in their possession." Because of this warning, Armalto buried his own chronicle and burned all of his Armenian and French books. On the last day of April, soldiers surrounded the Armenian Church, entered, and began to search for hidden weapons and demanded that Archbishop Maloyan show where the weapons were stashed. He denied that there were any arms, but the soldiers seized his "letters, papers, notebooks, newspapers, and archive" and took them to city hall from where they were sent to the vali of Diyarbekir for further investigation.[50]

After these events, Maloyan had a premonition of martyrdom. He gathered the church leadership on May 1 to inform them of his deep disillusion. He composed a letter to his congregation. This letter was later pre-

---

[48] Ibid.
[49] Ibid., 150; it has not been possible to find a copy of Zaki's publication.
[50] Ibid., 134.

sented to Tappouni and was published in full by Armalto and excerpted by Simon. In Armalto's version, Maloyan stated that in case anything happened to him, that is, "if the decisions by the highest authorities are realized, of whatever nature they may be—whether elimination or martyrdom," he named a successor. He added:

> I have never broken any of the laws of the Sublime Porte and I have always been upright, loyal as a Catholic archbishop should be. I urge all of you to follow my example in this matter. I commend you, dear children, to God. Pray to Him to give me the power and courage through His mercy and His love to carry me through this final time and the trials of martyrdom.[51]

The fear of a general massacre of Christians had been growing after Reshid Bey was installed in the spring of 1915. Simon used the term "general massacre" to sum up the dreadful climate of opinion in Mardin in April and May. It was believed that it would not just target the Armenians. Speculating wildly, he traced the origins of a conspiracy to exterminate all Christians to the formation in January of that year of a "Secret Committee" headed by Talaat together with "his chief lieutenant Reshid Bey." This "Secret Committee" aimed to create a single nation within the Fatherland, but it had to conquer all of the Christian elements within the six Armenian provinces. The conspiracy was against "Catholics of all rites and Schismatics [Orthodox Churches] of all sects." Here, much of Simon's text seems unsubstantiated, particularly when he asserts that a German officer had said to a Syriac notable that the German Reichstag had voted to annihilate the Armenians.[52] Although he is only repeating rumors, Simon points to several factors that were common in discussions of the massacres and were basically true: that they were coordinated, that Talaat and Reshid had close ties, that the Germans at first supported the anti-Armenian campaign, and that Christians of all faiths were at risk.

On Sunday, May 2, soldiers began to search through the remaining churches of Mardin. They thoroughly went through the Syriac Catholic Church buildings looking for weapons and bombs. On Sunday, May 9, the soldiers arrested the Chaldean priest Hanna Shouha under the trumped-up charge that he was hiding some deserters in his home. They put an iron ring around his neck and paraded him through the Muslim section of the town under humiliating conditions. When he arrived in Diyarbekir, he was beaten

---

[51] Ibid., 137; Simon, *Mardine*, 17–18, 56–57.
[52] Ibid., 39–40.

and tortured to death. After this ritual of dehumanization, the emboldened soldiers went freely in and out of Christian homes. Reshid sent one of his closest associates, National Assembly deputy Feyzi, to Mardin on May 15. He convened with Muslim notables to convey the plans of the vali. According to Armalto he said, "The time has come to save Turkey from its national enemies, that is, the Christians. We must be clear that the states of Europe will not protest or punish us, since Germany is on our side and helps and supports us."[53] The first step was to have the town crier broadcast the message "All Christians must within 24 hours deliver the shooting-weapons that they have to the commander" of the gendarmes. The thought behind this message was not that many weapons would be delivered, but rather the fact that few weapons had been turned over could be used as an excuse for further arrests. After this, the handful of Christian gendarmes were discharged, and all but two Christians who were public employees were fired from their jobs. News also came of the torture and dismembering of a young Syriac boy in broad daylight.

On May 25, Reshid paid a visit to Mardin to give personal commands to Hilmi Bey. He was ordered to arrest the Christian leaders and put them in the town's prison. Armalto states that Hilmi's refusal was worded, "I see no reason that Mardin's Christians need to be arrested. Therefore I cannot agree to your demand." According to Rhétoré, Hilmi added, "I am not without conscience [and cannot] cooperate in the massacre of Ottoman subjects who are innocent and loyal to the government."[54] After this, Reshid looked for a way to get Hilmi Bey removed.

Hilmi, for his part, tipped off Maloyan, who smuggled a note to the American consul in Aleppo, Jesse Jackson, begging for help, but he received no reply. On June 1 he sought out his colleague Tappouni. He read the letter that he had written for his congregation on May 1, folded it, and gave it to Tappouni, saying,

> Keep this testament on you. ... I know for sure that I and my congregation will be condemned to torture and death. I expect them to come to arrest us any day. It is unavoidable. ... Pray for me. I suspect that this is the last time I will see you.[55]

Following the same procedure as in Diyarbekir, the authorities fabricated evidence of an Armenian revolt. Photographs were taken purporting

---

[53] Armalto, *Al-Qusara*, 141.
[54] Ibid., 145; Rhétoré, *"Les Chrétiens aux bêtes"*, 62.
[55] Armalto, *Al-Qusara*, 161.

to show that bombs and caches of weapons had been found inside the churches. This evidence was sent to Istanbul. "The local authorities also forged a letter, ostensibly written to Maloyan, the head of the Armenian Catholic community, by a young Armenian stating that an arms shipment had been sent to the Armenian Catholic Archbishopric." A group of militiamen was sent to make arrests in the town of Tel-Arman. The accusation was that Sarkis, a local headman, had smuggled 25 rifles and 5 bombs into the Armenian church in Mardin. They arrested a priest and several other leading men and took them to the Mardin prison. From this moment, elaborate fabrications of accusations of intent to revolt were set in motion. Torturers interrogating prisoners in the jail focused on this charge. In the end, the searches did turn up a solitary cache, but not in the cathedral. Suspiciously, it was found on the land of Muhammed Farah, a Kurd.[56]

DISASTER

On June 3, Hilmi Bey had been lured away from Mardin and a delegation of officials arrived from Diyarbekir with orders from the governor. With them they had documents with prepared allegations, and they demanded the arrest of persons named in the accusations. Members of the Al-Khamsin militia were sent out to make the arrests, and among the first arrests were Maloyan and his secretary. The military cordoned off Mardin and prevented anyone from leaving. Further waves of arrests took place on the following days and resulted in the imprisonment of, according to Armalto, 662 adult males of all Christian denominations. They were squeezed into the Mardin prison and one barrack. Among them were the richest and most educated lay notables of the community plus many religious leaders. The main charge was that they aided France, an enemy of the Ottoman Empire. Anything written in French or sounding French could be used as evidence. In the Capuchin church, the semiliterate militia discovered a register of the "Franciscan Brothers" association, and that was enough for them to prove that they had discovered a pro-French conspiracy.[57]

A very confused week occurred as several groups vied for control over the local administration. On the evening of June 7, Hilmi returned to Mardin and began energetic arguments to set the Christians free, but he was immediately deposed from his office by one of the conspirators, Halil Adib, the criminal court judge and CUP leader.[58] The local Christians were in the

---

[56] Sarafian, "Diasters of Mardin," 263.
[57] Marie-Dominique Berré, "Massacres de Mardin" (1997), 85.
[58] Armalto, *Al-Qusara*, 166.

dark as to who was in power, and most Christian witnesses state that Hilmi was temporarily replaced with Shefik Bey, who might have been Hilmi's predecessor, who had moved south to take up a post in Baghdad. However, unbeknownst to the Mardin Christians, Talaat Pasha had already appointed Bedri Bey on June 8 to be mutasarrif.[59] Why the Christians were kept in the dark about this appointment is not easy to understand. Shefik was probably just a high Ottoman official in transit, but he acted as a free agent without any real jurisdiction. He may have been seen as a savior, as many sources relate that he demanded a stop to the general massacre of Christians.[60] It was said that Reshid tried to have Shefik assassinated, but that Nazif, the vali of Baghdad, stopped the plan.[61] According to Rhétoré, Shefik sent telegrams to the government and other influential persons protesting against the massacres. It is not clear how long Shefik was in Mardin, but it could only have been a few days. Already on June 11, Armalto recorded, although Shefik was gone, the Syriacs were still petitioning him to intervene for the release of prisoners while the government was still pressuring him to issue orders of deportation of Archbishop Tappouni. He refused to sign the order of deportation and sent a message personally guaranteeing Tappouni's "upright loyalty and trust in the state."[62]

Even members of the Syriac Orthodox Church had been arrested, although there was no evidence of contact with the French. After an intervention, and a large bribe, the Syriac Orthodox prisoners were released.[63] On their way out of the prison, they expressed gratitude to the government and wished it victory. Armalto stated that the reason the Syriac Orthodox prisoners were set free was to calm the anxiety of the Syriac community. They formed a very large part of the population; it was important that they not sympathize with the other Christians and mount a common front. In this way, the conspirators felt free to concentrate on the various Catholic denominations and deal with the Syriac Orthodox later.[64] However, the release of the Syriac Orthodox created very bad blood between them and the other Christians. An anonymous account repeats the rumor that the

---

[59] BOA. DH. ŞFR 53/291 Ministry of Interior to Diyarbekir vilayet June 8, 1915.

[60] Ternon, "Mardin 1915," 129; Jean Naslian, *Les Mémoires de Mgr. Jean Naslian sur les événements politico-religieux en Proche-Orient de 1914 à 1928* (1951), 323–27.

[61] Sarafian, "The Disasters of Mardin," 264.

[62] Armalto, *Al-Qusara*, 308.

[63] Ternon, "Mardin 1915," 119–20; Rhétoré, *"Les Chrétiens aux bêtes"*, 63; Sarafian, "Disasters of Mardin," 264.

[64] Armalto, *Al-Qusara*, part 3, chap. 4.

Orthodox leaders had signed false accusations against the Armenians prepared by the authorities. They had

> joined local Muslims to sign a statement regarding the alleged guilt of Armenians. Four days later, around June 9, 1915, 85 Jacobites were released by the authorities. Syriac Catholic and Chaldean Christians also expected to be released but were not afforded the same treatment.[65]

Archbishop Tappouni intervened to get the imprisoned members of the Syriac Catholic Church free, but he did not succeed. The American missionary Alpheus Andrus tried but failed to get the Protestant prisoners released.

Remaining in prison were, according to Rhétoré, 410 persons: 230 Armenian Catholics, 113 Syriac Catholics, 30 Chaldeans, and 27 Protestants. Among them were ten clerics, the most prominent of them being Maloyan. A large number of the prisoners were tortured in a special cell. During the torture they were interrogated about caches of weapons and explosives, or membership in terrorist associations. All were pressured to convert; all refused. Tortures involved beatings, bastinado, being tied upside-down for hours on end, or being thrown off the roof of a low building. Sometimes toenails were pulled off and beards ripped out. Maloyan suffered through nearly all of these tortures, including having his toenails pulled off and being thrown off the roof. He was accused of having received two boxes of weapons and hiding them in his church. He was also accused of being the organizer of a terrorist cell.[66] As an act designed to terrify the rest, the prison guards doused Sa'id Wazir with gasoline and set him on fire, and he burned to death. Armalto heard of these beatings, tortures, and other atrocities from one survivor, a nineteen-year-old schoolboy, Boulos, the son of Rizqallah Shouha. At the last moment he managed to argue his way out since he could speak Turkish and could prove that he had been in school in Diyarbekir all of the previous year and thus could not have been the secretary of a secret Armenian society in Mardin, which was the charge against him.[67]

On June 10, the more than four hundred prisoners were chained and roped together and paraded from the prison high above the town, through the streets, and out by one of the main gates, guarded by Memduh in charge

---

[65] Sarafian, "The Disasters of Mardin," 264.

[66] Armalto, *Al-Qusara.*, part 3, chap. 5, gives a detailed account of the interrogation of Maloyan under torture.

[67] Ibid., part 3, chap. 4.

of one hundred militiamen. At the front of the parade limped a 75-year-old Syriac Catholic archpriest supported by a younger colleague, and the final prisoner in the parade was Maloyan—according to Simon bareheaded and barefoot—held upright by two policemen. The prisoners were tied together in groups of forty, each group including a priest. In the Muslim quarters, the inhabitants jeered and children threw stones. In the Christian quarters, the inhabitants looked on in silence from the windows and roofs. It was said that the prisoners were being marched to Diyarbekir for trial.

These prisoners were then killed at places outside the town along the main highway: a small number of notables were pressed for money and then killed at Akhtachké, about 2 hours by foot from Mardin; about one hundred were murdered at the caves of Sheikhan, a religious shrine about 6 hours from Mardin; another hundred died near the castle ruins of Zirzawan; and the remainder met their fate at a ravine in a valley about 4 hours outside Diyarbekir. We know the details of the killings because the column passed through Kurdish villages where witnesses later spoke about the events. One of the militiaman guards also gave testimony to Hyacinthe Simon.[68] At the Sheikhan caves, Memduh read out what he claimed was an imperial decree declaring the prisoners traitors and condemning them to death. Those prisoners who chose to convert could return free to Mardin. Otherwise they would be executed within the hour. Maloyan began to improvise religious services, and the archbishop and the priests circulated among the prisoners celebrating Holy Communion. Maloyan was marched off alone and executed apart from his flock—after refusing to convert. More than a month later, Talaat Pasha sent a telegram wondering whether the provincial governor had any information about what had happened to Maloyan.[69]

On June 11, several hundred more Christians were arrested among the various congregations. On June 14, a second death march paraded through the streets of Mardin. At daybreak they were led in chains out of the town. Simon stated that the group contained 278 persons including 12 priests, Rhétoré counted 266 prisoners, and Armalto said that they numbered 309.[70] Rhétoré counted 181 Armenian Catholics, 50 Syriac Catholics, 19 Chaldeans, and 4 Protestants. According to Armalto, some prisoners from Tel-

---

[68] Simon, *Mardine*, 65–66.
[69] BOA. DH. ŞFR 54A/178 Ministry of Interior to Diyarbekir vilayet July 30, 1915.
[70] Simon, *Mardine*, 71; Rhétoré, *"Les chrétiens aux bêtes"*, 72–74; Armalto, *Al-Qusara*, 209.

Arman and Mardin were bound with iron rings around their necks; the rest were tied with thick ropes or handcuffs. At the Sheikhan cult-place the column rested close to a place of pilgrimage, the shrine of Sheikhmous. Kurdish tribesmen brandishing knives, axes, swords, butcher's knives, and clubs surrounded the prisoners. They pressed to attack the Christians as if to make living sacrifices. The soldiers guarded the Christians and hid them in a large cave, and the officer in change said he would protect them if they turned over all their money and valuables to him for safekeeping. At 8 o'clock in the evening, all who had iron rings around their necks or had handcuffs were ordered to stand up and leave the cave. This group of 84 prisoners bade farewell. As they left the entrance, a struggle began between the militia and the Kurds over who was to spill the blood. The militia marched away with the prisoners, whom they proceeded to shoot as soon as they were out of sight. When the soldiers returned, they ordered the rest to come out of the cave. They were told that they could drink water, but when they approached the watering place, they were shot at and 15 more prisoners died.

According to survivors, the column was on its way to the next point of execution when Ottoman cavalrymen crying "Afou, afou!" (Pardon, Pardon) approached with an order to stop the killing, waving a piece of paper: the "pardon from the Sultan."[71] Soon after, a militia company from Diyarbekir arrived and took over command from the Mardin militiamen. The new commander forced the Mardin militia leader to return the money and valuables to the prisoners. He also criticized the militia for murdering some of the prisoners and commanded them to return home, which they did. However, instead of dispersing the convoy, which would have been the logical result of a pardon, it was hurried off to Diyarbekir. Here all stayed incarcerated at a caravan station. Armalto received his information from one of the survivors, the elderly Syriac Catholic priest Matta Kharimo. While incarcerated, Kharimo was taken by a guard and locked in the latrines. There he saw three large baskets of human noses, ears, teeth, nails, hair, eyes, and fingers. He also saw corpses and dying prisoners half buried in the filth. On June 21, the prisoners were allowed to return to Mardin. They were still bound together with ropes when they arrived, and they were placed under guard in barracks. Kharimo underwent extreme torture and interrogation. He was accused of having received five wagonloads of weap-

---

[71] Ternon, "Mardin 1915," 133; Rhétoré, *"Les chrétiens aux bêtes"*, 74; Sarafian, "The Disasters of Mardin," 264, states that the pardon was a result of a telgram from Shefik to Talaat.

ons and having distributed them. He was beaten and hung by the feet upside down. Suddenly there was a turn of events. On June 26, Memduh appeared at the barracks and called out, "All Syriacs, Chaldeans, and Protestants, hold up your hands and give your names." These prisoners were then released, but the Armenians remained.[72] The Armenian prisoners continued to be tortured and murdered in the prison. They also formed part of the further convoys of Armenians that were sent away from Mardin during the following months.

Basing his narrative mostly on the testimony of Jacques Rhétoré, one of the interned French Catholic priests, Ternon gives a chronology of five or six separate major waves of deportation from Mardin ending in late October 1915.

Separate deportations of Catholic Armenian families from Mardin took place on July 2 (600 persons), July 17 (250 persons), July 27, and August 10 (600 persons), and continued on into the coming months, until the entire Armenian community was liquidated. Usually the caravans would be annihilated after one day's march from Mardin, but some of the final caravans in September did arrive at the concentration camps in the desert. Later in the war, these camps were exterminated—as a precaution against epidemics, it was said. Only a few individuals survived.[73] Memduh was the principal organizer, and he profited greatly from the wealth he took from the Armenians. Simon lists the number of families that Memduh robbed and gives the amount stolen. Even Reshid accumulated great wealth.[74]

WAS ANYONE SAFE?

During the initial phase of arrests and executions, the Syriac Orthodox in Mardin appeared to be secure. After the "Sultan's pardon," the remaining other non-Armenian Christians also seemed safe. They would not be subject to semipublic mass execution as was the case previously. However, according to Rhétoré, the local officials continued to arrest individuals on any number of charges, and while in jail people of all faiths were starved and maltreated to death. Some of those imprisoned were released if their families paid exorbitant sums of money to the officials.[75] A British officer, Ma-

---

[72] Armalto, *Al-Qusara,* part 3, chaps. 12, 13, 14, 15; Rhétoré also uses some of Kharimo's testimony.
[73] Ternon, "Mardin 1915," 139–55, gives details of each caravan.
[74] Ibid., 95; Simon, *Mardine,* 117–23.
[75] Marco Impagliazzo, *Una finestra sul massacro: Documenti inediti sullo strage degli armeni (1015–1916)* (2000), 152.

jor Edward Noel, reported in 1919 that the proclamation had been respected in the city of Diyarbekir, but that "in the districts, however, the Government very soon lost control of the passions they had let loose (if they had ever wanted to keep them in control), with the result that the Jacobites [Syriac Orthodox] suffered there as much as anybody else."[76] But, as chapter 8 shows, nearly all Syriacs of all denominations were wiped out, and in the countryside massacres were going on at the same time that some of the urban Syriacs were spared.

Talaat Pasha's telegram that purported to save the non-Armenian Christians was sent on July 12, on the eve of Ramadan. Attacks in the large Syriac town of Midyat in Tur Abdin began on July 19.[77] Seven thousand are believed to have died as the massacres there went on for a week and Christians shot back in defense. Attacks on the Syriac Christians in the town of Nisibin began on August 16; the bishop was among the first victims. Here the entire Christian population was exterminated. Massacres in the town of Jezire took place on the last days of August and the first days of September. Here more than 5,000 died. In Midyat, Nisibin, and Jezire, there were few Armenians. Obviously the proclamation by Talaat excepting the non-Armenian Christians and the Armenian Catholics was simply not respected.

As long as Reshid remained vali, Diyarbekir was a province of killing fields. On July 21, the consul Holstein reported the arrival in Mosul of about 600 women and children, "Armenian, Chaldean, Syriac," whose male relations had been massacred in Sa'irt, Mardin, and Pesh-Khabur, and more were expected to arrive in the next days. "The misery of these persons cannot be described, their clothes fall from their bodies; daily women and children die of hunger."[78] On September 9, Holstein communicated to the embassy, and on September 11 the ambassador wrote to the Reichskanzler of a massacre of "all the Christian inhabitants" of the town of Jezire. The military had participated and the civil authorities stood by passively.[79]

Even Ottoman officials were angered by Reshid's methods, since he assassinated opposition functionaries. After the war, Suleyman Nazif, the vali of Baghdad and a Kurdish member of the CUP, testified to the De-

---

[76] Noel, "Note on position of Syriac Jacobites," in his *Diary* (1919), n.p.

[77] Syriac oral testimony uses the old calendar and gives July 6, which is 13 days after the modern calendar.

[78] Holstein to German Embassy July 21, 1915, in Lepsius, *Deutschland und Armenien*, 107.

[79] Hohenlohe-Langenburg to Bethmann Hollweg September 11, 1915, ibid., 152.

partment of the Interior. He wrote, "the catastrophic deportations and murders in Diyarbekir were Reshid's work. He alone is responsible. He recruited people from the outside in order to perform the killing. He killed the kaymakams in order to scare all other opposition Muslim men and women—he displayed the corpses of the kaymakams in public."[80] According to Armalto and Berré, Nazif had tried to save an entire caravan of about 260 of Mardin's Armenian women and children that was traveling from Tel-Arman on July 16. But since he was outside his own jurisdiction, Memduh showed him Reshid's execution order and threatened to arrest him if he dared intervene. The caravan was then massacred the next day at the village of Abdul-Imam near Viranshehir.[81]

Jacques Rhétoré estimated that 200,000 Christians were killed within the province of Diyarbekir. Of that number, 144,185 (amounting to 82 percent of the Christian population) were native residents and about 55,000 were outsiders who had been killed when their deportation caravans were attacked. Victims came from all faiths, and the largest groups were from the Syriac Orthodox Church with 60,725 deaths and the Gregorian Armenians with 58,000 deaths.[82]

"Either Them or Us"

What happened in Diyarbekir during World War I had a terrifying and systematic character that indicates a wide and willing network of local collaborators and some form of high-level coordination, if not a detailed plan. However, the motive for why the ethnic cleansing actions also included the Syriacs and Chaldeans is not completely clear. The intentions of local politicians and Kurdish tribes need not be the same as those of the highest leadership of the CUP.

Perhaps some inkling of the geopolitical vision behind the total removal of all Christian groups can be seen in a congratulatory telegram addressed to vali Reshid Bey after the worst atrocities were over. The sender was a judge, the leading local CUP politician in Mardin Halil Adib: "Let me shake your hand, you who have regained the six [Armenian] vilayets and opened the way to Turkistan and Caucasus."[83] The context of this short

---

[80] This testimony is an appendix in Bilgi, *Şahingiray'* 168–71; Nazif also served as vali of Mosul until December 20, 1915.

[81] Armalto, *Al-Qusara*, 283; Marie-Dominique Berré, "Massacres de Mardin" (1997), 93; A. H. B., "Mémoires sur Mardine," 125.

[82] Rhétoré, *"Les chrétiens aux bêtes"*, 136–37. See appendix 3 below.

[83] Telegram from Adib to Reshid October 19, 1915, cited in Bilgi, *Şahingiray*,

congratulation would be the "Pan-Turanian" dream of a greater Turkey extending into central Asia. An ethnically cleansed eastern Anatolia made possible a very large and unbroken swath of Turkish-speaking settlements stretching far into the Russian Empire. In order for the congratulation to make any sense, Reshid must have spoken about this as his primary goal, even if this was not the program of the entire Ottoman government. Thus he targeted non-Armenian Christians in an area far from the front line, thereby arousing the wrath of the German diplomats but the support of the local politicians.

There are also some further traits that were systematic. There was the similarity in urban areas of the multistep pattern of shattering the Christian population. Also, the creation of conflicts between the denominations in order to discourage solidarity and united defense. Step one, the arrest and interrogation under torture of the male notables, including religious leaders. Step two, the killing of the notables about one week later. Step three, the deportation and killing of the remaining adult males. Step four, the formation of columns of women and children who were told that they were being sent to join their male relatives and marched out of the towns. Throughout, the Christians were extorted of their wealth. This procedure was used in Mardin and Diyarbekir.

Officials who refused to take part in the organization of massacres were removed from office. The mutasarrif of Mardin sanjak, Hilmi Bey (and perhaps Shefik Bey), refused to cooperate and was transferred elsewhere. There is information that some resistant kaymakams were murdered outright and others removed from office.[84] The kaymakams who were killed were those of Derike, Lije, Beshiri, and Midyat.[85] Obviously there was some dispute among the Ottoman officials about the legality, necessity, and morality of the actions against the Christians. Even though some clearly tried to protect them, there were many ways for local functionaries to continue a general anti-Christian policy.

Late in 1915, Reshid was summoned to Istanbul to be interrogated by the CUP general secretary Mithat Şükrü Bleda as to the reason for the massive killing, which appeared excessive in the eyes of the committee. Reshid

---

29.

[84] Ternon, "Mardin 1915," 112, 139–40.

[85] Holstein to German Embassy Istanbul July 16, 1915, in Lepsius, *Deutschland und Armenien*, 104; Taner Akçam, *Armenien und der Völkermord: Die Istanbuler Prozesse und die türkische Nationalbewegung* (1996), 69, 384; Bilgi, *Şahingiray*, 87–88.

was harshly questioned about how he could reconcile the extermination of Christians with his profession as a medical doctor. He defended himself:

> If you, like me in Diyarbekir, had had the opportunity to see at close quarters with what kind of secret plans the Armenians let themselves be possessed, in what prosperity they lived, what an awful animosity they felt toward the state, they you would not today be making any admonitions [against me]. The Armenians in the Eastern Provinces were so aggressive against us that in their areas, if they were allowed to remain in place, not a single Turk or Muslim would be left alive. I have studied the personal dossiers of many of them. In house searches, we found ammunition that would have blown up an entire army. They possessed a fantastic organization. We would soon need to use candles to find any Turks in Anatolia, if we allowed this widespread organization to exist in our country. Therefore—either them or us. In this situation, I thought to myself: Hey, Doctor Reshid! There are two alternatives. Either the Armenians liquidate [*temiz liyecekler*] the Turks, or the Turks them! Facing this necessity, I did not hesitate. My Turkishness triumphed over my medical identity. Before they did away with us, we should remove them, I said to myself. ... But this act neither pleases my personal pride, nor has it enriched me. I saw that the fatherland was on the verge of being lost; therefore with my eyes closed and without looking back I continued in the conviction that I acted for the well-being of the nation. ... The Armenian bandits were a bunch of dangerous microbes that infected the body of the fatherland. Is it not the duty of a doctor to kill microbes?[86]

After the war, Reshid was jailed, accused of crimes against humanity. Before the trial began, he was helped to escape. It was said he then committed suicide, which was convenient, for if he had admitted in court anything similar to what he gave to Bleda, it would have proved very compromising for the others who were accused. For they tried to claim innocence, while the unpredictable Reshid might well use the opportunity to take full responsibility as his patriotic duty to annihilate the dangerous enemy within.

---

[86] Cited from Salâhattin Güngör, "Bir Canli Tarih Konuşuyor" [A living oral history] (1953), 2444.

7 The Destruction of Midyat

The Syriacs of Tur Abdin first heard of the attacks on Christian villages from survivors coming from the provinces to the north. Word of the massacres spread quickly. Escaped Armenians, and even some escaped Syriacs, could be found hiding in nearly every town and large village. Alerted to the danger, Tur Abdin's Syriacs turned to their local authorities to find out what might be in store for them. Invariably, they were told that this was only a matter that concerned the Armenians, but from the stories told by the survivors, it became clear that that was not the case. There were actually very few Armenians living south of the Tigris River. When troops and tribes gathered menacingly, anxiety grew that the Syriacs would be attacked. And in June and July, all Tur Abdin, the core region of the Syriac Orthodox Church, had been set ablaze. Survivors and prisoners from Hasankeyf, Kfar-Boran, and Habses arrived in Midyat long before massacres took place in the latter town.[1]

The official assurances made some impression on the urban Syriacs who were attempting to integrate into Ottoman society and had learned the need to trust authorities. But in the countryside, the poorly integrated villagers prepared themselves for the worst. They could see Kurdish tribes assembling and heard rumors of secret plans. Already in the spring, villagers of Azakh took the precaution of building barricades and reinforcing walls. An Ottoman official from nearby Jezire heard of this and came to express the government's surprise. Did they not know that the vali himself insured that "Sayfo was declared against the Armenians above all?" he scolded. The skeptical villagers thanked the official and asked if he would be so kind as to send more weapons instead, as arms alone could give a feeling of safety.

When the gathering tribes did not disperse, the Syriacs asked the reason, as there were no Armenians living in the farm villages of Tur Abdin (but there were a few in the commercial towns). They were told that an attack was being planned on the *Frangoye* or *Faraniye* (Syriac and Arabic for "French"), a term that was common for Catholic and Protestant converts.[2]

---

[1] Gallo Shabo, appendix 1, no. 75.
[2] Ibid.

The inhabitants of Kfar-Boran used the term *Ajnabi* (Kurdish for "foreigners") to designate the same Christian groups.[3] In the towns of Midyat and Jezire, the Syriac ethnic community split, and the heads of the Syriac community were tricked into collaborating and helped to turn over the Catholics and Protestants. Although they believed they were saving the rest of the Syriacs, in reality they had only made their defensive capability weaker.

It is hard to judge the intention of the repeated declarations to isolate the Apostolic Armenians from the other Christians. These decrees have already been described in chapter 3. It may be that the German and Austrian allies attempted to rescue Catholic and Protestant co-religionists. With hindsight, it appears as if the Ottoman government issued these orders under foreign pressure and did not intend them to be universal exceptions, but rather temporary tactical measures. Although the orders did cause some confusion and slight delays, all of the Christian religions in eastern Anatolia suffered intensely and nearly equally. The main difference was that the Armenians were always the first to be arrested, so that fewer of them had a chance of surviving. After the Armenians of whatever denomination, sometimes even including Armenians who had converted to Islam, had been dealt with came the turn of the other Christian groups, using a popular Tur Abdin saying: "White or red—an onion is still an onion."[4]

The Syriac Orthodox population of Tur Abdin and its associated neighborhood (the kazas of Midyat, Beshiri, Jezire, and Nisibin) amounted to 64,540 persons, according to the list presented by Agha Petros (see appendix 2 below). To this should be added 13,500 Chaldeans included in Tfinkdji's statistics for that church in the dioceses of Sa'irt, Jezire, and Mardin (see appendix 2.3). The number of Armenians is not known. The regions of Bitlis, Sa'irt, Diyarbekir, Mardin, and Jezire were, according to one investigator, "the most annihilated because here the most systematic and organized massacres took place." Mar Severius Barsaum, an observer to the Paris Peace Conference sent by the Syriac Patriarch of Antioch, Elias III Shakir, presented a district-by-district list of destroyed Syriac Orthodox churches, murdered priests, and dead inhabitants. This was a calculation limited to his jurisdiction and only where the Syriac Orthodox church was active. Barsaum's list registered 156 destroyed churches and a total of 90,313 persons killed, including 154 clerics. The lists and figures included persons who belonged to the Syriac Orthodox faith but excluded Syriac

---

[3] Useve Wardo, interviewed October 1997 (appendix 1, no. 41).
[4] Danho Keno, interviewed July 1993 (appendix 1, no. 8).

Catholics and Chaldeans living in the same area.⁵ Of the victims in his list, 77,963 came from Diyarbekir vilayet, 8,500 from Bitlis vilayet, 3,500 from Mamuret-ul-Aziz vilayet, and 340 from Urfa sanjak in Aleppo vilayet.

TUR ABDIN: THE WEST SYRIAC HEARTLAND

Since late antiquity there had been a compact settlement of Christians in a tiny region of southeastern Anatolia named Tur Abdin. This is a small kaza of the Mardin sanjak of the Diyarbekir vilayet. Until this day, Tur Abdin itself has had only one major town, Midyat, but its borders approach the historically important towns of Mardin in the west, Nisibin in the south, Hasno (Hasankeyf) in the north, and Jezire in the east. The origin of the name is somewhat unclear; *ṭur* means "mountain" and *ʿabdin* indicates "servant" or "slave," so the geographical term is sometimes interpreted as "Mountain of the Servants [of God]"; this may have come from the fact that there was a great number of monasteries full of monks and hermits. An alternative interpretation is that it means "Mountain of the Slaves" because it was at one time populated with prisoners of war taken by the Romans during wars with Persia.⁶ The term Tur Abdin goes far back in time to the Roman fortress "Castle of Tur Abdin."⁷ In Ottoman tax registers the region was denoted by terms like *Tur*, *Tor*, or *at-Tur*. The term *Jebel Tur* came into use in the late eighteenth century—a strange combination, since the Arabic word *jabel* also means "mountain." Although this is indeed a mountainous area, with 56 percent of the area being rocky impediment unsuitable for agriculture, they are not the precipitous alp-like mountains of Armenia and Hakkari, but rather a series of surrounding mountains that vary between 900 and 1400 meters. In the north and east, mountains bend, following the deep gorge of the Tigris River to enclose a high plateau, which to the south slopes steeply down from a (then) thickly forested area to the semidesert *Chol,* which mediates between the high plateau and the desert, forming a relatively protected area. In the southern forest area, called Raite, Syriac partisans could operate, and the small and isolated villages were never systematically attacked.

---

⁵ PRO FO 371 E1242/16/118, Barsoum to , Prime Minister, March 8, 1920; Sébastien de Courtois, *The Forgotten Genocide: Eastern Christians, The Last Arameans* (2004), 239.

⁶ Helga Anschütz, *Die syrischen Christen vom Tur 'Abdin: Eine altchristliche Bevölkerungsgruppe zwischen Beharrung, Stagnation und Auflösung* (1985), 11.

⁷ Andrew Palmer, *Monk and Maṣûîson on the Tigris Frontier: The Early History of Tur ʿAbdin* (1990).

Christianity came to this area some time during the fourth century. From 363, this region was the border between the Roman and Persian Empires. For centuries, the Castle of Tur Abdin was one of the most easterly Roman fortresses and Nisibin was the most westerly Persian fortress. On the Roman side of the border, the Christian population was basically Syriac Orthodox (Jacobites) and on the other, East Syriac Nestorians. The border actually cut through the region, with Jezire and Nisibin in Persian territory and Midyat in Roman. Only after the Muslim conquest of 639–40 did this frontier cease to have importance and the Jacobite and Nestorian populations intermingle, to such a degree that Nisibin is normally considered part of Tur Abdin even though it was historically outside.

Through this area cross several language barriers, which have been flexible. The Christians traditionally spoke a local variant of the Syriac language called Turoyo. But by the time of the World War I massacres, many Christians in the villages to the north and east spoke Kurdish. In the western and southern villages, the language spoken was often Arabic. With only a few exceptions, no Nestorians could be found west of the Tigris, but Chaldeans, who shared their east Syriac origin, could be found in a handful of towns and villages to the west. During the late nineteenth century there was a great amount of Christian inmigration into the region, also spilling over into new colonization of villages south of the plateau.

The population was also mixed. There was a large Kurdish population that was both tribal-nomadic and settled in villages. The Kurdish presence was increasing through in-migration of tribes belonging to the Dakshuri confederation, who were favored by the Ottoman government and were permitted to push into the lands of the Christians and even encroach on the traditional grazing rights of the Kurdish tribes who were already present. There was also a very large number of Christian converts to Islam, known as the Muhallemi; according to legend, they traced their origin to a conflict with the patriarch over the need to fast during a severe famine.[8] The entire diocese converted to Islam, but they kept the memory of their Christian past and maintained many Christian practices. The main area of the Muhallemi is west of Midyat and northeast of Mardin, near the small town of Sawro, where they lived in villages surrounded by vineyards. A further religious minority were the Yezidis, often called "devil worshippers," remnants of an ancient local cult. They lived dispersed in a few forest villages, but the main body of Yezidis was outside Tur Abdin in the Sinjar Mountains a few days' walk to the south. Although many villages had a homogeneous ethnic

---

[8] Anschütz, *Syrischen Christen*, 17.

and religious population, some villages had mixed populations of Kurds and Christians.

Agricultural villages were normally compact, with an urban closeness. Fields, orchards, pastures, and vineyards were outside the villages. The ancient churches were large building complexes with few ground-floor openings, traditional places of refuge from an outside attack. The monasteries in particular were designed to withstand a siege, with high walls surrounding wells for water and storage rooms for supplies. The towns and largest villages often contained government-appointed officials, secular and religious judges, tax collectors, army representatives, and units of gendarmes quartered within. Merchants and craftsmen catered to the needs of the rural population and organized the caravan trade.

The Christians belonged almost exclusively to the Syriac Orthodox Church; there were practically no Armenians save the Catholics in the commercial towns along the trade routes. This Syriac Orthodox Church was well organized with 5 bishoprics in Tur Abdin—Midyat, Mor Gabriel monastery, Mor Malke monastery, Mor Quryakos (in Beshiri north of the Tigris), and Dayro da Şlibo—and deans serving the rural areas. By the start of the twentieth century, American and European missionaries had made some inroads, and there were numerous converts to Catholicism and some to Protestantism. In Midyat, the wealthiest families had become Protestants, and they possessed the newest and largest church building. In the immediate Midyat area, there were in 1890 just over 22,000 Christian inhabitants and about 22,500 Muslim inhabitants.[9]

Very many separate Kurdish tribes lived in the area (map 6). A local history of Mardin district lists 70 tribes for a swath of territory extending a little more than 200 kilometers from the town of Derike in the west to Silopi in the east. Some tribes are very large, some are very small. Some are confederations with adherents in many places, others live in only one place.[10] Ziya Gökalp listed 18 tribes in the Midyat region on the eve of World War I.[11] Many Kurdish tribes, for example the Rama and the Haverkan, suffered during the confused period after the war and fled to Syria.[12] After the war, new tribes moved into the area, taking advantage of the

---

[9] Ibid., 22.

[10] Suavi Aydin et al., *Mardin: Aşiret – Cemaat – Devlet* (2000), 462–63.

[11] Ziya Gökalp, *Kürt aşiretleri hakkında sosyolojik tetkikler* [Sociological studies of Kurdish tribes] (1992), 87–89.

[12] Martin van Bruinessen, *Agha, Shaikh and State: The Social and Political Structures of Kurdistan* (1992), 103–4.

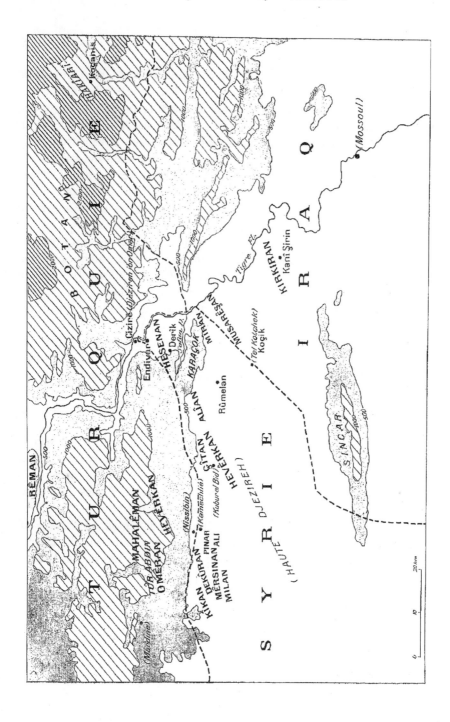

Map 6 *[opposite]*: Kurdish tribes of the Upper Jezire. From Pierre Rondot, "Les Tribus montagnards de l'Asie antérieur" (1937), 13. Reprinted with permission.

abundant vacant land and abandoned villages. The government helped the families of irregular Kurdish cavalry in Bitlis to settle in Mardin and Midyat. The tribes of Babay and the Zerikan tribe resettled in the town of Derike, and Circassians relocated in Tel-Arman.[13]

In Tur Abdin, the largest tribal confederations were the Dakshuri and the Haverkan. The chief of the Dakshuri lived in 'Arnas; this confederation was closely allied with the government, and the worst carnage went on in villages in its control. The larger Dakshuri tribes were the Cizbini, Hizar, Reman (Rama), Gercüs (Kfar-Gawze), and 'Arnas (Kurds and Syriacs)—these were mostly found in the north. The largest tribes in the Haverkan were the Alike, Alikan, Arbiyan, Baskili, Dalmakiyan (Kurds and Syriacs), Dumanan (Kurds and Syriacs), Durikari, Mzizah (Kurds, Syriacs, and Yezidis), Shemikan (Kurds, Syriacs, and Yezidis), and Seydan.[14] This confederation, the core of several pre-war anti-government uprisings, had a large and diffuse structure. At the time of the war it was split into two rival leading dynasties: the Hajo, whose chief resided in M'are outside of Nisibin; and the Chelebi, whose chief resided in Mizizah outside Midyat. Of the 18 tribes in the Midyat area, 11 belonged to the Haverkan and 5 to the Dakshuri. Normally, the Haverkan confederation was in opposition to the government and thus lacked a Hamidiye regiment. Historically they tended to protect the Christians, and some Syriacs were tribe members. When the war broke out, the main chiefs of both segments were in jail following the suppression of a Kurdish revolt early in the year. In their absence, the chief's nephew Sarokhano headed the Chelebi segment while Hasan, the eldest son, headed the Hajo segment.[15] At an early stage, both Haverkan leaders promised to safeguard the Syriacs. However, during the summer of 1915 the authorities somehow persuaded or forced Hajo to participate in the massacres, while the Chelebi subsection continued throughout to support the Christians, although with limited success. Other local tribes that sheltered individual Christians were the Tayy, an Arab Bedouin tribe living in the south, and the Yezidis of Mount Sinjar.

---

[13] Fuat Dündar, *İttihat ve Terakki'nin Müslümanları İskân Politikası (1913–1918)* [CUP Muslim Settlement Policy 1913–1918] (2001), 138–39, 143.

[14] Gökalp, *Kürt aşiretleri*, 87–89.

[15] Van Bruinessen, *Agha, Shaikh and State*, 102 fig. 4; these individuals can be identified as Hasan II and Sarokhan II in this genealogy.

With the exception of the administrative center of Midyat, most of the massacres in Tur Abdin were committed by Kurdish tribesmen together with local volunteer militia groups, often termed in Arabic Al-Khamsin death squads because they had 50 soldiers. The Al-Khamsin units were composed of Muslim males too old for the army or exempt for other reasons. They had uniforms and government-issued weapons and ammunition. The leaders were recruited among prominent Muslim families. In towns with garrisons or forts, soldiers from the regular Ottoman army would be present and could be used in massacres, but in the countryside they were present only when authorities expected strong and determined Christian defenses. Most of the initial attacks took place in June 1915, but there was continuous fighting in some of the defended villages through November 1915.

The anti-Syriac policy was unarticulated and confused. The central government was silent about their fate. But the provincial and local governments targeted them in the same way Armenians were targeted in the more northern provinces. The main difference between the genocide of the Armenians and that of the Syriacs was that in the Syriac case there were no deportation caravans but instead massacres in or near their homes. One possible reason would be that deportation to Aleppo or Mosul would have meant informing the central government. Massacres, on the other hand, meant that whatever information came to the government was very much delayed. A massive, more or less clandestine operation could wipe out the Syriacs within a few months.

A WEEK-LONG MASSACRE

Perhaps the most blatant case of dividing the Christians against each other was that of the town of Midyat (map 7). Here the Syriac Orthodox leaders were lured into believing that they would be saved only if they collaborated to turn over the Protestant families. In Midyat, the mayor (Reis Baladiya) was Galle Hermez, a Protestant, from a large and wealthy family. The Syriac Orthodox were led by Hanne Safar, who was so favored by the government that he was officially awarded the honorary title "pasha" and had a ceremonial sword. The large Kurdish population was led by 'Azizke Mahmado Agha. When the situation for the Christians darkened, all of the Christian religious leaders met and swore on the Bible that they would stick together and mount a common defense. When the kaymakam heard of this alliance, he summoned Hanne Safar to the town hall and explained that there must have been a misunderstanding. The Protestants and Catholics were the targets since they had foreign connections, but not the Syriac Orthodox, who would

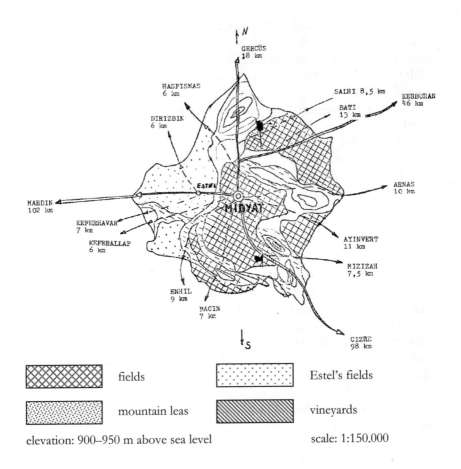

Map 7: Plan of Midyat. After Helga Anschütz, *Die syrischen Christen vom Tur 'Abdin* (1985), 240.

not be harmed. After this, Hanne Safar broke with the other religious leaders and even assisted in the arrest of the adult males in the Hermez family, who were executed before the main assault. However, only a few weeks later, Hanne himself was one of the first victims of the general massacre of Syriac Christians in the town. Very little documentary evidence is available about the events in Midyat, so the following narrative is composed of various oral testimonies.

Over the past centuries, the town of Midyat had grown and become known as a safe haven for many Syriac and Chaldean families who fled oppression in other regions. Whole large clans sought refuge in Midyat, such as the Rhawi, who arrived in Midyat from the city of Urfa; the Hermez family, who had fled from the city of Mosul; and the Ghanno family, who came from Hasankeyf. The important families of Chalma, Sa'ido, and Safar came to Midyat from Ka'biye, a village outside Diyarbekir. The family of Khalaf came to Midyat from the village of Ahlah, the family of Haydari fled from the village of Kfar-Shoma', and the Sawo'e family hailed from the village of Kfar-Gawze.

The Kurdish emirs of the region of Bohtan in the northern part of Upper Mesopotamia were cruel and merciless in their treatment of Christians. In the 1840s, Emir Badr Khan killed many Assyrians, particularly in Bohtan and in the Hakkari mountains, during his well-known revolt. What is less known is that the massacres also affected the Syriacs of Tur Abdin. This crisis prompted a prominent Syriac leader in Midyat, named Grigho, to attempt to solve the security problem in the long term, appealing for protection from Kurdish aghas residing in the valley of Nisibin. He asked them to provide Kurdish people willing to settle in Midyat and assist the population in defense against the recurrent attacks from the emirs. In consequence, two Kurds named Mahmado and Nahrozo agreed to settle in Midyat and brought their large clans with them. Grigho imposed a kind of local defense tax, called *khafirti*, on Syriac Christians.[16] This money went into a fund to pay the two Kurdish clans so that they could establish themselves in Midyat.

Sultan Abdul Hamid bestowed decorations and medals on important people in places where his influence was weak. The aim was to create personal allies out of these people. In Midyat, the head of the Safar clan, Hanne Safar, received such a distinction, the *Hamidi* medal. Hanne Safar always represented the Syriac inhabitants in formal ceremonies wearing his decorations, medals, and special sword. As a state-certified ethnic leader, Hanne Safar had considerable power and controlled the Syriac affairs of Midyat and its surroundings in accordance with the will of Sultan Abdul Hamid. The ultimate function of Hanne Safar was to thwart any subversive movements against the government. The Syriacs of Tur Abdin held him in awe and seldom dared challenge him. In 1905, a feud took place between the clans of Chalma and Safar. Hanne Safar was able, thanks to his unique

---

[16] *Khafirti* is a Kurdish term meaning "tax." In the modern history of Midyat, Mahmado and Nahrozo are considered the first Kurdish settlers in Midyat. Grigho initiated the custom that if a Syriac in Midyat died without an heir, all the wealth would go to the Mahmado and Nahrozo clans. These two families later became the rulers of Midyat.

political-administrative status, to banish all members of the Chalma family from Midyat; they lived in exile for seven years.[17] After the expulsion of the Chalma, Safar's main political rival was Galle Hermez, a popular Syriac Protestant and a member of district and provincial advisory councils.

In 1913, the Mardin priest Ishaq Armalto, of the Syriac Catholic Church, inspected Midyat and Tur Abdin. He observed that "in Midyat there lived between 6000 and 7000 people, the majority of whom were Syriac Orthodox but with 80 Protestant, 30 Syriac Catholic, Chaldean, Armenian families and 50 Muslim families."[18] Joseph Tfinkdji, a Chaldean priest from Mardin, estimated that there were around 180 Chaldeans living in Midyat.[19]

In 1913, an incident took place in Midyat that had deep repercussions for the climate of opinion among the Syriac Christians. It was connected with the banishment of Patriarch Abén from Midyat because of his unpopular attempts to reunite Tur Abdin with the rest of the Syriac Orthodox Church. Since 1364, the diocese of Tur Abdin had been autocephalic, with its own Patriarch of Tur Abdin, separate from the mother church, ruled by the official Patriarch of Antioch, who resided in the Za'faran monastery outside Mardin. The diocese of Tur Abdin appointed its own bishops and clergymen. Formally, Tur Abdin rejoined the mother church in 1839, but the rivalry continued. However, Patriarch Isma'il, who was then the head of the Antioch Syriac Orthodox Church, strove for reconciliation. A year before Sayfo, a series of friendly conferences took place between the bishop of Tur Abdin and the patriarch, and they were still in progress when war broke out.[20] Very little is known about the nature of the negotiations or the opinion of the people of Midyat toward them. Clearly, the local faithful were not happy about the thought of reunion, since they banished their Patriarch Abén just for beginning talks. It was common knowledge that Abén was very angry over leaving Midyat, and when he left the town, he uttered a curse. He said: "I hope and pray that Midyat will be turned upside down."

---

[17] Qayasa lies in the southern part of Midyat, near the Yezidi village of Bajénne. Here the Chalma family converted to Catholicism and built a church and houses. They lived here in exile until 1912.

[18] Ishaq Armalto, "Siyahati fi Turabdin" [My journey in Tur Abdin] (1913), 663.

[19] Josef Tfinkdji, "L'Église chaldéenne catholique autrefois et aujourd'hui" (1914), 511.

[20] Ignatius Ephraim Bet-Barsawmo, *Turabdin Tarihi* [History of Tur Abdin] (1996), 50–51.

In the summer of 1914, the Ottoman government ordered mobilization. It drafted men between the ages of 20 and 45 to join the army, but few were enthusiastic. The recruits from Midyat had to be chained together to be taken away. Few who were taken in this way ever returned.

In the late spring, Armenians and Syriacs fleeing from massacres around Diyarbekir found their way to Midyat after crossing the mountains. Many described the killings and the persecution occurring in their areas. The people of Hasankeyf, the northernmost town with mixed Armenian and Syriac population, heard about these killings as well, so they sent several men to Midyat to investigate whether these reports were really true. Those men survived because their arrival in Midyat coincided with the massacre of their home town on June 5, 1915. Some Syriac and Armenian escapees managed to make their way to Midyat. After listening to the Hasankeyf information, the Syriac headmen of Midyat went to the kaymakam, Nuri Bey, to ask him about these massacres; they told him that people were arriving in Midyat telling stories of horrible killings and atrocities taking place all over Anatolia. According to some versions, the kaymakam had his daughter sitting in his lap at that meeting. He answered: "That rumor is as false as if I am committing incest with my own daughter." He stressed: "It is the Armenians who took arms against the government, and the government for its part is taking measures to restore law and order."[21] Nevertheless, the arrival of considerable numbers of Syriac refugees in Midyat who escaped from local villages and who were attacked by local Kurdish tribes did not cease. Nothing about these massacres made sense if only the Armenians were to be punished. The leaders of Midyat became suspicious, but they had no clear idea of what to expect.

SOLIDARITY BREAKS DOWN

Early in 1915, the Syriac Orthodox and Protestant leaders of Midyat, Hanne Safar and Galle Hermez, assembled in the church of Mort Shmuni to discuss how to defend Midyat and themselves. They decided to prepare a common defense of Midyat by any means necessary. They put their hands on the Bible and uttered a solemn oath of solidarity and mutual defense.

---

[21] It is probable that this kaymakam was Nuri Bey and that he believed in the truth of what he said. Contemporaries believed that Nuri Bey refused to participate in the killings of Syriacs, so the vali of Diyarbekir had him removed. Holstein to Deutsche Botschaft July 16, 1915, in Lepsius, *Deutschland und Armenien 1914–1918: Sammlung diplomatischer Aktenstücke* (1919), 104. See also Uğur Ü. Üngör, "A Reign of Terror: CUP Rule in Diyarbekir Province, 1913–1923" (2005), 56.

However, there were informers among the Christians who told the authorities about the decisions and whereabouts of the influential people in Midyat. The authorities thus immediately learned the details of the agreement.

The informers were told to return and tell Hanne Safar that the planned actions were to be limited only to Midyat's Protestants and Catholics, and that the Syriac Orthodox could feel secure. Building on both class resentment and religious hatred, some Syriacs began to argue, Why should we help the Hermez clan, which is a large and rich family of Protestant converts that could defend itself and its possessions, at our expense? What can be gained by involving us in the fate that was awaiting them? Hanne Safar reversed his position after hearing this and told the Hermez clan that the agreement they had reached at Mort Shmuni was no longer valid. The Hermez answered by saying that, if this was the case, they would face their destiny alone without any help and without causing any problems for the other Christians. After that, some members of the Hermez family actually surrendered to the authorities, which used this as a pretext to imprison more than one hundred men from the same family. No adult male avoided imprisonment, except one who escaped disguised as a woman. The authorities said that these men would be sent to a court-martial in Mardin; but in reality they were killed during transport and thrown down the wells outside Astal, just west of Midyat.[22]

An obituary for Hermez calling him a Syriac patriot stresses his unselfish political activities:

> Galle Hermez [1859–1915] was born in Midyat in Mesopotamia. He lived 56 years and died at the hands of the Young Turks. Galle Hermez sacrificed his life for the sake of his people and fellow countrymen. In his area he was known as a great thinker. In Midyat he worked on the administrative council for 21 years. He was the mayor for a period of eight years. After that he became a representative for Midyat in the council that was yearly held in Amid. In Mardin Sanjak, he worked as deputy for the Sanjak council. This great man became a respected figure in the governmental circles. His name became well known among his people in Anatolia, Aleppo, Beirut, and in the whole of Mesopotamia for defending the rights of his people and the poor in particular. He

---

[22] The city of Midyat has two parts. The western part is Astal (Estel), about 3 kilometers from Midyat's center (see map 7 on p. 189). The majority of people who live there are Muslims. They use a particular dialect of Arabic called Muhallami. The eastern part is called Midyat and was inhabited mostly by Christians. Until the Sayfo, there was a church in Astal, but it lacked both a priest and a bell. After Sayfo the church was converted into a mosque.

fought against all kinds of oppression. He was a generous man, and his house was open to all people, which earned him the appreciation of - everyone. This man suffered a terrible death at the hands of the Young Turks together with 75 people from Midyat.[23]

In Tur Abdin, early June saw the start of attacks on rural villages and preparations for action against the large Syriac community of Midyat. The government sent a messenger to Midyat to announce that the Christians had to turn over all arms to the local authorities. The local Syriac leaders, Hanne Safar and a Syriac Orthodox priest, Isa Zatte, as well as Aziz Agha, Midyat's Kurdish headman, and Rauf Bey, the head of the Jandarma, called an assembly and ordered the Christians to surrender their weapons. On June 21, soldiers began house-to-house searches for hidden arms and arrested many of the Armenian and Protestant males they found. These persons were imprisoned, tortured, and then murdered; a group numbering either 104 or 113 was killed just outside of town on June 28/July 11.[24] Included in this mass execution were 20 or 30 escaped Armenians from Hasankeyf and Kfar-Boran, plus the prisoners from the Hermez clan. True to his promise of protection, Sarokhano of the Haverkan tribe made plans to rescue the Hermez family, but the kaymakam was informed and threatened Sarokhano with death if he intervened.[25]

ANNIHILATION OF THE SYRIACS

In late June, the kaymakam, Nuri Bey, simply disappeared, presumably because he had refused to organize the killing of Christians. Nuri had sworn many solemn oaths to the Christians that they would not be injured within his jurisdiction. Holstein, the German consul in Mosul, believed that he had been assassinated, but if so, that was not known in Midyat and is not part of Syriac oral testimony. Preparations for his removal began in May when he was appointed consul in Khoi in Iran, which given the Turkish retreat from Azerbaijan seems unrealistic. But it was a way of getting him out of town, and on his way east he vanished. A telegram sent from the Ministry of the Interior on June 27 reveals that he was missing and could not be found. Authorities in Bitlis were asked to search for him. Later an investigation

---

[23] Skandar, "A Syrian Patriot" (1916).
[24] Ne'man Beth-Yawno, interviewed November 1993 (appendix 1, no. 2).
[25] Ibid.; Sabri Hermez, interviewed November 1997 (appendix 1, no. 9); 'Abdo Ghanno-Gawweke, interviewed February 1997 (appendix 1, no. 18).

began into his alleged misuse of authority, but none of the documents indicate whether he was alive or dead, or what he was actually accused of.[26]

The new temporary kaymakam, Hajji Bashar Bey, summoned the heads of the local Kurdish tribes to his headquarters. They were ordered to take severe actions against the Christian inhabitants. However, the guard at the door was a Muhallemi who went to the heads of the Syriac Orthodox community and informed them of the plans discussed at that meeting. A second meeting was held at a mosque in Estel on July 2 with the kaymakam, some Muhallemi chiefs, and the heads of Midyat's Kurdish clans. Warning came to the Syriacs from Salimo, a Kurdish shepherd, who was present at the mosque.[27] The kaymakam and the Kurdish agha 'Azizke advised the Christian leaders to surrender themselves to the government, but all refused. In response to noncompliance, on July 6/19, 1915, the tribe of Omariyan, together with some of the Muhallemi and aided by regular soldiers, invaded the Christian sectors.

Even though they must have expected an attack for some time, the Christian resistance in Midyat proved rather weak. Sustained resistance was mounted in only two places. The first was the monastery of Mor Sharbel, where the large Rhawi clan and their clientele defended itself for one week.[28] Syriac warriors from the village of 'Ayn-Wardo, about 10 kilometers due east of the town, came to their support and escorted them back to their village. The second point of resistance was the building and yard of the 'Adoka clan. Many people from surrounding streets assembled there to hide in the underground tunnels leading to the monastery of Mor Abrohom in the eastern sector of Midyat.[29] Many saved themselves by fleeing through

---

[26] BOA. DH. ŞFR 52/344 Ministry of Interior to Van vilayet May 13, 1915; 54/210 Ministry of Interior to Bitlis vilayet June, 27, 1915; 55/123 Ministry of Interior to Baghdad vilayet August 21, 1915; 58/104 Ministry of Interior to Diyarbekir vilayet December 26, 1915

[27] Gorgis 'Abdiyo, interviewed July 2000 (appendix 1, no. 17).

[28] The old monastery of Mor Sharbel was north of Midyat, near the quarters of the Rhawi clan. Until the time of Sayfo, there were priests, monks, nuns, servants, and students living in it. After Sayfo, the government confiscated it and turned it into a military base. To keep the name alive, the Syriac Orthodox in 1955 built a church in the Rhawi quarters and called it Mor Sharbel.

[29] Under the city of Midyat there are many tunnels, called *khishe* in Neo-West Syriac. These tunnels lead to 'Ayn-Wardo and were common knowledge to the Christians, who tried to keep them a secret from the Turkish officials. These tunnels are very old and there is no information about the date of their construction. Perhaps these tunnels were the first cave-like habitations in Midyat. These tunnels

these tunnels to the monastery and could then travel onward to 'Ayn-Wardo. However, very many lost their lives in the last-ditch defense guarding the entrances to the tunnels.

Although the Christians of Midyat were outnumbered and outgunned, they managed to mount a number of difficult missions to eliminate government heads. Some particularly brutal Ottoman officials became the target of special missions. One Syriac death squad liquidated a Kurdish officer named Yusuf. He had been in charge of the squads that guarded the newly mobilized recruits on their way to the front. Oral testimony indicates that harassment of Christian recruits began during these marches. From Midyat, the recruits were led chained together in groups of three or four.[30] None of the 45 persons from 'Ayn-Wardo that he escorted ever returned.[31] Another official on the hit list was Sherif Efendi, the tax collector (*tahsildar*). He had ordered the murder of persons who could not pay their taxes. He was also observed taking an active part in the Midyat massacre and raping many women. Gallo Shabo's partisans eliminated him.[32] Beyond these particular officials, the Syriacs also stormed the town hall.

The once almighty secular head of the Syriac community, Hanne Safar, was beheaded with his own ceremonial sword. Syriac oral testimony alleges that he stopped several attempts to rescue the Hermez family, who were the first group massacred. After Safar's death, a crowd stuck his head on a long pole and paraded through the streets of Midyat chanting, "This is the head of the Syriac leader in Midyat, take care of him." After that they presented Safar's head to some Muslim boys to use as a football. In the middle of this chaos the Muslims started to plunder the abandoned homes. They stole not only valuable items but also the doors and windows. At the marketplace of Shaqfo, young boys were killed by throwing them headfirst from the roof of a tall building.[33]

---

have many entrances scattered about the town.

[30] Rume Lahdo-Antar, interviewed July 1993 (appendix 1, no. 3); Danho Keno, interviewed July 1993 (appendix 1, no. 8).

[31] Hanna Hawsho, interviewed August 1993 (appendix 1, no. 16).

[32] Hanna Bitar, interviewed February 1994 (appendix 1, no. 14).

[33] Habib Maqsi-Musa, interviewed August 2003 (appendix 1, no. 11).

8 SAYFO: THE GENERAL MASSACRE OF NORTHERN MESOPOTAMIA

The following list catalogues the Syriac testimony about the fate of 178 small towns and villages in the Mardin sandjak and its vicinity, such as Bohtan, Beshiri, Urfa, and the villages closest to Diyarbekir (map 8). Most of the entries tell a story of massacre, but in more than twenty cases Muslim neighbors gave substantial protection or help. The places are listed in alphabetical order. Most of the basic information comes from just a few sources (marked by an abbreviation so as to avoid repetitive footnotes: **H**, Hinno's oral history; **Q**, Qarabash's testimony; **A**, Anschütz's historical geography.[1] Names of villages are generally given in Syriac unless the place is better known under another name. The place names include alternative spellings in Arabic and Kurdish and the new Turkish names. With very few exceptions, villages and towns were renamed during the Turkish Republic, and it has not always been possible to find the new names, particularly for places outside Tur Abdin. A few of the places were so thoroughly destroyed that they have not been rebuilt.[2]

Concerning the population of the villages, reference is made to the typed list presented by Agha Petros to the Lausanne peace conference. It provides a village-level estimate of the "Assyro-Chaldean" population of

---

[1] Süleyman Hinno, *Günhe d Süryoye d'Turabdin* [The massacre of the Syriacs of Tur Abdin] (1987); Abed Mschiho Na'man Qarabasch, *Vergossenes Blut: Geschichten der Greuel, die an den Christen in der Türkei verübt, und der Leiden, die ihnen 1895 und 1914–1918 zugefügt wurden* (2002); Helga Anschütz, *Die syrischen Christen vom Tur 'Abdin: Eine altchristliche Bevölkerungsgruppe zwischen Beharrung, Stagnation und Auflösung* (1985).

[2] Villages are sometimes said to be "owned." With a Syriac owner, the reference is to recently colonized villages east of Nisibin, an area opened up in the late 19th century. An "owner" was one of the original colonizers and the others farmed land "owned" by him. With a Kurdish agha, this phrase indicates a type of feudal lord who extracts tribute or rent from the tenants.

Map 8: Tur Abdin region at the start of World War I (names in Aramaic). After Gabriele Yonan, *Ein vergessener Holocaust: Die Vernichtung der christlichen Assyrer in der Türkei* (1989), 272–73.

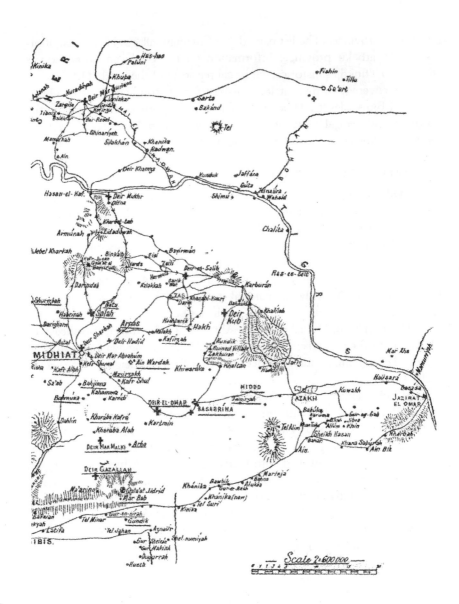

Diyarbekir province.³ The list named 345 Christian villages in and neighboring the Diyarbekir province. Information on the Chaldean population is taken from Tfinkdji's historical-statistical report published in 1914.⁴

The coverage of this catalogue is best for the southern parts of Diyarbekir and Bitlis vilayets. There are few detailed reports of the events in the northern and central parts of these provinces or in Mamuret-ul-Aziz, although it is known that carnage among the Syriacs was great there.

A Catalogue of Massacres

'**Abbase**. 'Abbase is a small Syriac village in the Anbart river area near Diyarbekir. Along with inhabitants of several other neighboring villages, the males were slaughtered on May 7, 1915. The women and children were put to forced agricultural work. The massacre was perpetrated by one of the Al-Khamsin death squads at the instigation of the owner of the villages, Qasem Bey. According to testimony of survivors, 114 men from these villages were killed. After the agricultural season was finished, the women and children had to convert to Islam or be killed. **Q**

Ahlah (Halah, Achlah, Narli). Ahlah is 13 kilometers northeast of Midyat. Only 3 or 4 Syriac families lived in Ahlah among a large number of Kurds. These families survived because their Kurdish neighbors protected them. **H, A**

Anhel (Yemişli, Enhil). Anhel was one of the largest villages in Tur Abdin. It is located 10 kilometers south of Midyat on the road to Nisibin. It had two Syriac Orthodox churches, Mor Quryaqos and Mor Eshayo, plus six chapels. This village was never attacked, and it came to serve as a concentration camp and swelled with Christian refugees. Armed guards stood watch and permitted entry but not exit. There were limited opportunities to get out, and the inhabitants believed that it was only a matter of time before they too would suffer attack. The leader of the Syriacs was named Beso. It is said that Aziz Agha of the Mahmado clan of Midyat instigated this form of guarded protection. The aggressors had insufficient force to attack both 'Ayn-Wardo and Anhel at the same time. They decided to concentrate on 'Ayn-Wardo first, but since they never managed to conquer that village,

---

³ "Liste des villages, des habitations et nationalités," PRO FO 839/23 82893 136, appendix to a cover letter of Agha Petros to Mr. Adam November 26, 1922, identifying it as enumerating "Assyrian villages north of Mosul." See appendix 2.2 below.

⁴ Joseph Tfinkdji, "L'Église chaldéenne catholique autrefois et aujourd'hui" (1914).

they found no opportunity to attack Anhel. The villagers of Anhel smuggled salt, food, and weapons to 'Ayn-Wardo.[5] **H**

'Arbaye (Alayurt). 'Arbaye is situated 34 kilometers northeast of Midyat and 7 kilometers west of Kfar-Boran. There lived 30 Syriac families in the village of 'Arbaye. They were slaughtered by Kurds led by Ali Musa of Dayvan. Only a few people survived. The parish church of Mor Sobo, said to be from the eighth century, was destroyed. **H, A**

Arbo (Taşköy). Arbo is situated 15 kilometers southeast of Midyat in the wooded area known as Raite. When the massacres broke out, Arbo had 70 Syriac families. They fled to the Mor Malke monastery and to Mor Eliyo monastery. **H**

Arkah-Kharabale (Arkah-Harabale, Üçköy). Arkah-Kharabale is 20 kilometers south of Midyat. Seventy Syriac families lived here. They sought safety in nearby Mor Malke Monastery. **H**

Armun (Ermuni). Armun lies northeast of Kfar-Gawze, and 10 Syriac families lived there. An unnamed government representative in Hasno came with soldiers and some Kurdish tribesmen and attacked the village. All but ten were murdered. **H**

'Arnas (Urdnus, Bağlarbaşı). 'Arnas is 9 kilometers northeast of Midyat. The village church, Mor Quryaqos, dates from 761. In 'Arnas lived 70 Syriac families, but the rest, probably a majority, were Kurds, including the leader of the Dakshuri confederation, Osman Tammero. The majority of the Christians belonged to the Syriac Orthodox Church, but 10 families were recorded as Protestant. When the Syriacs learned of the fate of nearby Saleh and heard gunshots from the direction of Midyat, they took as much as they could carry and left the village. The Kurds tried to stop them, but the Christians were many and they forced themselves past and came to 'Ayn-Wardo. Twenty-three Syriac men who had remained in 'Arnas were murdered the following day.[6] **H, A**

Artvena (Artoukh, Artoun). Upper and Lower Artvena were two villages with mixed population near Sa'irt. Upper Artvena had 29 Nestorian households and 310 Chaldeans, while Lower Artvena had 90 Nestorian

---

[5] Armalto, *Al-Qusara fi nakabat al-nasara* (1919), 406; 'Abdo Ghanno-Gawweke, interviewed February 1997 (appendix 1, no. 59); Ello 'Amno, interviewed September 2004 (appendix 1, no. 60).

[6] 'Abdo Ghanno-Gawweke, interviewed February 1997 (appendix 1, no. 54); Gawriye Beth Mas'ud, interviewed July 2002 (appendix 1, no. 55).

households and 160 Chaldeans. The villagers met their death during the massacres at Sa'irt in early June 1915. See the section on Sa'irt below.

'Ayn-Sare. 'Ayn-Sare is 15 kilometers south of Azakh. A mixed village, it had 15 Syriac and many Kurdish families. As the Kurdish neighbors met to plan a massacre, one of the Kurdish women, named Hinde, came to warn the Christians. Those who believed her fled to Azakh, those who remained were murdered.[7]

'Ayn-Wardo (Inwardo, Gülgöze). 'Ayn-Wardo is a large village built on a high hill 2 hours by foot from Midyat. It had 200 Syriac Orthodox families, but no Muslims except for servants. The name means "Source of the Rose." The church was surrounded by high walls and was built as a fortress. The Christians from many villages poured into 'Ayn-Wardo: they came from Bote, Habses, Kafarbe, Kafro, Midyat, and Zaz. An estimated 6,000 to 7,000 Syriac Christians from all over assembled there in the summer of 1915.[8]

In July, Kurds, Turks, and Muhallemi combined to attack the Christians of Midyat. Hearing the news, the people of Mizizah took their animals and valuables and headed for 'Ayn-Wardo. The people of 'Ayn-Wardo brought in their harvest earlier than usual. Mas'ud Shabo from Mizizah was chosen leader of the defense. He had experience dealing with the Kurds, Yezidi, and the Muhallemi tribes. Mas'ud began to set up a strategic plan to defend 'Ayn-Wardo. He started by strengthening relationships between Syriacs and the neighboring Yezidi. At the time there were some Kurds and Yezidi working as servants and shepherds in the village. Mas'ud decided to expel these men to avoid any complications. Although some left, the Syriacs hid others in the caves until the time of Sayfo was over.

In a relatively short time, Mas'ud assembled 700 men. At night they would dress in black and go out to rescue people who had survived execution squads or escaped from deportation convoys. They would carry the wounded to 'Ayn-Wardo and provide medical help. The majority of those saved were Armenians but ones who came from villages where they spoke Kurdish. Mas'ud would listen to their stories of how the tribes and government forces played tricks on them. First they might be told that they would be safe if only they handed over their weapons, but after complying, they were massacred. In June 1915, the government arrested the leaders of the Hermez family and other Protestant notables in Midyat. Mas'ud set up a

---

[7] Hanna Murat Hannouche, *Azekh "Beyt Zebde"* (2002?), 63.

[8] **H** gives the higher figure (p. 70), Armalto the lower figure (*Al-Qusara*, 406); otherwise the two narratives are similar.

plan to help them. In Midyat, Hanne Safar heard about his plans and notified the Turkish government about them. The plans were changed as a result, and Mas'ud failed in this particular mission.

Mas'ud sent help to the people of Midyat. Two places became the centers of Syriac resistance: the Monastery of Mor Sharbel, where the clan of Rhawi was in charge; and the large house of 'Adoka, from where underground tunnels led to 'Ayn-Wardo. Mas'ud sent 100 men dressed in black to Midyat to help. Some stayed to help the Rhawis, while the others went to the house of the tax-collector Sharif Afandi. They were ordered to kill Sharif Afandi and take the tax money. Sharif Afandi escaped, but they did get hold of the tax money. However, one of the Syriac leaders in Midyat, Isa Zatte, heard about this and confiscated the money. The men returned angry and upset. The Rhawi defenses grew steadily weaker, so the survivors left for 'Ayn-Wardo. In a final attempt to rescue the last Syriacs holding out at the tunnel entrances under the house of 'Adoka, a death squad was sent out. They did not make it and came back reporting that the wells outside the town were full of dead bodies.

After conquering Midyat, the Kurds, Turks, and Muhallemi prepared to attack both 'Ayn-Wardo and Anhel, where there were also many Christian refugees. Azizke Mahmado, Midyat's Kurdish leader, suggested that all join forces to strike against 'Ayn-Wardo as the first priority. Guards were placed around Anhel, and the mass of aggressors concentrated on 'Ayn-Wardo. Since the mass attack on 'Ayn-Wardo failed, it made possible the survival of Anhel, which never had to face a storming.

Mas'ud heard about the movements from the Yezidi, who supplied information, arms, and transport from their nearby villages: Kharabya, Kiwakh, Kochanes, Taqa, Bajenne, Daywanke, and Kavnas. They smuggled provisions at night to avoid detection.

The bishop, Mor Filiksinos Ablahad, preached in the Church of Mor Hushabo, telling his congregation that it was their sacred duty to resist even though they were outnumbered. He called upon the Holy Spirit to aid them in their ordeal while defending their Christian faith and their sacred soil. After that, he went up to the roof of the church, where he fasted and prayed for two weeks. When the Christians captured the Muslim flag, they went up to the bishop, who was very weak from hunger, to show him the flag and convey the good news. He asked them to burn the flag in front of him. Seeing the enemy's flag burning, the bishop was said to have died at peace.

The Turkish officials collected Kurdish tribes from the Midyat and Mardin areas, and some of the Muhallemi as well as the Rama tribe from further to the north, to surround 'Ayn-Wardo. It was said that this force amounted to 13,000 men. They received weapons, ammunition, and food supplies from the government warehouses. On an unspecified Friday in the middle of July, they surrounded 'Ayn-Wardo, and harsh battles began immediately. There were casualties on both sides. Thereafter the Syriacs staged a counterattack to split the enemy and, as already mentioned, even managed to seize their battle flag. Shooting continued daily, and the corpses of the dead lay rotting in the summer sun. The next Saturday, the Syriacs staged counterattacks under cover of darkness, and although they lost 26 men, the Turkish and Kurdish losses were much greater. The full-scale war continued for about 10 more days. The Turkish commandant ordered a final large-scale charge for Sunday morning when the church bells started to ring. This attack was partially successful; the soldiers seized a lookout point and killed 10 Syriac warriors from Kfarze. Again on Tuesday there was a new Turkish attack, but that failed completely. The Turks lost 50 men, including a high officer. This resulted in confusion and shock. The troops sent a message to Mardin for reinforcements, and the mutasarrif, Bedri Bey, sent what he could, including a large cannon. They began to fire at the village with this cannon, and the siege continued for twenty more days.

Armalto stated that the aggressors lost 200 men while the defenders lost 300. At that point the Turks prepared to negotiate an armistice. The Shaykh of Dara was used as mediator. The conditions were that the villagers must give up their arms and obey government orders. If they did this, they would be protected. The villagers were wary and refused to give up their weapons. After the refusal, a three-day battle began, but even with reinforcements and superior firepower, the Turks and Kurds could not break the defenses. Informed of the impossibility of storming the village, Bedri Bey sent two Syriac Orthodox clerics from Mardin, bishop Yesua and the priest Hanna. Their task was to persuade the defenders to capitulate, give up their arms, and obey the state. But the defenders refused to listen to the clerics. Other intermediaries were equally unsuccessful. Finally, the defenders said that if the Turks were serious about a cease-fire, they should send someone whom they trusted as guarantor of the peace. This had to be a person who was trusted by the Christians but who also had enough authority among the Kurds that his word would be respected. That ruled out any Christian cleric. The defenders suggested Shaykh Fathulla from 'Ayn-Kif, a Muhallemi Kurd. After some time, this shaykh arrived. The Syriacs placed themselves under his protection. He then persuaded the Turks to order the Kurds to go away and to guarantee the Syriacs free passage. After this, the shaykh collected weapons from the Syriacs, and the attackers were ordered away. The shaykh commanded the Muslims not to harm any Christians. The siege of 'Ayn-Wardo went on for either 52 (Armalto) or 60 days (Hinno). Despite the guarantee of amnesty, most of the Syriacs remained there and did not return to their original villages. A few who dared were shot on their way back to 'Arnas, Ahlah, and Mizizah.

After the cease-fire, Mas'ud asked to move to Anhel, but the Christian leaders advised him to go somewhere else, since the government was searching for him and they did not want to be involved. Mas'ud went to Kafro in Rayete. There he lived a short time in a tent on the roof of the local church. He was easy prey for the government, which had him shot. The number of Syriacs who were killed as they returned to their villages was greater than the number who died during the siege.[9] **H**

Azakh (İdil, Hezak, Hazak, Beth Zabday). See chapter 9 below.

Babeqqa (Babika, Babiqqa, Bebek). Babeqqa is 6 kilometers south of Azakh. Hinno states that 60 Syriac families who lived here fled to Azakh. However, the A. H. B. source states that there was first an attack and that only the survivors reached Azakh. Hendo's diary gives the date of the attack as June 20, 1915.[10] **H**

Bafayya (Bafawa, Bafova). Bafayya is a Christian village located 25 kilometers northeast of Mardin in a deep river valley. Before the war, 500 Assyro-Chaldeans resided here. The village was attacked by Hussein Bakro and his men on June 10 (Simon) or June 4 (Qarabash), 1915. All sources agree that this was one of the earliest massacres in the region. The Syriac Orthodox priest was burned alive and the village headman murdered. Only a handful of men escaped to Benebil, and two of them arrived at the Za'faran monastery after a week's journey.[11] **Q**

Bagh-Chejik (Baglit, Baggetshik, Bagdjaoljik). Bagh-Chejik is a small Syriac village in the Anbart River area near Diyarbekir. During the war, four Syriac families totaling about 50 persons who lived in Bagh-Chejik were murdered. One person survived. Along with inhabitants of several other villages, the males of this village were shot on May 7, 1915. The women and

---

[9] Armalto, *Al-Qusara*, 409; appendix 1 below, section C, nos. 21–40.

[10] A. H. B., "Mémoires sur Mardine (1915ss)" (1998), 186; Hannouche, *Azekh*, 42.

[11] Hyacinthe Simon, *Mardine la ville héroïque: Autel et tombeau de l'Arménie (Asie Mineure) durant les massacres de 1915* (1991), 135.

children were put to forced agricultural work. The massacre was perpetrated by one of the Al-Khamsin militias at the instigation of the owner of the villages, Qasem Bey. According to testimony of survivors, 114 men from these villages were killed. After the agricultural season was finished, the women and children had to convert to Islam or be killed. **H, Q**

Bara-Betha (Bara Beita, Bar-Abaysa, Brabite). This Chaldean village of 300 persons is 15 kilometers south of Jezire. The Esene Kurds attacked, and all villagers are believed to have died.[12]

Barlat. In Barlat, near Hasno and the Tigris River, there were ten Syriac families. During the massacres, some were killed and some survived. **H**

Bashok (Basak, Beth Ishok, Besük). Bashok is located 20 kilometers northwest of Azakh near the Wadi Salo. The fortress-like parish church was named after Mar Addai and is now used as a stable. In the late nineteenth century, the inhabitants were all Christians. Some of the villagers sought protection in the defended village of Basibrin. The village was destroyed during World War I. **H, A**

Basibrin (Basibrino, Beth Sorino, Besorino, Haberli). Basibrin and Sare are twin villages close to each other halfway between Midyat and Azakh. The villages lie east of Qartmin monastery. The people of the two villages did not get along very well with each other, and in the late nineteenth century, they kept up a long vendetta. Basibrin had about 250 families and Sare had 200, all Syriac Orthodox. When news of the massacres came, the people of Sare squeezed into Basibrin. Mor Dodo church had high walls and towers and could be used as a fortress. A guard of 40 Turkish soldiers was already quartered in the village, ostensibly to shield the Christians. When the Syriacs heard of the murder of the Hermez family in Midyat in late June or early July, they seized the rifles of the soldiers. After local attacks, villagers from Miden, Tamarz, Bashok, Zinawrah, Qanaq, and Bazar fled into Basibrin. According to Hinno, there were a reported 2,000 well-armed Syriacs assembled here. The leader of the Syriacs was a villager from Sare named Malke, son of Hanne Haydo and brother to the legendary Syriac warrior Shemun Haydo, who was then in prison. Some friendly Kurds from Araban and some Yezidis from Gali brought food, which they sold to the defenders. One day, however, Malke seized the delivery without paying for it and the supplies stopped coming. After this, Malke went out with some men, stole several herds of sheep from Araban, and distributed

---

[12] Yves Ternon, "Mardin 1915: Anatomie pathologique d'une destruction" (2002), 369.

the booty unequally, causing a deep split within the Syriac defenders. The opposition to Malke found its leader in the Kamsho family, which was from Basibrin. In secret, the Kamsho made contact with the Salihan Kurds to get rid of Malke and conspired to let the Kurds enter the village, promising some of the booty. They tried to trick Malke into a trap, but he escaped and killed three of the Kamsho family. The rest of the Kamsho left Basibrin, joined the Kurds, and according to Hinno's testimony took part in the siege of the village. A large number of tribes were called together to assault Basibrin. Turkish troops under the command of Ömer Naji Bey were also present, as well as a German officer.[13] After the rejection of Naji's ultimatum to surrender, fighting began. The defenders were initially successful in mounting a counterattack and they advanced outside the walls, but they became cut off from the village. The Syriacs lost many dead, but even the leader of the Salihan Kurds, Muhammed Amar, was killed. After this the Kurds became confused and the attackers disappeared, saying that they would return after they had buried their dead. Hostilities resumed and continued into November, when a general amnesty was negotiated with the government for the few remaining defended villages. After some weeks, the Syriacs began to return to their villages. The authorities, however, waited for a time to pay the Basibrin villagers back for taking the soldiers' weapons. Their revenge came in the spring of 1917, when the village headman, Malke, was captured and burned. Three months after Malke's death, half of the remaining Syriacs was massacred by their neighbors led by Awgin and the Kurdish tribes Salihan and Dumanan. The only Christians who survived were twenty families who had placed themselves under the patronage of Awgin.[14] **H, A**

Baspin (Besbine, Bespen). This Chaldean village had 200 inhabitants. It is located about 40 kilometers east of Jezire. Bohtan Kurds destroyed it.[15]

Bayaza (Beyaza). The village of Bayaza, near Nisibin, was owned by the families of Malke Sumoko from Zaz and Rohom from Hebob. A neighboring Kurdish chieftain, Ahmed Yusef of the Kaskan clan, summoned the Syriac village headman Malke. The leading Christian men of the

---

[13] Fehmi Bar Gello, *Seifo: Trakasserier och folkmord 1914 i Tur-Abdin* (2000), 41.

[14] Armalto, *Al-Qusara*, 394; Gabriele Yonan, *Ein vergessener Holocaust: Die Vernichtung der christlichen Assyrer in der Türkei* (1989), 280–82; A. H. B., "Mémoires sur Mardine," 188–89; Gawriye Beth Mas'ud, interviewed July 2002 (appendix 1, no. 58).

[15] Ternon, "Mardin 1915," 369.

owner-families followed their headman, and they were ambushed and killed at Lake Qiro near the village of Duger. Kurds from the neighboring villages of Sehya, Gutbe, Grisur, and others combined to attack Bayaza. They slaughtered and plundered in the village. Thirty persons survived by hiding in underground tunnels. They fled to the mountains. **H**

Bazar (Pazar). In Bazar, near Basibrin, lived 10 Syriac families. They were escorted to Basibrin by Syriac leaders. **H**

Bekhaire (Bkhireh, Bekéri, Buherki). Bekhaire is one hour by foot south of Mardin. The Agha Petros list stated that 200 Syriacs and Chaldeans resided here. The village belonged to the nearby Za'faran monastery. When news of the massacres came, the abbot asked the neighboring and usually friendly chief of the Omeran Kurds, Khalil Ghazale, to protect the village and asked whether extra guards from Mardin would be needed. The Kurdish chief said that extra guards would not be necessary and swore a solemn oath to protect the village and its inhabitants. However, Khalil Ghazale at some point was persuaded—Armalto states he was tricked—to collaborate with the provincial government. The mayor of Mardin apparently threatened him with death and loss of property, so he participated in the attack on Benebil. After returning from plundering that village, he invited the villagers of Bekhaire to eat with him. He then said that they should prepare to go to the monastery and that he and his men would provide an escort. But when they reached a deep well named Bir Mammo, he had 15 of the males killed and thrown into the well and kept the women as captives. Most of the women fled later to the monastery. According to Simon, 100 Christians from this village were slaughtered on June 2, 1915. This date seems to be too early, as Armalto indicates that the attack took place after the middle of June.[16] **Q**

Bekind (Bikin, Pékionde). Bekind was a village near Sa'irt with 85 Nestorian households and 80 Chaldeans. The inhabitants were exterminated in the massacres in June 1915 at the nearby town of Sa'irt. See the section on Sa'irt below.

Benebil (Banabil, Bülbül). Benebil is 10 kilometers east of Mardin. The village takes its name from the Byzantine fortress of Benabelon. According to Qarabash, 150 Syriac families lived here. There were two parish churches, the Mor Quryaqos and the Mort Shmuni. A pogrom occurred here on November 9, 1895. In 1915, news of massacres of Christians arrived in the middle of June when a few who escaped from nearby Ma'sarte

---

[16] Simon, *Mardine*, 134; Armalto, *Al-Qusara*, 425–27; A. H. B., "Mémoires sur Mardine," 181–82.

and Bafayya sought refuge. The villagers expected an attack and sent the women and children to Za'faran monastery while the men took their weapons and spread out in their orchards and vineyards. Various dates are given for the start of the siege: June 9 (Qarabash), June 10 (A. H. B.) and for the first battle: June 17 (Simon), June 30 (Armalto). There was a large gathering of tribes. At first, the village was surrounded by Ghamrian Kurds from Mahmoudkiye and the Reshmel Muhallemi. These made camp on the top of a hill overlooking Benebil. The Christians made contact with the Omeran Kurdish leader, Khalil Ghazale, who had promised to protect them. The Omeran sent 60 Kurdish warriors to protect the villagers. Also, a contingent of 18 Ottoman soldiers arrived and said that they had been ordered to protect Benebil. However, the Christians remained suspicious. The next day, the Kurds assaulted the village. Armalto states that the number of aggressors was 10,000 and speaks of 20 tribal chiefs and the presence of Bedouins. Qarabash, who observed from the roof of Za'faran monastery, states that the number was 5,000. Shooting began, and the soldiers, instead of protecting the village, joined the aggressors. However, the Omeran Kurds headed by Khalil Ghazale kept their promise and fought on the side of the Christians. The militia appealed to Khalil to help them instead, but he refused. Then Khalil received a written order purporting to come from Qaddur Jalabi, the mayor of Mardin and leader of the militia, that anyone who protected Christians would lose their property and be executed, but that those who killed Christians would enjoy the favor of the government. According to Armalto, Khalil saved this document and Armalto had seen it, and from that moment the Christians no longer had protection. Many of the Benebil villagers began to run and escaped to Za'faran, but many were murdered on the way. When they arrived at the monastery, the Ottoman guards refused to let them through the gateway, so three men climbed over the fortified walls. The chief of the guards, Nuri Badlisi, was angered and seized the three men and sent them to prison in Mardin, where they were sent on to Diyarbekir for execution. The other Benebil men, about 70, left the monastery and hid in caves for a few days and then returned and hid in a building in Benebil. One day they were discovered and attacked by Kurds, but they managed to shoot their way back to the monastery and were able to enter after bribing the guards with 35 liras. They remained for three months, paying further bribes each month. Later, a new chief of guards arrested them and sent them to Mardin, where they did slave labor for the government during harvest time. When harvesting was over, most of them were killed.[17] **Q**

Ben-Kelbe (Binkelb). Ben-Kelbe is one of the northernmost villages in Tur Abdin, being 22 kilometers north of Midyat. There were 35 Syriac families living here in a tract that was predominantly Kurdish already by the nineteenth century. Two Kurdish clan leaders lived in the village: Izzeddin, who was chief of the Tammero clan (part of the Jizbini tribe) and the Dakshuri confederation, and Shamdin from the clan of Hasan Shamdin. These clans were feuding with each other, and even the Syriacs were split in support of one or the other of the Kurdish clans. When the massacres broke out, Izzeddin took his closest Syriac allies and their family-members out of the village and escorted them to 'Ayn-Wardo. Shamdin did the same for his clients. But the rest of the Syriacs remained in the village and they were murdered. **H, A**

Benkof (Bingov). Benkof was a Chaldean village of 110 persons in the Sai'rt diocese. The villagers were exterminated in the massacres at Sa'irt. See the section on Sa'irt below.

Berke (Bir-ke). Berke had 120 Chaldean inhabitants. As part of the Sa'irt diocese, the villagers were annihilated at massacres there. See the section on Sa'irt below.

Berke (Peirik). Berke is in the Chaldean diocese of Jezire about 10 kilometers south of the town. It was massacred by the Esene Kurds.[18]

Beshiri (Bshiriyye, Zarjel, Beşiri). Beshiri was is a Syriac Orthodox enclave east of Diyarbekir. The administrative capital was Almedina, where 200 Syriacs lived. In the surrounding villages of the kaza were 4,690 Syriacs in 27 villages, plus 2,000 in 15 villages in nearby Bafaya nahiya.[19] The Syriac bishop resided in Mor Quryakos, Dera Kera. Very little is known of events in this tract, but attacks by Rama and Hazini Kurds were widespread in the autumn of 1914 and authorities replaced the kaymakam for passivity.[20] Much later, the substitute kaymakam of Beshiri, Ali Sabit es-Süveydi, was assassinated on the orders of the vali for refusing to implement the anti-Christian repression.[21] Qarabash records that a contingent of 70 Christian

---

[17] Armalto, *Al-Qusara*, 428; Rhétoré, *"Les Chrétiens aux bêtes"*, 120; Simon, *Mardine*, 136; A. H. B., "Mémoires sur Mardine," 179–82.

[18] Ternon, "Mardin 1915," 369.

[19] The names and population of these villages are given in appendix 2 below.

[20] BOA. DH. ŞFR 45/205 Ministry of Interior to Diyarbekir vilayet October 8, 1914.

[21] Abidin Nesimi, *Yılların İçinden* [During the years] (1977), 37; Nejdet Bilgi, *Dr. Mehmed Reşid Şahingiray'ın Hayatı ve Hâtıraları: İttihâd ve Terakki Dönemi ve Ermeni Me-*

captives from Beshiri was liquidated in the village of Sa'diye close to Diyarbekir. **Q**

Beth-Debe (Badibe, Dibek, Daskan). Beth-Debe lies on the top of Izlo Mountain northeast of Nisibin. At the start of the massacres there were 40 families here, but they were reinforced by refugees from many other places, among them 20 families from Sederi and 20 families from Kharabe-Mishka, and those who came from Nisibin's neighborhood. Sarokhano Agha, the temporary leader of the Chelebi fraction of the Haverkan Kurds, came and gave information, weapons, and ammunition. The villagers built defensive barriers. The night before the attack was planned, Sarokhano Agha sent information about it to the Syriacs. It was early in August, and the Kurdish tribes were the Hajo, Ali Batte, Doman, Chumaran, Dayre, Surgechi, Bunusra, Omaran, and Alike. Qaddur Bey also came with the Nisibin militia. The defenders at Beth-Debe received 100 armed men as reinforcements from Mor Malke monastery. Hard fighting went on for 15 days and nights, but the Kurds could not win, and the Kurdish losses were greater than those of the Syriacs. The Kurds retreated by the holiday of Saint Mary, which was celebrated in the middle of August. The Syriac losses were 18 deaths; of the Kurds, 30 deaths. When the Kurds went away, the Syriacs in Beth-Debe continued to the Mor Malke monastery. **H**

Birguriya (Balaban). Birguriya is 40 kilometers east of Nisibin along the road to Jezire. The name is derived from the Syriac word for well, *biro*. There were 5 Syriac families living in Birguriya. All of them were murdered by Kurds from Kfar-Gawze. **H, A**

Boqusyono (Bekusyono, Bakısyan, Bagssian, Kustan). Boqusyono lies half an hour by foot north of Hah. About 120 Syriac families lived here, and there were no Muslims. The villagers were escorted to Hah by a friendly Kurdish chief, Hajo of the Kurtak clan. They stayed in Hah for the whole war. After seven years, they returned to their village through the intermediary of Chelebi Agha of the Haverkan confederation, who had been in prison throughout the war. **H**

Bote (Boti, Bardakçı). Bote is a large village about 2 hours' walk north of Midyat. In it lived 300 Syriac Orthodox, 10 Syriac Catholic, and 15 Kurdish families. The village was famous for its pottery. The church of Mor Afrem is built like a fortress and was the traditional place of refuge from attack. The agha of the village was Saleh of the Dakshuri tribe. On July 4,

---

selesi [Dr. M. R. S.'s life and memory: The CUP period and the Armenian Questions] (1997), 34.

the authorities in Midyat sent 20 soldiers to guard the village. The soldiers took over the Syriac Catholic church and used it as their headquarters and barracks. After 6 days, the villagers occupied the church to induce the soldiers to leave. Instead, they called for reinforcements, who surrounded Bote. According to Armalto, these Kurds were Jamil and Nejim, the sons of Osman, the owner of Bote. These invaded the village, which was unprepared for defense. They stormed both the Syriac Orthodox and the Catholic churches and destroyed their outer walls. The Syriacs hid within the church itself. The church was besieged for 13 days, and the people in it had very little food. A few people managed to escape through a tunnel leading from the church and fled to 'Ayn-Wardo to get help. 150 partisans came from 'Ayn-Wardo to attack the Turkish-Kurdish forces from the rear. The beseigers fled after some losses, and the 'Ayn-Wardo warriors rushed to free the people in the church. However, it proved difficult to open the church door, and the Muslims returned to surround Bote; the 'Ayn-Wardo partisans retreated. About 70 of those in the church fled through the tunnel. Those in the church gave up and opened the door, hoping that the promises of personal safety they were given by the Turks were true. But they were tied together. One woman told of the people who were hiding in the tunnel: the enemy set fires in the entrances, and those inside died of the smoke. The others who were captured were taken outside the village and killed.[22] **H**

Boz-Pinar (Bospinar, Bos-Pouar, Beşpınar˙). Boz-Pinar was a small Syriac village of 50 inhabitants in the Anbart River valley southeast of Diyarbekir. Along with inhabitants of several other villages, the males of this village were slaughtered on May 7, 1915. The women and children were put to forced agricultural work. The massacre was perpetrated by one of the Al-Khamsin militias at the instigation of the owner of the villages, Qasem Bey. According to testimony of survivors, 114 men from these villages were killed. After the agricultural season was finished, the women and children had to convert to Islam or be killed. **Q**

Brahemiye (Abrahamiya, Ibrahimie). Brahemiye is 5 hours' walk southwest of Mardin and close to Tel-Arman. Agha Petros listed the Christian population before the war as 400 persons, and A. H. B. stated that it contained 60 families. It was mainly a Syriac Catholic village, but there were some recent Protestant converts also. Most of the inhabitants fled to Tel-Arman in late June, where they sought refuge in the Armenian Catholic

---

[22] Armalto, *Al-Qusara*, 410; appendix 1 below, section H, nos. 48–53.

Church building.²³ Simon recorded that the massacre took place there on June 25, 1915.²⁴

Chanaqchi (Tjanakji, Tschanaqtschi, Çarıklıfabrikasköyü). Chanaqchi was a Syriac village of 100 inhabitants in the Hawar River district near Diyarbekir. On May 3, 1915, a death squad led by Shakir Bey, with members of the Rama tribe headed by Ömer, perpetrated a massacre on the adult males of the many small villages here. The village males were collected in Chanaqchi and then taken to a pit near the village of Hawar-Dejla, where they were shot. Those from these villages who were murdered numbered 164, "all notable, strong, and rich men." **Q**

Charukhiye (Tjarugiye). Charukhiye was a Syriac and Chaldean village along the Tigris River south of Diyarbekir. On June 2, 1915, a detachment of the Al-Khamsin militia arrived from Diyarbekir under the command of Yahya Effendi. The soldiers surrounded the village and let no one out. In the evening they invaded the village and seized 35 men, who were all that were there. They were roped together and told they would be taken away to construct roads. When they arrived at the village of Gülla, the soldiers played a game of seeing whether one bullet could kill five men if they were standing behind each other. In this way, all were murdered. The women and children fled to the Chaldean Church in Diyarbekir. **Q**

Chelik (Çelik). Chelik is located 15 kilometers north of Kfar-Borna on the west bank of the Tigris River. It was very isolated and could be reached only by footpath. The Christians here spoke Kurdish, and it was the home base of the Kurdish Rammo tribal leader Mustafa Agha. In the mid nineteenth century, there were a reported 400 to 500 Syriac Orthodox living there. However, Hinno states that by the time of the massacres only 20 Syriac families remained; Agha Petros listed 100 Christian inhabitants. They were murdered by the Ali Rammo tribe.²⁵ **H, A**

Chemchem (Shim-Shim). This Syriac village of 800 inhabitants is within the kaza of Lije, northwest of Diyarbekir. A massacre took place here some time before the middle of July 1915.²⁶

---

[23] Ternon, "Mardin 1915," 160.
[24] Rhétoré, *"Les Chrétiens aux bêtes"*, 120; Simon, *Mardine*, 137.
[25] See also Useve Wardo, interviewed October 1997 (appendix 1, no. 41); Hanna Polos, interviewed November 1993 (appendix 1, no. 42).
[26] Joseph Naayem, *Les Assyro-Chaldéens et les Arméniens massacrés par les Turcs: Documents inédits recueillis par un témoin oculaire* (1920), 169–76.

Cherang. Cherang was a small Syriac village in the Anbart river area near Diyarbekir. Along with inhabitants of several other villages, the males of this village were slaughtered on May 7/20, 1915. The women and children were put to forced agricultural work. The massacre was perpetrated by one of the Al-Khamsin death squads at the instigation of the owner of the village, Qasem Bey. According to testimony of survivors, 114 men from these villages were killed. After the agricultural season was finished, the women and children had to convert to Islam or die. **Q**

Dara (Oğuz). Dara is located 23 kilometers southeast of Mardin. Situated on a ridge, it had been founded as a fortress during the reign of the Roman Emperor Anastasius on the main road between Mardin and Nisibin. The fort was already in ruins long before World War I, and the town had declined to insignificance. Dara is not included in the Agha Petros list. Dara was a town with 150 Catholic Armenians, who lived in a sector in the western part of town. The total Christian population was larger, as A. H. B. stated that there were also 120 Syriac Catholic families living there. Before the government's anti-Christian policies had become obvious, one of several interim mutasarrifs, the criminal court judge Halil Adib, sent the Al-Khamsin militia to Dara. The Christian heads of household were assembled and told that they had to leave Dara to do labor for the army. They were marched to a deep well about half an hour from the village. There they were murdered and the bodies thrown in the well. One person escaped and came to Bekhaire and told his story. This event took place on June 14, 1915. Simon recorded that 30 Armenian villagers had been killed.[27] **Q, A**

Darakli (Deragli). Darakli is a village half an hour by foot from Qarabash in a rural area near Diyarbekir. The Agha Petros list indicated that 50 Assyro-Chaldeans lived in this village. On April 22, villagers from Qarabash fled from a massacre and barricaded themselves in the houses of Darakli. The Kurds attacked this village and killed all they could get their hands on. A few persons escaped in the middle of the night and avoided the slaughter. **Q**

Dashta-Dere (Deştadarı). Dashta-Dere is 13 kilometers east of Azakh. Twenty Syriac families lived there, but all were killed. Kurds moved into the village and kept many Christian captives. In October 1915, Syriac warriors from Azakh invaded the village to release the hostages.[28] **H**

---

[27] Armalto, *Al-Qusara*, 417; Simon, *Mardine*, 136; A. H. B., "Mémoires sur Mardine," 111.

[28] Hannouche, *Azekh*, 66.

Dayro da Şlibo (Dersalip, Bethil, Çatalçam). The monastery in Dayro da Şlibo is one of the best known in Tur Abdin. The name means "the monastery of the Cross." The monastery complex and the village nearby are situated 2 hours by foot north of Hah on the slope of Mount Eloyo, halfway between Zaz and Kfar-Boran. At one time it had been the residence of a bishop of Hah, and therefore it had hundreds of rooms and a good well for water, but it was no longer a bishop's residence at the time of the massacres. Besides the monastery there was a village with 70 Syriac families. When the news of the massacres arrived, the villagers moved into the monastery with their valuables and animals and food supply. The monastery was surrounded by Kurds from the the area, among them the Chelik clan of the Ali Rammo tribe led by Mustafa, the Sa'irt, the Beth-Shiroye, the Rama, as well as some Ottoman troops. Hinno's witnesses state that the aggressors totaled 15,000 men. On the first assault against the monastery, 30 Syriacs were killed, but the Kurds could not force the walls. There were several other assaults with ladders, but even these were fought back with large losses for the aggressors. One of the Kurdish leaders, Mustafa of the Ali Rammo, came and said that he would withdraw since he had seen miraculous visions emerging from the monastery and was frightened. After the Rammo left, the other Kurdish tribes melted away. The battle for the monastery had lasted 3 months. At this point in time, Shaykh Fathulla of 'Ayn-Kif arrived with people from 'Ayn-Wardo, and they convinced the Turkish troops, who had remained in place after the Kurds disappeared, also to leave the area. But the Turkish officer, a major, would not leave until the defenders had given up their weapons, which they refused to do, so the major prepared for a new assault. Shaykh Fathulla made contact with the provincial government in Diyarbekir and complained about the major. The major was issued orders to obey the Shaykh and to withdraw with his troops, which he then did. The Syriacs in Dayro da Şlibo continued to live in fear of new attacks for the remainder of the war. They did not dare leave the village even to tend their fields. Those few who had done so had been killed or never returned. The government stationed 40 soldiers with the duty to protect the villagers from attack on the part of the Kurds. The soldiers stood guard when the villagers tended the fields or went to other villages to buy food. However, the soldiers obviously did not care much for this duty. On one occasion, they informed some Kurds of a planned trip to buy food in another village, and these Kurds ambushed the Syriacs and murdered 7 men but spared the women. When the people of Dayro da Şlibo heard of this, they chased the soldiers away. After a period of time, conditions appeared to have become normal, but a local Kurd, Ali Sagfan of Harmes, collected neighboring tribesmen and attacked the village at night and succeeded in occupying the monastery complex. A few villagers managed to escape. Those who were in the village were forced to the square, where they were burned alive in a large fire. Only 30 people survived, because they were outside the village at the time of the assault.[29] **H, A**

Dehok (Dihouk). Dehok was a village with 66 Nestorian households and 146 Chaldeans. As part of the Sa'irt diocese, the villagers were killed during the massacres that took place in early June 1915. See the section on Sa'irt below.

Dentass (Dantas, Dintass). Dentass had a mixed population with 18 Nestorian households and 80 Chaldeans. The villagers were killed in the Sa'irt massacres of June 1915. See section on Sa'irt below.

Der-Eliya (Chiftlik, Cheftelek, Tchifitlik, Çiftlik). Der-Eliya is about 3 kilometers south of Mardin. It had a Syriac Orthodox parish church dedicated to Saint Theodore. The Agha Petros list indicated that 200 Syriacs lived here in 1914, and A. H. B. wrote that there were 30 Christian families.[30] There is no specific information about the fate of this village, but all of the neighboring Christian villages were wiped out in June 1915.

Derike (Derké, Direk, Derik). Derike is an administrative town between Mardin and Viranshehir. Agha Petros listed 500 Syriac or Chaldean inhabitants; Tfinkdji stated that the Chaldean congregation numbered 40. On November 10, 1895, Kurds attempted to plunder Derike but were prevented by Ottoman soldiers. However, Simon recorded that on August 11, 1915, the entire Christian population, which included both Syriacs and Armenians, totaling more than 1,000 persons, was massacred.[31] Armalto stated that before the massacres the town was populated with 250 Armenian, Syriac, and Protestant families.[32]

Rhétoré informs us that the kaymakam, whose name is yet unknown, refused to cooperate in the anti-Christian operation. He insisted that Reshid show him a written order from the government, and Reshid requested his presence in Diyarbekir for that purpose. On the way the kaymakam was murdered, and Reshid cast the blame on the Armenians.[33]

---

[29] Armalto, *Al-Qusara*, 394.
[30] A. H. B., "Mémoires sur Mardine," 111.
[31] Simon, *Mardine*, 140.
[32] Armalto, *Al-Qusara*, 343.
[33] Rhétoré, *"Les Chrétiens aux bêtes"*, 46.

Armalto gives information gathered from a survivor named Gabriel Qas'e. On Monday, May 24, 1915, the vali, Reshid Bey, sent a delegate and two officers to Derike. He called the Armenian and Protestant priests to a meeting. This became a confrontation in which the priests expressed concern over the on-going killing, plundering, and atrocities. When they had returned to their churches, the delegate summoned seven Armenian Catholic notables. On arrival, these persons were accused of having hidden weapons, and they were mistreated when they denied that they had any arms. They were badly beaten; some were close to death when they were carried back to their homes. The delegate and the two officers returned to Diyarbekir two days later.

The local authorities summoned the Christian notables again. Again they were questioned about hidden weapons. Several were thrown into jail and subjected to beatings and torture. They were then called up and extorted: "We have orders to kill all of you. But those who can pay fifty liras can go free. Those who do not will be killed." Some who paid were liberated, but the others remained. One of the Ottoman judicial officials began to defend the Christians, but he was deposed by the vali.

On June 7, Touma Bahhe, a leading Armenian Catholic, was arrested together with several other Christians. Soldiers broke into the Armenian Catholic church, seized documents, and arrested the priest. They also searched the Syriac Catholic church and led the priest, Ibrahim Kuroum, by a rope arround his neck to town hall. He was forced to crawl on hands and knees with one of his tormenters on his back, while the others kicked and stabbed him and finally hacked him to pieces. On June 8, authorities arrested the Protestant priest Johannes and the schoolteacher Ibrahim. At sunset a show trial was held of the Armenian Catholic priest Andraos, and he was beaten badly before being thrown back into his cell. Then the turn came of the Syriac priest Sa'id, who was also beaten. Touma Bahhe received ninety lashes of the whip. According to Armalto, the Christians remained in prison for eight days, during which beatings and torture were daily occurences. On Sunday, June 20, the victims were taken in groups of ten to a place near Khawarouk, where they were tortured once again and then murdered.

A few remaining priests in the prison were murdered by their guards on June 27. However, that very day an officer arrived from Diyarbekir and announced that amnesty had been declared. The surviving Christians began to relax their guard, but the same evening, gangs in the streets began to grab any male Christians they found and take them to the prison. On June 28, one of the CUP deputies from Diyarbekir, sent by Reshid Bey, arrived. He began to interrogate the prisoners. They were roped together and taken to Zinare Sa'our and one other place, where they were slain. After this new decimation, only 23 men remained in the prison; 16 were set free after they paid their guards bribes of up to fifty liras. Some of those released were soon rearrested and killed despite having paid the enormous bribes. A small number of Christian artisans had never been arrested because they were not leading members of their communities and because they manufactured equipment necessary for the army. But during the feasts at the end of Ramadan, many of these artisans were seized and taken on the road to Farashiya, where they were slaughtered. In August, on the third feast day of Ramadan, Christian women and girls were marched out to a place identified as Gorta and were murdered there.

Der-Qube (Derkube, Dirkup, Karagöl). Der-Qube is very close to the large village of Hah, on a steep slope. Ten Syriac families lived in Der-Qube. Agha Hajo of the Kurtak clan escorted them to Hah. **H**

Der Shemsh (Der-Chemsch). Der Shemsh was a Chaldean village of 40 persons. It was in the Sa'irt diocese, and the inhabitants were killed in the great massacres at that town. See the section on Sa'irt below.

Deyr-Bashur. Deyr-Bashur was a small Syriac village in the Hawar river district near Diyarbekir. On May 3, a force of 150 militiamen led by Shakir Bey and members of the Kurdish Rama tribe headed by Ömer perpetrated a massacre on the adult males. The village males were collected in Chanaqchi and then taken to a pit near the village Hawar-Dejla, where they were shot. Those from these villages who were slain numbered 164, reputedly "all notable, strong, and rich men." **Q**

Deyr-Elayta (Deir-Elaia, Derajuri). This Chaldean village with a monastery had 400 inhabitants. It is located north of Jezire near the Tigris River. The Bohtan Kurds attacked the village.[34]

Deyr-Takhtayta (Deir-Tahtaia, Derajiri). This Chaldean village and monastery had 300 inhabitants. It is north of Jezire along the Tigris. The Bohtan Kurds destroyed the village.[35]

Deyr-Zor (Deir Zor). Deyr-Zor is a town in Syria along the Euphrates River on the edge of the desert. It had grown very rapidly at the end of the nineteenth century out of a small village. At the beginning of the twentieth century it had roughly 25,000 inhabitants, who were mostly Kurds.[36] Many

---

[34] Ternon, "Mardin 1915," 369.
[35] Ibid.
[36] Mark Sykes, "Journeys in North Mesopotamia" (1907), 394; Armalto, *Al-*

of the Christians were Armenian, Syriac, and Chaldean merchants who had moved south from Mardin. Each congregation had its own church and priest.

Deyr-Zor was to be the final destination for many columns of Christian deportees from all over Anatolia. Most of those who were deported in May to July died on the way and never arrived, but by August and September, deportees actually began to come through in sizable numbers. Rhétoré reckoned that as of November 1916 there were 160,000 deportees from Marash, 'Ayntab, Konya, Bursa, Ankara, and Sivas (chiefly women and children) staying in and around the town. Jalal ed-Din, the governor of this area, was universally praised for his humanity, but he was replaced in 1916 and a reign of terror began. Thus the original inhabitants of the town witnessed the treatment of the Armenians and Syriacs who arrived there. Orders were given in early 1916 that the "government will consider as outlaw anyone who gave lodging to the Armenians." After this, the local Christians did not dare to take in the refugees, who were then placed in tent camps or were slaughtered. About 15,000 Armenians came to the nearly village of Shahdadde, where soldiers shot them, saving only some attractive women and children who were held as captives. The reason given for the extermination of the camps was the need to contain an outbreak of typhoid fever.[37]

Dirhab. One Syriac family lived in Dirhab, a Kurdish village east of Nisibin. It was exterminated. **H**

Diyarbekir. See chapter 6 above.

Dufne (Difne, Üçyol). Dufne lies east of Hasankeyf on the southern bank of the Tigris River. This was the site of the Byzantine fortress Daphnoudis. Between Dufne and Hasno lie the ruins of a monastery. Dufne was a rich village that used irrigation from the river for growing cotton. Kurds from the Rama tribe under the leadership of Amin Ahmad attacked the Syriacs of Dufne, took them captive to the river, murdered them, and threw the bodies in the water. Only 6 people survived the massacres of Dufne. **H, A**

Duger (Duker, Dougueur, Dagra). Duger is located 20 kilometers east of Nisibin. This was a village with 50 Syriac and 4 or 5 Muslim families. Agha Petros listed the Christian population as 300. A Kurd named Muhammed Abbas owned the village. Most of the villagers were from Hebob in Tur Abdin. Because this was a friendly Kurdish village, many Christians

---

Qusara, 364.
[37] Rhétoré, *"Les Chrétiens aux bêtes"*, 165.

hid from the authorities here. Qaddur Bey sent 15 of his militiamen to attack Duger and the surrounding villages of Bayaze, Ger-Sheran, Mharka, Tel-Jihan, Qewetla, Helwa, and Siha. Together with Kurds, the militiamen captured all of the men who had remained in the village. Some were roped together and marched to the nearby village of Helwa, where they were killed and their bodies thrown into the river. Others were killed at nearby Lake Qiro. The priest had been murdered on the way, because he was old and could not walk so far. The women were assembled and taken to the Kurdish village of Nisran, where they met their deaths.[38] **H, Q**

'Emerin (Amirin, Ömerin). 'Emerin is 23 kilometers east of Azakh. Hinno states that there were 250 Syriac and some Chaldean families. The Agha Petros list attributed 300 inhabitants to the village. A Syriac landlord named Malke Rasho owned it. On June 1, 1915, the Esene, Mammi, and 'Alikan Kurds captured nearly all of the Christians.[39] Fifteen families managed to survive because a Kurdish shaykh, 'Abde from Batelle, protected them and escorted them to Azakh.[40] **H**

Esfes (Hespest, Isfis, Yarbaşı). Esfes is an old Christian settlement on a cliffside 9 kilometers north of Azakh. Close by are the ruins of a fourth-century Roman frontier fortress. Three hundred Syriac families lived in the village, and it had 5 priests. The Kurdish tribes of Ömerkan, 'Alikan, and Dörekan attacked the village on June 6, 1915. The village managed to withstand the agressors, and an Al-Khamsin detachment arrived saying it would shield the Christians. Instead, the militia also fired on the villagers. After three days, the priest 'Abdallahad Jebbo managed to bribe the militia commander with gold coins and a pocketwatch, to let the villagers flee to Azakh. As they went, they could see the village being plundered and burned.[41] The abandoned village was destroyed. **H, A**

Fum (Foum). This Syriac village of 700 is in the kaza of Lije northwest of Diyarbekir. The massacre occurred before the middle of July 1915.[42]

Garisa (Garisan, Garessa). Garisa is just over 10 kilometers east of Azakh. In fear of massacre, the twenty families fled to Azakh in April

---

[38] Gawriye Maqsi-Hanna Hamra, interviewed November 1997 (appendix 1, no. 70).
[39] Ternon, "Mardin 1915," 369.
[40] Hannouche, *Azekh*, 63.
[41] Ibid., 41, 60.
[42] Naayem, *Assyro-Chaldéens*, 169–76.

1915.[43] After the siege was raised, they did not return but instead left for Mosul. **H**

Gerdahol. In Gerdahol, east of Nisibin, lived 20 Syriac families, and the rest were Kurds. The Christians had heard of the on-going massacres and fled to the mountains at night. **H**

Gerke-Shamo (Guirke Châmou, Kergue-Chamo). Gerke-Shamo is 20 kilometers east of Nisibin. Here lived 35 families who were new colonists originating from Hebob. The Agha Petros list indicated that 450 Christians lived in the village. The owner was Mushel Quryo. Hinno stated that the inhabitants managed to flee to Hebob before an attack could take place. Qarabash, however, stated that all of the villagers were killed in a coordinated attack of Al-Khamsin militia under lieutenant Qaddur Bey and the Dakshuri Kurds in the second half of June 1915. **H, Q**

Gershiran (Gerchiran). Gershiran is near Nisibin. Agha Petros listed the Christian population as 400 persons. The owner, Suleyman Abbas, saved the Christians here. **Q**

Gidyanes (Guèdyanes). Gidyanes was a Chaldean village with a population of 55 in the Sa'irt diocese. Its congregation was massacred in connection with the large massacres at Sa'irt in June 1915. See the section on Sa'irt below.

Girefshe. Most of the 40 Syriac families who colonized Girefshe originated in Arbo. The owner was Jallo Hanna. The inhabitants managed to flee with their property and cattle to Mor Malke monastery. **H**

Giremira (Girmira). Giremira is 20 kilometers northeast of Nisibin. It had 70 Syriac and 10 Kurdish families. They managed to flee in time. **H**

Gösli. Gösli is a village near Diyarbekir with 300 Syriac inhabitants. On May 3/16, 1915, all of the adult Christian males were killed by soldiers of the Al-Khamsin militia led by Shakir Bey and some of the Rama tribe. Some of the women and children managed to flee to safety in Diyarbekir, and others were abducted. **Q**

Goliye (Göllü, Qesor, Kesor). Goliye is 7 kilometers south of Mardin along the main road. Until the late nineteenth century, this was a purely Christian village with 3 churches. It was subjected to a pogrom in November 1895. It had a very large Christian population. According to Qarabash, all of the villagers were Syriac Orthodox and had 400 households, but A. H. B. states that there were 500 or 550 Syriac Catholic families living here, Rhétoré recorded that there were 3,000 Christian residents, and Agha Pet-

---

[43] Hannouche, *Azekh*, 40.

ros listed 1,500 Syriac Orthodox and Chaldeans. The Protestant missionaries in Mardin were also active in the village. Qarabash states that on June 14/27, 1915, about 5,000 Kurds and Arabs "from the desert and mountains" prepared to attack. Armalto gives the date as July 2, 1915, and identifies the aggressor tribes as the Milli, Dakuri, Mersani, Kiki, Khalyi, Arbani, Mishkeni, Sevaraki, Derkavi, and Danbali coming from the west and the Afs, Ghara, and Sheykhan from the mountains. The Baghara, Khar'ayna, and Harb Arab tribes were also said to be present. 120 militiamen had already been posted, allegedly to protect the Christians. At first the soldiers did protect the village and fired back at the Kurds, but then they quickly changed sides and helped in the assault. A. H. B. and Armalto identify the instigators as Youssef Badlisi, the head of the militia, and Mohammed Bey, a chief of the Milli Kurds. The village was plundered and people were killed in their homes. For 8 days, fires raged in the village. Fire and smoke from the massacre could be seen from the roofs of houses in Mardin. A few escaped to Mardin. A Turkish official from Diyarbekir was sent to investigate the damage, and he reported that he found 1,700 corpses. He also identified Shaykh Ramadan as a leading plunderer. According to Simon, about 30 Syriac Catholics and some Syriac Orthodox villagers were able to save themselves, but there were 3,200 deaths. A few hundred survivors fled and were given shelter by Agha Halilo, in the nearby Kurdish village of Tomik, until the war was over.[44] **Q, A**

Grebya. Grebya is 20 kilometers east of Nisibin. The villagers of Grebya were saved by their Kurdish Agha, Hassan, who escorted them to Hebob. **H**

Gueratel. Gueratel was a village with 100 Chaldeans in the Sa'irt diocese. They were annihilated in the massacres that took place in early June. See the section on Sa'irt below.

Guerektha d'Badro (Guirguébadro, Guircnébédro). This Chaldean village is in the kaza of Jezire in the plain of Silopi. According to the Agha Petros list, 800 Syriacs lived here, while Tfinkdji counted 600. Suleiman Ismael and the Aghas of Şirnak and Silopi attacked on July 3, 1915. It was the festival day of St. Thomas the Apostle, and most villagers were slaughtered inside the church.[45]

Habses (Habsus, Hapisnas, Mercimekli). Habses lies 7 kilometers northwest of Midyat on a ridge. Here lived more than 100 Syriac families in

---

[44] Rhétoré, *"Les Chrétiens aux bêtes"*, 122–24; Simon, *Mardine*, 137; A. H. B., "Mémoires sur Mardine," 111, 178; Armalto, *Al-Qusara*, 432..

[45] Ternon, "Mardin 1915," 369; Rhétoré, *"Les Chrétiens aux bêtes"*, 320.

1915. On June 11, Kurds from the Rama tribe attacked the village during the night, and the battle continued into the following day. Some villagers managed to get to Midyat and report the situation. Midyat's Jacobite leaders, Efrem and Hanne Safar, went to the kaymakam and appealed for help. Soldiers were sent to Habses. They chased the Rama tribesmen away, and 15 soldiers remained to guard the village. However, when fighting broke out in Midyat itself, a Yezidi herdsman in the employ of Aziz Agha was sent to Habses with a message of warning to expect a new attack. The villagers assembled, and most of them took their movable property and went to 'Ayn-Wardo. The guards and members of the Rama tribe murdered the nearly 200 persons who remained.[46] **H, A**

Hah (Anıtlı). Hah is a large, old settlement located 22 kilometers east of Midyat. Its Syriac Orthodox church, named Yoldath Aloho (Mother of God), was one of the largest, most ornate, and most ancient in Tur Abdin. It is dated to the sixth century. Historically (up to 613 and again in the eleventh to thirteenth centuries) it had been the seat of a bishop ruling over half of the Tur Abdin villages. Around Hah there are numerous ruins of religious buildings.[47] In Hah there was a very large old building known as King Yuhanon's palace, which was surrounded by high walls, and the Syriacs sought protection behind the walls. About 100 Syriac families lived here at the start of the massacres. The village headman, Rasho, traveled into the Armenian regions to the north to see for himself what was happening and was able to confirm the stories about the atrocities committed against the Armenians. When he returned, the Syriacs began to prepare to defend themselves. They strengthened the walls, built barricades, and collected food and water. Persons from other villages arrived, and at the height 2000 persons were behind the walls, and of them 200 were armed adult men. Before the fighting began, a local Kurdish chief, Hajo of the Kurtak clan, came and warned them of what was coming and that the authorities probably would keep him from protecting them. Hajo escorted the villagers of Boqusyono and Der-Qube to Hah. In the middle of August, Kurdish tribesmen and some Turkish soldiers surrounded Hah. Fighting went on day and night. The siege of Hah lasted 45 days. Shaykh Fathullah, the Muhallemi religious leader, came to Hah after he had negotiated the cease-fire at 'Ayn-Wardo, and he made a similar cease-fire at Hah. **H, A**

---

[46] Skandar Sha'o-Murad, interviewed July 1993 (appendix 1, no. 57).
[47] Hans Hollerweger, *Turabdin: Lebendiges Kulturerbe* (1999), 165–75.

Hanewiye (Hanaviye, Hané). Hanewiye is a village in the diocese of Jezire. The Agha Petros list indicated that 400 Christians lived here. The landlord was the Syriac Chalo family. It is believed that all were murdered.[48]

Harbol (Herbol, Herbul). This Chaldean village of 500 (Agha Petros) or 300 (Tfinkdji) is 40 kilometers east of Jezire and northeast of Silopi. Rachid Osman, the agha of Şirnak, protected the inhabitants and moved them to mountain villages.[49]

Hasno (Hesno-d Kifo, Hasankeyf). Hasno is situated on the Tigris River, where there is a centuries-old bridge. It is 60 kilometers north of Midyat and forms the northern gateway to Tur Abdin. Settlement in caves along the riverbank dated back to ancient times. Its name means Rock Fortress. The town was built around a Roman fortress, and there are many ruins in the surroundings. The population was a mix of Christians and Muslims. The oldest mosque was built in the fourteenth century. Until the sixteenth century, a Syriac Orthodox bishop resided in Hasno. Among the inhabitants were 500 Christians of the Syriac Orthodox, Armenian, and Protestant denominations. The killing in this village began on June 5, 1915, on an order from the Turkish officials in Midyat to Ahmad Mudir, the government official in Hasno. Other interviewees state that the leading official was instead Jalal Rumi, a Muhallemi CUP member from Mardin. Local Kurds also took part. Amin, the son of the Eshkafte tribal chief Hajji Abdalla, played a leading role. A hundred Turkish troops also participated. Hasno was an ancient fortress, so the Christians might have had a chance to defend themselves, but the government official opened the gates for the Kurdish tribesmen. The slaughter went on for many days. Some Syriacs and Armenians managed to flee to Midyat. Women who were left in the town threw themselves into the river from the fortress walls. No Christians remained in Hasno, and although some Syriacs survived as refugees elsewhere, the Armenians vanished without a trace. **H, A**

Hassana (Hassan, Hessanna, Hossana, Kösrali). Hassana is 30 kilometers east of Jezire in Bohtan. Originally Chaldean, it had a large but recent Protestant congregation. The 300 inhabitants who were tenants of the Aghas of Şirnak and Silopi, who belonged to the Rahman dynasty. The village was massacred, and the Presbyterian pastor and the Nestorian priest were murdered. Some of the survivors of the massacre found asylum in the nearby Kurdish village of Gerçulaye.[50]

---

[48] Hannouche, *Azekh*, 67.
[49] Ternon, "Mardin 1915," 369; Rhétoré, *"Les Chrétiens aux bêtes"*, 309.
[50] Report of E. W. McDowell to Board of Foreign Missions of the Presbyterian

Hawar-Dejla and **Hawar-Khase** (Huardahle and Huarkhaseh). Hawar-Dejla and Hawar-Khase were two Syriac villages, each with 50 inhabitants, in the Hawar River district near Diyarbekir. On May 3, 1915, a force of 150 men headed by Shakir Bey with an Al-Khamsin death squad and members of the Rama tribe headed by Ömer perpetrated a massacre on the adult males of the various small villages here. The village males were collected in Chanaqchi and then with men from other villages taken to a pit outside Hawar-Dejla, where they were shot. Those from these villages who were murdered numbered 164, "all notable, strong, and rich men." **Q**

Hebob (Ehwo, Habab, Güzelsu). Hinno states that he has his information from a person who was in Hebob at the time. Hebob is located 25 kilometers southeast of Midyat. At the time of the massacres, 50 Syriac families lived in Hebob, because many persons had already left the village for more defensible places. This village had two Christian churches, of which Mor-Sargis-Mor-Bakos was very large and easily defensible. Outside of Hebob was the Mor Eliyo monastery, built on a high hill and surrounded by high walls. When news of the massacres came, the inhabitants collected provisions and took cover in the churches. Refugees came to the Mor Eliyo Monastery from other villages and even from Midyat. Musa Asso from Midyat was elected head of the defense. Early in August, Kurdish tribes surrounded the Hebob church and the monastery. These clans were the Omariyan, Bunusra, Elyan, Apshe, and even some Yezidis from their villages Mhuka, Dasekha, and Bajenne. The battle lasted 15 days, but the attackers were unsuccessful. One of the Kurdish leaders was Hassan Hajo. The Syriacs actually captured Hajo plus some of his men. These were then released, and the Kurds lifted their siege. The Syriacs lost 4 men during the battles. **H**

Hedel (Hedil, Hidil). Hedel was 12 kilometers northwest of Azakh, near Esfes, with 22 Syriac families. The Syriac Hano Basuski was landlord. These people fled to Azakh, where they stayed until the massacres were over. **H**

Helwa (Hlule, Heloua, Hilwa, Lilan). Helwa was a newly settled village about 15 kilometers east of Nisibin. Here lived about 40 Syriac Orthodox families who had originated in Tur Abdin, from the villages of Hebob, Hah,

---

Church March 6, 1915, in James Bryce and Arnold Toynbee, *The Treatment of Armenians in the Ottoman Empire, 1915–1916* (1916), 211–12; August Thiry, *Mechelen aan de Tigris: Het verhall van een dorp en een wereld* (2001), 104–7; Rhétoré, *"Les Chrétiens aux bêtes"*, 309.

and 'Ayn-Wardo, and who had recently begun to colonize the area. Agha Petros stated that the pre-war Christian population amounted to 300 persons. A Kurd named Ali Isa owned the village, and there were 10 Kurdish families living there. According to Hinno and Qarabash, after completing the massacre of Nisibin, Qaddur Bey took his Al-Khamsin militia unit and Kurds to Helwa. They surrounded the village and captured all of the men. They were taken to the river's edge, where they were killed and the bodies thrown into the water. The women were placed in a large house and were raped and then murdered. The house was then burned. The youngest children were allowed to live but were brought up as Muslims. Ali Isa seized the property of the richest Christian family, that of Eliyo Alyudo. A different version comes from Yeshue Samuel, who was a young boy at the time. He gives no account of a massacre of the villagers, but rather that the people killed were Armenian deportees. After epidemics decimated the village, the remainder managed to get to Mor Malke monastery, where they lived a precarious existence.[51] **H, Q**

Ided. Ided was a Chaldean village in the Jezire diocese that was attacked by Mamman Kurds.[52]

'Isa-Powar (Issa-Pouar). 'Isa-Powar was in the Bafaya commune of Beshire kaza northeast of Diyarbekir. Agha Petros wrote that there were 200 Assyro-Chaldean inhabitants and a further 1,800 in 14 surrounding villages, of which the largest was Sa'diye. There are no reports of survivors from this entire tract. The head of the village was a Syriac named Rais Bero, who was very influential in the tract. Prior to the general massacres, vali Reshid Bey had ordered him killed and for that purpose ordered him to come to Diyarbekir. On the way, he was confronted by an official and told to either convert or be killed. He and his son-in-law refused to convert and were killed. Kurdish friends of Rais Bero later took revenge and murdered the official.[53]

Jarahia (Chariha, Cerrahi, Djerahie). This Chaldean village along the Tigris River in the Jezire diocese had 100 inhabitants. The Mamman Kurds attacked the village on June 18, 1915.[54]

Jezire (Gziro, Jeziret-ibn-Ömer, Jizre, Cizre, Djezire). Jezire was a small, multireligious town on an island in the Tigris River close to the Syr-

---

[51] Athanasius Yeshua Samuel, *Treasure of Qumran. My Story of the Dead Sea Scrolls* (1968), 42–47.
[52] Ternon, "Mardin 1915," 369.
[53] Rhétoré, *"Les Chrétiens aux bêtes"*, 49–50.
[54] Ternon, "Mardin 1915," 369; Hannouche, *Azekh*, 62.

ian border. Its Syriac name is Gziro, but at that time official documents termed it Jezire and it would be confusing to use any other name. It was the ancestral base of the Badr-Khan dynasty. There were about 2,000 Christian residents of many faiths—Syriac Orthodox, Syriac Catholics, Nestorians, Chaldeans, Armenians, and converts to Protestantism.[55] The Chaldean diocese of Jezire had congregations in 17 towns and villages with a total membership of 6,400. It had 17 priests, 11 churches, 3 chapels, and 7 schools. The bishop in Jezire was Jacques Abraham (1848–1915).[56] According to the Chaldean Patriarch, the losses in this diocese were 5,000 of the faithful as well as the bishop and ten priests.[57] The secular leader of the Christian community was Gabro Khaddo, who attempted to appease the Ottoman authorities and collaborated to a great extent. He collected the sum of 1,500 gold coins and presented it to Osman Effendi in return for a promise of protection. Gabro Khaddo was instrumental in stopping attempts to form a self-defense unit and visited the neighboring villages giving assurances that they need not fear aggression. This attempt at appeasement ended in catastrophe.

In the short term, Gabro Khaddo's policy seemed successful, and Jezire alone in the Tur Abdin and Bohtan region survived the early summer intact. Probably it had the support of local authorities, although documentary evidence is lacking. However, very large massacres took place here in August and September 1915. Among those killed were many non-residents, since the town became a staging point for deportees trickling through from Van and Bitlis. Two groups of Al-Khamsin militia, led by Muhammed Resul and Haji 'Abdo, who had come from Mardin, organized a full massacre on August 24, 1915. All of the adult men, including secular and religious leaders, were killed at a place known as Chamme Sus on the banks of the Tigris River. The women and children were locked up in the Dominican monastery and the Syriac Catholic church. Here they were pressed for money, raped, and tortured. Some were taken captive, while others were sold as slaves. The remainder were murdered.

After the war, the Chaldean Patriarch accused the following individuals of instigating the massacres:

---

[55] Rhétoré, *"Les Chrétiens aux bêtes"*, 50.
[56] Tfinkdji, "L'Église chaldéenne catholique autrefois et aujourd'hui," 496, 502, 505.
[57] Ternon, "Mardin 1915," 368–70.

The Mufti; Feyzi Bey, the deputy of Diyarbekir [at the National Assembly]; Haji Nain Agha; Haji Zoraf; Mohammed-Arab; Haji Seif-el-din; Seid Nedjm-el-din; Seid Abdul-Hamid; the sons of sheik Mohammed-Amin; Said-Hindi; Yousouf Effendi; the sons of Mohammed-Kani; the sons of Reshid; Ahmed Nazo; Mohammed-Amin-Goro; Abdul-Manaf; Mousa Effendi; Sevi-ibn-Reshid; Haji Abdul-Hamid; Haji Sepho; Abdi-Hadjaj; Seid Mohammed; Seid Abd-Alsalam, Haji Hassan-Fattah.

The perpetrators of the massacres in Jezire and its immediate surroundings were: "the aghas of Sharnak [Şirnak], the Silopiya, the Bazamer, the Chapsia, the Hesné, and the Kochers."[58] But there were several aghas who protected Christians: Marho Oro, 'Azar, and Slayman Berho.[59]

The above-mentioned CUP deputy Feyzi Bey was instrumental in initiating and getting permission from Constantinople for the massacres in Diyarbekir and was a leading politician in the Committee for Union and Progress.[60] Armalto indicates that Zulfi, the Kurdish National Assembly deputy from Diyarbekir, was sent by Reshid Bey in April 1915 to assume the post of kaymakam and to organize the Kurds to massacre the Christians.[61] Hendo's diary stated that he was in Jezire from April 15 to 25.[62]

Armalto gave the following details:

> When the scorpions of massacre crawled over Armenia and Diyarbekir, the Jacobite archbishop Behnam Aqrawi [of Jezire] fled to Azakh. Both [Syriac and Chaldean] Catholic archbishops stayed in place in their dioceses until August 27 when a group of soldiers broke into the Syriac church. They arrested Filipos Mikhail Malke and the priests Shimun and Boulos Qestan Eframi and took them to prison. They then went to the Chaldean church and collected archbishop Ya'coub and the priests Hanna, Elias, Marqos, and Yousuf Sa'id and also put them in prison. Istayfo's daughter Elly went there to hear about it. Mikhail gave her his cross and said "Go home immediately!" One brute assaulted her on the way home, tore off the cross, and threatened to kill her. She hurried home and did not dare to go out again. The Christians were overcome by fear and they prayed through the night. On the night of August 28, the spokesmen of hypocrisy called archbishop Ya'coub to the court and interrogated him on whatever weapons he and his congregation pos-

---

[58] Ternon, "Mardin 1915," 369.
[59] Hannouche, *Azekh*, 57.
[60] Naayem, *Assyro-Chaldéens*, 57–59.
[61] Armalto, *Al-Qusara*, 383; Joseph Alichoran, "Un Dominicain témoin du génocide de 1915 le pére Jacques Rhétoré (1841–1921)" (2005), 315.
[62] Hannouche, *Azekh*, 40.

sessed. He laughed at them and assured them that neither he nor his congregation had anything like that. Those present went pale and became extremely wild. They took turns beating him and then shot him to death with three shots. He fell as a martyr. Each bullet-hole formed the sign of the cross on his forehead. Then they carried him out of town, stripped him, and left his corpse by the Tigris River and then returned. Then they called in Archbishop Mikhail and interrogated him in the same way about the same things. But he stood silent, since he understood the intention and saw through the intrigue. He was sure that he would meet the same fate as his colleague. His inhuman enemies threw him to the floor, tied his feet, and beat him until they tired and the prelate fainted and was half living, half dead. They then pulled him out and made an end of him with a shot. They left him there naked, prey for wild animals. Back at the government building they amused themselves with torturing a group of priests in various ways. When they were close to expiring, they were plundered of all they had on them and were killed. On August 29, the soldiers broke into the other Christians' houses, seized all the men, and took them to prison. There they stayed for four days with little food and great need. Then they were interrogated about what rifles and bombs they had. Most were beaten, tied with chains and ropes, and brought to a nearby place where they were shot. Their clothes and belongings were plundered as usual. At the start of September there was a new raid, and the women and children were seized. The soldiers said that they planned to take them to their relatives in Mosul. But they were only taken a short distance while crying and wailing. They were killed and robbed of their clothes and valuables. But before that, the killers chose some boys and girls who appealed to them, and they took them home.[63]

An American missionary in Urmia received the following information about the situation of the Protestant converts in the Jezire area.

> There was a general massacre in the Bohtan region, and our [Protestant] helpers, preachers, teachers and Bible-Women, with their families, fell victims to it among the rest. The man who brought the word is known to me personally. This young man tells the story of how, by order of the Government, the Kurds and Turkish soldiers put the Christians of all those villages, including Djeziré, to the sword. Among those slain were ... Muallim [teacher] Mousa, pastor of our church in Djeziré, and his sixteen-year-old son Philip. There are three preachers not heard from, and one of them is probably killed, as his village, Monsoria, was put to

---

[63] Armalto, *Al-Qusara*, 385.

the sword; another, Rabi Ishak, is possibly alive, as there is a report that his village has been preserved by the influence of a Kurdish agha. It is to be feared, however, that this agha would not be able to protect them for long, as from every source comes the word that the Government threatened such friendly Kurds with punishment, if they did not obey orders. The third man is reported as having fled to Mosul. Whether he reached there or not is not known. The women and children who escaped death were carried away captive. Among these were the families of the above mentioned brethren. The wife and two daughters of Muallim Mousa, the daughters of Kasha Elia, and Rabi Hatoun, our Bible-Woman, were all schoolgirls in Urmia [mission school] or Mardin. Kasha Mattai was killed by Kurds in the mountain while fleeing. ... The terrible feature about it was that, after the first slaughter, there were Kurds who tried to save some of the Christians alive, but the Government would not permit it. My informant had found refuge with an agha and was working for him, when a messenger from the Government came with orders to the Kurds to complete the work or be punished. Word was brought to my informant in the field, and he with a few others fled to the mountain and made their way to Van, and so came here. The villagers of Attil, where we had work also, all escaped to Van. Their Kurdish agha, who was a warm friend of our preacher and of our work, gave them warning that he would not be able to protect them, as the massacre was being pressed by the Government.[64] **H, A, Q**

Ka'biye. Ka'biye was a very large Christian village near Diyarbekir with a population of 1,650. In 1895, an anti-Christian pogrom took place here. Agha Petros declared the pre-war population to have been 1,600, and Qarabash stated the number of families to have totaled 160. Al-Khamsin militiamen under the command of three officers arrived from Diyarbekir and surrounded Ka'biye on April 10/23. They demanded of the headman that he force all males over 15 years of age to come out of the village. Otherwise he and his family would be executed. Therefore 125 men came out and they were tied together with ropes. The soldiers then demanded all of the weapons in the village, but the villagers insisted that they had none. The militia leaders refused to believe this and began to torture by the bastinado method of beating the soles of the feet in order to find out where the weapons were hidden. When torture did not have any effect, five leading villagers were selected and executed. Then two priests were tortured. The soldiers ordered the village women to feed them a large feast, and then they

---

[64] Report of E. W. McDowell to Board of Foreign Missions of the Presbyterian Church 6 March 1916, in Bryce and Toynbee, *Treatment of the Armenians*, 211–12.

marched the remaining men to a caravanserai named Misafir-Khana in Diyarbekir, where they were placed under close guard. Here they were imprisoned until April 15/28. On that day they were told that they would begin at forced labor making roads, but as they marched away they were taken to a hill near Igil village and killed and thrown into the Euphrates River. On April 20/May 3, Kurds attacked Ka'biye again, plundering more than they murdered. Some villagers ran away to the town of Male, but during their flight 50 were killed. In Male they found no refuge, and the authorities arrested them and sent them back to Ka'biye. After some time of living in terror, only 5 Syriac families remained. On May 30/June 12, Shakir Bey, the militia leader, arrived from Diyarbekir with members of the Rama tribe. In the evening they seized all of the men that they could find and demanded money. The sum of 1,500 gold dinars was collected and given them. Then the Kurds began to violate the women. The men were tied together and marched away. At a cliff generally known as Kurt Kaya (Wolf Rock), they were murdered and the bodies burned. The women and children were taken as captives and some managed to escape to the city. It came to the ears of the authorities that there were a number of Ka'biye refugees hiding in Diyarbekir. These were assembled and guaranteed their safety and taken back to Ka'biye, where they arrived in September. Almost immediately, Circassian soldiers and Al-Khamsin militia surrounded the village. The villagers were once again marched out, this time in the direction of Mardin. At Kurt Kaya, the men were shot and Kurds attacked the women and children. A few of the women and children survived. Qarabash asserts that only three children and two women were known to be alive after this final catastrophe. **Q**

Kafarbe (Keferbe, Keferbi, Fofyath, Güngören). Kafarbe is 27 kilometers southeast of Midyat, about 2 kilometers north of the Mor Gabriel monastery. According to the Agha Petros list, the prewar Syriac Orthodox population was 200. The parish church of Mar Estephanos dates from the eighth century. Villagers from here sought protection in the Qartmin monastery and were safe until 1917, when Kurds of the Azzam clan led by Shandi assaulted the monastery and captured the Kafarbe villagers. They were taken to their parish church and there they were murdered. Only a few persons survived. **H, Q**

Kafro-Elayto (Upper Kafro, Arıca, Kafri). Kafro-Elayto is 12 kilometers from Midyat, close to Bote. Before the massacres, 80 Syriac and 30 Kurdish families lived here. When the Syriacs heard of the massacres, they barricaded themselves in the Mor Ya'qub church. The Kurds, led by Yusuf

Agha, son of Hasan Shamdin, the owner of Kfar-Gawze, surrounded the village. The Syriacs were unprepared and could only hold out for five days. Yusuf promised them good treatment if they gave up voluntarily, which they did. They tied the leaders together, took them outside the village, and killed them. The houses of the village were destroyed. **H, A**

Kafro-Tahtayo (Lower Kafro, Elbeğendi). Kafro lies near the Mor Malke monastery southeast of Midyat. According to Agha Petros, it had a pre-war Christian population of 250. It was attacked, and the survivors fled to the monastery.

Kafshinne (Kefşin). Kafshinne is 10 kilometers northwest of Azakh and had 25–30 families. The landlord was Hano Basuski, a Syriac. When news of the atrocities came, the Muslim villagers warned the Christians, "We will not harm you in any way, but for your safety it would be better for you to go to Azakh." Therefore they all went with their property to Azakh. After the war, the villagers returned to Kafshinne but left it again for Iraq and settled in Mosul. **H**

Kavel-Karre (Kavel-Kerre). Kavel-Karre is northeast of Azakh near Khandad. Bafi, Arzaneh, and Awsar Kurds attacked on June 19, 1915. All inhabitants were killed and the bodies thrown into the Tigris River.[65]

Kfar-Boran (Kerburan, Karkh Buran, Dargeçit). Kfar-Boran lies 46 kilometers northeast of Midyat. It is one of the largest and richest villages in Tur Abdin and was more like a small town than a village. Because of many streams that flowed all year round, there were many water mills, which made the place a commercial and craftwork center. At the time of the massacres, there were 500 Christian and 60 Muslim families. The Christians belonged to the Armenian, Syriac Orthodox, Syriac Catholic, and Syriac Protestant denominations. Agha Petros stated that 2,000 Christians lived here before the war. The population, even the Christians, spoke Kurdish. The Syriac Orthodox bishop, Mor Antimos Ya'qub, had his residence here, as well as twelve Syriac priests and one monk.[66] The Ottoman regime was represented by a mudir (village-level government official) who commanded a detachment of 40 gendarmes quartered inside the village. Refugees from massacres in neighboring villages fled into Kfar-Boran and told of atrocities. The Syriac notables held council to decide how to act, but they could not agree. Some recommended capturing the Turkish troops and seizing their weapons and ammunition. Others said they should trust in the assurance that the mudir had given that the government would protect the vil-

---

[65] Hannouche, *Azekh*, 62.
[66] Hollerweger, *Turabdin*, 77.

lage. As a precaution, the official took the Syriac bishop to the town hall, and he eventually converted to Islam, thinking it would save his life. But contact was made with the Kurds led by Ömer and Mustafa, the sons of Ali Ramo, to attack the Christians. The residential quarters of Kfar-Boran are built on relatively flat land and lacked natural defenses. The Syriacs therefore took cover in seven large building complexes, popularly known as the "seven palaces." The Turkish mudir convinced some of the Syriacs to leave the buildings under promises of safety. These people were taken to the town hall and killed. One group that refused to leave its building was attacked by the troops and the inhabitants slaughtered. After this, full war broke out between the troops and the Syriacs. The battle went on for about a week, but the Syriacs had not had time to lay up supplies and soon ran out of ammunition. The troops could not attack all of the buildings at the same time, but rather stormed them piecemeal. After they stormed one building, they would bring the captives outside and there kill them in sight of the other defenders. Despite his conversion to Islam, Mustafa ibn Ali Ramo seized the bishop (apparently against the will of the mudir), who was taken up on a roof, where he was tortured before his throat was cut or he threw himself from the roof. Afterward, the bodies were collected and burned on a large fire. In total about 100 Syriacs survived the 1915 massacres. Some were outside the village when it was attacked, some had sought safety in Hah, and a number of children were saved to be servants in Muslim households. No exact date is known for the massacres, but the destruction predated the destruction of Midyat in mid July.[67] **H, Q, A**

Kfar-Gawze (Karjos, Gercüş). Kfar-Gawze is a small town and administrative center, about 20 kilometers north of Midyat, populated with Syriac and Chaldean families as well as Muslims. Agha Petros listed the Christian population as 150 persons. When the massacres began, the local Kurdish chief, Yusuf Hasan Shamdin, promised to help and protect the Christians. Members of his family had been imprisoned under Sultan Abdulhamid for rebellion, and they were normally opposed to the government. However, Yusuf Hasan Shamdin apparently changed sides and instead seized some adult male villagers and took them to a place called Zaghore and plundered them and threw them in a river. The rest of the Syriacs did forced labor and many of them ran away to Midyat. The oral history relates

---

[67] Armalto, *Al-Qusara*, 39,1; Useve Wardo, interviewed October 1997 (appendix 1, no. 41); Hanna Polos, interviewed November 1993 (appendix 1, no. 42); Gallo Shabo, appendix 1, no. 75.

that Shaykh Fathulla, the Muhallemi leader, came to Kfar-Gawze and forced the release of captive Syriac women and children.[68] **H, A**

Kfarze (Keferzi, Altınaş). Kfarze is an agricultural village 15 kilometers northeast of Midyat. Here lived 160 Syriac Orthodox families and 70 Kurdish families of the Ismail clan. Agha Petros listed the pre-war Christian population as 350. The Syriac church, named for Mar Azazael, was built in the tenth century. When news of the massacres arrived, the Christian villagers held a council. Some wanted to arm themselves, but the majority put their hopes in the promises of government authorities that they would be safe. The Kurds, however, prepared to massacre their neighbors, and news of this was leaked to the Christians. Hinno stated that this person was an anonymous official in Midyat, but Armalto named him as Yusuf Hassan Shamdin. The villagers sent word to 'Ayn-Wardo asking for help. On the night that the Kurds set for the attack, well-armed men from 'Ayn-Wardo arrived and helped the Christians to flee. The Kurds observed this flight, and there was hard fighting. Many survived and reached 'Ayn-Wardo, while others took refuge in the neighboring Muslim villages of Dermuske and Kafsange, where they were held hostage. The Syriacs sent out a detachment of 300 men to free the hostages held in Dermuske. They attacked the village and freed their relatives and neighbors and took the Kurdish leader Abdulrahman's sister captive in order to exchange her for the other Christians. But 86 Syriac hostages were still in Kurdish hands in Kafsange, and these were marched out of the village to be killed. At that moment, Abdulrahman sent a message not to harm the hostages. Instead, an exchange of hostages for his sister was agreed upon. The villagers remained in 'Ayn-Wardo throughout the war.[69] **H, A**

Khandaq (Kendek). This Chaldean village with 100 inhabitants was in the Jezire diocese near the Tigris River. Mamman Kurds attacked it on June 19, 1915.[70]

Kharabe-Mishka (Kharab-Meshka, Harab-Mechké, Harap-Mişki). Kharabe-Mishka is near Mor Malke monastery. The Agha Petros list stated that 200 Christians lived here. The villagers fled to the monastery.

Khezna (Hizna). Khezna is near Nisibin. Here lived 15 Syriac families. Most originated from Zaz. Ibrahim, the Kurdish owner of Khezna, took the Christians out of the village and killed them. Government authorities

---

[68] Hanna Bitar, interviewed February 1994 (appendix 1, no. 43); Brahim Maqsi-Musa, interviewed December 1995 (appendix 1, no. 44).

[69] Hanna Mure, interviewed November 1926 (appendix 1, no. 47).

[70] Ternon, "Mardin 1915," 369.

approached Ibrahim Halil and made a plan to annihilate the Christians in his village. The Christian men were taken captive and tied together. They plus the women and children were taken outside the village and killed. **H, Q**

Koshk (Keuck, Köschk). Koshk was a small Syriac village with 100 inhabitants in the Anbart river area near Diyarbekir. Along with inhabitants of several other villages, the males of this village were slaughtered on May 7, 1915. The women and children were put to forced agricultural work. The massacre was perpetrated by one of the Al-Khamsin death squads at the instigation of the owner of the villages, Qasem Bey. According to testimony of survivors, 114 men from these villages were killed. After the agricultural season was finished, the women and children had to convert to Islam or be killed. **Q**

Kubibe (Qoubik). Kubibe is 25 kilometers east of Nisibin. According to Qarabash, it was a village whose Christian inhabitants all fled before the massacre. **Q**

Kuvakh (Kofakh, Koufek, Küfah hr.).[71] Kuvakh is located 5 kilometers east of Azakh, and the site is now classed as ruins. The Agha Petros list indicated a Christian population of 400. Already in April 1915, the villagers fled to safety in Azakh.[72]

Laylan. This village is east of Nisibin. Laylan had 15 Syriac families. They were attacked by the Kurds of the Kasekan tribe headed by Ahmed Yusef. All of the Syriacs were assembled and taken outside the village, where they were killed. **H**

Lije (Lice). Lije is an administrative center in the district of Ma'den-Arghana, about 18 hours by foot northeast of Diyarbekir. It had 12,000 inhabitants, of which 7,000 were Christians. Information about the massacres comes from a survivor, Naaman Effendi, a member of the Chaldean church originally from Sa'irt, who was head of the local office of the Ottoman Public Debt Authority.[73] The Christian inhabitants belonged to many faiths: Armenian, Chaldean, and Syriac Orthodox. In spring 1915, a local militia was created of Muslim volunteers. After this, the Christians were ordered to collect all their weapons and leave them at the church. The militia then armed themselves with the weapons. During preparations for the massacres, the kaymakam Hüseyin Nesim Bey vociferously refused to par-

---

[71] "hr." in a place name stands for *harap* "ruins" or a deserted settlement.
[72] A. H. B., "Mémoires sur Mardine," 186; Hannouche, *Azekh*, 40, 61.
[73] Testimony of Naaman Effendi in Naayem, *Assyro-Chaldéens*, 169–76.

ticipate in the anti-Christian activities and was assassinated on the way to meet the vali.⁷⁴ At once, guards were placed outside the homes of all Christian notables, and all Christian civil servants were fired from their jobs. The following day, 50 representatives of the Christians were arrested, put in cells, and tortured with bastinado and other methods. After some days, they were tied together arm-in-arm in pairs with ropes. They were marched outside the town and slaughtered by Kurds at a place known as Dashta-Pis, near Diyarbekir, where the corpses were placed in caves. Among those killed were the Syriac priests from Qarabash and Ka'biye, who had been jailed in Lije. After this there was a second mass arrest, which included several priests, followed by mass executions. Gangs of *çete*s massacred and plundered the neighboring Christian villages: Fum, Chemchem, Jum, Tappa, Nagle, Pasor, and Khaneke. Only the first two of these villages are in Agha Petros's list of Assyro-Chaldean villages, and it names 8 other villages in the kaza of Lije that are not named by Naayem. It is possible that this confusion is based on alternative Syriac and Armenian place names. The total Assyro-Chaldean population of the kaza was given as 4,100 persons, and there was a larger Armenian settlement. The destruction was done before the holiday of Ramadan began (mid July), and during the holiday month no further massacres took place. However, when Ramadan was over, the murders resumed again. As the males had been disposed of, the activities focused on the women and children, who were deported.

Mansuri (Mansurije, Mansourie, Monsoria). This originally Chaldean village is 5 kilometers north of Jezire on the Tigris River. It had 350 inhabitants; 80 of them were Chaldean, and the rest had converted to Protestantism. The Chokh-Sora Kurdish tribe attacked this village. The Presbyterian preacher was reported missing and presumed dead.

> The three villages of Hassan [Hassana], Shakh, and Monsoria were Protestant, and it is to be feared that they were wiped out, as were all the other villages of the plain. Many of the women of Monsoria threw themselves into the river to avoid falling into the hands of the Kurds. ... The terrible feature about it was that, after the first slaughter, there were Kurds who tried to save some of the Christians alive, but the Government would not permit it.⁷⁵

---

⁷⁴ Nesimi, *Yılların İçinden*, 37.
⁷⁵ Ternon, "Mardin 1915," 369; Report of E. W. McDowell to Board of Foreign Missions of the Presbyterian Church March 6, 1916, in Bryce and Toynbee, *Treatment of Armenians*, 211–12.

Mansuriye (Mansuri, Yalim). Mansuriye is very close to Mardin, located about 4 kilometers to the north. It specialized in textiles and wool. On November 5 and 10, 1895, Kurds attacked the village. At the start of the World War, 400 families lived there; half were Christians and half were Kurds belonging to the Dashi tribe. Agha Petros listed the pre-war Christian population as 400 individuals, and A. H. B. stated that there were 250 Orthodox and Catholic Syriac families. Each community had a parish church. Many of the Christian youth had avoided conscription to the army and were hiding. Kurds surrounded the village on June 11, 1915. At first the Dashi Kurds merely pressed the Christians for money and took their property in exchange for not disclosing those in hiding, but they did not attack their Christian neighbors. The Syriac Orthodox, however, gave the names of some of the Syriac Catholic youth, particularly the recent converts. The authorities began to search for them. At the same time, a judge ruled that the Kurds must give back the wealth they had taken from the villagers. On the night of June 16, the Dashi Kurds attacked the Mansuriye Christians. Many Syriac Catholics fled to the church. One Kurdish leader, Chachano Sayrane, pretended to protect the Syriacs, but he used the opportunity to get into the church and open the doors for the aggressors. They killed 41 persons in the church and burned two men alive. Several other people were killed in the aftermath of this first attack. Simon recorded the number of Christian victims to have been 95. Soldiers from Mardin were sent out, ostensibly to chase the Dashi away but in actuality to join them. On June 17, the Christians all fled to Mardin to seek refuge in the Syriac Orthodox church. They stayed there for 10 days under great confusion. Archbishop Tappouni asked the authorities to let them go free. Seven soldiers were sent to escort them back to Mansuriye to collect their property; their safety would be guaranteed. Seventy women followed the soldiers, but Dashi tribesmen attacked the column, and all but two women were killed in a cave. A second group of 100 women was given guarantees of safety, and they went back to the village. But after a month, the Dashi again attacked and killed them and threw the bodies into a well. After that, no one dared to return to Mansuriye, but stayed in Mardin. According to Armalto, the leaders of the Dashi Kurds were Huseyin Ballo, Khalil and his brother Osman, Deli Bero Khalilo, Hassan Osmane, Haji Badro, Haji Bania, Shaykhi's family, Hese Haji Ali, Khalo Mastoke, Ali Jabali, and Farho Arfe.[76] **A**

---

[76] Armalto, *Al-Qusara*, 428; Simon, *Mardine*, 136; A. H. B., "Mémoires sur Mardine," 179.

Maqsi-Oglu. Maqsi-Oglu was a Syriac village with 100 inhabitants in the Hawar River district near Diyarbekir. Along with neighboring villages, on May 3, a death squad of 150 militiamen led by Shakir Bey and members of the Rama tribe perpetrated a massacre on the adult males. The males of the villages were assembled in Chanaqchi and then taken to a pit near the village Hawar-Dejla, where they were shot. Those from these villages who were murdered numbered 164. **Q**

Mar Bobo (Günyurdu). Mar Bobo was a village owned by Sarohan, chief of a subsection of the Haverkan. He allowed Christians to flee into his village and gave asylum and then escorted them to Beth-Debe, where they survived the massacres. **H**

Mardin. See chapter 6 above.

Mar Gurya. Mar Gurya, with a population of 182 Chaldeans, was in the Sa'irt diocese. The inhabitants perished during the great massacres in Sa'irt in June 1915. See the section on Sa'irt below.

Marwaniye. Marwaniye lies north of Dufne. Its ten Syriac Christians were murdered, but one person survived. **H**

Mar Ya'qub (Mar Yacoub, Mar Yaco). The small village of Mar Ya'qub lies south of Jezire about 12 hours by foot east of Pesh-Khabur in present-day Iraq. There was a large building complex belonging to the French Dominicans. However, because the village was in the Mosul vilayet, it was declared off limits for Christian persecution, by order of the vali. Despite this, Mohammed, a chief of the nomadic Artoshi (who used the area for grazing), began to attack the neighboring villages. The kaymakam of Dehok sent soldiers and discovered that Mohammed had taken possession of the Dominican building and had installed himself as owner. His men had pillaged the village. The agha was executed on the orders of the vali for disobeying his order not to persecute Christians within his province.[77]

Ma'sarte (Omariyan, Ömerli). Ma'sarte is a district town 20 kilometers northeast of Mardin on the border of the Muhallemi area. Here lived about 300 Syriac Orthodox Christians with a parish church, Mar Gewergis. Agha Petros listed the pre-war Christian population as 300. They were known for cultivation of grapes and weaving of wool. On June 12, 1915, a few men escaped from here and told the following story. Huseyin Bakkero, the owner of the village, went to Mardin and parleyed with the Kurdish tribal leaders Faris Chelebi, Mohammed Ali Chelebi, and the Dashit chief Ahakat, to get participation in the liquidation of the Christians. Huseyin rode back and summoned the villagers and gave a solemn promise that they would

---

[77] Rhétoré, *"Les Chrétiens aux bêtes"*, 133–34, 323.

come to no harm. However, when they arrived at his house, they were taken captive by large numbers of Kurds. They were tied together and murdered, and their bodies were thrown into wells. Qarabash gave the date as June 2, 1915. Simon recorded that 80 Christians were killed. Two men saved themselves by hiding in a cave, and one arrived at Za'faran monastery. Some of the Muslim women protected the Christian women and children and escorted them, after a few days of hiding, to the Church of the Martyrs in Mardin.[78] **Q, A**

Mazre (Marze, Mazraat, Mezre). This Chaldean and Syriac Catholic village with a population of 100 is about 10 kilometers south of Jezire along the Tigris River. The neighboring Esene Kurdish tribe stormed it in June 1915.[79]

Meshte (Mesti). Meshte village lies north of Kfar-Boran near the Tigris River. In this village lived 40 Syriac families who spoke the Turoyo dialect. Kurds from the Ali Rammo tribe slaughtered them. **H**

Mharkan (Mahreikane, Mahreke). Mharkan is situated 25 kilometers east of Nisibin. Agha Petros listed the pre-war Christian population as 600. This village had a Syriac owner who lived in Hebob. This village was attacked by groups of Nisibin's Al-Khamsin militia under Qaddur Bey's command and Dakshuri Kurdish tribesmen, who destroyed Helwa and Duger during the same operation. However, some managed to survive by hiding outside the village and escaped to the mountain villages during the night.[80] **H, Q**

Miden (Midun, Öğündük). Miden was a very large village with 500 Syriac families. It is 30 kilometers east of Midyat and 15 kilometers west of Azakh. Within the village were 10 churches. Miden suffered often from Kurdish attacks. The latest destruction had been during the Badr-Kahn uprising in the mid nineteenth century. The Kurdish tribes in the neighborhood surrounded Miden. Battles went on for a week, but the defense held. But because this village lay in the plain, it lacked good protection. Therefore, the villagers made plans to leave for Basibrino. Malke and other warriors came to escort them, and they took as much property as they could carry. The Kurds attacked the villagers as they were on their way, and some were killed. Kurds of the Dumanan tribe moved into the houses of Miden.

---

[78] Armalto, *Al-Qusara*, 425; Simon, *Mardine*, 136.
[79] Ternon, "Mardin 1915," 369; Hannouche, *Azekh*, 62.
[80] Gawriye Beth-Mas'ud, interviewed July 2002 (appendix 1, no. 65).

After the war, some of the Syriacs returned with the help of Chelebi Agha.⁸¹ **H, A**

Midyat. See chapter 7 above.

Mir-'Aziz (Mirazez). Mir-'Aziz was in the Jezire diocese and had 50 Syriac families. It was owned by a Syriac familiy named Chalo and was unmolested.⁸²

Miyafarkin (Miafarqin, Mefrektho, Silvan). Miyafarkin was a town northeast of Diyarbekir in the Silvan kaza. The population was 2,500 Gregorian Armenians and a combined total of 1,500 Chaldeans, Syriac Catholics, Syriac Orthodox, and Melchites. The Agha Petros population lists gave the size of Miyarfarkin as 1,270 Assyro-Chaldeans plus an additional 2,730 in 13 surrounding villages. Tfinkdji noted 500 Chaldeans here. The Christians were annihilated, but the circumstances are not known. In December 1915, the Ministry of the Interior ordered the area repopulated with Muslim refugees from Bayezit and Diyadin.⁸³

Mizizah (Mozizah, Doğançay). Mizizah had 70 Syriac and 50 Kurdish families. The village is 7 kilometers from Midyat. This was one of the richest agricultural villages in Tur Abdin. Normally, this was the residence of Chelebi Agha, the chief of one segment of the Haverkan confederation, who swore protection to the Christians. However, he was in prison when the massacres took place and was not released until 1917. The leading Syriac here was Mas'ud from the Musa Gebro family. He became the leader in the defense of 'Ayn-Wardo; he went to many surrounding villages and urged them to come to 'Ayn-Wardo for protection. All of the Christians from Mizizah took their possessions and went to 'Ayn-Wardo.⁸⁴ **H, A**

Mor Malke Qluzmoyo. The Mor Malke monastery was a very large building complex with several enclosed courtyards. It resembled a fortress, with high stone walls on all sides and only a few windows placed very high. It is located 25 kilometers south of Midyat in sight of the summit of Mount Izlo, which was the Roman-Persian frontier in Classical times. Since the fifteenth century it had been the residence of a Syriac Orthodox bishop. Many Christians from the nearby villages of Arbo, Arkah-Kharabale, Sederi, Kharabe-Mishka, Kafro, and Beth-Debe, along with survivors from other

---

⁸¹ Yonan, *Ein vergessener Holocaust*, 280–82.

⁸² Hannouche, *Azekh*, 67.

⁸³ Rhétoré, *"Les Chrétiens aux bêtes"*, 48–49; BOA. DH. ŞFR 59/7 Ministry of Interior to Diyarbekir vilayet December 14, 1915; Mikhayel Salmo, interviewed March 1996 (appendix 1, no. 71).

⁸⁴ For oral history, see appendix 1 below, section Q, nos. 66–68.

places, sought refuge in the monastery. During the summer of 1915, the monastery was left in peace by the Turkish forces, and the Kurds who had failed to capture Hebob and Beth-Debe did not even attempt to storm Mor Malke. While they were assembled in the monastery, the Christian warriors made attacks on Turkish and Kurdish forces. On one occasion they captured 30 Turkish soldiers, including a Syriac medical doctor. On August 21, several hundred Christians, mostly refugees from Kafro village, marched on Sheweske and attacked it as an act of revenge. Some time in September, about 900 Syriacs led by Shemun Malke of Beth-Debe surrounded and attacked the village of Mharkan to avenge themselves on the deceitful Yusef Hajo, who had not protected the Christians as he had first promised. On September 14, 1915, many of the refugees left the monastery and began to return to their villages. The mutasarrif in Mardin, Bedri Bey, received news of this event and sent a Syriac cleric with a message to the villagers, that they must give up their weapons and obey the state. Otherwise the government would continue to treat them as rebels. The bishop, however, informed the Syriacs that this was a trap, and they refused. The Christians returned to the monastery and remained there until winter. Yeshue Samuel tells of a group of Syriacs from Helwa who sought sanctuary in the monastery. His story is one of starvation under constant sniper fire.[85] After the war, the monastery was destroyed in fighting between Kurds and the Turkish army between 1924 and 1928.[86] **H, A**

Nehrivan (Nuhervan, Nahravan). This Chaldean village of 200 is sited 30 kilometers southeast of Jezire. It was attacked by the Bohtan Kurds.[87]

Nisibin (Nusaybin, Nsibis). Nisibin was a famous ancient town that during the early church was a center for learning and missions to the east. It is on the plain just to the south of the slope up to Tur Abdin, and the river Harmas flows through it. Today it is on the border between Turkey and Syria. By World War I it was a small, rather forgotten place, but when the Baghdad railway made it a station in 1916, it had strategic importance. According to Hinno, there were 100 Syriac Orthodox families in the town of Nisibin. The head of the Syriac Orthodox Church there was Istayfanos. About one third of the population of 8,000 was Christian, mostly Armenian Catholics and Syriac Orthodox. A Syriac Orthodox bishop resided in the town. The Agha Petros list of Syriac Christians gave the population as

---

[85] Samuel, *Treasure of Qumran*, 52–58.
[86] For oral history, see appendix 1 below, section O, nos. 63–64.
[87] Ternon, "Mardin 1915," 369.

1,200. Tfinkdji listed 160 Chaldeans in the local congregation. There was also a sizable Jewish community. As in the other Tur Abdin towns, when the persecution began, the first group to be arrested was made up of Armenian, Catholic, and Protestant males.

The town and its upland are among the oldest Christian settlements in Mesopotamia, dating from the second century. Lying at the foot of a steep incline, the town of Nisibin was a caravan stop on the flattest and most abundantly watered trade route between Persia and the Mediterranean Sea. The river Jaq-jaq runs through it. In antiquity it was a fortress town that was once Roman and then, after 363, became Persian; the frontier went through the neighborhood until the Muslim conquest. The pilgrimage church of Mar Ya'qub dates from the fourth century. From about 300 A.D. it had been a bishopric in a diocese named Beth-'Arbaye. After the Council of Ephesus in 431, Nisibin developed into a center for Nestorian Christianity, and it had a famous school of divinity. After the Ottoman conquest in 1515, it served for a period as provincial capital. On November 10, 1895, one of the Hamidiye pogroms occurred here, but the Tayy Bedouin tribe protected the Christians then, as they continued to do in World War I.

The Syriac archbishop in Homs, Efrem Barsom, named 50 villages in Nisibin's upland that were ruined. The affected Syriac Orthodox population was approximately 7,000, coming from about 1,000 families. The Syriac Orthodox farming population had recently migrated from Tur Abdin. Many of the villages in this district were on level ground and lacked the ability to defend themselves against outsiders. Therefore, those who could went to villages higher up on the nearby Izlo Mountain, which formed a steep slope up to the Tur Abdin plateau. Among those who fled from the town were about 30 youths.

During late Ottoman times, Nisibin was a garrison town for troops employed in stamping out Kurdish rebellions. By the start of the World War, Nisibin was planned to be a station on the railway to Baghdad. Here was the seat of the kaymakam. Many survivors of the 1915 massacres found work here finishing the railway line, cutting timber in the forested mountain slopes (the only wooded tract in the region), burning charcoal for the trains, and so on.

At the start of the troubles, a committee was formed to organize the atrocities in the Nisibin region. It was headed by Refik Nizamettin Qaddur Bey and Süleyman Majar. Qaddur Bey held the rank of lieutenant and commanded the local Al-Khamsin militia units. According to Armalto, the committee sent letters to the rural Kurdish chiefs ordering them to get rid of their Christian tenants. Among the Kurdish leaders who obeyed this summons were Ibrahim, the Agha of Khezna, Ahmed Yousuf, Muhammed Abbas Agha of Dawkar, and Ali Isa.[88] Gangs of "*çete*" were organized by Qaddur Bey to crush the rural villages. At first, the local authorities and Kurdish tribal chiefs assured the Syriac Orthodox population that the massacres and deportation that affected the Armenians would not be done to them. Some Syriacs did not believe these promises and fled to the mountains. Many Christian villages were completely annihilated.

The first notable to be killed was Gorgi (Gewargi) Abrat, who was arrested on June 4 and sent to Mardin, where he was included among the several hundred who were executed on June 10. There is some confusion as to the chronology of events in Nisibin, as orders and counterorders were given to local authorities. On June 13, all of the Armenian and Syriac adult men, including some from the neighboring villages, were arrested and put in jail. All of them believed they would be executed, as they already knew about the recent death march at Mardin. They were accused of belonging to secret Armenian revolutionary societies. On the morning of June 14, the authorities released all of the imprisoned Syriac Othodox men and told them to go home and be calm. The same afternoon, all of the other Christians were freed. A few immediately fled to Sinjar Mountain, which was only a few days' journey south. However, on June 15 the just-released Armenian, Syriac Protestant, and Chaldean men were again imprisoned, and that night they were executed. They were assembled, marched out of town, and slain at a stone quarry. At the same time as these events were going on, the Syriac Orthodox priest Istayfanos was summoned to the town hall. An official pretended to send the priest to the countryside to deliver the important message that it was now safe for the Syriacs to come out of hiding and return to town. Soldiers escorted Istayfanos, but once outside the town, they tortured and murdered him. The next day, all the Syriacs—men, women, and children—that the militia could find were assembled at the town hall and told that they would be marched to Mardin. When they came to a place called Nirbo d Afrasto, they were surrounded by the militia and slaughtered. The bodies were thrown into a well. On June 28, some remaining Armenian women in Nisibin were arrested, brought to the stone quarry, and slaughtered.[89]

As a consequence of the government policy of divide and conquer, at first some of the large population of Jacobite Christians had been spared,

---

[88] Armalto, *Al-Qusara*, 418.
[89] Ibid.

while the other Christians were exterminated. But on August 16, the Syriac Orthodox notables, including the bishop, were slain at a place outside the town. Hyacinthe Simon records that it was a "massacre of all Christianity, more than 800 persons."[90] The important clan of Shouha was transferred to Mardin to be tried by a judge. According to one account, all of the Christians of Nisibin had been killed except the handful who escaped to Mount Sinjar.[91] **H, Q, A**

Owena (Uuéna, Avina). This village is 2 days' walk west of Mardin, about 15 kilometers west of Sawro. It was a district administrative center. According to the Agha Petros list, there were 100 Assyro-Chaldeans living here, and A. H. B. asserted that there were 70 Christian families. A massacre of Christians took place on June 1, 1915.[92]

Pesh-Khabur (Peschabour, Peychabour, Feich-Khabour, Faysh Khābūr). Pesh-Khabur is 40 kilometers south of Jezire on the Tigris River, now in Iraq. On July 11, 1915, it was attacked by the sons of Mohamed Agha of the Artoshi (also known as Mestto). The German consul in Mosul, Walter Holstein, reported on July 15, 1915, that Kurds had just assaulted Pesh-Khabur. Pesh-Khabur was the largest rural Chaldean congregation in the region and had 1,300 members. The entire population, consisting "exclusively of Chaldean Christian population, was massacred." He added that as long as the government did nothing to control the vali of Diyarbekir, it was not possible to "reckon that the massacres would stop."[93] It is believed that 900 of the population were massacred that day.[94] Ternon states that Pesh-Khabur was attacked by the Miran tribe.[95]

Piros (Piron, Peroz). Piros was a mixed village with 62 Nestorian households and 300 Chaldeans. The inhabitants were killed in connection with the early June massacres at nearby Sa'irt. See the section on Sa'irt below.

Qal'at-Mara (Kalitmara, Hesno d'Athto, Qal'at al-Mar'a). "The Fortress of the Women" was a completely Christian village about 2 kilometers east of Mardin. Agha Petros listed the Christian population as 800 persons. The village was built on top of the ruins of an important Roman fortress.

---

[90] Simon, *Mardine*, 140; Rhétoré, *"Les Chrétiens aux bêtes"*, 129–30.

[91] Ternon, "Mardin 1915," 183; Gawriye Maqsi-Hanna Hamra, interviewed November 1997 (appendix 1, no. 70).

[92] Simon, *Mardine*, 134; A. H. B., "Mémoires sur Mardine," 112.

[93] Holstein to German Embassy 15 July 1915, in Lepsius, *Deutschland und Armenien*, 103.

[94] Rhétoré, *"Les Chrétiens aux bêtes"*, 321.

[95] Ternon, "Mardin 1915," 369.

The inhabitants were Syriac Orthodox and Syriac Catholics, who each had a parish church. There was also a Protestant chapel. The economy was based on production of wine and weaving. On Friday, June 11, 1915, the women of the village went to the Syriac archbishop and expressed fear of an expected massacre. He advised them to evacuate the village and seek refuge in the Za'faran monastery. On their way home, the villagers saw that Kurds were already plundering the houses. However, the Dashi Kurdish leaders, Ismail the son of Ali Mahmoudi and Ahmed Marzo, tried to calm them, but the villagers instead went on to the monastery about 3 kilometers away. On June 13, about 50 villagers returned to get back into their homes to collect property. Two Ottoman soldiers, Khallo and Abdi, escorted them and pretended to stand guard. The soldiers signaled to the Dashi Kurds, who were waiting in ambush, and all but two men, who managed to escape to Mardin, were slaughtered. One of the survivors, Gewargis, came to the Protestant hospital, where his wounds were treated. Simon recorded the Christian losses to have been 60 dead. On June 24, Nuri Badlisi, the chief of the Al-Khamsin death squad in Mardin, entered the monastery and arrested 450 persons and took them to Mardin. He stated that they were needed for forced labor. Among the arrested were 15 Armenian refugees from Pirane (in the north of the sanjak), and these persons were immediately selected out and shot at a crossroads just south of Mardin called Khajo, and the bodies were placed in a cave.[96] The Syriacs were set to slave labor at building roads, but one by one they ran away after bribing their guards. When they returned to the monastery, they had to continue to bribe Nuri al-Badlisi for safety. After the World War, the settlement had been completely destroyed and there were hardly any Christian survivors.[97] **Q, A**

Qanaq (Kanak, Kanuik). Qanaq is 30 kilometers east of Nisibin on the road to Jezire. In Qanaq lived 50 Syriac families. The inhabitants fled before the attackers arrived. They went to villages in the Izlo Mountain and to Basibrin. There they remained for two years before they returned to Qanaq. The place is now classified as a ruin. **H**

Qarabash (Karabash). The large village of Qarabash is situated about 10 kilometers east of Diyarbekir. The population was completely Christian, of the Syriac Orthodox denomination. It had been subjected to a pogrom that began on October 1, 1895, and lasted two days, and at that time the population was more than 1000. Agha Petros listed 600 persons who lived

---

[96] Ternon, "Mardin 1915," 77.
[97] Armalto, *Al-Qusara*, 423; Simon, *Mardine*, 136.

here just before the war. One of the first anti-Christian events of 1915 occurred here on February 18. Twelve young men from the village were arrested for desertion from the army. They had run away from the draft and hidden in a nearby place called Takhta Kala. When they were interrogated, the court official instead wrote Chanak-Kale, which was the famous fortress along the Dardanelles. It was made to appear that they had deserted in the face of battle, a more serious crime than draft-dodging, and this paved the way for a harsher punishment. They were condemned to death, and to make an example the execution took place in the major towns: two in Mardin, two in Almadina, two in Harput, two in Urfa, and four in Diyarbekir. The Christians considered these persons to be martyrs, and Syriac and Armenian bishops protested and held memorial services. On April 20, two persons from Reshid Bey's committee for the Armenian question arrived in Qarabash. They were Yahya Effendi (son of the agha of the village of Charohiya) and Sidki Effendi (a relative of the CUP National Assembly deputy Feyzi). Accompanying them came 50 militiamen from an Al-Khamsin detachment. They demanded that the villagers hand over all of their weapons. The soldiers went from house to house and collected swords, lances, knives, rifles, and pistols. In secrecy, Kurdish tribesmen had gathered around Qarabash now that it was disarmed. The militia seized 20 villagers and took them away to Diyarbekir, where they were put in the caravanserai Misafir-Khane, which served as a prison. After they had been imprisoned for 5 days, they were taken out and told that they would be put to work building roads. On the way to that site, they were killed at Sharabi and the bodies were thrown in the Tigris River. On April 22, the Al-Khamsin militia and its leaders returned to Qarabash. This time they arrested the rest of the adult males in the village and took them to Diyarbekir, where they were executed. Tribesmen then sacked the village, which was disarmed and without defenders. The priest Behnam and many of the women and children were killed, and some tried to escape to other villages but were hunted down and murdered. A few managed to get as far as the riverbank opposite Diyarbekir. Here soldiers stopped them and took them back to Qarabash. A friendly Kurdish shepherd, Haji Mustafa, attempted to help the survivors. He discovered that a newly appointed army officer named Ibrahim had an honest character. Ibrahim and Mustafa smuggled the villagers in small groups into Diyarbekir. As the village was abandoned, Muslim refugees then moved into the houses.[98] **Q**

---

[98] Testimony of Hanna Shamoun in Naayem, *Assyro-Chaldéens*, 152ff.

Qarte (Qarteh, Kerti). Qarte was a Syriac village with 150 inhabitants in the Hawar River district near Diyarbekir. Along with neighboring villages, it was surrounded on May 3 by a force of 150 men led by Shakir Bey with an Al-Khamsin death squad and members of the Rama tribe. They massacred the adult males of the various small villages here. The village males were collected in Chanaqchi and then taken to a pit near the village Hawar-Dejla, where they were shot. Those from these villages who were murdered numbered 164, "all notable, strong, and rich men." **Q**

Qartmin (Mor Gabriel monastery, Kartmin, Yayvantepe). Qartmin or Mor Gabriel monastery is the largest monastery in Tur Abdin. The oldest buildings date back to 397, but most were built in the sixth century. In the building complex were 33 persons, 6 of them monks. For some time, 70 refugees from Kafarbe found asylum here. But in the autumn of 1917, Kurds under the leadership of Shandi attacked the monastery and killed the refugees, except for 2 children. One of them fled to Basibrin, the other to 'Ayn-Wardo. Shandi's clan, the Azzam, moved into the buildings, and only after the war did the Syriac church get this property back. **H, Q**

Qatrabel (Qatarbel, Keterbel). Qatrabel is a village opposite Diyarbekir on the east bank of the Tigris River. In 1895, an anti-Christian pogrom took place here. Agha Petros listed the Christian population as 300 persons in 1914. On April 1, 1915, Osman, one of the officers of the Al-Khamsin militia, entered the village with a death squad. He called forth the headman and demanded that all weapons be handed over. The villagers insisted that they had no weapons and allowed the soldiers to search if they did not believe. A search was made and the soldiers found a hunting rifle. Osman arrested the headman and four other village leaders and sent them to Kharput to face a court-martial. On April 10, Yahya Effendi and another detachment of Al-Khamsin militia arrived and seized 23 men, tied them up, and took them to a caravanserai in Diyarbekir. There they were tortured for four days. They were taken to a hill named Kandalesur near the village Sharuki and murdered. When the women and children of Qatrabel heard of the executions, they fled across the Tigris and hid in Diyarbekir. **Q**

Qeleth (Killit, Qelleth, Dereiçi). Qeleth is a very large village close to Sawro, about 50 kilometers west of Midyat and 60 kilometers northeast of Mardin. It is on the old main road between these towns and lies in a valley surrounded by high hills. Agha Petros listed the pre-war Christian population as 2,500, and there were no Muslims. Here were Syriac Orthodox, Syriac Catholic, and Protestant parish churches. The church of Mar Yuhanon dates from the seventh century. Close by are the ruins of the monasteries of Mor Abay and Mor Dimat, who were Persian saints.[99] This is the only village in the Muhallemi tract that did not convert to Islam but instead remained Christian. Qarabash related that on June 3, 1915, Kurds appeared, and 25 militiamen said that they had been ordered to guard the village. The village headman Benyamin and his son were taken to Diyarbekir and murdered on their way back. The Christians barricaded themselves in large buildings, but they were slaughtered. Simon dated this event to June 10 and gave the number of victims as more than 2,000 persons.[100] **Q, A**

Qewetla (Khoueitla, Khvitla). Situated 20 kilometers east of Nisibin, Qewetla had 20 Syriac families originating in Arbo. Agha Petros listed a Christian population of 300. Here the villagers had become aware of the attacks on Nisibin and other villages. They fled to a Muslim village, Upper Qewetla. The Muslim chief, Halil, guaranteed their safety as long as they were in his village. Halil, however, went to fetch more tribesmen. The Christians, perceiving treachery, began to flee but were pursued by Halil and other Kurds. Hinno stated that they managed to get to the village of Qritho di' Ito and proceed from there to Beth-Debe. Qarabash stated that the Christians of Qewetla were all killed in a coordinated attack of Al-Khamsin militia under Qaddur Bey and Dakshuri Kurds. **H, Q**

Qritho di' Ito (Gündükschükrü, Odabaşı). The village of Qritho di'Ito is 20 kilometers east of Nisibin on the road to Jezire. Fifty Syriac families lived here before World War I. It lies in an open plain and was known as a producer of cotton. The owners were the Malke Gawriye family. Most of the Syriacs traced their roots to Hebob. Already in April, the Monday after Easter, the Turkish commander, Sheyhe Dolmaji, came here with 15 soldiers to round up deserters from the army. He tortured some, and the Christians attacked the Turks and killed the commander, and the soldiers were chased away. After this event the villagers took their valuables and fled to Hebob. **H**

Quwwal (Kovel). Quwwal lies east of Nisibin. The 10 Syriac families who lived here were all killed. **H**

Ras al-'Ayn (Rish-'Ayno). Ras al-'Ayn is now a medium-sized town on the Syrian-Turkish border on the Khabur River. It was about 18 hours' march over the steppe south of Mardin. This was an ancient but small settlement that had flourished during antiquity and early Christianity. The Ottomans were using it as a place to colonize Caucasian Muslim refugees. Before World War I there was a large concentration of Circassian refugees,

---

[99] Hollerweger, *Turabdin*, 143–49.
[100] Simon, *Mardine*, 135.

who were very hostile toward Christians of all denominations. It was the nearest train station on the unfinished Baghdad railway for the expelled in transit through Mardin and Diyarbekir. From here the deportees could be sent on to Deyr-Zor for transport into the desert.[101]

Ras al-'Ayn was designated one of the major collecting places for the deported Christians. At the beginning of the deportations and massacres, almost every Christian was killed near their home towns and villages or along the main roads, so few of the first deportation caravans actually reached this destination. However, by September 1915 the columns of surviving deportees began to arrive after the exhausting journey. The refugee population was usually made up only of women and children. Armalto stated that the local governor was well inclined, treating the Christians mildly and punishing those who attacked them. Near the end of September 1915, about 1,500 barefoot and badly clothed Armenians deported from Sivas and other places arrived. They were in such bad condition that nearly 200 died more or less immediately. The following days, the rest of them were killed by soldiers who had been sent from Deyr-Zor for this task. Columns kept coming from the distant provinces of Izmir, Konya, Ankara, Dörtyol, Mar'ash, 'Ayntab, Mersin, and Zeytoun.

A total of 70,000 were said to have passed through Ras al-'Ayn, and at its peak about 40,000 survivors were assembled. Some of them had managed to keep part of their valuables, and a large tent camp was erected. After two weeks in the tent camp, a large part of the Christians were selected and divided into four large groups. Two were sent in the direction of Deyr-Zor and two were sent to Mosul, where they apparently arrived safely.

In late January 1916, Rafi Bey, a Circassian, was appointed the new local governor. He ordered all Armenians in Ras al-'Ayn to prepare to be sent away without their food, clothing, or other property. For reasons unknown, this order was not put into effect, but in March 1916 a detachment of Circassian soldiers, led by their officer Hussein Bey, surrounded fifty tents, and the inhabitants were told to start marching without any baggage. They were beaten along the way until they arrived at the village of Jarjab, where they were murdered. Afterward, the soldiers returned to the tents and took all the property left behind. Five days later, the same procedure was repeated, and the inhabitants of another fifty tents were forced to walk to Jarjab, where they were killed. The murders continued for weeks until the tent

---

[101] Armalto, *Al-Qusara*, 360; P. V. M., "Autres documents sur les événements de Mardine" (1998), 57–58.

camp was empty. The motive for the extermination was said to have been to prevent an epidemic of typhus.[102]

A sizable group of Armenians converted to Islam and were allowed to build houses in the town. However, on May 1, 1916, even they were captured by Circassian soldiers and taken to Jarjab. The males and females were kept in separate groups. Bedouins who had been hiding nearby attacked and slaughtered both groups except for some of the attractive women. One man, Abd al-'Jalil Burghouth, managed to flee to Mardin, his hometown, to report what happened. After this event there were only 20 Armenian families left in Ras al-'Ayn, and they were all artisans except the family of the tobacco trader Wasif Effendi, who had bought false documents purporting that his religion was Syriac Orthodoxy rather than Armenian.

Sadath (Sadek, Sadakh). Sadath had 12 Nestorian households and 230 Chaldeans. As part of the Sa'irt diocese, the inhabitants were victim to the great massacres of June 1915. See the section on Sa'irt below.

Sa'diye. Sa'diye lies in the rural district of Diyarbekir about two hours' walk east of the city. Agha Petros listed the pre-war Syriac population as 350. The inhabitants were Armenians and Syriac Orthodox. It was subject to a major pogrom on October 1, 1895, and many people perished in the church when it was set on fire. Concening the events of 1915, Qarabash recorded the testimony of one of the militia soldiers. He said that an official from Almadia had taken 70 Christian captives from Beshiri to Sa'diye to execute them at a cliff overlooking the Tigris River. Observing that the village was intact, the official approached the militia and asked why they had not annihilated the Christians of Sa'diye, stating that it was an order. The Syriacs and Armenians gathered and took Holy Communion together. The soldiers searched the village and captured the priest, who was tortured and killed. **Q**

Sa'irt (Siirt, Seerd, Sahirt). The town of Sa'irt is along a tributary of the Bohtan River in the province of Bitlis. High mountains bound the region to the west, south, and east. Before World War I, the town and its surrounding villages were a Christian enclave, but with considerable variation. Immediately surrounding Sa'irt, the Christian communities belonged to the Chaldean Church. Tfinkdji noted a total population of 5,430 persons in the Chaldean diocese, with 21 priests, 31 churches, 7 chapels, and 9 schools. Of the Chaldeans, 824 lived in the town and the rest in 36 surrounding villages. The Agha Petros list noted 40 Nestorian Assyrian households in the town.

---

[102] Rhétoré, *"Les Chrétiens aux bêtes"*, 161.

To the northeast was an area of mixed Armenian and Syriac Orthodox villages with some Yezidi presence. To the east, beyond a mountain range, was a region of mixed Chaldean and Nestorian villages. According to Rhétoré there were originally 15,000 Chaldeans among the estimated 60,000 Christians living in the Sa'irt sanjak as well as 25,000 Armenians and 20,000 Syriac Orthodox.[103]

In June 1915, the armies of vali Jevdet Bey and general Halil Bey, who were retreating from Hakkari (see chap. 5), organized a general massacre that lasted throughout the month. People were killed in their houses and in the streets. "No one was spared," stated one account. Organized gangs of *çete* did the destruction in the town, while Kurdish tribes destroyed the rural villages. The mercenary officer Nogales asserted that the attack was premeditated, planned as an act of revenge for the defeat at the hands of the Russians.

> On the road to Sairt several officers of the Voluntary Battalion of Bash-Kaleh overtook me, and snatched time to explain with an air of great satisfaction how and when the authorities at Bitlis had everything in readiness, merely awaiting Khalil Bey's final order, to commence one of the most cowardly massacres in the contemporary history of Armenia. ... These fellows even advised me to hurry up if I wished to arrive in time to witness the great massacre of Sairt, which by that time must have already commenced under the direction of the Governor-General of the province, Jevdet Bey.

Nogales arrived at midday on June 18 and saw

> the atrocious spectacle afforded by a hill beside the highway. The ghastly slope was crowned by thousands of half-nude and still bleeding corpses, lying in heaps, or interlaced in death's final embrace. ... Overcome by the hideous spectacle, and jumping our horses over the mountains of cadavers, which obstructed our passage, I entered Sairt with my men. There we found the police and the populace engaged in sacking the houses of the Christians. At the Seraglio I met various sub-Governors of the province, assembled in council under the presidency of the chief of the local gendarmes, Nasim Effendi, who had directed the massacre in person. From their talk I realized at once that the thing had been arranged the day before by Jevdet Bey. Meanwhile I had taken up my lodging in a handsome house belonging to Nestorians, which had been sacked like all the rest. There was nothing left in the way of furni-

---

[103] Ibid., 225.

ture except a few broken chairs. Walls and floors were stained with blood.[104]

Just before the Sa'irt massacre, Jevdet Bey had left, proceeding to Bitlis to organize yet one more terrible slaughter.

The surviving women and children were forced to march to an unknown destination, sometimes in one direction, sometimes another, being beaten by the gendarmes along the way. The survivors arrived in Mosul. The loss of life was staggering: some one hundred persons managed to arrive from an area where there had originally been between 7,000 and 8,000 Chaldeans.[105]

> The massacres at Sa'irt preceded by three days those of Bitlis and were much more atrocious. I possess the very relevant details about the massacres which touch me very deeply, but it is impossible to relate them in this short report. In summary, one should know that our Chaldean diocese in Sa'irt has been completely exterminated. In fact, the government registers do not include the names of more than 767 men, but those are exceeded by the names of those who were shot on one single occasion, on the top of a hill that is to be found one hour north of the town. The number grows much greater if it includes those who were killed in their houses and in the streets. The massacres went on for more than a month. They commenced in the middle of May and were not finished until the month of June. No person was spared. The "chettis" attacked the Christians of the town, and the Kurds [attacked] those in the villages. The Armenian women of Sa'irt were the first to arrive in Mosul. They were 1,700 on departure, but only six or seven hundred arrived in a lamentable state, after a forced march of eight days. Those who arrived were mostly only older women. The young were ravished on the way by the Kurds, or sold and killed by the gendarmes. They were installed in a house of the apostolic delegate and were given new clothes by the German consul [Walter Holstein]. ... The Chaldean women of Sa'irt ended in a more unfortunate way, but conducted themselves heroically and with admirable dignity. After resisting for an entire month the indecent solicitations of the Turkish officers and their soldiers, they were abused without pity because of their virtue. They were told to leave their homes after the disappearance of their husbands and chil-

---

[104] Nogales, *Four Years beneath the Crescent*, 123–25.

[105] "Note adressée au Consulat de France en Mésopotamie par un ecclésiastique chaldéen," undated report appended to a letter of January 16, 1918, addressed to the French Foreign Minister Pichon, in Arthur Beylerian, *Les Grandes Puissants: L'Empire Ottoman et les arméniens dans les archives françaises (1914–1918)* (1983), 478–79.

dren. They sought protection through grouping together into five or six large houses in the Chaldean quarter. Finally, they were taken from their place of protection and conducted in an unknown direction. They left the town in a cortege, all dressed in black and silently. The Dominicans, six in number, preceded and sang pious songs. The superior, an old man, was killed by crushing blows when he could no longer walk. A certain number of them together with many young girls threw themselves into the river and tried to escape from their killers. The others were taken by the Kurds. A great number died on the road from the blows dealt by the gendarmes as they were pressed to march sometimes in one direction and sometimes in another. ... In all, about one hundred persons were all that was left of the Chaldean diocese of Sa'irt, which counted seven or eight thousand souls.[106]

One of the victims was the Chaldean bishop Addai Sher, who was a well-known scholar who had published his research in European journals.[107] The bishop had been arrested and locked up in May just before the massacres, but a Kurdish agha named Osman (said to be a client of the Badr-Khans) helped him escape disguised in Kurdish clothes. He hid in a Yezidi village named Tanzi. When he was discovered, he fled to a nearby mountain with a chief named Omar Agha, and they prepared to proceed toward Mosul. On the way south, gendarmes caught the bishop, who was shot after refusing to convert.[108]

Armalto related some futher details of the events in Sa'irt:

In the middle of June 1915, the enemy went into action and broke into the homes of the first group of Christians. They tortured them brutally and killed them directly afterward. Then they arrested the leading clans like the notworthy family Abboush, which had almost 60 members, Iwaz [Aywaz], Mousa Kourkis [Gorgis], Lousho and others, in total around 600 persons. They were thrown into prison. Their relatives were forbidden to visit them or bring food. The five Armenian priests and other leading men were taken to the torture-chamber where they were interrogated about weapons caches, were beaten and tortured. Ahmed Agha Koja al-Si'radi [Kocha Sa'irti] threw himself onto the Jacobite Syriac priest Ibrahim and cut off his head. Boys then played with it in

---

[106] Ibid., 478–79.
[107] Ternon, "Mardin 1915," 209.
[108] Letter of Philippe Chauris to Gonzalve Galland September 25, 1917, in Rhétoré, *"Les Chrétiens aux bêtes"*, 338–39. "The Killing of the Christians in Seert" (1993), 63–68, gives a slightly different version of events.

the streets of the town. Qasime and his evil companions assaulted the Chaldean priest and Dominican student Gabriel Kabo [Adamo] in his home and brought him, beating him all the way, to the government building. When they arrived, they stripped him and took turns beating him and stabbing him with knives. With each blow they urged him to convert to Islam. But the pious father refused and screamed as loudly as he could, "I die in the faith of the risen Christ," until he gave up his spirit. The enemy cut off his head and rolled it into a nearby ditch known as Beit al-Agha's dike. When the Christians had spent four days in prison, the enemy came in, tied them up, and brought them all at sunrise to Zaryab valley, an hour's walk north of Sa'irt. There they took out their weapons and daggers and prepared to kill. Then the Syriac priest Efram al-Qusurani [Afrem Qesorani] rose up and gave a short speech, fired up the other prisoners' faith, and strengthened them in their conviction to leave the port of life through love of their savior. At that the enemy attacked them and slaughtered them to the last man. Loud screams were heard all the way to town and they made the earth shake. Thereafter, the killers returned to town and drew lots for their clothes. Then they searched the houses a third time and seized the women, boys, and girls. They placed them in three columns and marched them away. Most of the women were raped. Hate and cruelty were such that they were forced to go naked, hungry, and thirsty along the most desolate roads in order to experience maximum fear and pain. The killers kept many of the youngest girls to satisfy their obscene lust. Remaining in town were some children, who for a time received food. But when the Russian troops approached, the remainder were attacked and killed at Sari Zine [Z'ayne].[109]

Jalila, another Sa'irt witness, was interviewed by Naayem in October 1917. She was the sister of the Chaldean archbishop's secretary and thus was well acquainted with the views of the Chaldean Church. She described the arrival in Sa'irt of the vali of Van, Jevdet Bey, with large contingents of soldiers. They were retreating, along with civilian Muslims from the Hakkari Mountains. Jevdet arrived in Sa'irt with 8,000 soldiers, including a detachment he always called the butcher battalion (*kassablar taburu*). When the first mass arrests occurred, the relatives were told that the Christian men would not be harmed but would be sent to forced labor. This did not calm the Christians, as they had heard of Kurdish tribes assembling outside the town. The Chaldean archbishop Addai Sher gave Jevdet 500 gold liras as a bribe to drive away the tribes. The local mayor, Abdul Ressak, protected the

---

[109] Armalto, *Al-Qusara*, 388.

Christians, but he was replaced by Hami Effendi, who was known as a fanatic. After this, Osman Agha helped the archbishop to flee disguised in Kurdish clothes. The destruction of the Chaldean community in Sa'irt, which was over by early July, had been organized by the local governor, the chief of police, the mayor, and other notables listed by name in Naayem's report. Jalil was put into a column of women and children and sent west. On the way, the exiles were attacked several times by tribesmen, who took their money, food, and clothing. They seized the attractive women, among them Jalil's eight-year-old daughter Ewdoksiya, her sister-in-law Salima, and her nieces Najima and Latifa. When the remains of the column reached Sawro, the survivors were stoned by waiting Kurds.[110] Jalil was knocked unconscious but was still alive, and an older Kurdish man took her to his house. From there she managed to get to Mardin, where a female relative lived. After about a year, she managed to find her daughter.[111]

A report from the Chaldean patriarch of Babylon, Joseph-Emmanuel Thomas, dated January 29, 1919, listed all of the destroyed Chaldean villages in the Bohtan dioceses.[112] For Sa'irt, the number of victims was 4,000 as well as the bishop and 12 priests. Beside the name of each village the report gives the names of those who executed the massacres. Then it gives the name of those who had "promoted" the massacres. Among the executioners were mostly local Kurdish tribes, but among the instigators there were well-known local politicians and officials.

The promoters of the massacres in Sa'irt were

> Hamdi Bey, the chief of the gendarmes; the sons of Haji Mohammed Agha; Abdul-Rassak [Abdul Rezzak]; Haji Abdallah; Hamed Effendi; Haji Mustapha Hetro; shaykh Mohammed; Ahmed Shakardji Beth Kedjki; Abdul Maula; Seid Hassan-Moukitar; Haji Yasin; Seid Haider; Hassan-Mohamé Beth Hamké; Beth Mamo; Haji Isa Kamo; Beth Haji Abdul-Karim; the sons of Haji Abdul-Rahim; Beth Haji Khalaf; Haji Mousa.

These were predominantly Kurdish tribal leaders. Naayem gave the following list of the organizers behind the Sa'irt massacres:

---

[110] Simon notes that this event took place on July 24 and that 250 women were stoned to death (*Mardine,* 138).

[111] Naayem, *Assyro-Chaldéens,* 48–96.

[112] Ternon, "Mardin 1915," 368–70.

Hilmi Bey, the mutasarrif; Hamdi Bey the chief of police; Hami Effendi, the mayor; Ali Effendi, policeman; Emin Basri, policeman; Fathulla Effendi; Haji Abdi Mussulli, merchant; Fardo Ibn Ibrahim, merchant; Aziz ibn Haji Ömer, a cousin of Fardo; Mullah Heder; Mullah Elyas; Haji Ibrahim Hasane; Hamid Agha and his four sons; Hamdi ibn Haji Mamad Effendi.[113]

The perpetrators of the massacres in and around Sa'irt were: "The sons of Haji Barkho, the head of Halenzi; Sheik Mohammed head of the Fiskin, Sheik Mohammed head of the Farsaf; the sons of Sheik Nuri head of the Toun; the sons of Selo head of the Djouankiye and their bands." Outlying villages were the victims of local tribes. The killers in the village of Hamidi were "Kelhoc, Bloris and Omer-Rivern of Kersia." The perpetrators at Gidyanes were "the sons of Taher-Haji-Djenguir." The leading attacker of Tel-Michar was "Mohammed-Resoul and his sons." At Mar Gurya, the assault was by "the chiefs of the Karan-Dara." At Der Shemsh, it was "Cheik Khierd [Shaykh Kheder] and his sons." At Benkof, it was "the sons of Ömer Agha." At Sadath, it was "the aghas of Gund, sheik Fakiy-Kasim Abdulkarim." At the villages of Berke and Bekind, it was "the sons of Faro-Ömer-Eskan." In the villages of Piros, Dentass, Eleloké, Upper Artvena, and Lower Artvena, the perpetrators were "the aghas of Aro and their bands." At Dehok, it was "the aghas of Bataviya," and at Gueratel, it was "the aghas of Garcia-Demany." Clearly, a very large number of the neighboring Kurdish tribes participated.[114]

Saleh (Salah, Barıştepe). Saleh had 40 Syriac Orthodox families. This village is about 8 kilometers north of Midyat, and nearby were the ruins of the ancient monastery of Mor Ya'qub. The name of the agha was Hassano. On July 3, 1915, soldiers and Kurdish clans instigated by Midyat's new kaymakam, Bashar Bey, surrounded the village. The Christians fought back in defense but were overpowered and killed in their homes. Muslim refugees displaced by the war settled in the empty houses. Gradually the surviving Syriac families tried to return, but there were many violent conflicts.[115]
H, A

---

[113] Naayem, *Assyro-Chaldéens*, 57–58.

[114] The villages of Artvena, Gueratel, and Piros are 30 kilometers east of Sa'irt; Mar Gurya is about 10 kilometers southwest. Isho' Qasho-Malke, interviewed November 1993 (appendix 1, no. 73).

[115] Armalto, *Al-Qusara*, 400; Use Malke-Sahyo, interviewed July 1995 (appendix 1, no. 56).

Sare (Gawayto, Istir, Sariköy). Sare is located 37 kilometers east of Midyat. Sixty Syriac families lived there. It had two parish churches, Mar Malke and Mort Shmuni. During the time of the massacres, the inhabitants took refuge in Basibrin, which is 3 kilometers away. For more information see the entry for Basibrin. **H, A**

Sawro (Sor, Sur, Savur). The town of Sawro is 48 kilometers north of Mardin on the ridge of a hill. A river runs in the valley and makes for good crops of fruits and vegetables. It is built on the site of an ancient fortress. For a period it was the seat of a bishopric. Many of the Christians converted to Islam together with the Muhallemi, and the town held many more Muslims than Christians. Before the World War, it contained 300 Armenian and Syriac Christians. The Agha Petros list gave a Syriac population of 200. The neighboring Kurdish tribes were the Diveran, the Dizveren, the Köse, and the Sürgücü.[116] In June 1915, the local Kurdish chiefs communicated with Mardin asking what should be done with the Christians. The government gave them freedom to do what they liked. The Kurds arrested the males and tortured them. Then they were taken out of jail and killed at a place known as Babein. Only four men were left in the prison, and as they were being taken on the highway to Mardin, they were also slain. The Kurds demanded gold, silver, and jewels from the Christian women. They arrested the women and put them under guard in a barracks without food or water. After two days, some were taken out and executed. Many women survived prison and were marched out of town. Along the way, local Kurds came up and seized boys and girls and took them away. They were marched all the way to Nisibin, where they rested. The next day they marched off and were attacked by Kurdish tribes, who took their clothes and killed them. The bodies were thrown into wells. Simon dated this massacre to July 20, 1915, and estimated the number of victims to be more than 650 persons.[117] **A**

Sederi (Sideri). Sederi is southeast of Midyat, very close to the Mor Malke monastery. Survivors from this village fled to the monastery.

Seruja (Srougiye). Seruja is in the Nisibin upland and had 30 Syriac families. The owner was Lahdo Barsavmo from Hebob. Here all of the Christians managed to flee to Hebob under the escort of armed Syriacs sent down from the mountains. **H**

---

[116] Suavi Aydin et al., *Mardin: Aşiret – Cemaat – Devlet* [Mardin: Tribes, communities, state] (2000), 462–63.

[117] Simon, *Mardine*, 138.

Sha'baniye (Sha'bane, Chabanié). This was a village in the Jezire diocese with 28 Syriac families. All of them were reported killed.[118]

Shahdadde (Chiddadi). Shahdadde was a concentration camp near Deyr-Zor by a bridge over the Khabur River. At its greatest extent it held 15,000 captives, mostly Armenians who had survived the caravans from the central and western provinces. Large exterminations took place on several occasions, and the bodies were thrown either into the river or into a salt-mine. Armalto reports that the Jabbur Bedouins tried to help the captives.[119]

Shakh (Chahk). This village of 300 lies 15 kilometers east of Jezire. Originally Chaldean, most inhabitants had converted to Protestantism by the outbreak of the World War, and 140 remained Chaldean. Turkish soldiers stationed there massacred the inhabitants.

> Kasha Mattai was killed by Kurds in the mountain while fleeing. Kasha Elia and Kasha Sargis, with other men of the village of Shakh, were killed by Turkish soldiers, who had been stationed in their village by the Government. The three villages of Hassan [Hassana], Shakh and Monsoria were Protestant, and it is to be feared that they were wiped out, as were all the other villages of the plain.[120]

Shehirkan. Twenty Syriac families lived in Shehirkan, near Hah. Half of them were massacred and half managed to get to Hah. **H**

Shelumiye (Chalhoumiye). Shelumiye lies in the colonization region 20 kilometers east of Nisibin. Fifty Syriac families lived in this village before the World War. The owner was Hasan Abbas, a Kurd of the Hajji Slaymani tribe. The Christians asked Hasan to ride out and find out what was happening in the other villages, since they had heard of massacres. On return, he confirmed the atrocities in Helwa and Duger. The authorities had said to Hasan that he should calm the Syriacs so that they would remain in the village, but instead he told them to flee to the mountains, which they did. They reached the village of Hebob, where they stayed throughout the period of massacres.[121] **H**

Shterako (Estrako, Hesterek). Shterako is 17 kilometers northeast of Midyat. Before the massacres, 20 Syriac families lived among 200 Kurdish

---

[118] Hannouche, *Azekh*, 66.

[119] Armalto, *Al-Qusara*, 365; Rhétoré, *"Les chrétiens aux bêtes"*, 169–70.

[120] Report by E. W. McDowell to Board of Foreign Missons of the Presbyterian Church March 6, 1916, in Bryce and Toynbee, *Treatment of Armenians*, 211–12.

[121] Gawriye Maqsi-Hanna Hamra, interviewed November 1997 (appendix 1, no. 70).

families. The parish church, Mar Addai, has been dated to the first century. It is now a mosque. From the nineteenth century, Shterako was the seat of a Kurdish agha. On July 3, 1915, the Kurdish neighbors murdered the Syriacs. Twelve youths survived and managed to get to Hah. **H, A**

Shufir-Anase. One Syriac family lived in the Kurdish village of Shufir-Anase, and it was annihilated. **H**

Siha (Sabha). Siha is in the Nisibin upland. It is not on the Agha Petros list, so it was probably a village that was predominantly Muslim. The Christians of Siha were murdered by the owner of the village, Ahmed Yusef. According to Qarabash, he was acting at the instigation of Qaddur Bey, the leader of the Al-Khamsin militia.[122] **Q**

Sinjar (Shigur, Sincar). The Sinjar Mountains are a broad ridge of high hills in the desert of northern Iraq, northwest of Mosul. It is a fertile region reputed to have contained about fifty villages with a population before World War I of 8,000 persons. At one time, Christianity was well established here, as the ruins of many churches and monasteries witness. However, from the end of the twelfth century the major population was the Yezidis, who had their own unique religion.[123] The Muslims persecuted the Yezidis, but they still survived in a few out-of-the-way places in Mesopotamia. Rhétoré considered the Yezidis to be the "only protectors" of the persecuted Christians. In November 1916, there were close to a thousand refugees living here: 500 Gregorian Armenians, 160 Catholic Armenians, 100 Syriac Orthodox, and 100 Chaldean and Syriac Catholics.[124]

The Yezidi religion is named after its founder, who is worshipped alongside the gods Shaykh 'Adi, Malik Tawus, Sharaf al-din, Shams al-din, and Fakhr al-din. The religion emerged as a sect in the seventh century. It is traditional to describe the Yezidis as "devil-worshippers," as their god Malik Tawus can be identified as a god of evil. The followers believe in reincarnation.

As fellow non-Muslims, Yezidis and Christians were on good terms with each other, and there was much trade and commerce between them. When the war began, some young Christian men, particularly from Mardin, fled to the Sinjar Mountains to avoid military conscription. Additional refugees started arriving when news of the massacres spread. This was mostly an in-flow of younger males. The combined secular and religious leader of

---

[122] Ibid.
[123] Armalto, *Al-Qusara*, 369–83.
[124] Rhétoré, *"Les Chrétiens aux bêtes"*, 142.

the Yezidis was named Shaykh Hamo Sharro, and he saw to it that the refugees were given asylum.

The situation for the Christians was not happy. They worried about the families and friends they had left behind. Also in the autumn of 1915, an epidemic of typhoid fever broke out, and the Christians were accused by some Yezidis of being the cause of the disease. The Christians were therefore collected and concentrated in one place on a hill, which was reserved for them and where they could build houses. The Chaldean priest Yousuf Tfinkdji fled from Mardin and served as minister to the Christians, who prayed and sang psalms in Armenian and Arabic. After a short while, Tfinkdji returned to Mardin and was succeeded as priest by Farjallah Kaspo, a teacher. According to Armalto, the Christian colony built about sixty dwellings in the Sinjar region. They also built a hospital.

In March 1916, deported Armenians arrived in Deyr-Zor, and some escaped to Sinjar's southern parts after they were forced into the desert. The Yezidis went out and collected the survivors that could be found wandering about, and they were brought to the Christian colony. Also, at that time a group of Armenian Catholics arrived from Mardin. In all, about 300 additional Christians received asylum during the spring of 1916. But it proved more and more difficult to feed and house the stream of new arrivals. Some Christians worked in the vineyards and gardens of the Yezidis, and some traded their agricultural produce with the Tayy Bedouin tribe.

In the spring of 1917, a motorway was opened leading to Baghdad, and it ran close to the Sinjar Mountains. A group of refugees from Mardin managed to get to Baghdad with the help of some Arabs, and they lived in the city in relative freedom. They wrote to relatives in Sinjar and told them that the danger was over, but many in Sinjar were suspicious. Some, however, left Sinjar to work on building the railroad.

In March 1918, there was a confrontation between the Yezidis and the Turks, who sent a small army to conquer the Sinjar region and punish the Christians and Yezidis. The Ottoman troops proved too great for the Yezidis and caused much destruction. The Christian colony was burned. The Christians fled, and most of the Yezidis capitulated. Hamo Sharro was sentenced to five years in prison at hard labor. **Q**

Sirmi (Sırımkesen). Sirmi was a village with 300 Syriac inhabitants. It is located south of Diyarbekir. On May 3, 1915, all of the adult Christian males were killed. Shakir Bey, of the vali's inner circle, and Ömer of the Rama tribe led the attackers. Some of the women and children managed to get to safety in Diyarbekir; others were captured by the Kurds. **Q**

Siwerak (Siverek). This administrative town is located northwest of Viranshehir. The Agha Petros list stated that it had 1,200 Syriac inhabitants and that there was a rural population of 6,550 Syriacs in 32 villages. The men and priests were killed and the women raped. The bishop Athanasios Danho was 79 years old. He was jailed, tortured, and then crushed to death under stones.[125] **H**

Tamarz (Temerzi, Üçarli). Tamarz lies 15 kilometers southwest of Azakh. Twenty Syriac families lived in Tamarz; these were originally East Syriac Nestorians, but they had joined the Chaldean Church in the nineteenth century. The Kurdish chief Muhamma 'Alo (also called Aliko) lived with his clan in the village. This tribe belonged to the Haverkan confederation. When they heard the shooting in neighboring Midun, the villagers went to Muhamma. He said that he would not harm them and they would be safe as long as they remained. But if they had to move elsewhere, he could not protect them in those places. However, if they wished to seek protection elsewhere, they would escort them. The Syriacs asked that he escort them to Basibrin. **H, A**

Taqiyan (Tahyan, Takyan, Takian). This Chaldean village with a pre-war population of 600 (Agha Petros) or 900 (Tfinkdji) is about 30 kilometers southeast of Jezire in the Silopi plain. It contained a large monastery church where the Christians tried to defend themselves. It was attacked on July 10, 1915, by the aghas of Şirnak and Silopi and Suleiman Ismael. The inhabitants were locked into the church and it was set on fire. The mayor, the priest, and 105 others were slaughtered.[126]

Tel-Arman (Kızıltepe). Tel-Arman was a very large Armenian Catholic village with a population of about 6,000 located 4 hours foot-march southwest of Mardin. Tfinkdji stated that 100 Chaldeans also lived here. It was subject to a pogrom on November 6, 1895, that was organized by the Hamidiye regiment belonging to the Kiki Kurdish tribe. According to Rhétoré, this was the most important tax district in the whole sandjak of Mardin. Its rich economy had its background as a major caravan stop with many merchants and craftsmen supplying the caravans. A. H. B. claims that no household had less than 200 head of cattle. The first measures against the Armenian Catholics came in April, when the village was surrounded by cavalry who demanded that 500 Armenians be recruited into the labor battalions. These persons were sent to Diyarbekir and disappeared without a

---

[125] Ibid., 47–48.
[126] Ibid., 321; Ternon, "Mardin 1915," 369; Thiry, *Mechelen aan de Tigris*, 104.

trace. Armalto stated that the initiative for the annihilation of the Armenians came from the Ottoman mudir in Tel-Arman, Darwish, who was the son of Qaddur Chelebi of Mardin. He had written to the vali accusing the Armenians. On June 7, the militia arrested Sarkis, one of the village headmen, accusing him of smuggling weapons and bombs into Mardin's Armenian church. On June 11, a detachment of soldiers arrived from Mardin and seized some priests and notables. These people were taken out of the settlement and killed. On June 18, the soldiers seized 10 more people and took them to Mardin, where they were imprisoned for many days. All men aged between 10 and 70 were arrested and placed inside the church. Kurds from the surrounding area began to assemble, waiting for an order from Darwish. The Armenian women appealed to him for an explanation but were told they had nothing to worry about. A detachment of soldiers was sent to nearby Brahemiye to capture Syriac and Armenian Christians there and bring them to Tel-Arman. However, some of the Syriac Orthodox escaped. The Christians being escorted were attacked by the Shahtana Kurds and troops led by Darwish. The males were murdered and the women placed in Tel-Arman church. A hundred men were selected from the church and bound together in groups of four. On July 1, they were marched out and executed. The Kurds then returned to the village and slaughtered those who remained in the church. Many of the bodies were burned. Women who survived were raped. A few persons managed to hide through the massacres. Simon recorded that the number of Christian deaths was 1,500 persons.[127]

The corpses were left lying on the ground. A few days later, a German major named Mikusch passed through and reported with disgust, "About a week ago the Kurds staged an Armenian slaughter (*Armeniermetzeleien*) in Tel-Arman and the surrounding villages. The large churches are in ruins. Herr von Mikusch saw for himself 200 corpses. The militia and gendarmes had tolerated, and probably participated in it." The major also met up with a group of released convicts and their regular army commander, who had just plundered an Armenian village and who were "beaming with joy" when they boasted of their exploits.[128] The German consul in Aleppo, Rössler, considered the presence of military personnel to show the implication of the Turkish government in the massacres despite continual denials.[129] Trav-

---

[127] Armalto, *Al-Qusara*, 435; Rhétoré, *"Les Chrétiens aux bêtes"*, 120–22; Simon, *Mardine*, 137, A. H. B., "Mémoires sur Mardine," 126–29.

[128] Wangenheim to Bethmann Hollweg July 9, 1915, in Lepsius, *Deutschland und Armenien*, 98.

[129] Rössler to Bethmann Hollweg July 27, 1915, ibid., 111.

eling between Mosul and Aleppo, vice-consul Walter Holstein stopped at Tel-Arman: he found the church filled with decapitated heads and severed limbs.[130]

Tel-Aryawon. Tel-Aryawon, east of Nisibin, had 20 Syriac and Kurdish families. The village leader was Sleyman Abbas, a Kurd. Half of the village belonged to the Syriac Abbo family. When news of the massacres spread, Sleyman rode off to Duger, which was owned by his brother, to see what was going on. When he returned, he confirmed that massacres were happening everywhere. He advised the Christians to get away quickly to the village of Mar Bobo. The men fled first, leaving the women and children under Sleyman's protection. Three days later, Sleyman organized an escort of Arabs, who took the women and children to safety in Mar Bobo. **H**

Tel-Bal (Telibel). Tel-Bal was in Jezire diocese and had 50 Syriac families. According to Hannouche, there were only 2 survivors, who had been hidden by their Kurdish servants.[131]

Tel-Dare (Teldare, Teldin). This Chaldean village with 250 inhabitants was in the Jezire diocese of the Chaldean Church about 10 kilomters south of the town. It also included 5 Armenian families. It was stormed by the Esene, a Kurdish tribe. **H**

Tel-Hasan. Tel-Hasan is 20 kilometers east of Nisibin. Fifteen Syriac families lived here. The owner was Ömer Osman, who killed the Christians. Hinno records that Ömer personally killed seven Christian widows and collected their blood. **H**

Tel-Jihan (Tell Cihan). Tel-Jihan is 15 kilometers east of Nisibin. Hinno stated that the 15 Syriac families who lived here fled in time. But oral history relates that some of the villagers were killed at Lake Qiro near Duger.[132] **H**

Tel-Khatun. Tel-Khatun is situated about 30 kilometers east of Nisibin. Agha Petros indicated a pre-war Christian population of 250. The testimony published by Hinno came from Hasan Abbas, the Kurdish owner of the nearby village of Shelumiye. The leader of the Nisibin militia, Qaddur

---

[130] Report of Hoffmann November 8, 1915, in *Die armenische Frage und der Genozid an den Armeniern in der Türkei (1913–1919)*, ed. Vardges Mikaelyan (2004), 276.

[131] Hannouche, *Azekh*, 67.

[132] Gawriye Maqsi-Hanna Hamra, interviewed November 1997 (appendix 1, no. 70).

Bey, owned half of the village, and Shaykh Isa owned the other half. Qaddur Bey assembled the Christians and said,

> There is neither an order nor a decision by the government to massacre and murder you, so you need not be afraid. But it is important that you each and every one of you write down all your property, because I must take you to Nisibin. If you stay here, the Muslims will kill you. For your safety, you shall stay with me in Nisibin under my protection until the danger is over. You are my villagers and I don't want anyone to hurt you.

Qaddur stayed in the village overnight, and the next day he assembled the Christians on the pretext of escorting them to Nisibin. The inhabitants were bound with ropes—supposedly to fool the Kurds into thinking that they were being taken to a killing site. They were moved to the Jareh River. Once there, Qaddur commanded them to choose either to convert to Islam or be killed. The Christians refused conversion and were killed. The women and children remaining behind in the village were also killed. **H**

Tel-Manar (Telminar). Tel-Manar is a village south of Izlo Mountain. Agha Petros gave a population of 150 Syriac Christians. Ten Syriac families lived here and they fled to Mharkan, but there they were murdered by Yusuf Hajo. **H**

Tel-Michar. Tel-Michar was a Chaldean village of 290 persons in the Sa'irt diocese. The inhabitants perished in the large massacres that took place at Sa'irt. See the section on Sa'irt above.

Tel-Qebbin (Tel Kebbin, Telkebbine). This village of 500 (Agha Petros) or 450 (Tfinkdji) is in the Chaldean Church diocese of Jezire, about 30 kilometers southeast of that town in the plain of Silopi. It was attacked by the Şirnak Kurds on July 10, 1915. Most of the inhabitants perished.[133]

Tel-She'ir (Tel-Cheir). Tel-She'ir is built on the slope of the Izlo Mountain, and the houses are partially caves. Fifty Syriac families lived here, and Agha Petros stated that the pre-war Christian population was 200. The fate of this village is unknown. **H**

Tel-Ya'qub. Tel-Ya'qub is on the slope of Mount Izlo. Ten Syriac families sought protection in Mharkan, where they were killed. **H**

Urfa (Ruha, Edessa, Urhoy). The town of Urfa, 120 kilometers southwest of Diyarbekir, and its vicinity made up a Christian enclave in the province of Aleppo. It was the final remnant of a much larger Christian population dating back to antiquity. Under the name of Edessa, this town was one

---

[133] Rhétoré, *"Les Chrétiens aux bêtes"*, 321.

of the first outside Palestine to have a Christian congregation. However, by the early twentieth century, Edessa was no longer a central place but was rather the western outpost of the Syriac Churches and one of the most southern of the Armenian Churches. This was a region of agricultural surplus, particularly of grain, and many merchants lived off of exporting foodstuffs to Aleppo and Lebanon. In 1895, the Christians of all faiths were victims of the Hamidiye massacres and pogroms. Prior to the war, according to the Agha Petros list there were 7,200 Syriacs in the town, and a further 8,800 lived in 10 outlying villages. Some of these villages were very large—Roum Kale, Serudj, Harran, and Biredjik had close to 2,000 Syriac residents each. Tfinkdji noted 200 Chaldean residents with 2 priests, 1 church, and 2 schools.

According to the Chaldean priest Josef Naayem, who was born there, the inhabitants of Urfa became aware of the on-going atrocities in March 1915, when some deported women, children, and elderly men reached the town. They were in a miserable state, and many died soon after arrival, some of hunger in the streets. Others wandered about in rags, sick and begging for food.[134]

In June 1915, authorities demanded that the Christians deposit all of their weapons in the government building. At first they refused, and the authorities threatened the death penalty for noncompliance. A large army, headed by two German officers, entered the town and set up artillery aimed at the Christian quarters. The cannons destroyed several buildings, and soldiers attacked the quarters. According to Naayem, the Armenian bishop, Ardawart, ordered his congregation to turn over weapons and ammunition, although a few kept the better weapons. After this the Ottoman authorities began to arrest and torture Armenian notables. Naayem stated that all Muslims in their mosques had been encouraged to take an oath not to help the Christians. On one occasion, Turkish soldiers searched the house of Naayem's father, a grain merchant, and found two Armenians from Siwerak, who were his employees, hiding in a corner of the kitchen. The Armenians were seized and Naayem's father was arrested for shielding rebels. Although Naayem's father was well integrated into Ottoman life and was the business partner of Urfa's Muslim mayor and a friend of the chief of police, he was kept in jail and his Muslim friends could not help him.

---

[134] Naayem, *Assyro-Chaldéens*, 10.

The priest of the Gregorian Armenian Church was seized, maltreated, and then taken to city hall, where he was sentenced to be hanged. According to Armalto, he made a statement in Turkish:

> I suspect that I have committed a crime, since I prevented my congregation from fighting the Turks, although I know that they easily could have defeated them. But we die, not because of our inability to fight against our enemies, but out of love for the Christian religion and our unhappy Armenia. God the just will make good all distasteful injustice.

He was immediately hanged. The authorities killed all of the Gregorian Armenians that they could capture and as many as possible of the captive "Syriacs, Chaldeans, Jacobites, and Armenian Catholics." Among the dead were the Syriac priest Hana Qandalaft and the Syriac monk Efram. Other clerics were put under house arrest.[135]

Vartabed Vartan, the Armenian Catholic leader, hid in the house of a Muslim friend. When he was caught, he was sent away to a prison in Adana, where he was sentenced to death. He appealed for a new trial and was sentenced to 101 years imprisonment, which was later reduced to 15 years. He was hanged on the order of the local governor after the armistice had been signed at the end of the war, only two days before the English and French troops arrived and took control.

A tribunal arrived in Urfa to interrogate and judge the Christian prisoners. But no trials began. After some time had elapsed, groups of prisoners, including Naayem's father, began to be sent away to Diyarbekir. Naayem knew that at least one group of about 50 persons was shot near the village of Karaköprü, about two hours by foot outside of Urfa. The soldiers sent to guard them returned with large sums of money in their pockets. These events took place early in August 1915, and Naayem's family decided to flee to Aleppo, while he remained.

On August 19, police and soldiers went to an Armenian house to arrest the owner. He was determined not to be caught and shot one policeman and two soldiers. After this, armed Turks spread in all directions through the streets killing all Christians they met. As was their custom, many Christians fled into the churches. Naayem estimated that 600 Christians were killed by evening, including some British and French civil employees of the Ottoman Debt Administration who had been interned at Urfa. The next day, the Jews of Urfa were ordered to collect the bodies and take them out of the town. About 500 Christian soldiers in labor companies

---

[135] Armalto, *Al-Qusara*, 336.

who were working on building roads near Urfa had also been slain. On August 21, Naayem left Urfa disguised as a Bedouin Arab and was smuggled by Muslim friends to safety in Aleppo.

On August 23, the highest Ottoman official ordered that all Armenians be deported. Since they knew what this meant, they refused and prepared to defend themselves in their homes. A siege of the Armenian quarter began, and a final week-long battle began on September 23. Reinforcements arrived under General Fahri Pasha to strengthen the Turkish troops, but the Armenians fought desperately and kept the enemy at bay. Naayem stated that several hundred Turkish soldiers died. Artillery, led by German military advisors, bombarded the Armenian houses, and the surviving defenders gave up. All Christians who were found in the ruins were killed regardless of sex or age. Several thousand women and children were held hostage in a large building near the Armenian cathedral, where they quickly died of disease and starvation.

Urmia. See chapter 4 above.

Viranshehir (Tel-Mawzal, Veran-Cheher, Viranşehir). Viranshehir is an ancient settlement, known through the nineteenth century under the name Tel-Mawzal. The 600 Christian families belonged mostly to the Armenian Catholic denomination and used a large church built in 1911; Syriac Catholics had the church named after Mar Afrem. The Gregorian Armenians and Syriac Orthodox had chapels. The Agha Petros list gave the Syriac population as 2,000 in the town with a further 1,700 living in 15 neighboring villages. Tfinkdji calculated the size of the Chaldean congregation at 90. Rhétoré stated that the town had 1,000 Gregorian Armenians, 650 Armenian Catholics, 250 Syriac Catholics, and 750 Syriac Orthodox residents.[136]

Viranshehir was the seat of the paramount chief of the Milli confederation, Ibrahim Pasha. During the Hamidiye pogroms, he protected the Christians. On November 3, 1895, the town was surrounded by Kurdish tribes, who began plundering and destroying Christian shops and market stalls but were stopped by Ibrahim Pasha. Because of this, many ruined Christian families from Urfa and Siwerak and even Mardin moved here, and the Christian population, particularly of Armenian and Syriac Catholics, having found asylum, expanded greatly in the two decades before World War I.

Anti-Christian violence first broke out on May 1, 1915, after soldiers broke into the Armenian Catholic church at night and seized its priest,

---

[136] Rhétoré, *"Les Chrétiens aux bêtes"*, 44.

Vartabed Ishaq Holozyan. They searched for weapons for three hours without finding any. The priest was taken before a judge, who released him. On May 2, the soldiers searched the Syriac Catholic church but found nothing incriminating. On May 13, the authorities summoned some leading Armenians and accused them of belonging to a secret revolutionary society. They were then confronted with aggressive representatives of the provincial government in Diyarbekir. They were beaten and threatened. On May 18, soldiers began to arrest the Christian notables and claimed to have discovered a large box of ammunition, which had been planted beforehand in a well belonging to Abd al-Ahad Salbo, a Syriac. The soldiers beat and whipped him terribly and threw him into jail. On May 27, once again soldiers arrested the Armenian priest Vartabed Ishaq. On May 28, some of the prisoners were tortured and executed. On June 3, Abd al-Ahad Salbo and eight other prisoners were executed at a place identified as Boughri. Vartabed Ishaq, however, was sent away to Diyarbekir guarded by six officers, and he was executed at the provincial capital on June 15, 1915.

Meanwhile, in Viranshehir on June 7, the soldiers arrested the rest of the Christian males aged between 12 and 70. The Syriac Catholic priest Gabriel Munashi Ahmardaqne was arrested, accused of sympathy for France. On that day, all of the 470 prisoners, Armenians, Syriac Catholics, and Syriac Orthodox, were tortured without exception. On the night of June 10, the men were roped together, and at sunrise they were marched out of town barefoot in groups of four to a place called Haftmala. There they were murdered; their clothes were taken back to town and distributed. Authorities then began to arrest the women and children. On June 11, about a thousand women and girls from the richest families were marched out of town to some caves and slain. A second column of women went out on June 14, and a third column was killed on June 16.

The few remaining Armenian women in Viranshehir were sent away to Ras al-'Ayn and their property was confiscated. Thereafter came the turn of the Syriac Catholic and Syriac Orthodox women. In return for confiscation of all of their jewelry and other valuables, they were allowed to stay in their houses. On June 21, 1915, the Syriac Catholic church was plundered of all valuable objects. Thus by the end of June all of the active Christian males of whatever denomination had been killed, all of the Armenian women were dead, and only the Syriac women and three aged Syriac men remained in Viranshehir. The Ministry of the Interior initiated an investigation into what had happened with the property of the Syrian Orthodox homes that were plundered, which had apparently not been turned over to the government as ordered.[137]

Wastta (Wahsad, Vahssed, Vasit). This Chaldean village was located in the Silopi plain about 40 kilometers southeast of Jezire with about 600 inhabitants (Tfinkdji stated that there were 520). On July 10, 1915, Suleiman Ismael and the aghas of Şirnak and Silopi with their tribes attacked. The villagers were slaughtered "like sheep."[138]

Yardo (Erdi, Yamanlar). Yardo is built on the slope of the Tur-Eloyo Mountain, 21 kilometers northeast of Midyat. *Yardo* is a Syriac word for "spring water." There were 70 Syriac and 30 Kurdish families. The Kurdish chiefs for the local tribes were Osman Tammero and Sleyman Shamdin. They conspired to trick the Syriacs, by making mutual promises that neither side would harm each other; they did not intend to keep these promises. One day, the Kurds lay in ambush around the village. They cried out that they needed help from the village to stop cattle from being stolen. The Syriacs heard the cries and grabbed their weapons and came out to help. When they were a bit distant from the village, they saw other people enter. The Syriac village headman, Malke Khatun, saw this and realized what was going on and that the Kurds planned to kill them when they returned. Instead, they took refuge in the ruins of a nearby fortress and demanded that the Kurds release the Christians captured in the village. The villagers were released and came to the fort. When the villagers proceeded to 'Ayn-Wardo, the Kurds attacked and all were killed except 40 boys, women, and girls who were held captive as slaves in Muslim households. **H**

Za'faran. The name *Za'faran* means the "Saffron Monastery." It is located a few kilometers east of Mardin, halfway up a mountainside. The most ancient buildings in this complex are from the sixth century. Some decorations are from the time of the Roman Emperor Anastasius and are presumed to be the remains of a Roman temple. From 1166, the monastery was the residence of the Syriac Orthodox Patriarch of Antioch. It once had a valuable library. When the authorities sent away and massacred the first column of prisoners from Mardin on June 10, 1915, about 700 Syriacs from Qal'at-Mara and Benebil fled to the monastery. They brought their weapons and ammunition. The Turkish authorities began to organize the storming of Za'faran, which soon housed more than a thousand refugees. They made

---

[137] Simon, *Mardine*, 134; Armalto, *Al-Qusara*, 358; BOA. DH. ŞFR. 58/147 Ministry of the Interior to Diyarbekir vilayet November 8, 1915.

[138] Ternon, "Mardin 1915," 369; Rhétoré, *"Les Chrétiens aux bêtes"*, 321.

contact with Khalil Ghazale, the leader of a local Kurdish Dashit subtribe, as well as the Kurdish villagers from Amrian, Reshmel, and Qabala, who agreed to launch an assault. The leader was the head of the militia, Nuri Badlisi. They arrived on July 4 and began shooting at the defenders from both the east and west sides. The refugees took up their weapons and fired back. Although some reached as far as the outside gardens, the Turks and Kurds found it impossible to force their way into the monastery complex, and the Kurdish tribes gradually drifted away. From Mardin, a group of Al-Khamsin militia was sent ostensibly to guard the monastery, but the leader of the militia, Farhan, accepted a bribe from the Kurds. A second group of 100 soldiers was sent as a guard, and they chased away the Kurds. The bishop ordered a feast of thanksgiving, and the soldiers stayed for two days. When they left, 10 soldiers remained as a guard for twenty days. After that, Nuri, who was quite corrupt, together with guards from Mardin remained and profited by taking money and valuables from the Syriacs in return for continued "protection." The Syriacs remained in the monastery until October, when it was deemed safe enough to return to their villages. During this time epidemics took the lives of about half of the refugees.[139] **Q**

Zangan (Zengan). Zangan lies along the Tigris River northeast of Kfar-Boran. Thirty Syriac families lived here, and they were murdered by the Ali Rammo tribe. **H**

Zaz (İzbırak). Zaz is four hours' foot travel northeast of Midyat. Before the massacres, 200 Syriac families lived here. The church of Mor Dimat was surrounded by high, thick walls and was defensible, as were two other large building complexes inside the village. The defenders were both in the church and in the building complexes. Kurdish tribes surrounded the village. These were the clans of Shterako, led by Latif, and the clans of Hitto and Haydaro, as well as the Kurds of Derhav tribe, led by Osman Sille. Fighting under a state of siege lasted twenty days, and the Christians suffered from starvation and thirst. At a critical moment, Osman Sille promised that if they gave up, they would be guaranteed safety. The Christians were suspicious but felt there was no alternative. The Syriacs hiding in one of the building complexes came out of the village and were first given water but then taken to a place known as Ferbume, where most were killed except for a few young women whom the Kurds took into their households. The number of inhabitants killed in this way was 366. Two men managed to flee and went back and informed those who were hiding in the church. The next day, the Kurds roped together the captive Syriac women

---

[139] Armalto, *Al-Qusara*, 421.

and forced them to shout up to the church that the other Syriacs had given up and had not been killed, but rather had been taken to Shterako, where they were safe. But the Syriacs in the church knew the fate of the others, so they were not tricked into coming out. The Kurds then stormed the churchyard from all sides. The Kurds also cut off an underground tunnel that the Syriacs in the church used to collect water from a well. They managed to get into the churchyard, and the Syriacs retreated and barricaded themselves in the church itself. The battle went on for three days, until the Kurds retreated. The Zaz villagers remained in the church for two more weeks and suffered from hunger and thirst. The authorities in Midyat were informed of the conditions in Zaz and that the Syriacs were receiving help from foreign countries. A Turkish major with heavily armed soldiers and artillery came to Zaz to investigate. When the troops arrived, they started to shoot at the church with a cannon, but the Syriacs did not fire back. The major proceeded up to the church door and asked to talk with those inside, and the Syriacs let him in. At that moment the major realized that the Kurds had lied and that the Syriacs were not helped by foreigners and did not have an enormous stockpile of weapons and supplies. He said to them: "You need not fear. What the Kurds accused you of was a lie. From now on you are under my protection; on my honor and conscience I will take you to safety." The Syriacs then said that they left themselves in his hands. After that, the troops chased the Kurds away and escorted the Syriacs from the church to the village of Kfar-Boran, where they stayed under military protection for a month. After that month, they were taken to a new place, the church of Mort Shmuni in the town of Midyat, which was then completely empty of Syriacs. The Zaz villagers continued to live in fear, hunger, and misery, and many died of disease and harsh conditions. By the end of the period of massacres, only 100 Zaz villagers were still alive, and they spread out in Tur Abdin to work in the Muslim villages. A little group of them was collected after the war by Chelebi Agha, who reinstated them in Zaz. **H**

Zinawrah (Zinavrah). During the massacres, 20 Syriac families lived in the Kurdish village Zinawrah, near Basibrin. The Kurdish leader Musa Fatme, chief of the Dayran clan, also lived here. According to the witness statements collected by Hinno, Musa Fatme gave asylum to 40 Syriacs during the massacres. Musa and his family escorted them in two groups to Basibrin. **H**

Zurafe (Surafe). Zurafe was a Syriac village of 100 inhabitants in the Hawar River district near Diyarbekir. On May 3, a death squad commanded by Shakir Bey with members of the Rama tribe headed by Ömer perpetrated a massacre on the adult males of the various small villages here. The village males were brought to Chanaqchi and then taken to a pit near the village Hawar-Dejla, where they were shot. Those from these villages who were murdered numbered 164, "all notable, strong, and rich men." **Q**

9 THE BATTLE FOR AZAKH

Humiliated, the former CUP Inspector General Ömer Naji Bey, the well-known orator, journalist, and intelligence operative, pondered the strange quirk of fate that had brought him off the beaten track to the village of Azakh,[1] just west of Jezire.[2] Halil Bey, his old spy comrade, had tricked him a month before into commanding a siege force against a small village with a few hundred defenders. Try as he might, his thousands of cavalry and foot-soldiers with all their modern equipment, even cannons, backed up by local tribes and militia, just could not budge the thorough defense. Even Enver Pasha, whom he knew well, had telegraphed that he wanted Azakh "suppressed immediately with the utmost severity." But nothing had worked, and then suddenly the rebels had crawled through tunnels in the night, surprised the sleeping army, and forced them to flee, losing masses of weapons and suffering hundreds of casualties. Now his two howitzers were out of order and his expedition was gravely diminished.

Naji's frustration was natural; after all, he was supposed to be in Iran accomplishing a secret mission with the Germans to instigate an uprising of Kurds, rather than wasting time and energy bombarding a Syriac village. In any case, Syriacs were supposed to be spared from the atrocities; why had the locals insisted on calling the rebels Armenians?

After this fiasco, Naji was replaced as siege commander. He had asked to give up the siege several times before but had always been refused because crushing the revolt was such a prestige issue. The only reason he had been made commander was Halil's plot to implicate the German officers who accompanied Naji's detachment in the Armenian massacres. But right from the start, the Germans had refused to take part in the siege and even brought the German government into the act. So Naji's defeat came to play

---

[1] Located very close to the Turkish-Syrian border, Azakh is the name used by the villagers, who spoke an Arabic dialect. Neo-Syriac speakers refer to it as Hazakh, and the modern Turkish name is İdil. Lahdo Beth-Lahdo Musa / Beth-Gorgis, interviewed May 1993 (appendix 1, no. 69), provides a lengthy oral history.

[2] On Naji see Fethi Tevetoğlu, *Ömer Naci* (1987). He was a deputy in the National Assembly and a member of the CUP inner circle.

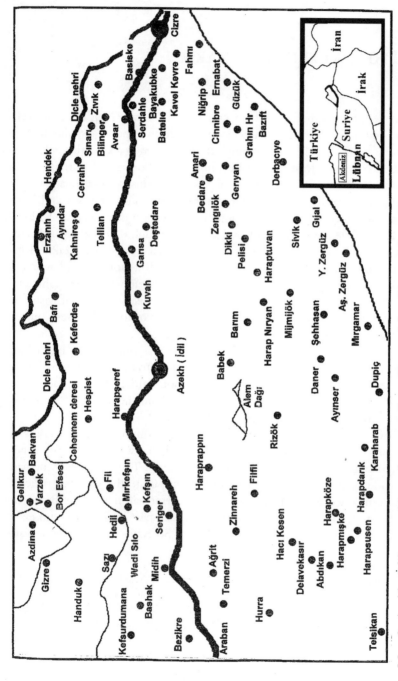

Map 9: Azakh (İdil) township and surrounding villages. After Hanna Murat Hannounche, *Azekh "Beyt Zebde"* (2002?), facing p. 4.

itself out on an international stage. This was a miserable end for east Anatolia's former political boss and legendary guerilla leader. But clearly he had actually been out of favor for quite some time because of his grumbling about the course of the war. He considered this expedition to Iran a form of exile, as far as possible from political influence. Within a few months he would be dead, under somewhat suspicious circumstances.

THE "MIDYAT REBELLION"

Against the background of intensive slaughter in the southeastern part of Diyarbekir province, local armed resistance began to form among the Syriacs, Chaldeans, and runaway Armenians. This was a considerable embarrassment to the Ottoman authorities, who had put great effort into pacifying the region. El-Ghusein wrote,

> The Syriacs in the province of Midiât were brave men, braver than all the other tribes in these regions. When they heard what had fallen upon their brethren at Diarbekir and the vicinity they assembled, fortified themselves in three villages near Midiât, and made a heroic resistance, showing courage beyond description. The Government sent against them two companies of regulars, besides a company of gendarmes, which had been dispatched thither previously; the Kurdish tribes assembled against them, but without result, and thus they protected their lives, honour and possessions from the tyranny of this oppressive Government. An imperial Irâdeh [decree] was issued, granting them pardon, but they placed no reliance on it and did not surrender, for past experience had shown them that this is the most false Government on the face of the earth, taking back to-day what it gave yesterday, and punishing to-day with most cruel penalties him whom it had previously pardoned.[3]

Walther Holstein, the German consul in Mosul, reported on July 28 that an uprising "both of Chaldeans and Syriacs" flared up and the telegraph line to Diyarbekir had been broken. "This uproar is a direct consequence of the extreme actions of the vali of Diyarbekir against Christians in general. They are trying to save their skins." He also reported that the Yezidis of Sinjar Mountains, who were friendly with the Christians, were also in revolt.[4] The German ambassador in Istanbul sent a message to

---

[3] Fâ'iz El-Ghusein, *Martyred Armenia* (1917), 31.
[4] Holstein to German Embassy July 28, 1915, in Lepsius, *Deutschland und Armenien: Sammlung diplomatischer Aktenstücke* (1919), 114.

Reichskanzler Bethmann Hollweg about the situation in the Tur Abdin region:

> At the beginning of this month, the vali of Diyarbekir, Reshid Bey, started a systematic extermination of the Christian population of his jurisdiction, without difference to race or confession. Of these particularly the Catholic Armenians of Mardin and Tel-Armen and the Chaldean Christians and non-Uniate Syriacs [that is Syriac Orthodox and Protestants] in the districts of Midyat, Jezire, and Nisibin have been victim. According to information obtained by the consulate in Mosul, the Christian population between Mardin and Midyat has risen up against the government and destroyed the telegraph lines.[5]

The main defended villages were Azakh (now İdil, not far from Jezire), 'Ayn-Wardo (now Gülgöze, near Midyat), Dayro da Ṣlibo (now Çatalçam, about 30 km northeast of Midyat), Hah (now Anıtlı, about 22 km northeast of Midyat), Basibrin (now Haberli, about 25 km east of Midyat), and Beth-Debe (now Daskan, just north of Basibrin) (map 9).[6] In addition, some of the larger monastery complexes could function as fortresses if needed: Mar Malke on Izlo Mountain, Za'faran monastery outside Mardin, Mar Gabriel near Midyat. Most of the defensible villages succeeded in fighting off the initial attacks of primarily poorly disciplined Kurdish tribes, but it proved impossible to leave the defended sites. The defenders remained in the villages throughout the summer and could not tend their fields and flocks. Instead, some of them began to raid Kurdish villages at night to get food. The raids inevitably led to killing, and this brought the situation in Tur Abdin to the attention of Ottoman authorities, who decided to bring in the army. The first order to pacify the region went to the Fourth Army, but they proved too far away to implement the order in time.

Because of the rich supply of documentation, it is possible to describe what happened to one village. Azakh had a large Syriac Orthodox and Syriac Catholic population of about a thousand inhabitants. Just before the massacres, several hundred Syriac families from surrounding villages sought shelter there, as did many escapees from the Armenian deportation caravans. According to the oral history compiled by Hinno, at the start of the sieges the headmen gathered under the leadership of the Syriac bishop Mar Behnam Aqrawi, who had fled from nearby Jezire, to select a leader. This

---

[5] Hohenlohe-Langenburg to Bethmann Hollweg July 31, 1915, ibid., 115.

[6] Hellmut Ritter, *Ṭūrōyo: Die Volkssprache der Syrianischen Christen des Ṭūr 'Abdîn* (1967), 331; Süleyman Hinno, *Günhe d Süryoye d Turabdin* [The massacre of the Syriacs of Tur Abdin] (1987), 60ff., 82ff., 109ff., 114ff., 156ff.

was done by lottery, and Yesua Hanna Gawriye drew the piece of paper with the cross on it and was acknowledged leader. He chose some adjutants; together, they built fortifications and made secret tunnels, and some made bullets for the flintlock rifles. According to oral testimony, they swore to uphold a traditional motto: "We all have to die sometime, do not die in shame and humiliation."[7]

Rumors of preparations for a general massacre of Christians had circulated for some time before Feyzi Bey, the National Assembly deputy, arrived in nearby Jezire on April 15, 1915. Reshid Bey had sent him to coordinate the Kurdish tribes. By the time he left Jezire ten days later, Kurdish tribes and military could be observed surrounding the Syriac villages of Garessa and Kuvakh. The villagers fled to Azakh, which was a traditional fortification famous for its defensive walls and aggressive inhabitants. Throughout history, it had been a place of asylum. In late Ottoman times, as a large village it had a government-appointed administrator, the *Bucak Müdürü*, who commanded a contingent of gendarmes quartered in the center.

The following information comes from a diary kept by a Syriac Catholic priest and schoolteacher, Gabriyel Qas Tuma Hendo, who lived through the siege of Azakh.[8] He tells of the slow realization that Azakh was going to be stormed and that the aggressors were carefully gathering support for their assault. In mid May, the kaymakam of Jezire and the kaza's highest military officer inspected Azakh. They asked that the tallest buildings be handed over to the Turkish soldiers, claiming they needed to defend the village from an expected Kurdish attack. On May 25, Muhammed Agha, chief of the Rama tribe, arrived ostensibly for a courtesy call on the Bucak Müdürü, but in reality to check out the defenses at first hand. The Ömerkan, 'Alikan, and 'Aliyan tribes besieged the nearby village of Babeqqa on May 30. The villagers of Azakh collected a large sum of money and paid those tribes to disappear. Instead, the same tribes plus the Dörekan tribe simply moved on to surround close-by Esfes, also a Syriac village, on June 6. The villagers there managed to defend themselves, and after some time a group of Al-Khamsin militiamen arrived from Mardin saying they would help defend the village. The soldiers were allowed inside, but when the Kurdish tribes charged, the soldiers began to fire on the villagers. After three days of fighting, the priest 'Abdallahad Jebbo succeeded in bribing the

---

[7] Ibid., 157.

[8] "Tarikh Azakh" ([1915]). Excerpts from this diary are published in Hanna Murat Hannouche, *Azekh "Beyt Zebde"* [Azakh or Beyt Zebde] (2002?), 36ff.

head of the Al-Khamsin, Sergeant Ilyas Chelebi, with a fine pocketwatch and ten gold coins. The villagers were allowed to flee to Azakh, while the tribesmen plundered and burned their homes.

Authorities made many attempts to reduce the number of Azakh defenders by luring the refugees into returning to their homes. An unnamed Turkish officer arrived on June 11 and asked to meet with the leaders of the refugees from Garessa and Kuvakh. He promised that if they returned to their villages, he would guarantee protection. But the refugees refused, suspicious that this was a step intended to weaken the resistance at Azakh. The officer went on to meet with Hasse Barakat, the head of the Botikan clan, because he refused to join the rest of the Kurdish tribes assembling to strike the Christian villages. Hasse Barakat had made a solemn pledge of peace with the village of Azakh as a reward for helping him fight the Miran nomads back in 1901, and he would not break his oath. However, he added, if removing the Christians really was a case of a religious duty, as the officer insisted, then he would stay at home and let his son Yasin lead the tribe, as the son was not personally bound by any pledge. Kurdish tribes from far and wide began to gather in the village of Rizo. They came from Midyat, Jezire, and Nisibin. Once more the village of Babeqqa was besieged, but after a short battle all the inhabitants managed to flee to Azakh.

On July 1, there was a large meeting of Kurdish chiefs to plan how to proceed with the assault. During the following week, there was a great buildup of enemy forces and considerable psychological warfare. The leading Syriac in the town of Jezire was Gabriyel Khaddo. He collaborated closely with the local authorities under the belief that his loyalty would save the Syriac community. On July 5, he arrived at Azakh together with other Jezire notables and a detachment of soldiers. As in other towns, authorities dealt with the Christians in piecemeal fashion and exterminated the Catholics and Protestants first. Khaddo demanded that the leaders of Azakh turn over all Catholics and Protestants. If they did that, he promised that the other Syriacs would be safe. Once again the villagers refused, asserting that all residents were Syriacs and they were all related to each other. This was not completely correct, as Azakh was filling with Armenian refugees and with runaways from the deportation caravans. The next day, July 6, a large detachment of Turkish soldiers arrived from Midyat and demanded to be billeted inside the village, saying they had been ordered to defend Azakh. They were refused entrance but could camp outside along the main road. Suspecting a sneak attack, the Azakh leaders also forced the gendarmes out of the village. On July 9, a group of Al-Khamsin militia under the command of Ahmed Nazo arrived from Jezire. He had lived in Azakh and could speak the local Arabic dialect.

From an early stage, the Kurdish–Syriac confrontation assumed a religious character. On July 10, the gendarmes posted inside the village made themselves invisible, and the military that had camped on the road did the same. But the Kurdish tribes were mobilized and had been whipped into a frenzy by their shaykhs. Azakh leaders met to organize the defense, forming committees with various tasks and listening to sermons from their priests. The most important tasks were building lookout points for sharpshooters and digging a secret tunnel to get in and out of the village once the expected siege began. A suicide group of fifty volunteers took the name *fedai*s[9] of Jesus and was placed under the charge of Andrawos Hanna Eliya and Ya'qub Hanna Gabre. Out of respect for the month of Ramadan, the expected attack did not come, as the tribes returned home to observe their religious obligations, but they returned as soon as the month was over.

On Saturday, August 14, a large fire was lit on top of the 'Alam hill, the signal for Kurdish tribesmen to amass. The next day, Azakh villagers were shot at as they tended their vineyards. A delegation of Jezire's town officials, the kadi court judge, a mufti, and the Al-Khamsin arrived on August 16. They brought modern weapons and ammunition, which were distributed among the tribesmen. The first skirmishes between Christians and Kurds took place with losses on both sides. On August 17, Azakh found itself surrounded by the Miran, Hamidi, 'Abdi Agha's clan, and townsmen calling themselves "Jezire's Hajjis." On the evening of the 18th, the tribes staged a frontal charge using *Muhammad Salawat* as a battle cry. The defenders said that the next morning they saw bodies and blood everywhere. In a surprise nighttime attack on August 26, the Jesus fedai captured the Kurdish strategic positions and destroyed them. By September 9, the Kurdish tribes had departed, leaving Azakh in peace. The villagers had lost 50 men, while the Kurdish casualties were believed to be much greater.[10]

Directing their wrath elsewhere, the Kurdish tribes in the area sacked most of the neighboring villages and were especially vicious in the nearby town of Jezire, where starting in August waves of large-scale massacres rocked the town. These massacres were organized by local notables and functionaries sent from Diyarbekir. In connection with the Jezire massacres,

---

[9] *Fedai* is a word of Persian origin, used by Armenians and Syriacs to denote nationalist or religious warriors.

[10] Hannouche, *Azekh*, 40–46.

the authorities began to discuss staging more concentrated efforts to deal with the Christians of Tur Abdin, who had not only survived the initial strikes but had now begun to raid Kurdish villages in search of food. Hinno states that the ringleaders in Jezire

> sent a report to the government and accused the Syriacs of being Armenians, rebels, and guilty of destroying the villages in the area. When the report came to the authorities, they sent commander Ömer Naji with 8,000 fully equipped soldiers to Azakh, and in addition these soldiers were joined by Kurdish rebels from the clans in Nisibin, Şirnak, and Tel-Afar.[11]

NAJI AND SCHEUBNER-RICHTER

Ottoman documents fill in many of the details of the oral history narrative and the Azakh diary. The oral testimony correctly identifies the leader of the Ottoman troops as Inspector-General Ömer Naji Bey. He is particularly interesting because of his national connections with the highest political leaders. He had been a long-time member of the Committee for Unity and Progress. He was the rabble-rouser who fired up the mob that backed the coup of January 23, 1913, that paved the way for the warlordship of Enver Pasha and Talaat Pasha. He was a member of the military branch of the Teskilat-i Mahsusa.[12] Formally, he was under the command of General Kamil Pasha, head of the Ottoman Third Army, based in Erzerum. After the war, he was named in the French list of suspected war criminals, but since he died of typhus (it was said) in 1916, he could not be tried.[13] One of the German officers who observed the events at Azakh, Paul Leverkuehn, described Naji as one of the most "remarkable figures of the Turkish political world," and it was his impression that Naji "enjoyed the unconditional trust of all the Young Turk politicians and had the authority, if one can say so, of a master prophet." As a Circassian, Naji's dream was to liberate his homeland from Russian domination.[14]

---

[11] Hinno, *Günhe d Süryoye d Turabdin*, 158.

[12] Naim Turfan, *The Rise of the Young Turks: Politics, the Military and Ottoman Collapse* (2000), 209, 280; Israfil Kurtcephe, "Birinci dünya savasinda bir süryani ayaklanmasi" [A Syrian revolt in World War I] (1993), 292.

[13] Bilâl N. Şimşir, *Malta Sürgünleri* [The Malta exiles] (1976), 76.

[14] Paul Leverkuehn, *Posten auf ewiger Wache: Aus dem abenteuerreichen Leben des Max von Scheubner-Richter* (1938), 54–55. During World War II, Leverkuehn returned to Turkey as a secret agent (Burkhard Jähnicke, "Lawyer, Politician, Intelligence Officer: Paul Leverkuehn in Turkey 1915–1916 and 1941–1944" [2002]).

Naji teamed up with another adventurer, the German officer Max von Scheubner-Richter, who for a short time had served as vice-consul in Erzurum. Scheubner-Richter handpicked some other officers, among them Paul Leverkuehn, an intelligence officer who later wrote a book on the expedition. Their idea was to take a joint German and Turkish expedition into Iran. There was already a large German and Turkish presence there, and this would be a welcome reinforcement. Their volunteer detachment amounted to over six hundred mounted soldiers and field artillery. The plan was to create an uprising of Muslims in Russia's east Caucasus provinces. Naji was the Committee for Unity and Progress's expert on Iran; he had been there during the brutal occupation of Persian Azerbaijan in January 1915.

On the way from Erzurum to Mosul, Naji's expedition met up with Halil Bey and his divisions at Sa'irt. The latter were marching south to form part of the new Sixth Army presently under construction near Baghdad. A mediocre soldier, Halil depended for his career on the fact that he was Enver Pasha's uncle. Halil had retreated from Persia after a major defeat at Dilman in May and had thereafter perpetrated the massacres of Christians in Sa'irt earlier in the summer. The German officer Leverkuehn described Halil as an "ambitious political and military dilettante," traveling in lordly style with a long caravan of wagons pulled by beasts of burden. One was heavily laden with a large bathtub, and the Germans speculated that this was not for his own sanitary needs, but rather was brought for the needs of the captive Armenian females Halil had seized.[15]

In the expedition, Scheubner-Richter served as military commander while Naji functioned as political commissar, which suited a former political boss. Regular army observers considered both outsiders and reckless adventurers.[16] That the militarily inexperienced Naji was placed in charge of the operation rather than Halil, who was an experienced general, is somewhat surprising. Naji had only an expeditionary force mentally prepared for guerilla warfare and sabotage, whereas Halil had a whole division, or whatever was left of it. However, Naji's force included many German officers, and the Ottomans attempted to entice the German military to get their hands dirty in the anti-Christian policies. Scheubner-Richter as vice-consul sent many reports protesting the harsh treatment of the Armenians, which he

---

[15] Leverkuehn, *Posten auf ewiger Wache*, 72–73.
[16] Aziz Samih, "Umumi Harpte Kafkas Cephesi Hatıraları" [World War I: Caucasian Front memoirs] (1935).

did not support. Although his reports show him to be a racist thinker, he protested against the annihilation of the Armenian population in Anatolia and intervened several times to aid Armenians. His opposition to the anti-Armenian policy caused disputes with the Turkish officers, although they were able to cooperate in most other matters. After returning to Germany he became a leading right-wing anti-Communist politician and died literally arm-in-arm with Adolf Hitler at the 1923 Munich Beer-Hall putsch.

Naji was ordered to coordinate the operations against the Christians of Tur Abdin. Purely by accident, at the end of October 1915, Naji's detachment was passing near Tur Abdin on its way to Persia. Turkish sources sometimes speak only of Azakh, but sometimes they talk in general about the "Midyat revolt." Because the villages of Azakh, 'Ayn-Wardo, and Basibrin presented such firm resistance, Ottoman troops became tied down for a long time. This brought the situation to the attention of the highest political and military circles. General von der Goltz, the main German officer in the area, became involved and had been ordered by Jemal Pasha, commander of the Fourth Army, to take charge of a detachment of the Third Army and restore order. Enver Pasha, the Minister of War and one of the two leading political figures, sent telegrams asking about the situation. In the end, in both Azakh and 'Ayn-Wardo, a cease-fire was reached and Ottoman troops pulled back after failing to defeat the defenders.

SYRIACS OR ARMENIANS?

Naji sent a telegram on October 29, 1915, stating that Syriac Christians had taken up arms in revolt in Diyarbekir, Jezire, and Midyat and were "cruelly massacring" the Muslim people in the area. He asked authorization to "chastise" the rebels. Because telegraph lines were cut, his message was sent first to the vali of Mosul, who then forwarded it to the Supreme Military Command in Constantinople. The telegram reads:

> I am in Jezire with a detachment of troops bound for Persia. In the districts of Diyarbekir, Midyat, and Jezire, which are situated one hour distant from here, the Syriac Christians have revolted and are cruelly massacring the Muslim people in the area. I will go there with my troops to punish the rebels who, it has been reported, have 4,000 arms, though I think this is an exaggeration. My troops consist of 650 cavalry and infantry soldiers. We have two mountain guns. I request that a battalion from the Fifty-first Division, which is due to arrive in Jezire, with a number of mountain artillery, be ordered to join our troops.

From this we can see that he was not at all convinced by the locals who claimed that the rebellious villagers were Armenian. But he called for reinforcements from Mosul and the possibility of using some of Halil's soldiers.[17] Afterward he would say that he lifted his siege of Azakh from the date he was convinced that the villagers were Syriacs, but he must have known that all along. Before any shooting began, he met with Azakh's headmen twice—he could converse with them directly as he was fluent in Arabic, having grown up in Baghdad. The first encounter was deemed friendly, the second, on November 7, hostile. On the latter occasion Naji demanded the villagers give up their weapons and submit to deportation.

Naji contacted Scheubner-Richter, who had gone ahead to order supplies in Mosul, to win the participation of the Germans in the fight. Leverkuehn describes Scheubner-Richter's negative gut reaction:

> In the mountains west of the Tigris, fleeing Armenians had fortified themselves in some villages inhabited by Syriac Christians that refused to obey the Turkish authorities to deliver requisitions of foodstuff and military recruits. The vali of Diyarbekir demanded of Constantinople that it order Naji's and Scheubner's troops to conquer these villages. Ömer Naji telegraphed Scheubner asking if he would place his detachment and the Germans under his command, as desired. Scheubner, however, was placed in a difficult situation by this demand. He was in no way convinced by the Turkish description [of the background]. Rather, he had the view that this was not a real rebellion but concerned a not unjustified defense by people who feared meeting the same fate as most Armenians. If the Germans participated now, the Turks would not shrink from intimating that it was they [the Germans] who had led the [atrocities] against the Christian Turkish subjects. ... Under these circumstances, Scheubner therefore placed all of the Turkish troops and Kurdish cavalry under Ömer Naji's command, but ordered Leverkuehn, Thiel, and Schlimme [the German officers] to come immediately to Mosul.[18]

Calling it an "inner Turkish" matter, however, Scheubner permitted the Turkish troops and Kurdish cavalry under his command to participate in full. General von der Goltz approved this step. The Ottoman authorities, however, expressed disappointment over the nonparticipation of the Ger-

---

[17] Appendix to cipher telegram of Haydar Bey to Supreme Military Command October 29, 1915, ATAŞE, Kol.: BDH, Kls.: 17, Dos.: 81/, Fih.: 27 (appendix 4.2, no. 1). Cf. Kurtcephe, "Birinci dünya savaşında bir süryani ayaklanması," 291–96.

[18] Leverkuehn, *Posten auf ewiger Wache*, 83.

man troops and officers, and Scheubner concluded that it really was an ill-disguised attempt to trick the Germans by "drawing them into the Armenian affair" through the back door.[19]

To what extent Armenian volunteer fighters were involved in the Tur Abdin resistance is uncertain. Their presence is not mentioned in the Syriac oral history recorded by Hinno, so they could not have played leading roles. The diary of Gabriyel Qas Tuma Hendo states that the villagers were hiding about eighty Armenians who had fled to Azakh after escaping from the deportation caravans.[20] Knowledge of the presence of Armenian refugees gave the local officials reason to exaggerate their involvement, as this was a sure way of getting the attention of the leadership. Naji always used the term *Süryani*—that is, Syriac Orthodox or Syriac Catholics—in his telegrams. But other officials tried to hide the facts by naming them Armenians or by using the generic term "rebels." An example: when General Halil Bey arrived in Jezire, he sent the following telegram to the Supreme Military Command:

> Upon my arrival in Jezire I found that, nearly 50 kilometers west of Jezire, in the village of Hazar [Azakh] from various neighborhoods and villages in the vicinity, up to 1,000 armed Armenians gathered lately and started an assault destroying Muslim villages nearby and massacred their inhabitants and cut the telegraph line between Jezire and Diyarbekir. As there is no force in this area to punish them, this assault will continue. Naji Bey from the Third Army with a force under his command, [who] is on his way to Iran, is currently in Jezire. I do not think he has pressing duties and [will wait] until the arrival of a formal order. I submit that if they are not to be relied on, I request it would be appropriate to order the Fifty-Second Division to punish them.[21]

Bedri Bey, serving as temporary vali in Diyarbekir, simply used the term "rebels" in a telegram dealing with casualties.

---

[19] Schuebner-Richter to Bethmann Hollweg December 4, 1916, in Lepsius, *Deutschland und Armenien*, 306. Holstein toyed with the idea of using Scheubner and himself as go-betweens, believing that the Syriacs would trust them more than the Turks. The ambassador and von der Goltz said no. Holstein to German embassy November 4, 1915, German Embassy to Consulate in Mosul November 8, 1915, PA-AA A53a/1915/6381.

[20] Gabriel Qas Tuma Hendo, "Tarikh Azakh" (n.d.).

[21] Cipher telegram Halil Bey to Supreme Military Command October 30, 1915, ATAŞE Kol.: BDH, Kls.: 17, Dos.: 81/, Fih.: 27-1 (appendix 4.2, no. 2).

> In the course of the punishment of the rebels in the Midyat region, they were first of all asked to give up their arms. [One] could not be certain about the accessibility of the terrain in such places as Basabriye [Basibrin] and Azakh where the rebels are in great numbers. Two or three villages that were isolated [did already] surrender and although they were forced to lay down their arms, [did so] with half-hearted confidence; they handed over to the government ineffective weapons and concealed the rest. Rebels in other places dared to respond to the proposal by firing guns and by means of patrolling [raiding?] Muslim [areas] and attacking and massacring the inhabitants. They fortified themselves in the village of Azakh and fortified the village with walls and trenches. Assigned to the punishment of about 10,000 rebels, Ömer Naji Bey, commander of the Iran expedition force, after the blockade of the village with the troops and the military, proposed peace and asked them to surrender their weapons. They had the insolence to respond to this proposition by causing 38 wounded, including two officers, and three *shahids* [martyrs] in the detachment.[22]

In reality, the number of defenders was much smaller, and the extent of Turkish casualties much greater.

Reassignments of troops and redirection of artillery had to be authorized by the Ottoman military headquarters and had to wait until formal orders arrived. This meant, of course, that the military and political leadership was kept informed on a day-to-day basis. There were also the special units of the Teskilat-i Mahsusa, which were under the control of the Minister of the Interior. The vali of Mosul commanded some volunteer units that he termed *mujaheddin*, headed by the notorious Çerkez (Circassian) Ethem. A short communiqué on November 7 to the Supreme Military Command suggested the redeployment of these units. "I submit that in order to assist Ömer Naji Bey, 500 fighters that have been organized under militia commander Edhem Bey could be moving within two days."[23] On the telegram another hand wrote: "It will be discussed with *Nazir* [Minister] Pasha." The next day, Talaat sent a telegram to the Supreme Military Command confirming that he had ordered the 500 mujaheddin to reinforce Naji's forces.

> In a telegram dated November 7, 1915, that has arrived from the province of Mosul… it was communicated that in order to assist Ömer Naji

---

[22] Cipher telegram Bedreddin to Supreme Military Command November 12, 1915, ATAŞE, Kol.: BDH, Kls.: 17, Dos.: 81/, Fih.:35 (appendix 4.2, no. 9).

[23] Cipher telegram Haydar Bey to Supreme Military Command November 7, 1915, ATAŞE Kol.: BDH, Kls.: 17, Dos.: 81/, Fih.: 31 (appendix 4.2, no. 4).

Bey, 500 fighters under militia commander Edhem Bey have been organized and they would be moving within two days. In this matter command belongs to Him to whom all commanding belongs.[24]

The commander, Edhem, was one of the Circassians whom Reshid Bey had recruited to staff his private army. He was also a Teskilat-i Mahsusa operative and well known for his brutality.[25]

An official order from Enver Pasha was sent to the commander of the Third Army in Erzerum, of which Naji's detachment was still part.

> Ömer Naji Bey reported that the Syriacs between Midyat and Jezire have united with the Armenians and cut the telegraph lines and attacked the Muslim people. To suppress them, Ömer Naji Bey's detachment, plus a battalion of infantry and two mountain artilleries, have departed from Urfa and are moving toward Jezire. ... The rebels and the districts they attacked [are located] within the jurisdiction of the Third Army, and because of this, the movement of the detachment [should be coordinated by] the headquarters of the Third Army. If the uprising of the rebels is warded off [and they] give up arms ... if they consent to be [resettled] in a locality selected by the government. Even if it is not true about their attack and massacres of Muslim people.[26]

Relying on Naji's communications, Enver too identified the villagers as Syriacs, and he also indicated some skepticism as to whether they actually had done the atrocities they were accused of. From the start Naji harbored doubts. Hinno's oral history records that when Naji's troops arrived, the Syriacs asked to meet with the commander. The Syriac bishop and some other notables came to his tent. They brought with them gifts of food for the soldiers. "The Syriacs explained to him that the accusations against them were false and groundless, and that they were neither enemies of the state nor traitors and that they were prepared to follow his orders with respect."[27] According to Hendo's diary, Naji asked if there were any Armenians in the village and asked to enter and make an inspection. Deceptively, the village headmen said bluntly that there were only Syriacs, not Armeni-

---

[24] Cipher telegram Talaat Pasha to Supreme Miltary Command November 8, 1915, ATAŞE Kol.: BDH, Kls.: 17, Dos.: 81/, Fih.: 31-3 (appendix 4.2, no. 6).

[25] Taylan Sorgun, *İttihad ve Terakki'den Cumhuriyet'e Halil Paşa Bitmeyen Savaş* [From the CUP to the Republic: Halil Pasha's unfinished war] (2003), 9; Çerkes Ethem, *Anilarim* [Memoirs] (1993); Leverkuehn, *Posten auf ewiger Wache*, 104–9.

[26] Cipher telegram Enver Pasha to Third Army Command November 9, 1915, ATAŞE Kol.: BDH, Kls.: 17, Dos.: 81/, Fih.: 32 (appendix 4.2, no. 7).

[27] Hinno, *Günhe d Süryoye d Turabdin*, 117.

ans, and there would be no need for an inspection. For a brief moment, it seemed as if the Syriacs had convinced him. However, according to Hinno's narrative the Kurds had given him a different version and they knew that there were Armenians inside, so he changed his mind again. The next time the Syriac notables came to meet Ömer, he would not see them. From this they concluded that a full attack was being planned.

Naji's first attempt to storm Azakh took place on November 7 and 8. One of the first casualties was the Turkish officer riding in front of the first charge. According to schoolmaster Hendo, the officer was shot in the forehead as he was urging his troops to show no mercy.[28] Many of the Turkish soldiers who tried to clamber over the outer walls died in the attempt. The army used artillery and shelled the walls and some of the strategic bunkers. After this failure, Naji adopted new tactics and had trenches dug zigzaging up to the village, and yet there was no breakthrough.

The German high command was aware of what was going on. Ambassador Neurath notified Bethmann Hollweg on November 12 at the request of General von der Goltz.

> As a result of his mission to the east Anatolian theater of war, Field Marshal von der Goltz asked me to let him see the copies of the records of the embassy concerning the Armenian question and at the same time to orient him on our standpoint on this question. I have sent him the attached notes. The request of the Field Marshal was caused by the Expedition against a number of Christians of Syriac confession that has been planned for a long time. They are allied with Armenians and have fortified themselves in difficult terrain between Mardin and Midyat in order to get away from the massacres of Christians that the vali of Diyarbekir has organized. Since the original detachment designated for this mission from the Fourth Army is too distant, he asked the Field Marshal for a detachment of the Third Army to be ordered to restore order there. The consul in Mosul, Holstein, for his part pointed out that this is not a real uproar, and with the understanding of the vali in Mosul wishes that negotiations take place with the besieged and that among other personalities Herr von Scheubner-Richter, whose troops are anyway participating in the mission, shall participate and take part in the negotiations. The Field Marshal rightly not wishing German officers to get involved in this

---

[28] Hendo, "Tarikh Azakh"; Lahdo Beth-Lahdo Musa / Beth-Gorgis, interviewed May 1993 (appendix 1, no. 69).

affair, has given the order that Herr von Scheubner's troops will not be included in the expedition in question.[29]

At its greatest, the combined Ottoman might amounted to several thousand—the Eighteenth Army Corps contributed Halil's Fifty-Second Division and a battalion from the Fifty-First Army Division, a unit of mountain howitzers, and the Naji-Scheubner expedition minus its German officers. They also received more reinforcements in the form of 500 mujaheddin marched up from Mosul. The Syriac oral history narratives estimate that the troops totaled 8,000 soldiers.[30] The situation probably seemed to be growing out of government control. Additional reinforcements came in the form of an infantry battalion from the Fourth Army, which was based in Syria.

NAJI'S DEFEAT

A turning point came on the night of November 13–14. On that date, the Jesus fedai crept through the secret tunnel and emerged in the midst of the Turkish soldiers, who were sleeping on the ground. Chaos broke out as the Turkish soldiers in the darkness could not see who was friend or foe. The fedai shot at the soldiers as they rose from their sleep. According to the Syriacs, they killed a few hundred Turkish soldiers and the rest fled in disarray, abandoning their equipment. In this way the Syriacs got possession of modern semi-automatic rifles and real ammunition instead of their flintlocks and gunpowder made of tree roots, charcoal, and boiled excrement. This defeat came as a great shock, and Naji pleaded for reinforcements from Halil in Mosul and Sami Bey in Midyat.

Events revealed Ömer Naji to be a better ideologist and orator than military strategist. During the siege there were heavy losses, and apparently the army was embarrassed by its failure to conquer a rural village. The actual size of the Ottoman losses was not known, but it must have been very great as the calls for reinforcements kept coming. This meant that the buildup of troops for the operation in Iran fell behind schedule. Naji's campaign complicated relations with the German military advisors, who looked on as bewildered bystanders, while their ally wasted time and energy pursuing an illusory victory of no value to the war effort but possessing great prestige for warlord Enver. Because of this defeat, discussions began of making a temporary armistice and dealing with the Syriacs at a later date, since they

---

[29] PAA. Neurath to Bethmann Hollweg November 12, 1915.
[30] Hinno, *Günhe d Süryoye d Turabdin*, 117.

were not a true military threat. However, it proved difficult to negotiate a truce that both sides could accept. Already in a state of semi-disgrace, Naji needed to save face, but the stubborn Syriacs refused deportation and disarmament, which were Enver's unconditional demands. So shooting resumed.

Perhaps in order to countervail truce negotiations, General Kamil Pasha, the commander of the Third Army, argued that the Midyat rebellion was spreading to other villages and towns, even to the Yezidis in the Sinjar Mountains in the province of Mosul. He intimated that the various rebel groups were in contact with each other and coordinated their efforts into a major revolt. He confirmed that he had sent a battalion to reinforce the troops already in place. The telegram read:

> The rebels in Midyat and Jezire, not only did they not respond to the proposal of Ömer Naji Bey, the commander of the detachment of troops set for the village of Azakh, to give up their arms, but they also answered, by shooting, a previous proposal to relinquish their arms, the aforementioned rebels responded by attacking Muslims and massacring Muslim people, and to a third proposal for peace [illegible] that it was not considered acceptable was understood from the correspondence with the Province of Diyarbekir. In the Mosul province the Armenians who took refuge in the Sinjar Mountains united with the local Yezidis and communicated with the Midyat rebels and [urged them] to persevere with their rebellion and [illegible] for encouraging the rebels in Sinjar [we request] an order to do what is necessary to punish and repress the rebellion.[31]

Naji started truce negotiations on November 16, 1915, by sending a message asking for a meeting with the Azakh leaders. But they were reluctant to talk, as they had no reason to trust his word. The next day, Naji sent a new message and promised to leave an officer and a doctor as hostage with the Syriacs if they would meet. This time the village headmen accepted. According to Hendo, Naji said,

> You have killed many of my soldiers. But it is only now that I know for absolutely sure that you are not Armenians but Syriacs. Therefore, I will raise the siege of Azakh and withdraw my force. I propose a truce from now on.

---

[31] Mahmut Kamil Pasha to Ministry of War November 15, 1915, ATAŞE Kol.: BDH, Kls.: 17, Dos.: 81/, Fih.: 35-3 (appendix 4.2, no. 12).

Azakh's leaders were believed to have replied:

> Commander Bey! We have only defended ourselves and that is why we shot. If you really stop shooting and raise the siege, we will not shoot back.

Naji asked that the villagers return the weapons and ammunition that they had captured, but the villagers denied that they had any. In this meeting, Naji lied about not knowing that the villagers were Syriacs, and the villagers in turn lied that they did not have the army's weapons. Still, this was not a good time or place for accusations of being untruthful, and Naji had to make the first move. On November 21, his troops began their pullback from the trenches surrounding the village, and three days later they seemed to have disappeared for good.[32]

ENVER INTERVENES

But things were not so simple that local negotiations were acceptable. From Constantinople, Enver Pasha let it be known that he was not ready for an armistice. Instead, he ordered the complete destruction of the village. He reacted by sending an order on November 17 to the commander of the Sixth Army.

> The Commander of the Third Army reports that the rebels who attacked in the Azakh village of Midyat [district] responded with fire against Ömer Naji Bey's detachment to his proposal of handing over their arms. And about 100 kilometers west of the area, in Sinjar, the Yezidis and the Armenians together are currently in a state of rebellion. In response [illegible] the detachment which transferred from the Fourth Army and Ömer Naji Beys's detachment if necessary, [is] to be immediately reinforced in order to suppress [the revolt] in the Midyat area. As yet no additional information has arrived about the circumstances in Sinjar. If required, I request that your high office order its investigation and that I be informed of the outcome.[33]

About the same time, he telegraphed the Third Army Commander, giving explicit orders:

> In accordance with the conditions about which I wrote to you and in the event of lack of consent [of the Azakh defenders] to immediately evacuate and repress. Ömer Naji Bey's detachment is still in the vicinity

---

[32] Hannouche, *Azekh*, 70–75.
[33] Enver to Halil November 18, 1915, ATAŞE Kol.: BDH, Kls.: 17, Dos.: 81/, Fih.: 35-4 (appendix 4.2, no. 13).

of the village of Azakh and the battalion of foot soldiers and the mountain artillery unit sent from the Fourth Army is in the Midyat region [illegible] from the Fourth Army and from Mosul another force [from the Sixth Army] which can be spared, if necessary these forces from your area [are] to reinforce the Azakh [operation]. Inform of the outcome of the operation.[34]

Naji hoped to get Enver's go-ahead to proceed to Iran, but he was refused authorization to leave the area. He was already pulling back when Enver ordered Naji to resume the siege. Enver's telegram reads:

> I have transmitted the following telegram to the Third Army Command and informed the Sixth Army. The Midyat rebellion should be suppressed immediately and with utmost severity. Accordingly, Ömer Naji Bey's detachment will remain there under the orders of the army.[35]

Obviously, Enver sought total destruction rather than peaceful settlement. He was probably considering the negative influence this defeat would have on the morale of the army. Even Kamil Pasha insisted that Naji stay put, as he was worried that the rebellion was spreading and that the Christians were not about to surrender. Kamil telegraphed back:

> The ciphered telegrams regarding communication for Ömer Naji Bey's detachment to depart for Mosul have arrived. In the telegram dated November 22 from the Province of Diyarbekir it is understood that the associates of the rebels are attracting attention [again] and in Midyat the rebellion is growing day by day [and that] they [the rebels] will not ask for mercy and if this matter is not taken care of, [and] in the case that the detachments are transferred to other places in the said district, there is a probability of important unexpected events happening. The foot soldiers of the Fourth Army on their own and without artillery cannot pacify the rebellion as demonstrated by the failure of Ömer Naji Bey's detachment.[36]

Naji, in desperation, defied Enver and unilaterally agreed to let the Azakh villagers remain in place and keep their arms. Shocked by news of an agreement, Enver demanded answers to four questions. He sent a telegram to the Third Army Command:

---

[34] Enver to Kamil November 15, 1915, ATAŞE Kol.: BDH, Kls.: 17, Dos.: 81/, Fih.: 35-6 (appendix 4.2, no. 14).

[35] Enver to [illegible] Command probably November 27 or 28, 1915, ATAŞE Kol.: BDH, Kls.: 17, Dos.: 81/, Fih. 35-14 (appendix 4.2, no. 17).

[36] Kamil to Enver, undated, ATAŞE Kol.: BDH, Kls.: 17, Dos.: 81/, Fih. 51:1.

Provide information about the following items. 1. Of what nation [*millet*] are the rebels in the Midyat area? If there are Armenians among them, where are they from and how many are they? 2. With whom, upon what conditions, and in what way did Ömer Naji Bey reconcile? 3. Have these conditions been agreed by the rebels? What is the current situation? 4. If you find this settlement problematic what measures do you propose? To what extent is it possible to carry them out?[37]

Kamil Pasha, Commander of the Third Army, answered November 28, 1915, with an urgent telegram. He stated:

> 1. The great part of the rebels in the Midyat region are Syriacs who are native to the area. They were joined by a small number of Armenians and Chaldeans who escaped from here and there. 2. Ömer Naji Bey and the vali of Diyarbekir have reported that the Syriacs in the village of Azakh had agreed to the conditions of handing over their arms, repairing the telegraph lines they destroyed, paying their debts to the government, and returning to their villages, and that they have solved the matter peacefully. However, they also stated that the arms the rebels handed over constituted an insignificant amount and that furthermore if their domiciles are to be changed [if they are to be deported] and their weapons are going to be destroyed, the rebels will revolt once again. 3. Upon orders from your high office, Ömer Naji Bey's detachment departed for the Mosul border. The commander of the detachment which remained there [in Azakh] in accordance with the condition stipulated in the second item continues to collect the settlement money from the Syriacs. 4. The matter has been settled in this way and in that region to stabilize order and make these rebels docile and completely obedient to the government, and come what may, the transportation and removal of the abovementioned people to other places will be necessary. At present, the province of Diyarbekir has been informed that if the enemy approaches, this would cause renewed rebellion and banditry. In the opinion of your humble servant, this state of affairs is not acceptable…However, Ömer Naji Bey's failed operation and the lack of available forces to send in that direction necessitate postponement of the engagement to a more opportune moment; … the matter of when to complete the destruction of the rebellion is a matter that is left to your discretion.[38]

---

[37] Enver to Third Army Command November 27, 1915, ATAŞE Kol: BDH, Kls.: 17, Dos.: 81, Fih.: 51-3 (appendix 4.2, no. 20).
[38] Kamil to Enver 28 November 1915, ATAŞE Kol.: BDH, Kls.: 17, Dos.: 81/, Fih.: 58-1 (appendix 4.2, no. 21).

In the end, Naji was willing to give up the siege at any price and let the Syriacs keep their weapons and remain in their home villages. Thus he ignored most of the conditions that the Ottoman government had established at the start of the campaign against the Christian villages. He did this for two reasons: one, because even with reinforcements he could not win battles over the villagers; the other reason was that the siege delayed his more important mission and the failed attacks decimated his troops and made his mission more difficult. However, Kamil Pasha the head of the Third Army and Enver Pasha the Minister of War appear only to see this settlement as an embarrassing setback that must be counterbalanced by a future victory. Kamil urged a complete suppression of the rebellion and deportation of the Christian population. He stated that Enver only needed to give a new order when time was ripe.

However, this was not the end to the aggression against the defended villages in Mesopotamia. Residual resistance and fighting continued for several months. Finally, on February 14, 1916 the German Ambassador in Istanbul could report to Bethmann Hollweg that "the difficulties between the Syriac Christians at Mardin and Midyat" had been cleared up, in part because of the influence of General von der Goltz on the Turkish military.[39] Although Azakh and other well-defended villages were spared, the territory of the Mardin *sanjak* had been greatly devastated. A telegram of November 7, 1915, from the Directorate of Settlement of Tribes and Immigrants ordered the "deserted" villages in the Mardin and Midyat region to be settled with the families of "immigrant members of the Division of Public Order Cavalry."[40]

The details of the sieges in the Mardin sanjak are important for many reasons. Without doubt the case of Azakh shows that population loss in the countryside could not be attributed to "tragic" events that were solely the responsibility of the Kurdish tribes, outside government control. Here, instead, the attack was done by regular troops from the Third, Fourth, and Sixth Armies plus a large death squad of the Teskilat-i Mahsusa. The determined opposition of a little village of about a thousand souls became a matter for discussion in the highest government circles in the Ottoman Empire

---

[39] Metternich to Bethmann Hollweg February 14, 1916, in Lepsius, *Deutschland und Armenien*, 238.

[40] BOA.: Dahiliye Nezareti, ŞFR 57: 328; Fuat Dündar, *İttihat ve Terakki'nin Müslümanları İskân Politikası (1913–1918)* [CUP Muslim settlement policy 1913–1918] (2001), 138–39.

and Germany. The triumvirate of Enver, Talaat, and Jemal took part in the decisions. Even the German Reichskanzler Bethmann Hollweg found it wise to intervene. Thus it was not an obscure event that went on without government knowledge. This case also indicates how close the German military came to direct involvement, and they were more than just passive bystanders.

Scheubner made a report on his activities after he returned to Germany in 1916. He described how when he and Naji were proceeding to Mosul, they received an order to

> attack and punish an Armenian [sic] village. I found out that the presumed "rebellious" people were those who had taken cover to save themselves out of fear of a massacre. ... I pulled myself out of this threatening conflict by saying that I and my German officers and men were needed in Mosul. The command over my Turkish troops was transferred to one of my Turkish officers under the motive that this was an "inner Turkish" affair and that it was not proper for Germans to command the "gendarme-service" that the Turkish troops were expected to do. General Field Marshal von der Goltz approved my position. Even the Turkish side admitted this afterward. The disappointment shown then proved the supposition that the order that I received was an attempt by Halil Bey to involve me and the Germans under my leadership, in a compromising way, in the treatment of the Armenians.[41]

The German officers realized that the Turks were spreading the rumor that they had "German approval for the expulsion of the Armenians," or even that the extermination was a German idea. Leverkuehn drew the conclusion that

> the enormous importance of Scheubner's denial in the so-called uprising near Jezire stands before my eyes in its full political sharpness. Everything that one afterward heard about it justified the stance that Scheubner then had made. The entire uprising was only a matter of the destruction of a telegraph line, and it was done in self-defense, while the Armenian [sic] villages were still under Kurdish attack, and an appeal for help to the kaymakam met with not the least response. Directly, and before he received Scheubner's order, Leverkuehn could not separate himself from the troops and became a witness of the gruesomeness that the kaymakam tolerated without intervention, in the destruction of peaceful villages and the abuse of the inhabitants.[42]

---

[41] Scheubner-Richter report December 4, 1916, in Lepsius, *Deutschland und Armenien*, 306.

[42] Leverkuehn, *Posten auf ewiger Wache*, 102.

10 IMPLICATIONS AND CONCLUSIONS

The ancient bazaars of Diyarbekir burned for three days and nights in late August 1914. The chief of police, Mehmed Memduh, prevented the merchants from putting out the fire or even saving their merchandise. The new vali, Mehmed Reshid Bey, installed one week before, refused to intervene, and he took the blame for the arson conspiracy. When all was over, 1,578 Diyarbekir shops and warehouses smoldered in ruins. The burned and plundered shops belonged mostly to Armenians and Syriacs adhering to various faiths. The Christians had some evidence that the local government had instigated the fire, and they complained to Istanbul.[1]

In peacetime, this act was too blatantly anti-Christian and the central government cracked down on Reshid. A new vali was named, and some weeks later, Reshid traveled on while the more pro-Christian personality of Hamid Bey moved into city hall. About the same time, police chief Memduh was sent packing to Adana. However, the memory of the bazaar fire was a premonition of worse times to come, when half a year later, on March 25, 1915, Reshid turned up again as vali and Memduh returned as provincial chief of police.[2] Then, under cover of wartime, the anti-Christian activities, which horrified contemporaries by their all-encompassing scale and bloody-minded nature, began with great intensity, reaching a peak the following summer. By the end of autumn 1915, very few Christians were left living in the province, and more than a hundred thousand were dead.

---

[1] Ishaq Armalto, *Al-Qusara fi nakabat al-nasara* [The calamity of the Christians] (1919), part 2 passim. Ankara's Armenian quarter burned down a week after Reshid was installed as vali in 1916 (Marie-Dominique Berré, "Masacres de Mardin" [1997], 98; BOA. DH. ŞFR 44/234 Ministry of Interior to Diyarbekir vilayet September 13, 1914).

[2] Nejdet Bilgi, *Dr. Mehmed Reşid Şahingiray'ın Hayatı ve Hâtıraları: İttihâd ve Terakki Dönemi ve Ermeni Meselesi* [Dr. M. R. S.'s life and memory: The CUP period and the Armenian Question] (1997), 23–24.

This series of events illustrates two themes in the anti-Christian genocide: the deep popular undercurrent of anti-Christian sentiment that even permeated some of the civil officials, coupled with the political expediency of ethnic cleansing. Growing anti-Christian resentment existed before the war. Whatever sort of religious tolerance characterized the timeworn millet system, it had rapidly withered away under the pressure of popular nationalism in the early twentieth century. Local officials and politicians found it easy to play on these feelings to set mobs in motion against non-Muslim lives and property. Christian soldiers experienced brutal harassment, and few returned to their home villages save those who dared to desert. In Hakkari, ethnic cleansing of the Nestorian Assyrians was planned to start in the short interval between mobilization and the declaration of war. This recurrent stream of religious hostility was a necessary, but not sufficient, cause of genocide. Low-intensity violence and occasional pogroms did not necessarily result in genocide, particularly if it lacked the backing of the central government.

However, by early 1915, systematic, government-sanctioned ethno-religious hostility gradually assumed a structured form.[3] This planning concerned the targeting of certain ethnic and religious groups, the dates at which specific areas would be evacuated, and whether certain non-Muslim groups would be temporarily excluded and for how long. The exact manner in which deportations and massacres would be carried out was the object of little high-level planning and was left to local initiative. Personalities like Reshid and Memduh had free rein. The Ministry of the Interior ordered deportations with little concern for the social consequences. It has been claimed that deportations took place in humane and secure conditions, but the lived experience of Christians in Diyarbekir province, as well as Hakkari and Sa'irt sanjaks, gives absolutely no support to that interpretation. In this region, ethnic cleansing, wholesale massacres, mass rape, and attacks on outnumbered villages were a daily occurrence throughout June, July, and August 1915. Tens of thousands of deportees from other provinces were slaughtered along the roads of Diyarbekir and the banks of the Tigris River as a matter of course. Perpetrators and instigators ranged from government officials, army officers, and local politicians to tribal aghas, brigands, local riff-raff, and released convicts. Only in the very final months of the anti-Christian policy (from September 1915) is there solid evidence that de-

---

[3] Donald Bloxham, *The Great Game of Genocide: Imperialism, Nationalism, and the Destruction of the Ottoman Armenians* (2005), chap. 2.

ported Christians from Diyarbekir province actually began to arrive at their stated destinations.

A characteristic of historical research is counterfactual thinking. For instance: What could prove that it was not the intention to exterminate the evacuated population? What sort of proof could there be that the Ottoman government had a true concern for the health and welfare of the deportees? The Ottoman Ministry of the Interior archive includes a series of important decrees known as the cipher telegrams. These are the most important and urgent decrees dealing with the appointment of high officials, urgent administrative and financial questions, orders of deportation, and so on. If the ministry interested itself in the survival of the evacuated population, a researcher would expect to find drawn-out bureaucratic discussions going back and forth about how to deal with the deportation caravans. There would be plans for collecting and stockpiling food, water, clothing, and medicine at convenient waystations. There would be discussions of how to transfer legal responsibility when caravans from one province crossed through another province. There would be masses of tricky questions about what authority is to finance the caravans: would it be the state, the province, the nearest larger town, or the people themselves? If financing is to be shared between several entities, how is that to be done: by the number of days' travel through a province, or by the number of people? Should the size of rations differ between males and females, old and young? What would be the sanction in case one province rushed the deportees so that they arrived in the next province in a state of total exhaustion and must rest for a long time? If tax funds were allocated, there should also be inspectors appointed to check the costs. In any compartmentalized administration there will be bitter conflicts between authorities over jurisdictions, responsibilities, and funding. One would expect decrees appointing officials temporarily in charge of security and being brought to task for failure to guarantee safety. None of this type of documentation is available in the series of cipher telegrams, and this is an indication that the Ottoman government had little concern for the fate of the deportees, particularly in the most genocidal period, the summer of 1915, and particularly in the Armenian and Syriac heartlands of eastern Anatolia.[4] One of the few telegrams that deal

---

[4] As an example, the Government dismissed the kaymakams of Tenos and Aziziye in Sivas vilayet in late October 1915 on accusations of "acting improperly during the Armenian deportation." The exact nature of the impropriety is not given: it could have been for plotting to massacre, but it could just as well have

with the practical side of refugee survival is a response to a request from Mosul. The vali had asked who was to be responsible for the welfare of the Syriac and Chaldean women and children who had arrived destitute from Bashkale and Sa'irt. Talaat Pasha informed him that their care and sustenance was the sole responsibility of their churches, and he made no offer to use government funds.[5] The official publication *Armenians in Public Documents* publishes two telegrams from October 1915, one inquiring as to whether funds were sufficient for feeding the Armenian convoys, and the other about food and lodging for deportees in Edirne province. These come very late in the chronology of the deportations, and they concern the western provinces. No published documents concern the early stages or the deportees from eastern Anatolia.[6]

In Europe, World War I was already well under way by late summer 1914, but the Ottoman government was split and hesitated to choose sides officially, but it had begun general mobilization on August 2 just in case. Able-bodied males between 20 and 45 were drafted, and beginning with the youngest they were sent off in all directions, sometimes in chains. The generals had to prepare the defense of far too many fronts: in Thrace, along the Straits, in the Caucasus, at the Suez Canal, and on the Persian Gulf. In Diyarbekir and Mardin, the army requisitioned or seized enormous amounts of supplies and transport animals of all conceivable varieties—horses, donkeys, mules, and camels. The call-up came at a bad time for villagers who were basically subsistence farmers busy in the middle of the growing season. Villages were emptied of their young males. Urbanites observed that every day new contingents of troops arrived, only to be sent out the next day. The air vibrated with rumors of European battles won or lost. Mobilization encompassed citizens of all classes, ethnic backgrounds, and religions, for the Ottomans, just like the other combatants, prepared for total war and demanded absolute loyalty and sacrifice of the citizens. At first some Christian soldiers were placed in fighting units, but as the war progressed they were disarmed and placed in slave-labor battalions building roads or serving as beasts of burden. Few of these soldiers survived the war

---

been that they pocketed the Christians' wealth instead of turning it over to the government. See Talaat to province of Sivas October 24 and October 25, 1915 BOA. DH. ŞFR 57/105, 57/116, in Turkish Republic. Prime Ministry, *Armenians in Ottoman Documents (1915–1920)* (1995), 124–25.

[5] BOA. DH. ŞFR 54A/154 Ministry of Interior to Mosul vilayet July 28, 1915.

[6] Turkish Republic, *Armenians in Ottoman Documents (1915–1920)*, documents BOA. DH. ŞFR 57/110 Talaat to Şükrü October 26, 1915 and BOA DH ŞFR 57/32 Ministry of Interior to vali of Edirne October 16, 1915.

as most of the labor battalions were being worked to death, at times even liquidated though the task was unfinished. In April 1915, the government ordered an assembly of 4,000 slave-labor soldiers for major road construction outside Diyarbekir and found that there were so few left that Christian women had to be pressed into filling out the ranks.[7]

Citizens were required to register to get new identity cards, and Armenians and Syriacs of various faiths were surprisingly classified simply as *khiristiyan* without the traditional terms designating the different religions. Quite a large number of young men hid to avoid conscription, and many others deserted once they had their first harsh taste of army life. Authorities had great problems and had to divert attention to catching the deserters, particularly if Christians, who soon became the scapegoats for the military setbacks. Syriac deserters returning to Azakh told of how their party of deserters was attacked by Muslim villagers once they realized that they were not Muslims.

After initial tribulation, the Ottoman Empire entered the war on the side of Germany and Austria-Hungary by opening provocations in October and after formal declaration of war in early November 1914. From that moment on, the already precarious position of the non-Muslims eroded rapidly. The core region for ethnic cleansing became the area along the Turkish-Iranian border, the southeast parts of the province of Van, and the occupied Iranian province of Urmia. Here military operations, occupation, and the constant movement of troops formed the background of the first military atrocities committed against defenseless civilian populations. Faced with constant provocation, the Armenians of Van and the Assyrians of Hakkari fought back; skirmishes escalated into massacres and then full ethnic war. Even in the short run, the small ethnic and religious minorities did not stand a chance against the better-equipped Ottoman army and the numerically superior local Muslims. In separate waves they came as refugees behind Russian lines. During this local ethnic war, the Assyrians were badly decimated. Only half of them survived and found refuge outside Ottoman clutches by 1916. Was this in any meaningful sense a civil war? The Assyrians do admit to having made a declaration of war in May 1915. This step was taken in desperation nearly seven months after the October order of evacuation and after repeated massacres of Assyrians in the Bashkale region and genocidal acts perpetrated on co-religionists on the Iranian side of the

---

[7] BOA. DH. ŞFR 51/186 and 51/231 Ministry of Interior to War Office April 1 and 8, 1915.

border. Historians reserve the term "civil war" for major political conflicts splitting the population more or less into half over the question of control over the national government. What happened in Hakkari cannot be termed civil war, since events took the form of forced evacuation of an ethnic and religious minority that had the misfortune of living on both sides of an international border defending its home territory against a government bent on removing it at any cost.

Diyarbekir was one of the regions where Christians, of whatever faith, had little chance of surviving the war. As the last province before the desert, the roads and pathways also became the killing fields where caravans of deportees from the northern provinces were attacked and hacked to pieces. In the northern provinces of Van and Erzurum, it was possible for some Armenians and Assyrians to flee into the Caucasus region. Although not unheard of, few of Diyarbekir's Christians could ever escape to Russia. Here over 90 percent of the Armenian and Catholic population was lost, and the Syriac Orthodox lost over 70 percent. These are very high losses for a province so far distant from any frontline. The case of Diyarbekir shows just how greatly the term "military necessity" was misused.

THE NUMBER OF VICTIMS

The 1948 United Nations declaration on the prevention of the crime of genocide does not designate any exact number or percentage of population loss as a minimum criterion for applying the term "genocide." However, in common-sense usage it is usual to speak of a significant proportion of a targeted population having been killed in order to speak of genocide. After the war, some of the witnesses and representatives of the Syriacs, Assyrians, and Chaldeans did try to establish the number of victims.

The Assyro-Chaldean delegation to the Paris Peace Conference presented table 6.

Table 6: Approximate population of Assyro-Chaldeans lost in battle or massacred between 1914 and 1919

In Persia	40,000
Vilayet of Van	80,000
Vilayet of Diyarbekir	63,000
Vilayet of Mamuret ul-Aziz	15,000
Vilayet of Bitlis	38,000
Vilayet of Adana, Der Zor and diverse	5,000
Sanjak of Urfa	9,000
Total	**250,000**

The same source reckoned the combined pre-war core Assyro-Chaldean population of Ottoman Turkey and Persia to have been 563,000. The indicated population loss thus amounted to about 45 percent. These figures are not easy to check because of the high level of aggregation, and there is also some uncertainty (as discussed in chap. 1) about whether the Chaldean Church is included in these figures, despite the name of the delegation.

Other calculations are limited to a single region or to one religious organization. The Ottoman official El-Ghusein observed that the slaughter was general throughout the Armenian, Protestant, Chaldean, and Syriac communities of Diyarbekir. "Not a single Protestant remaining in Diarbekir. Eighty families of the Syriac community were exterminated, with a part of the Chaldeans, in Diarbekir, and in its dependencies none escaped save those in Madiât [Midyat] and Mardin."[8] As the annihilation progressed, the size of the population loss grew. Large-scale killing in Diyarbekir province began in May and June and continued nearly unabated (except for the period of Ramadan in mid July to mid August) until September 1915, with only occasional outbursts of violence afterward, mostly dealing with attacks on the few defended Syriac villages. Most of the killing took place during the summer. However, local attacks on individuals and groups could recur throughout the remaining war years. Also, famine and typhoid fever struck the few survivors in concentration camps in the deserts. Several times, entire camps near Ras al-'Ayn and Der Zor were liquidated as a precaution against typhoid epidemics.

In September 1915, Reshid Bey sent a telegram to Talaat informing him that 120,000 Armenians had been removed from the province through late August, and he obviously included Christians of all faiths.[9] Witnesses living in the province of Diyarbekir told of very high proportions of victims. The French Dominican Jacques Rhétoré, who finished his manuscript in late 1916, gave the following population losses for the vilayet of Diyarbekir: Gregorian Armenians lost 58,000 (97 percent), Armenian Catholics lost 11,500 (92 percent), Chaldeans lost 10,010 (90 percent), Syriac Catholics lost 3,450 (62 percent), Syriac Orthodox lost 60,725 (72 percent), and the Protestants, who could be either Armenian or Syriac, lost 500 (67 per-

---

[8] Fâ'iz El-Ghusein, *Martyred Armenia* (1917), 30.
[9] Bilgi, *Şahingiray*, 48, reprints a telegram from Reshid Pasha to Talaat Pasha, BOA. DH. EUM 2Şb 68/71 Reshid to Talaat September 18, 1915. This was published in the Turkish newspaper *Memleket* on April 29, 1919.

cent). Overall this gave a Christian population loss of 144,185, amounting to 82 percent of the total. On top of this, Rhétoré reckoned that more than 50,000 Christians hailing from other provinces met their deaths within the jurisdiction of the vali of Diyarbekir.

Rhétoré commented that the population loss for the Catholic population was "enormous," amounting to 85 percent.[10] He also supplied figures for the sanjak of Mardin, where population loss for all Christians was 47,675 of 74,470 (64 percent). The breakdown into religious groups is as follows: Armenian Catholics lost 10,200 of 10,500 (97 percent); Chaldeans lost 6,800 of 7,870 (86 percent); the Syriac Catholics lost 700 of 3.850 (18 percent), the Syriac Orthodox lost 29,725 of 51,725 (57 percent), and the Protestants lost 250 of an initial 525 (48 percent).[11]

Another French Dominican monk, Hyacinthe Simon, arrived at slightly higher figures, and these were used after the war's end by Edward Noel, a British political officer in Iraq, who was on a special mission in the spring of 1919 to prepare a report that could be used for negotiating the new boundary lines.[12] Both calculated the total number of Christian victims for the province of Diyarbekir to amount to 157,000.[13] The main difference between Simon and Noel compared with Rhétoré is that they give higher losses for the Syriac Orthodox, 98,000 compared with 60,725. Rhétoré does state that the Syriacs claimed nearly a hundred thousand victims inside the province, but that he found that claim somewhat exaggerated; obviously, Simon and Noel did not share his doubts.[14]

The French Dominican Marie-Dominique Berré supplied statistics limited only to the Mardin sanjak, but he revealed an even greater proportional loss of life. His report on the massacres is dated January 15, 1919, and thus conceivably covers all of the war years. He estimated a loss of 127,700 Christians. Divided into the relevant denominations, the number of victims was: Syriac Orthodox 100,000, Chaldeans 18,000, Armenian Catholics 7,000, and Syriac Catholics 2,700.[15]

---

[10] Jacques Rhétoré, *"Les Chrétiens aux bêtes": Souvenirs de la guerre sainte proclamée par les Turcs contre les chrétiens en 1915* (2005), 136.

[11] Ibid., 138.

[12] *Review of the Civil Administration of Mesopotamia* (1920), 59, 66–71; Edward W. C. Noel, *Diary of Major E. Noel on Special Duty in Kurdistan* (1919).

[13] Hyacinthe Simon, *Mardine la ville heroique:Autel et tombeau de l'Arménie (Asie Mineur) durant les massacres de 1915* (1991), 146.

[14] Rhétoré, *"Les chrétiens aux bêtes"*, 136; see also appendix 3 below.

[15] Berré, "Massacres de Mardin," 93.

Severius A. Barsaum, the Syriac archbishop of Syria, was sent as Patriarchal delegate to the peace conference. In February 1920 he supplied figures for the losses of the faithful belonging to the Syriac Orthodox Church dioceses. His figures give losses of a total of 90,313 for the entire church, including 156 ruined churches and monasteries and the deaths of 154 priests including 7 bishops. The breakdown according to province is: Diyarbekir 77,963, Bitlis 8,510, Kharput (Mamuret ul-Aziz) 3,500, and Urfa 340 dead.[16] Barsaum thus confirms Rhétoré's suspicion that the number of Syriac Orthodox victims in Diyarbekir province was less than a hundred thousand. But we are still dealing with a very large proportion of an originally very small religious community.

Within the vilayet of Diyarbekir, there were few survivors. British intelligence officer Noel recorded in a memorandum of June 10, 1919, a reduction of the Christian population down to only 18,959. Speaking of them, he had discovered that there was a group of 12,981 composed of "widows and orphans in more or less destitute condition." The issue of the return of captive Christian children to their families proved very complicated. Over the years, some had become attached to their captors and some had turned Muslim. It appeared to Noel possible to force the Muslims living in the towns to voluntarily give up the children. However, in the villages it was a different matter. Some of the Kurdish families demanded to be paid a ransom; and if the authorities intervened, the action would only "result in the child being done away with."[17] As the oral history narratives in appendix 1 below indicate, it was sometimes possible for relatives to locate and retrieve captive children. Ten-year-old Asmar 'Adoka was taken by a Muslim family and given the name Ibrahim. According to him, there were many other Syriac captive boys in the village in a similar situation. He stayed in the household for about a year and became very attached to his Muslim captors and at first even refused to be reunited with his mother.[18]

INTENTIONS

The Assyrian, Chaldean, and Syriac victims were easy to single out because they belonged to a non-Muslim group and spoke non-Turkic languages. They were thus targeted for violent ethnic cleansing as religious and ethnic groups, but not as racial groups. Thus the reason for their extermination

---

[16] PRO FO 371E 1221 1920 Memorandum February 1920, f. 110-112.
[17] Noel, *Diary*, April 23, 1919.
[18] Asmar 'Adoka, interviewed September 1997 (appendix 1, no. 12).

should be sought against the background of their religious and ethnic deviation from the political standards held by the ideologues in power.

The research in this book has focused on the concrete details of the Ottoman ethnic and religious wars and the full-scale, religiously inspired massacres. Here are a wide array of hitmen, cutthroats, bureaucratic collaborators, political agitators, profiteers, and brigands. However, the form of killing in itself gives little clue as to why it was being done in the first place. Only in an indirect way is it possible to ascertain the degree to which the events were rationally planned by central decisions to solve an important social conflict, or whether they were spur-of-the-moment results of an epidemic of war psychosis using despised minorities as a scapegoat.

The degree of extermination and the brutality of the massacres indicate extreme pent-up hatred on the popular level. Christians, the so-called *gawur* infidels, were being killed in almost all sorts of situations. They were collected at the local town hall, walking in the streets, fleeing on the roads, at harvest, in the villages, in the caves and tunnels, in the caravanserais, in the prisons, under torture, on the river rafts, on road repair gangs, on the way to be put on trial. There was no specific and technological way of carrying out the murders like the Nazis' extermination camps. A common feature was that those killed were unarmed, tied up, or otherwise defenseless. All possible methods of killing were used: shooting, stabbing, stoning, crushing, throat cutting, throwing off of roofs, drowning, decapitation. Witnesses talk of seeing collections of ears and noses and of brigands boasting of their collections of female body parts. The perpetrators not only killed but humiliated the victims: the public display of archbishop Maloyan and the other priests of Mardin, the similar parading of the Nestorian bishop in Sa'irt, the execution of the Syriac leader Hanne Safar Pasha of Midyat with the ceremonial sword presented to him by the Sultan, the humiliation of the Chaldean bishop of Jezire, the slaughter of Christians as human sacrifices at the semi-pagan shrine of Sheikhan. In several instances, decapitated heads of well-known Christians, such as Hanne Safar of Midyat and Ibrahim the Syriac priest of Sa'irt, were used as footballs. In Diyarbekir, the Armenian bishop Andre Chelebian was saved to be killed last and forced to witness the extermination of his flock. Just before his death on September 18, his beard and hair were ripped off, then a group of Muslim women insulted him before he was stoned to death.[19] In Derike, the Syriac Catholic priest Ibrahim Qrom had his beard torn off and was then forced

---

[19] Yves Ternon, "Mardin 1915: Anatomie pathologique d'une destruction" (2002), 93.

to crawl on all fours with a tormentor on his back while others kicked him, stabbed him, and finally cut him to pieces.[20] Virtually every deportation caravan and village massacre was accompanied by serial mass rape of the women. Young girls were abducted as sex slaves and children as household servants. Even when they were not killed outright, the women were often stripped of their clothes. The homes of Christians were broken into, plundered, furniture smashed, windows and doors removed, set on fire. Sometimes a survivor had little to return home to.

The number of perpetrators of the local massacres was staggering. Apparently the local officials like Reshid and Bedri or the local politicians like Feyzi and Zulfi had no difficulty in motivating the populace for extermination. The officials established and recruited death squads from middle-aged Muslim men. National Assembly deputies Feyzi and Zulfi agitated among the Kurdish tribes and even managed to get notorious outlaws like Omar and Mustafa and their band of Rama to cooperate in return for loot, adventure, and a promise of amnesty. On a few occasions, Muslim women were present, for instance at the Sheikhan shrine or at the public humiliation of Christian dignitaries, but mostly the perpetrators were males. There were literally thousands of perpetrators, most of them locals. In the defended villages like Azakh and 'Ayn-Wardo, aggressors and defenders were neighbors and could recognize each other's voices and taunt one another over the barricades. As the oral history interviews reveal, there was a widespread belief among local Muslims that the Sultan had issued a decree ordering the extermination and that killing of the treasonous non-Muslims was morally justified. Although these beliefs were misinformed, they did gain hold on an illiterate and superstitious populace whipped into frenzy.

The intense extermination of the Christians was completed in a short period between June and September 1915. Throughout the southeast Anatolian provinces, bodies of the victims lay strewn everywhere: along the highways, outside the city gates, on hills outside town, in caves, in ravines, in wells and cisterns, in latrines, floating on the lakes and rivers. No traveler could miss them. In 1919, after the war, Edward Noel, the British political officer, observed corpses still rotting along the roads and noted that all the male corpses were on their stomachs but the corpses of women were lying face up on their backs.[21] It was as if an incurable plague of hundreds of Jedwabnes and Srebrenicas afflicted the region.

---

[20] Rhétoré, *"Les Chrétiens aux bêtes"*, 47.
[21] Noel, *Diary*, 10–11.

A single episode that shows most clearly the intention to exterminate rather than deport is one that was related by the vali of Baghdad, Suleyman Nazif. A loyal CUP member and Kurd, Nazif had forbidden all massacres of Christians in his province. In July 1915, Nazif was in transit on official business proceeding through the Diyarbekir countryside near Tel-Arman, when he encountered Memduh with a detachment of soldiers leading 260 Armenian women and children from Mardin. Nazif realized that they were marching to their deaths. He intervened, using his superior position as vali, and demanded that Memduh hand over the column so that it could be safely escorted to Mosul. Memduh refused, showing Reshid Bey's order that they were to be executed. He even threatened to arrest Nazif, who being outside his jurisdiction had no choice but to back down. The next day, local Kurds directed by one of Ibrahim Pasha's sons annihilated the column at a previously arranged spot.[22]

What is particularly unusual about the Mardin sanjak was that until World War I it was famed for being relatively free from Muslim–Christian conflict as a sort of model for everyday Ottomanist pluralism. Throughout the massacres of 1895–96, which devastated Diyarbekir and its surroundings, Kurdish and Bedouin tribes guarded their Christian neighbors so destruction was limited to only a few localities. Particularly famous for this was Ibrahim Pasha. His home base of Viranshehir, as well as Mardin and Midyat, were acknowledged havens for Christians who moved there after the massacres to find safer homes. In 1915, there were few protectors in this vast area. Even traditional allies of the Christians like the Haverkan confederation, the Muhallemi, and the Yezidis were split—some continued to help, but others took part in the extermination.

Tragically, the authorities succeeded in dividing the Christians between themselves so that suppression could proceed through a technique of divide and conquer. Initially, all of the Christian faiths experienced the same rising specter of persecution and put age-old quarrels aside; in Midyat they swore unity on the Bible. Solidarity between them proved fragile, at least in the larger towns, as some groups, in their terrified panic, accepted any promise at face value no matter how hollow it could seem to a more sober observer. At times it was said that the target was only the Armenians, not any of the other denominations. At other times it was said that the targets were only those who had contacts with the enemy, for instance the Armenians with the Russians, the Catholics and Protestants with the French, the so-called

---

[22] Armalto, *Al-Qusara*, 282; David McDowell, *A Modern History of the Kurds* (1996), 92, 123.

Farangoye. This ignited deep-seated mistrust between the rival Christian faiths. Sometimes the populace would be told that only the rich and influential families were being sought, not the ordinary people. Thus class hatred could also be set in motion.

In places like Mardin, Midyat, and Jezire, the Syriac Orthodox fell into this trap and watched as authorities dealt with persons belonging to other faiths. They had no contacts with foreign enemies, they had no political parties, and they had not demanded political autonomy; and they believed they just might be secure if they cooperated. In Mardin and Jezire, the Syriac leaders even amassed large sums of money to bribe authorities to leave the congregation in peace. Their leaders lulled themselves into a false sense of safety and assumed the role of bystanders. After the first waves of mass killing, the authorities were free to turn on the Syriac Orthodox communities. Sometimes the technique of dividing the Christians did not work, chiefly because of the stubbornness and inbred suspicion of the rural villagers. At Azakh, the first question the army commander asked was whether there were any Armenians in the village. Azakh's Syriac Orthodox leaders denied the presence of the runaway Armenians and Chaldeans and simply said no, adding that if the commander did not believe them he could consult the local archives. They gave a similar answer when ordered to hand over the Protestants and Catholics among them.

The Enver and Talaat warlord administration had come to power by violent means and held itself in place by even more violence. In World War I, the Committee for Union and Progress slid almost unnoticed into a military dictatorship. As Isabel Hull concludes, the immense destruction of military culture was deeply "goal-irrational," but within the near-sighted context of military life in total war this culture was actually "eminently institutional-rational." It worked professionally until the task was complete, without needing or even asking for an overarching explanation.[23] In the absence of any definite aim for the genocidal project, the local Ottoman organizers and perpetrators realized that they were to continue until someone with higher authority told them to stop, or until there was no one left to kill. No general order to stop ever came, although every so often Talaat inquired about how many Christians remained in any particular place, with a goal of under 10 percent allowed to remain. For Hakkari, he decreed in June 1915, no Assyrians could return. Those few defended Syriac villages

---

[23] Isabel V. Hull, *Absolute Destruction: Military Culture and the Practices of War in Imperial Germany* (2005), 4.

such as 'Ayn-Wardo and Azakh that held out as long as the late autumn of 1915 were grudgingly given an amnesty. However, during the rest of the war the inhabitants always ran the risk of assault as soon as they set foot outside their village walls. Here and there one could find pockets of refugees who as individuals had filtered in and made it to rescue in one of the few monasteries or churches still in operation.

Ethnic Cleansing

The massacres in Diyarbekir and the military attacks in Hakkari and Van made an enormous impact through massive violence concentrated in a very short period of time. The intensity of murder parallels that of the holocaust of the Jews of Lithuania, who were exterminated in less than half a year between July and December 1941. When World War I was over, entire provinces were empty of the ethnic non-Muslim population that had lived there for millennia. Here and there, a captive woman or child could be found in slave-like existence. Only a handful of families made it back to their ancestral home or village intact.

Michael Mann has created a sociological theory for ethnic cleansing, which can be used as a starting-point for discussion of the Anatolian experience. He compares the genocides of the Armenian and the Nazi holocausts, Bosnia, Rwanda, as well as the communist cleansings under Stalin, Mao, and Pol Pot. In his scheme, total ethnic cleansing escalates through several phases but was nowhere the original intention.[24] **Plan A** includes serious attempts from the side of the majority population to integrate, assimilate, or at least make an alliance with the minority guaranteeing neutrality. This aims at making a common political, social, and cultural front in which residual ethnic differences cease to be important. If Plan A does not work, then **Plan B** necessitates the deportation of the minority population to new settlements and under circumstances (such as wide dispersal) that are experienced as less dangerous for the majority. Usually these deportations are done strategically, and minorities are removed piecemeal in steps starting with the areas that are considered most risky, such as a border area, large towns, or near railroads. This involuntary resettlement is inherently problematic because many members of the targeted groups will automatically resist, making implementation by civil means difficult. If Plan B does not succeed, then **Plan C** takes effect. Now deportation becomes universal and more violent, often requiring the use of military force to get the obsti-

---

[24] Michael Mann, *The Dark Side of Democracy: Explaining Ethnic Cleansing* (2005); on the Armenian genocide, see 111–79.

nate minority population to begin moving. Civil administrations normally cannot manage Plan C and this task is assigned to the army, which employs its normal total ruthlessness to the effort, often considering the population to be moved as the enemy. Plan C easily slides into **Plan D**, namely genocide, since a military solution to the presence of minority populations almost always results in exaggerated violence, triggering instinctive self-defense and igniting a process that knows no natural limit.

Mann also identifies a number of key social groups and social situations that are instrumental in effectuating a total ethnic cleansing. "Key ministerial elites" need to make the initial decisions starting Plan A and Plan B. On this level, the necessary laws and decrees are made and measures are taken for the organization and administration of the alliances or deportations. Special departments need to be set up and state funds need to be allocated. "Factual struggles among officials" are also a necessary precondition. Mann points out that there was much dissent between Turkish military about the wisdom of going to war. Administrators vacillated between the ideals of Ottomanism, which taught gradual Plan A, peaceful integration of minorities, and the Young Turk ideals of Plan B, immediate forced assimilation. Many Ottomanist officials had to be replaced, some even assassinated, in order to implement ethnic cleansing. Dissident officials lived in terror while the ruling clique found that it needed to give cutthroats freedom of action to do the dirty work. "Paramilitary killers" were a third precondition, and the existence since the Balkan wars of the Committee for Union and Progress Teskilat-i Mahsusa special organization fitted this role very well. During the wars, this secret group initiated guerrilla wars behind the lines and assassinated difficult political opponents both within and without the CUP. Here was a core of unquestioning professional killers already connected to Enver Pasha, which was reinforced by Talaat Pasha with released convicts from the prisons. A final element was the existence of "ordinary Turks" who Mann theorizes were not engaged in the killing: "Villagers and townspeople were usually required to do little. Mobs might be useful, but a hundred or two rioting in a town of many thousands would suffice to put pressure on the Armenians. ... Nor were the perpetrators the Kurds."[25] In Mann's scheme, final responsibility for most ethnic cleansing rests with the political elites and their allied paramilitary forces, but not with ordinary people, despite their ethnic or religious hatred.

---

[25] Ibid., 167–69.

The Ottoman part of Mann's argument is based on what is known about the situation of the Armenians. Many of his points quite naturally also have bearing for the treatment of Assyrian, Chaldean, and Syriac Christians since they occurred at the same time and under the same dictatorship. But still there are some differences. Discussion can begin with the transitions from Plan A to Plan D.

Plan A. Prior to the war, the local Christian elite identified, at least in part, with Ottomanism and was loyal to the state. Several of the persons later slain had been decorated with medals and honors from the government. Ignace Maloyan received the Sultan's medal as an acknowledgment of meritorious service just two months before he was murdered. Hanne Safar in Midyat had not only medals but also the honorary title Pasha and his own office in the town hall. Galle Hermez represented the Syriacs on the town, regional, and provincial councils, working for reform through everyday politics. Mar Shimun received the Hamidi decoration, as did his archrival Nimrod Shimun, who was killed by his own people on suspicion of pro-Turkish feelings. Agha Petros, the future Assyrian general, had even served as the Turkish consul in Urmia. Hormuz Shimun was attending university in Istanbul when he was taken hostage. When the war broke out, as Armalto in particular shows, the Christians of Mardin sanjak allowed themselves to be registered and drafted.[26]

Plan B. In August 1914, Mar Shimun XXI Benyamin was summoned to Van to meet with the governor, who wanted assurances that the Assyrians would be loyal and useful to the state. But the Assyrians rejected mobilization into the army. This was a decision that immediately led to escalation to Plan B. For the Assyrians of Hakkari sanjak, Plan B began in October 1914—that is, before the declaration of war. A specific decree, pertaining only to Nestorians, arrived, commanding the vali to remove the Assyrians living along the border with Iran. The reason given was an accusation of being a tool of an unnamed foreign power—Russia, of course. Because the government no longer trusted them, they were to be "chastised" by resettlement in suitable areas like Ankara and Konya. Once in central Anatolia, the Assyrians were to be divided up so that families would be placed in overwhelmingly Muslim villages. The intention of this dispersal was to thwart the possibility of maintaining their Assyrian culture in the new settlement. As part of Enver's policy of drawing Turkey into war by provoking Russia, high-intensity violence was already occurring along the border area between Hamidiye cavalry regiments, Teskilat-i Mahsusa, and ordinary As-

---

[26] Armalto, *Al-Qusara*, 101f.

syrians. The Assyrians were not going to be an easy group to deport, as they had always been armed and were as ferocious as their Kurdish neighbors. Thus Plan B was never feasible. The order of deportation is unknown in Assyrian sources; instead they refer to mass arrests and executions in the administrative capital, Bashkale, beginning at the end of September. This violence continued throughout the winter of 1914 and early 1915, but it apparently had no other aim than to kill in retribution for alleged collaboration with the enemy during the occasional Russian occupations.

For the Syriacs and Armenians of Mardin sanjak, there simply never was a Plan B. No deportation order for the Syriac Orthodox, Syriac Catholic, Syriac Protestant, Chaldean, Armenian Catholic, or Armenian Protestant populations was issued, and there is not even indirect mention of such decrees in other sources. In truth, the only deportation decree at all was issued for the province when Talaat sent one, concerning only the Armenians, on June 21, 1915, about one month after the start of intensive universal killing.[27] However, since May, Christians irrespective of faith had been subject to the same sort of brutality. Churches of all denominations were searched for guns and bombs; private homes were turned upside down looking for books and papers in the French and Armenian languages; and Christian notables were arrested and imprisoned, tortured, and later executed. Possibly this was an effect of decisions made not in Istanbul, but in the provincial government. Talaat sent a telegram on July 12 to Reshid Bey insisting that the deportations should only focus on the Armenians and "are absolutely not to be extended to other Christians." This telegram arrived much too late for most of the rural Christians, who were already dead. It had only short-term compliance, limited to the larger towns and cities. General massacres continued unabated in parts of Tur Abdin and the nearby towns of Jezire and Nisibin.

Plan C. The violent and general deportation can be said to have arrived in Hakkari at the start of June 1915 when the vali of Mosul, Haydar Bey, was reassigned to amass heavily armed troops with artillery and machine guns plus four separate agglomerations of Kurdish tribesmen to invade the Hakkari mountains. The content of his orders is not known, but an invasion force of such magnitude cannot have intended to peacefully round up and transfer the Assyrians. Rather, this force must have intended either to annihilate the Assyrian population totally, or to drive them out of

---

[27] BOA. DH. SFR 54/87 Talaat to the provinces of Trabzon, Mamuret-ul Aziz, Sivas, Canik, and Diyarbekir June 21, 1915.

the area totally. The Assyrians found themselves in a no-win situation with few alternatives. Their hope for substantial protection from Russia proved fruitless because of their remoteness from lines of supply. With their traditional firearms they had no chance against a modern army, so they were gradually pushed out of their dwellings and took their families up into the wilderness of the mountaintops, where they could not survive more than a few months. They could watch down below as their houses, farms, fields, and animals were destroyed. There was thus little to return to. As the Assyrians were fighting for their very existence, Plan C slid directly into Plan D as Assyrians were killed wherever they were found—the soldiers took no prisoners.

Plan D. At the same time as the Hakkari mountains were being ethnically cleansed, a different strategy was being applied in Mardin sanjak. Plan D came into effect in early June, implemented by the provincial authorities without written orders from Istanbul. Throughout the broad region, Christian villages were plucked one by one. In these cases all persons were killed, except the few who were taken captive, usually children or young women. In a few villages, the populations were formed into deportation columns, but often they were cut down just outside their own village at the nearest convenient cliff or riverbank. The countryside was turned into one large killing field, with nearly the whole rural Christian population annihilated during the months of June and July. In the towns and cities, the Christian groups were arrested piecemeal. First the most important secular and religious leaders were taken to a point of execution in as large a group as was possible for a small detachment of militia to control. After the males, a similar procedure was done with the women, the only difference being that the women might not be first imprisoned and tortured like their husbands and sons. Throughout all of this, houses were plundered of valuable items and families pressed to pay extortion money. Reshid is said to have amassed over 100,000 liras and Memduh left Mardin with a reported 53,000 liras.[28]

Thus in the Assyrian case, the progression from Plan A to plan C was very swift; and Plan C in the mountainous circumstances could only be Plan D—that is, genocide. As for the Armenians and Syriacs of Diyarbekir, Plan A extended to April 1915 and then immediately turned into Plan C: generalized uncontrolled violence that was inherently genocidal.

Let us examine some of the sociological groups or situations that Michael Mann identifies as essential elements of ethnic cleansing. "Key ministerial elites" is probably not completely appropriate, in a semantic sense.

---

[28] Simon, *Mardine*, 118, 122.

However, Enver Pasha, along with his brother-in-law Jevdet Bey and his uncle Halil Bey, were the key elite network that staged the massacres of Armenians and Assyrians, first in Urmia in February to May and then in Van and Hakkari in April and May; and later the mass killings in the cities of Sa'irt and Bitlis. Enver, as Minister of War, and Jevdet, as governor of Van, were responsible for the concentration of undisciplined troops composed of Hamidiye irregulars, Jandarma, Teskilat-i Mahsusa, border guards, and Kurdish tribal volunteers. They were placed in an occupation that they were not trained for and attempted to control Christian civilians through sheer terror. As they retreated before a Russian advance, led by a Russian general of Armenian extraction, Nazarbekov, they slaughtered the Christian population as an extreme precautionary measure, possibly as a psychologically misconceived warning to others. Halil even had the Armenian and Syriac soldiers in his division shot using the freedom granted commanders on the frontline.

Within Diyarbekir, the genocide instigators crystallized around a provincial elite rather than a ministerial elite. Talaat Pasha's role was essential to appointing Reshid governor, despite his past history of anti-Christian violence, and to permitting him to stay at his post in face of the repeated complaints about the general Christian massacres. Reshid proved to have a flair for genocidal organization and established a network of central and local directories as well as death squads for implementing mass murder. It would seem that Reshid never bothered with Plans A and B: even before the war he instigated the fire in the bazaar, and immediately upon his arrival in Diyarbekir he began organizing general anti-Christian operations. Ka'biye and Qarabash, two Syriac villages, were slaughtered as early as April, only a few weeks after he moved into city hall. Without the network, the effort to liquidate so many people in such a short time would have been impossible. Enver's role in the province supported the activities of the regular army, attacking the handful of defended Syriac villages in Tur Abdin. Several times during November 1915, he sent messages about how to treat the defenders in Azakh. Once he ordered his forces to "evacuate and suppress" and later, after a lost battle, to "suppress immediately and with utmost severity." He was not satisfied with the truces and waited for a better opportunity to renew the ethnic cleansing of Tur Abdin.

Another essential element was the presence of "paramilitary killers." In Hakkari and Van, they were already in place in the expeditionary forces led by Jevdet, Halil, and Kazim. The professional mercenary Nogales characterized them as "ex-bandits and *comitadchis* [*komitaji*s, another term for Teskilat-i Mahsusa], who had been exiled ... as undesirables. ... I myself often had to go about, pistol in hand and sword in readiness, to prevent disorder and to check pillage."[29] In Diyarbekir, Reshid had in secret formed many local paramilitary death squads, known in the local Arab dialect as the Al-Khamsin because each unit had 50 men. The 50-man militias were unique for Diyarbekir. They had uniforms and armbands and had leaders holding military rank. They functioned much like the *Einsatz* groups of the Nazis; these would organize mass executions with the collaboration of local people. Thus the small units of Al-Khamsin were often accompanied by hundreds of Kurdish volunteers who would assemble at a spot designated in advance for an attack. Rudimentary planning involved setting priorities for the order in which the various villages would be attacked, which meant that some low-priority villages like Anhel had some respite.

What about the "ordinary" people? It appears that throughout the area, local people participated in the brutality. In truth, the whole area was violent even in times of peace, as Kurdish tribes fought internally and incessantly with each other and with their Christian neighbors. Haydar Bey had little difficulty in gaining the participation of the surrounding Kurdish aghas when he mounted the large invasion of Hakkari. Suto Agha of Oramar, the next-door neighbor to the Assyrian Jilu tribe, was particularly notorious for slaughtering Assyrians. Even the Hamidiye regiments that committed so much mayhem in the Bashkale area stemmed from the supposedly friendly Artoshi confederation. In Diyarbekir, neighbor fought neighbor, as the oral testimony bears witness. Horrendous atrocities occurred in face-to-face situations in which perpetrator and victim knew each other, at least by sight. Some of the worst instigators were descendants of previous persecutors: Hurshid Bey, the Hamidiye leader who terrorized the Bashkale area, was the grandson of Nur-Allah, who slaughtered ten thousand Assyrians in the 1840s; Feyzi, a CUP delegate and a prime mover behind the Diyarbekir genocide, was the son of Arif, the mayor who incited the pogroms of 1895.

But there were also "righteous" Muslim people, those who went out of their way to aid the Christians. There were the unnamed Kurdish leaders who tipped Mar Shimun that authorities intended to kill him. Numerous aghas escorted their Christian serfs to defended villages. There were Sarohan, Sarokhano, and Chelebi of the Haverkan confederation, who succeeded in protecting some of the villages in Tur Abdin. There were the Tayy Bedouin who smuggled Christians to Mount Sinjar, where Hamo Sharro, leader of the Yezidis, welcomed them and let them build new vil-

---

[29] Rafael de Nogales, *Four Years beneath the Crescent* (1926), 114.

lages. There was Shaykh Fathullah, the Muhallemi religious leader, who mediated the armistice at 'Ayn-Wardo and set his own family as hostages and guarantors of pledges. Then there were many old-school Ottomanist officials who insisted that the Christians were loyal and integrated citizens and who refused to obey orders to arrest and kill. In Mardin, the mutasarrif refused Reshid's orders and was removed. Special Organization operatives assassinated middle-level officials like the kaymakams of Lije, Beshiri, and Derike, and the kaymakam of Midyat simply vanished, for the same reason. The fate of dissenting lower officials can only be guessed.

This book has told a story of ethnic wars, innumerable retributions of suspected collaborators, and astounding genocidal projects throughout southeastern Anatolia. What happened was indeed the feared "general massacre" that the German diplomats in July 1915 warned the regime in Istanbul was imminent unless it lessened the brutality of the forced deportations and the Diyarbekir massacres. This term, "general massacre," along with others like "extermination" and "annihilation," was as close as the German diplomats at that time could come to formulating the modern concept "genocide," as defined by the United Nations in 1948. The Vatican expressed its fear for "the threatening destruction of en entire people," to which the Sultan replied on November 19, 1915, acknowledging the deaths of innocent people and explaining that it had unfortunately proved impossible to separate the "peaceful elements from those in rebellion." Already on May 24, 1915, at the very beginning of persecution, the Entente powers labeled them "crimes against humanity and civilization."

11 NOTES ON THE SOURCES

GENERAL SOURCES

On May 24, 1915, Britain, France, and Russia formally declared that they would hold the Ottoman government responsible for crimes against civilization and humanity. From about that time, the powers started collecting documents to be used for the purpose of prosecution or to create public opinion. Some of the English-language testimony was collected and published in the work edited by Arnold Toynbee (1889–1975) and Lord Bryce (1838–1922).[1] This was commissioned by Parliament and appeared in its official "Blue Book" series. It was the first of many official or semi-official collections of documents. It assembles 150 documents, chiefly letters, reports, and newspaper articles from missionaries or persons connected with agencies giving humanitarian aid to refugees. The collection was published in 1916 and builds mainly on documents from 1915. The lions's share of the material came from two organizations: the American Committee for Armenian and Syrian Relief, and the Board of Foreign Missions of the Presbyterian Church. The reason for the American dominance was that the United States was neutral and its nationals lived throughout the Ottoman Empire. Although the title only mentions Armenians, the entire section IV on Azerbaijan and Hakkari (135–222) and a few other scattered documents deal with East Syriac populations. There is, however, no information about Diyarbekir province or the West Syriac population.

The Germans were anxious to clear themselves of the accusation that they colluded with the Ottoman government in the massacres and deportation. Johannes Lepsius (1858–1926), the well-known leader of the Deutsche Orient-Mission and very pro-Armenian, was commissioned to edit a volume from diplomatic correspondence gathered in the archives of the Ger-

---

[1] James Bryce and Arnold Toynbee, *The Treatment of Armenians in the Ottoman Empire, 1915–1916* (1916; uncensored edition, 2000). The 1916 original omitted some of the names of persons and their places of residence if they were still living within Ottoman territory. This information has been included in the uncensored edition.

man Foreign Office.² Lepsius published 444 reports and messages covering 1914–18 from local consuls and ambassadors and, sometimes, military officers and private individuals. Some of this material deals with the Syriac population, particularly the consular papers from Mosul and Aleppo. Lepsius was not allowed free access to the archive but received the documents from the Foreign Office, and some documents had been doctored. Usually the reason for omissions was to remove information that would incriminate the Germans. A website now supplies the full version for the abbreviated documents (www.armenocide.net). None of the documents used here are among those that had been manipulated.

More recently, Arthur Beylerian published sources from the French Foreign Office archives.³ These comprise 757 reports sent in from Catholic missions, military personnel, and consular agents, which all came to rest at the foreign ministry. Considerable space is given to plans to organize an Armenian and Syriac volunteer legion for an invasion of the Anatolian coast. The material from the Catholic Church often deals with massacres and destruction of the Chaldean Church.

Armenian source publications as a rule do not deal with Syriacs, but sometimes both Armenians and Syriacs are mentioned in the same documents. M. G. Nersisiyan collected a massive volume published in 1982.⁴ This contains 267 sources selected from Russian diplomatic and military correspondence, material from the Armenian Church, newspaper articles, translations from documents printed by Lepsius and by Bryce and Toynbee, and contemporary books. This work also includes materials on massacres and pogroms during Abdul Hamid's reign (2–187) and during Young Turk rule prior to World War I (188–272). Another source publication collects 152 documents from the Russian Foreign Office and from newspapers.⁵ A very useful collection republishes 26 longer contemporary Russian-language publications (articles and pamphlets) about the Armenian persecutions.⁶ In

---

² Johannes Lepsius, *Deutschland und Armenien: Sammlung diplomatischer Aktenstücke* (1919).

³ Arthur Beylerian, *Les Grandes Puissants: L'Empire Ottoman et les arméniens dans les archives françaises (1914–1918)* (1983).

⁴ *Genotsid armyan v osmanskoi imperii. Sbornik dokumentov i materialov* [The Armenian genocide in the Ottoman Empire: Collection of documents and materials], ed. M. G. Nersisiyan (1982).

⁵ *Russkie istochniki o genotside armyan v osmanskoi imperii 1915-1916 gody (Sbornik dokumentov i materialov)* [Russian sources on the Armenian genocide in the Ottoman Empire 1915–1916], ed. G. A. Abraamyan and T. G. Sevan-Khachatryan (1995).

⁶ *Genotsid armyan i russkaya publitsistika* [The Armenian genocide in Russian pub-

particular, the article on the defense of Van contains information on the Syriacs as well.

For the Paris peace conference, Iran published a collection of 305 documents dealing with Ottoman and Russian infringements of Persian neutrality.[7] They deal with massacres of Iranian citizens (Muslim and non-Muslim), troop movements on Iranian territory, and the Ottoman occupation of Azerbaijan, January–May 1915. These come manly from the Iranian Foreign Office and include many interesting documents of correspondence with the Turkish ambassador in Tehran and the Persian ambassador in Constantinople.

Selected Ottoman sources have been published. The multivolume history of World War I made by the Turkish General Staff progresses army by army through each year and campaign of the war. It publishes or summarizes in Modern Turkish many of the actual documents in the military-history archives. The volumes for the Third Army, which was based in Erzurum and had jurisdiction over all of eastern Anatolia, is the most relevant for the Christian deportations and for the struggle against the alleged "Armenian revolt."[8] There is also a journal that publishes military history sources, and it always provides a transliteration and sometimes a translation into Modern Turkish. Some of the issues deal with the treatment of the Christians, deportations, and so on.[9] Most of these documents are short telegrams between the War Office and the local commanders. Being telegrams, they give little information other than a brief description of the situation or the actual order with a rudimentary explanation. Because of their brevity, the military-history documents lack the analytical depth of diplomatic sources, but they give insight into the thinking of the army leadership.

Archives in Turkey have become more accessible, and the papers of the Ministry of the Interior are essential for the period of the deportations. The series of so-called cipher telegrams (these are actually the originals before they were encoded) sent from the ministry contains decrees of depor-

---

lications] (1998).

[7] Empire de Perse, Ministère des affaires étrangers, *Neutralité Persane: Documents diplomatiques* (1919).

[8] Genelkurmay Başkanlığı, *Birinci Dünya Harbi'nde Türk Harbi Kafkas Cephesi 3 ncü Ordu Harekâti* [World War I, Turkish war on the Caucasus front, Third Army operations], 5 vols. (1964–93). The early volumes were compiled by Fahri Belen, but the later volumes do not give an author.

[9] *Askeri Tarih Belgeleri Dergisi*.

tation, orders freeing convicts from prison to join the gendarmes, and correspondence with the provincial authorities. As a rule, these telegrams are very short and do not give a motivation about the order being given. As yet the correspondence coming *from* the provinces has been litte used. The so-called Second Section, with the provincial correspondence on internal security, was opened to research in the summer of 2006 and was not available for this book. However, one telegram, that from Reshid to Talaat concerning the number of deportees from Diyarbekir, could be used since it is among the telegrams published on the Prime Ministerial Archive's homepage online document section on the "Armenian Issue."[10]

Sources on Urmia

Urmia was the place where the world first began to observe the wartime Ottoman atrocities. There are many sources for the events in Iranian Azerbaijan, and many of them were published during the war or during the peace negotiations. A major portion is the reports sent to their home countries by American and English Protestant missionaries, and similar reports by Roman Catholic clergy, which were usually sent to France. These reports could thus be several weeks old before they became public knowledge. Refugees began to cross into Russian territory by mid January 1915, and some managed to get by train to St. Petersburg. This meant that the first news and eyewitness reports became available by late January. At that time, however, most of the violence could only be attributed to local Kurdish anarchy and pogroms. The violence shifted toward genocidal actions at the end of February and beginning of March, with a noticeable increase in the number of victims and a greater role being played by Turkish civil and military authorities.

The news from the Urmia area was the first notice received by the outside world of systematic massacres of Christians instigated by a government against an unarmed civilian population at a time when the battles were over. The French reports were published in the journals of the missionary societies. During and after the war, several works written by Syrians were published. Among the most detailed is the book by the American-trained Baptist minister Yonan Shahbaz, who had worked and lived with his American wife in the large village of Gogtapa.[11]

---

[10] www.devletarsivleri.gov.tr "Arşiv belgelerine göre Ermeni konusu."

[11] Yonan Shahbaz, *The Rage of Islam: An Account of the Massacre of Christians by the Turks in Persia* (1918).

Members of the French and American missions kept chronicles of events and observations. Mary Lewis, who was the principal of the American School for Modern Girls in Urmia, wrote one of the journals. Another diary appears to be a collective work of the Sisters of the Saint-Vincent-de-Paul Catholic mission.[12] The French diary begins on January 2 and the Lewis diary on January 9, 1915. As a rule, the entries of Lewis are more detailed and express greater personal feeling than those of the French nuns. Another chronological report was made by one of the Lazarist missionaries, Abel Zayia, and this sometimes took the form of a day-to-day diary.[13] Archival material on the events can also be found in Russian archives. The Russian military-history archives include material on the situation and on the use of Syriacs as soldiers and scouts. The Russian Foreign Office holds correspondence with vice-consuls and consuls working in the area. Of particular interest is information about meetings with Mar Shimun, who was the leading Syriac figure at the start of the war, and with Agha Petros, who emerged as the Assyrian leader after the death of the patriarch.

In the Turkish military-history archive, there is a very large dossier taking the form of a bundle of detailed reports of Turkish–Russian conflicts along the Iranian border, as well as some reports about other fronts. The report records all unfriendly acts by the Entente powers against Turkey in the period leading up to the declaration of war but omits its own aggressive acts. It also includes a number of telegrams between the Russian Foreign Ministry and vice-consuls in Iran that had been captured by Ottoman troops, probably in connection with the assassination of the Russian consul in Sawuj Bulak, A. I. Ias, in December 1914. The report is anonymous and may have been prepared within the Ministry of War itself. Internal evidence indicates that several persons must have collaborated. A possible purpose of the report was as part of the diplomacy surrounding the Ottoman war claim that aggression on the side of the Entente powers before the war had forced the Ottomans to pursue the war on neutral Iranian territory and legitimated its occupation of the province of Azerbaijan. The report is not dated, but the last documents in the appendix are from February 1915, and

---

[12] *The War Journal of a Missionary in Persia*, ed. Mary Schauffler-Platt (1915), repr. in Boyce and Toynbee, *Treatment of the Armenians*, 154–82; excerpts of the mission journal are reprinted in Eugène Griselle, *Syriens et Chaldéens leur martyre, leurs espérances* (1917), 29–39.

[13] Published ibid., 40–59.

only the section dealing with Kuwait mentions events later than March 1915.[14]

Russian diplomats reported back to their government about the situation in the Ottoman occupied districts. Particularly useful are the reports and telegrams of Vvedensky, who served as the vice-consul from February 1914 to May 1915. During the Ottoman occupation he evacuated from Urmia and was stationed in Khoi.[15]

SOURCES ON HAKKARI AND VAN

The collection of testimonies assembled by Bryce and Toynbee, *The Treatment of Armenians in the Ottoman Empire 1915–1916*, has sections on the siege of the Armenians in the city of Van and on the Assyrian refugees from the Hakkari Mountains. These are letters, statements, and extracts from longer reports. There are several autobiographical works on the events in Van. Clarence Ussher, a physician at the American hospital, was well situated to observe both the aggressors and the defenders. Particularly valuable are the conversations he had with the vali Jevdet Bey.[16] Rafael de Nogales was a Venezuelan mercenary who arrived in Van at the start of the siege. He was made chief artillery officer for the Ottoman bombardment. His book reveals insights that only long military experience can provide.[17]

For the situation in the Hakkari district, there is much information in a book written by Lady Surma, the elder sister of Mar Shimun XXI Benyamin. As she knew many languages, she functioned as the Assyrian foreign minister and took part in many deliberations. This book, however, hides some of the conflicts between the mountain tribes and concentrates on the role of her brother and her side of the dynasty.[18] Malik Cambar, who later was a leader of the Assyrian refugees in Syria, wrote a pamphlet and an unpublished autobiography that give more information about the friction between Mar Shimun and Cambar's tribe, the Jilu.[19]

---

[14] ATAŞE, Kol.: BDH, Kls.: 1488, Dos.: 32/-, Fih.: 3-1, 3-2, 3-3, 3-4, 3-5, 3-6, 3-7, 3-8, 3-9, 3-10, 3-11, 3-12, 3-13.

[15] Vladimir Genis, *Vitse-konsul Vvedenskii sluzhba v Persii i Bukharskom khansive (1906–1920 gg.) Rossiskaya diplomatiya v sud'bakh* [Vice-consul Vvedensky's service in Persia and the Khanate of Bukhara 1906–1920] (2003).

[16] Clarence D. Ussher, *An American Physician in Turkey: A Narrative of Adventures in Peace and War* (1917), 236–45.

[17] Rafael de Nogales, *Four Years beneath the Crescent* (1926).

[18] Surma D'Bait Mar Shimun, *Assyrian Church Customs and the Murder of Mar Shimun* (1920).

[19] Malik Cambar, *Vie et coutmues des Maliks* (1924); "Autobiography."

Neither Germany nor the United States had any consular representation in Van and its province. The Russians, however, did have vice-consuls in Van before the war, and these officials invariably made military-political investigations of the strength and opinions of the Kurdish, Armenian, and Assyrian populations. The reports were printed in limited editions with limited distribution. They are very useful for information about the Kurdish irregular cavalry regiments and about the size of the Christian population down to the village level. Often these were based on quickly counting the number of houses. Italy did have a consular agent, Sbordoni, in Van, and some of his reports are printed in a book by a French war correspondent.[20]

Two works contain details of the military exploits of the tribes both while in Hakkari and after they went into exile. They are written by relatives of the leading tribal chiefs.[21]

SOURCES ON DIYARBEKIR VILAYET

There are comparatively many sources that deal with massacres in the Diyarbekir province. Many clerics inside monasteries composed chronicles of the events that affected the Christians; sometimes they collected verbatim testimony of survivors who sought sanctuary in the monasteries; sometimes they copied documents; and some of the more ambitious attempted to calculate the number of victims.

The most complete and detailed chronicle is that of Ishaq Armalto, the secretary of the Syrian Catholic vice-patriarch in Mardin, Gabriel Tappouni. Starting in July 1914, he kept a daily journal in Arabic. As the vice-patriarch's secretary, he participated in many discussions of the fate of the Christians and had some contact with Ottoman officials. Without revealing his name, he published this journal under the title *The Calamities of the Christians* in Lebanon just after the war. Armalto's work is particularly valuable as it gives insight into the rising fear and awareness of coming catastrophe among the Christian leadership before the massacres and deportations began.[22]

In December 1914, three French friars who had been working in the Dominican mission in Mosul arrived in Mardin, where they were interned

---

[20] Henry Barby, *Au Pays de l'épouvante: L'Arménie martyre* (1917).

[21] Hazqiyel Rayyis Gabriyel Beth-Malik Babane, *Tash'ita d Aturaye* [Assyrian history] (1975), 17–29; Rudolf Macuch, *Geschichte der spät- und neusyrischen Literatur* (1976), 230–61.

[22] *Al-Qusara fi nakabat al-nasara* (1919) .

under house arrest in a building belonging to the Syrian Catholic Church until November 1916. All three made use of their time to chronicle the events going on about them. The most important of the reports is that of Jacques Rhétoré, an elderly priest, who had started the Catholic mission in Van and who was a noted linguist and Syriac scholar. His long manuscript, *"Les Chrétiens aux bêtes"*, which originally contained 21 chapters, is deposited in the Dominican archives of Saulchoir in Paris. Unfortunately, several chapters, among them that dealing with the massacres of Tur Abdin, are now missing, although they are named in the list of contents. Rhétoré tried to be meticulous in establishing testimony about the perpetrators and the circumstances before and during the attacks; he also provided statistical information.[23] Hyacinthe Simon was another Dominican who wrote a chronicle of events in the Mardin area. His manuscript was completed in June 1916. His work is particularly valuable for the long chronological lists of massacres of towns and villages and attacks on deportees, as well as the many obituaries for priests who perished.[24] The head of the Mosul mission, Marie-Dominique Berré, wrote a short report dated January 15, 1919, which includes statistics and a discussion of the roles of the provincial and central governments in the genocide.[25] Bishop Jean Naslian of Trabizon published sections from these reports in his book about the political and religious conflicts of the war period.[26] As Catholics, all of the French chroniclers have much to say about the situation of the Armenian Catholics, who were numerous in Mardin and Tel-Arman. After the war ended, Efram Rahmani, patriarch of the Syrian Catholics, presented a memorandum to the peace conference giving a chronology and some new details, but as he resided in Lebanon it also contains inaccuracies about dates and events and is therefore not a very reliable source.[27] In addition, there are two anonymous reports which although short do supply some additional information.[28]

---

[23] Jacques Rhétoré, *"Les chrétiens aux bêtes": Souvenirs de la guerre sainte proclamée par les Turcs contre les chrétiens en 1915*, ed. Joseph Alichoran (2005), including many new documents; it was first published in Italian in *Una Finestra sul massacro: Documenti inediti sulla strage degli armeni (1915–1916)*, ed. Marco Impagliazzo (2000), 97–250.

[24] Hyacinthe Simon, *Mardine la ville héroïque: Autel et tombeau de l'Arménie (Asie Mineure) durant les massacres de 1915* (1991).

[25] Marie-Dominique Berré, "Massacres de Mardin" (1997).

[26] Jean Naslian, *Les Mémoires de Mgr. Jean Naslian sur les événements politico-religieux en Proche-Orient de 1914 à 1928* (1951).

[27] This document, dated July 18, 1919, is published in Sébastien de Courtois, *The Forgotten Genocide: Eastern Christians, The Last Arameans* (2004), 244–53, 347–52.

[28] Ara Sarafian, "The Disasters of Mardin during the Persecutions of the Chris-

Notes on the Sources

A young novice residing in the Syriac Orthodox monastery of Za'faran, Abed Mishiho Na'man Qarabash, kept a chronicle for 1915. This gives information that is similar in content to that of the other chronicles, but the coverage of Syriac Orthodox villages is more complete. Since he hailed from Karabash near Diyarbekir, he had access to unique knowledge of the events that took place in that region.[29] Another testimony focused on Syriac Orthodox communities is the oral history collected and edited by the priest Süleyman Hinno from refugees who were living in Syria. He collected information from 13 named survivors and attempted to document the massacres in as many villages as possible in the Tur Abdin region. Due to the nature of the witnesses, some descriptions are very short, while others are relatively detailed.[30] A unique source is the diary of Gabriel Qas Tuma Hendo, the Syrian Catholic priest and schoolteacher of Azakh (now İdil). This manuscript details the long siege of the village of Azakh by the Ottoman army in 1915. This document also has much to say of events in Jezire.[31]

Use of these sources can be difficult, since the chronicles of Catholic origin used the modern calendar, whereas Orthodox documents used the Old Style and were 13 days behind. Ottoman documents are in Hicri (A.H.; most of 1333 A.H. with its lunar months = A.D. 1915) or in Rumi (an alternative secular dating system; 1331 = A.D. 1915, with months corresponding to the European months) and must be converted into modern dates. There are also difficulties in the transcription of names written in the Ottoman, Arabic, and Syriac languages and in interpreting handwriting. Many place names have also since been changed, so in a few cases it is hard to identify the exact location of small villages. This is particularly so for isolated caves, quarries, and pits that were used as execution sites.

Some memoir literature gives insight into the thinking of the Ottoman side. The vali of Diyarbekir, Reshid Bey, prepared a written defense of his activities that was partially autobiographical. Long excerpts from this

---

tians, especially the Armenians, 1915" (1998); Vincent Mistrih, "Mémoires de A.Y.B. sur les massacres de Mardine" (1997).

[29] Abed Mschiho Na'man Qarabasch, *Vergossenes Blut: Geschichten der Greuel, die an den Christen in der Türkei verübt, und der Leiden, die ihnen 1895 und 1914–1918 zugefügt wurden* (1999).

[30] The original is in Syriac, Süleyman Hinno, *Günhe d Süryoye d Turabdin* (1987); there is also a German translation. I use the Swedish version, *Massakern på syrianerna i Turabdin 1914–1915* (1998).

[31] Gabriel Qos Tuma Hendo, "Tarikh Azakh" [History of Azakh] (1915).

document, published as *Mülâhâzat* [Explanation], as well as other official documents are printed in the biography by Nedjet Bilgi.³² The son of an Ottoman official in Lije whom Reshid had liquidated became a Turkish politician and wrote a book which included much information about the circumstances of his father's death.³³ An unpublished manuscript gives the modern history of the Kurdish Rama (in Modern Turkish referred to as the Rema) tribe, which was omnipresent in the Diyarbekir massacres. This manuscript tells of the negotiations between the tribal leaders, who were the author's uncles, and Reshid Bey when he recruited them to organize the killing and plundering.³⁴ Of Bedouin origin, Fâ'iz El-Ghusein was a former deputy of the National Assembly who was removed from his post as kaymakam accused of Arab nationalism. He was banished to Diyarbekir, where he lived relatively freely for seven months in 1915. As an official and politician, he socialized with other civil servants and military officers and thus had inside knowledge of the treatment of the Christians. He fled from Turkey and ended up in India, where he completed his manuscript in September 1916.³⁵

---

³² Nejdet Bilgi, *Dr. Mehmed Reşid Şahingiray'ın Hayatı ve Hâtıraları: İttihâd ve Terakki Dönemi ve Ermeni Meselesi* [Dr. M. R. S.'s life and memory: The CUP period and the Armenian Questions] (1997).

³³ Abidin Nesimi, *Yılların İçinden* [During the years] (1977).

³⁴ Hüseyin Demirer, "Haver Delal" [Help, my dear] (1983).

³⁵ Fâ'iz El-Ghusein, *Martyred Armenia* (1917).

APPENDIX 1
ORAL TESTIMONY ON TUR ABDIN 1914–15

Collected and edited by Jan Beṯ-Şawoce

This appendix contains the narratives of 35 men, eyewitnesses and their descendants, and they have been subdivided into 75 passages organized into 24 largely geographical sections, to achieve a somewhat coherent narrative. The individuals, in the order of their age, with their numbered passages are as follows:

Gallo Shabo (1875–1966), 75
Rume Lahdo-Antar (1893–1997), 3
Hanna Bitar (1903–2001), 14, 43, 63
Yawsef Babo-Rhawi (1904–1999), 5, 22, 26, 28, 50
Hanna Hawsho (1904–1993), 13, 16
Asmar 'Adoka (1905–2000), 10, 12
Useve Wardo (1906–1999), 41
Ello 'Amno (b. 1908), 15, 20, 21, 45, 60
Ne'man Beth-Yawno (1908–2001), 2
Resqo Gawwo-Afrem (1908–1996), 4, 29
Karmo Salma-Gawwo (1908–1995), 7, 30, 64
Hanna Ablahad (1909–2001), 6
'Abdo Ghanno-Gawweke (b. 1911), 18, 38, 54, 59
Isho' Qasho-Malke (1913–2004), 73
Sabri Hermez (1915–2002), 9
Danho Keno (1915–2000), 8, 40
Gawriye Maqsi-Hanna Hamra (b. 1918), 70
Hanna Polos (b. 1921), 32, 35, 42

Salim Beth-Bido (b. 1922), 72
'Abdo Yuhanun (1922–2003), 52
Mikhayel Salmo (1924–1997), 71, 74
Murad Maqsi-Murad (1925–1998), 53
Brahim Maqsi-Musa (1925–1998), 19, 23, 25, 27, 44, 46, 49
Gawriye Beth-Mas'ud (b. 1926), 24, 34, 55, 58, 65, 67
Hanna Mure (b. 1926), 37, 47
Lahdo Beth-Lahdo Musa / Beth-Gorgis (b. 1926), 69
Gorgis 'Abdiyo (1927–2001), 17, 39
Eliyo Gares (b. 1928), 61
Use Malke-Sahyo (b. 1931), 56
Skandar Sha'o-Murad (b. 1931), 57
Malke Gares (b. 1932), 48, 51
Lahdo Musa-Malaka (1932–1999), 36, 66, 68
Tuma Salmo (b. 1932), 1, 31, 33
Shaq Galle (b. 1938), 62
Habib Maqsi-Musa (b. 1948), 11

A. GENERAL STATEMENTS

1. Tuma Salmo (b. 1932), interviewed June 2003

My cousin [a Chaldean] Alyas Salmo [1923–1989] told me that at the end of 1880, the religious Muslim leaders in the Ottoman Empire went to Sultan Abdul Hamid II to warn him about the growing Armenian influence, that their "nails were getting longer and longer," as they put it. They asked him to restrict them in order to keep the supremacy of Islam and Muslims in the Ottoman Empire. After a long meditation, Sultan Abdul Hamid II assured them that as long as Christians adhere to separate denominations and go to different churches, the risk of threat from them is minimal. But in case Christians renounce their differences and start to pray in each other's churches, then Muslims should fear them and be on their guard.

2. Priest Ne'man Beth-Yawno (1908–2001), interviewed November 1993

In 1915, the Turkish government issued a decree signed by the Sultan, the Caliph of all Muslims, to systematically root out all the Christians in general and Armenians in particular. In our area the killings started in 1914.

The [East Syriac] Chaldeans and [West] Syriacs[1] in Gharzan and in Ramma, Hasno, Karme, Al-Aziz, Hesen-Mansur [Adiyaman], Siwerak, Besheriye, and Sa'irt and its surroundings were killed savagely and on a large scale. Before the killings, the procedure was that the Christians were chained and dragged to the banks of the rivers Tigris and Euphrates to be slaughtered like animals and thrown in the water. Pregnant women had their babies torn out of their bellies, killed, and thrown in the rivers. The young girls got raped in a horrific manner. Some girls committed suicide by throwing themselves into the rivers to avoid experiencing such demonic assaults. Many clergymen were mercilessly killed. Houses, churches, monasteries were barbarically destroyed. This wave of evil started to wane as it approached the area of Tur Abdin that was particularly famous at that time for its schools, monasteries, churches, and educational centers. Tur Abdin was considered a center of faith at that time. Many people from Tur Abdin, however, fled to avoid being killed at the hands of the Muslim fanatics.

---

[1] In this appendix, "[East] Syriac" refers to Chaldeans and Nestorians, "[West] Syriac" to Syrian Orthodox and Catholic and Protestant converts therefrom, and "[East and West] Syriac" to locations with mixed populations.

Those who made it to other areas suffered from other kinds of calamities, like hunger and disease. They were malnourished and exhausted. Lice and insects infested their bodies, and life was unbearable. Many prayed to God for help, wishing that death would put an end to their inhuman misery. The number of Christians decreased slowly but surely as many of them were ambushed on their way out of or into their villages. Many were mugged, killed, and left to be eaten by the birds of prey, with nobody having a clue about their fate. Many Christians lost their lives in this way. At that time it was not strange to come across parts of human bodies scattered all over. Those who survived this catastrophic plight experienced hunger and learned to survive mostly on grass, just like animals. The corpses were disposed of at random in the cities, from which emanated a terrible stench of death. In consequence, the villages became empty as their Christian inhabitants disappeared in a systematic eradication. Only two villages, Anhel and 'Ayn-Wardo [near Midyat], escaped the killings and devastation. In the towns of Karme [Kharput] and Omid [Diyarbekir], there were some pockets of Christians, but all in all their number was considerably reduced. The Christians' calamity was like a wave of severe frost that destroyed all greenness and serenity that characterized that place. In Besheriye and its Church of Mor Quryaqos, and in the city of Lije, all Christians were disposed of in one way or another. Those few who could escape sought refuge in other countries.

Midyat was the capital of the villages in Tur Abdin and contained many religions [Christians, Jews, Muslims, Yezidi] and nationalities. The Turkish fanatics tried at first to allay the fears of the Christians under the pretext that they were immune from any kind of persecution and that the Sultan himself was their protector. The idea was that the anger of the government would be vented on one group only; namely, the Armenians who were engaged in rebellion against the Turkish government. This argument alas convinced the rest of the Christians and calmed their worry. In fact, the gradual and systematic killings of all Christians were planned from an early stage, but the implementation of the killings took place step by step. After the Turkish government and its Kurdish allies got rid of a great number of Armenians, they took another step in the direction of disposing of all Christians in that area. They accused the [West Syriac] Protestants of supporting the Armenians and of having external contacts with countries that were enemies of the Turkish state. On June 22/July 5, some 113 persons were chained and taken to the outskirts of Midyat. These men were sure that their end was imminent, so they recited prayers and other religious hymns until the end. On June 28/July 11, they arrived at the Muhallemi village of Kfar-Hewer and were taken to a place called Sito where they were made to take off their clothes. They were tortured and then killed and thrown into deep wells.

After the killings of the Protestants, the Turkish government, the Muhallemi, and the Kurds were openly encouraged to set their whole plan in action with respect to disposing of all the [East and West] Syriacs in the area. They surrounded Midyat from all sides in vast numbers and started indiscrimnate killings of the Syriacs, destroying their houses, churches, monasteries, and palaces. The attack on the Church of Mort Shmuni and its neighborhood was extremely barbaric. They captured the Patriarch's representative, the priest Afrem, inside the church, tortured, and killed him. Then they slaughtered the Syriac leader Hanne Safar and his son Skandar. They murdered all his family including the women and children.

The quarter of Qasho-Aho was surrounded and set on fire. Those who were able to escape the fire were murdered on the spot. The Christians proceeded to the house of Malke Bette, who tried to put up some resistance, but the Kurds scaled the house, made an opening at the top of the house, and threw fire inside the house that set the house alight. All the people there were suffocated to death. When Malke went out to surrender, he was slaughtered like an animal. Yawsef Gawwo, who lived with his family in that area, was also attacked and killed.

In the quarter of 'Adoka, the Kurds surrounded the big house of the 'Adoka family, stormed it, and killed all the Syriacs hidden there. The big house turned red from the blood of thousands of Syriacs who were there to escape via an underground tunnel beneath that house that would lead them to the village of 'Ayn-Wardo. Then the raping of women and young girls began in front of everybody. As if all those atrocities were not enough, the Kurds went to the area of Gawwo and Barlate, where they repeated their savage acts, leaving death, chaos, and misery behind them. They went to the old monasteries surrounding Midyat: Mor Abrohom, Mor Hobel, Mor Ya'qub, and Mor Sharbel, and ordered the monks and nuns there to come out, then they started spitting at them and making fun of them. Some of them were crucified like their "Master" and killed. Some monks were able to escape to 'Ayn-Wardo, Anhel, and Mor Malke after enduring a terrible ordeal. As such, Midyat was turned into a mountain of dust, a town in ruins that was left to wither and be forgotten.

After the cease-fire between the Christians and the Muslims in 'Ayn-Wardo, peace still seemed far off as the Muslims adopted another policy for minimizing the number of Syriacs in the area. They decided to target the leaders in the Christian communities. Many influential figures lost their lives in mysterious ways while traveling or moving from one place to another. There was a kind of tacit policy between the Kurds and the Turkish forces to kill Christians. In fact, the number of Syriacs killed in accidents arranged by Muslims exceeds the number of Syriacs that died in the events of Sayfo.

After the cease-fire in 'Ayn-Wardo between the Christians and the Kurds who were aided and abetted by the Turkish government, the Christian leader Mas'ud lost his life in a mysterious way in 1916.[2] The whole Christian community was devastated at hearing of the loss of this great hero. Mas'ud had defended his people, organized them, and made them stay in their historical homeland.

B. MIDYAT

3. Rume Lahdo-Antar (1893–1997), interviewed July 1993

During the period of mobilization (1914), the Turkish government took a large group of [East and West] Syriacs from Midyat to Hasan-Qal'a to help them in their war against the Russians. The people taken for that purpose were countless. Groups of three or four were chained together so that nobody would escape. The line of people extended from the town hall (*Saraye di hkume*) to the Patriarchate.[3] Few of these people would ever return. Among the dead were my uncles Slayman, Musa, and Danho, who died, presumably killed on the way there. My uncle Shebo, however, did return, and one person survived from the family of Shabo Bahdo. Gorgis Asso returned but he died shortly after his return.

4. Resqo Gawwo-Afrem (1908–1996), interviewed July 1993

My uncle Isa was taken from Midyat to Hasan Qal'a during the war between Turkey and Russia. His prescribed task was to transport food to the soldiers, but he failed to come back. Our three donkeys at home were confiscated for the purpose of transporting food to the Turkish soldiers. I had three cousins named Dawud, Afrem, and Musa, and all of them disappeared and failed to come back.

***

---

[2] Ishaq Armalto, *Al Qusara fi nakabat al-nasara* [The calamities of the Christians], 405. Mas'ud was killed in January 1918 by members of the Hajo Kurdish tribe.

[3] More than a kilometer.

In Midyat we lived in a house situated in an isolated area [Guharre]. My father, Gallo, bought a rifle for 35 Ottoman liras and two belts of bullets for 5 liras. He hid them under the fireplace that we had in the yard. His mother asked him why he did that, but he didn't want to involve her in that matter. At the time the Turkish government and its Kurdish allies started their attacks on us, we had a neighbor named Hajji Bashar Bey who was staying at Ya'qub Shahho's house. Hajji Bashar Bey had a prominent position in the government [temporary kaymakam], and he had a servant who lived in the same area whose name was Khalaf. Khalaf's wife asked him to invite the neighbors to visit them. We accepted the invitation and went to pay them a visit. When my father saw the rifles hanging on the walls in Khalaf's house, he was tempted to take them. My uncle Zayto was a religious man, and he warned my father, Gallo, not to take them, nor to use any violence. At that time, Hajji Bashar Bey arrived with 40 soldiers. Khalaf's wife stopped him and asked him to vow not to hurt her Christian neighbors. Hajji Bashar Bey promised not to cause them any harm, since they seemed peaceful. He went up with 5 soldiers and saw the rifles all in place, and after that he promised them safety.

There were two routes leading to our house, one from the market and the other from [West Syriac] Fatrus Rhawi's house, which we took. Nevertheless we were shot at, and this caused the death of one of my cousins, Brahim. We sought shelter in the house of Gorgis Isa Gawriye. The shooting increased, and the Muslims seemed determined to kill us, so we escaped taking the small passages between the buildings. My cousin hid at home, but his father refused to let him be an easy prey to the enemy, so he risked his life to bring his son to join the fleeing Christians. The adults gave us children to a person named Mure Marre to be taken to 'Ayn-Wardo. The adults went first to the Monastery of Mor Sharbel and after that were reunited with us in 'Ayn-Wardo.

5. **Yawsef Babo-Rhawi** (1904–1999), interviewed June 1993

During the mobilization, I was 10 years old. I witnessed how groups of [East and West] Syriac young men were taken to participate in the so-called war against Russia; in fact, this implied a death sentence to all the Christians who were forced to participate. My uncle As'ad, my brother Isa, the children of my uncle Sham'un, and the children of my uncle Gawwe were taken for that purpose. It was estimated that around 20 young men were taken from the Rhawi family. Only two or three were able to return safely. Some of those who failed to come back settled in Russia. Many young men were taken at random, and the majority of them didn't come back. After that, Sayfo started.

***

In Midyat, the events started by gathering the leaders and the important people from the Protestant community, such as Xoja Galle Hermez, the mayor [*Risho di baladiye*]. The government gave the impression that the [West Syriac] Orthodox community was safe and that her aim was to restrain the other communities, such as the Chaldeans, the Armenians, and the [West Syriac] Protestants only. These prominent figures were taken to 'Ayn-Senje near the Muhallemi village of Dayro-Zwino that is situated to the west of Midyat. There these people were shot dead and thrown in the wells. The government seemed to buy time to get rid of the existing Christians in a gradual manner, step by step and community after community, playing on their differences, as it were. After restraining the Protestants, the government turned to the Orthodox community and started its shrewd policy of weakening the Christians by collecting the leaders of this particular community, such as Isa Zatte and others. The process was carried out without the intervention of other Christians, who were bitter and disappointed with the passivity of the Syriac Orthodox Christians. The Syriac Orthodox Christians believed in the empty promises given to them by the government and didn't extend the hand of solidarity to their fellow Christians in their time of need. At noon, when everyone was at work and at a time when there were few young men around, some forces were sent to arrest Isa Zatte. The Syriac Orthodox leader knew they were going to arrest him so he took his rifle and shot at them.

Meanwhile, Midyat's Kurdish Agha, 'Azizke, started to gather forces from the Kurdish and Muhallemi villages. He took advantage of the prevailing chaos in the region, and as a result the killings and bloodshed increased in Midyat. The Rhawi family took refuge in the monastery of Mor Sharbel to protect themselves as the government forces plundered the houses and killed Christians at random. From the top of the monastery we could see how they started taking our animals, possessions, and our other valuables. We went out: me, my uncle Hobel, Ishaq 'Abdiyo, my uncle Makko, and my brother Shabo, and waited outside to stop the attackers. We killed two of them while the others escaped. We took back some of our valuables and animals and went into the monastery of Mor Sharbel.

We got some help from the village of 'Ayn-Wardo. This help was headed by Gallo Shabo, who called on my father and informed him that they intended to help the Christians in Midyat. They first went down to assess the situation. They arrived at the house of Bero Sharro and saw three [West] Syriac men lying dead. Some corpses were seen in front of the house of my cousin Abdulmasih Rhawi. All in all, Midyat seemed very still, soundless, and empty.

My uncle Dahho remained in the house of Malke Hermez and continued to put up some resistance. He addressed the enemy in Kurdish: "I am the deacon, I serve in the church and I am the father of Isa, Musa, and Bahde." He did that to boost his own morale. His three sons were killed during military service. My father assured Dahho that they had gotten some reinforcements and that he didn't need to fear anymore. Dahho became so glad that he proclaimed himself to be a Pharaoh upon hearing this good news. We occupied the buildings for the purpose of defense. Dahho said that two families—the Mexxe and the Abraham—were responsible for the defense of three houses, and because of this the Muslims were prevented from carrying out their plundering and killings.

***

The people coming from 'Ayn-Wardo attacked the town hall [*Saraye di hkume*] in Midyat. In that building there was a soldier named Badraddin from Kfar-Gawze. The Kurdish Agha 'Azizke told him that he should flee. Badraddin answered that he was from a respectable family named Hasan-Shamdin [from Kfar-Gawze], and that he was a Hajji and wanted to stay. As a result of the confrontations here, three people from 'Ayn-Wardo died and Gallo Shabo was wounded. The people from 'Ayn-Wardo gradually retreated. In the Monastery of Mor Sharbel, we met a person who survived by pretending to be dead among the corpses. He asked for some water. The man advised us to leave because at that stage resistance seemed pointless. We left Midyat and headed for 'Ayn-Wardo together with our animals. Gallo Shabo, who was wounded, rode a donkey to 'Ayn-Wardo.

6. Hanna Ablahad (1909–2001), interviewed February 1994

Our house was situated in Guharre quarter. Gallo Hawike came to my uncle Ya'qub and said that the situation was terrible and advised him to move to 'Ayn-Wardo. I was too little to understand at that time. The Kurds, supported by the government forces, attacked the houses, and from the top of Barsawmo's house we could see the killings. We saw a Turkish captain who cursed the attackers and ordered them [the Muslims] to stop the shooting.

In the quarter of Chalma, which was near the town hall [*Saraye di hkume*], many horrible events took place where girls were raped and pregnant women were killed after their babies were taken from their bellies. Many men died too. We escaped these atrocities thanks to the location of our house on the outskirts of town. I returned home to tell my father, Ablahad, about what was going on. When I got back, the house was empty. I went to the house of Hanne Antun, which was near our house, where they had a secret tunnel leading from the village to 'Ayn-Wardo. I stayed there, and then I saw our neighbor Qedso and her little brother Shabo. I went with them to Abraham's house, which was full of Syriacs. My family arrived at 'Ayn-Wardo, and there my father asked my brother about me and then he sent my brother to look for me. My brother arrived with five armed men at Abraham´s house, and they escorted some of the people to 'Ayn-Wardo at night. But we could not discover the fate of the rest of the Christians who stayed behind.

7. **Karmo Salma-Gawwo** (1908–1995), interviewed July 1993

The Christians suffered a massacre every twenty years. In 1914, killings occurred on a large scale, and our people suffered horrible kinds of death and were scattered on the roads.

***

My father Afremo was a Jandarma serving his military service under the command of Rauf Bey. Rauf Bey lived in the house of the Besse family in Midyat. He himself was supervising and organizing the massacres of the [East and West] Syriac Christians. My father escaped and sought refuge in 'Ayn-Wardo too. He first came to Midyat with the other volunteers to help the people hiding in Mor Sharbel. Due to the ordeal he had experienced, my father could not see properly any longer, so he needed medical help.

In the house of my uncle Mehe lived a Turkish clerk. He had a German flintlock rifle. My father forced him to hand over that rifle. He took it and went to the house of Hanne Mure and from there went to As'ad and then through the underground tunnels to 'Ayn-Wardo, taking the rifle with him.

I remember very well how we went to the house of Hanne Antun along the same street. Standing in the back yard, we were planning our escape when gunfire started to rain down upon us. It came from a military depot in the neighborhood. A [West] Syriac person named Habib helped us to enter the house by breaking down the door. We took a ladder and proceeded to the house of Abraham and then to the house of Mbaydono, where we saw some defenders arriving from 'Ayn-Wardo and joined them. They took the small children and showed them the way to safety. There was a person, Selo Wardane from Kfar-Gawze, who recognized me at once because he was our neighbor. He put me on his shoulders and went to 'Ayn-

Wardo. Thanks to the 'Ayn-Wardo defenders and to the mercy of God, we were able to save ourselves.

Midyat gradually became rather empty because its inhabitants fled for fear for their lives. When the Muslims saw that, they took the opportunity to loot the houses freely and without any scruples. Then they came to the house of 'Adoka, which was full of people. They surrounded it and set the pieces of wood surrounding the house on fire. It became a tremendous fire, which caused the death of many women and children. During the chaos that resulted from the blaze, the defenders that were there in the house decided to use their weapons even if it meant the death of many of them. After a terrible confrontation and exchange of fire, some of them died but some were able to escape.

***

After the cease-fire that was declared between the people of 'Ayn-Wardo and Turkish forces, my family moved to Anhel. On the road, the Yezidis started to shoot at us. My uncle Salim was wounded and could not carry me any longer. He left me and escaped to Anhel, so I hid myself somewhere. When Salim arrived at Anhel, my grandmother asked him about me. He told her what had happened. She rebuked him, saying that what he did was wrong. My mother decided to fetch me, whatever the risk this might entail. She asked the people if anybody would follow her to Bajenne. She heard that the situation there was tense, and nobody dared to go due to conflict between the Yezidis in Bajenne and the Christians in Anhel. Then a man named Hapsuno Shebo told her that he would go because he was on good terms with the people of Bajenne. My mother thanked him and prayed for him, and she cried all day long. Before the events of 1915, we had a shepherd in our house named 'Abdeko, and when she met him in Bajenne, the shepherd recognized her. She told him the story of her lost son and her intention of finding him. 'Abdeko told her that there was a risk that she might lose her life and promised to help her. 'Abdeko went around calling my name: Karmo! Karmo! I was at first afraid to respond, but when I saw that it was our shepherd who was calling, I went toward him. He gave me some grapes and took me to my mother, Salma.

Our world is always a mixture of good and evil people. My mother was worried at the time, so Namaye, 'Abdeko's sister, came to her and offered to read her palm and tell her future. Namaye told my mother that she would soon meet her son again, and at that very moment I popped into the room along with our shepherd 'Abdeko. My mother grabbed me and decided to leave for Anhel. 'Abdeko accompanied her to the village of Anhel. There he bade her farewell by waving his rifle. When we arrived at Anhel we began to experience the terrible conditions there from which the people suffered in the form of lice, dirt, poverty, and starvation.

***

After Sayfo, the government imprisoned the [West] Syriac 'Isa Zatte, 'Azizke Mahmado, and the head of the Kurdish tribe of Deravari, named Isa Hamo. Shortly after that, they took the three men to a place named 'Awjet al-Semmaq near Sawro, where they were killed.

A Turkish prosecutor named Fuat Bey [from Nigde] lived in the neighborhood, and he was kind to us. My mother helped him sometimes by cooking for him, and in return he was very mild and thankful. Rumours were abundant at that particular time that the Kurdish tribe of Hajo [the Hajo branch of the Haverkan] would attack Midyat and kill its Christian inhabitants. My uncle Brahim was visiting us at the time. Upon hearing the news, he started crying, overcome by memories of the previous Syriac massacres that were fresh in his mind. My mother, Salma, comforted him and told him that she would ask for Fuat Bey's help. She went to Fuat Bey and told him about the rumors. He calmed her fears [by saying] that the government was targeting the leaders of the community to get rid of them, but that the ordinary people would not be affected at all.

8. **Danho Keno** (1915–2000), interviewed July 1993

My uncle Dawud and my father, Hanne, were mobilized together with many [East and West] Syriac Christians. They were taken to Hasno [Hasankeyf] and put in a mosque. They were chained in groups of two or three. They were imprisoned and guarded by Turkish forces. My father, Hanne, was responsible for taking care of the horses belonging to the Turkish officers. Once he told the soldier watching him that the captain's horse needed some feed. This was a pretext for him to flee. He fled heading for Midyat by crossing the mountains. At that time the custom was that those who fled faced a special punishment. The wife would be taken, then they would bind her hands and feet and make her stand in the pond. Then they would put some puppies, rats, or other animals in her dress or in her underwear. In winter women froze to death, or they would be saved in case the husbands surrendered to the authorities.

My uncle Isa ran away from the army, so the Turkish officers paid us a visit and threatened to take my father, Hanne, and hang him by his moustache. Upon hearing the punishment waiting for him, my father avoided returning to Midyat. He waited for the farmers to come to Huwle (Mount Qeno di Dabco). When the farmers arrived, he introduced himself to a farmer from the [West Syriac] Rhawi family. My father Hanne told the farmer to notify his parents what happened to him. He sent a message to them that they should flee to Anhel and then to the village of Neben, where they could be reunited. The family stayed there for five years until the Sayfo came to an end.

My uncle Dawud was in Hasno with the other Christians, but for some reason he was lost. Only four men came back. A survivor who was Shabe's father knew the whereabouts of Dawud. He explained how they were tortured on the way, how many were killed. That prompted him and Dawud to flee. They were pursued by the Turkish forces. They had to split up. Shabe's father arrived in Russia, where he stayed seven years and after that went back to Midyat.

***

In Midyat before Sayfo the government promoted a [West] Syriac leader, Hanne Safar, to the rank of Pasha. He enjoyed the power of decision-making at that time. This man approved the government decision to kill over 70 persons from the Protestant family of Hermez.

At that time, my grandfather had a fertile piece of land. Our Muslim neighbors wanted it for themselves, so they killed my grandfather. An old man from our family named Babo Haydari sought to take revenge on the killers, aided by some other men. On the way, they passed the Hermez family being led to their death by two Turkish soldiers. One of Babo Haydari's children asked permission to shoot the two soldiers and free the Hermez family.

It seemed very likely that the plan of the government was to get rid of all of us in small groups. Babo Haydari refused to give his permission for fear that Hanne Safar would be enraged, as he was considered the government representative at that time. When the chaos broke out in Midyat, the son of Babo Haydari who wanted to help the Hermez family was the first to die. He got a bullet in the head while returning from the harvest. A Muslim named Arif, associated with Shekhmus Agha's house, killed him.

One day the Mufti and his Muslim colleagues met and decided to arrest Hanne Safar, saying, "No matter whether they were red or white, onions remain onions." This saying meant that all Christians deserve the same treatment: that is, death.

***

The waiter who was in charge of serving at the [Mufti's meeting] was a [West] Syriac. He overheard the decision adopted against all Christians. He hurried to inform Hanne Safar before he arrived at his job. Hanne Safar didn't believe him, but Hanne was arrested shortly after he came to his office. After that, random shooting took place in Midyat. My father was in Anhel and my uncle Barsawmo was working as a farmer in a place named Shalwo. They decided not to go into Midyat. Instead they headed for 'Ayn-Wardo. My uncle Ya'qub, who lived in Midyat, gathered his family, about 45 persons, and left Midyat for 'Ayn-Wardo. When we passed by the pond, the Muslims started shooting at us. My uncle's first wife and Stayfo Haydari's wife were killed. She was carrying her son Ishaq at the time. He was 5 months old. Brahim, one of our relatives, was taken to 'Ayn-Wardo by his aunt. On the way to 'Ayn-Wardo, they met some Kurds. They hid, fearing for their lives. The aunt told him to keep silent. They stayed in a field until the Kurds disappeared, and in that way they were able to arrive safe and sound in 'Ayn-Wardo.

***

After Sayfo, the Muslims got rid of many Christians, three times as many as in the time of Sayfo. The Christians would file complaints against these killings and disappearances, but to no avail. When the [East and West] Syriacs went out to sell their products, for example, the Muslim Kurds in particular took their goods, their money, and even killed the people themselves. After Sayfo, when I was young, I remember an incident that happened in the church of Mor Barsawmo when my father, Hanne, and Makko Kettek took it upon themselves to prepare the coffee for the worshipers after the mass. Suddenly the Mufti and a Kurd named Mehika stormed the church and picked out 72 people to dig trenches for the Turkish forces, who were engaged in a war with Russia at that time. There, two people were said to have been killed and the others could barely survive because of mistreatment and malnutrition.

9. Sabri Hermez (1915–2002), interviewed November 1997

The old people at home told me the following as regards the events of 1915. My grandfather, Galle Hermez, was the mayor of Midyat. Before Sayfo, my grandfather was informed that Christians were being killed in Edessa [Urfa, Urhoy], Erzurum, Adana, Diyarbekir. He went to the other [West] Syriac leaders and discussed the need for unity among Christians to face the imminent threat. Hanne Safar found it a good idea and they agreed in the Church of Mort Shmuni to stand united. There the priest Isa brought forth the Bible to make their vow holy. After some days, the government heard about this agreement. In response, it spread rumors that the Orthodox community was an accepted and respected community and were not threatened at all. Hanne Safar went to the kaymakam, local governor, and asked him about this rumor and requested assurance. The local governor replied that because the Orthodox had no major European country to defend them like the other communities, therefore the [Syriac] Orthodox were under the patronage of the Ottoman Empire. The firman [order to arrest] was directed against the Protestant community only. Hanne Safar went directly to meet the Protestant leaders—Galle Hermez, my grandfather; my father, Hermez; my uncles Isa and Shabo—and told them that the agreement was no longer binding because the Orthodox didn't want to be involved in a trouble that was not directed against them.

I was 2 weeks old when the government arrested my uncles Isa and Shabo; my father, Hermez; and grandfather Galle Hermez; and others from our family, about 15 persons all in all. They were disappointed with their former ally Hanne Safar. They waited a week in prison and were resigned to the fate awaiting them.

***

My uncle Dawud fled to Anhel, and there he contacted the Kurdish tribe of Sarokhano [the Chelebi section of the Haverkan confederation]. He told them what had happened to his family and asked them to help him free them while they were being transported from Midyat to Mardin by the government. For that he would pay them 200 gold liras. They accepted the deal. My uncle Dawud sent a message home about the plan—that when it was time for the transportation of the arrested men, the family should give a signal by setting a tent on fire, a tent that we had on the roof of the house, thus signalling that the men were on their way. At that time, we had a daughter-in-law from the [West Syriac] Galle-Sayde family who overheard the plan. She went to Hanne Safar and informed him about the rescue plan for the Hermez family. Hanne Safar went directly to the kaymakam and told him about the plan. The kaymkam warned the Kurdish tribe of Sarokhano that they would suffer the same fate as the Hermez family should they help. The kaymakam changed the route as a result, and the transport took place in the daytime, going through the Omariye area in the direction of Mardin. The guards were locals, Kurds and Muhallemis; one of them was Karme Mahmado, one from the [Muhallemi] Mefti family. The latter told me what happened in detail. He told me that after they killed the 15 persons from the Hermez family, one of the guards, Karme Mahmado, saw that Galle Hermez had a beautiful ring on his finger that he wanted for himself. When he couldn't remove the ring from the finger of the dead Galle Hermez, the Kurd Karme took his dagger and cut off the dead man's finger to get the ring. Karme Mahmado lived 30 years after Sayfo, but he lived as a madman because he lost his mind. All in all, 104 persons were shot dead; among them were 20–30 Armenians who came from Hasno and Kfar-Boran.

Two weeks after the killings, the kaymakam came to Hanne Safar and told him that some soldiers were to be placed at his house. Hanne Safar interpreted this as a declaration of war. He warned his community about the imminent danger. Soon after that, Hanne Safar was killed together with 17 persons from his family. Hanne Safar tried to defend himself with the sword with which he was beheaded. Those who survived from Hanne Safar's family went to 'Ayn-Wardo.

My uncle Dawud took the women and children to 'Ayn-Wardo. He had 15 German rifles with him. He participated in the battles that were waged against 'Ayn-Wardo. In 'Ayn-Wardo many Kurds died. When the government realized that it was impossible to win the war against 'Ayn-Wardo, it suggested that the villagers could surrender their arms in exchange for safety.

***

Miss Agnes Fenenga was an American missionary in Mardin [belonging to the American Board of Commissioners for Foreign Missions, ABCFM]. She helped all the Christian parents that lost their children or fell into the hands of the Muslims for one reason or another. My cousin Gorgis Musa-Shamosho as a child used to wear a red hat. He was captured by Omariyan [a Kurdish tribe] and taken to Goliye near Mardin. When Hanna Esqef went to Goliye, he saw this child and asked him his name. "Mohammed," answered the child. And the name of your father? "Musa-Shamosho" was the answer. Hanna Esqef returned to Mardin and sought Miss Fenenga and told her what he had encountered. The vali sent a force to seek the child, and luckily the child was later reunited with his family.

After Sayfo, in 1925, Shaykh Sa'id initiated a revolt against the government in Omid [Diyarbekir]. The Muslims in Midyat told the authorities that my uncle Dawud collaborated with the rebels. As a punishment, my uncle Dawud was exiled for two years to Akhisar and Antalya.

10. Asmar 'Adoka (1905–2000), interviewed September 1997

On Wednesday, July 6[/19], 1915, I went to school early in the morning. Then I went with my sister to the threshing floor. From there we began to hear shooting and loud noises coming from Midyat. My older sister told me to go home and that she would follow me later with the cows. In the street of Chalma, people gathered in Isa Zatte's and Adoka's house. The house was shot at for a period of ten days. In the house some people, Hanne Safar and the priest Afrem, were killed. We sought shelter in the underground caves beneath the houses. The Muslims started to shoot at random. My father, brother, and my younger sister were killed and we continued to hide in these caves. We stayed there a week, feeling both hungry and thirsty. Then our remaining relatives took off my clothes and told me to play dead under the scattered corpses. I saw the Muslims coming toward us with candles in their hands. I didn't have time to play dead, they saw me and people from 'Arnas and among them were Hanne's two sons [Yusuf and Selo]. They escorted us out of the cave. One Muslim stabbed Yusuf, then he brought a long piece of wood and started beating him on the head until the boy died. They took me and the other son to the house of Gharibo. We got two shirts to cover ourselves and from there we went to the caravanserai of Musa-Shamosho that was full of captives, the majority of whom were children and women. They gathered the young boys to be taken out by soldiers to be killed. Women and girls were sent to Anhel. My mother and my uncle's wife were taken to Anhel and they were able to survive.

11. Habib Maqsi-Musa (b. 1948), interviewed August 2003

My uncle [a Chaldean] Musa was six years old in Sayfo. When I was a young boy I heard this story that he told us about Sayfo.

In the market of Midyat there was a place named Shaqfo, near the house of the [West Syriac Protestant] Nateqo family, and there I saw how the Turkish forces killed the young Christian boys. They would throw [from the roof] young boys headlong from that high building to fall down and die at once. Many Christian caravans arrived at Midyat; and they were filled with women and children. They were taken to the mosque's yard. The yard would become overcrowded. To reduce the number of hostages, the Turkish forces gathered the boys, around 500–600. They told them to lie down, face down. Then they took some thick sticks and beat them on the head. Then some 40 to 50 Turkish soldiers riding horses rode back and forth over the boys' heads until they died.[4]

12. Asmar 'Adoka

In the caravanserai I met one of my relatives, Malke Haydari. I asked him for some food, so he pointed to some sacks of chickpeas. I went there to fetch some. The guard by the door saw me and asked me to come to him.

---

[4] The commander of the forces is identified as Sami Bey of the Teşkilat-i Mahsusa, who was in Midyat with a contingent of "mujahedin" recruited from released convicts.

There stood a man named Shekhmus from the village of Tenat [Tinat]. He took me with him to Astal [Estel, west of Midyat] to the Muslim family Na'alband, where we ate a delicious meal of bulgur, and after that I went with Shekhmus to Tenat the next day. Tenat had about 100 families. I stayed with them for 9 months. The man had two sons, Hasan and Huseyin, and they named me Ibrahim. I saw many [West] Syriac boys there. I saw Malke Malle, who became Muslim with his whole family. They had relatives who refused to change their religion, and for that they were killed. Malke Malle changed his faith to stay alive with his family. Malke Malle has two sons, Aziz and Karmo. His wife changed her name from Hese to 'Aysha. I met a boy named Abdike from the Sa'ido family there. After three months my family heard about my whereabouts and wanted to fetch me, but I refused. After 1916, my uncle's wife Saro came to the village where I was staying and bought me back. On the way home from the village of Tenat to Meqre [Mikri], we met the Omariyan Kurds who killed my mother Majo and my uncle's wife Saro. They took the clothes and the money. And I fled to the village of Meqre.

13. Hanna Hawsho (1904–1993), interviewed August 1993

Before Sayfo in 1914, two relatives of ours, Ya'qub and his son, were taken to participate in the mobilization. Our neighbor Afrem, father of the lame Tuma, was taken, too. They were told that they would take part in the war against Russia. They were taken to cities like Van, Erzurum, Bitlis, and their surrounding suburbs. It was common knowledge that they were Christians, and that would explain why none of them survived.

14. Hanna Bitar (1903–2001), interviewed February 1994

In the midst of the chaos and turbulence in Midyat, many groups arrived from 'Ayn-Wardo to aid and assist the Christian people of Midyat. One of them had the task of killing the tax collector [*tahsildar*], Sharif Afandi.[5] This particular man was responsible for the killing of many men and women who could not pay taxes to the Turkish government. This group asked about the whereabouts of this man. My [West Syriac] uncle Sa'ido heard about this, and he sought out the group to tell them about the "son of a bitch," as he called him, the one he served for three years so that his two brothers would avoid the obligatory military service. He told the group that

---

[5] He was both tax collector and state registrar.

this man stayed with his guards near the church of Mort Shmuni. Sharif Afandi used to pick up people passing by, torture them, and throw them in the wells, taking advantage of the state of chaos and lawlessness that dominated the town. My uncle told the group from 'Ayn-Wardo that the best way to get rid of this savage man would be to set the stable on fire; then they could confront him emerging from the nearby house of the Barsawmo Qasho-Gorgis. The group carried out the task successfully and went back to 'Ayn-Wardo. My father and my uncle Sa'ido went with them.

15. Ello 'Amno (b. 1908), interviewed September 2004

When the shooting started in Midyat, many units came from 'Ayn-Wardo to help the Christian people of Midyat in their calamity. There was a man named tax collector Sharif Afandi who was responsible for collecting money and taxes from the Christians to be paid to the Turkish state. One group from 'Ayn-Wardo attacked him. The man fled, leaving all the money at his house. They found a big box full of money. One of the [West] Syriac leaders, Isa Zatte, went to the group who had the money and told them that this money belonged to the people of Midyat, so he took it. The group tried to negotiate with Isa Zatte, but he refused to negotiate. They got angry and left for 'Ayn-Wardo and never came back.

16. Hanna Hawsho

A Kurdish officer named Yusuf [from Siwerak] in Midyat had the job of escorting the Christians [draftees] to Sa'irt, Van, and other places. He would stay over in the house of Danho in the quarter of Chalma. When the turbulence and the shooting broke out in Midyat he was sick and stayed home. One of our relatives snuck into his room and took him to my uncle's house. They took his horse and his rifle, a Mauser. Then they broke into the house of a Turkish officer and took his wife, who was given to the Kurdish family of Nahrozo.

At that time, the groups coming from 'Ayn-Wardo heard that Yusuf, the Kurdish officer, had been captured by the [West] Syriacs and they wanted him. My father, Yawsef, however, refused to surrender him. The group didn't take that for an answer, so they broke into the room where he was staying and took him. This Kurdish officer was responsible for taking 45 persons from 'Ayn-Wardo under the pretext that they would transport food and help the army, but none of them had ever returned from such missions. Malke Mbaydono heard that Yusuf was in the hands of the Syriacs. He was grieving the death of his nephew, who was arrested by the authorities on the way to 'Ayn-Wardo and beheaded at the doors of the government building on the same day that chaos broke out in Midyat. The boy, Ya'qub, was only 15 years old. Upon seeing Yusuf, Malke Mbaydono took his dagger and stabbed him, screaming, "Ya'qub, my child, this is your revenge!"

At night, warriors from 'Ayn-Wardo broke into the house of Sherif Afandi, killing him and his family. After these events, we fled to 'Ayn-Wardo, but my father, Yawsef, stayed in Midyat. After two days, the Muhallemi from Taffe [Tafo] killed my father, Yawsef.

***

There were some 30 [West Syriac] men from the village of Zaz in Midyat who were arrested by the Turkish authorities. These were ordered to carry corpses and to throw them in the wells. When these men arrived at the 'Adoka house, they were confronted with a horrible scene: many corpses of men, women, and children were without heads and burnt beyond recognition.

17. Gorgis 'Abdiyo (1927–2001), interviewed July 2000

Before the shootings in Midyat, our Kurdish shepherd Salimo from Kfar-Gawze came to pay us a visit. My uncle Brahim was cleaning threads and preparing them for weaving. Salimo called him and Abdiyo, the head of the house. Salimo was really astonished to see someone weaving at this critical time. Abdiyo was a butcher and was not at home at the time. He was summoned from his work to meet Salimo. The shepherd said that on Friday [July 2, 1915], while he was in the mosque in Astal [Estel], to the west of Midyat, he saw Muhallemis, the kaymakam, and the two big Kurdish families in Midyat, the Nahrozo and Mahmado. He witnessed how all of them vowed to kill the Christians and that they intended to keep the agreement secret. They did that by putting their hands on the Qoran. Salimo said, "Because you had been generous and kind to me, I felt that I should warn you in advance." Salimo told Abdiyo that if anybody should hear about this, that was disclosing the secret, the result would mean Salimo's certain death. Abdiyo said in Kurdish that Midyat could defend itself, that people had the resources and the means to defend it. Salimo left wishing him and his family safety and health. Abdiyo took some 90 goats and sheep and sent them with his nephews Ne'mo and Selo to the Yezidi village of Bajenne. With them he sent my aunt Merame and his sister Sade, who was lame and could not go properly. So they were saved.

***

When chaos spread in Midyat, 92 persons from our family and our neighborhood sought refuge in the house of Ello Heshshe. The Turkish soldiers headed by a captain[6] discovered their hiding place. They went onto the roof of the house and threw burning dried grass down on them. Many were suffocated to death and others were compelled to go out. The soldiers took them to the roof of the house and slaughtered them like animals.

18. 'Abdo Ghanno-Gawweke (b. 1911), interviewed February 1997

In 1914, before mobilizing, my father did his military service in Bitlis. After some time, he fled and stayed in Anhel. The government searched for him. In July 1915, the government started to mobilize Muslim people for Sayfo. A day before that, my father sent a woman named Nisane and gave her a majidi [a silver coin worth 20 piasters] to fetch his son from Midyat so that he would be saved. He told her that his son used to have yellow boots on him. Nisane recognized me, put me on her back and took me to Anhel.

***

Meanwhile, the government was prepared to put its plan as regards the Christians in action. It took advantage of the fact that there were some Kurdish and Muhallemi men [from Midyat] doing military service there to arrest the Christians and imprison them. These men could speak [Neo-West] Syriac and were acquainted with many Christians in the area. These men were: Sadeq As'ado and his brother Bakkere, Ahmad Hatleke [Nahrozo], and other Muhallemi. They were nearly 15 Muslims. The kaymakam asked them about the Christians and their denominations. He was told that the Protestant community was the wealthiest and the most influential in comparison to the other communities: the [Chaldean, Syriac, and Armenian] Catholics and the [Syriac] Orthodox. The kaymakam instructed them therefore to concentrate on the Protestants. At night these Kurdish and Muhallemi men went and gathered 104 Protestant men. Among them was Galle Hermez, the mayor. The mission was finished by daytime. The kaymakam asked the Kurds and Muhallemi to take these men and get rid of them.

After this incident, Hanne Safar assured the Orthodox Christians that they didn't need to be anxious or worried about any mishap because this action was directed only against the Protestant community. Two weeks after this, the shootings and killings became indiscriminate. Our house in Midyat was situated in the quarter of Guharre. In our yard they killed my sisters Stire, Nila, and Basse. My mother was saved.

---

[6] Sami Bey.

19. Brahim Maqsi-Musa (1925–1998), interviewed December 1995

At the same time that the shooting started in Midyat, my [Chaldean] uncle Abdelkarim Maqsi-Musa was in Midyat. After that he went to Kfar-Gawze. My grandmother Saro had her son Musa, who was 5 or 6 years old, with her. He had pretty clothes on him at the time because they were intending to pay a visit to somebody. They arrrived at Shaqfo, near the market that was by the house of the Nateqo family. They saw armed people preparing to attack Midyat. They were tribes coming from Omid, Mardin, and Sa'irt. Musa got lost but then he saw [Syriac] people gathering and running in the direction of the shop of Yusuf Ello. He followed suit. They went to the house of the priest Gawriye. They hid where the family used to pile the hay for winter. Musa and the people hid there. After a while, the place was overcrowded. This happened in the month of July, and people were thirsty, hungry, and sweaty. A baby on the shoulder of his mother started to cry. It was no use calming him down. One man told the woman to leave for fear that they would be discovered. The woman squeezed the baby's throat until it died. This didn't help, as the soldiers came to the house and saw the people. They set the hay on fire. People suffocated and died. But the young boy Musa escaped to the marketplace where he met some Kurdish Muslims who stopped him and took him with them. On the way, a Kurd from Midyat named Heso Mahmado, the father of Saleh Chawish and Khalil, saw Musa with them and asked them to leave the boy alone because he knew the family. They kept the boy with them after a little fight. At the Kurds' house, the boy was asked if he was hungry, and he was given some water. He drank a whole jug of water. He asked for more but one old person gave him food instead. The Kurds asked Musa about where his parents used to hide their money and valuables.

20. Ello 'Amno

In 1915, when Sayfo occurred in Midyat, my father's aunt Shmuni was in the house of the family Shakkere. The Muslims saw her there and killed her. This was the fate of many Christians who happened to be in the way of the Muslims at that time. Midyat couldn't resist long, so it surrendered.

C. 'AYN-WARDO (northeast of Midyat, 11 km)

21. Ello 'Amno

The people of 'Ayn-Wardo felt long before Sayfo that something sinister was going to happen. The killings first started in Besheriye [east of Diyarbekir], where many Armenians and Chaldeans were killed. As a result, people started to buy weapons to defend themselves if needed.

22. Yawsef Babo-Rhawi

Before Sayfo in 'Ayn-Wardo, men, women, and their cattle used to go to the Yezidi village of Taqa [Taka] to wash there. Once, on the way back, Mure Marre bought some grain, maize, chickpeas, and other kinds of crops to be loaded on his donkeys. We saw some Turkish soldiers so we rushed to avoid any confrontation with them. My uncle Hobel called the people of 'Ayn-Wardo at the top of his voice to take arms and defend the village. Wasting no time, the people of 'Ayn-Wardo started to build barricades of stone and prepare for the attack. The first assault, however, was very violent. My uncle Tuma took refuge in the church of Mor Hushabo. He called on the people he saw to help his brother, who was trapped resisting alone in Grighos's house. I together with Mas'ud and other men from 'Ayn-Wardo started shooting and engaging the enemy. The women encouraged us all the time. Together we joined forces to stop the advance of the Turkish forces. My uncle Hobel was helped too.

Before these tragic incidents, Sa'deko Kurke and Hanne Maqsi-Galle had experience interpreting the [bugle] signals made by the enemy, having spent seven years in military service in the Turkish army. Thanks to that experience, we could understand the enemy's intended moves.

23. Brahim Maqsi-Musa

When the Turkish forces and the Kurdish tribes decided to attack 'Ayn-Wardo, they made a peculiar signal. 'Ayn-Wardo warriors came forward and explained what each particular sound meant and that they were preparing themselves to attack. After a while, the horn sounded again and the fighters of 'Ayn-Wardo understood that a full-scale attack was under way. Before the imminent attack, Gallo Shabo and Mas'ud positioned some warriors in a deserted house on the outskirts of 'Ayn-Wardo. They opened some holes in the wall and they waited for the enemy to come. This proved very effective. Then we heard another sound, and it was interpreted as a withdrawal. Three times the Christians stopped the assaults.

24. Gawriye Beth-Mas'ud (b. 1926), interviewed July 2002

Ahmad Agha, the chief of the Kurdish tribe of 'Owena, together with 600 persons from his tribe went to see his nephew Ismail Beg, the head of the Muhallemi. Ahmad Agha addressed him in Kurdish, asking him to gather as many forces as he could to eradicate the remaining Christians in 'Ayn-Wardo. He said that contemptuously, ridiculing the Christians. Ismail Beg's father replied that the forces fighting the Christians were estimated to be more than 20,000 Kurds, aided by the government forces, and that should be enough to eliminate the Christians. He didn't need to bother [to go]. He meant that such a big force would not give up until they had accomplished their mission. Ahmad Agha became very angry and said that the Muhallemi had the same blood as the [West] Syriacs as they were Christians before. So he left for Midyat.

25. Brahim Maqsi-Musa

The village of 'Owena is situated on the top of Sawro [near Mardin]. It had a chief named Shaykh Ahmad Agha. He came to Midyat with a large force together with his two sons. He came to take part in the war against the Christians in 'Ayn-Wardo. He rode toward the Monastery of Mor Abrohom in Midyat. He entered the church and chained his horses to the columns of the altar and closed the door of the church after him.

The Kurd Azizke heard that Shaykh Ahmad Agha had arrived from 'Owena and was on his way to visit him. Azizke prepared lunch for his guests. Azizke asked Shaykh Ahmad Agha about where he put his horses. Shaykh Ahmad Agha answered him that he put them in the church. Azizke told Shaykh Ahmad Agha that this deed could be bad luck, that is, to put horses in a church. Shaykh Ahmad Agha ate lunch with his men and left for 'Ayn-Wardo to fight the Christians. The following day, Shaykh Ahmad Agha returned to Midyat because his son had been killed. Azizke saw him another time, and Azizke reminded him that it wasn't a wise move to put horses in a church.

26. Yawsef Babo-Rhawi

One day, Shaykh Ahmad Agha came from 'Owena heading for 'Ayn-Wardo. He was chief of 32 villages. When he arrived at 'Ayn-Wardo, there were already 12,000 men ready to fight. Among those fighting in the battle for 'Ayn-Wardo was a man named 'Azaddin Tamo-Gawre from the district of Habisbin. He called to the Christians on the other side and told them that Shaykh Ahmad Agha had arrived from 'Owena vowing to capture 'Ayn-Wardo and was not going to leave until he did so. He told the Christians to be ready. Mas'ud responded by preparing his men, positioning them in the house of Grigho. Meanwhile, the Muslim attack started. Women encouraged the men and started to throw stones at the attackers. The Muslims were able to remove the fortifying stones on the side where Mas'ud was positioned. Mas'ud's men hid, killing the approaching Muslims. Shaykh Ahmad Agha lost 60 men, and he withdrew after this.

Then 'Azaddin Tamo-Gawre called to Hobel from the Christian side and asked him about the Christian casualties. Hobel told him that they had only one wounded, but that he could count 60 Muslim dead.

***

To dampen the spirits of the Christians, Azizke Mahmado started to boast in Kurdish about his many titles, saying that he was the father of Rashid, the defender of the country, the butcher of the enemy, and that he was so generous that he could kill for the sake of a friend. In response, a man named Sawme Kettino started to lament him and his imminent fate on the hands of the Christians. He told him that he hoped his words could reach Kharput, where humane Kurdish Aghas [Chalabiyo, Alike Batte, and Sarokhano] were imprisoned by the government to keep them from helping the Christians, implying that Azizke was deviating from the general friendly Kurdish line vis-à-vis Christians. Sawme Kettino continued that Azizke was a worthless figure and would meet death and that his mission was doomed to fail. Azizke looked around to make sure nobody heard that. Alyas Bahdo and Gorgis Gharibo said similar things to Azizke: that he would die if the imprisoned Kurdish Aghas should hear about his war against Christians. My father, Ya'qub, addressed Azizke in Kurdish telling him to think about God and that he should contribute to stopping the bloodshed instead. Being an Agha he should work to implement peace instead of war. After all, the Christians and the Muslims were neighbors. Azizke replied that the Christians should no longer think of returning to Midyat and that the time of coexistence was over. He told them to fight to the bitter end.

Ya'qub replied by boasting in the same way, that he could be as savage as the Tatars, that he was the father of many sons, the brother of many brothers, the fish of the pond of Edessa, the defender of the hostages, the butcher of the enemy, and the selfless friend. Azizke told him that he forgot to add one thing to his list of merits: that he was from the family of Shurwaqi [that is, that they were new to the area and had taken a new surname].

27. Brahim Maqsi-Musa

One day, some Aghas from Kfar-Gawze came to join in the war against the Christians in 'Ayn-Wardo. They were Badraddin and his cousins Brahime Ismail and others. Before attacking, Badraddin boasted that he was the partridge [*qaqono*] of the Tal'a area and the valley of Kfar-Gawze.[7] Abdelkarim Maqsi-Musa was on the Christian side and was also from Kfar-Gawze. Recognizing each other's voices, Abdelkarim Maqsi-Musa replied that it was he who was the partridge of the whole of Kfar-Gawze.

The supply needs of 'Ayn-Wardo, such as arms and food, came from the villages of the Yezidis and the Rayete region [south of Midyat]. The Yezidis took the Christians' side.

28. Yawsef Babo-Rhawi

For a period of two months, the battles were ceaseless. The family of Rhawi saved 72 people who were stuck under the piles of dead bodies. We were able to take our money and belongings with us to 'Ayn-Wardo. My uncle Tuma used to give money to Dahho Khalaf to buy grain and meat for the people so they could survive. Meanwhile, the government sent two people, a priest named Hanna and a bishop from Mardin, to act as mediators. Upon arriving, they appealed to the people in 'Ayn-Wardo to surrender and said that they would guarantee everyone's safety. My father, Ya'qo, replied that surrender like this would mean the death of the Christians in 'Ayn-Wardo together with the bishop and the priest Hanna. He suggested the name of another mediator, namely, Shaykh Fathallah from '''Ayn-Kifo ['Aynkaf northwest of Midyat], a respectable figure whose mediation could be trusted and accepted on both sides. Shaykh Fathallah went to the Turkish vali and asked for serious obligations, demanding lasting peace and cease-fire, or otherwise he would not be involved in this task. Shaykh Fathallah came to 'Ayn-Wardo riding a horse. Before entering the place, he rested outside under a tree. When the Christians saw him, they rejoiced and sent a delegation to welcome him. Shaykh Fathallah was happy too. He requested a priest and two respectable men for discussions. He asked the Christians to take his nephew and five persons from his side as hostages. Should the government not keep its word and obligations, the Christians had the right to kill these people.

---

[7] Partridges had a particular meaning for local hunters. They would take a tame partridge into the fields to lure the other partridges out of their nesting places.

Before Sayfo, my father, Ya'qo, had been in 'Ayn-Kifo, the village where Shaykh Fathallah lived. He worked there building some houses and circular covers for tombs. So there was a kind of acquaintance between them. Ya'qo hurried to welcome Shaykh Fathallah's nephew. The latter told him that his uncle would exert sincere efforts to solve the problem and bring peace to this tormented region. My father was one of the delegates who went to see Shaykh Fathallah. He warmly welcomed him. Shaykh Fathallah asked them to bring him all the broken rifles so that they could be handed over to the government. This would be considered a gesture of good will. He promised to stay with them until the threat was over. The delegation came back with the useless rifles. In consequence, the withdrawal began, and the Christians could see the besiegers withdrawing from 'Ayn-Wardo to Midyat [about 11 kilometers]. The delegation was very happy to see this happening, and Gallo Shabo asked Shaykh Fathallah to pay them a visit in 'Ayn-Wardo. The Shaykh replied that what he did was prompted by pure human and religious values. He told them that he would accompany those who returned home to Midyat and other villages so that they would arrive safe and sound. Dawud Galle Hermez, my father Ya'qo Rhawi, Isa Awrohom, and others went with Shaykh Fathallah when he left 'Ayn-Wardo. On the way home he told the Christians that their homes had been looted but comforted them that God had not forsaken them. Typhus and other fatal diseases spread among us, presumably because of the lack of salt in our food. Tur Abdin was full of Muslim immigrants that Russia displaced at the time, and a lot of them died because of the terrible conditions.

29. Resqo Gawwo-Afrem

It was two weeks after we arrived in 'Ayn-Wardo from Midyat. The government troops advanced toward us. They reached the Church of Mor Hushabo. We had a bishop named Mor Filiksinos Ablahad who instructed the people of 'Ayn-Wardo not to start shooting because they had no mandate from God to do such a thing. The bishop stayed 17 days and nights on the roof of the church praying and meditating. [There] he died of starvation and thirst and not of any military action. The battle for 'Ayn-Wardo lasted 62 days and it didn't cease even at night. When the Kurds attacked the Church of Mor Hushabo, one of them raised a green flag, the symbol of Islam, in the churchyard. The Christians lost heart and women started to wail. The Christian leader Mas'ud stood up and tried to boost their morale; he called on the memory of their courageous ancestors in Midyat, Mzizah, 'Ayn-Wardo, and all the people of Tur Abdin.

APPENDIX 1

[in Neo-West Syriac]

Bashel babe medhyoye!
Bashel babe mzizaxiye!
Bashel babe ciwarnoye!
Bashel babe turoye!

Hay hawaryo, qumu hjamu!
Kloyo layt! Li raghlo qumu!
Dlo kloyo, nishe mhalhelu!
Dlo kloyo, gawre mhawu!

Bak kefe, alxune mhawu!
B qarce du kurmanj mhawu!
Twaru u kurmanj, twaru!
I malkutho athyo lu tarco du bayto!

"Come on, everybody! You Midyatis, you Mizizakhis, you 'Ayn-Wardis, you Tur Abdinis! This is a cry for help. Stand up ready for attack! Move forward all the time! Women, rejoice! Men, be firm! Throw stones against them, at the Kurds! Beat the Kurds! Victory is ours! Paradise is near, close to our homes!"

He ordered the men to stand up and fight, and the women to cheer and encourage with their songs. He prompted them to fight and stop the approaching enemy even if that meant throwing stones on the heads of the Kurds, as paradise was near and they had no choice but to fight. After this, the Christians surrounded the Kurds and started fighting. A Christian man named Makko Hattina ran toward the man waving the green Muslim flag. The Kurd stabbed him five times, three in the back and two in the breast, but he managed to stop the Kurd from flying the flag. The Kurds and the Turks were impressed by this heroism and started to withdraw. Outside 'Ayn-Wardo there were about 10,000 government soldiers aided by 12,000 Kurds. The Christians estimated that they had about 750 armed men whose 300 rifles were very primitive and not modern at all, and some of them were held together by string to make them work. The small children would creep up on the roofs of the houses, collecting used bullets to be refilled and reused.

***

To make gunpowder, the Christians went down to the caves and collected the excrement of the dogs and the white mould on the walls, which they then mixed with charcoal. They would test the mixture by putting some of it in a hole. If it exploded when fired on, then the process was considered a success. In 'Ayn-Wardo there was sufficient food. On the outskirts of 'Ayn-Wardo there was a Yezidi village named Taqa [Taka] whose inhabitants supplied the Christians with food. The Christians harvested all the grain in the fields just before the expected attacks. The people of Midyat who took refuge in 'Ayn-Wardo brought their food with them too. This meant that the Christians had food in 'Ayn-Wardo. Mas'ud, the Christian leader, mobilized even the young boys in the war for 'Ayn-Wardo. He gave us sticks that suited our height. We would use them to bang the garbage bins and sing songs like [in Neo-West Syriac] *Hema w haye / Hema w ha / Duqu berghel / Duqu ha! / Ha haye, ha haye!* (Come on, come on! Beat and beat the coscos!)—the songs we used to sing in harvest time. We did that to give the enemy the impression that we were not suffering from any shortage of food whatsoever. This had a tremendous effect on the Muslims, who were led to think that the Christians had an abundant harvest and intended to resist them to the end. I was seven years old at the time.

Mas'ud was rather dark, tall and thin. He behaved like a real politician. We had many such courageous and creative men working with him. Mas'ud's brother Shabo was a great man. In Midyat there emerged such men as [the Chaldean] Abdelkarim and his brother Mikhayel Maqsi-Musa, Malke Mbaydono, my father Gallo, my uncle and my cousin Hobel, Ya'qo, Makko, and Tuma Rhawi. Isa Gawriye was killed by friendly fire. He had a black suit on and was mistaken for an enemy. When he was killed and his rifle taken from him, the Christians realized their mistake. Strong and effective women played a positive role, such as Tarzo Nabat and Mas'ud's sister, who used to boost the fighters' morale by singing songs, reciting poems, and making sounds that would create a good atmosphere.

***

The Kurd 'Azizke Mahmado [from Midyat] was a sworn enemy of the Christians. In 'Ayn-Wardo my uncle Zayto, Slayman and his son, and two of my cousins were killed. My father and his brothers were wounded. A Kurd who was the head [*mukhtar*] of the town of Hasno [Hasankeyf] came to fight the Christians in 'Ayn-Wardo. He had with him a Russian rifle and lots of bullets. Taking a position on top of a tree on a hill called Qawro di Shelha, this Kurd could kill lots of Christians. The Christians sent 3 men to stop him; one of them was Musa Abraham. They were able to kill him and took the rifle.

After the war, our family went to Anhel and the Kurds didn't stop their attacks. They killed many Christian people on the road when traveling or moving from one place to another. In Anhel, my father, Gallo, my mothe,r Farida, my sister Setto, my brother Antun, and my sister Hana died of typhus and the lack of healthy and proper food. Lice spread all over the place. This disease took the lives of many people. In Anhel we stayed with our relative Aho Malke. We stayed there six months and returned to our houses in Midyat, where the houses were empty and plundered. The Kurds didn't leave anything in them.

30. Karmo Salma-Gawwo

On the road between 'Ayn-Wardo and Midyat, a lot of fighting took place between the people of 'Ayn-Wardo and the Muslims. Nevertheless, many people could be led to safety in 'Ayn-Wardo. After this, the Muslims realized that 'Ayn-Wardo had become a fort—a kind of refuge for the Christians. The Muslims decided to surround 'Ayn-Wardo and put it under siege. Their number steadily increased, so that they needed 13,000 loaves of bread a day to feed them. The Turkish forces had their own food, and the other Kurdish tribes did too. This might give an idea of the immense number of Muslims there. Every Turkish officer and Kurdish chief vowed to be the one who would conquer the Christians and take 'Ayn-Wardo. It must be mentioned here that, given these enormous numbers of attackers, 'Ayn-Wardo could resist only thanks to the help of a divine power. It was God who inspired Mas'ud. He was a magnificent organizer, so that everything seemed to be done in great precision and seriousness.

My family stayed in 'Ayn-Wardo for 45 days. I remember that the over 100-year-old Ablahad Haloqo was responsible for making bullets. He had a mould in which he filled chickpeas with gunpowder. I used to be fascinated by him. Mas'ud used to go round and gather men who for some reason stayed home with their wives reminding them that the war was so critical for the Christians; it was about their honor and the future of their children. They'd better stay on the front line rather than go to church or sleep with women.

The Muhallemi tribe of Rashdiye consisted of two groups that took turns fighting the Christians in 'Ayn-Wardo. When the Rashdiye came to 'Ayn-Wardo, they boasted that they were the ones who would invade and capture 'Ayn-Wardo. Mas'ud heard that they were on their way, so he told his men that the war would start when he fired the first shot. Mas'ud went round and made sure that everything was in place. When the Rashdiye started to climb over the walls of 'Ayn-Wardo, Mas'ud fired the first shot, giving the signal. The Christians fought back, and 15 persons from Rashdiye were killed. Seeing the number of casualties, the rest of the Rashdiye started to withdraw. The Christians chased them, and at that point people on both sides were killed.

We had a bishop who stayed on the roof of the Church of Mor Hushabo and the Muslims could see him. He fasted and prayed to God to extend a hand to his people. The Kurdish tribe of Ali Rammo, who came from the village of Chelek [Çelik] to participate in the war against 'Ayn-Wardo, testified how they saw strange scenes; how the bullets they fired at 'Ayn-Wardo appeared to come back at them as if there was a divine hand defending 'Ayn-Wardo. So they told the Christians not to fear.

There were Syriac women who played decisive roles in the war. They stood on the front line, cheering on the fighters and boosting their morale. Some of them would throw themselves in the way wherever they saw a big group about to attack them and their people.

***

The Christian village of Basibrin asked for help from 'Ayn-Wardo in the form of strong fighters. Among those who volunteered to help were Isa Polos and Galle Gejo and others. My father, Afremo, lost his voice because of the vehement nature of events. He was urged to join them by his uncle Mehe. Afremo abstained due to his weak voice and bad eyesight. His uncle asked him to hand in his rifle. Afremo refused and at last decided to go with them. The fighters from 'Ayn-Wardo were confronted by some Yezidis from Bajenne and started to exchange fire. They spread out and, as Afremo could not communicate with his fellow fighters, he got caught by the Yezidis. The Yezidis told the government in Midyat that they had captured Afremo Gawwo, and the instruction was that he should be killed. Shebliyo killed Afremo as a result. ... After the death of my father, some Yezidis later killed Shebliyo and his son-in-law. These Yezidi informed my mother about how they took revenger for the killing of her husband. She rewarded them for that.

***

In 'Ayn-Wardo, I had two uncles and three sisters, two of whom, Nazo and Jamila, died of typhus, which was incurable at that time. We used to eat our food without salt. The stench from the scattered corpses worsened the situation. Sarokhano [son of Sarhano], the chief of the Kurdish tribe in Mar Bobo, belonged to the family of Chalabiyo [a branch of the Haverkan], and he supported the Christians by providing them with whatever they would ask for. The government wanted to make peace with the people of 'Ayn-Wardo. The [East and West] Syriacs refused because they had no confidence whatsoever in its promises. However, the Syriacs named one person whom they would trust as a mediator; he was Shaykh Fathallah. When

Shaykh Fathallah came to the Christian side, he was warmly welcomed by the Syriacs, and peace was accomplished thanks to his efforts.

When we left Midyat for 'Ayn-Wardo, my mother stayed behind. She was taken as a hostage and put with other hostages in the caravanserai of Musa-Shamosho. There, a Turkish officer, Rauf Bey, who had worked for a while with my father, saw my mother and asked her about my father, Afremo. In fact nobody experienced any mercy from the government forces. The officers who guarded the hostages were Muslims from Midyat such as Skandarko and Karme Mahmado. They were told to take the hostages to Anhel, and so my mother Salma arrived there.

31. Tuma Salmo

In the time of Sayfo, the Muslim tribes were united in their decision to attack 'Ayn-Wardo. They besieged it and surrounded it like a ring. As a result, the resistance needed a continuous supply of bullets, and they lacked salt. Mas'ud, the Christian leader, called for a meeting and asked his men to nominate four men to bring gunpowder and other supplies that were needed. One of them was [the Chaldean] Abdelkarim Maqsi-Musa. Mas'ud told the four men that there was a weak concentration of Muslims in a certain place. They would take advantage of it to sneak out and head for Qameshli [now in Syria]. There they would meet some people and get the needed things and come back the same way so that the resistance could resume.

32. Hanna Polos (b. 1921), interviewed November 1993

In 'Ayn-Wardo, my father, [the Chaldean] Isa Polos, had the opportunity to get acquainted with Mas'ud. As salt was lacking in 'Ayn-Wardo, we used to sneak out to Anhel [about 10 km south of Midyat], taking advantage of darkness to fill our bags with salt. Once, my father did, that but as they approached 'Ayn-Wardo they heard some Kurds boasting. One of them was saying that he was from Khaltan and that he was here to get himself a Christian bride and that he was there for the sake of her eyes. Isa became very angry and wanted to see where the voices came from. They saw seven people smoking, and one of them was talking and boasting. Isa told his companions to halt. He wanted to do something to the Kurd who was so eager to capture a Christian woman; a wish that had stimulated the Kurds to wage war against Christians. Isa swore by Christ to fulfill the Kurd's dream. He told his friends to be prepared. Isa Polos took a rifle and shot him. The man fell, saying, "They fucked my mother." His companions fell into confusion and were easily killed. They took their rifles from them before the group went back to 'Ayn-Wardo.

In 'Ayn-Wardo, there were many strategically placed openings from which the Christians could shoot at the enemy. They could also listen to the Muslims making plans. Once my father heard that the Muslims attributed the Christian resistance to divine intervention; that it was Mor Hushabo himself who was fighting on the side of the Christian people. Before Sayfo, my father, Isa Polos, was in Kfar-Gawze working for Yusuf Agha; as such, he was acquainted with the Agha's cousin, Azdin, and his assistant, Shaker. The two men heard that Isa was in 'Ayn-Wardo, so they came to 'Ayn-Wardo to provide him with bullets and gunpowder from Kfar-Gawze. Isa set specific times and gave the password to get help from them.

33. Tuma Salmo

The Christians in 'Ayn-Wardo closely watched the Muslims' movements. Isa Polos used to sit and listen to the enemy talking. He heard how the Muslims were longing to capture 'Ayn-Wardo. They said they would slaughter the men first, then they would divide up the women among themselves. Isa Polos sought out Mas'ud and told him about the plans. He asked Mas'ud's permission to do something to destroy the enemy's morale. He went down to the caves and brought some thick mallets and asked them to bang the ground with them while singing "Come on, Come on" (*Hema w Haye*). Meanwhile women would utter sounds of joy so that the enemy got the impression that the Christians were not lacking anything as they were preparing food for the winter. The Muslims got the message and started to lose confidence that the Christians would give up soon.

***

After the battles at 'Ayn-Wardo, the Muslims realized that they were incapable of taking 'Ayn-Wardo. The Turkish commandant sent a message to Mas'ud calling for negotiations. Mas'ud asked for some guarantees in the form of 12 soldiers and a captain to stay with the Christians during the negotiations. The commandant consented. Mas'ud and a companion went out to meet him. The Turkish commandant had a Kurdish assistant working under him named Selo Maskane from the Omariye area [near Mardin]. As our family was acquainted with Selo Maskane's family, we got some interesting details about this meeting that were told to my father, Musa Salmo. When Mas'ud came to meet the commandant, he looked manly and professional. He had a long sword and a bag hung from his shoulder. The commandant asked Mas'ud when the Christians would surrender their arms. Mas'ud answered that the Christians would never unconditionally surrender and that they would fight to the bitter end if necessary. Selo Maskane thought to himself that this reaction was right and appropriate. To expess his admiration, Selo put his hand in his pocket and found some tobacco, so he gave it to him in secret as a token of admiration and encouragement.

34. Gawriye Beth-Mas'ud

The enemy, who was relentlessly attacking the Christians in 'Ayn-Wardo, began to seek peace thanks to the heroic resistance displayed by the Christians. At first the calls for peace were not serious and were intended to be a trick. Azizke, a Kurdish Agha, advised the Turkish commander to bring Sarokhano, the chief of the Kurdish tribe in Mar Bobo [in Rayete], since he was a friend of the Christians. Sarokhano belonged to the Osmano family, who had good relations with the Christians. It is worth mentioning that the three Kurdish Aghas, Chalabiyo, Alike Batte, and Sarokhano, had been imprisoned by the government [for rebellion before the war] and remained there to prevent any possible help from them to the Christians. The plan, however, was arranged in such a way that when the villagers would come out to negotiate with Sarokhano, the Kurds would sieze the opportunity, attack, and kill them all.

Sarokhano came to 'Ayn-Wardo carrying a white flag, and the Christians in 'Ayn-Wardo recognized him. He was seemingly aware of the foul play. Sarokhano addressed the Christians in Kurdish, urging them to listen to him and heed his words. He advised them to be careful and insinuated that the plan was to eradicate the Christians by killing the men and taking the women for themselves. The Christians got the message and therefore refused the Turks' and the Kurds' appeals for peace, saying they had no confidence in the honor of these people.

***

In the Sayfo of 1895 that occurred in Omid [Diyarbekir] and Sa'diye [near Diyarbekir], Christians were killed on a large scale. Shaykh Brahim, Shaykh Fathallah's father, stayed in Midyat and opposed those who initiated the massacres against Christians. He swore to commit suicide if the killings of the Christians did not cease. He said that Muhammad himself had instructed his followers to defend the Christians.

35. Hanna Polos

The Muslims suggested the names of many persons to accomplish peace between the Christians in 'Ayn-Wardo and the Turks and their allies the Kurds. My father told Mas'ud not to accept such suggestions because the names were not trustworthy. He told him to trust one person only; namely, Shaykh Fathallah from 'Ayn-Kifo ['Aynkaf]. Mas'ud asked my father, Isa Polos, for some information regarding Shaykh Fathallah. Mas'ud wanted to know the background of this eminent figure. My father, Isa Polos, told Mas'ud that originally our family came from Sa'irt. Due to a conflict with the Kurds, our family was compelled to seek refuge in 'Ayn-Kifo, where Shaykh Fathallah was the religious leader.

[Before 1915,] one of Shaykh Fathallah's brothers fell in love with a girl, but her parents wanted her to marry her cousin instead. Shaykh Fathallah's brother met the girl once and wanted to talk to her. But her parents and relatives attacked him and broke his shoulder. Isa Polos said that his family was represented by Gorgis and took the side of the Shaykh and his brother. Gorgis gathered his men and sought revenge on the girl's family. Gorgis's men killed three of the girl's relatives. As a result, her family had some kind of vendetta against Shaykh Fathallah's family. The conflict worsened, and the girl's family started to gather dried leaves, paper, and wood to set Shaykh Fathallah's place on fire. Gorgis called his family and Shaykh Fathallah's family to a meeting to decide their next move. Gorgis divided the men into two groups and asked the women to take care of the children. They decided to attack before being attacked and after that to escape to Kfar-Gawze seeking shelter at Yusuf Agha. Ten of our men stayed with Shaykh Fathallah to help him.

***

Isa Polos told Mas'ud that this incident strengthened the relations between the Christians and Shaykh Fathallah. Mas'ud agreed to take this suggestion, and Shaykh Fathallah was suggested as a mediator. Shaykh Fathallah was summoned to 'Ayn-Wardo, and when he arrived there, he stayed in a white tent together with his Yezidi servant. The servant beat his little drum to signal the start of negotiations, telling the Christians of 'Ayn-Wardo to come down and meet Shaykh Fathallah. Isa Polos was among the delegation to meet Shaykh Fathallah, who warmly greeted them with tears in his eyes. The meeting was emotional. Shaykh Fathallah said to Isa Polos that it was painful for him to see the Christians in this terrible situation but promised to do his best to help them. He asked them to bring about 20 rifles that were either worn out or not properly functioning. After the handing over of weapons, the Shaykh flew a white flag of peace, showing the other side that the Christians had performed a good-will gesture. Then he spoke Kurdish to tell the other side the terms of peace agreed on with the Christians. The rifles were loaded onto two donkeys and sent to the Shaykh. The Yezidi servant then beat his drum, signaling that peace had been achieved. Shaykh

Fathallah addressed the Muslims, saying that now it was forbidden to kill Christians, and those who would violate that order would answer to him and his men. He reiterated the word "peace" many times.

Thousands and thousands of Muslims started to withdraw, and they seemed more numerous than the leaves of the trees. Shaykh Fathallah called for my father, Isa Polos, and told him not to believe that this could be a total peace. Shaykh Fathallah advised them not to trust the promises of the Muslims, and that Christians should not wander outside the villages alone on the roads. Shaykh Fathallah left 'Ayn-Wardo for Kfar-Gawze after that. In fact, after Sayfo many Christians were killed while travelling or moving from one place to another. Many Christians died that way, actually more than the number who died in Sayfo itself.

36. Lahdo Musa-Malaka (1932–1999), interviewed June 1993

My father, Muro, was made a fighter in 1915 at 'Ayn-Wardo. He was 15 years old at the time. He told me the following: They were divided into two groups, and one group would fight when the other rested. While my father was asleep, the priest Dawud from the village of Zaz tried to enter 'Ayn-Wardo. He had black clothes on and so was mistaken for a Turkish officer. They shot at him many times. They woke my father up to help them get rid of the "Turkish" officer. Muro shot him and Dawud was hit in the neck. Between the enemy and the village was a boundary where the wounded and dead were placed. The Muslims notified the fighters of 'Ayn-Wardo that they had wounded their own priest. The Muslims asked for a short cease-fire so they could carry the priest to the boundary, where he could be brought to 'Ayn-Wardo. However, the priest lived for a long time after this incident with the bullet-scar on his neck.

Mas'ud was a good leader, and Muro accompanied him when he gathered men who had stayed home with their women, saying that they should first and foremost focus on victory over the enemy, to save their people and honor. From Mizizah some 7 or 8 men were killed in 'Ayn-Wardo; among them were Saffo Barse and Isa Mesqob.

37. Hanna Mure (b. 1926), interviewed November 1996

In 'Ayn-Wardo, Mas'ud positioned 10 or 15 men in key positions and told his men to guard them with their lives. Some men from Kfarze [Keferzi] were placed in a spot named the Strategic Fig Point [*Kozeke dat Tene*], which was on top of a mountain. There were two good fighters, Galle Maroge, Ishko, and some others. During the battle in 'Ayn-Wardo, the Muslims attacked this point and captured it. Mas'ud heard the bad news and told the men who had been positioned there to rest for a night, and they would get reinforcement in the form of another 20 men who wouild retake the point to avoid running the risk that Muslims would enter 'Ayn-Wardo from that point. Around 50 men engaged in clashes with the Muslims. Galle Maroge was killed and two Kurds also, but the Christians recaptured the position.

The Muslims believed it was not the Christians who were fighting, but that some divine hands were defending them. Some white figures were seen roaming around 'Ayn-Wardo that prevented the Kurds from entry, as they maintained.

38. 'Abdo Ghanno-Gawweke

The Ottoman forces that came from Midyat had a cannon with them. They fired at 'Ayn-Wardo twice, but it broke down and they could not use it any longer.

39. Gorgis 'Abdiyo

My father told me that at one time the Christians ran out of weapons, so they appealed to a [West Syriac] blacksmith from the Haddo family in Midyat, who came up with the clever idea of stuffing chimney pipes with gunpowder; he manufactured them in such a way that they were used and sounded like a real piece of artillery when fired. The effectiveness of this weapon inspired many songs that were sung both in Kurdish and in [Neo-West] Syriac:

> *Athen athen armenoye*
> *Nahiti mture celoye*
> *Sidayna fadawiye*
> *Amtalle top acmayye*
> *Ucdo ged muqdhina*
> *Babe d ha b ha minayye*
>
> "The Armenians came from high above to us fighters to help us get rid of all of our enemies."

He used that weapon many times, and the Muslims believed that Armenians had joined forces with the Christians and began to fear that the Christian side was growing stronger and more sophisticated in its resistance. Mas'ud came and told the blacksmith to stop that, as the device consumed a lot of gunpowder.

The Kurdish Agha Sarokhano helped the Christians by providing them with weapons and gunpowder that he secretly placed under the Church of

Mor Hushabo so that the Christians could fetch it at night. He told the Christians to take care of themselves and fight, and he openly threatened that any Yezidi who collaborated with the Kurds and the Turks would die at his hands. He was a great help to the Christians.

My father-in-law had a Muhallemi friend from 'Ayn-Kifo named Murad who took the side of the Muslims in 'Ayn-Wardo. He swore that he saw a vision of a hundred people dressed in white fighting and assisting the Christians.

40. Danho Keno

After Sayfo, a Muhallemi told me the following about 'Ayn-Wardo. In a group of 33 persons, he went to 'Ayn-Wardo. From the neighboring villages, tens of people did the same. He and his two brothers went to 'Ayn-Wardo, which at the time was full of people. The place was so full of volunteers that they could not see the ground. First they aimed at attacking the Church of 'Ayn-Wardo. They saw a man on the roof of the church whom they tried to shoot, but amazingly the bullets seemed to return to their guns, to burst or burn in their faces. As a result, 31 persons died, including his two brothers. Only two were able to return safely.

Rashido, the son of Azizke Mahmado, told me that an agha from the tribe of Habisbin came to Midyat. He ridiculed the Muslims of Midyat, saying that it was shameful that a little village like 'Ayn-Wardo could resist them. He had 100 men with him and promised to capture it in no time and to do what the others failed to do. Rashido showed them 'Ayn-Wardo and the great number of people besieging it. Rashido addressed the Christians in Syriac that one more agha had arrived vowing to take 'Ayn-Wardo. The Christians welcomed him reluctantly. The door of the Church of Mor Hushabo was special and very strong and could be locked from the outside. The Kurds stormed the churchyard, calling on the name of their Prophet Muhammad [*Muhammad Salawat*] to help them. The doorway of the Church had slots [for locking the door from the outside with a beam], and many Christians waited there until all the Kurds went in. The porter got the signal to close the door of the Church, and the Kurds were trapped inside, facing certain death. Then the door of the Church was opened and the corpses rolled down, to be taken away by the Muslims. From our family, 22 persons died of hunger and diseases. 32 persons returned to Anhel.

D. KFAR-BORAN (Kerburan; northeast of Midyat, 46 km)

41. Useve Wardo (1906–1999), interviewed October 1997

In Kfar-Boran, there were 500 Christian houses and around 30 Muslim houses. The Christians belonged to many denominations: [West] Syriacs, Protestants, Catholics [some of them were Chaldean]. Among the Syriac Orthodox leaders were Brahim Sham'un and Malke Hano. From the [West Syriac] Protestant group there were Useve Danho and Useve Lahdo. We suffered a lot from the Kurdish tribe of Rama, who lived in the village of Chelek [Çelik] outside Kfar-Boran. Their chief, Ali Rammo, had four sons: Darwesh, Abdelkarim [knicknamed 'Amar or Ömer], Khalil, and Mustafa. Ali Rammo used to impose taxes on the Christians. The people complained that it was an unbearable burden for them to pay taxes both to him and to the government; it was like carrying two melons in one hand, as they put it. Before Sayfo, Ali Rammo came to Kfar-Boran to collect taxes, and Bishop Antimos Ya'qub was there. The Christians refused to pay taxes to him. Before he went to Mecca to perform pilgrimage, he instructed his sons Mustafa and Khalil to inflict punishment on the Christians. Ali Rammo died during his pilgrimage.

***

When they heard of the massacres of Christians and the atrocities they suffered, the people of Kfar-Boran started to ask questions about the real culprit: the Turkish government or the Kurds? Meanwhile, my stepmother, Sade, needed some medical treatment. She went to Midyat, where we had some relatives; Gorgis Isa-Gawriye told Sade to return home because a Turkish captain said that Sultan Rashad had issued three decrees [from Istanbul] to get rid of the Christians. He emphasized that she ought to spread the news that the Christians should take precautions to avoid killings, such as seeking refuge in Hah, 'Ayn-Wardo, or Dayro da Ṣlibo. Sade went back to Kfar-Boran and told them of the imminent dangers.

The Christians called for a meeting; it was attended by Brahim Sham'un, Malke Hano, Useve Lahdo, and others. The [Orthodox] Syriacs reminded the Protestants of the Armenians' fate, how they were thrown in the wells of Sita [west of Midyat], implying that this time it was the Protestants' turn. The Syriacs maintained that they had assurances from the state that the Syriacs should not fear as no harm would come to them. The decree was directed against the foreigners ["ajnabi"], namely, the Catholics, Protestants, and Armenians, as foreign countries were backing them. Useve Lahdo, the leader of the Protestant community, decided to leave for Hah.

***

The local administrator [*nahiya mediri*] informed the Kurdish aghas that Kfar-Boran was ready to be taken. It was a Saturday in July when the tribe of Rama, headed by Mustafa Agha, attacked Kfar-Boran. The Christians sought refuge in a place called the Seven Palaces. Each day the Kurds and the Turkish forces attacked one of the palaces, until all the remaining Christians were killed. The walls of the places were full of blood. Women and children were forced to become Muslims, to be servants or wives for the invaders.

When the attacks on Kfar-Boran began, we had a friend named Hajji Ahmad, who helped us by taking us to the village of Baseqel [Basikil]. We stayed there for three months until the government issued a pardon so that we could return to Kfar-Boran. The pardon mentioned the killings of Christians and that the government had taken pity on them. The government took it upon itself to allow the dispersed Christians to come back. However, those who became Muslims were free to go and live wherever they found it convenient. A new kaymakam arrived at Kfar-Boran, and Useve Lahdo joined forces to allow the displaced families to come back to Kfar-Boran.

42. Hanna Polos

My father and mother told me the following. Before Sayfo, my father, Isa Polos, lived in Kfar-Boran. There lived a Muhallemi [from Astal, a section of Midyat] sergeant, Tawfiq, from the Mefti family. Tawfiq wanted my father to work with him. Tawfiq had 22 soldiers with him; 21 of them were Muslims and one was Christian, my father. My father led a jolly life; he would roam around, often drunk, with Tawfiq, singing and enjoying themselves. Tawfiq used to ask my father's advice about aghas and their personalities, and my father would give him his opinions about the different aghas and others. The killings of the Christians started in the areas adjacent to Russia and gradually started to threaten us.

***

In the village of Chelek [Çelik] lived Agha Mustafa Rammo, who went to the nearby Chaldean village of Meshte [Meşti], where he gathered 30 families to kill them so that the village would be his. The Christian village was situated on the banks of a river and the soil was fertile. The Syriac Orthodox Bishop Antimos Ya'qub of Kfar-Boran went to Chelek to rescue the Christians from death. The government was not the key actor at that time; rather the Kurdish Aghas were the ones with the real power. The bishop went to Mustafa Rammo and demanded to have the Christians back. He took the Christians with him to Kfar-Boran. There Isa Asmar's palace was empty at the time, so the families could stay there. News of the imminent attacks on the Christians grew by the day. The aghas became greedier and greedier, and they were preparing to attack the Christians, seizing the land and taking their belongings and their families. Shortly after that, the Turkish forces and their Kurdish allies began to kill Christians at random wherever they could find them. The 30 families in the above-mentioned palace died too.

The leader of the Syriac Orthodox, Brahim Sham'un, and Bishop Antimos Ya'qub went to the local administrator to seek refuge. That official liked Brahim Sham'un and wanted to help him. He told him that he could save only him but not the bishop, as the latter had exchanged harsh words with the agha, who was reluctant to let him go free. The government had little influence compared to the power of the aghas. Brahim Sham'un insisted on keeping the company of the bishop and not giving him as easy prey to the Kurds. Brahim Sham'un had many Kurdish friends in Kfar-Boran who took his family to Khalila and then to Baseqel. The local official hid the two men in the town hall. Mustafa Rammo, the Kurdish agha, came to Kfar-Boran and asked if there was anything left to be taken. The answer was that it was already plundered. Mustafa Rammo was standing in front of the Church of Mor Gorgis and was preparing to go back home. There stood the Kurd Faqqa Shahin, a wicked man who was a fanatic Muslim. He had killed many Christians and was a very despicable figure. He stopped the agha, saying metaphorically that "the snake had lost her tail but not the head," implying Brahim Sham'un and the bishop, who were hiding at the town hall. The agha went there and asked the local administrator to hand over the two men and especially the bishop.

The local administrator told Brahim Sham'un to save himself and give up the bishop to the waiting agha. Brahim Sham'un refused. So both men went out and saw the Kurds waiting to seize them. They feared torture, so they asked the local administrator to help them die in a dignified manner, to have the soldiers adjust the bayonets of their rifles vertically. The two men jumped from the roof onto the sharp bayonets and died at once. The agha and his men searched the village of Kfar-Boran looking for survivors. They killed many and took the small boys to be their servants.

***

Sergeant Tawfiq summoned my father and told him to find himself a safe place because he could neither defend him nor guarantee his safety. My father wanted to go to Hah, and Tawfiq promised to help him. My father asked him for two Kurdish escorts. Khalile Qaqati and Slaymane Hoski swore to help him. My father, Isa Polos, and my mother prepared to go to Hah with the two Kurds protecting them. Upon approaching Hah, my father told the two men to leave them, as there was exchange of fire in the area surrounding Hah. My father, Isa, started to sing in [Neo-West] Syriac that he was one of them so that the Christians in the palace of Hah would get the message to open the doors for him.

> *Ftahulli u tarco*
> *D cubarno*
> *Eno felan ha'no*
> *Kathino d cubarno*
> *De ftahulli ftahulli u qusro*

"Open the port, I want to get in. I'm the renowned, I want to come in. Hurry up, let me into the Castle!"

He went up to the palace and fired some shots in the air while producing sounds of joy as a signal for the two men that he had arrived safely. My father, Isa, stayed there, but there was not enough water or food in the palace, so at night they went to the wells in the houses surrounding the palace to fetch water.

Between the village of Hah and the village of Shterako [Heşterek] there was a valley named Valley of Doves [*Shalwo da Yawne*]. It was full of barley. Men used to go there to cut it and put it in parcels to be taken to the palace to be cooked as a kind of soup. The situation worsened by the day, so Isa told my mother to prepare to leave. He had a Greek rifle and 87 bullets, and he taught my mother how to use it. They went to 'Ayn-Wardo by crossing the mountains, and there he met most of Tur Abdin's people.

E. KFAR-GAWZE (Karjos; northwest of Midyat, 20 km)

43. Hanna Bitar

This happened in the Sayfo of 1895. My grandparents belonged to the family Sawme Hadodo. My mother went to Kfarze to see her parents. In Kfar-Gawze in her family's house there was a Kurd named Abdeke, who lived with them and treated them well. Abdeke, together with other Kurds, killed my grandparents on their way to Kfar-Gawze. They also killed three people from the family of Maqadese [from Mardin] who were with them. They killed them with daggers and threw their bodies into the wells.

***

Before Sayfo, Agha Yusuf summoned the heads of the Kurdish villages surrounding Kfar-Gawze to meet a Kurdish religious shaykh at his place. The religious shaykh adressed the aghas and told them that the Turkish government had issued a decree to get rid of all the Christians in this area. He asked them to vow to comply with the wish of the government and eradicate the Christians.

My uncle Sa'ido, of the family of Na'alband, was at Yusuf Agha's house shoeing the horses. When he heard what the Kurds agreed upon, he stopped working, went home, took his family and me too, and headed for Midyat. There my uncle Sa'ido went to see Galle Hermez and told him about what he heard in Kfar-Gawze. The next day the government announced a curfew in Midyat. Turkish forces spread throughout Midyat gathering the leaders of the Protestant families and putting them in prison. My father, Brahim, told his cousin Sa´ido to take the children and leave for Rayete. There we had a Yezidi friend called Hantushko who helped us to reach Arkah [Kharabale] and after that Mor-Malke, where we stayed for three months. In Mor-Malke we met Bishop Samuel, who came from Midyat and stayed in Mar Sharbel. The bishop died of old age and cold weather.

***

The shaykh [in Kfar-Gawze] said that the Turkish pashas issued a decree that the Christians must die and from a religious point of view it was legitimate to kill them. Anyone who killed Christians would be rewarded because he was consolidating Islam and Muslims. In consequence, the aghas and their men went out to plunder and kill Christians without any moral scruples whatsoever. The Turkish government didn't bother to arm the Kurds; referring to some religious texts was enough to inflame the Kurds. Greed was a factor, and the Kurds wanted to prove that they were good, obedient allies to the Turkish state. Thousands of Christians died at the hands of the Kurds, who emptied many villages and left them deserted. One day, a Kurd got 10.000 golden liras from plundering a group of Christians. Another got a beautiful Christian girl.[8]

***

After peace returned in 'Ayn-Wardo, we were the first to arrrive in Midyat. There we saw how the Kurds were selling the Christians' belongings in the caravanserai of Musa-Shamosho. My father bought from them some necessary items for us. The kaymakam knew my father, Brahim, and told him to go to Anhel and to order the [West] Syriac leader Besso to obey the Turkish

---

[8] See also the Kurdish poet Cigerxwin, *Jinenenigariyamin* [translation] (1995), 46. He was born in Kfar-Gawze and was an eyewitness.

state. My father did that. On his way back, the Kurds from the village of Kfar-Shoma' took his money and nearly beat him to death. However, he was able to get back to Midyat, where he met the kaymakam and told him what happened to him. Soon after that, my father died and I became an orphan.

44. Brahim Maqsi-Musa

Sayfo started at the end of July 1915 in Kfar-Gawze. Part of our [Chaldean] family was still staying in Kfar-Gawze. But many of them lived in Midyat. In Kfar-Gawze, Sayfo started with the arrests of men. From our family they took 45 men. My father, Hanna, and his two brothers, Abdelkarim and Mikhayel Maqsi-Musa, escaped to the mountains. My uncle Resqo was chained together with his three sons, Ne'man, Gorgis, and Hermez. They were taken with other Christians to a place called Zaghore on the way to 'Ayn-Tal'a, where they were killed. They were about to kill the women and children but as it was sunset they decided to postpone the killings until the next day.

The next day, Shaykh Fathallah came from 'Ayn-Wardo to Kfar-Gawze. Kfar-Gawze was adjacent to 'Ayn-Kifo. There was a Kurdish woman called Fatem who took pity on the Christians. When she heard that Shaykh Fathallah was in the village, she went to the remaining hostages, who were expecting death, and told them that she would bring the benevolent Shaykh Fathallah. She told the Christians that when the Shaykh passed by, they should attract his attention by crying and pleading for help. Fatem went to Shaykh Fathallah, who was riding a horse. She approached him and kissed his hand. He asked her the direction to Yusuf Agha's house. Fatem agreed to show him the way. She took him to where the Christian hostages were. There he heard the people crying and begging for water, since it was hot. He asked Fatem about these people, and she told him the whole story. Shaykh Fathallah was angry with Yusuf Agha because the Christians were productive people, supporting the agha and his people. Shaykh Fathallah dismounted and pitched a tent and stayed there. Some people went to Yusuf Agha and told him that Shaykh Fathallah was in the area. Yusuf Agha went to see him and asked him to stay with him. Shaykh Fathallah discussed with him the brutal way he had treated and killed the Christians. Agha Yusuf had no answer. Yusuf Agha told him that the local administrator in Hasno, Jalal Rumi, was to blame because he instigated the mischief. Yusuf Agha told him how Jalal Rumi told the aghas about the decree after coming back from Omid [Diyarbekir].

Yusuf Agha showed som repentence. Shaykh Fathallah ordered him to take care of the women and children until they could be reunited with their families. Yusuf Agha had two brothers, Hajji Osman Agha and Nuri Agha, and they were ordered to take care of the detained Christians.

***

At that time, Shaykh Ahmad Agha from Owena participated in the battle for 'Ayn-Wardo. He came to pay Yusuf Agha a visit. There he saw how women and children were serving in the house. A [Chaldean] girl named Warde caught his eye. Yusuf Agha told him that these were Christians and revealed the whole story. Shaykh Ahmad Agha told Yusuf Agha in Kurdish that he desired Warde for himself. Yusuf Agha told him that he would give him one or two of his daughters but not Warde, since the girl was his hostage and doing that would smear his reputation. Shaykh Ahmad Agha left angrily.

***

In Kfar-Gawze, there was a Kurdish field guard named Heso Taqe who was the father of Bero Asso [Brahim Chawish] from Midyat. This man helped all the Christians who could make it to the mountains by hiding them in the vineyards. He told the hiding Christians to be on their guard when he shouted at the top of his voice, "Who are you?" This indicated there was some sort of danger somewhere. He was thus able to help many Christians. My father, Hanna, hid in the mountains after Yusuf Agha took his cattle. One night he snuck into Hajji Osman's house. He climbed to the roof of the house, where the agha's family was sleeping since it was hot at that time of year. The agha had a little baby, so my father, Hanna, pinched him to attract attention. His intention was to awake the family by the cries of the baby. The mother woke up and recognized him. He wanted her to wake up her husband to accompany him to Aqabe, a linking point between Kfar-Gawze and Midyat. The agha agreed to accompany him to the village of Derendeb. The agha advised him in Kurdish to avoid the high roads and travel through fields and mountains to avoid attention. if he saw somebody passing by, he should sit down and keep a low profile. My father, Hanna, heeded the agha's advice and arrived safely in Anhel.

He heard the Syriac guards near Anhel whistling to each other upon hearing him approaching. They asked him his identity and he told them in [Neo-West] Syriac that he was Syriac and intended to visit his two brothers, Abdelkarim and Mikhayel Maqsi-Musa. After getting permission from Besso, the leader of the Syriacs at that time, my brother Abdelkarim let him in. Hanna entered Anhel and saw how Mikhayel was suffering from typhus.

Many people died of this disease. However, my brother got better after a while and went with Abdelkarim to 'Ayn-Wardo.

F. KAFRO-ELAYTO (northwest of Midyat, 12 km)

45. Ello 'Amno

My daughter's father-in-law, Barsawmo Gharib, came from Upper Kafro. He told me he was 10 years old during the time of Sayfo. The Kurds took them hostage together with many Christians. We had a Kurdish friend at that time called Darbaso who took them outside the village to help them escape from certain death. With them went two monks. On their way out of the village they met a Kurdish force that wanted to kill them. But Darbaso stepped between them and told them they had to kill him first. The Kurds told him that, being a Kurd, he shouldn't sacrifice himself for the sake of Christians. Darbaso refused again. The Kurds demanded the two monks. Darbaso refused again, but the monks decided to sacrifice themselves to ensure the safety of the group. The two monks, dressed in black, voluntarily went to the Kurds, and they were killed on the spot. They saw some mysterious lights coming down on the two bodies. The Kurds, however, stated that it was fire coming from above to burn them.

46. Brahim Maqsi-Musa

Armun is a village that lies behind Kfar-Gawze. It contained 10 [West] Syriac houses. During Sayfo, the Kurds killed all the men. They took the women and children to work as slaves. In September, when they needed fire to boil the grains, especially bulgur, they would use the Christian women as fuel.

The local administrator in Hasno was Jalal Rumi, who was a Muhallemi from Mardin.[9] He hated Christians and Christianty and was their declared enemy. In Hasno there were 500 houses, [West] Syriac, Armenian, and Chaldean. He mercilessly killed all of them. After Sayfo, and due to old age, he became a pensioner. One day he went to the public bath. As usual the floor there was wet, and people wore wooden sandals. Jalal Rumi had to go to the toilet wearing the wooden sandals, he fell down, broke his neck, and died there, and nobody could help him at the time.

---

[9] He was a member of the Mardin CUP.

G. KFARZE (northeast of Midyat, 15 km)

47. Hanna Mure

We had four Turkish soldiers stationed in our village at the time. Two of them stayed at Danho's and the other two at Skandar's [the priest Aziz Beth-Khawaja-Gunel's father]. These two Christian men were revered and regarded as the leaders of the [West] Syriacs. When they heard what was happening to the Christians in Midyat, Danho suggested to Skandar that they take the soldiers' rifles and flee to 'Ayn-Wardo. Skandar refused to do that, as he believed the Syriacs were safe and no harm would come to them. The next day, the Kurds came to them and told the Christians to leave or they might be hurt.

***

The aghas in our village who participated in the killings are the following: Hasan and Hus'ayn from the family of Ismailo, Hado from the family of Hamke, and a lame agha named Muhammad Saleh. These were originally not from Kfarze, but the Syriacs brought them to live among them to protect them from the other Kurds and Muslims. Gradually the aghas took over and dominated the village. After a while, the agha warned the Syriacs that a group of Kurds and other Muslims intended to come and attack Kfarze. They claimed that it would be difficult for them to defend the Syriacs. In consequence, a considerable group of Syriacs headed for 'Ayn-Wardo, but the others preferred to take the risk and stayed. Those who stayed in Kfarze suffered very much; men were first gathered and killed. Danho, the Syriac leader, was taken hostage with his wife and children. The children were killed in front of their parents, and then Danho and his wife were killed and thrown into the wells.

The remaining 72 were taken to Kfarze, where they were enslaved to some prominent aghas. There was another village adjacent to Kafsange called Dermuske, headed by Sayyid Khalil, who had seven Christians to work for him as slaves and shepherds. The Muslims destroyed the Church Mor 'Uzoziyel and killed the Christian men. There was a Christian man called Gorgis who converted to Islam and took the name Murado; this man participated in the destruction of the Church's walls and valuables. After Sayfo, Murado did not convert back to Christianity.[10] His family, three sons, a daughter, and his wife, remained Muslims. When Syriacs started returning to the village, the man remained Muslim while the rest of the family con-

---

[10] He remained Muslim until 1941 when he was on his deathbed.

verted back to Christianity. When the wife went to the priest Yuhanun to take Holy Communion, the priest refused, saying that it was inappropriate because her husband was Muslim. He consulted Bishop Tuma in Midyat. The wife got permission and continued to be a Christian wife to a Muslim husband.

***

The [West] Syriac hostages from Kfarze served the Muslims for three months. The other Syriacs at 'Ayn-Wardo wanted to help their people. They knew they were in the villages of Kafsange and Dermuske and that the Kurds refused to release them. They called for a meeting and decided to attack the four houses in Dermuske to free the hostages. They planned to take hostages from the Kurdish side, and maybe some of their animals, to be used for bargaining, to liberate the rest of the Syriacs in Kfarze. They eventually asked the help of Mas'ud in putting the plan into action, for fear that the hostages might be killed. Mas'ud agreed. At night they went to the village of Dermuske and took a Kurd called Abdo, his sister, and his wife as hostages. His wife was the sister of the agha Abdurrahman Khallo from the family of Ismailo. The plan was successful; the Kurds and the Syriacs exchanged hostages, and that is how the Syriac hostages were liberated and then went to 'Ayn-Wardo.

Among the 72 hostages in Kafsange was a 12-year-old boy named Gallo Qacho who told how they were taken from Kafsange to Kfarze to be killed. The aghas in Kfarze demanded it. On the way they passed a valley [Gubo das Safrune] between Kafsange and Kfarze, and there they halted to be killed. A Kurd called Yusufe Zurek who had killed many Syriacs began to chain them together and told them that he would experiment to see how many could be killed with one bullet. At that moment Abdurrahman Agha appeared and told Yusufe Zurek to stop.

***

In Sayfo time, Maryam [Merame], a married [West] Syriac woman with a child, was abducted by a Kurd named Tayyip [Tayyupko]. After three months, Maryam and Tayyip's first wife left the village to bathe in the river. Maryam had a plan to escape: she put lots of soap on the first wife's head and eyes. She took her daughter and escaped to 'Ayn-Wardo. The Kurdish woman washed herself and notified Tayyip. Maryam climbed the mountain of Kefsure near 'Ayn-Wardo, and the Kurd was following her. As Maryam realized that she wouldn't be able to make it carrying her daughter, she left the child somewhere on the mountain and ran. Tayyip, who was following her, stabbed the daughter and put her on the tip of the dagger and told

Maryam that this would be her destiny if she didn't stop. Maryam ran and started to call to the people at the Strategic Fig Point [*Kozeke dat Tene*] in 'Ayn-Wardo to help her. Thus she was saved.

***

The Syriacs who sought refuge in 'Ayn-Wardo stayed there for seven years. They then returned to Midyat and the other villages. Seven years after Sayfo, and after the Kurdish agha Chalabiyo was released from prison, many Christians were able to get their houses and property back.

H. BOTE (northeast of Midyat, 9 km)

48. Malke Gares (b. 1932), interviewed December 1999

In 1914, my father, Gares, was mobilized. He was taken with my uncle Shabo, who failed to come back. My father returned together with seven other men; among them were men called Hawsho and Yawsef. They went on foot, crossing the mountains until they arrived safely at the village. The Kurdish agha in our village, named Saleh, brought some 40 Turkish soldiers and stayed in the Chaldean church.[11] Hawsho suggested giving them some food, and while they were eating, they would steal their rifles, kill them, and hide in the Church of Mor Afrem. The priest Galluno wanted to discuss the situation with the Kurdish agha Saleh. The agha calmed him down, saying that the soldiers were for the safety of the Christians. Next day the soldiers killed most of the men in the village. Women and children sought refuge in the church. Some Christians fled the village heading for 'Ayn-Wardo. The church was full, with about 300 people staying there; 60 of them were children.

49. Brahim Maqsi-Musa

The Kurds put the village under seige and started shooting. They came to the churchyard. They brought some musicians who provocatively played songs of death. Inside the church, Hawsho was saddened by the music heralding their imminent death, so he took his dagger and snuck out of the church. Hawsho killed the musician and fled quickly and disappeared. The soldiers failed to capture him. Hawsho went to 'Ayn-Wardo.

---

[11] In Tur Abdin it was normal for Syriac Orthodox to refer to Syriac Catholics as Chaldeans.

50. Yawsef Babo-Rhawi

The Rhawi family was in 'Ayn-Wardo. News came to 'Ayn-Wardo that the village of Bote was being threatened by the Kurds. The people there had no food and feared for their lives. There were five from the Rhawi family, among them my cousins Selo, Hanna, and Tuma and my uncles Makko and Barsawmo. These men went with other volunteers from 'Ayn-Wardo to help the people in Bote. There they were able to free some Christians.

51. Malke Gares

Kurds from the Rama tribe took many children with them. Among them were my uncles Malke and Aziz. From the Sayidko family they took Ya'qo and Murad. From the Mirza family they took Ya'qo and many others. My aunt Maryam was made Muslim. My father, Gares, told me how they walked across dead bodies on their way out of the church to be taken by the Kurds. Some of them stayed there for more than ten years.

52. 'Abdo Yuhanun (1922–2003), interviewed December 1999

Many people from our family lost their lives in Sayfo. My mother, Basna, was in the church with the hostages. She told me how the Kurdish Saleh Agha took 60 persons out of the church and promised not to kill them. She said that her family refused to go out, refusing to trust Saleh Agha, as they were not on good terms with him. Saleh Agha sent a message to the neighboring Kurdish agha, Hajji Abdalla-Sabri in 'Arnas, to help him persuade them to go out. Hajji Abdalla-Sabri Agha from 'Arnas complied with his wish. When the Christians went out, they were taken directly to a cave called Zerqe between Bote and 'Arnas and shot at. The Christian hostages were hit and died. My mother, however, survived despite the nine bullets fired at her. She was hit but her wounds were not fatal. She crawled to the entrance of the cave and waited there for help. A Kurdish farmer called Mahmude Shahin took her to his house in 'Arnas after that.

***

The people who fled from Bote to 'Ayn-Wardo stayed there for seven years, and I was born in 'Ayn-Wardo. Some of our people went to Astal, west of Midyat, to seek work. The Kurdish Agha Saleh heard about them and asked them to return to Bote, promising that he would help them regain their lost property. They didn't trust him and refused to comply with his wish. My father, Yawsef, told me that Saleh was a Dakshuri, one of a group of Kurds who were known for their hatred and intolerance of Christians. The Heverki {Haverkan] Kurds, on the other hand, used to be friends with the Christians. Saleh went to Chalabiyo and Brahime Ismail in Kfar-Gawze and told them that the Christians who fled Bote refused to come back and asked for their help. Chalabiyo went to Astal [probably a mistake for Anhel] and met the Christians and urged them to return, but they refused due to the suffering inflicted on them by Saleh. Chalabiyo himself gave them guarantees that he would be responsible for their safety. The [East and West] Syriacs returned. In fact, the reason Saleh wanted the Syriacs back was that the supplies the Kurds took from Christians during Sayfo were running out and, being incapable of producing such things themselves, the Kurds wanted the Christians back to work and produce for them again. Saleh had a cousin who imposed a tax on every Christian who came back, the payment of 10 majidi [a silver coin worth 20 piasters].

My father, Yawsef, used to weave clothes and other things together with a [West] Syriac companion. One day, on his way home to eat lunch, my father met Saleh's cousin, who summoned him and demanded that he pay the tax. My father told him that he was a newcomer and hadn't established himself yet. Saleh's cousin hit him and kicked him until he couldn't stand up, then looked around to find a stone to kill him. A Kurdish woman called Halimke, from the village of Bahware, prevented him from doing that and, thanks to her, my father survived.

53. Murad Maqsi-Murad (1925–1998), interviewed October 1993

In the Sayfo of 1895 in Omid [Diyarbekir] and the villages surrounding it, the Kurd Shaykh Sa'id, aided and abetted by the Turkish forces, worked to kill many Christians: Armenians, Chaldeans, and Syriacs. Some of our Chaldean relatives fled to Midyat as a result.

***

In 1914, at the time of mobilization, two of my uncles were taken, and neither returned. The next year, my uncle Brahim was killed on the way to Talat, and they threw his body into a well. My uncle Ne'man was arrested while he was with the family of [West Syriac Protestant] Polos by four Kurds, who placed a big stone over his face and hit the big stone with smaller stones until he died. As was their custom, they disposed of the body by throwing it into a well.

***

My grandfather Yawsef, my uncle Musa, and his wife Sette were killed during the time of Sayfo in Bote. From our family, a man called Hermez was killed in a terrible way. The two Kurdish Aghas, Najo and Abdallako from 'Arnas near Bote, took the children that were in the Church of Mor Afrem to the roof of the church to be killed by throwing them headlong onto the stony ground of the church. After that, the Kurds went after Syriacs hiding in caves, wells, and cellars of houses. Abdallako, the Kurdish Agha, saw my aunt in a well. He liked her and took her to his house.

I. 'URNES ('Arnas; north of Midyat, 9 km)

54. 'Abdo Ghanno-Gawweke

Najo, the Kurdish agha, came from the family of Tammero. When he was a young boy, the [West] Syriacs took care of him, feeding him, and he lived among them. During the time of Sayfo, Najo attacked the very household where he was brought up. When the lady of the house reminded him of this, his answer was, "Yesterday is yesterday and today is today." Najo was a cruel man and turned against all Christians. Killing a Christian was something very easy for him. Many boys lost their parents and became orphans and came to Midyat to live there. Najo took many Syriac women to work for him as slaves after killing their husbands, fathers, and brothers. The women whom he no longer found desirable would be given to his men or be killed. Five years after Sayfo, while he was traveling in a caravan, bandits attacked him and his company. They took their belongings and killed them.

55. Gawriye Beth-Mas'ud

As a result of the turmoil and chaos that prevailed, some of the [Orthodox] Syriacs fled from 'Arnas to 'Ayn-Wardo. Others sought refuge in the Church of Mor Quryaqos. Only a few continued their occupations on the outskirts of the village. The cruel and merciless Agha Saleh [the lawyer Abdullah Timur´s father] asked a Syriac man named Ya'qo to go and ask the Christians to come back. To make his promises solemn, he swore that he would "sleep with Fatima [the daughter of Muhammad] on the back of a pig" before harming any Christian who came back to the village. Ya'qo was moved by the oath and brought the Syriacs back; 38 men returned. First the Kurds took all the weapons the men had on them. Then they were chained and dragged to the cave of Fero (which is located in a triangle connecting the three villages of 'Arnas, Bote, and Ahlah). In the cave the Kurds put out their eyes and severed their arms and opened their bellies, and the poor men suffered a slow and horrible death.

J. SALEH (north of Midyat, 8 km)

56. Use Malke-Sahyo (b. 1931), interviewed July 1995

My father was named Abdalla. Before Sayfo he went to Nisibin to the village of Sha'bane to hide from military service. There he worked as a farmer, chopping wood to sell to the Germans, who had a military base in the area. My uncle Use [Yawsef] was a chief figure [mukhtar] before Sayfo in Saleh, and the government killed him by having him beaten to death in front of the villagers.

***

In 1915, my father, Abdalla, worked for a Kurdish agha who demanded that he and other Syriacs become Muslims or face death. He didn't kill them, but he made them change their names and take Muslim names instead. And they survived after doing that.

***

In Tur Abdin, the killings officially started in Saleh. My father himself witnessed how the Muslims killed Armenians and Christians at random and on a large scale. He sent his mother to Saleh to tell the [Orthodox] Syriacs to run away; otherwise, they would face the same terrible fate. She came to Saleh and warned the Christians, but they didn't heed her advice for fear of losing their properties. While my mother was still in the village, two Syriac men, Filo and Isa, were attacked by Kurds, who first took their rifles and then killed them. After this incident, the Kurds stormed the village and killed all the Syriacs they met in their way. Other Syriacs fled to 'Ayn-Wardo, Bote, and Midyat. The Kurds who perpetrated the killings were the following: Hassano, the chief of Saleh, who initiated and instigated the killings; Saykho; Hajji Selo; Hajji Ali; Ismaile Mahmude; and Osmane Mahmude. The Turkish government gave the houses deserted by the Christians to Muslim immigrants whom Russia displaced at that time.

***

In 1916, my father, Abdalla, came back to Saleh after Sayfo and asked the Kurds to give back our property and help us return. One Kurdish leader, Brahimke Murado, answered contemptuously that we wouldn't get back our houses but we could live in the ruins of the village. My father accepted that and told him he would return to the ruins, and one day perhaps he would take revenge on him. In Midyat he was greeted by the people of Saleh, who advised him to return to Saleh in spite of the reluctance of the Kurds. Abdalla indeed went back with some [West] Syriacs. In 1917, the Kurds and Syriacs had a conflict because Syriacs reclaimed some of their property. Gradually the Syriacs were able to reestablish themselves in the village, and many Syriacs returned to the village. In 1918, another conflict broke out between the Kurds and Syriacs, and 33 men were killed on both sides. My father, Abdalla, captured Brahime Murado in the conflict and killed him in the ruins.

K. HABSES (northwest of Midyat, 7 km)

57. Skandar Sha'o-Murad (b. 1931), interviewed July 1993

In Habses, the old people told me the following about the mobilization that took place in 1914. My uncle Antar was summoned to military service but failed to come back. My mother, Farida, and her mother, Khatune, told me the following about the Sayfo of 1915. Before Sayfo, the Kurdish tribe of Rama attacked Habses, and a terrible conflict took place between the Syriacs and the Kurds. As a result, two Kurds died and the Kurds withdrew.

***

Azizke Mahmado, the Kurdish agha [of Midyat], had a shepherd. While on the mountain of Qroho near Habses, the shepherd was able to call to his people and warn them that the massacres had started in Midyat. The people of Habses met and discussed the necessity of leaving Habses as soon as possible. My uncle Gawriye suggested getting rid of the four Muslim families to ensure the safety of those who intended to stay in Habses. Many [West] Syriacs from Habses left their village, heading for 'Ayn-Wardo. My grandparents, who were old and wanted to stay, were killed and thrown into a well.

L. BASIBRIN (east of Midyat, 37 km)

58. Gawriye Beth-Mas'ud

Sarokhano`, the Kurdish agha, came to Basibrin\f "v" on his way back from 'Ayn-Wardo. He wanted to meet the family of Haydo, a prominent [West] Syriac family. He met with Malke Haydo even though they were not on good terms with each other.[12] Sarokhano told Malke Haydo that the Christians should not trust the Turkish government and its promises. He confirmed that the situation was such that the government's goal was to kill all the Christians who were in the hands of Muslims. It was not a matter of

---

[12] The cause of enmity was that Chalabiyo and Sarohano were involved in the killing of Malke Haydo's father before the war.

conflicts among different tribes any more; it was a war of religions. It was very possible, he added, that Christians might be killed by their own friends and neighbors. The Turkish government employed a shrewd plan by stirring up the Muslims and their aggressive religious instincts to fight the Christians in 'Ayn-Wardo. He said that he had a strong tribe and that he did not fear attacks. But in case other tribes wanted to cause harm and mischief, Sarokhano swore to save Basibrin. If the Kurds and the Turks succeeded in defeating the Christians in 'Ayn-Wardo, the possiblitity of helping Basibrin would be rather slim. He advised the Syriacs to defend themselves and that he would provide them with grain and other supplies needed to stay strong and defend themselves. He left 200 men to protect the village, and these would stay on the outskirts of the village. Malke Haydo didn't like these insinuations and suggestions, and Sarokhano left angrily.

In the Church of Mor Dodo in Basibrin, there was a Turkish Jandarma station. The sergeant there tried to attack a [West] Syriac woman. Malke Haydo killed the sergeant and then sought refuge in the Church of Mor Dodo. This prompted a terrible attack on Mor Dodo from all the Muslims in the area. They went onto the roof of the church and threw some burning dry grass into the church. When the doors of the church opened at last, a Muslim friend of Malke Haydo, [Imam] Malla Taher, took a dagger and stabbed him fatally. The army and the Kurds entered the village and assured the people that if they left their houses, they wouldn't be harmed. The people believed them when they heard them swearing by their prophet Muhammad. When the Syriacs went out, the Kurds and the Turks killed all the males and took the women and children to be distributed among them.

M. ANHEL (south of Midyat, 10 km)

59. 'Abdo Ghanno-Gawweke

We stayed in Anhel for four years. Azizke, the agha of Midyat, wouldn't allow the Turkish forces or the Kurds from other tribes to enter Anhel. There were armed guards protecting Anhel constantly. Nobody was allowed to enter the village of Anhel without a thorough search. Many people found it a safe haven. Many wounded and sick sought refuge in Anhel, and this led to the spread of disease, so many people died. Women and girls who had lost their parents and husbands were another problem. The [West] Syriac leader in Anhel, Besso, decided to solve this particular problem by gathering all the people in the village center. Besso addressed the men who were widowers or bachelors and asked them to choose a wife. Many marriages took place, and one problem was solved.

Many people in Anhel would smuggle salt, food, and weapons to the Christians in 'Ayn-Wardo so that they could keep up their resistance.

60. Ello 'Amno

Anhel was a refuge for many people. In our house we had two families [from Midyat] staying with us. A year after Sayfo, the Muslims in the Kurdish village of Daline plotted to kill people from Anhel. One day, the Kurds came to the Syriac Christians of Anhel and told them that somebody was stealing their cows while they were grazing in the mountains. Many men went to check this out. They searched the whole area [Qusro dah Hermeza] but didn't find anything. They realized that this was a trick played on them by the Kurds. On their way home, the Kurds ambushed them and killed 40 men. Among those killed were the following: Sohdo Afqede, Sa'do, Bahe, and Isho. My uncle Antar tried to shoot back with his Greek rifle but it failed to fire, so he fled to the mountains only to be captured by Muhallemi, who killed him and threw his corpse down from the mountain. The shepherds found his dead body and my mother went to collect his bones and buried him properly.

N. Mor Awgin (northeast of Nsibin, 30 km)

61. Eliyo Gares (b. 1928), interviewed January 1999

A [West Syriac] monk called Lahdo told me the following story.

After Sayfo, the Turkish government issued a decree expelling the Christians. The Kurds filed some complaints against me and another priest, and as a result the government escorted the two of us outside Nisibin. There we were obliged to take off our clothes and walk toward the mountain. I told the priest that we must find a way to run away before we met a certain death. He refused and was killed, but I made it up the mountain. I came to the little Nawale River. As I couldn't swim, I started to pray to God to help me cross the river. I threw myself into the river and found myself safe on the other side. I wandered naked until I arrived at the village of Dera-Chomara, adjacent to Kartwe, on top of a mountain. I knew a Kurd there so I went to him, knocked on the door, and asked for some clothes. I came in and told him my story.

***

I heard another story from a person who experienced remarkable events in the village of Rayete. I was told that, thanks to the Kurdish agha Sarokhano, the village was preserved intact. In 1914, the Turkish army took me at mobilization. The officers saw that I was rather short, so they rejected me and put me aside and I was forgotten. However, I was able to witness how the others were killed on the way. I escaped to the mountains and was able to find my way back to my village. But I didn't dare enter it, for fear that the army would take me again to send me off to war. Instead I went to Sarokhano's village of Mar-Bobo, and I was welcomed there and could see for myself how many Christians sought refuge there. I saw that Sarokhano was ordered to get rid of the Christians. Sarokhano didn't comply with that wish. The Turkish government sent Qaddur Bey to Sarokhano to threaten him. Sarokhano had to do something. He sent his men to the Syriac Christians of Rayete and told them to prepare themselves, as an attack on them was imminent. He sent some men to help the Syriacs. Qaddur Bey [leader of the Al-Khamsin militia] and his men took hostages while Sarokhano surrounded Mount Izlo and set fires all around the mountain to enable them to see, as it was night. Qaddur Bey asked Sarokhano to launch an attack on the Christians. Sarokhano asked him to wait until daylight, but Qaddur Bey insisted on attacking the Syriacs as soon as possible. The Syriacs resisted bravely with many fatalities on the Turkish side. Hence, Rayete was saved from the atrocities of Sayfo.

62. Shaq Galle (b. 1938), interviewed August 2003

There was a Chaldean called Isa Hakim living in our village. He was from the village of Basa in Bohtan. He told me the following. He said that 15 men armed themselves and went to the mountains. Their task was to help the wounded and the hostages fleeing from the caravans of death—the Christians taken by the Kurds and Turks to be killed. We got information from them about the whereabouts of the officers who tortured the Christians and indeed we found some of these murderers and killed them. We had no food or water, so we would steal some from the surrounding villages. One day we went to the village of M'are, where there was a well in the Church of Yoldath Aloho [Mother of God]. We were shocked to see piles of corpses in it. Now this well is called the "well of death." When we heard some sounds coming from the well, we were afraid. Then one of us went down to see where the sounds were coming from. To his shock and surprise, the man found his own son alive among the dead bodies. The son told his father how the Imam in the village of Sheweshke killed many [East and West Syriac] Christians and took him to be his son. Then he changed his mind and threw the little boy into the well and left him to die. The father decided to go to Sheweshke and take revenge on the Imam. So the father and his companions went to the village of Sheweshke. They stood by the lake on the outskirts of the village. They saw some people spending the night outside the village. They came nearer and saw that the Imam and his family were there. Some of the men took their daggers and attacked the Imam and his family and killed them.

O. MOR-MALKE (southeast of Midyat, 20 km)

63. Hanna Bitar

This happened before peace was negotiated in 'Ayn-Wardo [November 1915]. A [West Syriac] monk from Mardin, accompanied by Turkish forces, came to Mor-Malke. The [West] Syriac leader Sham'un Hanne ordered the people to be prepared. He wanted to put on a show of force to impress the Turks that the village was armed and ready to fight. He told the men to go up to the roofs of the houses with their rifles, and those who had no weapons at all would use sticks that looked like rifles. The monk addressed the Christian people to calm their fears, saying that they need not fear because the Christians of Mardin were all sound and well. The Syriacs sensed some sort of foul play and decided not to heed his words. It turned out later that he wasn't a monk at all, but a deceitful man. The monk tried to assure them. The people refused to listen, and the monk and the Turkish forces withdrew.

64. Karmo Salma-Gawwo

Mor-Malke was attacked again by the Kurdish tribe Hajo, supported by 35 Turkish soldiers. An exchange of fire broke out. The Syriacs were able to defend themselves and capture many Kurds and Turks. Sarokhano, the Kurdish agha, was informed about the situation and was asked to give his advice about the captured Hajo. Sarokhano advised the Syriacs not to kill the hostages, as that would inflame the feelings of hatred and revenge even more. Among the Turkish forces there was a Syriac who was a doctor doing his military service. His name was Salim Bakoz [from Mardin], and he was captured by the Syriacs of Mor-Malke. The Syriac officer told them that he lived in Midyat and that he had no intention of going back to military service. He asked them to spare his life, as he could help them take care of the wounded. The Syriac leader in the village of Musa Asso was contacted, and he gave his permission for the Syriac doctor to stay in the village.

P. M'ARE (northeast of Nisibin, 20 km)

65. Gawriye Beth-Mas'ud

My grandparents lived in the village of M'are. They were rich. The children suggested to their parents that they move to the region of Rayete, to Badebbe near Mor-Malke, to avoid being killed. Their father assured them that he was given the word of honor of the Kurdish agha, Hajji Yusuf, that no harm would come to them. Yusuf swore that he would sleep with Fatima [the daughter of Muhammad] in Ramadan on the skin of a pig before any harm would happen to the Christians there. The children decided to leave. They took some animals and food and headed for Badebbe. In the morning, the Kurdish agha, Hajji Yusuf, gathered the [West] Syriacs and chained them and butchered them like animals. The Kurdish agha, Hajji Yusuf, himself went and sought out the butchered body of the Syriac priest Qasho Yawsef. He took some of his blood and wiped his chest with it in a very sadistic manner. He did all of that in spite of the vows he swore that the Christians would be safe and protected.

Q. MIZIZAH (southeast of Midyat, 7 km)

66. Lahdo Musa-Malaka

In 1914, the Turkish government picked six men to join the war against Russia. Only a few were able to survive, such as Hanne Safarko, his brother Stayfo, and Sha'o Hanne. With them they had a companion who was lost on the way back. When I was a young man, these two men who managed to survive told us how they were taken to Hasan-Qal'a [a large fortress outside Erzurum]. They swallowed their gold liras for fear of having them confiscated by the army. They were able to desert from the army. In daytime they hid among the bushes and in the mountains, and at night they walked. It took them ten days to arrive at 'Ayn-Wardo. They went directly to the house of Gawriye Shmuni. The lady of the house immediately recognized them, and they stayed there.

***

On July 6, the news spread in Mizizah about the killing of Syriacs in Midyat. The [West] Syriacs in the village of Mizizah decided to flee before it was their turn. Meanwhile, the Kurds of Mizizah were preparing to kill their Syriac Christian neighbors. At dawn, the Syriacs left the village and headed for the mountains. The Kurds hastened to the mountains to stop them from fleeing. Tuma Sa'do addressed them, saying that the two communities knew each other quite well, and the Syriac Christians would not hestitate to fight them and that they intended to leave the village. He added that the Syriac Christians left the village to them, and in return they should allow the Syriac Christians to leave in peace. The Kurds eventually allowed them to leave for 'Ayn-Wardo.

***

My father, Muro, told me this story about the ordeal experienced by our family. In 1916, after the events of 'Ayn-Wardo, he and some other Christians moved to the outskirts of Nisibin, to a place called Shalwo dab Bunisriye, and they stayed there for two weeks with nothing to eat at the time. Sometimes they ate raisins and sometimes they ate the bellies of goats and sheep that he got as a kind of payment for slaughtering animals for the locals there. A Muslim from Maye dab Bunisriye [C'ayno-Hewarto] approached him one day and asked him to cut down some trees. The Muslim saw his knife and wanted it for himself. Muro gave it to him in return for a loaf of bread.

At that time, the Germans [stationed at Nisibin] needed charcoal. So that was an opportunity for Muro to earn some money. He would go to the mountains, cut wood from the trees, burn it, bury it underground, and after some days pack it in bags to be sold to the Germans. After delivering charcoal to the Germans, he used the same bags as a kind of blanket at night. Muro even used the same bags on his wedding night. Before Sayfo, his fiancee was left with the Kurdish tribe of [Alike] Batte. When they learned Muro's whereabouts, they sent her to him. There was no priest to wed them because all were killed during Sayfo. They went to Kharabe-Meshka, where they found an old priest who was really astonished to see people wishing to get married in the then terrible circumstances. The couple had two children who died, and even their mother died after them.

***

My father had two brothers, Eliyo and Gallo, who stayed in the Yezidi village of Kavnas. He lost his parents and after a lot of searching he found the brothers in the village of Baqesyane, where he discovered them still alive. My father asked about the Christians living in that village. He was taken to see some survivors. He met a woman, a girl, and three children. They all looked miserable. The woman was astonished when he spoke to her in Syriac. She started to cry because she was under the impression that this language had died forever as a result of the horrendous genocide inflicted on the Syriac Christians. A girl came to welcome him and all started to weep, because she turned out to be his sister Maryam. The next day, my father made the woman the offer of helping him in his new job, and in return she would get some grain that would help her to eat and survive. Gradually the woman's situation improved, as she could bake and eat fresh bread with her children. After the harvest, my father decided to take his sister and leave.

***

My father's second wife was called Hana. She was from the family of Bughdo in Midyat. The German need for charcoal increased, and many Muslim immigrants arrived there and were able to earn their living working for the Germans. Hana told me that her family lived in the empty caves of Shalwo dab Bunisriye for security. Hana was first married to another man, and when she heard from Mizizah that her father-in-law was sick, she went there with her first husband, Makko. The couple was shocked to find the old man lying on a thin layer of leaves, covered with lice. His son Makko started to remove the lice with his knife. The old man opened his eyes, recognized his son, and died. Hana and her husband stayed there.

67. Gawriye Beth-Mas'ud

When Chalabiyo was released from prison in Kharput, he took the train to Nisibin and was welcomed by thousands of Kurds. Some [West] Syriacs from Mizizah went to welcome him too. Chalabiyo asked to meet his fellow Kurds. Chalabiyo seemed sympathetic and kind after spending seven years in prison. He was imprisoned by the Turkish government, along with Sarokhano and Alike Batte, lest he help and protect Syriac Christians during Sayfo and the killings of the Christians. He asked Shabo, Mas'ud's brother, about the condition of the survivors. Shabo replied that there was no use talking about the past, and it would be better to ask about the miserable conditions of the Syriac Christians at that time, who were suffering and even dying of hunger, lice, and disease. His men told Chalabiyo that during his stay in prison the Kurdish aghas failed to keep their promises to protect the Syriac Christians and proved to be deceitful. They became allies of the Turkish government and turned against their Syriac Christian neighbors, plundering their houses, taking their property, raping their women, and destroying their churches. Chalabiyo confided to Shabo that Christians should never trust Muslims and they should not heed their words or promises. He put it in a metaphoric way, a saying that is still circulating among Christians almost everywhere: "If a Muslim seems as bright and as smooth as an apple, a Christian must not take him to heart, but put him in his pocket and let him fall through the hole." Chalabiyo promised Shabo to do his best to compensate the Syriac Christians.

68. Lahdo Musa-Malaka

Chalabiyo advised the Syriacs from Mizizah to leave 'Ayn-Wardo. At first the Christians were apprehensive, but Chalabiyo declared himself to the reluctant Kurds in the village to be a friend of Christians. Chalabiyo demanded even that all confiscated properties be returned to their legitimate owners. A Kurd called Rashido Khalaf in the village challenged Chalabiyo and refused to comply with the sympathetic measures that Chalabiyo stipulated in favor of the Christians. Rashido Khalaf and his men captured eight [West] Syriacs in the mountains and killed them there. A Christian man called Sawme was able to escape and went to the Yezidi village of Kavnas. Another Syriac named Saffo Barse, who was stabbed many times in the belly, did not die at once but dragged himself to the Yezidi village of Taqa, where some young men helped him. The young men who helpd him were the sons of a Syriac woman married to a Yezidi. He didn't want to stay in the village, so as not to cause them any trouble, and continued to 'Ayn-Wardo, where he died after a short time.

***

The Turkish government instituted a new policy after Sayfo: to get rid of Christians discreetly. They would capture Christian men at random to expel, to take for military service, or just to kill. My uncle Makke Muro was chained and taken to Omid [Diyarbekir]. On the way, the Kurdish soldiers started to swear at Christians and Christianity, calling the Christians bad names that made him sick. In Omid they put 45 men in a caravanserai. My uncle saw some men discussing an escape plan, and he joined them. At night my uncle and some prisoners escaped. The soldiers shot at them, but in the dark many were able to make it to safety.

R. HAZAKH (Azakh; East of Midyat, 60 km)

69. Lahdo Beth-Lahdo Musa / Beth-Gorgis (b. 1926), interviewed May 1993

In 1840, Badir-Khan Beg, along with Mire Kor Ahmad, arrived in Gziro [Jezire, Cizre]. They planned to attack and plunder Hazakh. As a result, many men were killed, while the women and children were seized by the attackers, who, after this terrible incident, then headed for Esfes. In the village of Esfes, the two amirs followed the same code of conduct: killing the men; about forty men lost their lives. Women and children were taken with them as they went to the monastery of Mar Gabriyel. The two amirs showed no respect whatsoever toward this sacred place. They killed the people and destroyed all the Christian symbols they encountered there. They continued their advance toward two [West] Syriac villages, Gawayto and Basibrin. There they met some resistance that compelled the two amirs to leave for Midyat. There they killed, plundered, and destroyed. Then they went to Kfar-boran. In Kfar-boran, the two amirs met some resistance, and Mire Kor Ahmad died in the clashes there. This didn't put an end to the ambitions of the advancing Kurds, who continued their advance in the direction of Hasno. The consequence of this Kurdish alliance was that Tur Abdin and its Syriac inhabitants were seriously affected and weakened

Before Sayfo, and more precisely before 1915, our family lived in Bafayya, near Hazakh. The village was inhabited by [West] Syriacs only. The Syriac inhabitants needed shepherds, so they employed some Kurds to take care of their cattle. The number of Kurds increased steadily. One day, something remarkable happened. Gawro, the brother of the priest Saliba, was about to take his cattle to graze in the mountain when he saw that the Kurds had occupied a church in the village. He saw that a Kurdish imam was chanting *Allah hu Akbar* at the top of his voice to proclaim the church a Muslim place of worship. Gawro ran to inform his brother the priest. The priest Saliba had three brothers. After that, Gawro hurried home and grabbed his rifle and went to the church. There he killed the chanter and seven Kurds and then ran away. This incident made it impossible for the priest and his brothers to stay in the village any longer, so they left for fear of acts of revenge. The priest Saliba went to Hazakh. Gawro went to Upper Kafro, and a third brother settled in Sa'irt.

Before 1914, some eight men from Hazakh were doing their military service in the village of Jaranja-Telane, near Sa'irt. Among them was the head of Hazakh at the time, Malke Gorgis. He was at the time accompanied by Hanna Sallo, Isa Basse, and others. On Sundays, the eight men would go to Sa'irt to do their shopping and look around. One day, as the eight men were talking to each other, a shoemaker seemed to listen attentively to them as the men were conversing in the distinctive Arabic of Hazakh. He approached them and introduced himself as the brother of the priest Saliba in Bafayya.

One day in 1914, the men met an Armenian man who was in military service with them. The Armenian confided to them how the Turkish officers would choose Christians and send them on strange missions from which nobody ever returned. The men decided to desert, fearing for their lives. At night the eight men escaped, walking overnight and resting during the day until they arrived in Basibrin. There they notified their relatives in

Hazakh of what had happened to them and of their intentions to return to Hazakh. The men were advised not to come back to Hazakh, as tensions between Kurds and Syriacs were escalating. The Kurds were trying to besiege Hazakh, while the government was at the same time trying to recruit men for the general *safarbarlik* [mobilization] it had declared. The conflict with the Kurds ended after forty days of clashes. The Syriacs in Hazakh sent some armed men to fetch the eight deserters and bring them back to Hazakh.

These sporadic conflicts gathered momentum, and the Kurds and Turks joined forces and declared a kind of holy war against the Christians. Massacres were committed in Sa'irt, Badlis, Hakkari, and Van. In this horrific and indiscriminate war against Armenians and Syriacs, the priest Saliba's brother the shoemaker was killed. The Turkish army, aided and abetted by the Kurdish tribes, was responsible for uprooting many Syriac villages and for killing thousands of Christians. This war expanded to include [East] Syriac Christians in Beth-Slux [Kirkuk] and Slaymaniye [Suleymaniyeh]. Chaldeans and Syriacs, who were the major inhabitants of these areas and their surroundings, suffered most. Their numbers decreased considerably as a result.

Malke Gorgis, my grandfather, was the head of Hazakh. He told me the following about Sayfo in Hazakh. He said that news reached the Christians in Hazakh about the genocide, or Sayfo, proclaimed against Christians in general. Fearing for their lives and families, the people in Hazakh met to discuss the precautions they could take to protect themselves from the imminent threat. They decided to build a fence around Hazakh. They sought the help and expertise of four workers from Midyat. The workers' answer was that such a precaution was unrealistic. They suggested a kind of a wall instead to be built around the Church of the Virgin, as the church was rather spacious with a well inside. The plan was put in action. Meanwhile, an investigator named Gabro Khaddo arrived in Hazakh. He expressed astonishment at how people were busy fortifying their houses. The investigator assured them that he himself had had assurances from the Turkish vali that Sayfo was declared against the Armenians above all. Based on his formal authority, no wrongdoing would befall the Syriacs. He ridiculed them and told those who were suspicious to come to him in Gziro. In Gziro lived around 700 Christian families. Chaldeans, Armenians, and Syriacs lived there side by side. The people in Hazakh thanked the investigator and asked him to send them arms and fighters to help them. For them, only these could generate safety.

After a short time, some Kurdish tribes from Badlis, Van, and the Mountain of Shigur [Sinjar] joined forces and attacked Hazakh. They beseiged Hazakh for forty days, but their evil mission failed.

Meanwhile, the Turkish army suffered major losses and withdrew along the Tigris River toward Mosul and Gziro. The Kurds in Gziro welcomed the army and offered them food and presents. The heads of the Kurds hurried to meet the Turkish commander, the Circassian Ömer Naji Bey. They asked him to do them a favor, namely, to eradicate the town of Hazakh. The commander agreed, and he was accompanied by some Kurds who would show him Hazakh.

The next day, the Turkish army and its allies the Kurds arrived in Sensele, alongside Hazakh. One blew his bugle, commanding the soldiers to halt. A man from Hazakh who had done military service recognized the sound and told the people to prepare themselves. Fear began to spread in Hazakh, and the people went to see the bishop, Behnam 'Aqrawi. They suggested negotiating with the Turks and adopting peaceful means of dealing with the matter. The bishop along with his deacons went on foot to meet the commander. The bishop addressed the commander kindly and treated him as a guest. He also offered to provide the guests with food and whatever would make their stay in Hazakh comfortable. The commander thanked them for their hospitality.

The bishop and the people went back to Hazakh and gathered all kinds of food for the commander and his soldiers. They went back to deliver them. The commander ordered his guards not to allow the bishop and his companions into his tent. When the guards and the Syriacs started to argue, the commander appeared. He told the bishop that he would be frank with him about the reason for his stay near Hazakh. The commander told the bishop that he intended to attack Hazakh. He gave the bishop and the people in Hazakh seven days to surrender; otherwise the attack would occur after the formal blowing of the bugle.

The bishop and his compnions went back to Hazakh. The people wanted some guidance, so they went to the bishop to discuss defenses. The bishop gave them simple, valuable advice. He told them that they ought to resist the strong enemy, and if they should die, it would be for the sake of their Christian faith. He told them to make holes in the walls but not to start shooting,, as bullets were scarce and their weapons insufficient. Two prisets, Yawsef [Shahin] and Samuel, prayed with the people and urged the believers to defend themselves and their faith. They urged them not to hesitate to direct their rifles at the hearts of the Turkish invaders.

APPENDIX 1

After seven days, the attack on Hazakh began. The Turkish army used heavy artillery to conquer Hazakh. They first bombarded Hazakh from all angles until the place was in ruins. When the Syriac Christians did not respond to the attacks, the commander ordered the soldiers to enter Hazakh on foot. Leading the troops was a Turkish officer riding a horse. He exhorted the soldiers in Turkish to be merciless, to kill, and to take Hazakh at any cost. At that moment, a bullet from Hazakh killed the officer at once. The morale of the soldiers was affected negatively by this incident. And after some clashes, the Turkish army retreated to a place called Kherbe. The people of Hazakh followed them and collected the dead soldiers' rifles. The commander sent a messenger to Omid [Diyarbekir] asking for assistance and reinforcement. The people in Hazakh also received outside help from the bishop in Mosul. The bishop went to the Chaldean Patriarch Emanuel Thomas II.

***

The two Christian leaders went to see Shawkat Pasha, the Turkish vali in Mosul. They told the vali that the people in Hazakh were loyal to the Turkish state and there were no Armenians among them. Shawkat Pasha sent a telegram to the military headquarters in Omid, which in turn sent a telegram to the Turkish commander in Hazakh ordering him to withdraw. Thus after forty days of conflict, the war came to end.

After the cease-fire, a group of Turkish officers visited Hazakh. There were some German officers with them too. One Turkish officer demanded the cannon the people of Hazakh had used during the conflict. The people of Hazakh were confused because they had no cannon at all. The officers went upstairs to inspect for themselves the place from which artillery-like fire had hailed onto them during the conflict with Hazakh. They saw an open Bible and a burning candle beside it. The German officer [identified by others as Bernard Püls] who was taking notes during the conversation, writing down what he was seeing, intervened. He confirmed that he himself had seen a strong fire emanating from a little window. He came to the conclusion that there had been some sort of heavenly intervention; probably the Virgin herself was protecting the people of Hazakh, maintained the officer. The German officer was touched by the deep faith the people of Hazakh had in the Virgin and in their Christianity.

The German officer resigned from the army to become a Catholic monk and spent the rest of his days at the Vatican. Apparently what happened in Hazakh had a tremendous effect on his life. He served in the Vatican and assumed important positions and responsibilities. One day the

Vatican held an international conference in which even many clergymen from the East took part. Among them was the Chaldean bishop, Stephan Ballo, who served as a bishop in Aleppo. In a break during the conference, the German officer who had become a Catholic monk approached Stephan Ballo. He told Ballo that there was a resemblance between him and the bishop in Hazakh. He even asked Ballo about Hazakh and its people. Ballo heard about the remarkable incident in Hazakh.

The villages surrounding Hazakh suffered immelsely during Sayfo. Many Christians lost their lives because of the indiscriminate killings at the hands of the Turkish forces and their allies the Kurds. Many Christians were obliged by force to change their religion. The names of the villages were changed to sound Kurdish, and in a short time these Christian villages began to lose their cultural, historical, and religious identity. The villages that were usurped by the Kurds are: Kherabe-Rappen, Heddel, Kafshenne, Esfes, Kherbe, Felfel, Zemmarakh, Tamarze, Babeqqa, Rizo, 'Ayn-Sare, Hajji-Hasan, Telle-Bal, Tizjare, Sevveke, Debkiye, Zangellor, Garessa, Telela, Lower Khandaq, Upper Khandaq, Arzarakh, 'Emerin, Bafayya, Kuvakh, and Babeqqa.

After Sayfo, a peculiar belief spread among the people of Hazakh. They believed strongly that blue-eyed young lions would come and save them from their misery. By this they meant the approaching Russians, who were at the outskirts of Sa'irt and Badlis. The people of Hazakh believed that the Russians would set the Christians free from the cruel fist of the Turks and the Kurds. They were tempted by the hope that with Russian help they could build a little state named Asuristan [Assyria].

During the war, three men from Hazakh were taken by the Russians. One of them, 'Isa, would send letters from Moscow to tell his people that he was safe and sound. When I was young, the Kurds killed my father. My widowed mother had a difficult time raising us.

S. NISIBIN AND GOZARTO (the region around Qamishli)

70. Gawriye Maqsi-Hanna Hamra (b. 1918), interviewed November 1997

In 1915, the massacres started in Tur Abdin. From Nisibin, the Muhallemi Qaddur Bey [head of the Al-Khamsin militia in Nisibin], who was a Turkish officer at the time, invaded the villages of the Gozarto region. He killed all the Syriacs he encountered until he came to the village of Tel-Khatunke, which housed 150 Christian families. Everybody was killed and only one woman, called Nasme, escaped death because she was outside the village at the time. When she came back, she saw the village on fire, people killed and burnt. She escaped to the village of Zinawrah and stayed there after marrying a man called Gawriye Hado.

The Kurdish agha Slaymane Abes gathered the [East and West] Syriacs of Bayaze, Ger-Sheran, Mharka, Tel-Jihan, Qwetla, Helwa, Siha, and the other villages. He brought them to his village, Dagra. My grandfather Sallo was among the people brought to Dagra. They were taken to a lake called Qiro. The Syriacs were tied up, shot dead, and thrown into the water. Many years after this incident, people went to collect the bones of the dead. My grandfather Sallo was shot at, but the bullet hit the rope and he and his companion were only wounded and pretended to be dead. They hid among the bushes and were able to survive. They went to the village of Dagra, where Kurds killed them on the spot.

The news of the massacres spread to the village of Shelumiye. My uncles had gone to Adana [in Cilicia] before Sayfo. The village was owned by a Kurd named Hasane Abbas from the tribe of the Hajji Slaymani. The Kurdish chief sent his brother Hus'ayn to Adana to observe the situation of the Christians. Hus'ayn told him that the Christians were being killed on a large scale. Hasane Abes gathered the Christians and told them to leave before they were killed by the other Kurds and Turks. He told them to take their valuables with them, and as a gesture of good will he offered to accompany them to the village of Seruja. He said that he would mislead the approaching Kurds and Turks by claiming that the Christians tied him up and left for Turkey [from the province of Syria].

The Syriacs continued to walk until they arrived at the village of Ehwo [Hebob] in Tur Abdin, and they stayed there until the massacres were over. They lived like prisoners there as the people were short of food and water. The spread of lice became a difficult problem for them. Half of them died of typhus.

Before leaving the village of Shelumiye, my father, Hanna, hid our food supply in the well and covered it with a bucket. He asked some men in Ehwo to go back to the village and bring the supplies, and in return we would share the food equally with them. After Sayfo, the people went back to their villages and were shocked to find Kurds occupying their houses, married to and served by Syriac Christian women. Syriac Christians in general became the slaves of the Kurds, working cheaply for them. Women who weren't good-looking were either sold or killed.

My father became the slave of the Kurd Abbase Ose. He witnessed how a Syriac woman called Khaneme, married to a [West] Syriac man named Lahdo from the family of Qasho, was about to be raped by the Kurd Abbase Ose. When the woman resisted him, he grew angry, killed her, and hung the naked dead body on the wall. Nobody dared defend her. At night he [my father] took down her dead body and threw some earth over her. In the morning the Kurd became angry to find that her body had been removed. He was angry and started asking her family questions. The family denied any involvement, and the Kurd accused Hanna. The religious head of the tribe, Hajji Isaye Ali, intervened and stopped the trouble resulting from burying the woman. Hanna told the man that it was a human duty to bury the body of a naked woman. The religious man was touched and slapped the Kurd on the face. Another day, Hanna and the Kurd were playing a kind of cricket. The Kurd cursed Christianity and Hanna cursed back. The religious head of the village, Hajji Isaye Ali, summoned them and told the Kurd not to curse the Christians: they paid heavily to preserve their faith and honor, so the Kurds must respect the Syriac Christians for that, he declared.

T. MIYAFARQIN (Silvan; east of Diyarbekir)

71. Mikhayel Salmo (1924–1997), interviewed March 1996

After Sayfo, and when we were young, the Chaldean bishop Timotheos used to come from Omid [Diyarbekir] to hold masses for the believers in Midyat. He used to tell them about the events of Sayfo in Omid. One day, while walking in the streets, a Kurdish man approached him and wanted to talk to him about a remarkable incident that he had experienced. The Kurd said that he was previously a soldier, ‚and one time they had captured a group of men and their priest to be killed. When they arrived at a hill, the priest asked in Kurdish if the end was near, as a strong smell of death and of rotten corpses emanated from that place. The soldier told the priest that after the killing they would be thrown into a well, as was the custom. The priest asked them if he could pray for one last time with his group. The priest started to pray and his men approached him with open mouths. The priest put some soil in their mouths. Some of the soil was thrown in the soldiers' eyes so that they couldn't see. They asked the priest for help, so he continued his prayers until they could see again. The Christians were killed and the Kurd wondered about the soil and its significance. Timotheos told him that it served as the Holy Communion, as bread was not available at the time.

U. TEL-GHAZ (near Diyarbekir)

72. Salim Beth-Bido (b. 1922), interviewed September 2004

Tel-Ghaz was near the village of Qarabash. After Sayfo, ten [West] Syriac houses were there with no Muslims whatsoever. We were 30 persons in our family. The elderly told us that 10 people were taken from this village during the mobilizing of [1914]. Nobody returned, and many believed that the government killed them. A person who did survive the mobilizaion was Malfono Abdelmasih Qarabashi. When he saw how his fellow Christians were killed, he fled to the mountains, where he stayed for a month and survived by eating grass.

***

During the time of Sayfo, the Kurds killed all the men in Tel-Ghaz. My two uncles, Gabriyel and Osyo [Asya], were killed. The Kurds set the village on fire. Two men survived, and the Kurds took the women and children with them, as they tended to do when attacking Christians.

***

After Sayfo, some Turkish cavalrymen visited the village and saw people planting tobacco illegally. Those caught were taken to the roofs of the houses and beaten to death in front of the rest of the villagers to set an example.

***

I was six years old in 1928. The Kurds committed atrocities in our village, which made us leave it. We went to the Tigris River and continued to Qameshli [Syria] with the help of some Kurdish smugglers. And we have stayed there ever since.

V. SA'IRT

73. Isho' Qasho-Malke (1913–2004), interviewed November 1993

Before the military rule in Turkey [1980], I used to go to Sa'irt every now and then. From there I would arrange passports for the Syriac Christians in Tur Abdin who wanted to seek political asylum in the West. In Sa'irt I became acquainted with a tailor called Adib who was kind and friendly. He told me that he knew a woman whose father had been a clergyman. This woman was a blind widow and had some valuable books she wanted to leave in safe hands. I went to her and presented myself to her, and I was impressed by the books that seemed very old. The books were about the church, written in Classical Syriac and Chaldean. I asked her to tell me her story, and at that point she began to cry and told me that she had been around ten years old when Sayfo took place.

In Sa'irt, the government began by gathering men. Rumors abounded at that time of the whereabouts of the men. When they failed to return to the village, we knew that the men of the village had been killed. After a while, the killings ocurred openly, and we started to hear that we ought to leave the village. Groups and groups of Christians were expelled. The old woman said that she was expelled in a group led by some Kurds. Christians didn't care to ask, because they felt that death was in sight. Thirsty and hungry they stayed on top of a mountain. The Kurds asked the women in the group if they knew where the supplies were kept in the [Chaldean] Dayr-Salib Church.[13] A woman raised her hand and asked for some companions to help her fetch supplies from the church. Two Kurds, two women, and I went to fetch supplies. The woman led them to the place where the food was kept. A Kurd kicked the door open and they found large jars of wine, pickles, and syrup. They refused the two large jars of wine, saying it was the drink of the infidels. They ate and took food to the others. A Kurd saw a door leading to larger rooms full of old books. It was the Church library [and archive]. He called his Kurdish friend and whispered something in his ear. The other nodded. They told the women to take the books and put them in the churchyard while they would go to bring the whole group. When the group arrived, the Kurds asked them to help take the books out of the library and put them in the churchyard. At sunset, we were told to stand around the pile of books that we had carried out. They set the pile of books on fire and took children from their mothers and threw them into the fire while the women wailed and screamed. Those who tried to flee were shot down and devoured by the ferocious fire. When the Kurds ran out of bullets, they started killing us with daggers until they became very tired and couldn't kill any more. So they left us to die slowly. I was thrown into the fire, but I survived. The books that we took out were more than twenty or thirty thousand books.

After hearing this horrific story, I contacted the priest Malke in Omid, who went to Sa'irt to see the woman and take the books she had back to the Church.

---

[13] This monastery belonged to the Nestorian Church until 1551 and had a very rich archive and library.

W. Gziro (Jezire, east of Midyat, 90 km)

74. Mikhayel Salmo

The [Chaldean] 'Abdelkarim Maqsi-Musa had a Muhallemi friend from Astal, west of Midyat. After Sayfo, this friend came to buy dyestuffs from him. The custom in Midyat was that people used to talk during the haggling process. The Muhallemi told 'Abdelkarim that he had something he must reveal. During Sayfo, he was a soldier ordered to kill the Chaldean bishop, Ya'qub Abraham. He didn't know who he was. He went to the bishop's headquarters without knowing that the intention was to kill. When they arrived at the churchyard, they called the name of the bishop in Arabic. We saw a man looking at us from the window. The soldiers hurried to him and hit him on the head with the bayonets of their rifles. They took him out and kept beating him so brutally. They dragged him to the market to be crucified and burnt, witnessed by both the Christians and Muslims alike. Seeing other Christians around, the soldiers went after them to kill them. As the Muhallemi was alone with the bishop, he took his rifle and shot the bishop dead to put an end to his agony. 'Abdelkarim thanked the Muhallemi for helping the bishop.

X. Diyarbekir, Midyat, 'Ayn-Wardo

The following is not based on an interview but rather is a transcription of a tape-recorded reading of a manuscript composed by one of the major figures of the events in Midyat and the defense of 'Ayn-Wardo, Gallo Shabo. The manuscript *Mimro d Gallo Shabo* was originally written in western Classical Syriac by Gallo Shabo himself. A priest by the name of Yuhanun Sham'unki decided to make the manuscript accessible by translating it into vernacular Neo-West Syriac. His reading was recorded on tape in Hannover, Germany, in 1981, and is translated here.

Gallo Shabo was born in 1875 in 'Ayn-Wardo. He went to school there and studied religion and the major languages, including Classical Syriac, Arabic, Persian, and Osmanli Turkish. When he was imprisoned in Midyat and Mardin, he translated and revived many religious works, especially those of Grigorios John Bar-Hebraeus. Gallo Shabo wrote the following narrative interspersed with poems (most of them religious in nature, and omitted here) about Sayfo, the East and West Syriacs' calamities in 1914–15. In this essay, he presented a detailed description of the experiences of the East and West Syriacs during the period of *Sayfo*.

75. Gallo Shabo (1875–1966)

The Ottoman Sultan and the Muslim Caliph Muhammed Reshad issued a decree against all Christians. The Sultan had a grudge against the Armenians in particular, a grudge so intense and bitter that it expanded to include the Syriacs and Chaldeans as well as the Armenians.

The Sultan sent the decree to all the Muslim heads in the Ottoman Empire. In the decree he specified that the Christians were traitors who usurped uncounted pieces of land. The Sultan depicted them as a group of people who intended to take power from the Muslims throughout the country. The decree concluded with a sinister insinuation regarding what ought to be done to curb the Christians and their influence.

The valis and the military heeded the decree and its message and started to create a negative atmosphere against the Christians in the press. Tangible unrest grew as regards the Christians and their situation in the Ottoman Empire. At first, a wave of arrests took place against the Armenian community. Many young men were imprisoned without any charge whatsoever. The Armenians questioned that move, and the answer was deceitful. They were led to believe that it was not a serious matter, a trifling misunderstanding that would be resolved sooner or later. Although the Christians had experienced the cruelty and harshness of Muslims, at that time they did not suspect that the arrests were the prelude to genocide.

The selective arrests of the religious leaders and some important figures among the Armenians escalated to massive arrests, until the prisons became overcrowded. To decrease the number of prisoners, the Armenians were taken at night to unknown destinations to disappear for good. The same tactics were used against the so-called Frangoye [French], that is, the Catholics and Protestants. Gradually even the East and West Syriacs living in the Armenian area were killed and disposed of. Those who were able to escape from Armenia to Tur Abdin [in Upper Mesopotamia] reported their terrible ordeal. An Armenian who managed to flee met Gallo Shabo and told him what he had witnessed. The Armenian began by searching for words to describe the inhumanity and cruelty of the Muslims. He said that the killings occurred indiscriminately and that the corpses were piled on each other. Hungry children roamed the streets, some of them looking for the breasts of their dead mothers. The Armenian told Gallo Shabo that pregnant women had their bellies slit open and babies taken out to be crushed like grapes under the feet of soldiers. The Armenian was short of words to convey the calamities of the Christian Armenians at the hands of the Ottomans. He continued with how soldiers raped the pretty girls and women in front of their families.

Omid [Diyarbekir]

Omid was the capital of our region. The Christians living there were known to be productive and hard-working. Omid was so prosperous that many had the impression that Omid was fortified and could resist any threat. The Muslims dreaded invading Omid. The vali [Reshid Bey] and his men deployed special tactics. They summoned the influential figures and the heads of the big families in Omid to meet the vali. Under that pretext they were able to gather around 700 persons, who shortly after that were arrested and imprisoned.

The Armenians wanted to protect themselves, so they complained to the Europeans about the maltreatment they suffered at the hands of the Turks. The Turks reacted by more persecutions and cruelty against all the Christians in general and the Armenians in particular. Gradually, the hatred and desire for vengeance accelerated to the extent that the Turks seriously planned to get rid of the Christians in one way or another.

The Turks put their plan in action by gathering and killing as many Armenians as possible. The conflict that started in Omid expanded to include the entire surrounding region. In Omid, the Turks did not spare the lives of either women or children. Heaps of dead bodies were left to rot and to be witnessed by the survivors. About 700 persons were killed at the hands of Turks. The first wave of killings was directed against the intelligentsia, the influential and educated people in the Christian community. Those who survived reported the following:

While we were sitting on the banks of the Tigris River, we witnessed groups of notables transported in small boats. One of the guards accompanying the groups was seen taking the gold, the money, and even the clothes of the doomed men before he and the others shot them dead. The guard was called 'Amar [Omar], son of 'Ali Rammo [Kurdish tribal leader] and Perikhane [his mother]. This ignoble guard did not have any scruples whatsoever about robbing and killing the Christians. The corpses were disposed of in the Tigris River. The Christians in Hasno [Hasankeyf] saw the corpses floating on the surface of the river and began to fear for their safety. In spite of all these atrocities, the Christians could not believe that genocide would occur on so large a scale. There was a kind of tacit belief that these atrocities were directed at some categories of Christians. But the renewed killings indicated that the Turks' aim was to get rid of all the Christians. The Kurds were a willing ally to the Turks in their despicable pursuits.

In the prison at Midyat

As many people filed complaints against me, I was particularly afraid of the kaymakam and the general prosecutor. One day I went out to hunt in the mountain in 'Ayn-Wardo. I saw three soldiers coming from Midyat to 'Ayn-Wardo. The soldiers were riding horses and seemed in a hurry. I asked them the reason for their visit, but they did not give me an adequate answer, and that made me very suspicious. I returned home to see the soldiers in my house searching among my collection of books. They did not find anything; nevertheless they tied my hands and took me with them. I asked them why I was being taken in this way; the soldiers ridiculed me and made me follow them. The next day, I was put in prison in Midyat among some animals. A guard was left on the door. In the evening I was taken to be interrogated and beaten. In the interrogations, I was asked about my religion and about an Armenian man called Kirkor. As a result of the violent beatings, I told them that I knew Kirkor, the baker, who at the time was with me in the prison. They left me and went to Kirkor, the baker, and beat him. I was taken back to my cell and there I stayed for forty days, during which we were subject to insults, curses, and recurrent beatings. At night we were left to be tormented by the scorpions that left us wounded and deprived us of sleep.

One day, we witnessed many Christians from Kfar-Boran arrive in prison. The people seemed hungry and exhausted and were ordered not to speak with anybody in prison. That day we saw how the guards were on alert and whispering to each other. After some days, I secretly got in touch with one of the newcomers. The man told me how Christians were about to be uprooted in Kfar-Boran and that the same fate would be experienced by all the Christians in the region. I went back to my fellow prisoners, and there I met a young man lamenting Hasno, as it was devoid of its Christian inhabitants. The young man confirmed that in Habses the sound of weapons and the weeping of Syriac Christians resounded.

As a consequence of these devastating events, the people in Midyat became fearful and went to see the general prosecutor. They complained of the rumors they had heard and asked him to do something. The general prosecutor sent a force to Habses to seek information. The force saw the Kurds attacking Habses and tried to repel them. Three Kurds were killed and the others fled. The force returned to Midyat, and the Turks tried to allay the fears of the Syriac Christians in Midyat that anything of the sort would happen to them.

The fanatic Kurds were inflamed with desire for revenge and sought permission from the Ottoman state to attack the Christians. Hanne Safar, the head of the Syriac Christians at that time, along with a priest went to the city hall to meet the kaymakam. The latter confirmed that nothing would happen to the Syriac Orthodox. He confided to the two men that Syriac Orthodox Christians were appreciated by the Turkish state. He continued cunningly, saying that the Turks were only opposed to the other Christians [Catholics and Protestants] whose denomination was different from theirs. The kaymakam confirmed that the Turkish state was against those whose allegiance was not to the Turkish state. The meeting was attended by a Kurd called Abdul-Aziz [Azizke], the Kurdish Agha of Midyat, who listened attentively to the conversation.

The same night, we heard turbulence and lots of noise around the prison. We heard the troops arriving and taking positions. Then the guards started to separate the Frangoye from the rest of the prisoners. These were taken away. At dawn, two Syriac men, along with the Kurdish Agha Abdul-Aziz, took 36 men to give evidence to the general prosecutor. Then a clerk came to the prison and asked about the remaining eight Syriac prisoners, and I was among the eight left who were set free.

'Ayn-Wardo

I went back to the village, and on my way there I rested at a place where I could see the church of Mor Hushabo. I sat there to meet the people who came to welcome me. I was amazed at the sheer number of new faces. I did not recognize many of them, as many were not originally from 'Ayn-Wardo. I asked these people about their places of origin and the reasons that prompted them to leave. One man told me he came from Farqin [Silvan near Omid]. Another man said he came from Kafarzo [near Sa'irt]. A third man told me that he came from Gziro near the Tigris River. A fourth man told me he came from Hasno. It seemed to me that these people were like birds fleeing their original places, seeking safety. I was almost certain that no Christians were left in these places. The men confirmed that no Armenian dared to wander freely in Armenia. These people would walk at night and hide in daylight.

Midyat

Midyat experienced a terrible war, as it was attacked by many fanatic Muslims and its people were forced to leave it in search of safety.

On Monday, July 6, [1915,] at dusk we heard sounds of people appealing for help. Twenty-five armed men responded, leaving 'Ayn-Wardo to help the people of Midyat. A bloody conflict took place at night between them and the Muslim attackers. The conflict went on until dawn, and both sides suffered casualities.

On Tuesday, July 7, I gathered 100 strong men and took them to Midyat. On the outskirts we waited until dark, and we saw a thick column of smoke emerging from Midyat and interpreted it as a bad omen. We felt that the situation in Midyat was really bad and that the Syriac Christians were engaging in a terrible war against the fanatical attackers. We resolved to intervene, and our plan was to enter from the northern part of Midyat, near the monastery of Mor Sharbel. When it was dark we attacked, and a horrible confrontation occurred.

On Wednesday, July 8, we were in the market in Midyat where the confrontations and the killings reached their peak. We killed many; among them was the Turkish clerk, Sharif Afandi. At night, the government decided to send a huge force to take disciplinary measures against 'Ayn-Wardo. We retreated to 'Ayn-Wardo to defend it, for fear of retaliations against our people in 'Ayn-Wardo.

On Thursday, July 9, a little force of ten men, including myself, decided to stay in Midyat. We were a bunch of experienced fighters. The rest left for 'Ayn-Wardo. The conflict in Midyat resumed unabated between us and the Muslims. The sound of rifles was ceaseless, and we could see the corpses of the people scattered in the streets. The Muslims would gather the corpses and pile them up. Blood was everywhere, and we encountered horrible scenes, such as people trembling with half-cut throats. Muslims seemed uncontrollable as they went on the rampage. They were like wild rats in their enormous numbers, attacking everywhere. Firewood was common in houses at that time. The Muslims would set them on fire, and the sight of flames made them madder as they shouted *Allah hu Akbar!* They threw any Christian they could capture into the fires. The inhuman killings resumed until night fell. A Syriac man called Yawsef was seen to open his house to give refuge to the frightened and fleeing Christians. The Muslims locked the house from the outsider and set the house on fire. All the Christians died of burning or suffocation. The cries for help still reverberate in our ears. Our situation deteriorated and we became desperate, with no help whatsoever in prospect. We resisted using every possible means. But the number of Muslims seemed to increase all the time.

The large numbers of Muslims and their relentless will to continue the fight frightened us. Sa'id, the Syriac priest, intervened to allay our fears. He addressed us, saying that the arrogance displayed by the Muslims would lead to their downfall. He encouraged us to be patient and to fight for the sake of our Christian faith. He boosted our morale that our death in such circumstances meant that we would be rewarded in paradise.

I gaborutho d Aloho 'yo!
Qumu! Lo zaycutu!
Hanoyo u darbo di sohdutho!
Sayberu ahunone!
Mqadamla i malkutho,
Tubo l ayna d menher lajan i macmoditho!

"Courage comes from God! Stand up! Don't be cowards! This is the right way to martyrdom. My brothers! Have patience! We are near the gates of paradise. Blessed are those who sacrifice themselves for Christianity."

After three hours, the Muslims staged a terrible attack on us. Many Syriac Christians died. Those who were captured alive by the Muslims met a terrible death. We heard the ceaseless sounds of rifles and the cries for help. At night people fled on a large scale, the majority in the direction of 'Ayn-Wardo. I was hit by three bullets. We had no choice but to resist. When we started to change our positions, we caught a glimpse of the heaps of corpses, the sight of which was intolerable, so I opened my hands and prayed to God to rescue me. We witnessed how the Syriac priest Afrem was captured by the Muslims and beheaded on the spot. Midyat gradually fell into the hands of Muslims who killed all the Christians they met. Later they looted the houses and the shops, taking everything they could grab. We were obliged to flee to 'Ayn-Wardo.

'Ayn-Wardo

The Kurdish tribes and the Turkish soldiers attacked 'Ayn-Wardo in the middle of July at three o'clock in the afternoon. They launched the attack from the high mountain. They were dressed in white. Some young men tried to resist the attack, and the result was an immense loss of life in a place called Adro d Shoco. The Muslims grew more violent at the sight of the death and started to shoot and shoot at random. The attack resumed overnight, and we were almost sure that the village had no chance but to fall in the hands of the Muslims. Many people fled. Priests and clergymen in 'Ayn-Wardo started to pray for the safety of the village; especially the Syriac bishop Filiksinos, who came from Upper Kafro. Both East and West Syriac Christians joined forces to stop the attackers and their aggression. The Christian men seized the war banner from the Muslims, and that implied a moral triumph for the Christians. A man took the banner and brought it to the church of Mor Hushabo and showed it to the bishop, who commanded the people to start praying and thanking God. Then he instructed the people to burn the banner in the earth oven. He told the people that the might of God helped the Christians in their ordeal, and he prayed that the enemy would turn to smoke and disappear. The confrontations lasted from Friday to Sunday. The Muslims waged psychological warfare against the Christians, taunting them that their end was imminent and that no life would be spared. We suffered from the loss of weapons and we grew weaker as our number steadily decreased.

On Sunday night, we decided to launch our major attack. We lost men, women, and even children but we were able to return to the village and we started to build a wall around the village to defend ourselves. Four houses that we couldn't include within the range of the wall were seized by the Muslims, and from there they shot at the Syriac Christians. This situation lasted for ten days.

On Sunday, we were ready to go to church, and we observed that the Muslims were preparing to attack us. We heard the sound of the horns and trumpets while we were in church. People started to ask God for help. The Muslims captured an important position that we had in the village and killed ten men from Kfarze. That night we decided to recapture the vital eastern position that we had lost, and we succeeded in our mission. The Muslims disappeared after that. The next night the Muslims came back with the intention of retaking the strategic position. We responded, and about fifty causalities among the Muslims could be counted by us. The Muslims brought a little artillery piece with them, and the aim was to destroy the church of Mor Hushabo, which the Syriac Christians were using as a shelter. After firing the artillery many times, the artillery broke down and the Muslims started to retreat. The war lasted sixty days. The Muslims seemed to arrive from everywhere keen to fight in 'Ayn-Wardo.

The Muslims had had modern weapons whose sounds were so terrifying that we experienced them like thunder. The Muslims realized that they would not be able to capture 'Ayn-Wardo, so they retreated. However, the consequences of this war were devastating. Families were split as they fled everywhere. Fatal diseases spread among the Christian people. Poverty and hunger meant certain death to many Syriac Christians. Some of them became servants to Muslims in their different categories [Kurds, Turks, Arabs, Persians, Azeris, Zazas, Circassians] to survive. This made them easy prey for the Muslims to ridiculed and victimize. The slavery degraded the Christians and some lived like animals. They were forced to eat grass to survive. Many Syriac Christians emigrated to remote countries to avoid these inhuman sufferings.

APPENDIX 2
DOCUMENTS ON THE SYRIAC POPULATION

1. STATISTICS PROVIDED BY THE ASSYRO-CHALDEAN DELEGATION TO THE PEACE CONFERENCE

From Said A. Namik and Rustem Nedjib, *La Question assyro-chaldéenne devant la Conférence de la Paix* (dated July 16, 1919).

Table of the population of the vilayets of Mosul, Diyarbekir, the sanjaks of Aleppo, Urfa, Deyr-Zor, Sa'irt, Hakkari, and the regions of Urmia and Salmas (in Iran) in 1914 (excluding the areas on the right bank of the Muradsu and Euphrates Rivers in the vilayet of Diyarbekir and the sanjaks of Aleppo, Urfa, and Deyr-Zor)

This table should be compared with the table published by the Armenian Patriarchate of Constantinople for other, more northern, parts of eastern Anatolia.[1] In principle, the two tables should supplement each other geographically and give a complete picture of the ethnic and religious divisions in eastern Anatolia, the northernmost Arab provinces, and northwestern Iran. The Armenian Patriarchy calculated that there were 123,000 "Nestorians, Jacobites, Chaldeans" living in regions to the north of the region included in the figures provided by the Assyro-Chaldean delegation. In both cases, the original data must come from an Ottoman ethnographic investigation, as the regions delimited do not correspond with church dioceses, and there is no natural reason for the Armenians or the Assyro-Chadeans to count other religious-ethnic groups, such as nomadic Kurds and Arabs, Zazas, Yezidis, and so on.

---

[1] Statistical analysis of the racial elements in the Ottoman vilayets of Erzurum, Van, Bitlis, Mamoure-ul-Aziz, Diyarbekir, and Sivas, drawn up in 1912 by the Armenian Patriarchate at Constantinople, in James Bryce and Arnold Toynbee, *The Treatment of Armenians in the Ottoman Empire* (1916), 656. These statistics exclude areas of the above-mentioned provinces that had few Armenians.

Table 7: Population of the Mosul, Diyarbekir vilayets; Aleppo, Urfa, Deyr-Zor, Sa'irt, Hakkari sanjaks; and Urmia, Salmas regions, in 1914

Nationalities and religions	Mosul	Diyar-bekir	Urfa & Aleppo	Deyr-Zor	Sa'irt	Hakkari	Urmia & Salmas (Iran)	Total
Turks and Turkmen	18,000	45,000	24,000	2,000	2,000	30,000	80,000	**201,000**
Circassians	—	8,000	—	5,000	—	500	—	**13,500**
Settled Kurds	41,700	48,000	13,000	4,000	15,000	60,000	38,000	**219,700**
Nomadic Kurds	4,000	24,000	—	3,000	—	8,000	—	**39,000**
Settled Arabs	43,000	14,000	6,000	11,000	13,000	—	—	**87,000**
Nomadic Arabs	20,000	22,000	8,000	14,000	—	—	—	**64,000**
Iranians	300	—	—	—	—	1,500	10,000	**11,800**
Zazas	—	20,000	—	—	—	—	—	**20,000**
Kamavends	1,000	—	—	—	—	—	—	**1,000**
Assyro-Chaldeans	122,000	117,000	16,000	4,000	61,000	165,000	78,000	**563,000**
Armenians	200	73,000	18,000	1,000	6,000	20,000	20,000	**138,200**
Greeks	100	10,000	6,000	—	—	—	—	**16,100**
Latins	200	200	500	—	—	—	—	**900**
Jews	6,000	2,000	500	500	—	6,000	4,000	**19,000**
Kizilbashes	—	11,000	8,000	1,000	—	2,000	—	**22,000**
Yezidis	25,000	10,000	3,000	2,500	—	5,000	—	**45,500**
Shabaks	15,000	—	—	—	—	—	—	**15,000**
Sarlis	3,000	—	—	—	—	—	—	**3,000**
Bablis	1,000	—	—	—	—	—	—	**1,000**
Gypsies	—	3,000	1,000	2,000	—	2,000	—	**8,000**
Total	**300,500**	**407,200**	**104,000**	**50,000**	**97,000**	**300,000**	**230,000**	

2. LISTE DES VILLAGES, DES HABITATIONS ET NATIONALITÉS

From Appendix to a letter of Agha Petros 1922
PRO FO 839 23 82893 (see pp. 20–21 above).

Part A. This 17-page list deals with Hakkari (including Sarai) in Van vilayet, Bohtan, a province in Biltlis vilayet, and Urmia in Iran. The names of the districts are probably dioceses of the Nestorian church. The Agha Petros list for the Assyrian regions of Turkey and Iran is typewritten in French. The names of the villages are in the French transliteration used by the Assyro-Chaldean delegation, which can explain why some well-known places were given odd spellings.

The version published here is formatted somewhat differently from the original source for practical reasons.

APPENDIX 2

Several things complicate the interpretation of this list. The nationalities Assyrian, Kurds, Armenians, and Jews were written in a column to the extreme right after the name and number of households. As a rule, the first time a nationality is named, it is followed by ditto marks for the successive villages with the same ethnic population. However, at some point Agha Petros, using pen and ink, adjusted the list, changing the attribution of some villages and sometimes giving ditto marks in ink, sometimes not. Therefore, in publishing the list here, the nationality is written out rather than indicated by ditto marks. Another complication is that certain letters on the typewriter were very worn, which means that some letters can have been misread. This affects the reading of M and N, G and C, c and e, which can have been confused. On a few occasions the typist wrote over a letter that was wrong, trying to correct it, but this process could result in an illegible symbol.

The register is presented in its original order. Why the districts come in this order is hard to say. Also, the villages are neither in alphabetical nor numerical order. Perhaps there is a geographic reason, following a mountain valley.

Table 8: District Haute Baroude

Villages	N°. de - maisons	Nationalités	Villages	N°. de - maisons	Nationalités
Khardalanis	15	Assyrien	Guidajory	Sainte-Marie	Assyrien
Kotranis	50	Assyrien			
Aconis	20	Assyrien	Hartice	Sainte-Marie	Assyrien
Chamoninice	25	Assyrien			
Auride	10	Assyrien	Aknice	Sainte-Marie	Assyrien
Civini	60	Assyrien			
Ispine	30	Assyrien	Bittkamolou	Sainte-Marie	Assyrien
Saline	10	Assyrien			
Gouranice	25	Assyrien	Nirwa	Sainte-Marie	Assyrien
Kirmi	15	Assyrien			
Kotchonice	120	Assyrien	Nittnanou	Saint-Georges	Assyrien
Bygar	10	Assyrien			
Sourinice	15	Assyrien	Pirvany	10	Kurdes
Tarmil	20	Assyrien	Kaliss Haute	10	Kurdes
Bittlihajdijde	10	Assyrien	Kaliss Basse	60	Kurdes
Pikhy	8	Assyrien	Salmonuvan	20	Kurdes
Kharouss	25	Assyrien	Khalilon	30	Arménien
Tircounice	40	Assyrien	Pagui	70	Arménien
Babanice	Raban - Hourmouz	Assyrien	Khourzaï	100	Arménien
Diriky	Raban - Hourmouz	Assyrien	**Total**	**608 Assyrien** 200 Arménien 100 Kurde	

Table 9: District Jilou

Villages	N°. de maisons	Nationalités	Villages	N°. de maisons	Nationalités
Alsan	50	Assyrien	Roma diorca	65	Assyrien
Nédii	30	Assyrien			
Zirinii	260	Assyrien	Ichatzine	85	Assyrien
Imoud	32	Assyrien	Sarpil	100	Assyrien
Saint Zaïa	200	Assyrien	Boubaba	28	Assyrien
Tallona	65	Assyrien	Chamsika	30	Assyrien
Yohra	80	Assyrien	Bittbakhchi	100	Assyrien
Bittpatchou	52	Assyrien	Ourmaï	19	Assyrien
Zeir	200	Assyrien	Mouspiran	50	Assyrien
Bittboukra	45	Assyrien	Awtichar	62	Assyrien
Auri	50	Assyrien	**Total**	**1683**	
Nirchak	80	Assyrien			

Table 10: District de Nirwa

Villages	N°. de maisons	Nationalités	Villages	N°. de maisons	Nationalités
Ourmar Saint Mamou	150	Assyrien	Tchii	45	Kurde
			Chouca	30	Kurde
Kimi de			Abro	25	Assyrien
Frizarii	60	Assyrien	Artiss	30	Kurde
Kharta	80	Assyrien	Kinyaniche	16	Kurde
Tamitowan	30	Kurde	Randlan	18	Kurde
Chatouniss	25	Kurde	Nirbakki	92	Kurde
Byra	60	Kurde	**Total**	**315**	**Assyrien**
				346	**Kurde**

Table 11: District de Doustican

Villages	N°. de maisons	Nationalités	Villages	N°. de maisons	Nationalités
Roma d'Ayra	50	Assyrien	Sronguil	18	Kurde
Razky Guipa	30	Assyrien	Bachkararan	32	Kurde
Ayri Zavissor	18	Assyrien	Mabichla	10	Kurde
			Gawani	23	Assyrien
Khaïcanaï	60	Assyrien	Khanikhigina	18	Assyrien
Chagoulvard	12	Kurde	Ourgueuzal	13	Assyrien
Bactazan Goulourd	35	Kurde	**Total**	**212**	**Assyrien**
Sarmargui	62	Kurde		**169**	**Kurde**

Table 12: District de Baz

Villages	N°. de maisons	Nationalités	Villages	N°. de maisons	Nationalités
Haute - Village	100	Assyrien	Arwanteuss	50	Assyrien
Argab	45	Assyrien	Koon	60	Assyrien
Bittsaïah	30	Assyrien	Toubi	70	Kurde
Kougulan	15	Assyrien	**Total**	**370 Assyrien**	
Chwawouta	70	Assyrien		**70 Kurde**	

Table 13: District de Livon-Bas

Villages	N°. de maisons	Nationalités	Villages	N°. de maisons	Nationalités
Vill. St. Georges	30	Assyriens	Bittkara	35	Assyriens
Kharguil	100	Assyriens	Bittguiry	36	Assyriens
Arka	12	Assyriens	Nispac	80	Assyriens
Kasra	62	Assyriens	Kwaly	12	Assyriens
Gnisky	32	Assyriens	**Total**	**399**	

Table 14: District Haut Livon

Villages	N°. de - maisons	Nationalités	Villages	N°. de - maisons	Nationalités
Eglise de Zanguil	150	Assyriens	Anitriss	100	Assyriens
Sadikhon	28	Assyriens	Payaniss?? [sic!]	19	Assyriens
Eydawan	30	Assyriens	Bily	45	Assyriens
Gouviky	14	Assyriens	Kalya	32	Assyriens
Warkoniss	60	Assyriens	Mapikun	16	Assyriens
Baden	18	Assyriens	Khidky	19	Assyriens
Marcoussine	25	Assyriens	Balakhon	27	Assyriens
Jaroniss	37	Assyriens	Koumonyta	32	Assyriens
Koublon	31	Assyriens	Naghbijan	60	Assyriens
Nicha	14	Assyriens	**Total**	**757**	

Table 15: District de Noddiss

Villages	N°. de maisons	Nationalités	Villages	N°. de maisons	Nationalités
Aras	32	Assyriens	Houstaia	35	Assyriens
Deriky	70	Assyriens	Maruvanan	62	Assyriens
Kodoum	52	Assyriens	Tchargalii	72	Assyriens
Parkhilan	100	Assyriens	Bichik	18	Assyriens
Rihawy	190	Assyriens	Awalma	50	Assyriens
Skouniss	29	Assyriens	**Total**	**710**	

Table 16: District de Sarii et Temou

Villages	N°. de maisons	Nationalités	Villages	N°. de maisons	Nationalités
Sarii	150	Assyriens	Aghsan Sainte		
Kharbas souro	25	Assyriens	Croix	56	Kurdes
Khino	38	Assyriens	Hundistan	200	Kurdes
Kouchissor	30	Assyriens	Ziwiky	108	Kurdes
Toun	40	Assyriens	Paguy	36	Kurdes
Gdalwa	35	Assyriens	Saint		
Kharachic	40	Assyriens	Audichou	72	Kurdes
Sariban	25	Assyriens	Adiman		
Aguidtcha	25	Assyriens	(Saint-		
Rachon	35	Assyriens	Etienne)	53	Kurdes
Sile	50	Assyriens	Ramikhnon	48	Kurdes
Klissa Saint-			Chkarodkan	64	Kurdes
Georges	4	Assyriens	Van (Saint-		
Poukhniss	10	Assyriens	Cyr)	—	Arménien
Armaniss	30	Assyriens	Satibagh	105	Assyrien
Pircaïf	18	Assyriens	(Saint-	entre les mains	
Darmonkoy	45	Kurdes	Marie)	des Yezidi	
Gridi	60	Kurdes	Kissaran	37	Kurdes
Caratchoukh	37	Kurdes	Poutt	16	Kurdes
Yarimkaïa	100	Kurdes	**Total**	**660 Assyrien**	
Tirraron	68	Kurdes		**1000 Kurde**	

Table 17: District Chamisdinon

Villages	N° de maisons	Nationalités	Villages	N° de maisons	Nationalités
Balakan	12	Assyrien	Saint-Cyr	75	Assyrien
Karwanon	18	Assyrien	Soursari	72	Assyrien
Goulanky	32	Assyrien	Tisse	36	Assyrien
Talana	72	Assyrien	Hallon	18	Assyrien
Daryon	19	Assyrien	Biduirdy	16	Assyrien
Saint Skil	39	Assyrien	Rabouniss	19	Assyrien
Déraii	42	Assyrien	Alwi	12	Assyrien
Beytour	14	Assyrien	Rouwan	14	Assyrien
Zikha	81	Assyrien	Bonowaky	80	Assyrien
Yardoucha	63	Assyrien	**Total**	**826**	
Dwary	92	Assyrien			

Table 18: District de Zazon

Villages	N°. de maisons	Nationalités	Villages	N°. de maisons	Nationalités
Sararou	62	Assyrien	Bibaba	30	Kurde
Saint Ichou	65	Assyrien	Kmiba	60	Kurde
Bikary	60	Assyrien			Assyrien-
Badawi	35	Assyrien	Chikhan	18	Kurde
Battimou	108	Assyrien	Pissani	106	Assyrien
Bimlata	100	Assyrien	Gahhara	29	Kurde
Nahrii	200	Kurde	Chivawouta	39	Assyrien
Nahrii	120	Assyriens	Hallona	60	Kurde
Nahrii	30	Juif	**Total**		**713 Assyrien**
Aton	—	Assyrien			**379 Kurde**
Katouna (Eglise Saint-Simon Bar Sablaah	—	Assyrien			**30 Juif**

Table 19: District de Guardian

Villages	N°. de maisons	Nationalités	Villages	N°. de maisons	Nationalités
Bitt Touci	50	Assyrien	Villages détruit	2	Kurde
Chapittnaii	38	Assyrien	Villages	1	Kurde
Pari	100	Assyrien	Saro	60	Assyrien
Villages	13 églises	Kurde	Jarwo	12	Assyrien
			Total	**260**	

Table 20: District de Galia de Derianai

Villages	N°. de maisons	Nationalités	Villages	N°. de maisons	Nationalités
Sarou	100	Kurde	Alwar	39	Kurde
Siardiki	25	Kurde	Pibohrine	75	Kurde
Khaliki	50	Kurde	Moznawa	77	Kurde
Almassan	40	Kurde	Nouchine	62	Assyrien
Koubaki	60	Kurde	Kolbani	54	Kurde
Bajraga de Cassari	80	Assyrien	Yagmala Haute	49	Kurde
Cassaraï	38	Assyrien	Yagmala Bassse	18	Assyrien
Tchilikha	92	Assyrien	Dara	100	Assyrien
Hilontchi	70	Assyrien	Pagui	120	Assyrien
Gulagriwi	50	Assyrien	Tiloran	10	Kurde
Iscon	16	Kurde	Mitchik	30	Kurde
Chahii	150	Kurde	Nachkon	35	Kurde
Deirikha	150	Assyrien	Hirmii	70	Kurde
Ziwor Saint-Georges	32	Assyrien	Noutirbon	15	Kurde
Sourean	100	Assyrien	Aliabad	19	Kurde
Nazrassli	55	Kurde	Marbichou	200	Assyrien
Moura	49	Kurde	Avitch	39	Kurde
Zirili	100	Kurde	Paguie	60	Kurde
Bassan	35	Kurde	Ile	160	Assyrien
Bilanbasson	62	Kurde	Parie	26	Assyrien
Avian	16	Kurde	Halinki	82	Assyrien
Razouki	80	Kurde	Bittzidki	50	Assyrien
Sourian	60	Kurde	Banowati	53	Kurde
Pirblona	30	Kurde	Barazar	16	Kurde
Kalia Daroucha	35	Assyrien	Arbili	70	Kurde
Bardkha	62	Assyrien	Bittgowsi	38	Kurde
Koulladarah	18	Assyrien	Peysani	75	Kurde
Dayalzi	200	Assyrien	Kourtakawa	25	Assyrien
Dibarkhi	100	Kurde	Thambassou	20	Kurde
Doudinan	120	Assyrien	Charmilon	32	Kurde
Boucharwaran	39	Assyrien	Balankonie	19	Assyrien
Chouchamasdin	75	Assyrien	Bardarchouki	20	Assyrien
Daryssani	20	Assyrien	Taalini	25	Assyrien
Khorikan Haute	120	Assyrien	Karsarie	7	Assyrien
Khourikan Basse	180	Kurde	Liguinie	30	Kurde
Kalaa de Chirkharir	30	Kurde	Kowlanie	25	Kurde
Kharindje	60	Assyrien-Kurde	Bittkwari	100	Kurde
			Dazguiran	20	Kurde
Bouloug	16	Kurde	Kachki	90	Kurde
Noudian	70	Kurde	Chkawtan	29	Kurde
Sakiran	39	Kurde	Kharbata	35	Kurde
Pizouki	85	Kurde	Bachirma de Panta	36	Kurde
Harcki	42	Kurde	Bazar	75	Kurde
Koukouze	16	Kurde	**Total**	**2374**	**Assyrien**
Pakhlan	99	Assyrien		**2822**	**Kurde**

Appendix 2

Table 21: District de Valtou

Villages	N°. de maisons	Nationalités	Villages	N°. de maisons	Nationalités
Sainte-Marie	28	Assyrien	Mazirgoumera	14	Assyrien
Khidiana	70	Assyrien	Tchomissiodi	25	Assyrien
Sirta	20	Assyrien	Bittmirigo	37	Assyrien
Balmazida	19	Assyrien	Tchamieta d'Kourca	30	Assyrien
Brin	5	Assyrien	Chinna	18	Assyrien
Ziba	37	Assyrien	Bouh	67	Assyrien
Sadionon	40	Assyrien	Bittmarasni	53	Assyrien
Didirki	29	Assyrien	Har	90	Assyrien
Ouriai	30	Kurde	Bsinbir	87	Assyrien
Drissa	80	Assyrien	Kotoss	17	Assyrien
Skita	65	Assyrien	Maronice	35	Assyrien
Bittloni	42	Assyrien	Anitos	62	Assyrien
Kiwrini	50	Kurde	Aina Dzidoni	14	Assyrien
Kanta Zargoni	30	Assyrien	Tchamba d'Hasso	18	Assyrien
Bira	48	Kurde	Tchta-dyahra Deacha	29	Assyrien
Zarowa	32	Kurde	Navlontz	50	Assyrien
Darawa	20	Kurde	Kambo d'Mallik	30	Assyrien
Roma Samouka	90	Assyrien	Kaletan	77	Kurde
Thomba - Dwalton	100	Assyrien	Tchomtouvan	20	Assyrien
Khan Babouche	20	Assyrien	Richegallia	100	Assyrien
Thomikta	30	Assyrien	Kourkha	50	Assyrien
Mabouor	34	Assyrien	Billsahmonon	67	Assyrien
Darouche	50	Assyrien	Gubara	79	Assyrien
Bittdaliati	70	Assyrien	Pircucaran	80	Assyrien
Tchomba de Jadrora	62	Assyrien	Ida	15	Assyrien
Kalaïta	63	Assyrien	Tchamba dbithiou	63	Assyrien
Bitt Nahri	45	Assyrien	Sarpsidon	100	Assyrien
Rounita	80	Assyrien	Siadir	82	Assyrien
Mazronca (Saint Sava)	62	Assyrien	Tchamba disbo	18	Kurde
Riche Nohra	39	Assyrien	**Total**	**2699**	**Assyrien**
Douza Haute	37	Assyrien		**275**	**Kurde**
Dirza (Saint-Georges)	70	Assyrien			

Table 22: District de Tal

Villages	N°. de maisons	Nationalités	Villages	N°. de maisons	Nationalités
Arouvan (village Babilonien)	250	Assyrian	Baïkta	100	Assyrien
			Nadari	95	Assyrien
			Saint-Audichon	39	Assyrien
Talna	100	Assyrian			
Rabat	30	Assyrian	Saint-Etienne	100	Assyrien
Bittazia	100	Assyrien			
Bittkoura	29	Assyrien	**Total**	**843**	

Table 23: District Tiari Haute

Villages	N°. de maisons	Nationalités	Villages	N°. de maisons	Nationalités
Achita	500	Assyrien	Bitt-Alta	100	Assyrien
Zavita	100	Assyrien	Cassara	98	Assyrien
Ravoula de Barua	80	Assyrien	Ouriata Tchomba de	100	Assyrien
Mintoniche	30	Assyrien	Bitt Sousiani	100	Assyrien
Margui	150	Assyrien	Bitt Nalou	105	Assyrien
Kourkha	170	Assyrien	Bitt Ravouli	20	Assyrien
Eijivon	80	Assyrien	Bitt-Mirou	180	Assyrien
Lizan	90	Assyrien	Bitt-Marou	19	Assyrien
Saint-Georges	100	Assyrien	Bit Titva	200	Assyrien
Tchamissor	300	Assyrien	Tchomikta	150	Assyrien
Darava	190	Assyrien	Gumani	30	Kurde
Coundie	100	Kurde	Ziva	172	Kurde
Bourache	50	Assyrien	Calien de Salavion	80	Kurde
Zarni	65	Assyrien	Soucidan	50	Kurde
Maiadan	72	Assyrien	**Total**	**3107 Assyrien**	
Bittzizou	39	Assyrien		**432 Kurde**	
Lakipa	19	Assyrien			

Table 24: District de Albac

Villages	N°. de maisons	Nationalités	Villages	N°. de maisons	Nationalités
Kharaba	60	Kurde	Malcava	70	Arménien
Migalva	50	Assyrien	Karatoum	65	Arménien
Omarabad	80	Kurde	Haspistan	36	Arménien
Sionva-Haute	45	Assyrien	Eglise d'Albac	78	Arménien
Sionva-Basse	68	Kurde	Porte Katous	95	Arménien
Khtivava	95	Kurde	Bachingar	36	Kurde
Richan Titar Aga	42	Kurde	Achkitan	73	Assyrien
Richan Klipa	63	Kurde	Babassan	100	Kurde
			Souradir	89	Kurde
Ouzan	37	Assyrien	Calanis	56	Assyrien
Poucine	18	Arménien	Thahardiran	78	Kurde
Souran	19	Arménien	Babis	38	Kurde
Bachcala	100	Arménien	Houzi	78	Assyrien
Alanian	30	Assyrien	Ardja	15	Assyrien
Arissan	85	Assyrien	Amouss	60	Assyrien
Achoutan	92	Assyrien	Rassoulan	62	Kurde
Keilagoum	17	Kurde	**Total**	**659 Assyrien**	
Kanjonice	65	Kurde		**481 Arménien**	
Arak	38	Assyrien		**893 Kurde**	

Table 25: District de Gavar

Village	N°. de maisons	Nationalités	Village	N°. de maisons	Nationalités
Dizza (Saint-Marie)	250	Kurde	Daras	10	Kurde
Dizza	100	Juifs	Dadan	80	Kurde
Dizza	250	Arménien	Zava	80	Assyrien
Dizza	100	Assyrien	Souliki	50	Kurde
Khakbak	60	Assyrien	Halsa	63	Kurde
Kartinis	50	Assyrien	Chakiton	27	Kurde
Khoulkous	80	Kurde	Hissa	62	Assyrien
Goulniki	62	Kurde	Goulcoulissan	18	Assyrien
Pouliniki	13	Kurde	Birabira	30	Assyrien
Zokhan	17	Kurde	Kiat	50	Assyrien
Hassarikhi	60	Kurde	Karpil	60	Arménien
Kaniadachi	25	Kurde	Kharvata	12	Assyrien
Yazran	63	Kurde	Zarmas	18	Assyrien
Mouza	14	Kurde	Zarova	20	Assyrien
Khoublan	100	Kurde	Ouricha	50	Assyrien
Sissark	50	Kurde	Manwanan	36	Assyrien
Gouhichni	60	Kurde	Kadian	72	Assyrien
Salniki	39	Assyrien	Khaladabad	18	Assyrien
Asmaïlki	75	Assyrien	Alihona	90	Assyrien
Bolissa	10	Assyrien	Monnican	33	Assyrien
Diraki	20	Assyrien	Djouyan	62	Assyrien
Charvan	12	Assyrien	Alivana	45	Assyrien
Chvavouta	7	Kurde	Gourika	62	Assyrien
Sakron	3	Kurde	**Total**	**1140**	**Assyrien**
Yaziran	20	Kurde		**310**	**Arménien**
Birindjin	14	Kurde		**1068**	**Kurde**
Avirde	16	Assyrien		**100**	**Juif**

Table 26: District d'Ourmiah*

Villages	N°. de maisons	Villages	N°. de maisons
Digula	500	Sari	60
Dizza de Khiari	40	Hassir	50
Vazirawa	130	Bihna	30
Aglija Kala	40	Mar Sarguiss	50
Goulpachon	500	Ali Kounii	50
Hassar	10	Gardabatt	100
Tarmoni	120	Kizlachouk	100
Tchragouchi	200	Djamalawa	300
Bourhanlouwi	50	Ada	300
Toutrache	30	Sipirghan	300
Karaghadj	70	Tchamakii	300
Saralan	100	Karadjalouwi	300
Saatlouwi	200	Michwa	300
Aliawa	120	Hassar Babagaga	20
Dizza	60	Hissalouwi	106
Tazakont	50	Abdlakandi	40
Khoumabatt	60	Badilou	100
Saribadjalouwi	60	Anhar	100
Dizzagorsoulman	100	Alwatch	70
Balaniche	300	Balawe	50
Gouka	20	Sangar	100
Toumatar	20	Sangar Bourzikhan	70
Baladjigh	20	Tchitaklouwi	50
Boïatri	12	Abadjalouwi	120
Chritanawa	150	Karaguss	100
Topouzawa	40	Jriaba	60
Nouli	10	Sangar	40
Toutrache	60	Borachon	50
Karassanlowive	58	Kanichan	150
Sirabadjalouwi	20	Kourrana	50
Saridjoukh	20	Mawana	160
Baridjoukh	20	Djandjatchin	250
Chamelladjion	120	Babadjidji	100
Kossabatt	70	Baloulan	200
Dizzatakia	500	Gamiliana	120
Mouradlouwi	50	Gawilan	200
Khidrawa	13	Kama	150
Khidrawa	30	Nakda	200
Darhari	100	Chitanawa	70
Babari	130	Toubasnoui	20
Mouruchkari	20	Oukhsar	60
Albakh	30	Rahtaki	60
Kourtapa	50	Moumtir	100
Cheinabot	60	Hassalowi	30
Takka	300	**Total**	**10,148**
Orduchaï	300		

*The list only contains Assyrian villages, so the space for nationality was not filled in.

Table 27: District de Gavar (all listed villages are Assyrian)

Villages	N°. de maisons	Villages	N°. de maisons
Malrijan	50	Habiban	85
Soucian	60	Zizan	62
Sinava	100	Tchardiwar	35
Mimabara	250	Pirzalan	42
Ziva	35	Maskhoudabad	80
Badana	100	Bachirga	50
Kharvaranki	60	Pazirabad	35
Hariki	33	Gagouran	60
Sardacht	57	**Total**	**1089**

Table 28: District de Haut Barwar

Villages	N°. de maisons	Nationalités	Villages	N°. de maisons	Nationalités
Bigouba	72	Assyrien	Dargali	80	Assyrien
Tchacala	58	Assyrien	Bicoulki	56	Assyrien
Tchalik Haute	35	Assyrien	Gadida	72	Assyrien
Tchalik Basse	62	Assyrien	Alcouchki	100	Kurde
Karourquiwar	34	Assyrien	Toular	150	Kurde
Kista	65	Kurde	Ourmana	35	Kurde
Koukria	38	Kurde	Ourmondavid	62	Kurde
Akirsouria	100	Kurde	Rabina	80	Kurde
Darchiriche	30	Kurde	Ouri	65	Kurde
Guirki	65	Kurde	Bido	30	Kurde
Baripoka	70	Kurde	Hidnia	75	Kurde
Kharchkhacha	80	Kurde	Binabia	85	Kurde
Tachiche	50	Kurde	Maïa	62	Assyrien
Kanibalabi	55	Kurde	Drichaki	38	Assyrien
Chiklou	35	Assyrien	Darichki	92	Assyrien
Garagou	49	Assyrien	Guinount	70	Assyrien
Ourmila	60	Assyrien	Casri	65	Assyrien
Babiri	35	Assyrien	Toutchamaï	84	Assyrien
Boulizanki	48	Assyrien	Tchni-bilki	80	Assyrien
Baz	150	Assyrien	Moussaka	55	Assyrien
Balida	30	Kurde	Bchila	60	Assyrien
Kanimazini	90	Kurde	Dargala	12	Assyrien
Tchamissaïdan	85	Kurde	Carrouki	19	Assyrien
Sparila	65	Kurde	Kalki	50	Assyrien
Sarro	49	Assyrien	Zicaraïa	80	Assyrien
Adine	35	Assyrien	Assa	37	Assyrien
Kassistark	37	Assyrien	Bittwapi	52	Assyrien

Villages	N°. de maisons	Nationalités	Villages	N°. de maisons	Nationalités
Nadjalani	64	Assyrien	Sarzir	48	Kurde
Chlaza	10	Assyrien	Tarnaniche	65	Kurde
Yagmala	100	Assyrien	Boutari	49	Kurde
Piss	50	Assyrien	Khawari	52	Assyrien
Kharaba	55	Assyrien	Halwa	63	Assyrien
Mirgadjaï	49	Assyrien	Mikharabian	32	Assyrien
Jiatt	32	Assyrien	Malikhta	80	Assyrien
Galia	100	Kurde	Ikrie	50	Assyrien
Doura	80	Kurde	Sardachta	62	Assyrien
Barbouri	10	Kurde	Tchami-doutina	100	Assyrien
Bichmiai	55	Kurde	Avsarik	62	Assyrien
Bittnoura	49	Juif	Bibalouk	10	Assyrien
Boukdnoudan	62	Assyrien	**Total**	**2788**	**Assyrien**
Galiki	17	Assyrien		**1947**	**Kurde**
Dacht	15	Assyrien		**49**	**Juif**
Doustkan	35	Kurde			

Table 29: District of Tkhouma

Villages	N°. de maisons	Nationalités	Villages	N°. de maisons	Nationalités
Pir	90	Assyrien	Houndi	[included	
Goundikta	200	Assyrien	Misgawt	in the	
Gouzirache	50	Kurde		above]	Assyrien
Mazraïa	80	Assyrien	Sigoundan	142	Assyrien
Tkhouma			Kasrana	65	Assyrien
Gavayo	450	Assyrien	Birizar	200	Assyrien
Kichatt	300	Assyrien	Khana de Tkhouma		
Zowita	250	Assyrien	partie orientale	156	Assyrien
Biridja	60	Assyrien	**Total**	**2484**	**Assyrien**
Khom de Tkhouma				**50**	**Kurde**
partie occidentale	491	Assyrien			

Table 30: District de Barwar de Bohtan

Villages	N°. de maisons	Nationalités	Villages	N°. de maisons	Nationalités
Chaminiss	60	Assyrien	Bidara	50	Kurde
Gouchaniss	80	Assyrien	Awbin	17	Kurde
Ari	25	Kurde	Akouchan	53	Arménien
Kouratch	60	Assyrien	Dachtik	32	Arménien
Arichcass	50	Assyrien	Valace	50	Arménien
Parkhikhi	100	Kurde	Malik	60	Arménien
Armakh	180	Kurde	Banidjan	95	Arménien
Casrouki	18	Kurde	Sagoukir	40	Kurde
Oussian	13	Assyrien	Sarap	88	Kurde
Caival	9	Assyrien	Khaskir	150	Kurde
Houl	20	Arménien	Pakh	11	Assyrien
Karmiance	50	Assyrien	Kep	25	Assyrien
Ourtch	65	Assyrien	Khoumar	36	Arménien
Yourachine	72	Assyrien	Sloupia	70	Arménien
Bourbe	30	Assyrien	Moullagbeïro	52	Arménien
Kidia	80	Assyrien	Village - Charnak	63	Arménien
Chwita	52	Assyrien	**Total**	**727 Assyrien**	
Bindoui	70	Assyrien		**691 Arménien**	
Alkip	35	Arménien		**668 Kurde**	
Armichatt	63	Arménien			
Ouzim	62	Arménien			

Table 31: District d'Ispirad

Villages	N°. de - maisons	Nationalités	Villages	N°. de - maisons	Nationalités
Piron	80	Kurde	Arkhanaïa	92	Kurde
Kantarou	50	Kurde	Awal	52	Kurde
Kasra	63	Kurde	Balo	100	Kurde
Radragoum	23	Kurde	Badjiri	30	Kurde
Yourva	72	Kurde	Satoriïa	60	Kurde
Pilanice	52	Kurde	Karnicise	50	Kurde
Kouvdi	30	Kurde	Kotor Rabta	30	Assyrien
Koutiace	62	Kurde	Ramoran	60	Assyrien
Koumazir	50	Kurde	Mata de Samki	50	Assyrien
Idra d'Hirian	100	Kurde	Hachtion	100	Kurde
Akir	80	Kurde	Chakhi	32	Assyrien
Saint Mathieu	90	Kurde	Hablar	62	Assyrien
Mihir	60	Assyrien	Hassand	50	Assyrien
Hawy	39	Assyrien	Narhouse	50	Assyrien
Abamaï	5	Kurde	Takia	44	Assyrien
Nachkhounaï	80	Kurde	Beyrian	33	Kurde

APPENDIX 2

Villages	N°. de maisons	Nationalités	Villages	N°. de maisons	Nationalités
Biguirzan	27	Kurde	Bassi	62	Assyrien
Djipona	85	Kurde	Haltou	35	Assyrien
Guilmidour	68	Kurde	Dachhalkou	49	Kurde
Chinraki	50	Kurde	Sanguirgue	55	Kurde
Dihouk	66	Assyrien	Ikwal	65	Assyrien
Dirgouli	44	Kurde	Ichbitt	72	Kurde
Bird	37	Assyrien	Ikroun	20	Kurde
Nanid	56	Assyrien	Khirwi	80	Kurde
Djiid	72	Assyrien	Hilta	50	Kurde
Bikdin	85	Assyrien	Bilon	60	Kurde
Anal	63	Assyrien	Asnakh	152	Assyrien
Nigue	78	Assyrien	Eglise de		
Mansouria	74	Assyrien	Chiche	100	Assyrien
Gzira	100	Kurde-Assyrien	Saint Sauvrichou	40	Assyrien
Bassorin	55	Kurde	Bindjou	16	Assyrien
Gurik	15	Kurde	Marga	32	Assyrien
Tilkabin	68	Assyrien	Artoukh		
Guirikta	56	Assyrien	Haute	29	Assyrien
Pista	37	Assyrien	Artoukh Basse	90	Assyrien
Bicheiri	44	Kurde	Piron	62	Assyrien
Sourbitania	102	Kurde	Dantas	18	Assyrien
Bittsapoun	100	Asyrien	Ali	42	Kurde
Hida	50	Assyrien	Anz	50	Kurde
Charzouk	36	Kurde	Koup	30	Assyrien
Koulia	20	Kurde	Koupratch-nice	60	Assyrien
Dirsor	50	Kurde			
Guitta	15	Kurde	Dih	18	Assyrien
Narbouli	8	Assyrien	Aro	27	Kurde
Harbichiche	2	Kurde	Sadek	12	Assyrien
Dirahouni	16	Kurde	Sahirt	40	Assyrien
Iskirad	130	Assyrien	Saint-Jacques	25	Assyrien
Imchine	15	Assyrien	Samkhom	30	Assyrien
Derki	44	Assyrien	**Total**	**2577**	**Assyrien**
Ilan	??	Assyrien		**2488**	**Kurde**
Ichiss	45	Assyrien			

Part B. Nombre des villes, bourgs et villages, habités totalement ou partiellement par les Assyro-Chaldéens en 1914 dans tout le vilayet de Diarbekir et le sandjak d'Ourfa.

The 13-page register is stamped with the seal of the Assyrian-Chaldean delegation in Paris, but it is not signed. This list presents few of the problems that made Part A so difficult. The names of the towns and villages are typewritten on a clean typewriter in bold letters. There are no handwritten changes. The list only deals with the Syriac population. The places are presented according to the administrative units of the Ottoman government, and the villages are listed more or less in order of size.

Table 32: Ville de Diarbekir et des environs

Place	Population	Place	Population
Diarbekir	8,000	Kerti	150
Kabié	1,600	Kara-Kilissa	200
Tjarchié	600	Tjanakeji	100
Karabach	600	Mekdessi-Oglou	100
Keterbel	300	Havara-Dejla	50
Satié	350	Havara-Hasse	50
Alipounor	100	Sirimi	300
Kaves	100	Deragli	50
Aincor	100	Tavogli	150
Kadié	200	Harnek	50
Telgaz	200	Bos-Pouar	50
Ancha	200	Bagdjaoljik	50
Cabasaccal	100	Keuchk	100
Arzi-Oglou	100	Mulla-Tjabir	150
Holan	50	Chehkend	150
Careh	50	**Total**	**14,450**
Selimi	100		

Table 33: Kaza (District de Silivan)

Place	Population	Place	Population
Miafarkine	1,270	Gheh-Davoud	300
Bochas	680	Aslo	200
Navdacht	200	Harzo	200
Zéré	200	Mir Alié	100
Attché	100	Germo	50
Guzel-Déré	100	Bachirik	200
Bavodine	100	**Total**	**4,000**
Gulémiré	200		

Table 34: Kaza (district) Lédjé

Place	Population	Place	Population
Lédjé	500	Chemchem	800
Foum	700	Yabtin	300
Halhel	200	Harbekne	100
Mellaha	800	Hererdem	200
Bamêtni	100	**Total**	**4,100**
Bachnic	400		

Table 35: Kaza (district) Dérék

Place	Population
Derek	500

Table 36: Argana Madan (sandjak)

Place	Population
Argana Madan	100

Table 37: Kaza (district) de Palou

Place	Population
Palou	50

Table 38: Sandjak (département) Severak

Place	Population	Place	Population
Severek	1,200	Agoin	300
Boudjah (Hédro)	300	Kafardis	300
Halokend	300	Avyous	500
Amespine	200	Kergere	400
Beyouk-Bagh	100	Vankok	100
Koudjak	50	Temsias	150
Ourbiche	200	Golek	150
Tjatag	100	Vanek	400
Mzreh	150	Kafar-Diche	300
Krbik	100	Machraca	100
Bekdjeri	100	Hachour	150
Bagdjajik	150	Pichoual	50
Pirchn-Chiro	100	Peterké	300
Pirchn-Babek-Chiro	100	Parisso	400
Amroun Chiro	300	Karatout	300
Bakesno	200	Dere-Peri	100
Chotam	100	**Total**	**7,750**

Table 39: Kaza (district) de Veran-Chéhér

Place	Population	Place	Population
Veran-Cheher	2,000	Achhine	50
Tel-Djafar	300	Délopérine	100
Drj [sic!]	100	Mahfouta	50
Olacdji	300	Altak	50
Hadji-Zeid	200	Kodjagui	100
Krme-Kor-Kahia	100	Tel-Goran	50
Anabi	100	Ibrahimié	50
Rikanié	100	**Total**	**3,700**
Tocli	50		

Table 40: Sandjak (département) de Mardine

Place	Population	Place	Population
Mardine	10,000	Mansourié	400
Golïé	1,500	Maassarté	300
Ibrahimié	400	Tjeftelek	200
Kalet-Mara	800	Békiré	200
Bénébil	300	**Total**	**14,100**

Table 41: Kaza (district) de Avnié (ou) Savour

Place	Population	Place	Population
Savour	200	Avine	100
Kellêt	2,500	Kordilik	100
Bafava	500	Tezian	100
Kherbé	200	**Total**	**3,700**

Table 42: Kaza (district) de Nissibin

Place	Population	Place	Population
Nissibin	1,200	Lilan	300
Mahricat	500	Bergorié	300
Kergué-Chamo	450	Lima	300
Merbab	400	Mrzé	300
Halvat	300	Koleké	250
Chomiah	300	Bazaré	300
Douger	300	Tel-Sefan	300
Gerchiran	400	Srganée	200
Tiz-Harab	300	Astouran	200
Khoutilé	300	Sirouan	300
Kerzerine	300	Krdim	300
Amchaoula	250	Chmohené	200
Karparer	250	Hachirlu	200
Kenké-Kanek	300	Benodeké	200
Seroujé	400	Keremaré	250
Mahreké	600	Tel-Husni	200
Aznavr [sic]	350	Peroulé	100
Tel-Chéir	200	Mendaré	150
Kerefché	400	Derouné-Kolteké	300
Kerpia	300	Cheïh-Hader	100
Teljihan	250	Knaneké	100
Krémira	400	Amarine	300
Kundek	250	Tel-Yacoub	300
Kundéré-Déré	400	Terbessé	300
Kerzoyne	100	Alian	100
Tel-Manar	150	Vavardé	200
Kre Super	200	Kerdahoul	150
Mla-Abbas	250	Sndé [sic !]	150
Tel-Hatoun	250	**Total**	**16,700**
Biazé	300		

Table 43: Kaza (commune) de Habab (attaché à Nissibin)

Place	Population	Place	Population
Habab	300	Badabé	250
Marine	400	Tdbo [sic !]	500
Sporé	250	Harabali	300
Kopeké	150	Harab-Mechké	200
Kafro	250	**Total**	**2,600**

Table 44: Kaza (district) de Djeziret-ibn-Oumar

Place	Population	Place	Population
Djeziret-ibn-Oumar	2,500	Tel-Kebbine	500
Telibel	300	Kenzumere	500
Amrine	300	Harbol	500
Kardié	200	Gurcnébédro	800
Koufek	400	Nahravan	200
Der-Babat	350	Tsché	300
Tafes	500	Raz	200
Kendek	100	Haltoun	100
Djerahié	100	Akol	200
Chak	300	Dissioum	200
Brebit	200	Mar-Sevricho	200
Mansourié	350	Chakh	200
Chabanié	100	Deran	200
Marzé	100	Deïr-Elaïa	400
Mirazez	100	Deïr-Tahtaïa	300
Takian	600	Handak	300
Dachte-Dare	100	Bara Beïta	300
Cafchené	200	Fendek	400
Hané	400	Fénék	400
Kéyouyé	300	Bosnaïé	400
Teldare	250	Ekval	300
Hodlé	100	Besbine	200
Mosié	100	Beïr-Mar-Avraham	300
Aïsaré	150	Maraké	200
Dayazé	100	Kochtana	200
Azék	1,000	Hossana	300
Pechabour	1,600	**Total**	**17,800**
Vahssed	600		

Table 45: Kaza (district) de Midiat (Djébel Tour Abédine)

Place	Population	Place	Population
Midiat	4,000	Hk [Hah]	500
Habsnas	450	Behvoir	100
Bati	700	Yerd	250
Azbas	350	Yenquels	150
Mzezak	350	Kefré	400
Kafarzé	350	Aylouz	100
Kafarbé	200	Abrimona	200
Basserine	900	Chabsand	100
Sari	300	Ylova	150
Arbaïe	120	Beïr-Kébé	100
Habis	100	Hassan-Kêf	400
Meddé	1,500	Cherrigan	100
Zenarek	120	Défné	200
Kerboran	2,000	Deïr-Avv	150
Bassac	120	Rjoké	100
Tjélek	100	Kerjoz	150
Haraba-Mechké	120	Harab-Allé	400
Tamziri	120	Badebé	400
Mechté	100	Arbo	300
Arbaya	250	Suleh	250
Deïr-el-Salib	400	Saliha	100
Araben	100	Anhel	700
Zaz	700	Aaïn-Ward	800
Bagssian	500	**Total**	**20,550**

Table 46: Kaza (district) de Bechérie

Place	Population	Place	Population
El-Medine	200	Bassourké	150
Kiresepra	200	Davoudié	50
Yliga	100	Kani-Kulna	50
Halkamié	300	Kodjan	50
Barsel	120	Sinoné	150
Kafarzo-Oulia	100	Helpélié	100
Kafarzo-Sufla	700	Kunda-Jano	50
Zerjel	300	Kiridié	200
Gueduk	250	Echcastik	150
Genesfer	320	Blior	100
Azek	100	Talmassas	150
Memounia	200	Telmergé	300
Chnaderk	50	Zevek	200
Kanireval	50	**Total**	**4,890**
Kureké	200		

Table 47: Nahie (commune) de Bafavoi

Place	Population	Place	Population
Yssa-Pouar	200	Frdilek	50
Kara-Pouar	100	Gunda-Abdi	100
Sadié	400	Alouzé	100
Harbé-Hanna	100	Belli	100
Mola-Davouda	50	Arakend	100
Feclé	100	Matri	150
Zré	200	Sildoun	50
Serperé	200	**Total**	**2,000**

Table 48: Sandjak (département) d'Ourfa

Place	Population	Place	Population
Ourfa	7,200	Dukerlu	100
Biredjik	1,500	Ounin Agai	150
Roum Kalé	2,200	Tjai Kapou	100
Seroudj	1,800	Boz-Abar	50
Harran	2,000	Kaïv-Haider	100
Kermouche	800	**Total**	**16,000**

3. THE SIZE OF THE CHALDEAN CHURCH IN JUNE 1913

The following list aims to calculate the size of the Chaldean Church, a Roman Catholic Uniate organization whose primate resided in Mosul. The task was given to Joseph Tfinkdji, a priest in Mardin, and he published the figures in a long article in a major Roman Catholic yearbook. Most of the figures come through correspondence in 1912 and 1913 with the various dioceses. Only in the case of Sa'irt, where the archbishop, Addai Sher, was a scholar, are the statistics exact; all of the other dioceses supply figures that are rounded off. As a small but widespread religious organization, the diocese combined places that normally were not part of the same Ottoman territorial divisions. The order in which the dioceses and parishes are listed is not alphabetical, or by size, but it follows the order used by Tfinkdji.

From Joseph Tfinkdji, "L'Eglise chaldéenne catholique autrefois et aujourd'hui" (1914), 449–525.

Table 49: Statistique générale de l'archidiocèse patriarcal

Place	Population	Place	Population
Bagdad	7,000	Le Caire (Egypte)	400
Amara	160	Téhéran (Perse)	120
Koutt	100	Carminchah (Perse)	320
Mosul (Résidence)	4,500	Ahwaz (Perse)	230
Alkosch	7,000	Constantinople	300
Telkèf	8,000	Basora (Babylonie)	500
Batnayé	2,500	Achchar	450
Bacofa	1,500	Dor-el-Zor (Syrie)	60
Télèskof	3,500	Alep (Syrie)	400
Caramless	4,000	Beyrouth (Syrie)	300
Bendawaïa	100	Damas (Syrie)	300
Pioz	100	Adana (Cilicie)	350
Nessaria	700	**Total**	**42,890**
Rome (Italy)	7		

Table 50: Statistique de l'archevêché d'Amida et de ses villages

Place	Population	Place	Population
Amida ou Diarbékir (résid.)	2,500	Navdacht	100 (néo-convertis)
Miafarkine	500	Zéré	120 (néo-convertis)
Djarokhié	150		
All-Poir	80	Attché	30
Bochatt	500 (néo-convertis)	Orfa (Mésopotamie)	200
		Total	**4,180**

Table 51: Statistique de l'archevêché de Kerkouk

Place	Population	Place	Population
Kerkouk (résid.)	800	Armota	100
Souleymanié	200	Koï-Sinjak	200
Arbelles	50	Koria	200
Aïn-Kawa	3,000	Rawandouz	90
Schaklawa	1,200	**Total**	**5,840**

Table 52: Statistique du diocèse de Séert

Place	Population	Place	Population
Séert	824	Dintass	80
Kotmès	326	Haute-Artoun	310
Mar-Gouria	182	Basse-Artoun	160
Guèdyanés	55	Goubarlanès	75
Tall-Michar	290	Tall	59
Bingov	110	Azar	50
Birkah	30	Guératel	100
Dehok	146	Mar-Anèche	70
Ramouran	126	Mar-Chanès	60
Dah-Rabban	142	Sadakh	230
Dah-Mazène	152	Mar-Yacoub	200
Ardjikanès	45	Marie-Chmoni	30
Koridj	100	Hadidi	200
Ouridj	20	Bir-Ké	120
Borim	282	Pékinde	80
Chwithá	95	Der-Chèmsch	40
Rauma	110	Kibb	50
Hakh	70	Einith	120
Péroz	300	**Total**	**5,430**

Table 53: Statistique de l'archevêché d'Urmiah

Place	Population	Place	Population
Urmiah (resid.)	500	Bardischok	80
Goulfakha	600	Snakak	200
Djarakosch	500	Mawan, Gubbachian	300
Koklafa	700	Chachajihan	320
Ardichaï	330	Tarcader	180
Djarlak	450	Bébaré	120
Désa	350	Anhar	270
Digal	400	Djamarbasch	200
Ada	700	Nazi	300
Spourkhan	350	Atlakindi.etc.	800
Takoi	150	**Total**	**7,800**

Table 54: Statistique de l'évêché d'Akra

Place	Population	Place	Population
Akra	250	Douré	50
Kherpa	200	Artoun	100
Hirdèz	120	Béchèmcha	150
Niram	100	Beit-Noura	80
Scharmin	250	Guéssa	60
Cahulpalan	120	Guépa	40
Kourkouran	80	Barzéné	90
Nouhawa	150	Bir-Sapra	30
Aréna	300	Mallabirwan	120
Sanïé	100	**Total**	**2,390**

Table 55: Statistique du diocèse d'Amadia

Place	Population	Place	Population
Amadia	400	Beit-Aïnatha	150
Aradène	650	Bibouzé	120
Téna	450	Asakh	300
Daoudié	300	Harmach	310
Minguèche	1,100	Théla	340
Hamzié	200	Birta	60
Ineschk	250	Dézé	80
Mézé	100	Tell-Hasch	100
Comané	60	**Total**	**4,970**

Table 56: Statistique du diocese de Gézirah

Place	Population	Place	Population
Gézirah	600	Mansourié	80
Takiann	900	Esché	200
Péchabour	1,300	Baz	150
Wahsad	520	Haltoun	100
Tell-Kebbin	450	Akol	180
Hoz-Umer	500	Dissioun	160
Harbol	300	Mar-Sauriché	100
Guirguébadro	600	Chakh	140
Nahrwan	120	**Total**	**6,400**

Table 57: Statistique du diocèse de Mardin

Place	Population	Place	Population
Mardin	1,100	Véranchahér	90
Nisibe	160	Déréké	40
Médéath	180	**Total**	**1,670**
Tellarmène	100		

Table 58: Statistique du diocèse de Salmas

Place	Population	Place	Population
Salmas	500	Khnakà	270
Khousrawa (résid.)	3,700	Zifajouk	280
Balarour	2,800	Satoura	240
Karilann	1,000	Serna	490
Ola	400	Colamar, etc.	230
Kuisàn	300	**Total**	**10,460**
Chahàra	250		

Table 59: Statistique du diocèse de Séna

Place	Population
Séna	900

Table 60: Statistique du diocèse de Van et des Missions nestoriennes

Place	Population	Place	Population
Van	100	Achita	350
Dizza	200	Zerné	100
Marbichó	250	Salamacca	150
Sat	300?	Autres localités	1,400?
Ibró	800	**Total**	**3,850**
Jolamérk	300?		

Note: Question marks are in the original text.

Table 61: Statistique du diocèse de Zakhô

Place	Population		
Zakhô	50	Marga	760
Bédaro	400	Bellonn	300
Bersevé	400	Asnakh	600
Chéranésch	600	Dehoc	350
Alanésch	70	Chioz	210
Yarda	250	Mar-Yacoub	150
Oumra	200	Garmavé	40
Bédja	500	**Total**	**4,880**

APPENDIX 3
DOCUMENTS ON THE NUMBER OF VICTIMS

1. THE APPROXIMATE NUMBER OF VICTIMS BELONGING TO THE VILAYET OF DIYARBEKIR

by Jacques Rhétoré (1841–1921)

From *"Les Chrétiens aux bêtes": Souvenirs de la guerre sainte proclamée par les Turcs contre les chrétiens en 1915* (2005), 135–39 (translated by David Gaunt).[1]

Five-sixths of the Christian population of the vilayet of Diyarbekir fell victim to the persecution. Those who survived are the non-Armenians for whom the Padishah, in his inexhaustible clemency, gave his pardon, after they were exterminated in great number and all the rest were ruined.

We have tried to give the number of the Christian subjects who were victims in the vilayet by confession, without counting the foreign deportees who also perished or disappeared inside the vilayet. This work is no more than an approximation because the troubles of the war precluded exact or complete information. I have based myself on an evaluation of public opinion, a task to extract from the vague and variable news what was closest to reality.

I combine the number of victims under the general name of Disappeared because there is not enough information to make a distinction between the killed and the captive. This distinction cannot be made with exact certainty until after the peace each returns to their home. …

I have prepared two tables: one gives the number of victims in the vilayet, the other the number of victims in the sanjak of Mardin. I had no information for the sanjak of Argana to put into the table. This I know—and it is true, I believe—that it is very important to include them in the table of the victims of the vilayet.

---

[1] This manuscript was completed some time in late 1916 or early 1917, with some minor additions made in June 1919.

**Table 62: Christians of Diyarbekir vilayet
who disappeared during the persecution of 1915–16**

	Number of persons before the persecution	Disappeared	Remaining after the persecution
Armenian Gregorians	60,000	58,000	2,000
Armenian Catholics	12,500	11,500	1,000
Chaldean Catholics	11,120	10,010	1,110
Syriac Catholics	5,600	3,450	2,150
Syriac Jacobites	84,725	60,725	24,000
Protestants	725	500	225
Total	**174,670**	**144,185**	**30,485**

The Jacobites said that they were just below 100,000 in the vilayet of Diyarbekir. This figure was too high, so I have given this, which I consider more reasonable.

Comments to table 62:

1. Among the 144,185 disappeared, almost all of the males should be reckoned as killed. In general, the women and children were captured by the Kurds, but there are also many among them who were killed. Also almost all of those remaining, save for the Jacobites, are women and children only.
2. The number of disappeared Catholics is enormous, 24,960 out of 29,220, and there are no more than 4,260 remaining—that is to say, about one seventh.
3. The non-Armenian disappeared exceed the number for the Armenians: 69,500 for the Armenians and 94,685 for the non-Armenians.
4. Only the Jacobites have more disappeared than the Gregorian Armenians, 60,725 compared to 58,000 Gregorian Armenians.
5. Among the remaining 2,000 Gregorian Armenians, there are 1,250 who come from the 250 families who converted to Islam.

About the foreign deportees who perished or disappeared inside the vilayet, it was never possible to make a count. Chapters XVI and XVII[2] give some idea of the great number of foreign victims lying in this inhospitable territory. It is possible to give the figure 55,000. I believe that this is close to the truth but more likely under than over the mark. This makes, then, with the vilayet's own victims, about 200,000 Christians who became victims of the persecution solely in the vilayet of Diyarbekir.

---

[2] This refers to chapters in Rhétoré's book. The title of chapter 16 is "The Armenian Deportees from Other Provinces: The Fate of Their Convoys in the Vilayet of Diyarbekir," and chapter 17 is "The Convoys of Foreign Deportees in Transit through Mardin."

Table 63: Disappeared Christians in the Sanjak of Mardin during the persecution of 1915–16

	No. of persons in Mardin before the persecution	No. of persons in the kazas and villages before the persecution	Total of persons before the persecution	Disappeared	Remain after the persecution
Gregorian Armenian	—	—	—	—	—
Armenian Catholic	6,500	4,000	10,500	10,200	300
Chaldean Catholic	1,100	6,770	7,870	6,800	1,070
Syriac Catholic	1,750	2,100	3,850	700	3,150
Syriac Jacobites	7,000	44,725	51,725	29,725	22,000
Protestants	125	400	525	250	275
Total	**16,475**	**57,995**	**74,470**	**47,675**	**26,795**

For the Jacobites, who were also attacked outside of the vilayet of Diyarbekir, the number of known disappeared is 96,000 (including those from the vilayet of Diyarbekir). Those who are not known are those who were from the vilayets of Bitlis and Kharpout.

It is estimated that after their disaster, the Jacobites, who had been about 200,000 in the empire, are not more than 60,000 or 70,000, of which 30,000 to 40,000 are in the vilayets of Diyarbekir, Bitlis, and Kharpout, and 30,000 in Mosul, Urfa, and Aleppo.

Comments to table 63:

1. There remain in the sanjak about one fifth as many Catholics as existed before.
2. The total number of Jacobites, 51,725, includes the 30,000 Jacobites of Jebel Tur.
3. The Armenian Gregorians, the prime object of the massacres, are missing [do not live] in this sanjak.[3]

It is interesting to reveal the losses suffered by the clergy of the churches, because we know that the clergy were particularly targeted in this persecution and no one was saved.

---

[3] This information is not correct, as there were Gregorian Armenians living in the towns of Hasankeyf, Kfar-Boran, and Jezire.

The Jacobites maintain that for their entire territory, there were 96,000 disappeared. Among them 2 bishops and 156 priests were killed, and 111 churches or monasteries were occupied or destroyed by the Kurds.

The Armenian Catholics have 2 bishops killed in Diyarbekir and Mardin and about 30 priests killed throughout the vilayet, 19 of whom were in Mardin. Four Armenian nuns of the Immaculate Conception were deported, 3 of whom were probably killed and one held captive by the Muslims.

The Chaldeans lost 3 bishops, those of Sa'irt, Artvena in Bohtan, and Jezire. We know of 10 priests killed at Jezire and Sa'irt, but there should be at least 20 others. One nun of the third order of Saint Dominique was killed at Jezire, 2 others at Sa'irt, and 5 were deported, whither no one knows.

The Syriac Catholics of Mardin diocese lost 29 priests killed. In the diocese of Jezire, they lost a bishop and many priests killed.

2. HECATOMBS AND MORE HECATOMBS

by Hyacinthe Simon (1867–1922)

From *Mardin, la ville heroique: Autel et tombeau de l'Arménie (Asie Mineure) durant les massacres de 1915* (1991), 133–43 (translated by David Gaunt).[4]
Eyewitness and oral testimony, I do not report anything but confirmed facts and authentic narratives. May I tell this in laconic brutality, but still an eloquent list of martyrs.

June

1 At Palu, 3 hours from Diyarbekir, massacre of 1,200 Christian soldiers constructing the road since November 1914.
- At Viranshehir, massacre of Abbé Jebrail Manaché, alumnus of the seminary at Mosul, with more than 1,000 of his parishioners.
- At Owena, 2 days from Mardin, massacre of the Christians, who were 200 persons.
- Convoy, on the waters of the Tigris, of 1,060 Christian notables from Diyarbekir and massacred on the banks of the river.

2 At the village of Bekarie, 1 hour from Mardin, massacre of 100 persons.

9 At Sa'irt, Bitlis vilayet, massacre of the Christians in the town and its surroundings, about 4,000 faithful. Among the perished, outside the town: Monsignor Addai Scher, born March 3, 1867, Chaldean

---

[4] Simon's manuscript is dated Mardin, June 1916.

archbishop since 1902, alumnus of the Dominican seminary in Mosul. Monsignor Thomas, Nestorian bishop who converted [to Catholicism] and resided in the village of Gueratil. The Sisters Suzanne, Anna, Saide, Radji, and Warda, Tertiaires Dominicaines. In the town: the Chaldean priests Jibrail Gorguis (alumnus of the Dominican seminary in Mosul), Mikail Kurio, Joseph Makdasi, Father Ephrem (Syriac monk from the monastery of Mar Ephrem in Mardin).

10 At the village of Qeleth, 8 hours from Mardin, massacre of all the Christians, more than 2,000 persons.

- At the village of Bafayya, 7 hours from Mardin, massacre of Christian villagers, said to be 600 persons.

11 At the village of Sheikhan and surroundings, 6 hours from Mardin, massacre of the first convoy of male notables from Mardin, said to be 405 persons, among them the archbishop and 9 Catholic priests. We invoke their names: Monsignor Ignace Maloyan, born April 15, 1869, Armenian Archbishop of Mardin since 1911. Father Léonard Baabdathi, Capuchin missionary, Lebanese. The abbots: Kouri Raphaïl Berdoa, Syriac Catholic archpriest. Petros Issa, Syriac Catholic, alumnus of the Dominican seminary in Mosul. Armenian Catholic clergymen: Boghos Gasparian, Ignace Chahadian, Augustin Baghdian, Léon Nazarian, Athanas Batanian, Antoine Ahmarian.

- At Mush (Bitlis vilayet), massacre of Monsignor Jacques Topouzian, Armenian Catholic bishop plus his diocese and the Gregorian Armenians.

12 At Harput, massacre of Monsignor Etienne Israelian, Armenian Catholic bishop and his diocese and the Gregorian Armenians.

- At the village of Ma'sarte, 6 hours from Mardin, massacre of 80 Christians.

14 At the village of Dara, 5 hours from Mardin, massacre of 50 Armenian Catholic villagers.

15 Near Sheikhan, 6 hours from Mardin, massacre of the second convoy of males from Mardin, said to be 75 persons, among them 4 Catholic priests. The abbots: Gabriël Catmardjian, Catholic Armenian; Matta Malache, Syriac Catholic; Joseph Mamarbachi, Syriac Catholic; Hanna Tabi, Syriac Catholic, alumnus of the Dominican seminary in Mosul.

16 At the village of Mansuriye, half an hour from Mardin, massacre of 95 Christians.

17 At the village of Benebil, 3 hours from Mardin, massacre of 70 Christians.

19 At the village of Qal'at-Mara, 1 hour from Mardin, massacre of 60 Christians.
20 Between Diyarbekir and Mardin, massacre of more than 12,000 Christians exiled from the north of Armenia who were on convoy to Mesopotamia. Slaughtered and thrown into the water at Gök River.
21 At Sivas, massacre of Monsignor Léon Ketchedjian, Armenian Catholic bishop and his diocese.
23 At the village of Brahemiye, 5 hours from Mardin, massacre of 400 Christians.

July

1 At the village of Tel-Arman, 4 hours from Mardin, massacre of all the Armenian Catholic villagers, said to be 1,500 persons.
3 At the village of Goliye, 1 hour from Mardin, massacre of all the Christian villagers, said to be 3,200 persons.
11 At the village of Dara, 5 hours from Mardin, massacre of a convoy of Christians exiled from Erzurum, all were thrown into the pits (ancient underground prisons of Darius).
13 At the above-mentioned village, massacre of two convoys of rich women from Diyarbekir, said to be 510 persons. Admirable bearing of an Armenian Catholic lady, Madam Cazazian, where her beauty provoked bestial passion, and she preferred death to a shaykh's promise of marriage if she converted to Islam.
14 At Mardin, murder of 3 Catholics who had observed the police making wine.
17 At the village of Abdul-Imam, 7 hours from Mardin, massacre of a convoy of rich women from Mardin, said to be 250 persons.
• Along with the above-mentioned victims died Der Ohannès Sarkian, Armenian Catholic priest aged 90 years, Monsignor Maloyan's general vicar.
19 At Midyat, 2 days from Mardin, massacre of 16 Catholic priests, one Jacobite bishop, 46 Jacobite priests, one convoy of 70 Christian notables, and 7,000 Christians from the neighboring villages. Among the notables are Dr. Na'aman Caragulla, Armenian Protestant, and his wife, Madam Stella, of the Catholic religion and Armenian nationality.
20 At the village of Sawro, 9 hours from Mardin, massacre of all Christianity, more than 650 persons.
24 In the surroundings of the above-mentioned village, stoning of 250 Catholic women deported from Sa'irt.

26 At the village of Dara, 5 hours from Mardin, massacre of a convoy of 300 Armenians deported from Mardin, among them 7 Armenian Catholic priests. The abbots: Nersès Tcheroyan, Mgrditch Kalioundjian, Stéphan Holozian, Boghos Chidian, Vartan Haddadian, Minas Naamian, Hagop Tell-Arménavian.
27 At Mardin, the murder of 2 young notable girls from Diyarbekir who were forced into a Muslim harem but refused to convert. Their corpses were found in a brook near the town.

August

8 Near Jezire, massacre of 15 Chaldean villages. Among the perished are many Catholics, notably 2 Chaldean priests, the abbots Augustin Murdjani and Thomas Chérin, both alumni of the Dominican seminary in Mosul.
10 At the village of Kikié, 9 hours from Mardin, attack on a convoy of 500 persons, women and children from Mardin exiled to Ras ul Ayn. More than 350 persons were massacred by the Kurds.
- About 50 women already robbed of their clothes and nearly dead had escaped. They went into the desert and got lost. Their killing took place in the same day as the Muslim holiday.
11 At the village of Derike, 10 hours from Mardin, massacre of all the Christians, more than 1,000 persons.
12 In the gardens of Zennar, formerly the fortress of Mardin, massacre of 50 labor-battalion soldiers, Armenian Catholics from this town. Their corpses were thrown into the pits.
16 At Nisibin, 14 hours from Mardin, massacre of all the Christians, more than 800 persons.
20 At Jezire, 4 days from Mardin, massacre of all the Christians, among them 2 bishops and 10 Catholic priests, 3 Jacobite priests, and 5,000 of the faithful. Among the prelates: Monsignor Jacques Abraham, Chaldean bishop, born January 3, 1848, bishop since 1882; Monsignor Michel Melki, Syriac Catholic bishop, born 1862, bishop since 1913; also 3 Chaldean priests, all of them alumni of the Dominican seminary in Mosul, the abbots Elias Issa, Marcos Thomas, Hanna Khatoun; finally the Syriac Catholic priests, Khouri Chamoun, arch-priest; Paul Castan, Ephremite monk; among them died the nun Radji Ritto, Tertiaire Dominican, and Abdulkerim Georgis, a seminary student at home on vacation with his family.
21 At Urfa, massacre of a convoy of 465 Christian soldiers.

22 In the suburbs of Mardin, massacre of 500 Christian women deported from Sawro and its neighborhood.
23 At Salakh, 4 hours from Mardin, massacre by the soldiers who were escorting the convoy of 300 women and children from Mardin who were being deported to Ras ul Ayn.
24 At Mardin, at the foot of Mar Michel monastery, 10 minutes outside the town, massacre of 12 Armenian Catholic slave-labor soldiers.

September

10 Between Diyarbekir and Mardin, massacre of 8,000 women and children convoyed from Harput and Erzurum. The convoy included 12,000 persons.
14 On the outskirts of Nisibin, massacre of 2,000 other foreigners in the above-mentioned convoy.
15 On the outskirts of Mardin and near Harrin (4 hours from Mardin), massacre of 125 women and children from Mardin on their way to Mosul.
17 Murder of an American Protestant missionary from Bitlis, between Harput and Diyarbekir.[5]
18 In a ravine near Diyarbekir, massacre of Monsignor André Tchelebian, Armenian Catholic archbishop of Diyarbekir, aged 67 years. Amsih Sabbahian, Armenian Catholic notable of that town, died at his side.
19 Bombardment of the village of Urfa. Ruin of the town, massacre of the Christians to the number of more than 25,000. Among them 2 Syriac Catholic priests, Youhanna Kandeleft and Ephrem Rahwali, and a French exile named Robert Germain.
22 At 3 hours southeast of Jezire, massacre of 200 males from Erzurum under the eyes of Halil Pasha, during a military inspection.

October

20 The first convoy of women from Urfa, 2,000 persons, on its way to Mardin.
28 Second convoy of Urfa Christians, 3,500 persons, directed, so they say to Mosul. The convoys followed one after another during the next month.
30 North of Diyarbekir, massacre of 2 convoys of Armenian soldiers, the one of 400 persons, the other of 600.

---

[5] This was George Perkins Knapp. See Grace H. Knapp, *The Tragedy of Bitlis* (1919).

3. Christian Massacres of 1915 in Diyarbekir Vilayet

From *Diary of Major E. Noel on Special Duty in Kurdistan* (1919), 10–11.

Entry for April 25, 1919

The account set forth is from material obtained during a short visit to Mardin. The opinions expressed reflect the merely local point of view, and are, therefore, likely to be distorted in many particulars, especially as regards the general political situation, which led to the massacres.

Very soon after Turkey's entry into the war, signs were forthcoming that the future for the Christian was full of presage. ... The first tangible presage of the storm was a cryptic agency telegram "The people themselves must deal with traitors." Who were the traitors referred to?

Among the Christians at Mardin it was at first thought that the allusion referred to the Armenian soldiery who were said to have deserted *en masse* to the Russians on the Caucasus front. No apprehension seemed to exist in the minds of the Mardinis that their town would be accused of disloyalty. Had not two mutasarrifs, Shafiq Bey and Hilmi Bey, vouched to Constantinople for its loyalty? Not more that 2 per cent of its Armenian citizens were members of the great Armenian organization, the Dashnaksaksio. The Roman Catholic Bishop, the spiritual head of the Armenian community, had from the pulpit warned his flock against joining secret societies.

Whether, in point of fact, proofs of active Armenian disloyalty were discovered at Mardin is difficult to state. The Turkish officials of '14 and '15 have disappeared. The records are not at present available, and the evidence of Christians is biased. The latter maintain that no secret supplies of arms and ammunition were disclosed as a result of the frequent house to house searches carried out by the Turks. (An Armenian store of arms was discovered at Diyarbekir in May, and this seems to have provided the tar with which to brush all and sundry.)

But even if Armenian treason could be proved to the hilt, there could scarcely be any contention, even on the part of the Turks, that the other Christian communities, Jacobite, Chaldean and Syrian, were parties thereto.

The people were not left long in doubt as to whom the word "traitor" referred to. Orders were received from Constantinople to disarm any Christian soldiers and gendarmes. Officers were told to dismiss their Christian servants and in future to allow no Christian to have any access to them. In January 1915 all Christians were dismissed from Government employ. In February and March, Turkish officials, including even deputies, visited the tribes under the guise of purchasing transport animals, and openly preached the doctrine of death to the infidel. This was followed in April and May, by a more sinister measure—the formation of a Moslem militia recruited from men from 50 to 60 years of age not already called to the colours. They were armed with a rifle and sword and wore a red badge on the arm.

These successive events pointed to the existence of a policy previously decided upon and worked out in all its details. It is said in fact that in December 1914 a Secret Commission was formed with Talaat at its head and Rashid Bey, the Vali of Diyarbekir, as one of its principal members. The Commission's instruction had to be obeyed implicitely on the pain of dismissal from Government service, or possibly a severer form of punishment. It is this which explains why two Mutasarrifs were removed from Mardin in quick succession.

Openly the policy adopted was to: 1. Deport suspects. 2. Put to forced labour anybody found in possession of arms. 3. Put to death anybody convicted of treason. In practice, however, the secret procedure laid down was to arrange for the massacre of all three of the above classes under the following circumstances.

A convoy of deportees was collected and told to prepare to start for an unknown destination in a few hours. After proceeding one or more stages under an escort of the local militia already referred to, they found themselves surrounded by local Kurds. The officer in charge of the convoy the read out a sentence of death purporting to have been signed by the Sultan, and the intended victims were offered their lives at the price of apostasy. On a refusal, which would seem to have occurred in the majority of cases, the convoy was split up into parties of a hundred to points where wells were available or deep trenches had previously been dug. They were then made to undress and this was followed by a general carnage in which the local Kurds participated. The rifle was not much used: the sword and a Kurdish dagger being preferred. In many cases the victims were hacked about without receiving the *coup de grace*.

Such would appear to have been the procedure officially laid down and more or less adhered [to] in the case of the first few massacres in June. The following variations, however, soon crept in. The local officials before dispatching a convoy squeezed their victims as much as possible with a hope of reprieve. (Mamdouk [Memduh] Bey, the Commissioner of Police at Mardin, is said to have made L.T. 50,000 in this manner. He is now at Diyarbekir conducting vigorous anti-British propaganda under the guise of a Kurdish national movement. He should certainly be brought to book.) On the day of departure by means of effusive promises of safe conduct and even a show of courtesy, the victims were induced to load themselves with jewels and ornaments, which were removed from them on leaving the town. The formality of reading the death sentence disappears, as before reaching the local Golgotha swarms of Kurds have collected and an impromptu carnage commences in which the militia escort participates. The women are stripped and raped. Some of the younger ones are spared to adorn Moslem harems, or be sold as slaves. The instructions to cover up traces of their deeds are disregarded. The bodies are left naked on the plains—a curious detail—the men on their stomachs, the women on their backs.

It is difficult to understand the mentality or follow the logic of the authors of these standing instructions. One can only conjecture that they were actuated by the following considerations, childish as some of them may seem. They hoped to give a stimulus to the jihad by whetting the peoples' taste for blood, and they calculated that once having started the ball rolling in the manner indicated, the infection would spread and the Mahomedan population would carry on the massacre automatically until the Christian population entirely ceased to exist. It would moreover seem that the Turks wished to give a veneer of legality to the opening massacres hoping to throw the responsibility for its continuance on the tribes' religious frenzy and national feelings excited by Armenian perfidy. It has also been suggested that by conducting the massacres in lonely spots far from the towns some time would elapse before the news of them would spread and the other Armenians awaiting their turn would not disperse to the country side or be driven into active opposition. Further that the tidings would take the maximum of time to reach the outside world and America in particular.

The outstanding feature, which is free from all element of conjecture, is that the massacres were scientifically organized from Constantinople, and the local ignorant Moslem was only used as a tool. It is not he who should be punished, but the Turk in high places, and again the local Turk who acted as his willing agent, and who filled his pockets in the process.

APPENDIX 4
TURKISH ARCHIVAL DOCUMENTS ON DEPORTATIONS AND SIEGES

by Dr. Racho Donef

The references to the documents are given in Turkish, rather than in English, to facilitate future research. In the translations of the documents, "..." indicates that a passage is illegible in the original

1. THE DEPORTATION OF THE ASSYRIANS IN OTTOMAN DOCUMENTS

The deportation of the Armenians in the Ottoman Empire in 1915 is a well-documented historical event. Many Armenian scholars have meticulously collected documents to prove that these deportations were part of a well-orchestrated campaign to annihilate the Armenian population.

As far as the deportation and genocide of the Assyrians is concerned, a great deal of research still needs to be carried out. The Ottoman archives have many documents, which need to be identified and studied in their historical context.

The following five documents from the Ottoman Archives, which, to my knowledge, have never been published before, contain the deportation of Assyrians as a connecting thread. All of them are telegrams sent from the Ministry of the Interior of the government of Ittihat ve Terakki (Union and Progress), usually known as the Young Turks. The telegrams were sent to the governors in the provinces of Van, Mosul, Diyarbakir, Mamuretü'l Aziz, Halep (Aleppo), and Bitlis. The documents show that all Assyrian denominations, be they Nestorian, Chaldean, or Syriac Orthodox or Catholic, were affected by the turmoil of deportation. Although the telegrams make no mention of massacres, the telegram of October 7, 1915 (no. 5), acknowledges that many villages around Mardin, Midyat, and Diyarbakir were empty. No doubt these villages were once populated by Christians. The term used in the telegram, "deserted," somewhat masks the turmoil that preceded. The Christian inhabitants of the "deserted" villages were either massacred or had to flee to avoid the fate decreed by the Young Turks. The government, having caused evacuation of the villages through physical elimination, then sought to repopulate them with Turks from the Balkans, inevitably altering the ethnic makeup of the region.

These documents are translated into English and Modern Turkish and appended below. Great care and research has been undertaken in rendering the content from the Ottoman Turkish to English.

FROM THE PRIME MINISTERIAL OTTOMAN ARCHIVES
Department of the Interior
Cipher office

1. BOA.Dahiliye Şifre Kalemi Nu:46/78

Babiali[1]   **Ministry of the Interior**
Office of the Directorate of Public Security
General ....
Private: Number: 104
Ciphered telegram to the Province of Van
It is very urgent.

The position of the Nestorians has always remained doubtful for the government [due to] their predisposition to be influenced by foreigners and become a channel and an instrument. Because of the operation and efforts in Iran, the consideration of the Nestorians for the government has increased. Especially those who are found at our border area with Iran, due to the government's lack of trust of them resulting in punishment ... their deportation and expulsion from their locations to appropriate provinces such as Ankara and Konya, to be transferred in dispersed manner so that henceforth they will not be together in a mass and be [settled] exclusively among Muslim people, and in no location to exceed twenty dwellings, and on the issue of settlement, with the proviso that the government will not undertake to provide any type of support, to be permitted to stay and transmit the communication to the appropriate Province and after the dispensation of the matter to depart from Van.   October 26, 1914[2]
   Minister

Şimdiye kadar vaziyetleri hükümet için daima daima iştibah bir halde kalmaktan kurtulamayan ve tahrikatı ecnebiyeye pek büyük bir vasıta ve alet olmakta ki istidatları İran'daki harekat ve teşebbüsatı ahıreleri münasebetiyle nazar-ı hükümette bir kat daha tevzih eden Nesturilerden bilhassa İran hududuna civar menatıkımızda bulunanlarının mücerred hükümetin kendilerine karşı adem-i itimadından münbais bir cezaya mahsus olmak üzere işarı alileri vechiyle bulundukları yerlerinden ihrac ve tardlarıyle Ankara ve Konya gibi münasip vilayete müteferrik surette sevkleri ve badema toplu bir halde bulunamamaları içün de münhasıran İslam kurrasında olmak ve hiçbir mahalde azami olarak yirmi haneyi tecavüz etmemek ve iskan hususunda hükümetçe bir guna muavenet ve taahhüdü (teaddi-i) tazammun itmemek şartıyle kalabilmelerine müsaade edilmesi ve icab iden vilayete tebliğkeyfiyet olunmak üzere işarı ve bu husus icab iden tedabirin ittihazından sonra Van'dan mufareket olunması
Fi 13 Teşrinievvel 330   Nazır

---

[1] Another name for the Sublime Porte, the central office of the Imperial Government of the Ottoman Empire.

[2] The dates in the original documents are given in the *Rumi* calendar, a fiscal-year calendar used in the Ottoman bureaucracy in its later period. This is an alternative Islamic calendar, which starts in the year 584 but it is a composite. The dates here have been converted to the Julian/Gregorian calendar.

2. BOA.Dahiliye Şifre Kalemi Nu: 54-A/154

Babiali
Ministry of the Interior
Office of the Directorate of Public Security
General: ....
Private: 62
Ciphered telegram to the Province of Mosul

It is appropriate for the care and sustenance of the Syrian and Chaldean women and children who are not Armenians, who reportedly have arrived from Başkale and Siirt on July 23, 1915, to be undertaken by their own community.
July 28, 1915
Başkale ve Siirt'ten geldikleri bildirilen Ermeni olmayan Süryani ve Keldani kadın ve çocuklarının kendi cemaatlerince terbiye ve iaşelerinin deruhte olunması münasiptir.
15 Temmuz 331

3. BOA.Dahiliye Şifre Kalemi Nu: 55/273

Babiali
Ministry of the Interior
Office of the Directorate of Public Security
General: ....
Private: 5310
Ciphered telegram to the Provinces of Diyarbakır, Mamuretü'l Aziz,[3] and Aleppo

It has been understood from the submission from the Command [?] that some members of the Syrian Catholic Community have been removed from their localities. Inform on whether or not these events took place.
August 28, 1915   Minister
Süryani Katolik Cemaati efradından bazıları hakkında uygulanan yerlerinden kaldırılma ve tebid olunma hadiseleri hakkında bilgi verilmesine dair Emniyet-i Umumiye Müdürlüğünden Diyarbakır, Mamuretü'l Aziz ve Halep vilayetinden çekilen telgraf.

4. BOA.Dahiliye Şifre Kalemi Nu:57/293

Babiali
Ministry of the Interior
Office of the Directorate of Public Security

---

[3] Presently Elazığ.

General: ....
Private: 91
Ciphered telegram to the Province of Mosul
It has been observed that the October 16, 1915, dated, edition [number] 684 of "Zuhur Newspaper," printed in Baghdad, has published a telegram regarding the removal of the Nestorians sent from your Most High Province to the Province of Bagdad and henceforth [?] ... the need not to give the opportunity for publication of official correspondence and telegrams of this sort has been communicated to them and the matter has been given serious consideration.

Date December 5, 1915   Minister

Bağdat'ta münteşir "Zuhur Gazetesi"nin 3 Teşrin-i Evvel 1331 tarihli 684 nüshasında Nasturilerin te'dib olunduğuna dair Vilayeti Aliyelerinden Bağdat Vilayetine keşide olunan bir telgrafnamenin münderic olduğu görülmüş ve bade....bu kabil mahrum mahiyette bulunan resmi muharrerat ve telgrafnamelerin neşrine meydan verilmemesi lüzumu vilayet-i müşarun ileyhümaya tebliğ kılınmış olmakla oraca da bu husus itina olunmuş fi 22 Teşrin-i Sani 331   Nazır

5. BOA.Dahiliye Şifre Kalemi Nu:57/328
Babiali
Ministry of the Interior
Directorate of Settlement of Tribes and Immigrants[4]
59
Ciphered telegram to the Province of Bitlis
Date October 30, 1915
As there are deserted villages around Mardin and Midyat, the Province of Diyarbakir has been informed that the immigrant members[5] of the Division Public Order Cavalry may settle [there] and that efforts to be made to dispatch them.

Ministerial Correspondence
Date November 7, 1915

fi 17 Teşrin-i Evvel sene 331 Mardin ve Midyat cihetlerindemetruk karyeler olduğundan Aşayir süvari fırkalarına mensup muhacirinin vurudlarında iskan idilecekleri bilmuhabere Diyarbekir vilayetine bildirilmiş olmakla sevkiyatına germi (gayret) verilmesi
Nazırname
fi 25 Teşrin-i Evvel 331

---

[4] This is an organization established in 1913 to assimilate the Kurdish tribes, as well as to settle Turkish refugees from the Balkans.

[5] More than likely Turks who have emigrated from Balkan countries.

2. Documents Related to the Siege of Hezak (Azakh) in the Turkish Military History Archives

Hezak is also spelled Azak or Hazax and is İdil in Turkish, while it is also known by its Aramaic name of Bet-Zabday.

1. Gnkur. ATAŞE Arşivi, Kol.: BDH, Kls.: 17, Dos.: 81/ , Fih.: 27

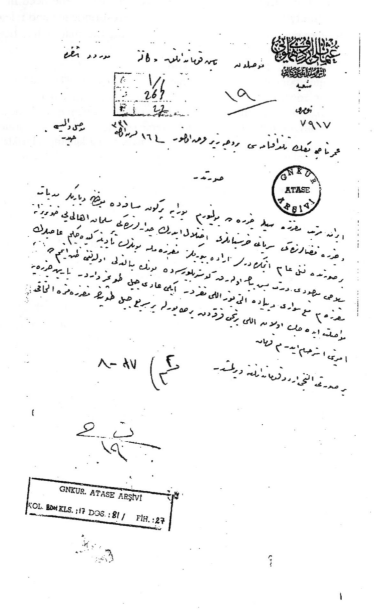

APPENDIX 4

Ottoman Imperial Army
Supreme Military Command
Branch: 19
Number: 7917
Ciphered telegram to the Supreme Military Command, received from Mosul

Ömer Naci Bey's telegram is submitted [and is] as follows. Date October 29, 1915[6]

                                                    Haydar, Governor of Mosul

                           Copy

I am in Cizre with detachment of troops bound for Persia. In the districts of Diyarbekir, Midyat, and Cizre, which are situated one hour distance from here, the Süryani Christians have rebelled and are cruelly massacring the Muslim people in the area. I will go there with my troops to punish the rebels who, it has been reported, have four thousand arms, though I think this is an exaggeration.

My troops consist of six hundred fifty cavalrymen and foot soldiers. We have two mountain artilleries. I request that a battalion from the fifty-first division, which is to arrive in Cizre, and a number of mountain artilleries be ordered to join our troops.

A copy has been given to the Command of the Sixth Army.
Section 8-17

Ömer Naci begin telgrafnamesi ber vechi zir arz olunur. fi 16 Teşrin-i Evvel 331
Musul Valisi Haydar

                         Surettir

İran'a mürettip müfrezesiyle Cizre'de bulunuyorum. Buraya bir gün mesafede bulunan Diyarbekir Midyat ve Cizre kazalarına ki Süryani Hıristiyanları ihtilal iderek civarlarındaki Müslüman ahaliyi hunrızane (hunharca)bir surette katliam itmektedirler. Orada büyüyenler müfrezemle te'dibine gideceğim asilerin silah-ı mevcudu dört bin beyan olarak gösteriliyorsa da bunun mübalağalı olduğunu zannettim. müfrezem maa süvari ve yayada altı yüz elli neferdir. İki adi cbl topumuz vardır. Yayaya Cizre'de muvasalat idecek olan elli birinci fırkadan bir taburla bir seri cbl topunun müfrezemize iltihakı emrini istirham iderim ferman
Bir sureti altıncı ordu kumandanlığına verilmiştir.
Kısım 8-17

---

[6] Unless otherwise noted, the dates in the documents are in the Rumi calendar. They have been converted to the Julian/Gregorian calendar by the translator.

2. Gnkur. ATAŞE Arşivi, Kol.: BDH, Kls.: 17, Dos.: 81/ , Fih.: 27-1

Ottoman Imperial Army
Supreme Military Command
Branch: 19
Number: 7904
Ciphered telegram to the Supreme Military Command, received from Cizre

Upon my arrival in Cizre I found out that up to fifty kilometers west of Cizre, in the village of Hazar, from various neighborhoods and villages in the vicinity, up to one thousand armed Armenians gathered lately [and] started an assault destroying Muslim villages nearby and massacred their inhabitants and cut the telegraph line between Cizre and Diyarbekır.

As there is no force in the area to punish them, this assault will continue. Naci Beg from the Third Army with a force under his command, [who] is on his way to Iran, is currently in Cizre. I do not think he has pressing duties and [will wait] until the arrival of the full order.

I submit that if they are not to be relied upon, I request that it would be appropriate to order a regiment from the Fifty-Second Division to punish them [the rebels].

Date October 29, 1915
Commander of the Eighteenth Army Corps Halil
(A copy has been provided to the Sixth Army Command)
Section: 8-17

Muhtelif mahallerden ve civar köylerden toplanmak suretiyle Cizre'nin elli kilometre kadar garbında Hazar karyesinde tecemmu' eyleyen ve bin kadar müsellah olan Ermeniler son zamanlarda tadiyata başlayarak civar Müslüman köylerini tahrib ve ahalisini katl ittiklerini ve Cizre ile Diyarbakır arasındaki telgraf hattını kat' ittiklerini Cizre'ye muvasılımda öğrendim. Bu havalide bunları te'dib idecek kuvvet mevcut olmadığından bu tadiyat devam idecekdir. Üçüncü ordudan Naci Begin taht-ı emrine verilmiş ve İran'a gitmekte olup elyevm Cizre'de bütün emrinizin vuruduna kadar tevekkuf ve vazifelerini müstacel zan itmediğim kuvvetle. Bunlara itimat buyurulmadığı takdirde elli ikinci fırkanın bir alayıyla te'diblerinin emir buyurulmasının münasip olacağı mütalasında bulunduğumu arz eylerim. Fi 16 Teşrin-i Evvel 331
On sekizinci Kolordu Komutanı Halil
(Bir sureti altıncı ordu kumandanlığına verilmiştir.)
Kısım.: 8-17

3. Gnkur. ATAŞE Arşivi, Kol.: BDH, Kls.: 17, Dos.: 81/ , Fih.: 27-2

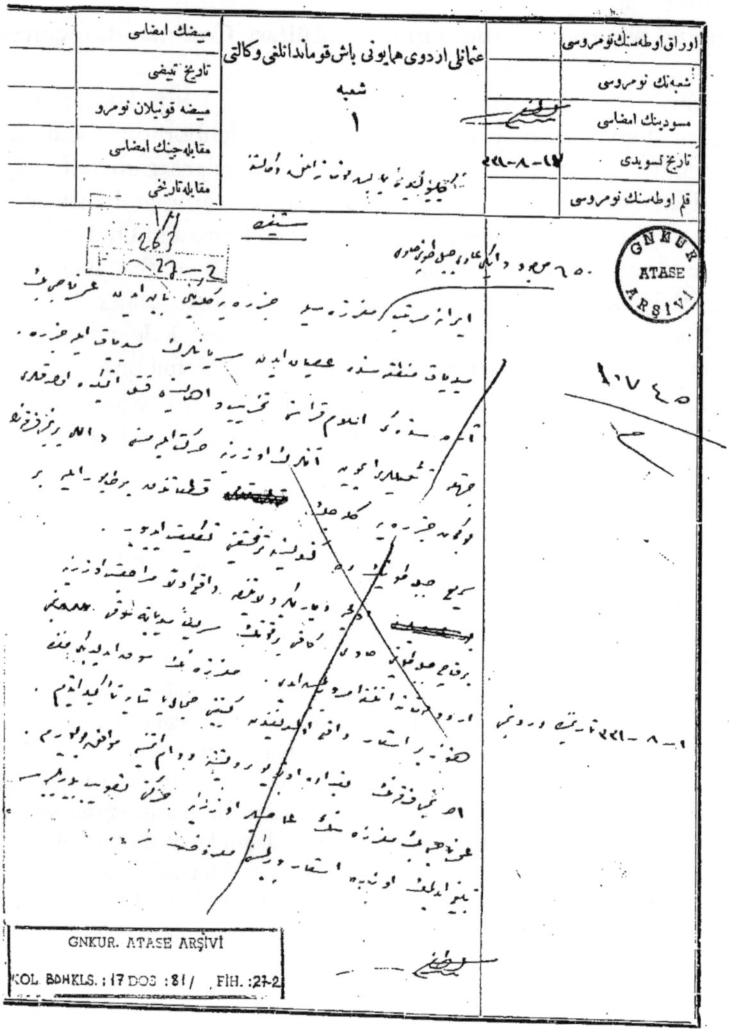

Imperial Ottoman Army
Supreme Military Command
Branch: 1
... Ciphered telegram to the Supreme Military Command
Date of draft: October 30, 1915
10745
Ömer Naci Beg, who reported his arrival in Cizre with detachment of troops bound for Iran, [consisting of] an effective force of 650 and two mountain artilleries, is proposing one battalion and a number of mountain artilleries from ... the Fifty-First Division, which is to arrive to Cizre, to join his troops, to [set upon] the Süryani who rebelled in the area of Mardin to punish them for destroying Muslim villages and massacring their inhabitants.

... according to a request which arrived in Diyarbekir to dispatch a number of mountain artilleries ... . Was ordered to transfer to Mardin immediately. If the detachment is dispatched, and as no communiqué has arrived as yet, circumstances ... ... I strengthened.
Of the Third Division
Ömer Naci Beg
transmission
on October 14, 1915
Tarih-i tesvidi: 17.8.331
10745
İran'a mürettib 650 mevcut ve iki adi cbl topu havi müfrezesiyle Cizre'ye geldiğini beyan iden Ömer Naci Beg Midyat mıntıkasında isyan iden Süryanilerin Midyat ile cizre arasındaki İslam kurrasını tahrib ve ahalisini katl itmekte oldukları cihetle te'dibleri için onların üzerine sevk eylemesini ve elli birinci fırkanın mevkice Cizre'ye gelecek. --- ...dan bir tabur ile bir seri cbl topun da koluna terfikini teklif ediyor.
... Diyarbekir vilayetine vaki olan müracaat üzerine birkaç cbl topunu sevk ... . Serian Midyat'a sevki ordu emir verilmiş idi. Müfrezenin sevk edildiği halde henüz bir istar vaki olmadığından keyfiyeti ... ... te'kt ettim.
Üçüncü fırkanın
Ömer Naci Beg
tebliğ
1.8.331 tarihinde

4. Gnkur. ATAŞE Arşivi, Kol.: BDH, Kls.: 17, Dos.: 81/ , Fih.: 31

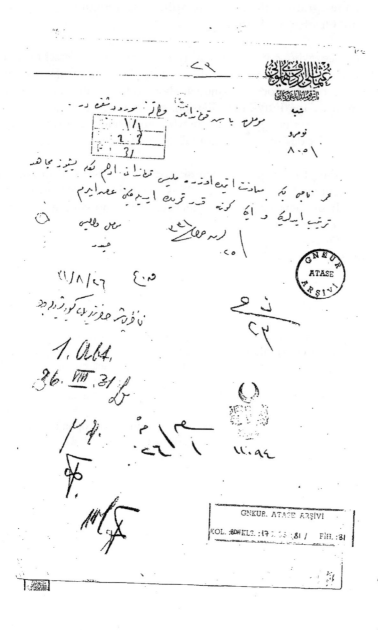

APPENDIX 4

Imperial Ottoman Army
Supreme Military Command
Branch:
Number: 805/
Ciphered telegram received at the Supreme Military Command from Mosul

I submit that in order to assist Ömer Naci Beg, five hundred fighters have been arranged with militia commander Edhem Beg, and that they would be moving within two days.
November 7, 1915
Governor of Mosul, Haydar
November 8, 1915
It would be discussed with Nazır Pasha

Ömer Naci Beg'e muavenet itmek üzere milis kumandanı Edhem Begle beşyüz mücahid tertib idildiği ve iki güne kadar tahrik eyliyeceğin arz eylerim.
25 Teşrin-i Evvel 331
Musul Valisi Haydar
26/8/331
Nazır Paşa İle Görüşülecek

5. Gnkur. ATAŞE Arşivi, Kol.: BDH, Kls.: 17, Dos.: 81/ , Fih.: 31-2

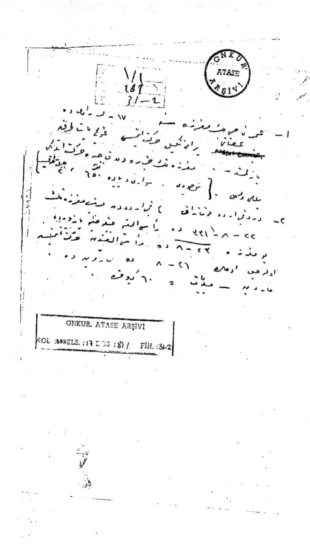

1. To Ömer Naci Beg's detachment [of troops] on October 30, 1915
Has departed to repress the rebellion ... It was communicated to Pasha. It is not clear when the detachment departed from Cizre (there are 650 cavalrymen and foot soldiers, and two mountain artillery men available).
2. The commander of the Fourth Army ... detachment arranged from the army.
on November 4, 1915
... October 25
... October 29
Mardin-Midyat=60 ...
1. Ömer Naci Beg müfrezesine 17-Teşrin-i Evvelde Usat -ı beray-ı tenkil hareket itmiş ... Paşa tarafına yazılmıştır. Müfrezenin Cizre'den kaçda hareket ettiği belli değil. {mevcud süvari ve yaya 650 nefer, 2 cbl topçu}
2. Dördüncü ordu kumandanı 4 ... ordudan mürettip müfrezenin
22-8-331'de
... 12-8'de
... 16-8'de
Mardin-Midyat=60 ...

6. Gnkur. ATAŞE Arşivi, Kol.: BDH, Kls.: 17, Dos.: 81/ , Fih.: 31-3

Babıali
Ministry of the Interior
Office of the Directorate of General Security
General: ....
Special: Office 371
To the Imperial Army Supreme Military Command
Your excellency
In a telegram dated November 7, 1915, that has arrived from the Province of Mosul ... Although it was communicated that in order to assist Ömer Naci Beg five hundred fighters with militia commander Edhem Beg have been arranged and that they would be moving within two days, in this matter command belongs unto him to whom all commanding belongs.
Date November 8, 1915[7]
Minister of the Interior
A copy has been sent to the Province of Mosul./8-27
Devletlü Efendim Hazretleri
Ömer Naci Beg'e muavenet itmek üzere milis kumandanı Edhem Begle beşyüz mücahid tertib idildiği ve iki güne kadar sevk olunacağı Musul vilayetinden varid olan 25 Teşrin-i Evvel 331
tarihli telgrafnamede izbar kılınmış olmakla olbabda emrü ferman hazreti men lehül emrindir. Fi 30 Zilhicce sene 333 ve fi 26 Teşrin-i Evvel 331   Dahiliye Nazırı
Bir sureti Musul Vilayetine gönderilmiştir./8-27

---

[7] The scribe in this document cited both the Hijra and Rumi dates.

7. Gnkur. ATAŞE Arşivi, Kol.: BDH, Kls.: 17, Dos.: 81/ , Fih.: 32

Ottoman Imperial Army
Ministry of Supreme Military Command
Branch: 1
Ciphered telegram to the Third Army Command
Date of draft: November 9, 1915
1. Ömer Naci Beg reported that the Süryanis between Midyat and Cizre have united with the Armenians and cut the telegraph lines and attacked the Muslim people. To suppress them, Ömer Naci Beg's detachment and a battalion of footsoldiers and two mountain artilleries have [departed] from Urfa and are moving toward Cizre; and that it has been understood that this matter was communicated to you [in writing] by the Sixth Army Command.

The rebels ... and the districts they attacked in the area of the Third Army and ... because of this, the movement of the detachments ... the administration of the Third Army ...

2. If the uprising of the rebels is warded off, giving up arms ... In a locality selected by the government ... [they] will consent .... Even if it is not true about their attack and massacres of Muslim people ... inform the Provinces of Diyarbekır and Mosul that I also agree that the matter should be followed up. Apparently we can make use of the Metropolitan in Mosul in this matter. Inform us of the outcome.

Signature
Tarih-i tesvidi: 27.8.331

1. Midyat ile Cizre arasındaki Süryanilerin kararı Ermeniler ile birleşerek telgraf hududunu kat' ve kurrayı islamiyeye taarruz ittikleri Ömer Naci Beg tarafından bildirildiğinden tenkili içün Ömer Naci Beg müfrezesi Cizre'den ve bir yaya taburu ile iki cbl topu Urfa'dan Midyat istikametine tahrik olmuş ve bu hususun Altıncı ordu kumandanlığından tarafınıza yazıldığı anlaşılmıştır. Usatın ... ve tecavüz ittikleri mahaller üçüncü ordu mıntıkası ve ... olmak hasebiyle işbu müfrezeler harekatına üçüncü ordu idaresi ...

2. Usatın muhafazai isyanları def idildiği halde teslim-i silah iderek Hükümetce takarrür idecek mahalde ... muvafakat idecekler... Bunların kurrayı islamiyeye taarruz ve katliam tasdiri vaki değil ise bu şart ve halde daha ... takib ittirilmesini ben de muvafık bulurum diyarbakır ve Musul Vilayetlerine muhabere ediniz. Musul'daki metropolitten de bu hususda istifade olunabilirmiş. Neticeyi bildiriniz.
İmza

8. Gnkur. ATAŞE Arşivi, Kol.: BDH, Kls.: 17, Dos.: 81/ , Fih.: 32-1

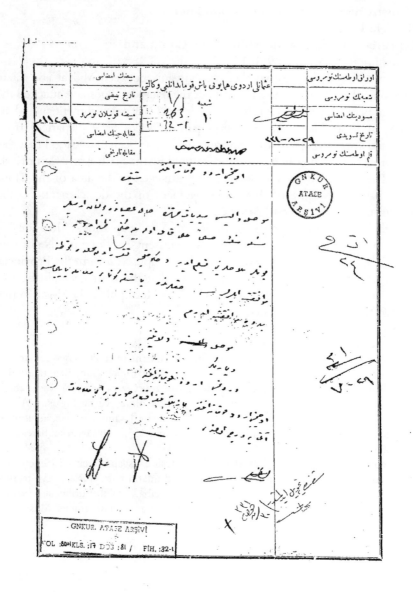

Imperial Ottoman Army Supreme Military Command
Branch: 1
Ciphered telegram to the Third Army Command
Date of draft: November 11, 1915   311291
The Governor of Mosul thinks that those who are presently rebelling in Midyat could be .... Armenians.
    If they give up their arms and in a locality to be determined by the government ...
    ... different treatment ... I agree in the place.
To the Province of Mosul
Diyarbakır
To the Fourth Army Command
For your information, copy of the telegram communicated to the Third Army Command ...
as follows.
The code has been transferred /12 November 1915
Tarih-i tesvidi: 29.8.331   311291
Musul valisi Midyat cihetine hali isyanda bulunan Ermeniler
.... olabileceğini zannediyor.
Bunlar silahlarını teslim ider ve hükümetce takarrür iden mahalde ... muvafakat iderler ise ... başka guna bir muamele ...
yerde muvafakat iderim.
Musul Vilayetine
Diyarbakır
Dördüncü Ordu Kumandanlığına
Üçüncü Ordu Kumandanlığına yazılan telgrafname sureti berayı ...
Şifre tahvil edilmiştir./30 Teşrini Evvel 331

9. Gnkur. ATAŞE Arşivi, Kol.: BDH, Kls.: 17, Dos.: 81/ , Fih.: 35

Imperial Ottoman Army, Supreme Military Command
Branch: Number: 8174
Ciphered telegram 82142, Diyarbekir to Supreme Military Command
Cipher dated November 12, 1915
In the course of the punishment of the rebels in the Midyat region, they were first of all asked to give up their arms. [One] could not be certain about the inaccessibility of the terrain, and in such places as Basabriye and Hezak, where the rebels are in great numbers, two, three villagers who were isolated surrendered, [and] although they were forced to lay down their arms, with half-hearted confidence they handed over to government useless weapons and concealed the rest. Rebels in other places dared to respond to the proposal by firing guns and by patrolling Muslim [areas] and attacking and massacring the inhabitants. They fortified themselves in the village of Hezak and fortified the village with walls and trenches, assigned for the punishment of about ten thousand rebels Ömer Naci Beg, commander of the Iran Expedition Force, after the blockade the village with the troops and the artillery proposed peace and asked them to surround their weapons. They had the insolence to respond to this proposition by causing thirty-eight wounded, including two officers, and three martyrs in the detachment. These scoundrels who [demonstrated] such boldness and such insolence could not appreciate this compassion and affection, and it is submitted that your command has been communicated to the civil service.

Date November 13, 1915   11332
Diyarbekır Province Acting Governor Bedreddin
Date of receipt of the cipher at the office November 14. 1915

Fi 30 Teşrin-i Evvel sene 331 şifredir.
Midyat mıntakasındaki usatın te'dibi esnasında evvelemirde asilereterk-i silah itmeleri teklif idildi. Mevkinin menaatından emin olamayan ve Basabriye ve Hezak gibi usatın kesretle bulunduğu mevakiiden tecrid idilen iki, üç karye ahalisi terk-i silahta muzattar kaldıkları halde hükümete nîm bir emniyetle silahlarının işe yaramayanlarını tevdi', diğerlerini ihfa ittiler. Mevaki-i sairedeki asiler bu teklife silahla mukabelede bulunmak ve karakollarla kurray-ı islamiyeye tecavüz ve katl-i nüfuse cüret itmek suretiyle cevap virdiler Hezak karyesinde mütehassın ve karyenin etrafını duvarla, hendeklerle tahkim iden on bin kadar usatın te'dibine memur idilen İran heyet-i seferisi müfreze kumandanı Ömer Naci Beg de müfreze ve toplarla karyeyi abluka ittikden sonra usata terki silahla sulh teklifinde bulundu. Bu teklife de silahla mukabele ve müfrezeye ikisi zabit olmak üzere otuz sekiz mecruh ve üç şehit verdirmek suretiyle red itmek küstahlığında bulundular. Bu kadar cüretkar ve bu kadar küstah olan eşrarın bu merhamet ve şefkati de takdir idemiyecekleri ve irade-i devletleri memuriyeyi mülkiyeye de tebliğ idildiği maruzdur.

Fi 31 teşrini evvel 331   11332
Diyarbakır Vali Vekili Bedreddin   Şifre kalemine vurudu fi 1 Teşrin-i Sani

10. Gnkur. ATAŞE Arşivi, Kol.: BDH, Kls.: 17, Dos.: 81/ , Fih.: 35-1

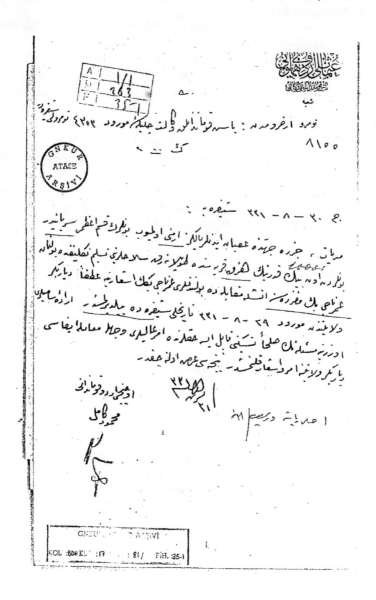

Ottoman Imperial Army
Supreme Military Command
Branch:
Number: 8155
Ciphered telegram number 4353 received at the Supreme Military Command from Erzurum
November 12 ,1915, [dated] cipher:
Those who rebelled in the Midyat, Cizre region, are not Armenians, but the majority are Süryanis.

In Ömer Naci Beg's ciphered communiqué dated November 11, 1915, which arrived in the Province of Diyarbekir, he reported that about ten thousand of these [people] who gathered in the village of Hezak responded by firing on Ömer Naci Beg's detachment. Upon your order, the Province of Diyarbekir was commanded and notified, if it is possible, to settle the issue peacefully. Its outcome will be reported.
November 13, 1915
Commander of the Third Army
Mahmut Kamil

30-8-331 şifredir:
Midyat, Cizre cihetinde isyan idenler yalnız Ermeni olmayıp bunların kısm-ı azamisi Süryani'dir.

Bunlardan on bin kadarının Hezak karyesinde toplanarak silahlarını teslim teklifinde bulunan Ömer Naci Beg müfrezesine ateşle mukabelede bulundukları Ömer Naci Beg'in işarına atfen Diyarbakır Vilayetinden mevrud 29-8-331 tarihli şifrede bildirilmiştir. İrade-i samileri üzerine meselenin sulhen teslimi kabil ise haklarında emri alileri vecihle muamele ifası Diyarbakır Vilayetine emir ve işar kılınmıştır. Neticesi arz olunacaktır.
31 Teşrin-i Evvel 331
Üçüncü Ordu Kumandanı
Mahmut Kamil

11. Gnkur. ATAŞE Arşivi, Kol.: BDH, Kls.: 17, Dos.: 81/ , Fih.: 35-2

Ottoman Imperial Army
Supreme Military Command
Branch:
Number: 8155
Ciphered telegram number 4353 received at the Supreme Military Command from Erzurum

Those who rebelled in the Midyat, Cizre, region are not Armenians but the majority are Süryanis.

In Ömer Naci Beg's ciphered communiqué dated November 11, 1915, which arrived in the Province of Diyarbekır, he reported that about ten thousand of these [people] who gathered in the village of Hezak responded by firing on Ömer Naci Beg's detachment. Upon your order, the Province of Diyarbekir was commanded and notified, if it is possible, to settle the issue peacefully. Its outcome will be reported.

November 13, 1915
Commander of the Third Army
Mahmut Kamil
11332 /7050

30-8-331 şifredir:
Midyat, Cizre cihetinde isyan idenler yalnız Ermeni olmayıp bunların kısm-ı azamisi Süryani'dir.
Bunlardan on bin kadarının Hezak karyesinde toplanarak silahlarını teslim teklifinde bulunan Ömer Naci Beg müfrezesine ateşle mukabelede bulundukları Ömer Naci Beg'in işarına atfen Diyarbakır Vilayetinden mevrud 29-8-331 tarihli şifrede bildirilmiştir. İrade-i samileri üzerine meselenin sulhen teslimi kabil ise haklarında emri alileri vecihle muamele ifası Diyarbakır Vilayetine emir ve işar kılınmıştır. Neticesi arz olunacaktır.

31 Teşrin-i Evvel 331
Üçüncü Ordu Kumandanı
Mahmut Kamil
11332 /7050

12. Gnkur. ATAŞE Arşivi, Kol.: BDH, Kls.: 17, Dos.: 81/ , Fih.: 35-3

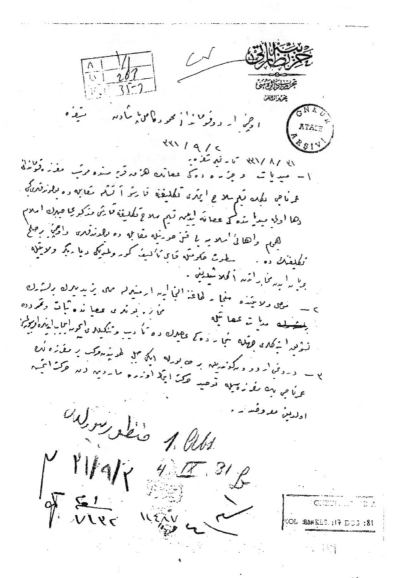

War Ministry
Office of Correspondence
Secretariat
Cipher from the Commander of the Third Army Mahmut Kamil Paşa
November 15, 1915
Cipher dated November 13, 1915
1. The rebels in Midyat and Cizre, nor only did they respond to the proposal of Ömer Naci Beg, commander of the detachment of troops set for the village Hezak, to give up their arms, by firing; to a previous proposal to relinquish their arms, the aforementioned rebels responded by attacking Muslims and massacring Muslim people; and to a third proposal for peace ... ...; that it was not considered compatible was understood from the correspondence with the Province of Diyarbekır.
2. In the Mosul province, the Armenians who took refuge in the Sincar Mountains united with the local Yezidis and communicated with the Midyat rebels and [urged them] to persevere with their rebellion and .:. for encouraging the rebels in Sincar; [we request] an order to do what is necessary to punish [the rebels] and suppress the rebellion.
3. And that it is known that a detachment composed of a battalion and two mountain artillery and sent from the Fourth Army has departed from Mardin to coordinate action with Ömer Naci Beg's detachment.
2-9-331
31-8-331 tarihli şifreye
1. Midyat ve Cizre'deki usatın Hezak karyesinde mürettip müfreze kumandanı Ömer Naci Beg'in teslim-i silah itmeleri teklifine karşı ateşle mukabelede bulundukları gibi daha evvelce Midyat'da usata idilen teslim-i silah teklifine karşı mezkur asilerin islama hücum ve ahali-i islamiyeye katl suretiyle mukabelede bulundukları ve üçüncü bir sulh teklifinin de ... hükümetle kabil-i te'lif görülmediği Diyarbakır vilayetiyle cereyan iden muhaberattan anlaşıldığı.
2. Musul Vilayetinde Sincar Dağı'na iltica iden Ermenilerle mahalli Yezidilerin birleşerek Midyat usatıyla muhabere bunları isyanda sebat ve ... teşvik ittikleri cihetle Sincar'daki asilerin de te'dib ve tenkilleri için icab idenlere emir buyurulması
3. Dördüncü ordudan gönderilen bir taburla iki cbl topundan mürekkep bir müfrezenin de Ömer Naci Beg müfrezesiyle tevhid-i hareket itmek üzere Mardin'den hareket itmiş olduğunu marufdur.

13. Gnkur. ATAŞE Arşivi, Kol.: BDH, Kls.: 17, Dos.: 81/ , Fih.: 35-4

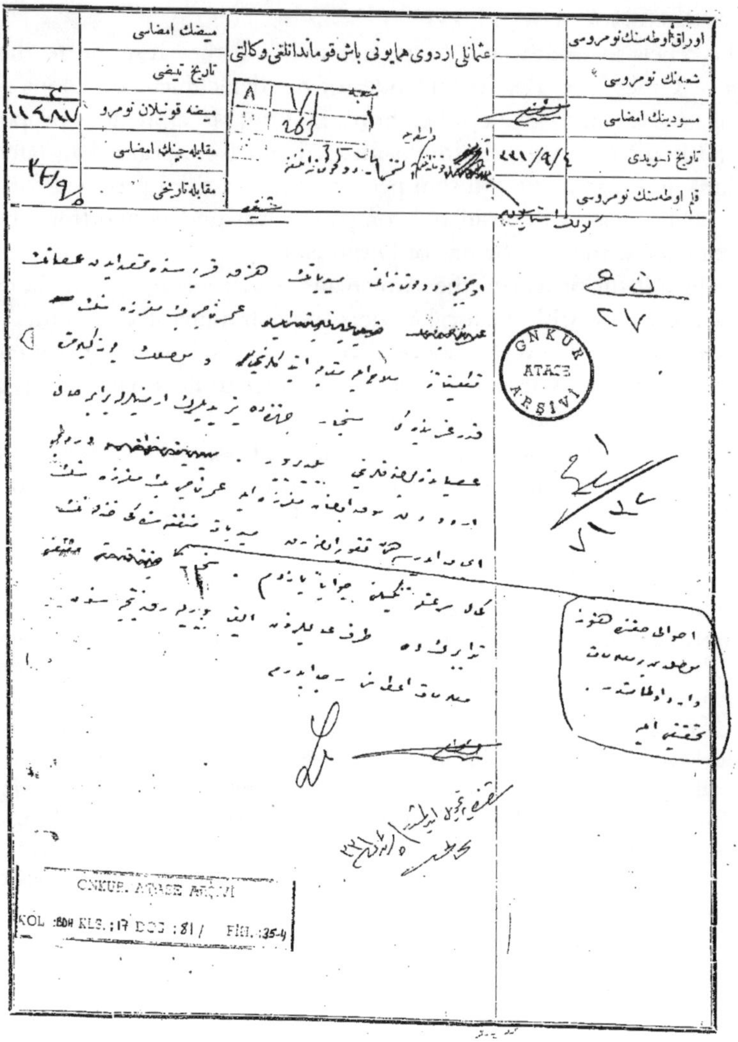

عثمانلی اردوی همایونی باش قوماندانلغی وكالتی

اوراق اوطه‌سنك نومروسی	میضك امضاسی
شعبه‌نك نومروسی	تاریخ تبیض
مسوده‌نك امضاسی	میضه قونیلان نومرو
تاریخ تسویدی	مقابله‌جینك امضاسی
قلم اوطه‌سنك نومروسی	مقابله تاریخی

GNKUR ATAŞE ARŞİVİ

GNKUR. ATAŞE ARŞİVİ
KOL :BDH KLS. :17 DOS :81/ FİH. :35-4

13

Supreme Military Command of the Ottoman Imperial Army
Branch: 1
Ciphered telegraph to the Sixth Army Command via the ... ... Command
Date of draft: November 17, 1915
The Commander of the Third Army reports that the rebels who attacked in the Hezak village of Midyat responded with fire against Ömer Naci Beg's detachment to his proposal of handing over their arms; and about a hundred kilometers west of the area, in Sincar, the Yezidis and the Armenians together are currently in a state of rebellion.

In response ... the detachment which transferred from the Fourth Army and Ömer Naci Beg's detachment if necessary, to be immediately reinforced in order to suppress ... in the Midyat area. As yet no additional information has arrived about the circumstances in Sincar. If required, I request that your high office order its investigation and that I be informed of the outcome.
The cipher has been transferred. November 18, 1915
signature
Tarih-i tesvidi: 4.9.331
Üçüncü ordu kumandanı Midyat'ın Hezak karyesinde taarruz iden usatın Ömer Naci Beg müfrezesinin teklifatına silah ile mukabele ittiklerini ve mahallin yüz kilometre kadar garbındaki Sincar cihetinde Yezidileri n Ermenilerle beraber hal-I isyanda bulunduklarını bildiriyor.
Dördüncü ordudan sevk olunan müfreze ile Ömer Naci beg müfrezesinin icab iderse hemen takviye olunarak Midyat mıntakasındaki müfrezenin kemali süratle tenkilini cevaben yazdım Sincar (ahvali hakkında henüz mevsıl bir malumat varid olmamıştır. Tahkiki ile) mukteza tedabirinde taraf-ı alilerinden emir buyurularak neticeyi sizin malumat itasını rica iderim.
Şifre tahvil olunmuştur. 5 Teşrin-i sani 331 imza.

14. Gnkur. ATAŞE Arşivi, Kol.: BDH, Kls.: 17, Dos.: 81/ , Fih.: 35-6

Supreme Military Command of the Ottoman Imperial Army
Branch: 1
Ciphered telegram to the Command of the Third Army
Date of draft: November 15, 1915
November 13, 1915 [dated] cipher
In accordance with the conditions of which I wrote to you, and in the event of lack of consent to immediately evacuate and suppress [them].

Ömer Naci Beg's detachment is still in the vicinity of the village of Hezak and the battalion of foot soldiers and a unit sent from the Fourth Army is in the Midyat Region. In respect to the general situation, another force from the Fourth Army and from Mosul which are not needed, if necessary, to reinforce immediately these forces from your area and inform of the outcome of the operation.
Additional cipher to the Province of Diyarbekir
November 13, 1915, [dated] cipher
For your information, eleven copies given to the Command of the Third Army.
As follows.
8055
Tarih-i tesvidi: 2.9.331
31 Teşrin-i Evvel 331 şifre
Usatın size yazdığım şerait dahilinde ve dalleten ademi muvafakatleri halinde süraten muhalla ile tenkilleri muktefidir.
Ömer Naci Beg müfrezesi halen Hezak Karyesi civarında ve Dördüncü ordudan gönderilen yaya taburu ile cîl takımı Midyat cihetindedir. Vaziyet-i umumiyete nazaran dördüncü ordudan ve Musul'dan başka bir kuvvet ifraza mahal olmadığından icab iderse bu kuvvetleri mıntakanızdan hemen takviye ediniz ve netice-i icraatı bildiriniz.
Diyarbakır Vilayetine mevsıl şifre
31 Teşrin-i evvel 331 şifre
Üçüncü Ordu Kumandanlığına verilen on bir sureti berayı malumat Atiye derc olunur.
8055

15. Gnkur. ATAŞE Arşivi, Kol.: BDH, Kls.: 17, Dos.: 81/ , Fih.: 35-8

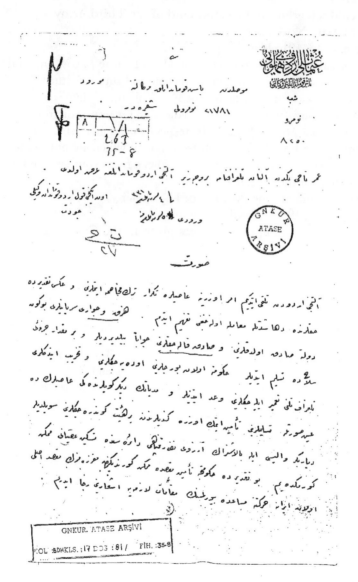

APPENDIX 4

Imperial Ottoman Army
Supreme Military Command
Branch:
Number: 8250
Cipher number 21781 from Mosul received at Supreme Military Command
The telegram received from Ömer Naci Beg has been submitted to the Sixth Army Command as follows.
November 17, 1915　　　　　Acting Commander of the Twelfth Army Corps, Cevdet
received on November 18, 1915

Copy

Upon the order I received from the Sixth Army, I communicated to the rebels to abandon the hostilities and that otherwise they would be dealt with more severely. In reply, they stated that the Süryanis in Hezak and the surrounding areas are loyal to the state and that they will remain loyal and they also surrendered a number of insignificant weapons. They promised to repair the telegraph line they destroyed and pay their debts to the government, and that they will send a delegation to the rebels in the other Midyat villages to arrange their surrender in the same way.

With the participation of the Governor of Diyarbekır ... I think it is possible to pacify the rebellion. If so, [and] since it seems possible for the government to ascertain [this] intention, I request permission to depart for Iran for the original purpose of our detachment and to communicate this to the appropriate authorities.

Ömer Naci Beg'den alınan telgrafname ber vech-i zir Altıncı Ordu Kumandanlığına arz olundu.
4 Teşrin-i Sani 331　　　　　Onikinci Kolordu Kumandan Vekili Cevdet
vurudu 5 Teşrin-i Sani
Suret

Altıncı ordudan telakki ettiğim emir üzerine asilere tekrar terki muhasıme etmelerini ve aksi takdirde haklarında daha şiddetle muamele olunacağını tefhim ettim. Hezak ve civarı Süryanileri bu gün devlet-i sadık olduklarını ve sadık kalacaklarını cevaben bildirdiler ve bir miktar cüz'iy-I silah da teslim ettiler. Hükümete olan borçlarını ödeyeceklerini ve tahrib ettikleri telgraf telini tamir eyliyeceklerini vaad ettiler ve Midyat'ın diğer köylerindeki asilerin de aynı suretle teslimlerini temin etmek üzere kendilerinden bir heyet göndereceklerini söylediler.
Diyarbakır valisi ile bil iştirak arzuy-ı nezaretpenahi dairesinde teskin-i isyanı mümkün görmekteyim. Bu taktirde hükümetçe te'min-i maksada mümkün göründüğünden müfrezemizin maksadı asli olan İran'a hareketine müsaade buyurulmasının makamatı lazımeye işarını rica ederim.

16. Gnkur. ATAŞE Arşivi, Kol.: BDH, Kls.: 17, Dos.: 81/ , Fih.: 35-12

Appendix 4

Imperial Ottoman Army
Supreme Military Command
Branch: Number: 8280
Cipher received at Supreme Military Command from Mosul
Urgent
The telegraph received from Ömer Naci Beg as follows has been submitted to the Sixth Army Command.

November 19, 1915   Acting Commander of the Twelfth Army Corps Cevdet

Copy

The rebels in Hezak ... surrendered. The other Süryani in Midyat villages ... that they are ready to show loyalty is conveyed in the report sent by the commander of the detachment from the Fourth Army. If it is authorized and ordered, our detachment will enter Iran via the Mosul–Rowandiz road. And on the occasion ... ... I thought it was suitable to unite. Our effective force ... ... and in the surrounding areas is suitable for action.

... expedition I undertake to take advantage of all the experience and reach locations that would please you. Just that our two artilleries have broken down and our effective force has been weakened even further. If it is ordered and permitted, the battalion and the artillery from the Fourth Army, which joined our detachment for the punishment of ..., to fully join our detachment, I promise and assure you that I will endeavour to enter Tabriz after a month.

....

Müstacel

Ömer Naci Beg'den alınan telgrafname ber vech-i zir Altıncı Ordu Kumandanlığına arz olundu.

6 Teşrin-i Sani 331   Onikinci Kolordu Kumandan Vekili Cevdet

Suret

Hezak'taki asiler ... teslimiyet eylediler. Midyat'taidiğer köylerdeki Süryanilerin de ... sadakate hazır oldukları Dördüncü Ordudan gönderilen müfreze kumandanının raporunda bildiriliyor. Müfrezemiz tesbit ve irade buyurulur ise Musul Revandez tarikiyle İran'a dahil olacaktır. Ve bir münasebetle ... ... birleşme olarak muvafık gördüm. Mevcudumuz ... ... ve civarında faaliyet bulunabilmeye müsaittir

... (iki nokta-boşluk) harekatın her türlü tecrübeden istifade ederek çalışacağımı ve zat ı fehimanelerini memnun edecek mevkilerde bulunacağımı emir ediyorum. Yalnız iki adi cîl topumuz bu hareketimizde bozulduğu gibi mevcud-u ferdde daha zayıfladı. Eğer Dördüncü Ordudan (iki nokta)lerin te'dibi münasebetiyle müfrezemize iltihak eden taburun toplarıyla birlikte tamamıyla müfrezemize iltihakına irade ve müsaade buyurulursa bir ay sonra Tebriz'e girmeye çalışacağımı vaad ve temin ederim.

....

17. Gnkur. ATAŞE Arşivi, Kol.: BDH, Kls.: 17, Dos.: 81/ , Fih.: 35-14

APPENDIX 4

Imperial Ottoman Army
Supreme Military Command
Branch:
Number:
From Papaslı   Ciphered telegram received at ...... Command.
I have transmitted the following telegram to the Third Army Command and informed the Sixth Army.
a. The Midyat rebellion should be suppressed immediately and with utmost severity. Accordingly, Ömer Naci Beg's detachment will remain there under the orders of the army.
November 26, 1915 [?]
11932
14.IX.31 [November 27, 1915]
Je crois, les télegs ne son't pas nécessaire[8]
Atideki telgrafı Üçüncü Ordu Kumandanlığına tebliğ, Altıncı Orduya da malumat verdim.
a.: Midyat isyanı derhal ve kemal-i şiddetle basdırılmalıdır. Bunun içün Ömer Naci Beg'in müfrezesi kema fissabık orada ordunun emri altında kalacaktır.
26 Teşrin-i Sani 915
11932

---

[8] Translation from French: "I think the telegrams are not necessary."

18. Gnkur. ATAŞE Arşivi, Kol.: BDH, Kls.: 17, Dos.: 81/ , Fih.: 35-15

A la 4ème Armée

Omer Nadji Bey qui partira pour Peru avec son détachement propose de donner sous son ordre le bataillon d'infanterie et 2 pièces de la 4ème armée qui se trouvent à l'environs de Midiat. Prière d'écrire, est-ce que vous êtes d'accord.

APPENDIX 4

Supreme Military Command of the Imperial Ottoman Army
Branch: 1
Ciphered telegram to the Command of the Fourth Army
Date of draft: November 20, 1915   9/11651
Ömer Naci Beg who is to ... depart to Iran with his detachment ... and the battalion of foot soldiers of the Fourth Army in the Midyat Region with ... unit ... is proposing its transfer. If you consent, I request that this be communicated immediately.
Included in the cipher ....
Tarih-i tesvidi: 7.9.331   9/11651
Müfrezesiyle İran'a ... azimet olan Ömer Naci Beg ve dördüncü Ordunun Midyat cihetindeki yaya taburu ile cîl takımınında ... itasını teklif ediyor. Muvafakat buyurulursa heman istarını rica ederim.
Şifreye dahil ..... .
Sağtarafta Ömer Naci Bey diye başlayan Fransızca bölüm var.
[The document contains a French translation in the margin.]

19. Gnkur. ATAŞE Arşivi, Kol.: BDH, Kls.: 17, Dos.: 81/ , Fih.: 51

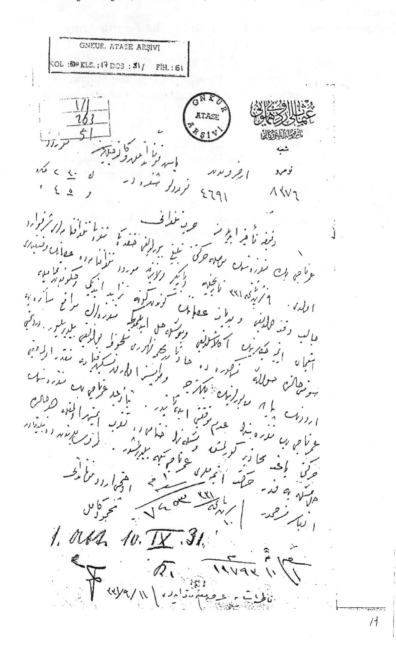

Appendix 4

Imperial Ottoman Army
Supreme Military Command
Branch: Number: 8376
Cipher number 4691 received at Supreme Military Command from Erzurum

...

The ciphered telegrams regarding communication for Ömer Naci Beg's detachment to depart for Mosul have arrived. [According to] the telegram dated November 22, 1915, from the Province of Diyarbekir, the associates of the rebels are attracting attention, and in Midyat the rebellion is growing day by day [and that] evidently they [the rebels] will not ask for mercy,[9] and if this matter is not taken care of, [and] in case the detachments are transferred to other places in said district, there is a probability of important unexpected events proceeding. The footsoldiers of the Fourth Army on their own and without artillery cannot quell the rebellion, as demonstrated by the failure of Ömer Naci Beg's detachment. Consequently, the expedition of Ömer Naci Beg's detachment is seen as fraught with danger, and Ömer Naci Beg was told not to proceed ... until the conclusion of the matter.
November 23, 1915
Cipher 7453
Commander of the Third Army Mahmut Kamil Nazır Paşa has been informed
November 24, 1915
Harb Telgrafı Dakika tehir eylemiyesiz. Ömer Naci Beg müfrezesinin Musul'a hareketini tebliğ buyurulduğu hakkındaki şifre telgrafnameleri şerefvarid oldu. 9 Teşrin-i Sani 331 tarihiyle Diyarbakır Vilayetinden mevrud telgrafnamede isyanın refikleri calib-i dikkat olduğu ve Midyat isyanının günden güne tezayüd ettiği ....in tamamıyle isti'man (aman dileme, sığınma) etmeyeceklerinin anlaşıldığı ve bu mesele halledilmedikçe müfrezelerin mevaki-i sairelere sevki halinde havali-i mezkurede hadisat-ı mühime zuhuru melhuz bulunduğu bildiriliyor. Dördüncü ordunun piyade taburlarının yalnızca ve topsuz olarak teskin-i kıyama mukadder olmadığı Ömer Naci Beg müfrezesinin adem-i muvafakatiyle şayandır. Binaenaleyh Ömer Naci Beg müfrezesinin hareket-i baisi mahzur görülmüş ve meselenin hitamı dertekarrub etmiş olmağla her halde hall-i meseleye kadar hareket etmemeleri Ömer Naci Beg'e bildirilmiştir. Taraf-ı samilerinden ... inbası ...dır.
10 Teşrini Sani 331; Şifre: 7453
Üçüncü Ordu Kumandanı Mahmud Kamil Nazır Paşa'ya arz-ı malumat edildi. 11/9/331.

---

[9] The word used, *istiman*, refers to an alien asking for safety of life and limb from a Muslim power.

20. Gnkur. ATAŞE Arşivi, Kol.: BDH, Kls.: 17, Dos.: 81/ , Fih.: 51-3

Supreme Military Command of the Imperial Ottoman Army
Branch: 1
Ciphered telegram to the Third Army Command
Date of draft: November 27, 1915
Number: 11932
Date of reply: November 28, 1915
Provide information about the following items.
1. Of what millet[10] were the rebels in the Midyat area? If there are Armenians among them, where are they from and how many are they?
2. With whom, under what conditions, and in what way did Ömer Naci Beg reconcile?
3. Have these conditions been agreed to by the rebels? What is the current situation?
4. If you find this settlement problematic, what arrangements are you proposing? To what extent it is possible to carry it out?
The cipher has been transferred. November 27, 1915
Tarih-i tesvidi: 14.9.331
Numero: 11932
Mukabele tarihi: 15.9.31
Mevad-ı atiye hakkında tafsilat veriniz.
1. Midyat mıntakasındaki asiler hangi milletten idiler. Bunlar meyanında Ermeniler de var idiyse nereli ve miktarları ne kadardır?
2. Ömer Naci Beg bunlardan hangileriyle ne gibi şerait dahilinde ve ne suretle uyuşdu?
3. Bu şerait asiler tarafından kamilen emin olundu mu? Bu günkü hal ve vaziyet nasıldır?
4. Siz bu suret-i tesviyede bir mahzur görüyor iseniz nasıl bir suret teklif ediyorsunuz. Bunun halen icrası ne dereceye kadar mümkündür.
Şifre tahvil edilmiştir. 14 Teşrin-i Sani 331

---

[10] The term *millet* in modern Turkish means "nation." However, in the Ottoman administration it meant "religious community."

21. Gnkur. ATAŞE Arşivi, Kol.: BDH, Kls.: 17, Dos.: 81/ , Fih.: 58

APPENDIX 4

Ottoman Imperial Army
Supreme Military Command
Branch:
Number: 54
Ciphered telegram from Erzurum to Supreme Military Commander His Excellency Enver Pasha
Very Urgent
11932
November 28, 1915, dated cipher:

1. The great part (majority) of the rebels in the Midyat region are Süryanis who are located in the area. They were joined by a small number of Armenians and Chaldeans who escaped from here and there.

2. Ömer Naci Beg and the governor of Diyarbekır have reported that the Süryanis in the village of Hezak had agreed to the conditions of handing over their arms, repairing the telegraph lines they destroyed, paying their debts to the government, and returning to their villages; and that they [Ömer Naci Beg and the governor of Diyarbekır] have resolved the matter peacefully. However, they additionally communicated that the weapons the rebels handed over constituted an insignificant number and that furthermore if we force them to change domicile and destroy their weapons, the rebels will revolt again.

3. Upon orders from your high office, Ömer Naci Beg's detachment departed for the Mosul border. The commander of the detachment which remained there ... ... Beg in accordance with the condition stipulated in the second item, the amount given by the Süryanis ... continue(s) to collect.

4. The matter has been settled in this way and in that region for the stabilization of order and to make these rebels docile and completely obedient to the government, and come what may, the transportation and removal of the above-mentioned people[11] to other places is necessary. At present, it has been communicated to the Province of Diyarbekır that if the enemy approaches, this would cause renewed rebellion and villainy. In the opinion of your humble servant, currently the state of affairs is not satisfactory; as the matter stands, the removal of the said [people] is in [progress]. However, Ömer Naci Beg's operation and the lack of availability of forces to send in that direction has necessitated postponement of the engagement at an inopportune time.

(Continued on page 2)

---

[11] The term "above-mentioned people" is used contemptuously.

21a. Gnkur. ATAŞE Arşivi, Kol.: BDH, Kls.: 17, Dos.: 81/ , Fih.: 58-1

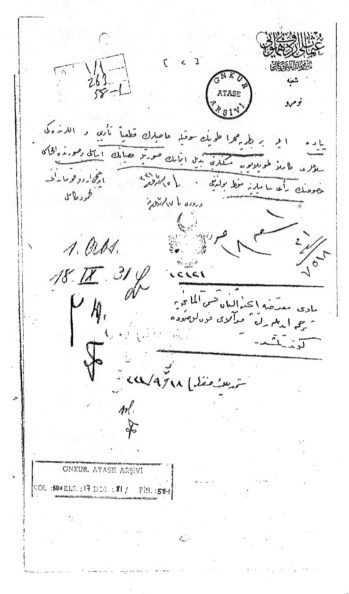

APPENDIX 4

With the transfer of two battalions of foot soldiers from the Fourth Army and a field artillery, the irrevocable punishment of the rebels, and the complete collection of their weapons without changing their domiciles, the matter of the complete destruction of the rebellion is a matter that is bound by your judgment. Date November 28, 1915
Received on November 30, 1915
Commander of the Third Army Mahmut Kamil
\/ 8517
12121
blue ... the section included was translated from German and the colonel ... was sent.
At present ... date December 1, 1915
Signature

Gayet Müstaceldir
11932

[15-9-331 şifredir:
1. Midyat mıntıkasındaki asilerin kısm-ı küllisi o havalide bulunan Süryanilerdir. Bunlara öteden beriden firar eden az miktarda Ermenilerle Keldaniler de iltihak etmişlerdir.
2. Ömer Naci Beg ve Diyarbakır Valisi bunlardan "Hezak" karyesindeki Süryanilerin silahlarını teslim ederek kendi köylerine avdet etmek ve tahrip ettikleri telgraf hududunu tamir etmek ve hükümete olan borçlarını ödemek şeraitine muvafakat ettiklerini ve bu suretle meseleyi sulhen hallettiğini bildirmiş ve fakat teslim ettikleri silah cüzi olup ayrıca meskenlerinin tebdiliyle ellerindeki umum silahların teharri ve ehazı cihetine gidildiği taktirde usatın yeniden isyan edeceklerini ilaveten işar etmişlerdir.
3. Makamı samilerinden aldığı emir üzerine Ömer Naci Beg müfrezesi Musul hududuna hareket etmiştir. Orada kalmış olan diğer müfreze kumandanı ... ... Beg ikinci maddede arz edilen şerait mucibince Süryanilerin verdikleri miktar ... toplamakta devam ediyor.
4. Mesele bu suretle tevkii hal edilmiş olup o mıntıkada asayişin istikrarı ve bu asilerin hükümetin emrine tamamıyle mutiğ ve münkad olmaları için behemehal ahali-i merkumenin mevaki-i saireye nakl ü teb'idi mukteza olup halihazırda düşmanın takribi halinde mübeddeli isyan ve şekavet olacağı Diyarbakır vilayetine işar etmektedir. Bendenizin mütalaamda şimdi suret-i halin gayr-ı kafi bulunduğu, merkumunun teb'id tevzi'leri merkezindedir. Ancak Ömer Naci Beg'in hareket ve o cihete gönderilecek kuvvet bulunmaması icratı vakt-i müsaide ta'like mecburiyet etti] binaen aleyh müsait zamanda Dördüncü ordudan iki tabur
(Sayfa İkide Devam)
piyade ile bir batarya sahra topunun sevkiyle asilerin katiyyen te'dibi ve ellerindeki silahları kamilen toplayıp meskenlerini tebdil etmemek suretiyle isyanın esaslı bir surette imhası hususunun rey-i samilerine menut bulunduğunu. Fi 15 Teşrin-i Sani

331
Vurudu fi 17 Teşrin-i Sani 331
Üçüncü Ordu Kumandanı Mahmut Kamil
/ 8517
12121
mavi ... içine alınan kısmı Almancadan terceme edilerek miralay .... gönderilmiştir.
Şimdilik ... fi 18-9-331
İmza

BIBLIOGRAPHY

Abraamyan, G. A., and T. G. Sevan-Khachatryan, eds. *Russkie istochniki o genotside armyan v Osmanskoi imperii 1915–1916 gody* [Russian sources on the Armenian genocide in the Ottoman Empire 1915–16]. Sbornik dokumentov i materialov. Erevan: Areresum-Ani, 1995.

A. H. B. "Mémoires sur Mardine (1915ss)." In *Studia Orientalia Christiana Collectanea* (Cairo: Franciscan Centre of Oriental Studies) 29–30 (1998): 59–189.

Ainsworth, William. "An Account of a Visit to the Chaldeans, Inhabiting Central Kudistan; and of an Ascent of the Peak of Rowánduz (Túr Sheikhíwá) in the Summer of 1840." *Journal of the Royal Geographic Society* 11 (1841): 21–76.

Akçam, Taner. *Armenien und der Völkermord: Die Istanbuler Prozesse und die türkische Nationalbewegung.* Hamburg: Hamburger Edition, 1996.

Alichoran, Joseph. "Assyro-Chaldeans in the 20th Century: From Genocide to Diaspora." *Journal of the Assyrian Academic Society* 8, no. 2 (1994): 30–55.

———. "Un Dominicain témoin du génocide de 1915 le père Jacques Rhétoré (1841–1921)." In Rhétoré, *"Les chrétiens aux bêtes"* (2005), 215–327.

Allen, W. E. D., and Paul Muratoff. *Caucasian Battlefields: A History of the Wars on the Turco-Caucasian Border, 1828–1921.* Cambridge: Cambridge University Press, 1953.

Anschütz, Helga. *Die syrischen Christen vom Tur 'Abdin: Eine altchristliche Bevölkerungsgruppe zwischen Beharrung, Stagnation und Auflösung.* Würzburg: Augustinus Verlag, 1985.

Armalto, Ishaq. *Al-Qusara fi nakabat al-nasara* [The calamities of the Christians]. Beirut: Al Sharfe, 1919. Reprint, Beirut, 1970.

———. "Siyahati fi Turabdin." [My journey in Tur Abdin]. *Al-Mashriq* 6 (1913): 562–78, 662–75, 739–54, 835–54..

Armenians in Ottoman Documents (1915–1920). Ankara: General Directorate of State Archives), 1995.

Arutinov', A. "K' antropologii aisorov'" [On the anthropology of the Assyrians]. *Russkii antropologicheskii zhurnal* 1902, no. 4: 81–100.

Attwater, Donald. *The Churches of the East.* 2 vols. St. Helens, England: Thomas More and Geoffrey Chapman, 1961.

Aver'yanov', P. I. *Etnograficheskii i voenno-politicheskii obzor' aziatskikh' vlad'nii ottomanskoi imperii.* [Ethnographic and military-political description of the Asian provinces of the Ottoman Empire]. St. Petersburg: Glavnoe Upravlenie General'nogo Shtaba, 1912.

Aydin, Hanna. *Die Syrisch-Orthodoxe Kirche von Antiochien.* Glane-Losser, Netherlands: Bar Hebräus Verlag, 1990.

Aydin, Suavi, Kudret Emiroğlu, Oktay Özel, and Süha Ünsal. *Mardin: Aşiret – Cemaat – Devlet* [Mardin: Tribes,- communities, state]. Istanbul: Tarih vakfi, 2000.

"The Azizan or the Princes of Bohtan." *Journal of the Central Asian Society* 36 (1949): 249–51.

Babane, Hazqiyel Rayyis Gabriyel Beth-Malik. *Tash'ita d Aturaye* [Assyrian history]. Trichur, India: Mar Narsay Publishing House, 1975.

Babakhanov, I. *Sirokhaldeitsy, ikh istoriya i zhizn'* [Syro-Chaldeans: Their history and life]. St. Petersburg: Lopukhina, 1899.

Balakian, Peter. *The Burning Tigris: the Armenian Genocide and America's Response.* New York: HarperCollins, 2003.

Barby, Henry. *Au pays de l'épouvante: L'Armenie martyre.* Paris: Albin Michel, 1917.

Bardakçı, Murat. "Tehcir edilen Ermeniler 924 bin 158 kişiydi" [The deported Armenians were 924,158]. *Hürriyet*, April 24, 2005.

Bar Gello, Fehmi. *Seifo: Trakasserier och folkmord 1914 i Turabdin.* Jönköping, Sweden: Assurbanipal, 2000.

Benjamin, Yoab. "Assyrian Journalism: a 140-Year Experience." *Journal of the Assyrian Academic Society* 7, no. 2 (1993): 1–16.

Berré, Marie-Dominique. "Massacres de Mardin." *Haigazian Armenological Journal* 17 (1997): 81–106.

Bet-Barsawmo, Ignatius Ephrem. *Turabdin Tarihi* [History of Tur Abdin]. Södertälje, Sweden: Nsibin, 1996.

Beylerian, Arthur. *Les grandes puissants: L'Empire Ottoman et les arméniens dans les archives françaises (1914–1918).* Paris: Sorbonne, 1983.

Bihl, Wolfdieter. *Die Kaukasus-Politik der Mittelmächte*, part 1: *Ihre Basis in der Orient-Politik und ihre Aktionen 1914–1917.* Vienna: Böhlaus, 1975.

Bilgi, Nejdet. *Dr. Mehmed Reşid Şahingiray'ın Hayatı ve Hâtıraları: İttihâd ve Terakki Dönemi ve Ermeni Meselesi* [Dr. M. R. S.'s life and memory: The

CUP period and the Armenian Questions]. (Izmir: Akademi Kitabevı 1997).

Bloxham, Donald. *The Great Game of Genocide: Imperialism, Nationalism, and the Destruction of the Ottoman Armenians*. Oxford: Oxford University Press, 2005.

Braude, Benjamin, and Bernard Lewis, eds. *Christians and Jews in the Ottoman Empire: The Functioning of a Plural Society*. 2 vols. New York. Holmes and Meier, 1982.

Bryce, James, and Arnold Toynbee. *The Treatment of Armenians in the Ottoman Empire, 1915–1916*. Uncensored edition. Princeton, N.J.: Gomidas Institute, 2000. 1st ed., 1916.

Cambar, Malik. "Autobiography." Manuscript in East Syriac, [1960?], in possession of Juliana Jawaro, Chicago.

———. *Vie et coutmues des Maliks*. Marseilles: Guiran, 1924.

Chalabian, Andranig. *General Andranig and the Armenian Revolutionary Movement*. Southfield, Mich.: Author, 1988.

Chabot, J.-B. "État religieux des diocèses formant le patriarcat chaldéen de Babylone au 1ᵉʳ janvier 1896." *Revue de l'Orient chrétien* 1 (1896): 433–53.

Chevalier, Michel. *Les Montagnards chrétiens du Hakkâri et du Kurdistan septentrional*. Paris: Publications du département de Géographie de l'Université de Paris-Sorbonne, 1983.

Coakley, J. F. *The Church of the East and the Church of England: A History of the Archbishop of Canterbury's Assyrian Mission*. Oxford: Clarendon, 1992.

Dadrian, Vahakn. "The Armenian Genocide: An Interpretation." In *America and the Armenian Genocide of 1915*, edited by Jay Winter, 52–100. Cambridge: Cambridge University Press, 2003.

———. "Documentation of the Armenian Genocide in Turkish Sources." In *Genocide: a Critical Bibliographic Review*, edited by Israel Charny, 2:93–95. London: Mansell, 1991.

———. *The History of the Armenian Genocide: Ethnic Conflict from the Balkans to Anatolia to the Caucasus*. Providence, R.I.: Berghahn, 1995.

———. "The Role of the Special Organization in the Armenian Genocide during the First World War." In *Minorities in Wartime: National and Racial Groupings in Europe, North America and Australia during the Two World Wars*, edited by Panikos Panayi, 50–82. Oxford: Berg, 1993.

Davison, R. H. "Tanzīmāt." *Encyclopaedia of Islam*. 2nd edition. 10:201–9. Leiden: Brill, 1998.

D'Avril, Adolphe. *La Chaldée chrétienne: Étude sur l'histoire religieuse et politique des Chaldéens-Unis et des Nestorians*. Paris: Benjamin Duprat, 1864.

de Courtois, Sébastien. *The Forgotten Genocide: Eastern Christians, The Last Arameans.* Piscataway, N.J.: Gorgias Press, 2004.
Decroo, Georges. "En Perse: Pillages et massacres." *Les Missions catholiques* 47 (1915): 207.
Demirer, Hüseyin. "Haver Delal" [Help, my dear]. Unpublished typed manuscript (March 15, 1983), 199 pages. Mesopotamian Collection, Södertörn University College.
Driver, G. R. "The Religion of the Kurds." *Bulletin of the School of Oriental Studies* 2 (1922): 197–213.
Dündar, Fuat. *İttihat ve Terakki'nin Müslümanları İskân Politikası (1913–18)* [CUP Muslim settlement policy 1913–18]. Istanbul: İletisim Yayınları, 2001.
El-Ghusein, Fâ'iz. *Martyred Armenia.* London: Arthur Pearson, 1917.
Emîri, Ali. *Osmanlı Vilâyât-i Şarkiyyesi* [The eastern Ottoman vilayets]. Ankara: Ilâhiyât, 2005.
Empire de Perse, Ministère des affaires étrangeres. *Neutralité Persane: Documents diplomatiques.* Paris: Georges Cadet, 1919. Reprint in full, appendix to *Wer hat die persische Neutralität verletzt?* by Wilhelm Litten, 1–163. Berlin: Walter de Gruyter, 1920.
Erickson, Edward J. *Ordered to Die: A History of the Ottoman Army in the First World War.* Westport, Conn.: Greenwood, 2001.
Ethem, Çerkes. *Anilarim* [Memoirs]. Istanbul: Berfin Yayınları, 1962.
Die Europäischen Mächte und die Türkei während des Weltkrieges: Konstantinopel und die Meerengen. 4 vols. Dresden: Carl Reissner, 1930–32.
Findley, Carter. "The Acid Test of Ottomanism: The Acceptance of Non-Muslims in the Late Ottoman Bureaucracy." In Braude and Lewis, *Christians and Jews in the Ottoman Empire* (1982), 339–68.
Gatrell, Peter. *A Whole Empire Walking: Refugees in Russia During World War I.* Bloomington: Indiana University Press, 1999.
Gehrke, Ulrich. *Persien in der deutschen Orientpolitik während des ersten Weltkrieges.* 2 vols. Stuttgart: Kohlhammer, 1961.
Genelkurmay Basımevi, *Askeri Tarih Belgeleri Dergisi* [Review of military history documents]. Ankara: ATASE, 1983–85.
Genelkurmay Başkanlığı. *Birinci Dünya Harbi'nde Türk Harbi Kafkas Cephesi 3 ncü Ordu Harekâtı* [World War I, Turkish War on the Caucasus Front, Third Army operations], vol. 2, part 1. Ankara: Genelkurmay Basım Evi, 1993.
Genis, Vladimir. *Vitse-konsul Vvedenskii sluzhba v Persii i Bukharskom khanstve (1906-1920 gg.): Rossiiskaya diplomatiya v sud'bakh* [Vice-consul Vvedenski's service in Persia and the Khanate of Bukhara 1906–20: The fate

of Russian diplomacy]. Moscow: Izdatel'stvo Sotsialno-politicheskaya Mysl', 2003.

Genotsid armyan i russkaya publitsistika [The Armenian genocide in Russian publications]. Erevan: Muzei-institut genotsida armyan, 1998.

Goddard, Hugh. *A History of Christian–Muslim Relations*. Chicago: New Amsterdam Books, 2000.

Gökalp, Ziya. *Kürt Aşiretleri Hakkında Sosyolojik Tetkikler* [Sociological studies of Kurdish tribes]. Istanbul: Sosyal Yayınlar, 1992.

Grant, Asahel. *The Nestorians; or, the Lost Tribes*. New York, 1845.

Griselle, Eugène. *Syriens et Chaldéens: Leur martyre, leurs espérances*. Paris: Bloud et Gay, 1917.

Güngör, Salâhattin. "Bir Canli Tarih Konuşuyor" [A living oral history]. *Resimli Tarih Mecmaası* [Illustrated history magazine] 4, no. 43 (July 1953), 2442–45.

Guse, Felix. *Die Kaukasusfront im Weltkrieg bis zum Frieden von Brest*. Leipzig: Koehler & Amelang, 1940.

Haddad, Eva. *The Assyrian, Rod of My Anger*. N.p.: Author, 1996.

Hannouche, Hanna Murat. *Azekh "Beyt Zebde"* [Azakh or Beyt Zebde]. Paris?: author, 2002?.

Hellot-Bellier, Florence. "Chronique de massacres annoncés: Les Assyro-Chaldéens de Perse, la Perse et les puissances europeennes 1986–1919." Doctoral thesis, Université de la Sorbonne nouvelle Paris III, 1998.

Hendo, Gabriel Qas Tuma. "Tarikh Azakh" [History of Azakh]. Undated Arabic manuscript, 231 pp. Mesopotamian Collection, Södertörn University College.

Hinno, Süleyman. *Gunhe d Suryoye d Turabdin* {The massacre of the Syriacs of Tur Abdin]. Glane-Losser, Netherlands: Bar Hebräus Verlag, 1987. Swedish translation, *Massakern på syrianerna i Turabdin 1914–1915*. Örebro, Sweden: Syrianska riksforbundet, 1998.

Hoetzsch, Otto, ed. *Die Internationalen Beziehungen im Zeitalter des Imperialismus: Dokumente aus den Archiven der Zarischen und der Provisorischen Regierung*, ser. 2, vol. 6. Berlin: Reimar Hobbing, 1934.

Höjer, N. F. "Till armeniernas vänner." *Missionsförbundet* 1897, 330–33.

Hollerweger, Hans. *Turabdin: Lebendiges Kulturerbe*. Linz: Freunde der Tur Abdin, 1999.

Hull, Isabel V. *Absolute Destruction: Military Culture and the Practices of War in Imperial Germany* Ithaca: Cornell University Press, 2005.

Hultvall, John. *Mission och vision i Orienten: Svenska missionsförbundets mission i Transkaukasien-Persien 1882–1921*. Studia missionalia Uppsaliensia 53. Stockholm: Verbum, 1991.
Impagliazzo, Marco, ed. *Una Finestra sul massacro: Documenti inediti sulla strage degli armeni (1915–1916)*. Milan: Guerini, 2000.
Ineichen, Markus. *Die Schwedischen Offiziere in Persien (1911–1916)*. Bern: Peter Lang, 2002.
Jäckh, Ernst. *Die deutsch-türkische Waffenbrüderschaft*. Stuttgart: Deutsche Verlags-Anstalt, 1915.
———. *Kiderlen-Wächter der Staatsmann und Mensch: Briefwechsel und Nachlass*. Stuttgart: Deutsche Verlags-Anstalt, 1924.
Jähnicke, Burkhard. "Lawyer, Politician, Intelligence Officer: Paul Leverkuehn in Turkey 1915–1916 and 1941–1944." *Journal of Intelligence History* 2 (winter 2002): 69–87.
Jedin, Hubert. *Atlas zur Kirchengeschichte*. Freiburg: Herder, 1970.
Joseph, John. *The Modern Assyrians of the Middle East: Encounters with Western Christian Missions, Archaeologists, and Colonial Powers*. Leiden: Brill, 2000.
———. *Muslim–Christian Relations and Inter-Christian Rivalries in the Middle East*. Albany: SUNY Press, 1983.
Kansu, Aykut. *Politics in Post-Revolutionary Turkey, 1908–1913*. Leiden: Brill, 2000.
Karpat, Kemal H. *Osmanlı Nüfusu (1830–1914) Demografik ve Sosyal Özellikleri* [Ottoman population 1830–1914: Demographic and social characteristics]. Istanbul: Tarih Vakfı Yurt Yayınları, 2003.
Kévorkian, Raymond. "La Cilicia (1909–1921) des massacres d'Adana au mandat français." Special issue, *Revue d'histoire arménienne contemporaine* 3 (1999).
Kieser, Hans-Lukas. *Der Verpasste Friede: Mission, Ethnie und Staat in den Ostprovinzen der Türkei 1839–1938*. Zürich: Chronos, 2000.
"The Killing of the Christians in Seert." *Aram* 6 (1993): 63–68.
Knapp, Grace H. *The Tragedy of Bitlis*. 1919. Reprint, London: Sterndale Classics, 2002.
Kocahanoğlu, O. S. *İttihad-Terakki'nin Sorgulanması ve Yargılanması,1918–1919*. [CUP inquiries and trials, 1918–19]. Istanbul: Temel Yayınları, 1998.
Koohi-Kamali, Farideh. *The Political Development of the Kurds in Iran: Pastoral Nationalism*. New York: Palgrave Macmillan, 2003.
Korsun, N. G. *Alashkertskaya i khamadanskaya operatsii na kavkazskom fronte mirovoi voiny v 1915 gody* [The Alashkert and Hamadan operations on

the Caucasus Front in World War I in 1915]. Moscow: Gosudarstvennoe Voneenoe Izdatel'stvo, 1940.

Kurtcephe, İsrafil. "Birinci dünya savaşında bir süryani ayaklanması" [A Syrian revolt in World War I]. *Osmanlı Tarihi Araştırma ve Uygulama Merkezi Dergisi* 1, no. 4 (1993): 290–305.

Laloyan, E. A. "Aisori vanskago vilaiet" [Assyrians in Van Vilayet]. *Zapiski kavkazskago otd'la imperatorskago russkago geograficheskago obshchestva* 28, no. 4. Tiflis, 1914.

Landau, Jacob. *Pan-Turkism: From Irredentism to Cooperation*. Bloomington: Indiana University Press, 1995.

Lazarev, M. S. *Kurdistan i kurdskaya problema (90-e gody XIX veka – 1917 g.)* [Kurdistan and the Kurdish Question 1890–1917]. Moscow: Izdatel'stvo Nauka, 1964.

Lehmann-Haupt, C. F. *Armenien Einst und Jetzt*. 3 vols. Berlin: Behr's, 1910.

Lepsius, Johannes, *Deutschland und Armenien 1914–1918: Sammlung diplomatischer Aktenstücke*. Potsdam: Tempelverlag, 1919.

———. *Le Rapport secret du Dr. Johannes Lepsius sur les massacres d'Arménie*. Paris: Payot, 1918.

Leverkuehn, Paul. *Posten auf ewiger Wache: Aus dem abenteuerreichen Leben des Max von Scheubner-Richter*. Essen: Essener Verlagsanstalt, 1938.

Lewis, Mary E. *The War Journal of a Missionary in Persia*, edited by Mary Schauffler-Platt. New York: Board of Foreign Missions of the Presbyterian Church in the U.S.A., 1915.

Litten, Wilhelm. *Wer hat die persische Neutralität verletzt?* Berlin: Walter de Gruyter, 1920.

Lohr, Eric. *Nationalizing the Russian Empire: The Campaign against Enemy Aliens during World War I*. Cambridge: Harvard University Press, 2003).

Ludshuveit, E. F. *Turtsiya v gody pervoi mirovoi voiny 1914-1918 gg. Voenno-politicheskii ocherk* [Turkey in the years of World War I 1914–1918: Military-political study]. Moscow: Izdatel'stvo moskovskogo universiteta, 1966.

Macuch, Rudolf. *Geschichte der spät- und neusyrischen Literatur*. Berlin: Walter de Gruyter, 1976.

Maevskii, V. T. *Voenno-statisticheskoe opisanie vanskogo i bitlisskogo vilaetov'* [Military-statistical report on Van and Bitlis vilayets] Tiflis: Izdanie Shtaba Kavkazskogo Voennago Okruga, 1904.

Majd, Mohammed Gholi. *The Great Famine and Genocide in Persia, 1917–1919*. Lanham, Md.: University Press of America, 2003.

Mann, Michael. *The Dark Side of Democracy: Explaining Ethnic Cleansing.* Cambridge: Cambridge University Press, 2005.
Matveev, K. P., and I. I. Mar-Yukhanna. *Assiriiskii vopros vo vremya i posle pervoi mirovoi voiny* [The Assyrian Question during and after World War I]. Moscow: Izdatel'stvo Nauka, 1968.
McDowell, David. *A Modern History of the Kurds.* London: Tauris, 1996.
Menteşe, Halil. *Halil Menteşe'nin Anıları* [H. M.'s memoirs]. Istanbul: Hürriyet Vakfı Yayınları, 1986.
Meyrier, Gustave. *Les massacres de Diarbekir: Correspondance diplomatique du Vice-Consul de France 1894–1896.* Paris: L'Inventaire, 2000.
Mikaelyan, Vardges, ed. *Die armenische Frage und der Genozid an den Armeniern in der Türkei (1913–1919).* Yerevan: Institute for History, 2004.
Minorsky, V. "Kurds, Kurdistān, iii: History, A: Pre-Islamic History; B. The Islamic Period up to 1920." *Encyclopaedia of Islam.* 2nd edition. 3:447–64. Leiden: Brill, 1981.
———. "Urmiya." *Encyclopaedia of Islam* 4:1032–38. Leiden: Brill, 1934.
Mistrih, Vincent. "Mémoires de A.Y.B. sur les massacres de Mardine." In *Armenian Perspectives: 10th Anniversary Conference of the Association Internationale des Etudes Arméniennes,* ed. Nicholas Awde, 287–92. London: Curzon, 1997.
Naayem, Joseph. *Les Assyro-Chaldéens et les Arméniens massacrés par les Turcs: Documents inédits recueillis par un témoin oculaire.* Paris: Bloud et Guy, 1920.
Namik, Said A., and Rustem Nedjib. *La Question assyro-chaldéenne devant la conférence de la paix.* [Paris], July 16, 1919.
Naslian, Jean. *Les Memoires de Mgr. Jean Naslian sur les événements politico-religieux en Proche-Orient de 1914 à 1928.* Vienna: Méchithariste, 1951.
Nersisiyan, M. G., ed. *Genotsid armyan v osmanskoi imperii: Sbornik dokumentov i materialov* [The Armenian genocide in the Ottoman Empire: Collection of documents and materials]. 2nd ed. Erevan: Izdatel'stvo Aiastan, 1982.
Nesimi, Abidin. *Yılların İçinden.* [During the years]. Istanbul: Gözlem yayınları, 1977.
Nikitine, Basile P. "Une Apologie kurde du sunnisme." *Rocznik orientalistyczny* 8 (1933): 116–60.
———. "Les Kurdes et le Christianisme." *Revue de l'Histoire des Religions,* 1922, 147–56.
———. *Kurdy* [The Kurds]. Moscow: Izdatel'stvo Progress, 1964.
———. "Nestorians." *Encyclopaedia of Islam* 3:902–6. Leiden: Brill, 1936.
———. "Une Petite Nation victime de la guerre: Les Chaldéens." *La Revue des Sciences Politiques,* October–December 1921, 602–25.

Noel, Edward. "The Character of the Kurds as Illustrated by their Proverbs and Popular Sayings." *Bulletin of the School of Oriental Studies* 1, no. 4 (1920): 79–90.

Noel, Edward W. C. *Diary of Major E. Noel on Special Duty in Kurdistan.* Basra, 1919.

Nogales, Rafael de. *Four Years beneath the Crescent.* London: Charles Scribner's, 1926.

Ogandzhanyan, Artem. *1915 god neosporimye svidetel'stva. Avstriiskie dokumenty o genotside armyan* [1915 unquestionable evidence: Austrian documents on the Armenian genocide]. St. Petersburg: Armyanskoi apostol'skoi tserkvi, 2005.

Ovakiyan, Vakharshak. "V pokhode s Andranikom" [On the road with Antranik]. *Armyanskii vestnik* nos. 30, 34 (1916). In *Russkie istochniki o genotside armyan v Osmanskoi imperii 1915–1916 gody* [Russian sources on the Armenian genocide in the Ottoman Empire 1915–1916], edited by G. A. Abraamyan and T. G. Sevan-Khachatryan, 34-42.. Erevan: Areresum-Ani, 1995.

P. V. M. "Autres documents sur les événements de Mardine." *Studia Orientalia Christiana Collectanea* 29 (1998): 5–220, 30 (1998): 33–77.

Palmer, Andrew. *Monk and Maṣûîson on the Tigris Frontier: The Early History of Tur' Abdin.* Cambridge: Cambridge University Press, 1990.

Parhad, Sam. *Beyond the Call of Duty: The Biography of Malik Kambar of Jeelu.* Chicago: Metropolitan Press, 1986.

Qarabash, Abed Mschiho Na'man. *Vergossenes Blut: Geschichten der Gruel, die an den Christen in der Türkei verübt, und der Leiden, die ihnen 1895 und 1914–1918 zugefügt wurden.* Holland: Bar Hebraeus Verlag, 1999. Syriac original, *Dmo zliho.* Augsburg: ADO Publikationen, 1997.

Rahme, Joseph G. "Namik Kemal's Constitutional Ottomanism and Non-Muslims." *Islam and Christian-Muslim Relations* 10, no. 1 (1999): 23–39.

Review of the Civil Administration of Mesopotamia. London: His Majesty's Stationery Office, 1920.

Rhétoré, Jacques. *"Les Chrétiens aux bêtes": Souvenirs de la guerre sainte proclamée par les Turcs contre les chrétiens en 1915.* Étude et présentation du document par Joseph Alichoran. Paris: Cerf, 2005.

Riccardi, Andrea. *Mediterraneo: Cristianesimo e islam tra coabitazione e conflitto.* Milan: Guerini, 1997.

Ritter, Hellmut. *Ṭūrōyo: Die Volkssprache der syrianischen Christen des Ṭūr 'Abdîn*, part A: *Texte*, vol. 1. Beirut: Franz Steiner, 1967.

Robinson, Chase. *Empire and Elites after the Muslim Conquest: The Transformation of Northern Mesopotamia.* Cambridge: Cambridge University Press, 2000.

Rockwell, William Walker. *The Pitiful Plight of the Assyrian Christians in Persia and Kurdistan.* New York: American Committee for Armenian and Syrian Relief, 1916.

Rondot, Pierre. "Les tribus montagnards de l'Asie antérieure: Quelques aspects sociaux des populations Kurdes et Assyriennes." *Bulletin d'études orientales de l'institut français de Damas* 6 (1937): 1–50.

Runciman, Steven. *A History of the Crusades.* 3 vols. Cambridge: Cambridge University Press, 1951.

Saint Vincent de Paul Annales de la Mission 80 (1915).

Samih, Aziz. "Umumi Harpte Kafkas Cephesi Hatıraları" [World War I: Caucasus Front memoirs]. *Kurun,* April 10 and 22, 1935.

Samuel, Athanasius Yeshua. *Treasure of Qumran. My Story of the Dead Sea Scrolls.* London: Hodder & Staughton, 1968.

Sarafian, Ara, ed. "The Disasters of Mardin during the Persecutions of the Christians, Especially the Armenians, 1915." *Haigazian Armenological Review* 18 (1998): 261–71.

Shahbaz, Yonan. *The Rage of Islam: An Account of the Massacre of Christians by the Turks in Persia.* Philadelphia: Judson Press, 1918.

Shedd, Mary Lewis. *The Measure of a Man: The Life of William Ambrose Shedd, Missionary to Persia.* New York: George Doran, 1922.

Shedd, William A. "The Syrians of Persia and Eastern Turkey." *Bulletin of the American Geographical Society* 35 (1903): 1–30.

Simon, Hyacinthe. *Mardine la ville heroique: Autel et tombeau de l'Arménie (Asie Mineure) durant les massacres de 1915.* Jounieh, Lebanon: Maison Naaman pour la Culture, 1991.

Şimşir, Bilâl N. *Malta Sürgünleri* [The Malta exiles]. Ankara: Bilgi Yayınları, 1976.

Skandar. "A Syrian Patriot." *Beth-Nahrin Magazin* 24, No. 1 (December 5, 1916).

Soane, Ely Bannister. *To Mesopotamia and Kurdistan in Disguise.* 2nd edition. London: John Murray, 1926. Reprint, Amsterdam: APA Academic Publishing, 1979.

Sonyel, Salahi. *The Assyrians of Turkey: Victims of Major Power Policy.* Ankara: Türk Tarih Kurumu, 2001.

Sorgun, Taylan. *İttihad ve Terakki'den Cumhuriyet'e Halil Paşa Bitmeyen Savaş* [From the CUP to the Republic: Halil Pasha's unfinished war]. 2nd edition. Istanbul: Kum Saati Yayınları, 2003.

Sundvall, Elin. "Missionen i Persien." *Missionsförbundet* 1911, 60–63.
Surma D'Bait Mar Shimun. *Assyrian Church Customs and the Murder of Mar Shimun*. London: Faith Press, 1920. Reprint, New York: Vehicle Editions, 1983.
Sykes, Mark. "Journeys in Northern Mesopotamia." *Geographical Journal* 30 (1907): 237–54, 384–98.
Termen, R. I. *Otchet' o poezdke v sandzhak Khekkiari, vanskago vilaiet v 1906 gody* [Report of travel in the sandjak of Hakkari, Van vilayet in 1906]. Tbilisi: Shtaba kavkazskago voennago okruga, 1910.
Ternon, Yves. "Mardin 1915: Anatomie pathologique d'une destruction." Special issue, *Revue d'Histoire Arménienne Contemporaine* 4 (2002).
Tevetoğlu, Fethi. *Ömer Naci*. 2nd edition. Ankara: Kültür ve Turizm Bakanlığı Yayınları, 1987.
Tfinkdji, Joseph. "Le Catholicisme à Mardin (Mesopotamie)." *Les Missions Catholiques* 46 (1914): 29–31.
———. "Le Christianisme à Tour-Abdin." *Les Missions Catholiques* 46 (1914): 450–53.
———. "L'Église chaldéenne catholique autrefois et aujourd'hui." *Annuaire Pontifical Catholique* 17 (1914): 449–525.
Thiry, August. *Mechelen aan de Tigris: Het verhaal van een dorp en een wereld*. Mechelen, Belgium: CIMIC-EPO, 2001.
Trumpener, Ulrich. *Germany and the Ottoman Empire 1914–1918*. Princeton: Princeton University Press, 1968.
Turfan, Naim. *The Rise of the Young Turks: Politics, the Military and Ottoman Collapse*. London: Tauris, 2000.
Turkish Republic. Prime Ministry. *Armenians in Ottoman Documents (1915–1920)*. Directorate of Ottoman Archives Publication 25. Ankara: General Directorate of the State Archives, 1995.
Üngör, Uğur Ü. "A Reign of Terror: CUP Rule in Diyarbekir Province, 1913–1923." Master's thesis, University of Amsterdam, 2005.
Ussher, Clarence D. *An American Physician in Turkey: A Narrative of Adventures in Peace and War*. Boston: Houghton Mifflin, 1917.
van Bruinessen, Martin. *Agha, Shaikh and State: The Social and Political Structures of Kurdistan*. London: Zed, 1992.
———. "Kurdish Tribes and the State of Iran: the Case of Simko's Revolt." In *The Conflict of State and Tribe in Iran and Afghanistan*, edited by Richard Tapper, 364–400. London: Croom Helm, 1983.
Waterfield, Robin E. *Christians in Persia: Assyrians, Armenians, Roman Catholics and Protestants*. London: George Allen & Unwin, 1973.

Weber, Frank. *Eagles on the Crescent: Germany, Austria and the Diplomacy of the Turkish Alliance.* Ithaca: Cornell University Press, 1970.
Werda, Joel E. *The Flickering Light of Asia; or, the Assyrian Nation and Church.* N.p.: Author, 1924.
Wigram, Edgar T. A. "The Ashiret Highlands of Hakkiari (Mesopotamia)." *Journal of the Central Asian Society,* 1914, 40–59.
Wigram, W. A. *Our Smallest Ally.* London: Society for Promoting Christian Knowledge, 1920.
Wigram, W. A., and Edgar Wigram. *The Cradle of Mankind: Life in Eastern Kurdistan.* London: Adam and Charles Black, 1914.
Yapp, M. E. *The Making of the Modern Near East 1792–1923.* London: Longman, 1987.
Yerevanskaya statisticheskaya komissiya. *Odnodnevnaya perepis bezhentsev iz Turtsii, Persii i iz mest pogranichnikh s Turtsiei (armyan, aisorob, grekov i pr.)* [One-day census of refugees from Turkey, Persia, and places along the border with Turkey (Armenians, Assyrians, Greeks, etc.)]. Yerevan: Tipografiya Luis, 1915.
Yonan, Gabriele. *Journalismus bei den Assyrern: Ein Überblick von seinem Anfängen bis zur Gegenwart.* Berlin, 1985.
———. *Ein vergessener Holocaust: Die Vernichtung der christlichen Assyrer in der Türkei.* Göttingen: Gesellschaft für Bedrohte Völker, 1989.
Zirinsky, Michael. "American Presbyterian Missionaries at Urmia during the Great War." *Journal of Assyrian Academic Studies* 12 (1998): 6–27.
Zürcher, Erik J. *Turkey: A Modern History.* London: Tauris, 1998.

INDEXES

TOWNS AND VILLAGES

Page numbers in **boldface** refer to the entry in the Catalogue in chapter 8. Page numbers in *italics* refer to entries in appendix 2.

'Abbase, **200**
'Arbaye, **201**
'Arnas, 187, **201**, 205
'Ayn-Sare, **202**, 392
'Ayntab, 219
'Ayn-Wardo, 160, 195, 196, 200, **202**, 212, 223, 226, 240, 247, 276, 282, 329, 330, 332, 333, 334, 335, 343, 344, 348–63, 397–404
'Emerin, **220**, 392
'Isa-Powar, **226**
'Urnes, 377
Aaïn-Ward, *427*
Abadjalouwi, *417*
Abamaï, *420*
Abdlakandi, *417*
Abdul-Imam, 438
Abrahamiya. *See* Brahemiye
Abrimona, *427*
Abro, *408*
Achchar, *429*
Achhine, *424*
Achita, *414*, *432*
Achkitan, *415*
Achlah. *See* Ahlah
Achoutan, *415*
Aconis, *407*
Ada, 92, 113, *417*, *430*
Adana, 44, 45, 66, 266,
393, *429*
Adiman (Saint-Etienne), *410*
Adine, *418*
Adiyaman, 328
Adrianople, 45
Aghsan Sainte Croix, *410*
Aglija Kala, *417*
Agoin, *423*
Aguidtcha, *410*
Ahlah, **200**, 205
Ahwaz, *429*
Aina Dzidoni, *413*
Aincor, *422*
Aïn-Kawa, *430*
Aintab, 66
Aïsaré, *426*
Akhadja, 145
Akir, *420*
Akirsouria, *418*
Aknice, *407*
Akol, *426*, *431*
Akouchan, *420*
Akra, *431*
Alanésch, *432*
Alanian, 131, *415*
Alas, 131
Alashkirt, 60
Alayurt. *See* 'Arbaye
Al-Aziz, 328
Albak, 134, 137
Albakh, *417*
Alcouchki, *418*
Aleppo, 66, 73, 74, 77, 124, 169, *429*
Ali, *421*
Ali Kounii, *417*
Aliabad, *412*
Alian, *425*
Aliawa, *417*
Alihona, *416*
Alipounor, *422*
Alivana, *416*
Alkip, *420*
Alkosch, *429*
All-Poir, *429*
Almassan, *412*
Almedina, 210
Alouzé, *428*
Alsan, *408*
Altak, *424*
Altınaş. *See* Kfarze
Alwar, *412*
Alwatch, *417*
Alwi, *410*
Amadia, *431*
Amara, *429*
Amarine, *425*
Amchaoula, *425*
Amespine, *423*
Amida, *429*, *see also* Diyarbekir
Amirin. *See* 'Emerin
Amouss, *415*
Amrian, 270

507

Amrine, *426*
Amroun Chiro, *423*
Anabi, *424*
Anal, *421*
Ancha, *422*
Anhar, 99, *417*, *430*
Anhel, **200**, 203, 205, 329, 330, 336, 338, 340, 346, 354, 380–81, *427*
Anıtlı. *See* Hah
Anitos, *413*
Anitriss, *409*
Ankara, 219, 295
Antioch, 5, 6, 11
Antvat, 105
Anz, *421*
Araben, *427*
Aradène, *431*
Arak, 131, *415*
Arakend, *428*
Aras, *409*
Arbaïe, *427*
Arbaya, *427*
Arbelles, *430*
Arbili, *412*
Arbo, **201**, 221, 240, 248, *427*
Ardichaï, *430*
Ardichay, 103, 111, 119
Ardja, *415*
Ardjikanès, *430*
Ardshi, 133
Aréna, *431*
Argab, *409*
Argana Madan, *423*
Ari, *420*
Arıca. *See* Kafro-Elayto
Arichcass, *420*
Arissan, *415*
Arka, *409*
Arkah-Harabale. *See* Arkah-Kharabale
Arkah-Kharabale, **201**, 240
Arkhanaïa, *420*
Armakh, *420*
Armaniss, *410*
Armichatt, *420*

Armota, *430*
Armun, **201**, 371
Aro, *421*
Arouvan (village Babilonien), *414*
Artiss, *408*
Artoukh. *See* Artvena
Artoukh Basse, *421*
Artoukh Haute, *421*
Artoun, *431*, *see also* Artvena
Artvena, **201**, 256
Arwanteuss, *409*
Arzarakh, 392
Arzi-Oglou, *422*
Asakh, *431*
Ashita, 142, 143
Aslo, *422*
Asmaïlki, *416*
Asnakh, *421*, *432*
Assa, *418*
Astal, 193, 343, 345
Astouran, *425*
Atis, 134
Atlakandi, 111
Atlakindi, *430*
Aton, *411*
Attché, *422*, *429*
Attil, 230
Auri, *408*
Auride, *407*
Avak, 131
Avian, *412*
Avina. *See* Owena
Avine, *424*
Avirde, *416*
Avitch, *412*
Avsarik, *419*
Avyous, *423*
Awal, *420*
Awalma, *409*
Awbin, *420*
Awtichar, *408*
Aylouz, *427*
Ayri Zavissor, *408*
Azakh, 181, 273–94, 387–92
Azar, *430*
Azbas, *427*

Azek, *427*
Azék, *426*
Aznavr, *425*
Babadjidji, *417*
Babanice, *407*
Babari, *417*
Babassan, *415*
Babeqqa, 205, 277, 278, 392
Babika. *See* Babeqqa
Babiqqa. *See* Babeqqa
Babiri, *418*
Babis, *415*
Bachcala, *415*
Bachingar, *415*
Bachirga, *418*
Bachirik, *422*
Bachirma de Panta, *412*
Bachkararan, *408*
Bachnic, *423*
Bacofa, *429*
Bactazan Goulourd, *408*
Badabé, *425*
Badana, *418*
Badawi, *411*
Badebé, *427*
Baden, *409*
Badibe. *See* Beth-Debe
Badilou, *417*
Badjiri, *420*
Bafava, *424*
Bafawa. *See* Bafayya
Bafayya, **205**, 392, 437
Bafova. *See* Bafayya
Bagdad, *429*
Bagdjajik, *423*
Bagdjaoljik, *422*, *See* Bagh-Chejik
Baggetshik. *See* Bagh-Chejik
Bagh-Chejik, **205**
Baghdad, 11, 16, 47, 53, 68, 78
Baglit. *See* Bagh-Chejik
Bagssian, *427*, *See* Boqusyono
Baïkta, *414*
Bajenne, 203, 225, 336,

INDEX

345, 356
Bajénne, 191
Bajraga de Cassari, *412*
Bakesno, *423*
Bakısyan. *See*
   Boqusyono
Baku, 20, 93, 95, 100
Balaban. *See* Birguriya
Baladjigh, *417*
Balakan, *410*
Balakhon, *409*
Balaniche, *417*
Balankonie, *412*
Balarour, *432*
Balawe, *417*
Balida, *418*
Balmazida, *413*
Balo, *420*
Baloulan, 98, *417*
Bamêtni, *423*
Banidjan, *420*
Banowati, *412*
Baqesyane, 385
Bara Beita. *See* Bara-Betha
Bara Beïta, *426*
Bar-Abaysa. *See* Bara-Betha
Bara-Betha, **206**
Barazar, *412*
Barbouri, *419*
Bardakçı. *See* Bote
Bardarchouki, *412*
Bardischok, *430*
Bardkha, *412*
Baridjoukh, *417*
Baripoka, *418*
Barıştepe. *See* Saleh
Barlat, **206**
Barsel, *427*
Barzéné, *431*
Basak. *See* Bashok
Bashkale, 59, 60, 89, 95, 101, 122, 127, 129, 130–38, 142, 311
Bashok, **206**
Basibrin, 206, 245, 247, 257, 261, 271, 276,

282, 285, 356
Basibrino. *See* Basibrin
Basora, *429*
Baspin, **207**
Basra, 16
Bassac, *427*
Bassan, *412*
Basse-Artoun, *430*
Basserine, *427*
Bassi, *421*
Bassorin, *421*
Bassourké, *427*
Bati, *427*
Batnayé, *429*
Battimou, *411*
Batumi, 93
Bavodine, *422*
Bayaza, **207**
Bayaze, 220, 393
Bayazit, 59, 60
Baz, 144, *418*, *431*
Bazar, **208**, *412*
Bazaré, *425*
Bchila, *418*
Bébaré, *430*
Bebek. *See* Babeqqa
Béchèmcha, *431*
Bédaro, *432*
Bédja, *432*
Behvoir, *427*
Beïr-Kébé, *427*
Beïr-Mar-Avraham, *426*
Beit-Aïnatha, *431*
Beit-Noura, *431*
Bekarie, 436
Bekdjeri, *423*
Bekhaire, **208**, 214
Bekind, **208**, 256
Békiré, *424*
Bekusyono. See
   Boqusyono
Belli, *428*
Bellonn, *432*
Bellu, 132
Bendawaïa, *429*
Benebil, 205, **208**, 269, 437
Bénébil, *424*

Ben-Kelbe, **210**
Benkof, **210**, 256
Benodeké, *425*
Bergorié, *425*
Berke, 256
Berke (Jezire), **210**
Berke (Sa'irt), **210**
Bersevé, *432*
Besbine, *426*
Beshiri, 178, 185, **210**, 250, 328
Beşiri. *See* Beshiri
Besorino. *See* Basibrin
Beşpınar. *See* Boz-Pinar
Besük. *See* Bashok
Beth Ishok. *See* Bashok
Beth Sorino. *See*
   Basibrin
Beth Zabday. *See* Azakh
Beth-Debe, **211**, 238, 240, 248, 276
Bethil. *See* Dayro da Şlibo
Bet-Khiyo, 142
Beyouk-Bagh, *423*
Beyrian, *420*
Beyrouth, *429*
Beytour, *410*
Biazé, *425*
Bibaba, *411*
Bibalouk, *419*
Bibouzé, *431*
Bicheiri, *421*
Bichik, *409*
Bichmiai, *419*
Bicoulki, *418*
Bidara, *420*
Bido, *418*
Biduirdy, *410*
Biga, 66
Bigouba, *418*
Biguirzan, *421*
Bihna, *417*
Bikary, *411*
Bikdin, *421*
Bilanbasson, *412*
Billsahmonon, *413*
Bilon, *421*

Bily, *409*
Bimlata, *411*
Binabia, *418*
Bindjou, *421*
Bindoui, *420*
Bingov, *430*
Bira, *413*
Birabira, *416*
Bird, *421*
Biredjik, 265, *428*
Birguriya, **211**
Biridja, *419*
Birindjin, *416*
Birizar, *419*
Birkah, *430*
Bir-Ké, *430*
Bir-Sapra, *431*
Birta, *431*
Bit Titva, *414*
Bitkare, 128
Bitlis, 16, 66, 98, 131
Bitlo, 128
Bitt Nahri, *413*
Bitt Nalou, *414*
Bitt Ravouli, *414*
Bitt Touci, *411*
Bitt-Alta, *414*
Bittazia, *414*
Bittbakhchi, *408*
Bittboukra, *408*
Bittdaliati, *413*
Bittgowsi, *412*
Bittguiry, *409*
Bittkamolou, *407*
Bittkara, *409*
Bittkoura, *414*
Bittkwari, *412*
Bittlihajdijde, *407*
Bittloni, *413*
Bittmarasni, *413*
Bitt-Marou, *414*
Bittmirigo, *413*
Bitt-Mirou, *414*
Bittnoura, *419*
Bittpatchou, *408*
Bittsaïah, *409*
Bittsapoun, *421*
Bittwapi, *418*
Bittzidki, *412*

Bittzizou, *414*
Blior, *427*
Bochas, *422*
Bochatt, *429*
Boïatri, *417*
Bolissa, *416*
Bonowaky, *410*
Boqusyono, **211**, 223
Borachon, *417*
Borim, *430*
Bosnaïé, *426*
Bospinar. *See* Boz-Pinar
Bos-Pouar, *422*, *see also* Boz-Pinar
Bote, 202, **211**, 374–77
Boti. *See* Bote
Boubaba, *408*
Boucharwaran, *412*
Boudjah, *423*
Bouh, *413*
Boukdnoudan, *419*
Boulizanki, *418*
Bouloug, *412*
Bourache, *414*
Bourbe, *420*
Bourhanlouwi, *417*
Boutari, *419*
Boz-Abar, *428*
Boz-Pinar, **212**
Brabite. *See* Bara-Betha
Brahemiye, **212**, 262, 438
Brahimie, 164
Brebit, *426*
Brin, *413*
Bshiriyye. *See* Beshiri
Bsinbir, *413*
Bursa, 219
Bygar, *407*
Byra, *408*
Cabasaccal, *422*
Cafchené, *426*
Cahulpalan, *431*
Cairo, *429*
Calanis, *415*
Calien de Salavion, *414*
Caramless, *429*
Caratchoukh, *410*
Careh, *422*

Çarıklıfabrikasköyü. *See* Chanaqchi
Carminchah, *429*
Carrouki, *418*
Casri, *418*
Casrouki, *420*
Cassara, *414*
Cassaraï, *412*
Çatalçam. *See* Dayro da Ṣlibo
Çelik. *See* Chelik
Cerrahi. *See* Jarahia
Chabanié, *426*, *See* Sha'baniye
Chabsand, *427*
Chachajihan, *430*
Chagoulvard, *408*
Chahàra, *432*
Chahii, *412*
Chahk. *See* Shakh
Chak, *426*
Chakh, *426*, *431*
Chakhi, *420*
Chakiton, *416*
Chal, 143
Chalhoumiye. *See* Shelumiye
Chamba, 138, 142
Chamelladjion, *417*
Chaminiss, *420*
Chamoninice, *407*
Chamsika, *408*
Chanak-Kale *confused with* Takhta Kala, 246
Chanaqchi, **213**, 218, 225, 238, 247, 272
Chapittnaii, *411*
Chariha. *See* Jarahia
Charmilon, *412*
Charukhiye, **213**
Charvan, *416*
Charzouk, *421*
Chatouniss, *408*
Cheftelek. *See* Der-Eliya
Chehkend, *422*
Cheïh-Hader, *425*
Cheinabot, *417*
Chelik, **213**

INDEX   511

Chemchem, **213**, 236, *423*
Chéranésch, *432*
Cherang, **214**
Cherrigan, *427*
Chibane, 98
Chiddadi. *See* Shahdadde
Chiftlik. *See* Der-Eliya
Chikhan, *411*
Chiklou, *418*
Chinna, *413*
Chinraki, *421*
Chioz, *432*
Chitanawa, *417*
Chivawouta, *411*
Chkarodkan, *410*
Chkawtan, *412*
Chlaza, *419*
Chmohené, *425*
Chnaderk, *427*
Chomiah, *425*
Chotam, *423*
Chouca, *408*
Chouchamasdin, *412*
Chritanawa, *417*
Chvavouta, *416*
Chwawouta, *409*
Chwita, *420*
Chwithá, *430*
Çiftlik. *See* Der-Eliya
Civini, *407*
Cizre. *See* Jezire
Colamar, *432*
Comané, *431*
Constantinople, *429*
Coundie, *414*
Dachhalkou, *421*
Dacht, *419*
Dachte-Dare, *426*
Dachtik, *420*
Dadan, *416*
Dagra, 393, *See* Duger
Dah-Mazène, *430*
Dah-Rabban, *430*
Daline, 381
Damascus, 11, 124, *429*
Dantas, *421*, *see also*

Dentass
Daoudié, *431*
Dara, 9, 23, **214**, *412*, 437, 438, 439
Darakli, **214**
Daras, *416*
Darava, *414*
Darawa, *413*
Darband, 101
Darchiriche, *418*
Dargala, *418*
Dargali, *418*
Dargeçit. *See* Kfar-Boran
Darhari, *417*
Darichki, *418*
Darmonkoy, *410*
Darouche, *413*
Daryon, *410*
Daryssani, *412*
Dasekha, 225
Dashta-Dere, **214**
Daskan. *See* Beth-Debe
Davoudié, *427*
Dayalzi, *412*
Dayazé, *426*
Dayro da Ṣlibo, 160, 185, **215**, 276
Dayro-Zwino, 333
Daywanke, 203
Dazguiran, *412*
Debkiye, 392
Défné, *427*
Dehoc, *432*
Dehok, **216**, 256, *430*
Deir Zor. *See* Deyr-Zor
Deïr-Avv, *427*
Deir-Elaia. *See* Deyr-Elayta
Deïr-Elaïa, *426*
Deïr-el-Salib, *427*
Deirikha, *412*
Deir-Tahtaia. *See* Deyr-Takhtayta
Deïr-Tahtaïa, *426*
Délopérine, *424*
Dentass, **216**, 256
Der Shemsh, **218**, 256

Dera-Chomara, 381
Deragli, *422*, *See* Darakli
Déraii, *410*
Derajiri. *See* Deyr-Takhtayta
Derajuri. *See* Deyr-Elayta
Deran, *426*
Der-Babat, *426*
Derboder, 128
Der-Chemsch. *See* Der Shemsh
Der-Chèmsch, *430*
Dereiçi. *See* Qeleth
Derek, *423*
Déréké, *431*
Der-Eliya, **216**
Dere-Peri, *423*
Derik. *See* Derike
Derike, 24, 76, 77, 178, 185, 187, **216**, 439
Deriky, *409*
Derké. *See* Derike
Derki, *421*
Derkube. *See* Der-Qube
Dermuske, 234, 372
Derouné-Kolteké, *425*
Der-Qube, **218**, 223
Dersalip. *See* Dayro da Ṣlibo
Désa, *430*
Deştadarı. *See* Dashta-Dere
Deyr-Bashur, **218**
Deyr-Elayta, **218**
Deyr-Takhtayta, **218**
Deyr-Zor, 16, 27, 69, **218**, 260
Dézé, *431*
Diarbekir, *422*
Diarbékir, *429*
Dibarkhi, *412*
Dibek. *See* Beth-Debe
Didirki, *413*
Difne. *See* Dufne
Digal, *430*
Digula, *417*

Dih, *421*
Dihouk, *421*, *see also* Dehok
Dilman, 81, 83, 94, 95, 96, 104, 107, 108, 110, 122, 146, 147, 281
Dintass, *430*, *see also* Dentass
Dirahouni, *421*
Diraki, *416*
Direk. *See* Derike
Dirgouli, *421*
Dirhab, **219**
Diriky, *407*
Dirkup. *See* Der-Qube
Dirsor, *421*
Diru, 128
Dirza (Saint-Georges), *413*
Dissioum, *426*
Dissioun, *431*
Diyarbekir, 8, 9, 15, 16, 41, 42, 66, 71, 72, 74, 75, 76, 151, 152, 153, 154, 156, 157, 159, 160, 162, 163, 164, 166, 167, 168, 169, 170, 172, 173, 176, 177–79, 179, 192, 295, 323–26, 329, 397–404
Diz, 121
Diza-Tékia, 111
Dizza, *416*, *417*, *432*
Dizza (Saint-Marie), *416*
Dizza de Khiari, *417*
Dizzagorsoulman, *417*
Dizzatakia, *417*
Djamalawa, *417*
Djamarbasch, *430*
Djandjatchin, *417*
Djarakosch, *430*
Djarlak, *430*
Djarokhié, *429*
Djerahie. *See* Jarahia
Djerahié, *426*
Djezire. *See* Jezire

Djeziret-ibn-Oumar, *426*
Djiid, *421*
Djipona, *421*
Djouyan, *416*
Doğançay. *See* Mizizah
Dor-el-Zor, *429*
Dörtyol, 66
Doudinan, *412*
Douger, *425*
Dougueur. *See* Duger
Doura, *419*
Douré, *431*
Doustkan, *419*
Douza Haute, *413*
Drichaki, *418*
Drissa, *413*
Drj, *424*
Dufne, 160, **219**
Duger, **219**, 239, 258, 263
Duker. *See* Duger
Dukerlu, *428*
Dwary, *410*
Echastik, *427*
Edessa, 5, 6, 9
Eglise d'Albac, *415*
Eglise de Chiche, *421*
Eglise de Zanguil, *409*
Eglise Saint-Simon Bar Sablaah, *411*
Ehwo. *See* Hebob
Eijivon, *414*
Einith, *430*
Ekval, *426*
Elbeğendi. *See* Kafro-Tahtayo
Eleloké, 256
El-Medine, *427*
Enhil. *See* Anhel
Erdi. *See* Yardo
Erivan, 94
Ermans, 145
Ermuni. *See* Armun
Erzurum, 46, 55, 56, 57, 58, 59, 61, 100
Esché, *431*
Esfes, **220**, 277, 387, 392

Estrako. *See* Shterako
Eydawan, *409*
Faysh Khābūr. *See* Pesh-Khabur
Feclé, *428*
Feich-Khabour. *See* Pesh-Khabur
Felfel, 392
Fendek, *426*
Fénék, *426*
Fofyath. *See* Kafarbe
Foum, *423*, *see also* Fum
Frdilek, *428*
Fum, **220**, 236
Gadida, *418*
Gagouran, *418*
Gahhara, *411*
Galia, *419*
Galiki, *419*
Gallipoli, 60, 61, 78
Gamiliana, *417*
Garagou, *418*
Gardabatt, *417*
Garessa, 277, 278, 392, *see also* Garisa
Garisa, **220**
Garmavé, *432*
Gawani, *408*
Gawayto. *See* Sare
Gawilan, *417*
Gdalwa, *410*
Gelenkano, 99
Genesfer, *427*
Gerchiran, *425*, *see also* Gershiran
Gerçulaye, 224
Gerçüş. *See* Kfar-Gawze
Gerdahol, **221**
Gerke-Shamo, **221**
Germo, *422*
Ger-Sheran, 220, 393
Gershiran, **221**
Gézirah, *431*
Gharzan, 328
Gheh-Davoud, *422*
Gidyanes, **221**, 256
Girefshe, **221**
Giremira, **221**

INDEX

Girmira. *See* Giremira
Gnisky, *409*
Gogtapa, 92, 94, 103, 111, 138, 320
Golek, *423*
Golïé, *424*
Goliye, **221**, 341, 438
Göllü. *See* Goliye
Gose. *See* Houzi
Gösli, **221**
Goubarlanès, *430*
Gouchaniss, *420*
Gouhichni, *416*
Gouka, *417*
Goulanky, *410*
Goulcoulissan, *416*
Goulfakha, *430*
Goulniki, *416*
Goulpachon, *417*
Goundikta, *419*
Gouranice, *407*
Gourika, *416*
Gouviky, *409*
Gouzirache, *419*
Grebya, **222**
Gridi, *410*
Gubara, *413*
Gubbachian, *430*
Gueduk, *427*
Guèdyanes. *See* Gidyanes
Guèdyanés, *430*
Guépa, *431*
Gueratel, **222**, 256
Guératel, *430*
Guerektha d'Badro, **222**
Guéssa, *431*
Guidajory, *407*
Guilmidour, *421*
Guinount, *418*
Guircnébédro. *See* Guerektha d'Badro
Guirguébadro, *431*, *See* Guerektha d'Badro
Guirikta, *421*
Guirke Châmou. *See* Gerke-Shamo
Guirki, *418*

Guitta, *421*
Gulagriwi, *412*
Gulémiré, *422*
Gülgöze. *See* 'Ayn-Wardo
Gulpashan, 94, 107, 116, 119, 138
Gumani, *414*
Gunda-Abdi, *428*
Gündükschükrü. *See* Qritho di' Ito
Güngören. *See* Kafarbe
Günyurdu. *See* Mar Bobo
Gurcnébédro, *426*
Gurik, *421*
Guzel-Déré, *422*
Güzelsu. *See* Hebob
Gyarvilan, 92
Gzira, *421*
Gziro. *See* Jezire
Habab, *425*, *see also* Hebob
Haberli. *See* Basibrin
Habiban, *418*
Habis, *427*
Hablar, *420*
Habses, 160, 181, 202, **222**, 379
Habsnas, *427*
Habsus. *See* Habses
Hachirlu, *425*
Hachour, *423*
Hachtion, *420*
Hadidi, *430*
Hadji-Zeid, *424*
Haftevan, 81, 83, 84, 138, 147
Hah, **223**, 225, 233, 276, *427*
Hajji-Hasan, 392
Hakh, *430*
Halah. *See* Ahlah
Halhel, *423*
Halinki, *412*
Halkamié, *427*
Hallon, *410*
Hallona, *411*

Halokend, *423*
Halsa, *416*
Haltou, *421*
Haltoun, *426*, *431*
Halvat, *425*
Halwa, *419*
Hamidi, 256
Hamzié, *431*
Hanaviye. *See* Hanewiye
Handak, *426*
Hané, *426*, *See* Hanewiye
Hanewiye, **224**
Hapisnas. *See* Habses
Har, *413*
Harabali, *425*
Harab-Allé, *427*
Haraba-Mechké, *427*
Harab-Mechké, *425*, *see also* Kharabe-Mishka
Harap-Mişki. *See* Kharabe-Mishka
Harbé-Hanna, *428*
Harbekne, *423*
Harbichiche, *421*
Harbol, **224**, *426*, *431*
Harcki, *412*
Hariki, *418*
Harmach, *431*
Harnek, *422*
Harput, 437
Harran, 265, *428*
Harrin, 440
Hartice, *407*
Harzo, *422*
Hasan Qal'a, 331
Hasankeyf, 37, 152, 160, 181, 192, 194, 337, *see also* Hasno
Hasno, **224**, 328, 337, 341
Haspistan, *415*
Hassalowi, *417*
Hassan. *See* Hassana
Hassana, **224**, 236
Hassand, *420*
Hassan-Kêf, *427*
Hassar, *417*

Hassar Babagaga, *417*
Hassarikhi, *416*
Hassir, *417*
Haute Village, *409*
Haute-Artoun, *430*
Havara-Dejla, *422*
Havara-Hasse, *422*
Hawar-Dejla, **225**
Hawar-Khase, **225**
Hawy, *420*
Hay-Tepe, 103, 119
Hazak. *See* Azakh
Hebob, 219, 221, 222, **225**, 239, 241, 248, 257, 258, 393
Heddel, 392
Hedel, **225**
Hedil. *See* Hedel
Hédro. *See* Boudjah
Heloua. *See* Helwa
Helpélié, *427*
Helwa, 220, **225**, 239, 241, 258, 393
Herbol. *See* Harbol
Herbul. *See* Harbol
Hererdem, *423*
Hesno d'Athto. *See* Qal'at-Mara
Hesno-d Kifo. *See* Hasno
Hespest. *See* Esfes
Hessanna. *See* Hassana
Hesterek. *See* Shterako
Hezak. *See* Azakh
Hida, *421*
Hidil. *See* Hedel
Hidnia, *418*
Hilanek, 128
Hilontchi, *412*
Hilta, *421*
Hilwa. *See* Helwa
Hirdèz, *431*
Hirmii, *412*
Hissa, *416*
Hissalouwi, *417*
Hizna. *See* Khezna
Hlule. *See* Helwa
Hodlé, *426*
Holan, *422*

Hossana, *426*, *See* Hassana
Houl, *420*
Houndi Misgawt, *419*
Houstaia, *409*
Houzi, 132, 133, *415*
Hoz-Umer, *431*
Huardahle. *See* Hawar-Dejla
Huarkhaseh. *See* Hawar-Khase
Hundistan, *410*
Ibrahimie. *See* Brahemiye
Ibrahimié, *424*
Ibró, *432*
Ichatzine, *408*
Ichbitt, *421*
Ichiss, *421*
Ida, *413*
Ided, **226**
Idil. *See* Azakh
Idra d'Hirian, *420*
Ikrie, *419*
Ikroun, *421*
Ikwal, *421*
Ilan, *421*
Ile, *412*
Imchine, *421*
Imoud, *408*
Ineschk, *431*
Inwardo. *See* 'Ayn-Wardo
Iriawa, 116, 117
Iscon, *412*
Isfis. *See* Esfes
Iskirad, *421*
Ispine, *407*
Issa-Pouar. *See* 'Isa-Powar
Istir. *See* Sare
İzbırak. *See* Zaz
Jarahia, **226**
Jaranja-Telane, 388
Jaroniss, *409*
Jarwo, *411*
Jezire, 31, 32, 37, 76, 152, 159, 164, 176, 181, 182, **226**, 276,

277, 278, 279, 397, 439
Jeziret-ibn-Ömer. *See* Jezire
Jiatt, *419*
Jilu, 144
Jilu, 144
Jizre. *See* Jezire
Jolamérk, *432*
Jriaba, *417*
Julamerk, 125, 129, 140, 143, 146
Julfa, 94, 104, 105
Jum, 236
Ka'biye, 160, **230**, 236
Kabié, *422*
Kachki, *412*
Kadian, *416*
Kadié, *422*
Kafarbe, 202, **231**, 247
Kafarbé, *427*
Kafar-Diche, *423*
Kafardis, *423*
Kafarzé, *427*
Kafarzo-Oulia, *427*
Kafarzo-Sufla, *427*
Kafri. *See* Kafro-Elayto
Kafro, 202, 205, 240, *425*
Kafro-Elayto, **231**, 371
Kafro-Tahtayo, **232**
Kafsange, 234, 373
Kafshenne, 392
Kafshinne, **232**
Kaïv-Haider, *428*
Kalaa de Chirkharir, *412*
Kalaïta, *413*
Kaletan, *413*
Kalet-Mara, *424*
Kalia Daroucha, *412*
Kaliss Basse, *407*
Kaliss Haute, *407*
Kalitmara. *See* Qal'at-Mara
Kalki, *418*
Kalya, *409*
Kama, *417*
Kambo d'Mallik, *413*

INDEX

Kanak. *See* Qanaq
Kaniadachi, *416*
Kanibalabi, *418*
Kanichan, *417*
Kani-Kulna, *427*
Kanimazini, *418*
Kanireval, *427*
Kanjonice, *415*
Kanta Zargoni, *413*
Kantarou, *420*
Kanuik. *See* Qanaq
Karabach, *422*
Karabash, 154, *see also* Qarabash
Karadjalouwi, *417*
Karadjalu, 113
Karaghadj, *417*
Karagöl. *See* Der-Qube
Karaguss, *417*
Karakilissa, 98
Kara-Kilissa, *422*
Kara-Pouar, *428*
Karassanlowive, *417*
Karatoum, *415*
Karatout, *423*
Kardié, *426*
Karilann, *432*
Karjos. *See* Kfar-Gawze
Karkh Buran. *See* Kfar-Boran
Karme, 328
Karmiance, *420*
Karnicise, *420*
Karourquiwar, *418*
Karparer, *425*
Karpil, *416*
Kars, 59
Karsarie, *412*
Kartinis, *416*
Kartmin. *See* Qartmin
Karwanon, *410*
Kasha, 136
Kasra, *409*, *420*
Kasrana, *419*
Kassistark, *418*
Katouna, *411*
Kavel-Karre, **232**
Kavel-Kerre. *See* Kavel-Karre

Kaves, *422*
Kavnas, 203, 385
Kayseri, 66
Keferbe. *See* Kafarbe
Keferbi. *See* Kafarbe
Keferzi. *See* Kfarze
Kefré, *427*
Kefşin. *See* Kafshinne
Keilagoum, *415*
Kellêt, *424*
Kendek, *426*, *See* Khandaq
Kenké-Kanek, *425*
Kenzumere, *426*
Kep, *420*
Kerbala, 62, 100
Kerboran, 96, *427*
Kerburan. *See* Kfar-Boran
Kerdahoul, *425*
Kerefché, *425*
Keremaré, *425*
Kergere, *423*
Kergue-Chamo. *See* Gerka-Shamo
Kergué-Chamo, *425*
Kerjoz, *427*
Kerkouk, *430*
Kermouche, *428*
Kerpia, *425*
Kerti, *422*, *See* Qarte
Kerzerine, *425*
Kerzoyne, *425*
Kesor, 165, 166, *see also* Goliye
Keterbel, *422*, *See* Qatrabel
Keuchk, *422*
Keuck. *See* Koshk
Kéyouyé, *426*
Kfar-Boran, 55, 181, 182, 194, **232**, 271, 341, 364–67, 400
Kfar-Gawze, 211, **233**, 335, 345, 347, 358, 367–71
Kfar-Hewer, 330

Kfarze, **234**, 372–74
Khaïcanaï, *408*
Khakbak, *416*
Khaladabad, *416*
Khaliki, *412*
Khalilon, *407*
Khan Babouche, *413*
Khana de Tkhouma partie orientale, *419*
Khandaq, **234**
Khaneke, 236
Khanikhigina, *408*
Kharaba, *415*, *419*
Kharabe-Mishka, 211, **234**, 240
Kharab-Meshka. *See* Kharabe-Mishka
Kharabya, 203
Kharachic, *410*
Kharachique, 145
Kharafsorique, 145
Kharbas souro, *410*
Kharbata, *412*
Kharchkhacha, *418*
Khardalanis, *407*
Kharguil, *409*
Kharindje, *412*
Kharmad, 109
Kharouss, *407*
Kharput, 41, 329
Kharta, *408*
Kharvaranki, *418*
Kharvata, *416*
Khaskir, *420*
Khatune, 99
Khawari, *419*
Kherabe-Rappen, 392
Kherbe, 392
Kherbé, *424*
Kherpa, *431*
Khezna, **234**
Khidiana, *413*
Khidky, *409*
Khidrawa, *417*
Khinno, 145
Khirwi, *421*
Khnakà, *432*
Khoi, 89, 91, 94, 96,

102, 104, 107, 129, 139
Khom de Tkhouma partie occidentale, *419*
Khorikan Haute, *412*
Khosrowa, 81, 83, 92, 103
Khoublan, *416*
Khoueitla. *See* Qewetla
Khoulkous, *416*
Khoumabatt, *417*
Khoumar, *420*
Khourikan Basse, *412*
Khourzaï, *407*
Khousrawa, *432*
Khoutilé, *425*
Khtivava, *415*
Khvitla. *See* Qewetla
Kiat, *416*
Kibb, *430*
Kichatt, *419*
Kidia, *420*
Kikié, 439
Killit. *See* Qeleth
Kimi de Frizarii, *408*
Kinyaniche, *408*
Kiresepra, *427*
Kiridié, *427*
Kirkuk, 101, 142
Kirmi, *407*
Kissaran, *410*
Kista, *418*
Kiwakh, 203
Kiwrini, *413*
Kizlachouk, *417*
Klissa Saint-Georges, *410*
Kmiba, *411*
Knaneké, *425*
Kochanes, 8, 31, 125, 134, 138, 141, 144, 147, 203
Kochtana, *426*
Kodjagui, *424*
Kodjan, *427*
Kodoum, *409*
Kofakh. *See* Kuvakh
Koï-Sinjak, *430*

Koklafa, *430*
Kolbani, *412*
Koleké, *425*
Konya, 219
Koon, *409*
Kopeké, *425*
Köprüköy, 101
Korana, 98
Kordilik, *424*
Koria, *430*
Koridj, *430*
Köschk. *See* Koshk
Koshk, **235**
Kösrali. *See* Hassana
Kossabatt, *417*
Kotchonice, *407*
Kotmès, *430*
Kotor Rabta, *420*
Kotoss, *413*
Kotranis, *407*
Kotur, 89
Koubaki, *412*
Koublon, *409*
Koudjak, *423*
Koufek, *426*, *See* Kuvakh
Kougulan, *409*
Koukouze, *412*
Koukria, *418*
Koulia, *421*
Koulladarah, *412*
Koumazir, *420*
Koumonyta, *409*
Koup, *421*
Koupratchnice, *421*
Kouratch, *420*
Kourkha, *413*, *414*
Kourkouran, *431*
Kourrana, *417*
Kourtakawa, *412*
Kourtapa, *417*
Koutiace, *420*
Koutt, *429*
Kouvdi, *420*
Kovel. *See* Quwwal
Kowlanie, *412*
Kowsi, 119
Krbik, *423*
Krdim, *425*

Kre Super, *425*
Krémira, *425*
Krme-Kor-Kahia, *424*
Kubibe, **235**
Küfah hr.. *See* Kuvakh
Kuisàn, *432*
Kunda-Jano, *427*
Kundek, *425*
Kundéré-Déré, *425*
Kureké, *427*
Kustan. *See* Boqusyono
Kuvakh, **235**, 277, 278, 392
Lakipa, *414*
Laylan, **235**
Lédjé, *423*
Lice. *See* Lije
Liguinie, *412*
Lije, 178, **235**, 329
Lilan, *425*, *see also* Helwa
Lima, *425*
Liva, 142
Lizan, *414*
Lower Kafro. *See* Kafro-Tahtayo
Lower Khandaq, 392
M'are, 187, 382, 384
Ma'sarte, **238**, 437
Maassarté, *424*
Mabichla, *408*
Mabouor, *413*
Machraca, *423*
Mahabad, 91
Mahfouta, *424*
Mahreikane. *See* Mharkan
Mahreke. *See* Mharkan
Mahreké, *425*
Mahricat, *425*
Maïa, *418*
Maiadan, *414*
Malatya, 9
Malcava, *415*
Male, 231
Malik, *420*
Malikhta, *419*
Mallabirwan, *431*
Malrijan, *418*

INDEX

Mamuret-ul-Aziz, 42
Mansouria, *421*
Mansourie. *See* Mansuri
Mansourié, *424, 426, 431*
Mansouriya, 43
Mansuri, **236**
Mansuri². *See* Mansuriye
Mansurije. *See* Mansuri
Mansuriye, **237**, 437
Manwanan, *416*
Mapikun, *409*
Maqsi-Oglu, **238**
Mar Bobo, **238**, 263
Mar Efram monastery, 165
Mar Gabriel monastery, 276
Mar Gurya, **238**, 256
Mar Malke monastery, 276
Mar Sarguiss, *417*
Mar Ya'qub, **238**
Mar Yaco. *See* Mar Ya'qub
Mar Yacoub, 27, *See* Mar Ya'qub
Maraké, *426*
Mar-Anèche, *430*
Marash, 219
Marbichó, *432*
Marbichou, *412*
Mar-Chanès, *430*
Marcoussine, *409*
Mardin, 6, 9, 16, 24, 27, 28, 43, 62, 72, 73, 74, 75, 76, 122, 137, 152, 153, 159, 165–75, 170, 172, 175, 176, 177, 178, 182, *431*, 438, 439, 440
Mardine, *424*
Marga, *421, 432*
Mar-Gouria, *430*
Margui, *414*
Marie-Chmoni, *430*
Marine, *425*
Maronice, *413*

Mar-Sauriché, *431*
Mar-Sevricho, *426*
Maruvanan, *409*
Marwaniye, **238**
Mar-Yacoub, *430, 432*
Marze. *See* Mazre
Marzé, *426*
Maskhoudabad, *418*
Mata de Samki, *420*
Matri, *428*
Mawan, *430*
Mawana, 98, 99, *417*
Mazirgoumera, *413*
Mazra'a, 145
Mazraat. *See* Mazre
Mazrago, 143
Mazraïa, *419*
Mazre, **239**
Mazronca (Saint Sava), *413*
Mechté, *427*
Meddé, *427*
Médéath, *431*
Mefrektho. *See* Miyafarkin
Mekdessi-Oglou, *422*
Mellaha, *423*
Memounia, *427*
Mendaré, *425*
Meqre, 343
Merbab, *425*
Mercimekli. *See* Habses
Meshed, 63
Meshte, **239**
Mesti. *See* Meshte
Mézé, *431*
Mezre. *See* Mazre
Mharka, 220, 393
Mharkan, **239**, 241, 264
Mhuka, 225
Miafarkine, *422, 429*
Miafarqin. *See* Miyafarkin
Michwa, *417*
Miden, **239**
Midiat, *427*
Midun. *See* Miden
Midyat, 16, 25, 28, 37, 43, 55, 56, 76, 164, 176, 178, 181–96, 202, 271, 329, 331–47, 397–404, 438

Migalva, *415*
Mihir, *420*
Mikharabian, *419*
Mimabara, *418*
Minguèche, *431*
Mintoniche, *414*
Mir Alié, *422*
Mir-'Aziz, **240**
Mirazez, *426, see also* Mir-'Aziz
Mirgadjaï, *419*
Misafir-Khane caravanserai, 246
Mitchik, *412*
Miyafarkin, **240**, 394
Mizizah, 187, 202, 205, **240**, 384–87
Mla-Abbas, *425*
Mola-Davouda, *428*
Monnican, *416*
Monsoria, 229, *See* Mansuri
Mor Abrohom monastery, 195
Mor Eliyo monastery, 201, 225
Mor Gabriel monastery, 185, **247**, *see also* Qartmin
Mor Malke, 330
Mor Malke monastery, 185, 201, 211, 221, 226, **240**
Mor Quryakos monastery, 185, 210
Mor Sharbel monastery, 195, 203, 332, 333, 335
Mor-Awgin, 381–83
Mor-Malke, 383
Mosié, *426*
Mosul, 8, 11, 15, 16, 24, 32, 63, 73, 74, 119, 124, 152, 153, 163,

176, *429*
Moullagbeïro, *420*
Moumtir, *417*
Moura, *412*
Mouradlouwi, *417*
Mouruchkari, *417*
Mouspiran, *408*
Moussaka, *418*
Mouza, *416*
Mozizah. *See* Mizizah
Moznawa, *412*
Mrzé, *425*
Mulla-Tjabir, *422*
Mush, 61, 437
Mzezak, *427*
Mzreh, *423*
Nachkhounaï, *420*
Nachkon, *412*
Nadari, *414*
Nadjalani, *419*
Naghbijan, *409*
Nagle, 236
Nahravan, *426, see also* Nehrivan
Nahrii, *411*
Nahrwan, *431*
Najaf, 62, 100
Nakda, *417*
Nanid, *421*
Narbouli, *421*
Narhouse, *420*
Narli. *See* Ahlah
Navdacht, *422, 429*
Navlontz, *413*
Nazi, *430*
Nazrassli, *412*
Neben, 338
Nédii, *408*
Nehrivan, **241**
Nerdish, 128
Nessaria, *429*
Nicha, *409*
Nigue, *421*
Nihri, 32, 36, 63, 91, 97, 100, 125
Niram, *431*
Nirbakki, *408*
Nirchak, *408*
Nirwa, *407*

Nisibe, *431*
Nisibin, 6, 25, 35, 43, 76, 77, 159, 176, **241**, 392–94, 439, 440
Nispac, *409*
Nissibin, *425*
Nittnanou, *407*
Nouchine, *412*
Noudian, *412*
Nouhawa, *431*
Nouli, *417*
Noutirbon, *412*
Nsibis. *See* Nisibin
Nuhervan. *See* Nehrivan
Nusaybin. *See* Nisibin
Odabaşı. *See* Qritho di' Ito
Odessa, 54, 94
Öğündük. *See* Miden
Oğuz. *See* Dara
Ola, *432*
Olacdji, *424*
Omarabad, *415*
Omariyan. *See* Ma'sarte
Ömerin. *See* 'Emerin
Ömerli. *See* Ma'sarte
Orduchaï, *417*
Orfa, *429*
Oukhsar, *417*
Oumra, *432*
Ounin Agai, *428*
Ourbiche, *423*
Ourfa, *428*
Ourgueuzal, *408*
Ouri, *418*
Ouriai, *413*
Ouriata, *414*
Ouricha, *416*
Ouridj, *430*
Ourmaï, *408*
Ourmana, *418*
Ourmar Saint Mamou, *408*
Ourmila, *418*
Ourmondavid, *418*
Ourtch, *420*
Oussian, *420*

Ouzan, *415*
Ouzim, *420*
Owena, **244**, 349, 436
Pagaduk, 105
Pagui, *407, 412*
Paguie, *412*
Paguy, *410*
Pakh, *420*
Pakhlan, *412*
Palou, *423*
Palu, 436
Pari, *411*
Parie, *412*
Parisso, *423*
Parkhikhi, *420*
Parkhilan, *409*
Pasor, 236
Pasvah, 101
Payaniss, *409*
Paz, 131
Pazirabad, *418*
Pechabour, *426*
Péchabour, *431*
Pékinde, *430*
Peroulé, *425*
Peroz. *See* Piros
Péroz, *430*
Peschabour. *See* Pesh-Khabur
Pesh-Khabur, 176, **244**
Peterké, *423*
Peychabour. *See* Pesh-Khabur
Peysani, *412*
Pibohrine, *412*
Pichoual, *423*
Pikhy, *407*
Pilanice, *420*
Pioz, *429*
Pir, *419*
Pirane, 245
Pirblona, *412*
Pircaïf, *410*
Pirchn-Babek-Chiro, *423*
Pirchn-Chiro, *423*
Pircucaran, *413*
Piron, *420, 421, See* Piros

INDEX 519

Piros, **244**, 256
Pirvany, *407*
Pirzalan, *418*
Piss, 131, *419*
Pissani, *411*
Pista, *421*
Pizouki, *412*
Porte Katous, *415*
Poucine, *415*
Poukhniss, *410*
Pouliniki, *416*
Poutt, *410*
Qabala, 270
Qal'at al-Mar'a. *See* Qal'at-Mara
Qal'at-Mara, **244**, 269, 438
Qanaq, **245**
Qarabash, 214, 236, **245**
Qarte, **247**
Qarteh. *See* Qarte
Qartmin, **247**
Qartmin monastery, 231
Qatarbel. *See* Qatrabel
Qatrabel, **247**
Qeleth, **247**, 437
Qelleth. *See* Qeleth
Qesor. *See* Goliye
Qewetla, 220, **248**, 393
Qritho di' Ito, 248
Quwwal, **248**
Rabat, *414*
Rabina, *418*
Rabouniss, *410*
Rachan, 145
Rachon, *410*
Radragoum, *420*
Rahtaki, *417*
Ramikhnon, *410*
Ramma, 328
Ramoran, *420*
Ramouran, *430*
Randlan, *408*
Ras al-'Ayn, 77, **248**, 268
Rasoulan, 131

Rassoulan, *415*
Rauma, *430*
Ravoula de Barua, *414*
Rawandouz, *430*
Rayete, 101, 381
Raz, *426*
Razky Guipa, *408*
Razouki, *412*
Reshmel, 270
Rezaiyeh, 88
Richan Klipa, *415*
Richan Titar Aga, *415*
Riche Nohra, *413*
Richegallia, *413*
Rihawy, *409*
Rikanié, *424*
Rish-'Ayno. *See* Ras al-'Ayn
Rizo, 278, 392
Rjoké, *427*
Roma d'Ayra, *408*
Roma diorca, *408*
Roma Samouka, *413*
Rome, *429*
Roum Kale, 265
Roum Kalé, *428*
Rounita, *413*
Rouwan, *410*
Rowanduz, 108
Ruha. *See* Urfa
Sa'diye, 226, **250**
Sa'irt, 19, 142, 164, 176, 182, **250**, 328, 395–96, 436
Saatlouwi, *417*
Sabha. *See* Siha
Sadakh, *430*, *see also* Sadath
Sadath, **250**, 256
Sadek, *421*, *see also* Sadath
Sadié, *428*
Sadikhon, *409*
Sadionon, *413*
Sagoukir, *420*
Sahirt, *421*, *see also* Sa'irt
Saint Audichou, *410*
Saint Ichou, *411*

Saint Mathieu, *420*
Saint Sauvrichou, *421*
Saint Skil, *410*
Saint Zaïa, *408*
Saint-Audichon, *414*
Saint-Cyr, *410*
Sainte-Marie, *413*
Saint-Etienne, *414*
Saint-Georges, *414*
Saint-Jacques, *421*
Saint-Marie, *410*
Sakiran, *412*
Sakron, *416*
Salah. *See* Salah
Salakh, 440
Salamacca, *432*
Saleh, 201, **256**, 378–79
Saliha, *427*
Saline, *407*
Salmas, *432*
Salmonuvan, *407*
Salniki, *416*
Samkhom, *421*
Samsun, 42
Sangar, *417*
Sangar Bourzikhan, *417*
Sanguirgue, *421*
Sanïé, *431*
Sarai, 59, 60, 96, 101, 127, 130, 134, 135
Saralan, *417*
Sarap, *420*
Sararou, *411*
Sardacht, *418*
Sardachta, *419*
Sare, 206, **257**
Sarespido, 142, 143
Sari, *417*, *427*
Saribadjalouwi, *417*
Sariban, *410*
Saridjoukh, *417*
Sarii, *410*
Sarikamish, 59, 60, 65, 101, 102
Sariköy. *See* Sare
Sarmargui, *408*
Sarna, 105
Saro, *411*

Sarou, *412*
Sarpil, *408*
Sarpsidon, *413*
Sarro, *418*
Sarzir, *419*
Sat, *432*
Satibagh, *410*
Satié, *422*
Satoriïa, *420*
Satoura, *432*
Savour, *424*
Savur. *See* Sawro
Sawro, 77, 184, 255, **257**, 438
Sawuj Bulak, 63, 91, 101, *see also* Mahabad
Schaklawa, *430*
Scharmin, *431*
Sederi, 211, 240, **257**
Seerd. *See* Sa'irt
Séert, *430*
Segin, 128
Sele, 145
Selimi, *422*
Séna, *432*
Serarlu, 128
Serna, *432*
Seroudj, *428*
Seroujé, *425*
Serperé, *428*
Serudj, 265
Seruja, **257**
Severek, *423*
Sevveke, 392
Sha'bane. *See* Sha'baniye
Sha'baniye, **258**
Shahdadde, 219, **258**
Shakh, 236, **258**
Shalwo dab Bunisriye, 385
Shamdinan, 127
Shehirkan, **258**
Sheikhan, 437
Sheitan, 128
Shelumiye, **258**, 263, 393
Shemun Malke of Beth-
Debe, 241
Sheweshke, 382
Sheweske, 241
Shigur. *See* Sinjar
Shim-Shim. *See* Chemchem
Shterako, **258**, 271
Shufir-Anase, **259**
Siadir, *413*
Siardiki, *412*
Sideri. *See* Sederi
Sigoundan, *419*
Siha, 220, **259**, 393
Siirt. *See* Sa'irt
Sildoun, *428*
Sile, *410*
Silopi, 185
Silvan. *See* Miyafarkin
Sinava, *418*
Sincar. *See* Sinjar
Sinjar, **259**
Sinoné, *427*
Sionva-Basse, *415*
Sionva-Haute, *415*
Sipirghan, *417*
Sirabadjalouwi, *417*
Sirimi, *422*
Sırımkesen. *See* Sirmi
Sirmi, **260**
Sirouan, *425*
Sirta, *413*
Sissark, *416*
Sivas, 41, 42, 66, 219, 438
Siverek. *See* Siwerak
Siwerak, 35, 152, **261**, 265, 328
Skita, *413*
Skouniss, *409*
Sloupia, *420*
Snakak, *430*
Sndé, *425*
Sor. *See* Sawro
Soran, 131
Soucian, *418*
Soucidan, *414*
Souleymanié, *430*
Souliki, *416*
Souradir, *415*
Souran, *415*
Sourbitania, *421*
Sourean, *412*
Sourian, *412*
Sourinice, *407*
Soursari, *410*
Sparila, *418*
Sporé, *425*
Spourkhan, *430*
Srganée, *425*
Sronguil, *408*
Srougiye. *See* Seruja
Suleh, *427*
Suleymaniya, 101
Supurgan, 92, 93, 94
Sur. *See* Sawro
Surafe. *See* Zurafe
Taalini, *412*
Tabriz, 32, 60, 84, 88, 91, 94, 102, 104, 105, 106, 110, 115, 129, 144
Tachiche, *418*
Tafes, *426*
Tahyan. *See* Taqiyan
Takhta Kala *confused with* Chanak-Kale, 246
Takia, *420*
Takian, *426*, *See* Taqiyan
Takiann, *431*
Takka, *417*
Takoi, *430*
Takyan. *See* Taqiyan
Talana, *410*
Tall, *430*
Tall-Michar, *430*
Tallona, *408*
Talmassas, *427*
Talna, *414*
Tamarz, **261**, 392
Tamitowan, *408*
Tamziri, *427*
Tanzi, 253
Tappa, 236
Taqa, 203, 348, 354
Taqiyan, **261**
Tarcader, *430*

INDEX

Tarmil, *407*
Tarmoni, *417*
Tarnaniche, *419*
Taşköy. *See* Arbo
Tavogli, *422*
Tazakend, 111
Tazakont, *417*
Tbilisi, 20, 40, 93, 94, 120
Tchacala, *418*
Tchalik Basse, *418*
Tchalik Haute, *418*
Tchamakii, *417*
Tchamba d'Hasso, *413*
Tchamba dbithiou, *413*
Tchamba disbo, *413*
Tchami-doutina, *419*
Tchamieta d'Kourca, *413*
Tchamissaïdan, *418*
Tchamissor, *414*
Tchardiwar, *418*
Tchargalii, *409*
Tchifitlik. *See* Der-Eliya
Tchii, *408*
Tchilikha, *412*
Tchitaklouwi, *417*
Tchni-bilki, *418*
Tchomba de Bitt Sousiani, *414*
Tchomba de Jadrora, *413*
Tchomikta, *414*
Tchomissiodi, *413*
Tchomtouvan, *413*
Tchragouchi, *417*
Tchta-dyahra Deacha, *413*
Tdbo, *425*
Téhéran, *429*
Tel Kebbin. *See* Tel-Qebbin
Tel-Arman, 23, 24, 72, 165, 170, 174, 177, 187, 212, **261**, 306, 438
Tel-Aryawon, **263**
Tel-Bal, **263**

Tel-Cheir. *See* Tel-She'ir
Tel-Chéir, *425*
Teldare, *426*, *See* Tel-Dare
Tel-Dare, **263**
Teldin. *See* Tel-Dare
Tel-Djafar, *424*
Telela, 392
Télèskof, *429*
Telgaz, *422*
Tel-Ghaz, **395**
Tel-Goran, *424*
Tel-Hasan, **263**
Tel-Hatoun, *425*
Tel-Husni, *425*
Telibel, *426*, *see also* Tel-Bal
Teljihan, *425*
Tel-Jihan, 220, **263**, 393
Telkebbine. *See* Tel-Qebbin
Tel-Kebbine, *426*
Telkèf, *429*
Tel-Khatun, **263**
Tel-Khatunke, 392
Tell Cihan. *See* Tel-Jihan
Tellarmène, *431*
Telle-Bal, 392
Tell-Hasch, *431*
Tell-Kebbin, *431*
Tel-Manar, **264**, *425*
Tel-Mawzal. *See* Viranshehir
Telmergé, *427*
Tel-Michar, 256, **264**
Telminar. *See* Tel-Manar
Tel-Qebbin, **264**
Tel-Sefan, *425*
Tel-She'ir, **264**
Tel-Ya'qub, **264**
Tel-Yacoub, *425*
Temerzi. *See* Tamarz
Temsias, *423*
Téna, *431*
Tenat, 343
Terbessé, *425*

Tergawar, 140
Tezian, *424*
Thahardiran, *415*
Thambassou, *412*
Théla, *431*
Thomba Dwalton, *413*
Thomikta, *413*
Tiflis. *See* Tbilisi
Tikrit, 11
Tilkabin, *421*
Tiloran, *412*
Tircounice, *407*
Tirraron, *410*
Tisse, *410*
Tiyyari, 63, 121, 144
Tiz-Harab, *425*
Tizjare, 392
Tjai Kapou, *428*
Tjanakeji, *422*
Tjanakji. *See* Chanaqchi
Tjarchié, *422*
Tjarugiye. *See* Charukhiye
Tjatag, *423*
Tjeftelek, *424*
Tjélek, *427*
Tkhouma Gavayo, *419*
Tkhuma, 63, 121, 142, 144
Tocli, *424*
Tokaragua. *See* Tergawar
Tomik, 222
Topouzawa, *417*
Toubasnoui, *417*
Toubi, *409*
Toular, *418*
Toumatar, *417*
Toutchamaï, *418*
Toutrache, *417*
Trabzon, 58
Tschanaqtschi. *See* Chanaqchi
Tsché, *426*
Üçarli. *See* Tamarz
Uçköy. *See* Arkah-Kharabale
Üçyol. *See* Dufne

Upper Kafro. *See* Kafro-Elayto
Upper Khandaq, 392
Upper Qewetla, 248
Urfa, 25, 41, 66, 76, 142, 153, 163, 164, **264**, 439, 440, *see also* Edessa
Urhoy. *See* Urfa
Urmia, 15, 16, 17, 40, 63, 81–120, 122, 128, 129, 136, 137, 138, 320–22, *see also* Rezaiyeh
Urmiah, *430*
Uuéna. *See* Owena
Vahssed, *426, see also* Wastta
Valace, *420*
Van, 16, 57, 58, 61, 67, 71, 83, 95, 160, 322–23, *432*
Van (Saint-Cyr), *410*
Vanek, *423*
Vankok, *423*
Vasit. *See* Wastta
Vavardé, *425*
Vazirawa, *417*
Véranchahér, *431*
Veran-Cheher, *424, See* Viranshehir
Vill. St. Georges, *409*
Village Charnak, *420*
Villages, *411*
Villages détruit, *411*
Viranşehir. *See* Viranshehir
Viranshehir, 24, **267**, 306, 436
Wahsad, *431, See* Wastta
Warkoniss, *409*
Wastta, **269**
Yabtin, *423*
Yagmala, *419*
Yagmala Bassse, *412*
Yagmala Haute, *412*
Yalim. *See* Mansuriye
Yamanlar. *See* Yardo
Yarbaşı. *See* Esfes
Yarda, *432*
Yardo, **269**
Yardoucha, *410*
Yarimkaïa, *410*
Yayvantepe. *See* Qartmin
Yaziran, *416*
Yazran, *416*
Yemişli. *See* Anhel
Yenquels, *427*
Yerd, *427*
Yliga, *427*
Ylova, *427*
Yohra, *408*
Yourachine, *420*
Yourva, *420*
Yssa-Pouar, *428*
Za'faran monastery, 43, 165, 191, 205, 208, 239, 245, **269**, 276
Zakhô, *432*
Zangan, **270**
Zangellor, 392
Zarjel. *See* Beshiri
Zarmas, *416*
Zarni, *414*
Zarova, *416*
Zarowa, *413*
Zava, *416*
Zavita, *414*
Zaz, 202, **270**, 345, *427*
Zeir, *408*
Zemmarakh, 392
Zenarek, *427*
Zengan. *See* Zangan
Zéré, *422, 429*
Zerjel, *427*
Zerné, *432*
Zevek, *427*
Ziba, *413*
Zicaraïa, *418*
Zifajouk, *432*
Zikha, *410*
Zinavrah. *See* Zinawrah
Zinawrah, **271**, 393
Zirili, *412*
Zirinii, *408*
Zirne, 143
Ziva, *414, 418*
Ziwiky, *410*
Ziwor Saint-Georges, *412*
Zizan, *418*
Zokhan, *416*
Zor, 153
Zowita, *419*
Zré, *428*
Zurafe, **271**

PLACES OF EXECUTION

'Awjet al-Semmaq, 337
'Ayn-Senje, 333
Akhtachké, 173
Almadina, 246
Babein, 257
Baskale, 122
Boughri, 268
Chamme Sus, 227
Dara, 164
Dashta-Pis, 236
Diyarbekir, 246
Diyarbekir–Harput road, 164
Diyarbekir–Mardin road, 164, 165
Diyarbekir–Urfa road, 164
Farashiya, 218
Ferbume, 270
Fero, 377
Fort of Laborers, Argana, 164
Gök River, 438
Gorta, 218
Gülla, 213
Haftmala, 268

Harput, 246
Hawar-Dejla, 213, 218, 225, 238, 247, 272
Helwa, 220
Igil, 231
Ismail Agha's Kale, 136
Jareh River, 264
Jarjab, 249
Jewish Hill cemetery outside Urmia, 97, 98, 116, 119
Kala of Ismail Agha. *See* Ismail Agha's Kale
Kandalesur, 247
Karaköprü, 266
Khajo, 245
Khawarouk, 217
Kurdish Gate, Urmia, 115
Kurt Kaya (Wolf Rock), 231
Lake Qiro, 220, 263, 393

Mardin, 246
Nirbo d Afrasto, 243
Nisibin, 165
Nisran, 220
Sa'diye, 211
Sari Zine [Z'ayne], 254
Sharabi, 246
Sheikhan, 73, 173, 174
Shekevtan, 163
Sita, 364
Sito, 330
Tcharbash Gate, Urmia, 115
Urfa, 246
Zaghore, 233, 369
Zennar, 439
Zerqe, 375
Zinare Sa'our, 218
Zirzawan, 173

PERSONS

Syriacs

Page numbers in **boldface** refer to the testimonies in appendix 1.

Abbo family, half-owner of Tel-Aryawon, 263
Abd al-Ahad Salbo, 268
Abd al-Jalil Burghouth, 250
'Abdalla Sattuf, 165
'Abdallahad Jebbo, priest in Esfes, 220, 277
'Abdiyo, Gorgis, **345**, **362**
Abén, Patriarch of Midyat, 191
Ablahad, Hanna, **334**
Addai Sher, Chaldean bishop of Sa'irt, 253, 254, 429
'Adoka, Asmar, 303, **341**, **342**
Afremo Salma-Gawwo, 56
Agha Petros, Assyrian political and military leader, 20, 22, 92, 131, 137, 144, 182, 197, 310, 321
'Amno, Ello, 201, **344**, **347**, **371**, **381**
Andrawos Hanna Eliya, 279
Antimos Ya'qub, bishop of Kfar-Boran, 364, 365
Arsanis, Benyamin, 40

Asmar 'Adoka, 303
Athanasios Danho, bishop of Siwerak, 261
Babo-Rhawi, Yawsef, 55, **332**, **348**, **349**, **351**, **375**
Barsaum, Severius A., archbishop of Syria, 23
Baz, 143
Behnam Aqrawi, Jacobite archbishop of Jezire, 228, 276
Behnam, priest in Qarabash, 246
Beso, leader of Anhel Syriacs, 200
Beth-Bido, Salim, **395**
Beth-Lahdo Musa / Beth-Gorgis, Lahdo, 273, 287, **387**
Beth-Mas'ud, Gawriye, 239, **349**, **359**, **377**, **379**, **384**, **386**
Beth-Yawno, Ne'man, 194, **328**
Bit-Abraham, Feridoun, 40
Bitar, Hanna, 196, 234, **343**, **367**, **383**
Boulos Qestan Eframi, 228
Boulos son of Rizqallah Shouha, 172

Chalma family, 190, 191
Chalo family, owner of Hanewiye and Mir-'Aziz, 224, 240
Dera Kera, bishop of Beshiri, 210
Efram al-Qusurani, 254
Efrem Barsom, archbishop of Homs, 242
Elias III Shakir, patriarch of Syrian Orthodox Church, 182
Eliyo Alyudo, 226
*fedai*s, 279, 288
Filipos Mikhail Malke, 228
Gabriel Kabo Adamo, 254
Gabriel Munashi Ahmardaqne, priest in Viranshehir, 268
Gabriel Qas'e of Derike, 217
Gabriel Tappouni, archbishop, 165, 166, 169, 171, 172, 237
Gabro Khaddo, leader in Jezire, 227, 278
Galle Hermez, mayor of Midyat, 188, 191, 192, 193, 310, 333, 339, 346
Galle, Shaq, **382**
Gallo Shabo, 196
Gares, Eliyo, 55, **381**
Gares, Malke, **374, 375**
Gawwo-Afrem, Resqo, **331, 352**
Gewargis, survivor of Qal'at-Mara, 245
Ghanno family, 190
Ghanno-Gawweke, 'Abdo, 194, 201, **346, 362, 377, 380**
Girgis Sham'i, 166
Gorgi (Gewargi) Abrat, 243
Grigho, 190
Habib Jarwe, 43
Hamra, Gawriye Maqsi-Hanna, 220, 244, 258, 263, **392**
Hanna Shouha, 168
Hanna, priest from Mardin, 204
Hanne Safar Pasha, 188, 189, 190, 192, 193, 194, 196, 203, 223, 310, 330, 338, 339, 346, 400
Hano Basuski, owner of Hedel and Kafshinne, 225, 232
Hawsho, Hanna, 196, **343, 344**
Haydari family, 190
Hermez family, 189, 190, 193, 194, 196, 202, 206, 338
Hermez, Sabri, 194, **339**
Hormuz brother of Mar Shimun, 143, 310
Ibrahim Qrom, Catholic priest in Derike, 217, 304
Ibrahim, schoolteacher in Derike, 217
Isa Polos, 55, 357
Isa Zatte, 194, 203, 333, 337, 344
Isma'il, Patriarch, 191
Israel Audo, 165
Istayfanos, 241, 243
Jacques Abraham, bishop of Jezire, 227
Jacques-Eugène Manna, Chaldean bishop of Van, 138, 145
Jallo Hanna, owner of Girefshe, 221
Johannes, Protestant priest in Derike, 217
Joseph-Emmanuel Thomas, Chaldean patriarch of Babylon, 255
Judad Abdarova, 134
Keno, Danho, 196, **337, 363**
Khalaf family, 190
Lahdo Barsavmo, owner of Seruja, 257
Lahdo-Antar, Rume, 55, 196, **331**
Malek Ismael, 138
Malik Cambar, chief of the Jilu, 141
Malke Bette, 330
Malke Gawriye family, owners of Qritho di' Ito, 248
Malke Haydo, 379
Malke Rasho, owner of 'Emerin, 220
Malke-Sahyo, Use, 256, **378**
Maqsi-Murad, Murad, **376**
Maqsi-Musa, Brahim, 234, **347, 348, 349, 351, 369, 371, 374**
Maqsi-Musa, Habib, 196, **342**
Mar Ilya, Russian Orthodox bishop of Supurgan, 17, 119
Mar Khnanisho, 125, 127
Mar Sargis, bishop of Jilu, 126
Mar Shimun, 8, 12, 13, 17, 22, 29, 31, 32, 36, 57, 93, 125, 126, 127, 129, 133, 134, 137, 138, 139, 141, 144, 146, 147, 148, 310, 314, 321
Mar Shimun XXI Benyamin, 121, 310, 322
Mas'ud Shabo, leader of 'Ayn-Wardo defense, 202, 240
Matta Kharimo, 174
Mor Antimos Ya'qub, Orthodox bishop of Kfar-Boran, 232

Mor Filiksinos Ablahad, bishop of 'Ayn-Wardo, 203, 352
Mure, Hanna, **361**, **372**
Musa Asso, head of defense of Hebob, 225
Musa-Malaka, Lahdo, **361**, **384**, **387**
Mushel Quryo, owner of Gerke-Shamo, 221
Naaman Effendi, survivor of Lije, 235
Nimrod Shimun, chief of the Jilu, 126, 141, 310
Nisan, Y. M., 119
Polos, Hanna, 56, 213, 233, **357**, **359**, **365**
Qasho-Malke, Isho', 256, **395**
Qayasa, 191
Rahmani, Efram, 324
Rais Bero, head of 'Isa-Powar, 226
Rasho, headman of Hah, 223
Rushdouni, Y. K., 130, 131, 135
Sa'ido family, 190
Sa'id Wazir, 172
Sa'id, priest in Derike, 217
Safar family, 190, 191
Salma-Gawwo, Karmo, 56, **335**, **355**, **383**
Salmo, Mikhayel, 240, **394**, **397**
Salmo, Tuma, **328**, **357**, **358**
Sarkis, 170
Sawo'e family, 190
Severius Barsoum, 183
Sha'o-Murad, Skandar, 223, **379**
Shabo, Gallo, 181, 233, 333, **397**
Shamoun, Hanna, 246
Shimmon, Paul, 144
Shimun, 228
Shlemon son of Malek Ismael, 143, 144
Shlemon, Abraham, 109
Simon Lazarev, 133, 135
Suleyman Abbas, owner of Gershiran, 221
Surma d'Beit Mar Shimun, 129, 134, 143
tribes
  Baz, 126, 143
  Dez, 143
  Diz, 126
  Dumanan, 187
  Ishtazin, 126
  Jilu, 15, 99, 104, 126, 141, 143, 314, 322
  Tiyyari, 123, 126, 140
  Tkhuma, 123, 126
Wardo, Useve, 182, 213, 233, **364**
Ya'coub, Chaldean archbishop of Jezire, 228
Ya'qub Hanna Gabre, 279
Yesua Hanna Gawriye, 277
Yesua, bishop of Mardin, 204
Yuhannan Abdarov, 133, 134
Yuhanun, 'Abdo, **375**
Zayia, Abel, Catholic missionary in Urmia, 88, 98, 112–16, 118, 321

Kurds

'Abde, Shaykh, 220
'Abdi Agha, 279
Abdul Khadir, 33, 63, 72, 100
Abdul Rezzak, politician and collaborator with the Russians, 33, 36, 37, 48, 91
Abdul Salam, 36
Abdulhamid, 35
Abdulkarim Bey, 35
Abdulrahman, 234
Abdur Rahman Badr Khan, 36
Agha Hajo, 218
Agha Halilo, 222
Agha Hassan of Grebya, 222
Agha of Silopi, 222, 224, 261, 269
Agha of Şirnak, 222, 224, 261, 269
Ahakat, chief of the Dashit, 238
Ahmad Agha, 349
Ahmed Marzo, 245
Ahmed Yousuf, 243
Ahmed Yusef, 207
Ahmed Yusef, head of Kasekan tribe, 235
Ahmed Yusef, owner of Siha, 259
Ala al Din, 101
Ali Isa, owner of Helwa, 226, 243
Ali Musa of Dayvan, 201
Ali Sagfan of Harmes, 216
Amin Ahmad, leader of Rama tribe, 219
Amin Ali Badr Khan, 36

Artoshi confederation, 35, 314
'Azar, 228
Azizke Mahmado, leader of Midyat, 188, 194, 195, 200, 203, 223, 333, 337
Badr Khan, emir of Bohtan, 31, 32, 34, 37, 155, 190
Bayezid Agha, 101
Calipha Samad, 101
Chachano Sayrane, 237
Chelebi Agha of the Haverkan, 160, 211, 240, 271, 314
Cizbini, 187
Dakshuri confederation, 34, 184, 187, 201, 210
Dara Shaykh of, 204
dervish orders
  Nakshbandi, 30, 32
dynasties
  Chelebi, 187
  Hajo, 187
Faris Chelebi, 238
Fathulla, Shaykh of the Muhallemi tribe, 204, 215, 223, 234, 315, 351, 356, 369
Gercüs, 187
Haji Bey, 35
Haji Mustafa, 246
Hajji Abdalla, chief of Eshkafte, 224
Hajji Yusuf Agha, 384
Hajo chief of the Kurtak tribe, 211, 223
Halil, 35
Hamidiye regiments, 33, 34, 35, 36, 42, 60, 129, 131, 132, 133, 136, 187, 242, 261, 265, 267, 313, 314
Hasan Abbas, owner of Shelumiye, 258, 263
Hasan Shamdin, owner of Kfar-Gawze, 232
Hasane Abbas, owner of Adana, 393
Hassan Bey, 35
Hassan Hajo, chief of a subsection of the Havorkan tribe, 159, 160, 225
Hassano Agha of Saleh, 256
Hasse Barakat, head of Botikan clan, 278
Haverkan confederation, 34, 159, 160, 185, 187, 194, 211, 238, 240, 261, 306, 314, 337, 340, 356, 376
Herki confederation, 101
Hizar, 187
Husayin Rezzak, politician and collaborator with the Russians, 36
Huseyin, 37
Huseyin Bakkero, owner of Ma'sarte, 238
Hüseyin son of Emin, 152
Ibrahim Agha, owner of Khezna, 234, 243
Ibrahim Halil, 235
Ibrahim Pasha, leader of the Milli confederation, 30, 35, 36, 267, 306
Isa Hamo, head of Deravari tribe, 337
Ismael Agha, 143
Ismail son of Ali Mahmoudi, 245
Jalal Rumi, official in Hasno, 224, 371
Jamil son of Osman of Bote, 212
Jemal, 36
Khalil Ghazale, 270
Mahmado, 190
Mahmud, 35
Marho Oro Agha, 228
Mehmed Memduh Bey, chief of police in Diyarbekir, 73, 165, 172, 173, 175, 177, 295
Midhat Badr Khan, 36
Mohamed Agha of the Artoshi, 244
Mohammed, 101
Mohammed Ahmed, 101
Mohammed Ali Chelebi, 238
Mohammed Amine Agha, 101
Mohammed Bey, chief of the Milli, 222
Muhamma 'Alo, 261
Muhammed Abbas, owner of Duger, 219, 243
Muhammed Agha, chief of the Rama, 277
Muhammed Farah, 170
Muhammed Sadiq, 33
Musa Fatme, 271
Mustafa, 151, 152, 163, 305
Mustafa Agha of Rammo tribe, 213
Mustafa Pasha, 35
Mustafa son of Ali Ramo, 233
Nahrozo, 190
Najm ed Din, 101
Najo Agha, 377
Nejim son of Osman of Bote, 212
Nur-Allah, 31, 35, 314
Nuri Badlisi, 270
Omar Agha, 253

Omar Khan, 83
Ömar son of Ali Ramo, 233
Ömer head of Rama tribe, 213
Osman Agha, 255
Osman owner of Bote, 212
Osman Sille, 270
Osman Tammero, leader of Dakshuri confederation, 201, 269
Perihan, leader of the Rama, 151
Qaddur Bey, leader of the Al-Khamsin in the Nisibin area, 159, 211, 220, 221, 226, 239, 242, 248, 259, 264, 382, 392
Rachid Osman, agha of Şirnak, 224
Said Agha of Chal, 143
Said Agha of Julamerk, 143
Said Barzani, 37
Saleh, 101
Saleh Agha of Bote, 211
Salimo, 195
Sarohan, leader of the Chelebi section of the Haverkan, 160, 238, 314
Sarokhano, leader of the Chelebi section of the Haverkan, 160, 187, 194, 211, 314, 340, 379, 381, 383, 386
Shahin Agha, 134
Shandi, 231, 247
Shaykh Isa, half-owner of Tel-Khatun, 264
Shaykh Ramadan, 222
Shukri, 83
Sidki, 164
Simko Agha, chief of the Shikak, 83, 91, 92, 97
Slayman Berho, 228
Slaymane Abes Agha, 393
Sleyman Abbas, leader of Tel-Aryawon, 263
Sleyman Shamdin, 269
Suleiman Ismael, 222, 261, 269
Suleyman Nazif, vali of Baghdad, 171, 176, 306
Sureya Badr Khan, 36
Suto Agha, chief of the Oramar, 63, 123, 126, 143, 314
Taha, 33, 36
tribes
    'Alikan, 277

'Aliyan, 277
'Owena, 349
Afs, 222
Ali Batte, 211
Ali Rammo, 213, 215, 239, 270, 356
    Chelik, 215
Alikan, 187, 220
Alike, 187, 211
Apshe, 225
Arbani, 222
Arbiyan, 187
Artoshi, 126
Arzaneh, 232
Awsar, 232
Azzam, 231, 247
Babay, 187
Bafi, 232
Bahdinan, 126
Barzan, 126, 144
Baskili, 187
Beth-Shiroye, 215
Bohtan, 126, 207, 218, 241
Botikan, 278
Bucak, 35
Bunusra, 211, 225
Chelebi, 211
Chokh-Sora, 236
Chumaran, 211
Dakshuri, 211, 221, 239, 248, 375
Dakuri, 222
Dalmakiyan, 187
Danbali, 222
Dashi, 237, 245
Dayran, 271
Dayre, 211
Debokri, 101
Deravari, 337
Derhav, 270
Derkavi, 222
Dersim, 30
Diveran, 257
Dizveren, 257
Doman, 211
Dörekan, 220, 277
Dumanan, 207, 239
Durikari, 187
Elyan, 225
Esene, 206, 210, 220, 239, 263

Eshkafte, 224
Ghara, 222
Girdi, 126
Habisbin, 363
Hajji Slaymani, 258, 393
Hajo, subsection of the Haverkan, 211, 331, 383
Hamidi, 279
Hasankeyf, 126
Haydaranli, 37, 91
Haydaro, 270
Hazini, 210
Herki, 126
Hitto, 270
Jelali, 126
Karakechi, 35, 156
Kasekan, 235
Khalyi, 222
Khizan, 126
Kiki, 222, 261
Kiki-Kikan, 35
Köse, 257
Kurtak, 211, 218, 223
Mahmado, 200
Mamman, 226, 234
Mammi, 220
Mandalkaniya, 43
Mersani, 222
Milli, 30, 31, 35, 36, 222, 267
Miran, 35, 244, 278, 279
Mishkawiya, 43
Mishkeni, 222
Missuri, 126
Muhallemi, 29, 159, 184, 195, 202, 204, 209, 223, 224, 234, 257, 306, 315, 349
Mzizah, 187
Nauchai, 126
Nisanai, 29
Omaran, 211
Omariyan, 195, 225, 341, 343
Ömerkan, 220, 277
Omerli, 29
Oramar, 63, 123, 126, 143, 314
Pinyanish, 35, 133
Piran, 101
Rama, 151, 152, 160, 163, 164, 185, 187, 204, 210, 213, 215, 218, 219, 221, 223, 225, 231, 238, 247, 260, 272, 277, 305, 326, 364, 375, 379
Rawan, 126
Reman. *See* Rama
Ruzhaki, 126
Sa'irt, 215
Salihan, 207
Sevaraki, 222
Seydan, 187
Shahtana, 262
Shamdinan, 126
Shemikan, 187
Shernakli, 126
Sheykhan, 222
Shikak, 83, 90, 91, 97
Shterako, 270
Şirnak, 264
Surgechi, 211
Sürgücü, 257
Tawila, 101
Zebari, 126
Zerikan, 187
Ubaydallah, Shaykh of Nihri, 32, 33
Yahya Effendi, 246
Yasin son of Hasse Barakat, 278
Yusef Hajo, 241
Yusuf, 196
Yusuf Agha, 35, 232, 369
Yusuf Hajo, 264
Yusuf Hasan Shamdin, chief in Kfar-Gawze, 233, 234
Zazas, 19
Zulfi Bey, CUP National Assembly delegate from Diyarbekir, 155, 157, 158, 228, 305

Turks

Abdul Hamid II, 33, 34, 39, 43, 44, 45, 47, 48, 49, 55, 191, 318, 328
Abdul Ressak, mayor of Sa'irt, 255
Ahmad Mudir, official in Hasno, 225
Ahmed Bey, 131
Ahmed Nazo, 159, 279
Akçura, Yusuf, 50
Ali Emiri, 159
Ali Sabit es-Süveydi, kaymakam of Beshiri, 159, 211

INDEX

Al-Khamsin death squads, 159, 167, 170, 189, 201, 206, 213, 214, 215, 221, 222, 225, 226, 228, 231, 236, 240, 243, 246, 247, 248, 249, 260, 271, 277, 278, 279, 314
Arif Effendi, mayor of Diyarbekir, 46, 155, 314
Bashar Bey, 257
Bedri Bey, vice-vali in Diyarbekir, 66, 70, 115, 157, 158, 165, 171, 205, 242, 284, 285, 305
Behaeddin Shakir, 57, 58, 59
çetes, 57, 156, 237, 243, 252, 253
CUP, 37, 40, 45, 51, 57, 59, 71, 84, 87, 90, 91, 105, 121, 132, 153, 154, 155, 156, 157, 158, 159, 165, 170, 176, 177, 178, 218, 225, 229, 247, 273, 280, 281, 306, 309, 314, 371
Darwish, mudir in Tel-Arman, 262, 263
Emin, 151
Emîri, Ali, 23
Enver Pasha, CUP Minister of War, 36, 37, 40, 47, 50, 53, 54, 58, 59, 65, 71, 77, 87, 88, 90, 92, 95, 96, 100, 105, 106, 108, 142, 273, 280, 281, 282, 286, 288, 289, 290–94, 307, 309, 313
Ezurum, 59
Fahri Pasha, 267
Feyzi Bey, CUP National Assembly delegate for Diyarbekir, 45, 155, 157, 158, 159, 169, 229, 247, 277, 305, 314
Fuat Bey, 337
Haji 'Abdo, 228
Hajji Bashar Bey, kaymakam of Midyat, 196, 332
Hajji Zaki, 167
Hakki, 161
Halil, 92, 102, 105, 108, 109, 140, 142, 273
Halil Adib, CUP leader in Mardin, 165, 170, 177, 215
Halil Bey, General, commander of the Fifth Expeditionary Force, 83, 92, 100, 107, 118, 140, 252, 273, 281, 283, 284, 288, 290, 294, 313, 440
Halil Menteshe, Chairman of the National Assembly, 70
Hamdi, 155
Hamdi Bey, 256
Hami Effendi, mayor of Sa'irt, 255, 256
Hamid Bey, 154, 295
Harun, 156
Haydar Bey, vali of Mosul, 63, 121, 123, 141, 142, 143, 146, 283, 285, 311, 314
Hilmi Bey, mutasarrif of Mardinl, 158, 166, 167, 169, 170, 171, 178, 256
Hüseyin Bey, 135
Hüseyin Nesim Bey, kaymakam of Lije, 158, 236
Hussein Bakro, 206
Ibrahim Bedreddin Bey, 157, *see also* Bedri
Ibrahim Fouzi/Ibrahim Effendi, 88
Ibrahim Hakki Bey, 159
Ilyas Chelebi, 278
Inönü, Ismet. *See* Ismet
Ismail Mestan, 158
Ismet, general staff officer, 67, 68
Jalal ed-Din, 220
Jalal Rumi, official in Hasno, 369
jandarma, 55, 56, 60, 70, 72, 74, 75, 87, 89, 104, 108, 131, 132, 135, 136, 140, 156, 157, 158, 162, 165, 169, 185, 195, 233, 252, 253, 254, 256, 263, 275, 277, 278, 279, 294, 313, 320, 335, 380
Jemal, 40, 294
Jemal Pasha, 282
Jevdet Bey, vali of Van, 37, 57, 60, 82, 83, 84, 88, 89, 95, 98, 106, 109, 138, 139, 140, 252, 255, 313, 322
Kamil Pasha, 280, 289, 291, 292, 293
Kazim Karabekir, Commander of the First Expeditionary Force, 37, 57, 58, 60, 92, 130, 131, 132, 139, 140, 151, 313
Kemal, Namik, 49
Khzar Koomeli, 165
Mahmud II, 48
Mahmud V, 79
Mahmut Kamil Pasha, Commander of the Third Army, 37, 77, 289
Mehmed Ali, 135
Mehmed Ali Bey, 159
Mehmed Asim Bey, 162
Mehmed V, 45, 62

Mehmet Şefik, 137
Mithat Şükrü Bleda, General Secretary of the CUP, 178
Mohammed Hamdi Bey, 159
Muhammed Resul, 228
Mustafa, 135
Mustafa Bey, 155, 159
Nasim Effendi, 252
Nuri Badlisi, 159, 246
Nuri Bey, kaymakam of Midyat, 159, 193, 195
Omer Bey, 35
Ömer Naci Bey. *See* Ömer Naji Bey
Ömer Naji Bey, CUP Inspector-General for Eastern Anatolia, 51, 57, 58, 60, 87, 90, 92, 104, 112, 130, 131, 154, 208, 273, 280–94, 280, 390
Ömer Osman, owner of Tel-Hasan, 264
Qasem Bey, 201, 206, 213, 214, 236
Raghib Bey, head of occupation of Urmia, 87, 107, 110
Rauf Bey, head of the Midyat jandarma, 195, 335, 357
Reshid Bey, vali of Diyarbekir, 35, 66, 69, 70, 72, 74, 75, 112, 143, 151–70, 152, 171, 175, 176, 177, 178, 179, 217, 218, 227, 229, 247, 276, 277, 286, 295, 296, 301, 305, 306, 311, 312, 313, 314, 315, 320, 325, 399
Sait Halim, 54
Sami Bey, 115, 288, 342, 346
Shakir Bey, 165, 214, 219, 222, 225, 232, 238, 247, 261, 272
Sharif Afandi, tax collector in Midyat, 204, 343, 344

Shawkat Pasha, 391
Shefik Bey, mutasarrif of Mardin, 137, 171, 178
Sheref Bey, 131
Sherif Efendi, tax collector in Midyat, 197
Shevki Sheref, 157
Sheyhe Dolmaji, 249
Sidki, 159
Sidki Effendi, 247
Special Organization, 58, 84, 87, 92, 99, 130, 154, 280, 285, 286, 293, 310, 313, 314, 315, 342
Şükrü, 298
Süleyman Majar, 243
Taher, 135
Taher Pasha, 133
Tahir Effendi, 157
Tahsin Bey, 57
Talaat Pasha, CUP Minister of Interior, 36, 40, 41, 51, 57, 58, 65, 66, 67, 68, 69, 70, 71, 73, 74, 75, 77, 78, 90, 121, 128, 129, 132, 142, 143, 152, 153, 156, 157, 158, 159, 160, 168, 171, 173, 176, 280, 285, 286, 294, 298, 301, 307, 309, 311, 313, 320
Teskilat-i Mahsusa. *See* Special Organization
Tewfik, 72
Yahya Effendi, 214, 248
Young Ottomans, 49
Young Turks, 35, 36, 37, 39, 40, 44, 47, 56, 57, 79, 155, 156, 194, 280, 309, 318, 445
Youssef Badlisi, 223

Others

Adjzars, 65
Afshars, 51
Albanians, 37, 50
Americans, 15, 16, 27, 39, 78, 83, 111, 112, 117, 118
   Allen, E. T., missionary in Urmia, 113, 136, 137, 146, 147
   Andrus, Alpheus, missionary in Mardin, 165, 172
   Bryan, William Jennings, US Secretary of State, 120
   Caldwell, missionary in Urmia, 83

   Fenenga, Agnes, missionary in Midyat, 341
   Jackson, Jesse, consul in Aleppo, 169
   Jessup, F. N., missionary in Urmia, 82
   Knapp, George Perkins, 440
   Larabee, Robert M., missionary in Urmia, 84, 107, 139
   Lewis, Mary E., head of girls' mission school in Urmia, 112, 113–17, 321
   McDowell, E. W., missionary in Urmia, 116, 225, 231, 237

Morgenthau, Henry, US ambassador in Istanbul, 120
Packard, Dr., missionary in Urmia, 103, 114
Price, Philips, 147
Sargis, Jacob, medical missionary in Urmia, 104, 109, 137
Shahbaz, Yonan H., Baptist missionary, 111
Shedd, William A., head of Presbyterian mission in Urmia, 93, 97, 106, 118, 119, 120
Ussher, Clarence D., medical missionary in Van, 95, 139
Werda, Joel E., member of Assyro-Chaldean delegation to the Paris Peace Conference, 137
Arabs, 4, 9, 12, 34, 41, 50, 66, 264
  tribes
    Baghara, 222
    Harb, 222
    Jabbur Bedouin, 259
    Khar'ayna, 222
    Shammar, 30
    Tayy, 35, 43, 188, 243, 261, 314
Armenians, 4, 6, 12, 13, 15, 16, 18, 19, 20, 27, 29, 38–41, 41, 42, 43, 44, 45, 46, 49, 50, 56, 57, 61, 63, 65–71, 71, 72, 73, 74, 75, 78, 81, 83, 84, 90, 91, 92, 95, 96, 100, 101, 104, 106–10, 121, 123, 130, 131, 132, 138, 139, 140, 151, 152, 153, 155, 156, 160, 162, 163, 168, 175, 176, 177, 179, 181, 193, 195, 203, 215, 217, 220, 224, 225, 241, 250, 251, 258, 266, 267, 268, 276, 281, 282, 284, 290, 295, 306, 329, 333, 341, 348, 397
  Andraos, priest in Derike, 218
  Andre Chelebian, bishop of Diyarbekir, 304
  Antranik Ozanian, leader of volunteer brigade, 108, 131
  Ardawart, bishop of Urfa, 266
  Babikyan, Agop, 45
  Boghos Nubar Pasha, 68
  Dashnak party, 39, 40, 44, 56, 57
  Ishkhan, Michaelian, leader of Dashkan party in Van, 131, 132
  Maloyan, Ignace, archbishop of Mardin, 27, 72, 78, 165, 166, 167, 169, 170, 172, 173, 310
  Nerses, 147
  Tchobanian, 164
  Touma Bahhe, 218
  Tourian, Ghévond, 68, 164
  Vartabed Ishaq Holozyan, priest of Viranshehir, 268
  Vartabed Vartan, 267
  Vramian, Onnik, National Assembly delgate for Van, 131, 132
  Wasif Effendi, 251
  Zaven, patriarch of Constantinople, 69, 78
Austrians
  von Burian, Stephan, 78
Azeris, 50, 51, 56
Babis, 19
Bosniaks, 41
British, 39, 42, 46, 54, 62, 64, 78, 82, 91, 267
  Adam, Mr., 20
  Heazell, F. N., Anglican missionary, 119
  Lloyd George, David, Prime Minister, 183
  Tait, A. C., Archbishop of Canterbury, 16
  Wigram, W. A., Anglican missionary, 29, 137
Bulgarians, 78
Chechens, 50, 66
Circassians, 19, 38, 41, 50, 58, 66, 98, 99, 156, 158, 188, 232, 249, 250, 280
  Çerkez Aziz, 159
  Çerkez Ethem, 285
  Çerkez Harun, 158, 165
  Hachem, 98
  Hussein Bey, 250
  Rafi Bey, 250
  Rushtu, 157
Egyptians
  Muhammad Ali, 30, 48
Frenchmen, 15, 27, 39, 42, 43, 47, 51, 63, 66, 82, 83, 88, 112, 117, 118, 129, 138, 170, 239, 267, 306
  Bompard, 129

Chauris, Philippe, 254
de Sandfort, Barthe, 129
Decroo, Georges, head of mission in Khosrowa, 103, 117, 118
Delcassé, Théophile, Foreign Minister, 89, 130, 136
Galland, Gonzalve, 254
Guys, Albert, former consul in Aleppo, 74, 164
Paléologue, Georges, ambassador to St. Petersburg, 89, 130, 136
Pichon, Stephen, Foreign Minister, 253
Sisters of St. Vincent de Paul, 112–17
Sontag, Jacques, head of Catholic mission in Urmia, 63, 97
Germans, 16, 17, 47, 51, 53, 54, 59, 60, 64, 71, 72, 73, 75, 77, 78, 87, 90, 91, 104, 105, 116, 168, 178, 266, 268, 273, 315
   Bergfeld, 37
   Bethmann Hollweg, Theobald von, Prime Minister, 37, 74, 77, 78, 135, 176, 276, 284, 288, 293, 294
   Bismarck, Otto von, Prime Minister, 47
   Goltz, Colmar von der, Chief Military Advisor, 47, 105, 282, 283, 287, 293, 294
   Hoffmann, 263
   Hohenlohe-Langenburg, Ernst, temporary ambassador to Istanbul, 77, 78, 176, 276
   Holstein, Walter, consul in Mosul, 25, 37, 73, 74, 75, 109, 140, 141, 159, 163, 176, 178, 193, 195, 245, 253, 263, 275, 287
   Jäckh, Ernst, 51
   Kiderlen-Wächter, Alfred von, Undersecretary of State, 47
   Lepsius, Johannes, head of Deutsche Orient-Mission, 17
   Leverkuehn, Paul, military officer, 281, 283
   Litten, Wilhelm, consul in Tabriz, 102
   Mikusch, 263
   Mordtmann, Johannes, 77
   Neurath, Konstantin von, 288
   Püls, Bernard, 391
   Rössler, Walter, consul in Aleppo, 73, 74, 77
   Scheubner-Richter, Max von, vice-consul in Erzurum, 109, 281, 283, 287, 294
   Schlimme, noncommissioned officer, 283
   Thiel, lieutenant and military advisor, 283
   Wangenheim, Hans von, vice-consul in Erzurum, 25, 54, 72, 74, 75, 91, 105, 135, 140, 141, 263
Greeks, 41, 45, 49, 65, 66, 156
Gypsies, 19
Italians, 39
   Sbordoni, G., consular agent in Van, 131, 323
Jews, 4, 11, 12, 19, 20, 40, 42, 64, 94, 127, 267, 329
Kamavends, 19
Kizilbash, 19
Lazes, 19, 58
Niktitine, Basile, 104
Persians, 4, 6, 9, 12, 48, 51, 95, 116
   Azim al Saltaneh Sardar, 89
   Hossain-Rauf, 105
   Moaven od-Dowleh, 82, 83
   Mostovfi el-Memalik, 85
   Nasir-ul-Mulk, 91
   Salar al-Dawla, 90
Protestants, 3, 13, 15, 22, 24, 27, 28, 45, 69, 73, 77, 110, 161, 173, 175, 182, 185, 189, 194, 225, 276, 278, 306, 329, 333, 346, 398
Russians, 15, 17, 22, 35, 36, 37, 38, 39, 43, 46, 47, 50, 51, 54, 55, 56, 57, 59, 60, 61, 62, 63, 66, 72, 78, 83, 84, 85, 87, 89, 90, 91, 92, 93, 94, 95, 96, 99, 100, 101, 102, 103, 104, 105, 106, 108, 110, 111, 121, 122, 128, 129, 130, 131, 132, 135, 136, 137, 138, 140, 142, 144, 252, 255, 392
   Akimovich, consul in Khoi, 122, 146, 147
   Aver'yanov, P. I., staff officer, 22, 125
   Beliayev, 106, 144
   Benckendorff, Alexander von,

Index

533

ambassador to London, 102
Chernozubov, F. G., general, 100
Girs, M. N., ambassador to Istanbul, 17
Ias, A. I., consul in Sawuj Balak, 101, 321
Laloyan, E. A., 22
Maevskii, V. T., 133
Matikyan, K., officer, First Caucasus Army, 81
Nazarbekov, general, 108, 313
Nikitine, Basile, consul in Urmia, 29, 63, 103, 119, 120, 127
Orlov, 110
Sazonov, Sergei, Foreign Minister, 62, 96
Sergei, Archimandrate, 17, 93
Vegunin, Archimandrate, 69, 78
Vorontsov-Dashkov, Ilarion Ivanovich, Viceroy of the Caucasus, 64, 96, 100
Vvedenskii, Pavel, consul in Urmia, 81, 84, 95, 96, 97, 105, 107, 137, 139, 322
Yudenich, Nikolai Nikolaievich, Commander of the Caucasus Army, 61
Sarlis, 19
Shabaks, 19
Swedes, 16, 83, 91
Tatars, 50
Turkmen, 11, 12, 19, 50, 84
Vatican personnel
  Benedict XV, 79
  Dolci, Msgr., 79
  Gaspari, Cardinal, 79
  Scapinelli, Msgr., 79
Venezuelans
  Nogales, Rafael de, 110, 157
Yezidis, 15, 19, 30, 32, 36, 156, 184, 188, 192, 203, 204, 207, 223, 226, 251, 254, 260, 261, 275, 289, 290, 306, 329, 336, 351, 356, 363
  Shaykh Hamo Sharro, 260, 261, 314

Authors Cited

A. H. B., 154, 177, 206, 208, 209, 210, 215, 217, 223, 236, 238, 245, 263
Abraamyan, G. A., 69, 81, 318
Ainsworth, William, 31
Akçam, Taner, 2, 178
Alichoran, Joseph, 46, 63, 140, 229, 324
Allen, W. E. D., 62
Anschütz, Helga, 183, 184, 198
Armalto, Ishaq, 15, 35, 43, 73, 76, 137, 154, 158, 165, 166, 169, 170, 171, 172, 173, 175, 177, 192, 202, 203, 206, 208, 209, 210, 213, 215, 217, 219, 223, 229, 230, 234, 238, 240, 243, 246, 249, 255, 257, 259, 260, 263, 267, 269, 271, 295, 306, 310, 323, 331
Arutinov', A., 46
Askeri Tarih Belgeleri Dergisi, 37, 57, 67, 70, 77, 131, 132, 139, 161, 319
Attwater, Donald, 3
Aver'yanov, P. I., 22, 125
Aydin, Hanna, 13
Aydin, Suavi, 13, 35, 137, 185, 258
Babakhanov, I., 3, 93
Babane, Hazqiyel Rayyis Gabriyel Beth-Malik, 137, 141, 143, 323
Badger, George Percy, 16
Balakian, Peter, 2
Bar Gello, Fehmi, 208
Barby, Henry, 131, 135, 323
Bardakçı, Murat, 68
Barsoumian, Hagop, 13
Benjamin, Yoab, 40
Berré, Marie-Dominique, 170, 177, 295, 302, 324
Bet-Barsawmo, Ignatius Ephraim, 192
Beylerian, Arthur, 20, 68, 70, 72, 74, 89, 129, 130, 136, 139, 149, 164, 253, 318
Bihl, Wolfdieter, 53
Bilgi, Nejdet, 69, 155, 156, 157, 159, 161, 177, 178, 211, 295, 301, 326
Bloxham, Donald, 2, 296
Braude, Benjamin, 12
Bryce, James, 19, 57, 69, 71, 82, 83, 98, 104, 107, 109, 112, 118, 119, 130, 131, 135, 137, 139, 144, 145, 147, 225, 231, 237, 259, 317, 405
Cambar, Malik, 141, 322

Chabot, J.-B., 25
Chalabian, Andranig, 109
Chevalier, Michel, 8, 14
Coakley, J. F., 16, 93
D'Avril, Adolphe, 3, 13
Dadrian, Vahakn, 2, 58, 71, 108, 109
Davison, R. H., 49
de Courtois, Sébastien, 183, 324
Decroo, Georges, head of mission in Khosrowa, 88
Demirer, Hüseyin, 152, 164, 326
Driver, G. R., 29
Dündar, Fuat, 41, 51, 66, 188, 293
El-Ghusein, Fâ'iz, 152, 154, 164, 275, 301, 326
Emîri, Ali, 23, 159
Empire de Perse, 63, 83, 85, 88, 90, 97, 98, 99, 101, 102, 104, 105, 111, 319
Erickson, Edward J., 59, 62, 66, 88, 108, 158
Findley, Carter, 39
Gatrell, Peter, 56, 65
Gehrke, Ulrich, 62, 87, 90, 95, 96, 97, 100, 102, 105
Genelkurmay Başkanlığı, 59, 84, 88, 104, 106, 108, 110, 123, 139, 319
Genis, Vladimir, 22, 81, 84, 92, 97, 125, 137, 322
Genotsid armyan i russkaya publitsistika, 57, 78, 132, 318
Goddard, Hugh, 11
Gökalp, Ziya, 29, 185, 188
Grant, Asahel, 16
Griselle, Eugène, 88, 98, 108, 110, 112, 137, 139, 145, 321
Güngör, Salâhattin, 179
Guse, Felix, 60, 89
Haddad, Eva, 142
Hannouche, Hanna Murat, 203, 206, 215, 221, 224, 227, 229, 233, 236, 240, 258, 264, 277, 279, 290
Hellot-Bellier, Florence, 63, 88, 102
Hendo, Gabriel Qas Tuma, 277, 284, 287, 325
Hinno, Süleyman, 76, 198, 276, 280, 286, 288, 325
Hoetzsch, Otto, 63, 100, 101, 102
Höjer, N. F., 83
Hollerweger, Hans, 224, 233, 248

Hull, Isabel V., 53, 64, 71, 307
Hultvall, John, 16, 83
Impagliazzo, Marco, 175, 324
Ineichen, Markus, 91
Jäckh, Ernst, 47, 51
Jähnicke, Burkhard, 280
Jedin, Hubert, 7, 9, 11
Joseph, John, 13, 15, 16, 31
Kansu, Aykut, 40, 155
Karpat, Kemal H., 19
Kévorkian, Raymond, 45
Kieser, Hans-Lukas, 17
Knapp, Grace H., 440
Koohi-Kamali, Farideh, 91
Korsun, N. G., 59, 104, 108, 109
Kurtcephe, Israfil, 280, 283
Laloyan, E. A., 22
Landau, Jacob, 50
Lazarev, M. S., 17, 36, 37, 47, 90, 91, 95, 96, 97, 98, 104
Lehmann-Haupt, C. F., 94
Lepsius, Johannes, 25, 37, 57, 72, 74, 75, 77, 109, 110, 135, 138, 140, 141, 142, 159, 163, 176, 178, 193, 245, 263, 275, 284, 293, 294, 318
Les Missions catholiques, 103, 111, 117, 118, 119
Leverkuehn, Paul, 88, 104, 149, 280, 281, 283, 286, 294
Lewis, Bernard, 12
Lohr, Eric, 65
Ludshuveit, E. F., 103, 108
Macuch, Rudolf, 138, 143, 144, 323
Maevskii, V. T., 125, 127, 133
Majd, Mohammed Gholi, 122
Mann, Michael, 44, 308
Mar-Yukhanna, I. I., 81, 96, 101
Matveev, K. P., 81, 96, 101
McDowell, David, 31, 32, 35, 36, 37, 63, 306
Menteşe, Halil, 70
Meyrier, Gustave, 42
Mikaelyan, Vardges, 37, 74, 263
Minorsky, V., 32
Mistrih, Vincent, 325
Muradoğlu, Abdulla, 58
Muratoff, Paul, 62
Naayem, Joseph, 3, 76, 154, 156, 162, 214, 221, 229, 236, 247, 256, 266

INDEX 535

Namik, Said A., 18
Naslian, Jean, 171, 324
Nedjib, Rustem, 18
Nersisiyan, M. G., 69, 81, 318
Nesimi, Abidin, 156, 159, 211, 236, 326
Nikitine, Basile, 30, 40, 64, 89, 140, 144
Noel, Edward, 29, 176, 302, 303, 305, 441
Nogales, Rafael de, 59, 110, 140, 157, 162, 252, 314, 322
Ogandzhanyan, Artem, 78
Ovakiyan, Vakharshak, 108
P. V. M., 249
Palmer, Andrew, 183
Parhad, Sam, 141
Qarabasch, Malfono Abed Mschiho Na'man, 76, 154, 164, 198, 325
Rahme, Joseph G., 49
Review of the Civil Administration of Mesopotamia, 302
Rhétoré, Jacques, 25, 27, 76, 123, 142, 169, 171, 173, 174, 177, 210, 213, 217, 220, 223, 224, 225, 227, 239, 241, 244, 245, 250, 254, 259, 260, 263, 265, 268, 270, 302, 305, 324, 433, 434
Riccardi, Andrea, 79
Ritter, Hellmut, 276
Robinson, Chase, 7
Rockwell, William Walker, 3, 109
Rondot, Pierre, 29, 31
Runciman, Steven, 6, 11
Rushdouni, Y. K., 57
Saint Vincent de Paul Annales de la Mission, 97, 118
Samih, Aziz, 59, 281
Samuel, Athanasius Yeshua, 227, 242
Sarafian, Ara, 165, 170, 171, 172, 174, 324
Schauffler-Platt, Mary, 112, 321
Sevan-Khachatryan, T. G., 69, 81, 318
Shahbaz, Yonan H., 111, 129, 320
Shedd, Mary Lewis, 110
Shedd, William A., 94, 125
Simon, Hyacinthe, 76, 165, 168, 173, 175, 206, 209, 210, 213, 215, 217, 223, 238, 240, 244, 245, 246, 249, 256, 258, 263, 269, 302, 312, 324, 436
Şimşir, Bilâl N., 157, 280
Skandar, 195
Soane, Ely Bannister, 126
Sonyel, Salahi, 84, 97, 99, 140
Sorgun, Taylan, 92, 109, 142, 286
Sundvall, Elin, 83
Surma d'Beit Mar Shimun, 57, 126, 129, 134, 137, 138, 144, 322
Sykes, Mark, 4, 219
Termen, R. I., 35, 126
Ternon, Yves, 46, 155, 157, 162, 171, 174, 175, 178, 207, 208, 211, 213, 219, 221, 223, 224, 227, 228, 229, 235, 237, 240, 242, 245, 246, 254, 256, 262, 270, 304
Tevetoğlu, Fethi, 51, 58, 88, 90, 273
Tfinkdji, Joseph, 24, 27, 28, 92, 126, 192, 201, 227, 429
Thiry, August, 225, 262
Toynbee, Arnold, 19, 57, 69, 71, 82, 83, 98, 104, 107, 109, 112, 118, 119, 130, 131, 135, 137, 139, 144, 145, 147, 225, 231, 237, 259, 317, 321, 405
Trumpener, Ulrich, 53
Turfan, Naim, 280
Turkish Republic, 74, 298
Üngör, Uğur Ü., 157, 193
Ussher, Clarence D., 88, 95, 139, 322
van Bruinessen, Martin, 32, 34, 91, 185, 188
Waterfield, Robin E., 6
Weber, Frank, 53
Werda, Joel E., 127, 138, 142
Wigram, Edgar T. A., 29, 33
Wigram, W. A., 33, 140
Yapp, M. E., 50
Yerevanskaya statisticheskaya komissiya, 65
Yonan, Gabriele, 40, 90, 208, 240
Zayia, Abel, 111, 118
Zirinsky, Michael, 119
Zürcher, Erik J., 50, 58